contemporary
accounting

4th edition

mike **bazley**

phil **hancock**

aiden **berry**

robin **jarvis**

NELSON
TM
THOMSON LEARNING

Australia · Canada · Mexico · Singapore · Spain · United Kingdom · United States

NELSON

™

THOMSON LEARNING

102 Dodds Street
Southbank Victoria 3006

Email nelson@nelson.com.au
Website http://www.nelson.com.au

Adapted from *Accounting in a Business Context*, Third Edition,
A.J. Berry and R. Jarvis, 1997. Published in the U.K. by International
Thomson Business Press.

First published in 1993
Fourth edition published in 2001
10 9 8 7 6 5 4 3
05 04 03 02

National Library of Australia
Cataloguing-in-Publication data

Contemporary accounting.

    4th ed.
    Includes index.
    ISBN 0 17 010395 1

    1. Accounting – Australia. 2. Accounting – Australia –
    Problems, exercises, etc. 3. Accounting – Study and
    teaching (Higher) – Australia. I. Bazley, M. E.
    (Michael E.).

657.0994

Edited by Susan Lawrence and Carol Aikman
Text design by Kate Vandestadt
Cover design by Sonia Juraja
Cover illustration by Kim Roberts
Indexed by Max McMaster
Typeset in Garamond and Franklin Gothic EF by Modern Art Production Group
Printed in Australia by McPhersons Printing Group

Nelson Australia Pty Limited ACN 058 280 149 (incorporated in Victoria)
trading as Nelson Thomson Learning.

Contents

Appendices

Glossary   563

Preface

Contemporary Accounting, fourth edition, is designed to provide an introduction to accounting for students at universities and similar tertiary institutions. It is intended to cover the requirements of a one-semester course in accounting at the undergraduate and MBA level for both accounting and non-accounting majors. We believe that the approach to financial accounting taken in this book will provide a solid foundation on which accounting majors will be better able to understand the bookkeeping function. It also provides an excellent overview of the accounting function in business for non-accounting majors. The implications of accounting policies on managers are discussed wherever relevant throughout the book.

This book has been written with the objective of conveying an understanding of accounting without introducing unnecessary technical terminology and procedures. Rather, it builds on basic concepts to a clear understanding of financial statements, their uses and limitations. Accounting terms and concepts are defined according to the official pronouncements of the Australian Accounting Standards Board (AASB). In particular, the Statements of Accounting Concepts of the Conceptual Framework provide the conceptual basis of *Contemporary Accounting* and are used to analyse various issues in accounting. We have included in the text extracts from some annual reports to illustrate contemporary accounting practices. Also included are the 1999 financial statements of Woolworths Limited. These appear in Appendix 1 and students are referred to them frequently throughout the text.

To introduce accounting techniques and principles such as duality, we have used worksheets based on the statement of financial position equation. Students develop an understanding of concepts such as assets, liabilities, equity, revenues and expenses and see how financial statements are prepared. This approach avoids the problems often experienced by students in trying to understand debits and credits.

Chapters 1 to 14 provide an introduction to financial accounting where the needs of external users are most important. Chapters 15 to 21 look at the needs of internal users and provide an introduction to management accounting. A one-semester MBA course in financial accounting is likely to cover all the material in Chapters 1 to 14.

In each chapter key concepts are identified and highlighted and review questions and problems are provided. The problems are listed in order of difficulty. The more difficult problems are primarily intended for use in MBA courses, but instructors of undergraduate courses may also find them useful. The ethics case studies are intended for all students and are well suited to group discussion. We recommend that students refer to the comprehensive glossary as they work through the book.

Contemporary Accounting has been written in a manner which students find easy to read. The response to the first three editions of this book have been very positive. However, there are several changes in the fourth edition of the book. These changes have been made in response to comments from users of the book and also in response to changes occurring in education and business.

Summary of major changes

- Minor revisions have been made to several chapters to improve the content and to update material after changes in Accounting Standards and Corporations Law. A significant change has been the renaming of two of the key financial statements. From 1 July 2000, the profit and loss statement became the statement of financial performance, and the balance sheet became the statement of financial position. The section on accounting for taxation has also been rewritten.
- The 1999 financial report of Woolworths Limited has been included as an appendix. This replaces the extracts from various annual reports included in earlier editions. Reference is made to the Woolworths financial report throughout the financial accounting section of the fourth edition, enabling readers to acquire an appreciation of the financial report of a real company. There are questions relating to the report at the end of most chapters on financial accounting. The questions are intended to encourage students to read and familiarise themselves with financial reports.
- Newspaper articles have been included in most chapters to illustrate the various topics discussed in the book. Reference to newspaper articles adds realism to the subject matter and interest for students.
- The implications of accounting policies for managers and investors are addressed in some of the financial accounting chapters.
- Additional questions have been inserted in most chapters. The heading 'case studies' has been deleted and all questions are now either review questions or problems for discussion and analysis. Questions have also been ranked in order of difficulty. The ethics case studies remain.
- Chapter 16 has been substantially rewritten and the title of the chapter changed to 'Capital Investment Decisions'.

Learning and teaching aids

Various aids accompany the fourth edition of this book. These aids provide an educational package for both teachers and students. Available to students is:

Study Guide

The Study Guide provides material for the student to re-examine the concepts in the various chapters. It includes the learning objectives for each chapter, a summary of the major issues in each chapter, additional exercises, true/false questions and multiple choice questions. It will help the students as they prepare for tests and examinations on the material covered in the book. The Study Guide has been prepared by Di Van Rhyn of Murdoch University.

Available to teachers are:

Solutions Manual

The Solutions Manual contains suggested answers to review questions, problems for discussion and analysis, and ethics case studies.

PowerPoint® Slides

A set of slides using PowerPoint® software is available to help teachers in the delivery of lecture material for the book.

Testbank

A testbank of true/false questions and multiple choice questions is provided to assist teachers in the preparation of tests and examinations.

Acknowledgements

We wish to express our appreciation and gratitude to the following people who have contributed in some way to the development of this book: Professor Alan Davison at Murdoch University for his support and encouragement; Nicole Ladner, Stacey Porter and Andrew Macksey, our research assistants, for all their efforts; Colette Larsen and Lesley Murrish for the unenviable task of typing many drafts of the book; and to our wives Pam Bazley and Jenny Hancock for their patience, and for proof-reading early versions of the book.

We also acknowledge our debt to Aidan Berry and Robin Jarvis, the authors of *Accounting in Business Context* published in the UK. This book has been based on the British text, although the two books are now significantly different in the area of financial accounting, and we have introduced case studies on ethics at the end of all chapters. Responsibility for the opinions expressed and for any errors in this book is entirely our own.

Michael Bazley
Phil Hancock
Murdoch University

The authors and publisher would like gratefully to credit or acknowledge permission to reproduce the following:

AAP, pp. 221, 331; Bloomberg LP, pp. 472–3, Copyright 2000. Reprinted with permission. All rights reserved; Geoff Brayshaw ©, pp. 9–10; Gayle Bryant ©, pp. 268–9; *Business Review Weekly*, pp. 54–5; G. Carnegie, J. Gavens & R. Gibson ©, pp. 228–9, *Cases in Financial Accounting*, rev. edn, Harcourt Brace & Company, 1991, Case 86; Subrata N. Chakravarty, pp. 297–8. Reprinted by Permission of Forbes Magazine © 2001 Forbes Inc.; CPA Australia ©, pp. 75–6, 304. Reproduced with the permission of the copyright holder; R. Craven, I. Urquhart & R. Woolley, p. 255, *Case Studies in Accounting*, 3rd edn, 1985, VCTA Publishing, Case 3–3. Reproduced by permission of Macmillan Education Australia, copyright holder; Mark Fenton-Jones ©, p. 199, *Australian Financial Review*, 2/6/99; Financial Times Information Limited (UK), pp. 298–9; J. Godfrey et al., p. 387, *Accounting Theory*, 2nd edn, John Wiley © 1994, reprinted with permission of John Wiley & Sons Australia; I. Harrison, J. Horrocks & R. Newman, pp. 112, 253, 254–5, 412, *Accounting: A Direct Approach*, 1986, Pearson Education Inc, USA; Harvard Business Review, pp. 502–3. Reprinted by permission from 'Rethinking: Life without budgets' © 1999 by the President and Fellows of Harvard College, all rights reserved; J. Hoggett & L. Edwards, pp. 109, 131, 254, 256, 281, *Financial Accounting in Australia*, John Wiley © 1990, reprinted with permission of John Wiley & Sons Australia; W.J. Morse & P.H. Roth, pp. 410, 412–13, 440–1, 441, 457, 457–8, 481–2, 505–6, 507–8, *Cost Accounting: Processing, Evaluation and Using Cost Data* by Morse © 1986. Reprinted by permission of Pearson Education, Inc. Upper Saddle River, NJ, 07458, USA; C. Parker & B. Porter, p. 288, *The CPA Summary of Australian GAAP*, Parker Publishing, 2000, p. 30; T. Ravlic ©, pp. 96–7, 195–6, 291, *The Age*; Reuters Limited © 1998, p. 146; *South China Morning Post*, pp. 16–17, 246; *Sydney Morning Herald*, p. 10; The Times Newspapers Limited ©, pp. 26, 160–1, 404; Westpac, p. 218, Annual Report, 1999; T.D. Wise et al., pp. 270, 278–9, *Accounting in Australia* © 1990 by Houghton Mifflin Company. Adapted with permission; L. Wood ©, p. 384, *The Age*, 29/8/00; Woolworths Limited, pp. 513–46.

Every attempt has been made to trace and acknowledge copyright holders. Where the attempt has been unsuccessful, the publisher welcomes information that would redress the situation.

Introduction to Accounting

Learning objectives

At the end of this chapter you should be able to:

1   understand what is meant by the term 'accounting'

2   explain who are the main users of accounting information, and the main purposes for which the information is used

3   explain the difference between management and financial accounting

4   discuss the limitations of accounting information

5   discuss the factors that influence the choice of accounting systems for different types of organisations

6   discuss and appreciate the importance of ethics in accounting and business in general

7   explain what is meant by ethical behaviour

8   understand what should be considered appropriate ethical behaviour for accountants

9   explain what is meant by the term 'economic consequences'.

Introduction

This chapter discusses the role of accounting, its uses and its users. It will also give you an appreciation of the role of accounting within a business organisation and in its dealings with others. We introduce some ideas about the ways in which accounting helps managers to meet business objectives by, for example, providing the information necessary to make a decision about buying or renting premises. The way in which the size and type of the organisation affects its accounting will be discussed. For example, in a small family restaurant the accounting requirements are much less complex than in a large business such as Westpac Banking Corporation. Another factor that both affects and is affected by accounting is the commercial environment. The influence of the commercial environment on accounting can be through government legislation such as the adoption of a new Companies Act or through the introduction of a goods and services tax (GST). Besides government action, accounting can be affected at this level by changes in technology. For instance, the introduction of information technology has allowed accounting information to be provided quickly and efficiently, thus enabling different decisions to be taken than might otherwise have been the case. Finally, we look at the limitations of accounting information. As with most sources of information, there are imperfections. From this brief résumé we can see that the accounting activity interacts with all levels of business.

Accounts are normally seen as a series of figures, which may give the impression that they are only a form of commercial arithmetic. These figures are, in fact, a convenient way of summarising and reporting information that would be indigestible in narrative form. If you were asked to provide a report that gives details of the value of everything you own, it would be simpler to use figures to represent the value, rather than words. The value of some things is difficult to express in numerical terms: good health, lead-free petrol, or a qualification such as a degree. These examples do not lend themselves to numerical analysis, but this has not stopped people assigning a dollar value to them.

In order to understand the role and importance of accounting in the context of business organisations, it is necessary to decide what accounting means. If you were to look up the word 'account' in *Roget's Thesaurus* you would be directed to words such as 'report' and 'narration'. Further investigation would reveal that it is also referred to as commercial arithmetic, double-entry bookkeeping, etc. These alternatives imply totally different things: a report is something that conveys information for a particular purpose, while commercial arithmetic implies a mechanical exercise following agreed rules or principles.

Besides problems about what accounting can and should document, other issues need to be considered: for example, whether numerical format is the best format. We also need to consider whom the report is for and what its purpose is: for instance, you may give totally different accounts of your car's capabilities to a prospective buyer and to a mechanic to whom you have taken it for repairs. So we can see that the question of defining accounting has many facets: what you report, how you report, to whom you report and for what purpose you report. We shall look at these issues in more detail later in this chapter. First, in order to get a better idea of what accounting is generally understood to be about, let us examine some definitions contained in the accounting literature.

What is accounting?

There are a number of definitions of accounting and they have changed over time in response to the changing accounting environment. One definition that has stood the test of time is that given by the American Accounting Association in *A Statement of Basic Accounting Theory* (also known as *ASOBAT*), which defines accounting as:

the process of identifying, measuring and communicating economic information to permit informed judgement and decisions by users of the information.

First, this definition states the purpose of accounting. Second, it states that accounting has a number of components—some technical (such as measuring the data), some analytical (such as identifying the data), and some that require further information (such as the communication of this economic information to users: who are these users and what form does this information take?). Finally, the definition implies that the information has value in the decision-making process. The definition assumes that economics concerns any situation in which a choice must be made involving scarce resources.

Another definition was offered by the American Institute of Certified Public Accountants (AICPA), in the 1973 Trueblood Report, which looks to the role of accounting in decision making. The report lists 12 objectives which emphasise this decision-making process. They can be summarised as follows:

- to provide information, through financial statements, for the making of economic decisions
- to provide information for predicting, comparing and evaluating the effectiveness of management's use of scarce resources
- to provide information to predict and evaluate the going concern of an entity
- to provide information on earnings, cash flows, profitability and financial position of the entity.

The usefulness of accounting information for decision making is reinforced by the Statements of Accounting Concepts (known as the Conceptual Framework), which are discussed in more detail in Chapters 2 and 13.

This gives us a clue to the fact that accounting is closely related to other disciplines (we are recording economic data) and it also gives us some clue as to the uses of accounting information, i.e. for reporting on what has happened and as an aid to decision making and control of the enterprise.

A definition from the *Macmillan Dictionary of Accounting* states:

accounting, in broad terms, is the preparation and communication to users of financial and economic information. The information ideally possesses certain qualitative characteristics. Accounting involves the measurement, usually in monetary terms, of transactions and other events pertaining to accounting entities. Accounting information is used for stewardship, control and decision making.

This suggests that the role of accounting information within an organisation is at the very core of running a successful organisation.

The use of accounting information for business decision making is also brought out clearly in the definition given by the American Accounting Principles Board in 1970 (*APB* No. 4):

Accounting is a service activity. Its function is to provide quantitative information, primarily financial in nature, about economic entities that is intended to be useful in making economic decisions, in making reasoned choices among alternative courses of action.

The fact that accounting is described as a service activity reinforces the point made earlier: in order to understand the usefulness of accounting, we need to know who uses it and for what purpose.

Key Concept 1.1

Accounting

Important points made in these definitions are that:
- accounting is about quantitative information
- the information is likely to be financial
- it should be useful for decision making in the allocation of scarce resources.

For what purpose is accounting information used?

This question can be answered on at least two levels: that of the individual and that of the enterprise. At the individual level, individuals can use accounting information to help them control the level of their expenditure, to assist in planning future levels of expenditure and to help them raise additional finance (e.g. mortgages, hire-purchase, etc.) and decide the best way to spend their money. Thus we see that for the individual, accounting can have three functions, i.e. planning, controlling and decision support.

At the level of the enterprise it is used to control the activities of the organisation, to plan future activities, to assist in raising finance and to report upon the activities and success of the enterprise to interested parties.

You will note that the major difference between the two is that in the case of an enterprise, besides its uses in planning, controlling and decision making which are all internal activities or functions, accounting also has what we could describe as an external function, i.e. providing information to people outside the enterprise. The latter function is usually met through the medium of annual accounts or financial reports and is often referred to as financial accounting. The external users require the information contained in the financial reports to use in the decision-making process, or to evaluate what management has done with the money invested in the business.

Besides meeting the needs of external users, the system that produces the financial accounting reports also meets some of the needs of internal users. One need is to analyse the results of past actions. This requires information on the actual outcomes; these can then be evaluated against the projected outcomes, and reasons for differences can be identified so that appropriate actions can be taken. This is only one of a number of needs that managers have. Their other needs are met through other reports based upon information provided by the internal accounting system.

The internal accounting system, which may be in addition to the system which underpins the external financial reporting system, is often referred to as the management accounting function. The major difference between financial accounting and management accounting is that management accounting is primarily directed towards providing information of specific use to managers, whereas financial accounting information, which is often less detailed, has many users apart from managers. This leads us to the second question which we posed regarding the users of accounting information.

Who uses accounting information?

Whether accounting information relates to the activities of an individual or to a business enterprise, its users can be placed in two broad categories:

- those inside the enterprise—the managers or, in the case of a small business, the owner
- those outside the enterprise, including banks, the government, tax authorities, investors, creditors, trade unions, etc.

Internal users

The major internal user is the management of an enterprise. For a small enterprise this is likely to be the owner, or a small number of individuals in the case of a partnership. However, many businesses are much larger and are owned by numerous individuals or groups of individuals, as is the case with large enterprises such as Coles Myer, Woolworths, Western Mining Corporation or Gull Petroleum.

Often the major investors themselves are owned by others, as is the case with the major financial institutions. In such a situation it is extremely unlikely that the actual owners would or could take an active part in the day-to-day running of the enterprise. Consider the chaos if all the people who bought shares in Telstra tried to take an active part in the day-to-day running of that business. Instead these owners or share-holders delegate the authority for the day-to-day running to a group of directors and managers.

These directors and managers are involved in the routine decision making and are the equivalent of the owner in a small business in terms of their information needs. These needs are normally met by unpublished reports of various kinds, usually based on infor-mation provided through both the financial and the management accounting systems. The exact nature of the reports varies from enterprise to enterprise. A department store may require information about the profitability of each of its departments, whereas for a factory producing a small number of different products the information required is likely to be about the profitability of each product.

The form of the report will also vary according to its purpose. If the purpose of the report is to assist management, it needs to show the past transactions and performance, probably measured against some predetermined standard. For planning purposes, however, a forecast of what is likely to happen in the future is more important. These different forms of reports and ways of grouping information are normally referred to under the generic heading of management accounting and this form of accounting is the focus of the second half of this book.

At this stage it is worth briefly summarising the different categories of management accounting reports. To do this we need to make some broad generalisations about the needs of managers and to categorise those needs. In practice, of course, there is a certain amount of overlap between the categories but we need not concern ourselves with this at present. The categories are discussed in greater detail in Chapters 15 to 21. The broad categories that we have referred to in terms of the needs of managers are as follows.

Stewardship

Managers need to protect the enterprise's economic resources (normally referred to as assets) from theft, fraud, wastage, etc.

Planning

Managers need to plan activities so that finance can be raised, marketing and promo-tional campaigns set up and production plans made.

Control

Managers need to control the activities of the enterprise: this includes setting sales targets, managing human resources, ensuring that there are sufficient raw materials to meet the demands of production and sufficient goods in stock to satisfy customer demand, etc. It will also include identifying where targets can be set.

Decision making

Managers need to make specific decisions: Should we produce the item ourselves or buy it in? How much will it cost to produce a particular item? How much money will we need in order to run the enterprise? etc.

A moment's reflection leads us to the conclusion that management accounting is a vast area in its own right and so, rather than getting deeply involved at this stage, let us first look at the other broad area we identified—the needs of users outside the enterprise, the external users. We shall be returning to the needs of internal users in more detail in Chapter 15.

External users

We need to establish who the external users are. The Conceptual Framework, to be discussed in more detail in Chapter 2, lists the primary users of financial information. These primary users are divided into three groups, as follows:

- *Resource providers:* employees, lenders (those who lend money to the entity, e.g. bankers), creditors, suppliers (those who supply the entity with goods and services), and, in the case of business entities, investors (shareholders, i.e. the owners of the entity).
- *Recipients of goods and services:* those who benefit from the provision of goods and services by the reporting entity, i.e. customers.
- *Parties performing a review* or oversight function: government, trade unions, and special interest groups acting on behalf of the general public, e.g. Greenpeace.

These groups are normally provided with information by means of published annual reports. This type of accounting is generally referred to as financial accounting. In order to decide to what extent the annual reports meet the needs of the external users and to understand more fully the importance of accounting, we shall briefly discuss the needs of the external users listed above.

Owners and shareholders

As we have said, in the case of small enterprises the owners are likely to be actively engaged in the day-to-day operations of the enterprise. In these small enterprises the owners' needs are often met by the management accounting information and reports.

Key Concept 1.2

Financial accounting

Financial accounting can be thought of broadly as that part of the accounting system that tries to meet the needs of various external user groups. This it does by means of an annual report which includes statements of financial performance, financial position and cash flow, information requied by law and any additional information which the entity wishes to supply.

As the enterprise grows, however, it is likely that the owners will become divorced from the immediate and routine operations and will therefore not have access to the management accounting information, which in any case may be too detailed for their requirements. This is the case in companies listed on the Stock Exchange. (A listed or quoted company is one whose shares are traded in an open market where demand and supply govern the price of the share.) It is also the case in a number of other businesses where the functions of management are carried out by people other than the owners.

In all these cases the owner needs to know:

- whether the enterprise has done as well as it should have done
- whether the managers have looked after, and made good use of, the resources of the enterprise.

In order to evaluate whether the enterprise has done well and whether resources have been adequately used, it is necessary to compare the results of different enterprises. Information of this type is normally based on past results, and under certain conditions it can be provided by financial accounts.

Owners also need to know:

- how the enterprise is going to fare in the future.

Financial accounting is unlikely to provide this information for a variety of reasons, in particular because it is largely if not exclusively based on the past. Past results may be taken into account as one piece of information among many when one is trying to predict the future, but in a changing world it is unlikely that past results will be repeated because conditions will have changed.

Although there are limitations on the usefulness of the information in annual reports, they are often the only form of report available to an owner who is not involved in the day-to-day activities of the business. Owners therefore have to base their decisions on this information, despite its inadequacies. Thus, for example, a shareholder—who is, after all, a part owner—may use the accounting information contained in the annual report, by comparing the results of the business with those of another business, to decide on whether to sell his or her shares. In practice, the involvement of the shareholder in this process of making comparisons, in the case of a quoted company, is likely to be fairly indirect (for a discussion on this topic see Hines, 1986). This is because most of the information contained in the annual report has already been looked at by the owner's professional advisers—accountants, stockbrokers or financial analysts. The investor and owner are likely to base their decision on the professional advice they receive, rather than relying upon their own interpretation of the information contained in annual reports. This is not to say that they will rely exclusively on expert information or that they will not use the information provided in the annual reports to assist with their decision. The reality is likely to be a mixture, the balance of which will depend on the degree of financial sophistication of the shareholders or owners. The less sophisticated they are, the more reliance they will have to place on their expert advisers.

Lenders

People and organisations lend money in order to earn a return on that money. They are therefore interested in whether the enterprise is making sufficient profit to provide them with their return (usually in the form of interest). This information is normally provided in the statement of financial performance. They are also interested in ensuring that the enterprise will be able to repay the money it has borrowed; therefore they need to ascertain what resources an enterprise controls and what it owes. This information is normally provided in the statement of financial position.

Research in the UK (Berry et al., 1987, 1993) has shown that in practice bankers use a mixture of different approaches to arrive at a lending decision. The choice of approach has been shown to be related to the size of the enterprise. In the case of smaller enterprises the security-based approach, which emphasises the availability of economic resources to meet repayments in the event of business failure, predominates and the emphasis is clearly on the statement of financial position. However, with very large businesses the approach adopted is more likely to be the 'going concern' approach where the emphasis is on the profitability of the enterprise. The importance of published accounting information in the form of annual reports for this group cannot be overemphasised; nearly 100 per cent of respondents to a survey (Berry et al., 1987) said that the reports were very important and always used in making a lending decision. Other research, in Australia, has centred on the ability of bank loan officers to predict failure, using information collected over several years from annual reports (Houghton and Sengupta, 1984).

Suppliers of goods

Goods can be supplied on the basis either that they are paid for when they are supplied or that they are paid for at some agreed date in the future. In each case the supplier will be interested to know whether the enterprise is likely to stay in business and whether it is likely to expand or contract. Both these needs relate to the future and so they can never be adequately met by information in the annual report because this relates to the past.

Suppliers of goods who have not been paid immediately will be interested in assessing the likelihood of getting paid. This need is partially met by the annual report: the statement of financial position shows what resources are controlled by the entity and what is owed, and also gives an indication of the liquidity of the controlled resources. But the statement of financial position has limited usefulness for predicting the future: often the information is many months out of date by the time that it is made public, because in most cases it is only published annually.

Customers

Like suppliers, customers are interested in an enterprise's ability to survive and therefore to carry on supplying them with goods. For example, if you are assembling cars you need to be sure that the suppliers of components are not about to go bankrupt. The importance of this has increased with the introduction of techniques such as just-in-time management. (Briefly, this means that stocks of parts at the production centre are kept to a minimum, reducing the cost of storage space and parts. Parts are delivered to the production centre just in time before the stocks run out.) The customers in this situation need to see that the enterprise is profitable, that it has sufficient resources to pay what it owes, and that it is likely to remain in business and supply components efficiently and on time. Some of these information needs are met at least partially by the statements of financial performance and financial position.

Employees

Employees depend on the survival of the enterprise for their wages and therefore are interested in whether the enterprise is likely to survive. In the long term, an enterprise needs to make a profit in order to survive. The statement of financial performance may assist the employee in assessing the future viability of the company.

The employee may also be interested in ascertaining how well the enterprise is doing, compared with other similar enterprises, for the purposes of wage negotiations, although the accounts are only useful for this purpose if certain conditions are met. The accounts can also be used internally for wage negotiations because they provide evidence about the company's level of profitability and ability to pay.

The government

The government uses accounting information for a number of purposes, the most obvious of which is the levying of taxes. For this purpose it needs to know how much profit has been made. The profit a company reports to shareholders in its statement of financial performance is based on the application of accounting rules or standards, which we will refer to throughout this book. However, the profit upon which a company is assessed for tax purposes is based on the application of the tax rules and regulations. While these rules are often identical with accounting rules, there are instances where they differ. For example, a government may exempt certain income from taxation as an incentive to participants in that industry. This was the case with the gold industry in Australia for many years. Exempt income was not included in gold producers' calculation of their taxable income; however, as it obviously was still income, it was included in their statement of financial performance. The government also uses accounting information to produce industry statistics for the purposes of regulation, etc.

In certain cases, the government is both owner and customer (e.g. some state energy commissions) or public watchdog (e.g. the Environmental Protection Authority). It can combine any one of these roles with other roles, such as regulatory authority (e.g. Australian Securities and Investments Commission). For all these purposes the government uses accounting information.

The general public

The general public requires many different types of information about enterprises in both the public and private sectors. Much of this information is not supplied directly by financial accounts. For example, the public might be interested in the level of pollution resulting from a particular activity.

CASE STUDY 1.1

Good bottom line but how's the environment?

by Geoff Brayshaw

IN this financially driven era of e-commerce and stock trading online, shareholders are demanding more accountability. New and influential shareholders are evolving with an appetite for greater information on company performance.

This is not an issue of share price or dividend but rather a new challenge for companies to meet consumer concerns about environmental and social performance.

These new stakeholders not only hold stocks and research their progress on the Web but as consumers they also research company products and manufacturing methods. They are not satisfied purely by good financials.

...

Companies such as WMC, RGC, North and Body Shop Australia have taken the lead in this area.

More recently, Australian shareholders with issues of environmental performance have questioned North about its uranium mining and Amcor and Wesfarmers about logging.

Issues such as the uranium debate have driven a number of junior explorers from the industry rather than face a shareholder and community backlash.

To try to establish confidence between corporate management and stakeholder scrutiny of corporate ethics, governance statements have been introduced by the Australian Stock Exchange.

Unfortunately, in many cases, these have been viewed as corporate platitudes or motherhood statements with little substance.

…

However, most of the reports published so far are non-standardised and typically unaudited and rarely of any use to financial analysis. The challenge therefore is to adopt a wider range of criteria.

Corporations that seek to provide information relevant to shareholders must first understand how their company is being valued, what measures their shareholders use, how their environmental strategies affect those measures, and how best to gather and organise data that shows the effect of the strategies on the appropriate measures.

Australian, 13 July 1999

North feels the jab

THE move by 122 small investors in North to requisition an extraordinary general meeting (EGM) to question its investment in Energy Resources of Australia, the developer of the Jabiluka uranium project, heralds a new era of shareholder activism.

Last month the North Ethical Shareholders Group, which holds about $1 million worth of stock, called for an EGM, but North complained this would be a costly and unnecessary exercise given it would be held only a short time before the scheduled annual general meeting (AGM) on October 29.

A compromise has since been reached that will see the EGM held on the same day as the AGM.

The North shareholders are being co-ordinated by the Wilderness Society and the radical anti-mining lobby the Mineral Policy Institute (MPI).

'Companies are not always accountable to the broader community,' says the Wilderness Society's Chris Doran. 'But they are always accountable to their shareholders. The EGM process provides an avenue through which shareholders can empower themselves in regards to their ethical and financial concerns.'

On another front, MPI is also associated with the 'Goldbusters' campaign that aims to bring the gold industry to 'a grinding halt'.

Goldbusters wants to hammer 'a few last nails into the coffin of the gold-mining industry' by asking governments and individuals to sell their bullion holdings and consumers to no longer purchase gold jewellery.

'The mining of gold is one of the most environmentally destructive industrial activities presently blighting our planet,' Goldbusters says.

Sydney Morning Herald, Money Supplement, 21 July 1999

Commentary

Both these articles demonstrate the growing importance of shareholders' concerns about companies' treatment of the environment. More and more companies operating in environmentally sensitive areas are disclosing information about their environmental record, and many, like North, are discovering that environmental issues cannot be ignored if they wish to avoid a backlash from shareholders.

From this brief survey of the users of accounting information and the uses to which it can be put, it is clear that it has effects both within the organisation and in the wider commercial environment in which enterprises operate and in which we live. It should also be clear that the environment can use accounting as a tool for enterprise control. Before going on to consider in detail its impact upon the commercial environment and the impact of the commercial environment on accounting we should first consider the limitations of accounting information in order to put its potential impact in context.

Limits on the usefulness of accounting information

It has to be stressed that accounting is only one of a number of sources of information available to decision makers. Other sources of information might be just as important as, if not more important than, the information contained in the accounts available to decision makers. You will have the opportunity to examine this in more detail in 'Problems for discussion and analysis' at the end of this chapter.

However, to give you a flavour of what we are talking about, research into bankers' lending practices (referred to earlier) shows that a banker's personal interview with a client is as important as financial information. This is probably because accounting generally reports only on financial items, i.e. those that can be expressed in financial (monetary) terms, whereas the information that bankers are trying to derive from the interview is more qualitative, i.e. an impression of the ability of the applicant to run a successful business. It is also possible that the information which accounting provides is only of secondary importance: this would be the case where new technology has made the precise costing of a product irrelevant because the product is obsolete.

In general, financial accounting information relates to the past, whereas the decisions that need to be taken normally relate to the future. Thus, unless the past is a reasonable predictor of the future, accounting information will have limited value for this purpose. In the real world, because of the impact of such things as changes in technology, innovations, changing fashions and inflation, the past is unlikely to be a very good predictor of the future.

Besides these problems, there is also the question of what is and what is not included in the financial accounts. For instance, some items which it is generally agreed should be included in financial reports are difficult to measure with any accuracy and thus the figures become subjective. A good example of this problem is an unfinished building. How do we decide on a figure to represent something that is only half complete? Another example is the problem of deciding how long something is going to last. A motor car, for instance, clearly loses value the older it gets; the business might decide that a car ceases to be useful to it after four or five years, but this is to some extent an arbitrary decision because there are many older cars that still serve a useful purpose.

In addition to the problem of deciding how long things will last or what stage of completion has been reached, certain items are difficult to quantify in terms of value and are not easily included in financial reports. For example, the value of a football club is dependent on its ability to attract supporters; this in turn is dependent on its ability to succeed, which is dependent on the abilities of the players, and so on. However, it is difficult to decide what value to place on a player because this value will vary with the player's fitness, etc. Even so, certain football clubs in the Australian Football League attempt to quantify the value of their players. In the United Kingdom and the United States, several basketball, baseball, soccer and gridiron teams also follow this practice.

In addition to the questions raised above, there are many factors concerned with the natural and commercial environment which need to be taken into account but which cannot be adequately included in accounts, although they may be quantifiable in monetary terms. Examples are the potential market for the product, tariff restrictions, export subsidies and environmental issues. If information about these factors were included in the annual reports of a business, a loss of competitive advantage could result.

Finally we have to deal with the fact that accounting information is expressed in monetary terms and assumes that the monetary unit is stable over time. This is patently not the case. Although there has been much discussion on the problems of accounting in times of inflation, no agreed solution has yet been found.

We can conclude from this discussion that, while it is clear that accounting provides some information that is useful to decision makers, we must bear in mind the following important points:

- the information is only a part of that necessary to make 'effective' decisions
- accountancy is an inexact science and depends on a number of judgements and estimates
- the end result of the accounting process can only be as good as the inputs and in times of rising prices some of these inputs are of dubious value
- accounting systems can be counterproductive, e.g. the maximisation of a division's profit may not always ensure the maximisation of the profit of the enterprise.

Nevertheless, it is clear that accounting is vital to the running of a healthy and prosperous enterprise and arguably it is also an essential prerequisite for a prosperous economy. It will therefore be useful to look at accounting in the wider context of the business and its regulatory environment. We examine how the accounting function interacts with and is different from other business functions. We will also examine the various factors which influence the choice of an accounting system, including regulatory and environmental considerations.

Accounting as a business function

The accounting department, like the personnel department, theoretically operates in an advisory capacity only, providing information for managers to make the decisions. In practice, however, the financial elements controlled by the accounting function and the information it generates are so central to the operation of the enterprise that the influence of accounting is often pervasive. Although accounting is essential to the smooth running of the business it does not have as direct an impact as, for example, the buying department or the production line. Its effects are generally more subtle although they may in certain instances be very obvious. For example, if the accounting information indicates that expenses are too high, this may have dramatic repercussions in other functional areas. Training and recruitment budgets may be immediately frozen, affecting the work of the personnel department and other operating departments and possibly reducing both staffing and skills. Alternatively, a decision may be taken to stop expenditure on a current advertising campaign, thus having a direct effect on the work of the marketing department.

Accounting can have unintended effects; for example, if sales representatives are judged solely on their sales this may lead them to sell goods to customers who are unlikely to pay in order to achieve the sales targets set. It can also be a very dangerous tool if used in the wrong way; for example, targets could be set to achieve cost savings on a production line with no account taken of the effect on quality or employee safety.

Similarly, if accounting is used by people who do not understand its limitations it can lead to wrong decisions. If, for example, a person was unaware that accounting, as generally used, takes no account of rising prices, goods could be sold at less than they cost to produce.

The importance of accounting within a business should not be underestimated. It provides the basic information by which managers and owners can judge whether the business is meeting its objectives. Its importance is shown by the high salaries that accountants can command and by the prevalence of accountants on the boards of directors of our major public companies.

Accounting is also different from other business functions in that it is not only a function but also an industry. The accounting industry sells accounting and other advisory services to other businesses and is itself a major employer of graduate labour.

Choice of accounting systems

Accounting is used within business to evaluate alternative strategies such as making a component or buying it in from a supplier, thus shaping business plans and activities. At the same time it is itself a function of the type of activity that a business engages in and of the strategies a business adopts. In other words the accounting system not only influences business strategies but is itself influenced by the goals, size and structure of the organisation. For example, the accounting system that is appropriate for a local builder who does one job at a time and who can clearly identify the amount of time and materials being used on that job is not appropriate for a manufacturing plant which uses one building and many machines to produce multiple products all at the same time. In the latter case, to identify the materials used and the labour inputs for a specific product requires a much more sophisticated system of accounting. Accounting systems are variable and depend on the type of activity or activities in which a business is engaged and on the levels of activity.

Clearly, the organisation's goals will have a major impact on the accounting system it uses; for example, to develop an accounting system with the primary purpose of measuring profit would be wholly inappropriate for a charitable organisation. Similarly the requirements in terms of accounting reports will be very different in the case of a workers' co-operative, Medicare and a profit-oriented company. The co-operative's members are more likely to be interested in their pay and their share of the surplus generated than in the enterprise's profitability. Shareholders in a company, on the other hand, are likely to be more interested in judging overall profitability and comparing that with alternative investments. In the case of Medicare it may be that the owners, i.e. the general public, are primarily interested in the service received rather than its profitability.

Furthermore, the way in which an organisation is structured determines the type of accounting system that is needed. If a brewery operates all of its hotels by putting managers into them, it will need an accounting system that allows for the payment of regular salaries and bonuses based upon achieving preset targets. These targets are normally set in terms of barrelage and so it will need to know what the normal barrelage of each hotel is; it will also need to know the mark-up on spirits, soft drinks, etc. and the approximate mix of sales in order to ensure that its managers are not misappropriating the profits. If, however, it establishes its organisation so that each publican is a tenant of the brewery, a different accounting system will be required, because the publicans are not paid a salary or bonus—their remuneration comes from the profits they make from selling the beers, wines and spirits.

We have already alluded to the effect of the size of an organisation on its accounting system. The larger and more disparate the organisation, the greater the need for organisational controls through a system of accountability which makes managers responsible for the performance of their divisions and which provides reports that can be used by senior managers to evaluate the performance of their subordinates and of the organisation as a whole. As we have already mentioned, it is vital that the accounting system is tailored to the needs of the organisation; otherwise it will not allow management to control the organisation and, indeed, may have dysfunctional effects. Frequently in the case of a small business, little accounting information is available on a day-to-day basis. This may be because the operations are sufficiently simple not to warrant much information but is more likely to be because the owner does not have the skills to produce the information and the costs of hiring the necessary expertise are perceived as outweighing the potential benefits. It is often the case in small businesses that the only time that detailed accounting reports are produced is at the end of the year to meet the needs of the tax collector and when the bank demands them as a prerequisite to granting a loan or extending an overdraft facility.

Regulatory and environmental considerations

In general, the environmental aspects of a business which interact significantly with accounting are: the state, technology and labour. Accounting is also affected by and affects the economy; for example, a country such as Brazil suffering from hyperinflation out of necessity uses costs other than original costs in its accounting reports because the value of the monetary unit in which accounting information is expressed is changing so quickly. We have already discussed the potential uses of accounting information by employees and their organisations such as trade unions. We have mentioned different forms of organisation such as charitable organisations. In the case of the former, there is no requirement for the publication of accounting information, whereas for companies not only the form but also the content of their annual reports is laid down by legislation in the Corporations Law. The Corporations Law specifies Accounting Standards (AASBs) for companies which are reporting entities; the setting of these standards is discussed in Chapter 13. A similar situation prevails in most Western countries, although the importance of legislation in relation to accounting standards varies from country to country. Similarly, the reporting requirements are different in non-capitalist countries where the importance afforded to the statement of financial performance is considerably less. Technology has also had a major effect within the accounting function as accounting systems have been computerised. This has allowed accountants to free themselves from the mundane tasks of recording and to become more involved in decision support and strategic issues. At another level, however, new technology has imposed and is still imposing challenges to accounting thought. Systems that were appropriate in a labour-intensive environment are found to be lacking in the age of flexible manufacturing systems, such as just-in-time management and computer-controlled manufacturing environments.

Economic consequences of accounting information

The development of accounting standards is the responsibility of the appropriate accounting standard-setting board. We discuss the development of accounting standards in Chapter 13. The selection of appropriate accounting policies for a company is the responsibility of management. Where an accounting standard exists, the policies must comply with the standard. In some cases the standard allows a choice of policies and in other cases no standard may exist. In these instances the management of a company has a choice as to the appropriate accounting policy to select.

As we will see in Chapter 2, the primary objective for the standard setters in selecting particular accounting standards is to provide useful information to the users of financial statements. As preparers of financial statements incur costs in complying with accounting standards, the standard setters attempt only to impose requirements where the expected benefits exceed costs.

Managers do not necessarily adopt the same objectives in the way they select appropriate accounting policies for their company. Accounting policies affect the numbers which appear in the financial statements and these numbers can affect the wealth of managers and firms via:

- compensation plans
- debt contracts
- political costs.

Compensation plans

Many companies reward their managers through a fixed salary and an annual bonus. The bonus may be determined as a percentage of net profit. The bonus scheme, it is argued, provides an incentive to managers to increase net profit. Increases in net profit are in the best interests of shareholders. Therefore, the bonus scheme is intended to align the interests of managers more closely to the shareholders.

However, a consequence of the bonus scheme is that managers may also be motivated to increase reported profit by the appropriate selection of income-increasing accounting policies. Thus, this strategy may increase reported profit when the underlying profitability of the company has not increased. This has been described as a cosmetic increase in profits rather than a real increase in profits.

Debt contracts

Many lenders require a contract before lending money to a borrower. Such contracts may impose certain restrictions on the borrower. For example, a new loan contract may contain a clause which states that, if the borrower's level of debt exceeds a certain level, the loan must be immediately repaid in full. The measurement of the level of debt is based on the total liabilities figure as reported in the borrower's statement of financial position. Another common clause in debt contracts relates to the number of times the net profit covers interest expense.

These clauses in the debt contracts are based on accounting numbers as reported in the company's financial statements. Therefore, if a company is approaching the limits of a clause in a debt contract, there are incentives for managers to select appropriate accounting policies which allow the company to avoid being in violation of the debt contract.

Political costs

Political costs refer to the costs imposed on a company via regulation, taxation and closer public scrutiny of its affairs. Some accountants argue that bigger firms like BHP are subject to more political costs. Size is often measured in terms of net profit, total assets and total sales. These are all numbers determined by the application of accounting policies. Therefore, there are incentives for managers of large companies to select profit-decreasing accounting policies.

A further argument suggests that incentives exist for certain types of businesses, such as telephone or electricity organisations, to choose profit-decreasing accounting policies. This choice is made at a time when the organisation wishes to increase the charges for its service. It is politically more acceptable to increase charges when reported profits have decreased.

Therefore, political costs create incentives for managers of large organisations to select accounting policies which decrease reported profits. This clearly is the reverse of the argument under compensation plans. The compensation plans argument is where the manager's self-interest prevails. With political costs, it is the interests of the company which prevail. Ultimately, if the large companies attract lower political costs its managers will be rewarded.

The dual reason for selection of accounting policies

The selection of appropriate accounting policies may be based on the objective of providing useful information to users, or it may be based on economic consequences. These two objectives need not be mutually exclusive and, as you read the chapters which follow, you should consider the role of both these objectives. Shareholders and lenders may initiate strategies to mitigate against the incentives for managers to select accounting policies based on economic consequences.

In this event, the selection of accounting policies is more likely to be based on the objective of providing useful information to users. In the next section we discuss the important issue of ethics in business and accounting. A small ethics case study is located at the end of each chapter.

CASE STUDY 1.2

Fortune rings up earnings

by Hui Yuk-min

FORTUNE Tele.com Holdings' net profit in the first quarter to June 30 jumped nearly 10-fold to HK$42.6 million on the back of a change in accounting methods.

The mobile-phone distributor, however, attributed most of the increase to a HK$39.4 million exceptional gain from the valuation of its 9 per cent stake in PacificNet.com.

Revenue at the company, which is listed on the Growth Enterprise Market, increased 15 per cent from a year earlier to HK$365 million.

Fortune Tele.com cannot realise the HK$39.4 million paper gain until one year has elapsed because of a non-disposal agreement with PacificNet.com.

'We have a one-year share lock-up period for those shares, starting from July 21,' Fortune Tele.com financial controller Alik Yong said.

Stripping out the exceptional paper gain, Fortune Tele.com's net profit for the period was only HK$3.2 million, a 17.5 per cent drop in net earnings when compared with the previous corresponding period.

Mr Yong said the company was able to book the paper gain from the investment in PacificNet.com after it changed its accounting treatment of the stake by booking it as 'other investments' instead of 'investment securities' during the period.

Under the new accounting method the value of the securities would have to mark to the market price on the closing day of the accounting period. The difference between the carrying cost and the market price would then be booked into the profit and loss account.

However, if interest in listed securities were classified as 'investment securities', it would only be booked at cost of investment under the company's accounts. No exceptional paper gain or loss would be booked.

Mr Yong said the change in the accounting period was not intended to boost Fortune Tele.com's earnings during the period, but to better reflect the value of those securities in the company's accounts.

'We changed our accounting treatment only because our relationship with the company [PacificNet.com] has changed,' Mr Yong said.

'When we first bought into the company we intended it to be a long-term strategic partnership, but now we are considering it as an investment holding,' said Mr Yong.

Fortune Tele.com paid about HK$12 million for its stake in Nasdaq-listed electronic-commerce application solutions provider PacificNet.com.

Those shares were worth HK$55.7 million based on PacificNet.com's Wednesday closing price, compared with about HK$64 million valuation that Fortune Tele.com booked in its accounts during the period.

The counter has dropped 12.7 per cent since June 30 when Fortune Tele.com closed its first-quarter accounts for the financial year to March 30.

Shares in Fortune Tele.com yesterday eased five cents, or 2.6 per cent, to close at HK$1.87, compared with its HK$2.50 issue price.

South China Morning Post, Business Post,
11 August 2000

Commentary

The article shows how Fortune Tele.com Holdings was able to increase reported profit by a change in accounting rules. The company stated that the aim of this change was not to boost earnings for the year, but rather to better reflect the value of those securities in the company's accounts.

A recurring theme in this book is the impact of accounting rules on a company's reported results. By the time you complete the chapters on financial accounting, you should better appreciate how accounting rules impact on a company's financial statements.

You should understand that, while Fortune has changed the way it accounts for its investment in PacificNet.com, the actual investment has not changed. Does this change in profit, resulting from a change in an accounting rule, make Fortune more valuable? The answer is 'no', and there should consequently be no change in the value of Fortune's shares based on this higher reported profit. We will say more on this topic in Chapter 14.

Ethics in business and accounting

Figures show that corporate fraud now costs the US more than $400 billion per annum and in Australia it is $16 billion. Based on this amount, fraud in Australia is costing each household about $2500 per annum. How does a trader like Nick Leeson manage to run up billions of dollars in trading losses and bankrupt a bank like Barings Ltd? How do we solve problems of corporate fraud and embezzlement?

Dr Rushworth Kidder, president of the US-based Institute for Global Ethics, argues that this will not happen if companies adopt codes of ethics and create departments responsible for monitoring the codes. Employees must receive training about the codes of ethics and should be required to follow them.

Much has been written on business or professional ethics (see References on p. 23), but very few writers have attempted to define this term, perhaps believing that it needs no definition. What do we mean by ethics?

One could go back several thousand years and note that the word is derived from the Greek *ethikos* (from *ethos* meaning 'custom' or 'usage'). As employed by Aristotle, the term included both the idea of 'character' and that of 'disposition'. Ethics means, according to the *Macquarie Dictionary*, 'pertaining to morals'. From the foregoing it would appear that ethics is concerned with moral behaviour, and by 'moral' we mean that part of human behaviour that is formed primarily by national culture, parental influence, peer groups and religion.

A review of some of the literature on ethics provides some interesting insights into the important area of ethics. Some writers refer to business ethics, which in itself suggests that a particular set of ethics exists for business. This, in fact, is totally untrue as ethics apply to all parts of life and to think that you discard one set of ethics and adopt another as you enter the office is false. Ethics are like your skin: they go everywhere with you.

While it may be difficult to define ethics, Dr Michael Josephson, in an essay entitled 'The need for ethics education in accounting' (1992), identified the following characteristics of an ethical person:

- *honesty and integrity:* honesty is obviously important but we should really be referring to complete honesty or perhaps to not being dishonest. For example, a six-year-old student, when asked by his teacher if he had eaten any of the chocolates she had left on her desk, replied 'No'. The fact was that he had taken the chocolates but had not eaten any. It could be argued that he did not actually lie, but he was still dishonest. Integrity refers to having the courage of one's convictions and acting on principle. Further, it is important that we have *good* principles. A serial killer who believes all prostitutes are evil is acting in accordance with his own convictions, but he is not a person of integrity
- *promise keeping:* fulfilling a commitment
- *fidelity or loyalty:* the need to be loyal. But loyal to whom or what? The problem of conflicting loyalties is often the cause of ethical problems. In a company an employee could be loyal to his immediate boss, the general manager, the board of directors or the shareholders. The company itself exists in law but it is the people within a company that give it life. In a family relationship, for example, one person can be a mother, a wife, a daughter, a sister, a daughter-in-law, a sister-in-law, an auntie, a cousin and a niece. These different roles invariably lead to situations where being loyal to one party may involve disloyalty to another
- *fairness:* again this is a subjective term and what is fair to one party may be unfair to another. Consider an umpire in a football game. When he awards a penalty against one side, the supporters of that side often consider the decision unfair while the supporters of the side awarded the penalty consider the decision to be fair
- *caring:* caring for others is perhaps best summed up by the rule 'Do unto others as you would have them do unto you'
- *respect:* while you may not care for everyone you should give them respect
- *responsibility:* complying with the laws of the country and being part of a community
- *excellence:* we endeavour to do our job as well as we possibly can. We expect a surgeon about to remove our appendix to be competent to do this
- *accountability:* to be ethical means to be accountable for your actions.

It is probably no coincidence that Josephson has identified ten characteristics of an ethical person in the same way as Moses descended from Mount Sinai with the Ten Commandments. Some would argue that an individual's ethical values are better taught in a church than in a business school. A survey on professional ethics was conducted for CPA Australia by Leung and Cooper in 1994. The 1500 respondents to the survey indicated that family upbringing, conduct of peers and practices in the accounting field were the most important factors affecting the ethical conduct of accountants.

Why then do we have huge problems of fraud and embezzlement? Why do people not behave in an ethical manner? Josephson (1992) identified the following five reasons:

- *self-deception:* to believe somehow that because it is business it does not matter. Phrases such as 'everybody does it' or 'to get along go along' reflect self-deception. A common example is cheating on one's income tax return on the assumption that everybody else does. Just imagine what the streets of a city would be like if everybody dumped rubbish on the street because 'everybody does it'
- *self-indulgence:* the defence for unethical behaviour is the assertion that it was done for someone else's benefit
- *self-protection:* many examples of fraud start from one incident and grow from there. In his book, *Rogue Trader*, Nick Leeson contends that his first illegal trade was done to cover a small error by a colleague. This small error grew to a $16-billion loss
- *self-righteousness:* the assertion that one is right no matter what others think. No doubt Adolf Hitler considered he was right
- *faulty reasoning:* not correctly estimating the costs of being ethical versus unethical.

Generally the costs of being ethical ('I will lose my job') are overestimated while the costs of being unethical ('I won't get caught' or 'I will repay this later') are underestimated. In his paper 'Why I compromised my professional code of ethics', McKinley L. Tabor recounts the costs to his life of unethical behaviour. The costs included imprisonment, loss of family and friends, respect and other costs, all of which were in excess of what he embezzled from his employer.

What is the relationship between business and ethics? Is ethics good for business? The answer to such a question depends on how we assess what is good for business. If we use short-term profitability then it may be that on some occasions doing what is ethical may not enhance short-term profitability. It may well improve long-term profitability, but if you are not going to be in the company in the long term, then what is the incentive to be ethical? This raises issues about the objectives of business. Is there some conflict between the goal of profit maximisation and ethical behaviour? Is there a conflict between self-interest and ethical behaviour?

Two frameworks developed by ethicists which are relevant to our discussion on ethics are *utilitarianism* and *deontology*. *Utilitarianism* judges the moral correctness of an action based entirely on its consequences. The action that should be pursued is the one where the favourable consequences to all parties outweigh the unfavourable consequences. The consequences to all parties that will be affected must be included.

In *deontology* the underlying nature of the action determines its correctness. There are two types of deontologists. Some feel the action itself is the only thing to be considered and so lying, for example, is always unacceptable. Other *deontologists* are of the opinion, for example, that the nature of the action and its consequences in a particular situation should be considered and so lying in particular circumstances may be acceptable.

Given the enormous costs of fraud and embezzlement, the potential gains to society of ethical behaviour are significant. The difficulty is in developing an appropriate code of ethical behaviour which is adhered to by all people in business.

Business or professional behaviour is governed by sets of rules laid down by the controlling bodies; members of the organisation or profession are expected to follow these rules. In some professions, 'ethics' has come to mean these rules. Professional ethics should be regarded as 'standards of professional conduct (the ethics of lawyers)' (Statsky, 1985).

The problems of the 1980s can in part be attributed to some accountants substituting 'the rules' for genuine 'ethical behaviour'. For example, it was acceptable to follow the requirements of the Corporations Law, even when, by following the strict letter of the law, one was able to gain an unfair advantage which did not reflect the spirit of the law.

Business or professional ethics is a marrying of the rules of society with the moral principles by which a society is judged. The question of business ethics is well illustrated in this story by W. Albrecht (1992).

> There was once a very wealthy man who loved his money so much that he did not have many friends. In fact, he had only three friends. First, he had a lawyer friend who helped him structure his transactions to take advantage of other people. Second, he had an accountant friend who helped him count his money. And third, he had a minister of religion to whom he went every Sunday to confess the fact that he had taken advantage of others during the week. When he got old and was about to die, he called his three friends together and said, 'I have been wealthy all my life and I cannot stand going to the grave poor. I am going to give you each an envelope with $50 000 in it. I want you to promise me that when I die you will go to my casket and each deposit the envelope in the casket'. They all promised that they would. A short time later the rich man died. As the three friends passed by the casket, each deposited an envelope. The casket was sealed and the body was buried. Not long after, the minister developed a guilty conscience; he called the other two and said, 'We have to meet and talk about this'. When they met he said, 'You know, I thought about the poor members of my congregation. I thought about that money rotting down there in the grave and I just could not do it. I only put $25 000 in and I kept $25 000 to help the poor'. Then the lawyer said, 'If you really want to know the truth, he had asked me for free legal advice so often that I felt he owed it to me, so I kept $25 000 and only put $25 000 in'. Finally, the accountant said, 'You know I cannot believe you would do that. I cannot believe you would both be unethical. I want you to know that in my envelope was a cheque for the full $50 000'.

As this is a text about accounting, let us look at three of several choices available to the accountant:

- he could have put an empty envelope in the grave, as the deceased only asked him to deposit the envelope. This would have been following the letter of the request but not the spirit
- he could have done what he did in the story. Here he followed the letter of the request and some would say a small measure of the spirit of the request. Of course, we know the cheque will never be cashed and that the accountant is $50 000 better off. Is the accountant guilty of stealing the money?
- he could have carried out the deceased's wishes to the full, following the letter and the spirit of the request: that is, deposited the full $50 000 in cash in the casket.

As a professional person, the accountant was obliged to carry out in full the wishes of his client and friend regardless of his personal feelings or beliefs. Business or professional ethics means just that: clever or smart alternatives are not acceptable.

Remember, one of the characteristics of an ethical person referred to by Josephson (1992) was promise keeping. All three individuals should not have promised to put the envelope in the grave if in fact they knew they could not do it. The lawyer should have asked for his unpaid time to be paid by the wealthy friend. The minister should have asked the friend to consider donating to the church. The accountant did not comply with the spirit of his friend's request and all three acted unethically.

As noted earlier, in some way, the lack of ethics was responsible for some of the gains made by some of the high fliers in the 1980s. However, they have all since paid high costs for being unethical.

Professional accountants, in the many spheres in which they are of service to the general public and business community, should always be seen to be ethically correct. To this end, each of the major professional accounting bodies in all countries has developed a code of professional ethics. The code is to assist members in dealing with different types of situations in their professional lives. The CPA Australia survey on professional ethics asked respondents to rank various types of ethical issues. The results showed that the issues of greatest concern were:

- client proposal for tax evasion (83.3 per cent)
- client proposal to manipulate financial statements (80.2 per cent)
- conflict of interest (79.3 per cent)
- presenting financial information in the most proper manner so as not to deceive users (76.3 per cent)
- failure to maintain technical competence in the discharge of duties (71.3 per cent)
- coping with superior's instructions to carry out unethical acts (70.6 per cent).

The rules of the professional bodies are intended not only to guide, but in some ways to provide protection from the above types of ethical dilemmas for accountants. However, there are always some who are tempted to move around the rules for personal gain, and in the long run the profession and society are the losers. When dealing with accountants, individuals expect, and deserve to receive, conduct which will enhance the status of all who belong to that profession. Ethics in business and accounting is a matter of judgement based on rules and moral obligations.

There are a number of good texts available on this issue and reference to them is made at the end of this chapter. Before completing this chapter we briefly examine careers in accounting and professional membership.

Careers in accounting

Accountants are employed in many different areas in both the private and public sectors. This section provides only a brief overview of the different careers for accountants.

Accounting firms

Most accounting firms operate as a sole proprietorship or a partnership. The most significant firms are large firms like Arthur Andersen, PricewaterhouseCoopers and Ernst & Young. Large firms provide services in the areas of auditing, tax and management consulting.

Accountants in accounting firms are working in public accounting. They are members of either the Institute of Chartered Accountants in Australia or CPA Australia.

Industry and commerce

All companies, both large and small, employ accountants to perform many different duties. These duties include the preparation of financial statements for external reporting purposes. Large- and medium-sized companies also employ accountants in internal auditing. The internal auditor's role is to ensure that the internal controls in the company are adequate to safeguard the company's assets. Large- and medium-sized companies also often employ tax accountants to do all the work involved with income tax, payroll tax, goods and services tax, and other indirect taxes. They also employ cost accountants, whose job is to generate information about the behaviour of costs, help establish budgets and generally assist management in controlling costs and establishing appropriate prices for the company's products.

Government

The government is also a large employer of accountants, who work in all areas at the local, state and federal levels. Accountants can be found doing similar work to their private sector counterparts: preparing financial reports, auditing, tax work and cost accounting. Departments such as the Treasury and the Auditor-General's Office obviously employ many accountants. Other departments, such as Health, Housing and Local Government; Employment, Education and Training; and Tourism, also employ accountants to carry out all types of accounting work.

Professional membership

Most accountants in Australia are members of either the Institute of Chartered Accountants in Australia (ICAA) or CPA Australia (CPAA). Graduates in accounting from the TAFE sector tend to become members of the National Institute of Accountants (NIA).

The ICAA and CPAA have different categories of membership. Graduates are initially admitted as associates. They must then complete a postgraduate program and have three years' practical experience before advancing in their membership. Finally, a public practice certificate is required for all principals in public accounting firms.

Summary

In this chapter we have tried to give an idea of what accounting is and how it pervades both the internal workings of organisations and the external commercial environment. It can be seen to be at one level a functional area of business and at an external level an important determinant of business survival through its effect on shareholders, lenders, employees, etc. We have shown that there is no perfect accounting report that will meet the needs of all users, and that the needs of users vary. For example, in the case of a small business the owner may wish to show a low profit to reduce the potential tax bill, but may need to show a high profit in order to persuade a banker to lend the business money. We have shown that accounting will be useful only if it is used correctly and if its limitations are understood. A failing business will still fail even though it has an excellent accounting system; on the other hand, potentially successful businesses have been allowed to go bankrupt because the accounting system did not give any warning signs or gave them too late to allow management to take action to rectify the situation.

The issue of ethics in accounting and business was then discussed. It is difficult to define ethics, but ten characteristics of ethical behaviour were identified. Ethics are like your skin, they go everywhere with you. It is not something you adopt just for the work place. The important principle is that business and professional people should act in an ethical manner. Accountants have a professional code of ethics and this should help accountants to deal with ethical dilemmas, and guide them with regard to what is appropriate ethical behaviour.

The economic consequences of accounting policies can influence a manager's choice of accounting policies. Accounting numbers are used in various contracts and this, it is argued, creates incentives for managers to choose accounting policies based on their impact on the numbers in the contracts. Managerial compensation and debt contracts create incentives for managers to favour income-increasing accounting policies. Political costs create incentives for managers of large companies to favour income-decreasing accounting policies.

References

Accounting Principles Board, 1970. *Statement No. 4: Basic Concepts and Accounting Principles Underlying Financial Statements of Business Enterprises*, AICPA.

Albrecht, W.S. (ed.), 1992. *Ethical Issues in the Practice of Accounting*, South-Western.

American Accounting Association, 1966. *A Statement of Basic Accounting Theory*.

American Institute of Certified and Public Accountants, 1973. *Objectives of Financial Statements*.

Berry, A., Citron, D., and Jarvis, R., 1987. *The Information Needs of Bankers Dealing with Large and Small Companies. Certified Accountants Research Report 7*, Certified Accountants Publications.

Berry, A., Faulkner, S., Hughes, M., and Jarvis, R., 1993. *Bank Lending: Beyond the Theory*, Chapman and Hall.

Hines, R.D., 1986. 'Are annual reports used by shareholders?', *The Chartered Accountant in Australia*, March, pp. 46–52.

Houghton, K.A., and Sengupta, R., 1984. 'The effect of prior probability disclosure and information set construction on bankers' ability to predict failure', *Journal of Accounting Research*, vol. 22, no. 2, pp. 768–75.

Josephson, M.S., 1992. 'The need for ethics education in accounting', in *Ethical Issues in the Practice of Accounting*, Albrecht,W.S. (Editor), South-Western.

Leung, P., and Cooper, B.J., 1994. *Professional Ethics: A Survey of Australian Accountants*, Ethics Centre of Excellence, Australian Society of CPAs publication.

Parker, R.H., 1986. *Macmillan Dictionary of Accounting*, Macmillan Press Ltd.

Statsky, W.P., 1985. *West's Legal Thesaurus/Dictionary: A Resource for the Writer and the Computer Researcher*, West Publishing Company.

Tabor, M.L., 1992. 'Why I compromised my professional code of ethics', in *Ethical Issues in the Practice of Accounting*, Albrecht, W.S. (Editor), South-Western.

Review questions

1   For what purposes is accounting information used
    a   by the individual?
    b   by the enterprise?

2   Who are the users of accounting information and which accounting reports do they normally use?

3   What are the needs of internal users? Can you identify any other needs of internal users? If so, can you suggest how these would be met?

4   What are the limitations of accounting information?

5   Examples were given of certain limitations. Can you give examples of your own?

6   What are the major determinants of a useful accounting system?

7   What are the challenges for ethics in business? Are they different for accountants?

8   Is there a conflict between self-interest and ethical behaviour?

9   How do you think you will handle your future ethical problems? Can you do anything now to make it easier to handle your future concerns?

10   If you work for an accounting firm, whose perspective should you take—the firm's, the client's, the user's, or your own?

11   What are the economic consequences of accounting policy choice?

Problems for discussion and analysis

1 Refer to the 1999 consolidated figures in the Woolworths financial statements in Appendix 1.
   a What is the name of the auditing firm?
   b In 1998 and 1999, how many executives earned more than $1 million?
   c Is there an employee share plan? Who is eligible?

2 In fewer than 100 words, detail your understanding of the word 'ethics'.

3 Corporate fraud is estimated at $16 billion per annum in Australia. Is it possible to regulate against fraud?

4 Discuss what information you believe would be useful to the following groups of report users:
   a employees
   b investors
   c regulators
   d suppliers of goods and services
   e customers.

5 It was pointed out that accounting information is only a part of the input to the decision-making process. In order to expand your understanding of the role of accounting information, for the situation outlined below, identify
   a the accounting information that would be relevant
   b any other information that would be relevant.

   Head & Co. is in business making navigation equipment and wishes to diversify into the production of hang gliders. The business is based in Sydney but the owners may be willing to move. The owners have little knowledge about the market for hang gliders but feel that there is money to be made in that field.

6 You are considering buying a small retail store selling electrical equipment. The selling agent is very enthusiastic. What non-financial information should you be requesting?

7 Tom was left some money in his mother's will and decided that he should give up his job and go into business for himself. While the lawyers were still sorting out his mother's estate, he started looking round for a suitable business. After a short time, he identified a small boat-building business that he felt was worth investing in. He was still uncertain how much his mother had left him but thought that it was probably between $80 000 and $100 000. The boat-building business was for sale for $200 000 and so, assuming that he could finance the remainder, he engaged an accountant to check the books of the business and report back to him. As proof of his good faith, he deposited with the business agents $2000 which he had in savings.

   The report from the accountant confirmed his initial impression that the business was worth investing in and so he paid the accountant's modest fee of $1000 in full. At this stage he discussed his plans more fully with his bank manager, who was duly impressed with the professional approach taken by Tom.

   The bank manager pointed out that Tom had no business experience and therefore was a high risk from the bank's point of view. However, in view of their long-standing relationship the bank was prepared to take a chance and said that it would lend Tom 40 per cent of the purchase price.

On the basis of this, Tom signed a conditional agreement to buy the boat-building business. A short time after this he received from the lawyers a letter stating that his inheritance from his mother amounted to only $60 000. He could not raise the additional finance to purchase the boat-building business and so withdrew from the agreement, recovered his $2000 deposit, and purchased a yacht with the intention of doing charter work to the Caribbean.

Required:

Discuss the point at which, in your opinion, the accounting process should begin, giving reasons for your point of view. Pay particular attention to the dual needs of Tom as an owner and as a manager.

8   The No-Returns Rubber Company is considering setting up a new manufacturing plant which will produce rubber arbuthnots to be used in the manufacture of nuclear-powered frisbees. Discuss what information the managers are likely to require in order to make an informed decision about the viability of this project. Factors to be taken into account should include financial issues, health and safety considerations and also the possible social and legal issues which may arise from the manufacture of non-biodegradable substances, such as rubber arbuthnots and nuclear items. Discuss how you think these considerations can be incorporated into a costing of the project.

9   Non-financial information was identified in this chapter as an aid to evaluating an enterprise. These days, numbers are frequently assigned to various things. If the persons/things listed below were crucial to your enterprise and had to be insured, how would you value them? What financial information would you require to assist you in your decision making?
    a   An elite football player
    b   The *Mona Lisa*
    c   The Sydney Opera House
    d   The Prime Minister

10   Scasboro Beach is a beautiful beach in Bondavia. The surrounding residential area is very attractive because of the beach and the lovely views out to the ocean. After a great deal of negotiation, the Coastal Development Company obtained a permit from the local shire council to erect a 12-storey five-star hotel, which would encroach onto the lovely beach and sand dune area. Prior to this approval, the highest building permitted at Scasboro Beach was three storeys.

Construction began immediately. At this time a legal challenge to the hotel was lodged by a local ratepayers' association and environmental groups. They wanted the permit declared void because the planned structure would obstruct views of existing property owners as well as cause damage to sand dunes in the area.

After the Coastal Development Company had invested $500 000 in the Scasboro Hotel project, a court held with the plaintiffs and ordered demolition of the site as well as total restoration of the area. This would cost approximately $200 000. The company lost an appeal to a higher court.

(Adapted from R.G. May, G. Mueller and Williams, *A New Introduction to Financial Accounting*, Prentice Hall, 1975, Chapter 1, Exercise 1–2.)

Required:

    a Discuss how you might measure the economic worth of the project before the decision of
        i the lower court
        ii the higher court.
    b What problems do you envisage in making such measurements?
    c What losses were sustained and who sustained the losses in this case?

11 At the beginning of time there was a small dwelling of cave men and women who elected themselves a leader called Ugg. Ugg's responsibilities were to restore peace and order into the dwelling which had become unsettled due to a recent outbreak of stealing.

Ugg was a very intelligent cave man and he began thinking that if every cave person accounted for their belongings, then less stealing would happen. Furthermore, if cave people paid him some kind of 'due' in respect of their belongings, thieves would be deterred because the more belongings a cave person had, the more in dues he or she would have to give Ugg. Ugg decided to call this due the 'rock tax'.

The next day Ugg announced the rock tax to the dwelling. He explained to the cave people his thoughts from the previous day and asked for grunts of approval for the rock tax. These outweighed the grunts for disapproval so he then proceeded to outline the rock tax guidelines. These were:
a one large brown fur equalled 50 morsels of meat
b one small brown fur equalled 30 morsels of meat
c one large black fur equalled two large brown furs
d one small black fur equalled three small brown furs
e for every ten morsels of meat, one large rock had to be given to Ugg, which would help to build a wall around the whole dwelling. The tax would be paid once every 300 days commencing from the next day.

Ugg also said that he would personally check every cave person's rock-cave to make sure truthful accounts were given.

Two of the oldest members of the dwelling, Thug and Olga, thought Ugg's rock tax was the best announcement they had ever heard and proceeded to add up their furs and morsels. Thug calculated he had six large brown furs, two small brown furs and five small black furs in addition to the 34 morsels of meat he had stored in his rock-fridge. Thug had exchanged three small brown furs for his rock-fridge some 400 days ago. Olga counted two large brown furs, ten large black furs and nine small black furs in her rock-cabin. She also counted 22 meat morsels in her rock-fridge. Olga had exchanged one large black fur for the rock-fridge 200 days ago.

Required:

Imagining you lived in this dwelling, calculate:
a the amount of tax that Thug and Olga should give Ugg
b how Thug and Olga would pay their tax to Ugg.

(Adapted from R. Anthony and J. Reece, *Accounting: Text and Cases*, 8th edn, Richard D. Irwin Inc., 1988, Chapter 1, Case 1–2, and R.G. May, G. Mueller and Williams, *A New Introduction to Financial Accounting*, Prentice Hall, 1975, Chapter 1, Exercise 1–2.)

Ethics case study

You have been hired by Jim's Towing Service, a sole proprietorship, to prepare the tax return for the business. Upon checking the bank statements and the cash books of the business you discover that Jim has not included in the revenue any cash received when customers paid cash. Only the amounts received from insurance companies have been included in the revenue.

Discuss:

what you should do.

The Conceptual Framework

Learning objectives

At the end of this chapter you should be able to:

1 explain what is meant by the term 'conceptual framework'

2 understand some of the reasons for establishing a Conceptual Framework

3 discuss the stages in the Australian Conceptual Framework

4 explain the terms 'reporting entity', 'general-purpose financial report', 'asset', 'liability', 'expense', 'revenue' and 'equity'

5 understand the objective of general-purpose financial reporting and the role of relevant and reliable information.

NOTE TO INSTRUCTORS: Instructors may wish to defer consideration of this chapter until later in the course. However, the following terms, defined in this chapter, are used throughout the text: assets, liabilities, expenses, revenues, equity. These terms are restated in Chapter 4.

Introduction

In Chapter 1 we discussed the objectives of accounting reports and the influences of users on financial reporting. We also discussed the limitations of accounting information and the role of accounting in business, its effect on business and some of the factors which influence accounting. We mentioned the Conceptual Framework which the accounting profession in Australia has been developing since 1987. Other standard-setting bodies, including the International Accounting Standards Committee (IASC) have also developed their own conceptual frameworks.

The purpose of this chapter is to briefly examine what is meant by the term 'conceptual framework'; the development of the Conceptual Framework in Australia; and definitions of key accounting terms from the Conceptual Framework. The chapter concludes by briefly examining the need for and the impact of the Conceptual Framework.

What is the Conceptual Framework?

The Conceptual Framework is an attempt to develop a theory of accounting in order to assist accountants in determining how a particular transaction ought to be accounted for. As we indicated in Chapter 1, the preparation of financial statements involves many decisions about how to record certain transactions. To assist accountants in making these decisions, certain rule-making bodies (we refer to these as standard-setting bodies) have been established in most Western countries. In Australia we have the Australian Accounting Standards Board (AASB). Standard-setting bodies are responsible for developing standards (rules) to assist accountants in recording certain difficult types of transactions.

We would expect standards to be developed from some underlying theory, but in practice they have been determined on an *ad hoc* basis. Often a principle or practice is declared to be 'right' because it is generally accepted; but a principle or practice may not necessarily gain general acceptance even though it is 'right' (Solomons, 1986). We will discuss the standard-setting process in Chapter 13.

In recent years, standard-setting bodies have been concerned with developing a conceptual framework to provide the theory from which accounting standards can then be developed. For example, in 1978 the Financial Accounting Standards Board (FASB) in the US defined the Conceptual Framework as:

a coherent system of interrelated objectives and fundamentals that is expected to lead to consistent standards and that prescribes the nature, function and limits of financial accounting and reporting.

In Australia the purpose of the Conceptual Framework is similar, according to the statement in *ED42: Guide to Proposed Statements of Accounting Concepts*:

The Conceptual Framework is a set of interrelated concepts which will define the nature, subject, purpose and broad content of financial reporting. It will be an explicit rendition of the thinking which is governing the decision making of the Accounting Standards Board (AcSB) and Public Sector Accounting Standards Board (PSASB) when they set down requirements, including accounting standards. The issuance of Statements of Accounting Concepts will fundamentally alter the nature of accounting requirements in this country. [AARF, 1987]

Key Concept 2.1

The Conceptual Framework

The Conceptual Framework is a set of interrelated concepts which define the nature, subject, purpose and broad content of general-purpose financial reporting.

Key Concept 2.2

A general-purpose financial report

A general-purpose financial report is a financial report intended to meet the information needs common to users who are unable to command the preparation of reports so as to satisfy, specifically, all of their information needs. (SAC 2, para. 5)

Therefore a Conceptual Framework attempts to establish concepts or ideas which determine how financial reports are prepared for general users. It is an attempt to establish the foundations for the preparation of general-purpose financial reports. It addresses basic questions like: What is the purpose of financial reporting? What entities should prepare general-purpose financial reports? Who are the users of general-purpose financial reports? What are assets, liabilities, revenues, expenses and equity? How should these items be measured and displayed?

In the next section we examine the Conceptual Framework in Australia and its development. The definitions of 'assets', 'liabilities', 'revenues', 'expenses' and 'equity' are explained and the definitions are used throughout this book.

Objectives of the Conceptual Framework

Fewer Accounting Standards

Statements of Accounting Concepts are expected to provide a framework which will enable the resolution of accounting problems without the need to issue an Accounting Standard on every occasion. This should result in fewer Accounting Standards and help to minimise what some see as the problem of 'standards overload'. This problem is concerned with the time and costs involved in preparing general-purpose financial reports which must comply with a large number of Accounting Standards.

More consistent Accounting Standards

Some Accounting Standards will still be required; because they conform with the Conceptual Framework, they will be more consistent with each other.

Improved communication

There is already improved communication among accountants and between the standard-setting bodies and their constituents in Australia as a result of the Conceptual Framework project. All parties are now using common definitions for items such as assets, liabilities, revenues, expenses and equity.

Defence against politicisation

As we will discuss in Chapter 13, the standard-setting process often involves lobbying by interested parties to try to influence the standard-setting bodies. A set of concise and well-defined concepts should enhance the credibility of financial reporting and enable the standard-setting bodies to defend particular Accounting Standards on the basis that they are consistent with the Conceptual Framework. The setting of Accounting Standards will always be a political process to some extent. However, a Conceptual Framework should serve to reduce the ability of lobby groups to influence the standard-setting process to achieve their own self-serving objectives which are not in the public interest.

The Australian Conceptual Framework

The development of the Conceptual Framework in Australia commenced in 1987. The approach adopted is illustrated in Figure 2.1.

The Conceptual Framework will evolve in Australia through the release of Statements of Accounting Concepts. Statements of Accounting Concepts should be followed by members of the accounting profession when preparing general-purpose financial reports.

Compliance with Statements of Accounting Concepts was changed from mandatory to non-mandatory from 1 January 1994. The definitions of the elements of financial statements are already incorporated into several Accounting Standards. It is expected that other aspects from the Statements of Accounting Concepts will be incorporated into the Accounting Standards. This, together with the knowledge that the standard-setting boards will continue to use the Conceptual Framework to help resolve new issues, attests to the importance of the Statements of Accounting Concepts.

Although compliance with Statements of Accounting Concepts is not mandatory, members of the profession must comply with Statements of Accounting Standards when preparing general-purpose financial reports. Accounting Standards are more specific than Accounting Concepts and prescribe certain accounting and disclosure requirements for certain types of transactions, e.g. depreciation or goodwill, or for certain types of industry, e.g. the mining industry. We will discuss Accounting Standards in more detail in Chapter 13.

Figure 2.1 shows the stages involved in the development of the Conceptual Framework. The various stages are now considered in turn.

Stages of development of the Conceptual Framework

Definition of financial reporting

This stage involves determining what constitutes financial reporting and therefore the scope of Statements of Accounting Concepts and Accounting Standards. What type of information should be reported in general-purpose financial reports? This question should be resolved after taking into consideration the skills of the accountant and the expectations of the users of general-purpose financial reports. For example, should they contain information about the impact of the entity's operations on the natural environment? This and other questions should be resolved in this stage of the Conceptual Framework.

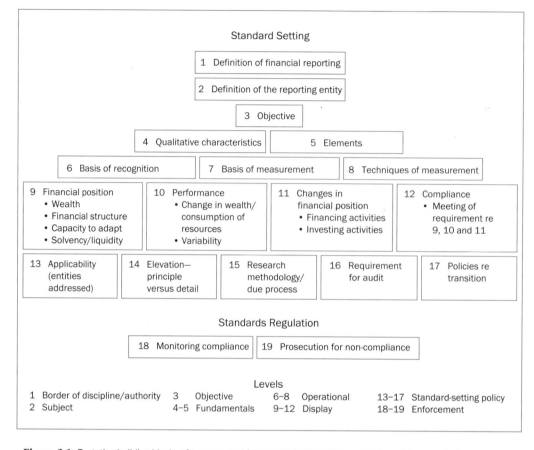

Figure 2.1 *Tentative building blocks of a conceptual framework for general-purpose financial accounting.*

Definition of the reporting entity

This part of the framework examines which entities should be required to prepare general-purpose financial reports. *Statement of Accounting Concept No. 1 (SAC 1)* was released in 1990 and addresses this particular issue. We will examine *SAC 1* in more detail later in this chapter.

Objective of general-purpose financial reporting

Having defined what financial reporting is and which entities should prepare general-purpose financial reports, the next question to address concerns the purpose of financial reporting. The users, their information needs and the type of reporting appropriate to those needs are examined in this stage. *SAC 2,* also issued in 1990, deals with the objective of general-purpose financial reporting and is covered later in this chapter.

Qualitative characteristics of financial information

This stage is concerned with the qualities which financial information should have if it is to meet the objective of general-purpose financial reporting. Should information be relevant? reliable? consistent? understandable? *SAC 3,* issued in 1990, addresses this aspect of the project and is covered later in this chapter.

Elements of financial statements

Definition and recognition

This stage of the project is concerned with establishing definitions and criteria for the recognition of assets, liabilities, revenues, expenses and equity. These are the elements which should be included in general-purpose financial reports to satisfy the objective of general-purpose financial reporting and the qualitative characteristics of financial information. *SAC 4*, re-issued in 1995, deals with the elements of financial statements and is examined later in this chapter.

Measurement

This part of the project identifies the basis and techniques for measurement of the elements of financial statements. Without doubt this stage of the project is the most critical. In Australia an accounting theory monograph on measurement was published in 1999; however, no Statement of Accounting Concept has been issued.

The central issue in the measurement phase is whether historic cost should continue to be the primary measurement method or whether some alternative current-value method should be preferred, given the objective of general-purpose financial reporting, the qualitative characteristics and the manner in which the elements have been defined. We will look at the impact of different methods of measurement on financial reports in Chapter 3.

At present in Australia we see examples of both cost and market values being used in general-purpose financial reports.

Display of financial information

The final stage in the project is concerned with how the information should be disclosed in general-purpose financial reports. The information is examined under the headings of financial position, performance and changes in financial position. Currently information on these matters is provided by the statements of financial position, financial performance and cash flow respectively. These financial statements will be discussed in later chapters which also consider whether these statements in their current format are the best means of disclosing financial information.

Compliance with the requirements to disclose financial information in the appropriate format will also be considered in this part of the project. There is little point in having detailed requirements if adherence to them is not enforced in some way.

Administration and enforcement

Levels 13 to 19 deal with administrative arrangements and enforcement of compliance with Statements of Accounting Concepts.

The Conceptual Framework to date

At the time of publication of this book the following pronouncements had been released.

- *SAC 1: Definition of the Reporting Entity*
- *SAC 2: Objective of General-purpose Financial Reporting*
- *SAC 3: Qualitative Characteristics of Financial Information*
- *SAC 4: Definition and Recognition of the Elements of Financial Statements.*

We will highlight the major concepts from each of these statements in relation to private-sector entities but you should be aware that these concepts are also applicable to public-sector entities. We will be using many of these concepts throughout this book.

SAC 1: Definition of the Reporting Entity

Key Concept 2.3

Reporting entity

Reporting entities are entities (including economic entities) in respect of which it is reasonable to expect the existence of users dependent on general-purpose financial reports for information which will be useful to them for making and evaluating decisions about the allocation of scarce resources. (*SAC 1*, para. 40)

From the definition we note that for an entity to be a reporting entity, there must be a demand from users—other than those users who receive special-purpose financial reports, such as a bank—for general-purpose financial reports. We have already looked at who the users of financial statements are in Chapter 1.

The identification of users is critical and is considered in *SAC 2*. Once an entity is identified as a reporting entity, it is required to prepare general-purpose financial reports in accordance with Accounting Standards. If an entity is deemed not to be a reporting entity, then normally, unless it is a disclosing entity, it need not comply with Accounting Standards in preparing financial reports. A small family company is not likely to be a reporting entity and is therefore not required to incur large costs involved in preparing detailed general-purpose financial reports. If Mum and Dad run the family company, they normally know how the business is performing and do not require general-purpose financial reports.

SAC 2: Objective of General-purpose Financial Reporting

Key Concept 2.4

Objective

The objective of general-purpose financial reporting as stated in paragraph 43 of *SAC 2* is to 'provide information useful to users for making and evaluating decisions about the allocation of scarce resources'.

We have already discussed in Chapter 1 the importance of providing information to assist users in making decisions. We also noted in Chapter 1 that *SAC 2* lists the primary users of external financial reports as:

- resource providers, including creditors, shareholders, lenders, employees and suppliers
- recipients of goods and services, primarily customers and beneficiaries
- parties performing a review or oversight function, including government, unions, analysts, media, employer groups and special-interest groups such as Greenpeace.

While the needs of these different groups vary, *SAC 2* states that they overlap to the extent that all users are interested in whether the entity is operating efficiently and achieving its objectives. General-purpose financial reports should provide sufficient information to enable users to assess the performance, financial position and the financing and investing of the reporting entity. We consider the analysis of financial statements in Chapter 14.

SAC 3: Qualitative Characteristics of Financial Information

This statement examines the qualities which financial information should possess to be included in general-purpose financial reports. *SAC 3* states that relevance and reliability are the primary qualitative characteristics. Information is relevant when it influences investors' decisions about the allocation of scarce resources. Information is reliable when the information can be depended on to represent faithfully, without bias and with minimal error, the transactions it is supposed to represent. Some information, such as forecasts of future profits, may be relevant but cannot be measured with an acceptable degree of reliability to be included in general-purpose financial reports. Conversely, some information may be reliable, such as the historical cost of an asset 20 years ago, but is it of relevance to users? We look at different measurement attributes in Chapter 3 and should keep in mind the concepts of relevance and reliability when considering the advantages and disadvantages of each attribute.

In addition to being relevant and reliable, information must also pass the materiality test. This essentially means that if the information is not likely to affect the users' decision adversely, the information is immaterial and need not be separately disclosed in the general-purpose financial report. In other words, we can ignore it for decision-making purposes.

Key Concept 2.5

Relevance and reliability

General-purpose financial reports should provide all financial information which satisfies the concepts of relevance and reliability and which passes the materiality test.

SAC 3 also requires that the relevant and reliable information be presented in such a way that it is both comparable and understandable to the users of general-purpose financial reports. As we will see in the chapter on analysing financial statements, it is important for users to be able to compare general-purpose financial reports of different entities.

SAC 3 also requires that general-purpose financial reports be prepared on a timely basis. It is of no use to a punter in 2001 to be told which horse won the 1997 Melbourne

Cup. The same applies to financial information about a reporting entity. However, for large organisations there is inevitably a delay of two to three months from the balance date until the release of the general-purpose financial reports.

Traditionally, accountants have tended to overstate liabilities, understate assets, recognise unrealised losses and defer unrealised gains. This approach is known as conservatism. *SAC 3* does not regard conservatism as an appropriate qualitative characteristic in deciding the type of information to be disclosed in general-purpose financial reports. You will notice as we proceed through this book that certain current accounting practices are based on the concept of conservatism.

SAC 4: Definition and Recognition of the Elements of Financial Statements

SAC 4 establishes the definitions and recognition criteria for assets, liabilities, revenues, expenses and equity. Each of these elements is discussed in turn and the definitions are identified as key concepts to be used in later chapters.

Key Concept 2.6

Assets

Assets are future economic benefits controlled by the entity as a result of past transactions or other past events. (SAC 4, para. 14)

Assets

Before an item qualifies for inclusion in the financial statements (in this case the statement of financial position), it must not only meet the definition of an asset, it must also pass certain recognition criteria. Firstly, it must be probable that the future economic benefits will eventuate and it must be possible to reliably measure the asset. Only when an item satisfies the definition and meets both recognition criteria will it qualify for inclusion on the statement of financial position.

The essential characteristics of an asset from the above definition are as follows.

- *Future economic benefits:* This is the essence of assets and relates to the scarce capacity to provide benefits to the entities that use them. It does not depend on physical form.
- *Control:* The entity must have the capacity to control the future economic benefits. Many earlier definitions of assets used the words 'legally owned' instead of 'controlled'. While control often arises from legally enforceable rights, the absence of legal ownership does not automatically deny the existence of control. An example of this is a noncancellable lease, where the lessee has control over the economic benefits embodied in the goods but the lessor maintains legal title to the goods. Thus, the lessor can resume possession of the goods but only if the lessee is unable to meet the lease payments.
- *Past transactions or other past events:* Only present abilities to control future economic benefits are assets. A decision at balance date to buy a new machine next year does not itself create an asset. However, if the entity has entered into an irrevocable contract to acquire the machine then a right might have been obtained and an asset created as a result of the contract. The signing of the contract is in effect the past event.

CASE STUDY 2.1

Man Utd takes a beating

by James Doran

MORE than £25 million was cut from the market value of Manchester United yesterday as the row over the abolition of transfer fees continues to dog the world's biggest football club.

Shares in the club tumbled 9.75p to 392p, one of the biggest losers in the FTSE 250 index, as European Commission plans to scrap lucrative transfer fees were digested by the market.

Manchester United is worth £750 million on the stock market with an estimated £200 million attributed to the value of players. If the new rules are enforced it is feared that the club could lose all of that value.

United shares are now well adrift of a record 412.5p, struck in April, when the company was dubbed the world's first £1 billion football club.

Yesterday Manchester United opened its first merchandising store in Singapore—operated by FJ Benjamin Holdings, a luxury brands and retail firm—and outlined plans to open other stores across South-East Asia.

The Times, 2 September 2000

Commentary

The article raises the interesting question of whether a football player is an asset. The £200 million attributed to the value of Manchester United's players is based on transfer payments. Consider whether in this case the definition of an asset is satisfied. Manchester United controls the services of a player because of the contract it has with him. The future economic benefits relate to the value of the player's services and his resale value by way of the transfer payment when he moves to another club. If transfer payments are outlawed by the European Commission, then a significant component of the future economic benefits is removed. Of course, the value of the playing services remains. The past event would be the signing of the contract.

Before being recorded on the statement of financial position, an item that meets the definition of an asset must also satisfy the recognition criteria. It must be probable that the future economic benefits will flow to the entity and there must be a cost or other value that can be reliably measured. The transfer payment would be an amount which could be used to report the value of the player. This would decline to zero if the system of transfer payments were outlawed. The probability of the economic benefits flowing to the club depends on a number of issues, including a player's age, risk of injury, performance on the field, and so on.

While it is common practice for some sporting clubs to report players on statements of financial position, it is not common practice with most entities to report their staff. Study the Woolworths statement of financial position (balance sheet) in Appendix 1 to see if you can locate any value for employees.

Key Concept 2.7

Liabilities

Liabilities are defined as the future sacrifices of economic benefits that the entity is presently obliged to make to other entities as a result of past transactions or other past events. (SAC 4, para. 48)

Liabilities

As is the case with assets, an item that meets the definition of a liability must also satisfy the criteria for recognition before being admitted to the statement of financial position. It must be probable that settlement of the liability will be required and the amount required can be reliably measured.

The essential characteristics of a liability from the above definition are as follows.

- *Existence of a present obligation:* This means that a transaction or event in the past has created an obligation which has not yet been satisfied. As with assets, the word 'legal' is not used in the definition of a liability. The view adopted is that legal obligations alone do not give rise to liabilities. There may be other social or moral reasons which create a present obligation. For example, an entity may decide to rectify faults in one of its products even though the warranty period has expired. The entity is not legally obliged to rectify the faults but the decision to do so imposes an obligation on the entity and the sacrifices required to honour the obligation constitute a liability.
- *Future disposition of economic benefits:* The obligation must result in the entity having to sacrifice economic benefits in the future to discharge the obligation.
- *Past transactions or other past events:* Only present obligations to sacrifice economic benefits in the future are liabilities. An obligation that may arise in the future is not a liability.

Key Concept 2.8

Expenses

Expenses are defined as consumptions or losses of future economic benefits in the form of reductions in assets or increases in liabilities of the entity, other than those relating to distributions to owners that result in a decrease in equity during the reporting period. (SAC 4, para. 117)

Expenses

Before expenses are recognised in the statement of financial performance, it must be probable that the consumption or loss of economic benefits has occurred and that the amount can be reliably measured.

Unlike the FASB Conceptual Framework, *SAC 4* does not differentiate between expenses and losses. When an asset is sold, the total carrying value of the asset is recorded as an expense. The proceeds from the sale of the asset will result in an increase in economic benefits and are recorded as revenue. The FASB approach is to treat the net amount of this transaction as a gain or loss and record it separately from other revenues or expenses. *SAC 4* states that any separate identification of losses is a display issue and will be considered when that stage of the Conceptual Framework is being completed.

Key Concept 2.9

Revenues

Revenues are inflows or other enhancements, or savings in outflows, of future economic benefits in the form of increases in assets or reductions in liabilities of the entity, other than those relating to contributions by owners, that result in an increase in equity during the reporting period. (SAC 4, para. 111)

Revenues

As with the other elements, revenue is recognised in the financial statements only when it is probable that the inflow, or other enhancement, or saving in outflows of future economic benefits has occurred and can be reliably measured.

The definition of revenues is consistent with that of expenses and does not differentiate gains from other revenues. This is a display issue and beyond the scope of *SAC 4*.

Key Concept 2.10

Equity

Equity is the residual interest in the assets of the entity after deduction of its liabilities. (SAC 4, para. 78)

Equity

This is a similar approach to the one adopted by the FASB. The identification of equity is therefore dependent on the recognition of assets and liabilities. Consequently, unlike the other four elements of financial statements, the definition of equity does not require recognition criteria.

An appendix to *SAC 4* provides examples of items which have created problems of classification because they have exhibited characteristics of both liabilities and equity. The definition and the recognition criteria for liabilities and equity are then used to resolve the classification of these items. We will refer to some of these examples in later chapters.

Future development

From Figure 2.1 we can determine that the following stages of the Conceptual Framework are still to be completed:

- definition of financial reporting
- basis and techniques of measurement
- display and compliance.

Clearly the most critical phase is the one dealing with measurement. The FASB Conceptual Framework in the United States received the most criticism on the issue of measurement. It remains to be seen whether the AASB will adopt a strategy similar to that of the FASB and permit different measurement attributes, or whether they will require the use of only one measurement attribute. At present in Australia there are several different measurement attributes in use.

Impact of the Australian Conceptual Framework

The reporting entity concept, as defined in *SAC 1*, has been incorporated into Accounting Standards with the result that certain entities may no longer have to comply with the onerous reporting requirements and costs associated with some standards.

The requirements in *SAC 2* and *SAC 3* in relation to the objective of general-purpose financial reporting and the qualitative characteristics of financial information are sufficiently subjective for it to be unlikely that they will have any significant effect on accounting practice.

The definition and recognition criteria on the elements of financial statements have already had an impact on Accounting Standards and Proposed Accounting Standards. As a result there have been some significant changes to accounting practice in various areas, particularly in relation to the recognition of assets and liabilities.

There are potentially even more significant changes to accounting practice in relation to the treatment of contracts equally proportionately unperformed, as discussed by Henderson and Goodwin (1990). As is evident from Hancock (1990), the application of the recommended treatments of these contracts to financial instruments may result in the recognition of assets and liabilities which is generally contrary to current practice. Whether such assets and liabilities should be offset for display purposes is an issue to be addressed in the display stage of the Conceptual Framework.

The Conceptual Framework project in Australia has already had a significant impact on accounting practice. This has not occurred without a great deal of controversy and debate, especially in relation to the Accounting Standards on superannuation funds (*AAS 25*) and general insurance activities (*AASB 1023*).

Without doubt, the greatest test of the Conceptual Framework will come with respect to the issue of measurement.

Summary

In this chapter we have identified what is meant by a conceptual framework of accounting. It is a series of statements which will assist all parties involved in the preparation of general-purpose financial reports. The proposed benefits of having a conceptual framework include:

- fewer Accounting Standards will be required
- more consistent Accounting Standards will be produced
- communication among parties involved in the preparation of general-purpose financial reports will be improved
- it will provide a defence against the actions of lobby groups.

We have noted that the Conceptual Framework project in Australia is well advanced, but the important stage on measurement is still to be completed. Statements of Accounting Concepts have been released on the reporting entity, the objective of general-purpose financial reporting, the qualitative characteristics of financial information and the definition and recognition of the elements of financial statements. The definitions stated in this chapter are followed in subsequent chapters, where appropriate.

The Statements of Accounting Concepts have already had an impact on accounting practice and we noted that the proposed treatment of contracts equally proportionately unperformed could potentially have a significant impact on current statements of financial position, especially for entities which have large dealings in financial instruments.

References

Accounting Standards Review Board and Public Sector Accounting Standards Board. *Statement of Accounting Concept No. 1: Definition of the Reporting Entity*, August 1990.

Accounting Standards Review Board and Public Sector Accounting Standards Board. *Statement of Accounting Concept No. 2: Objective of General-purpose Financial Reporting*, August 1990.

Accounting Standards Review Board and Public Sector Accounting Standards Board. *Statement of Accounting Concept No. 3: Qualitative Characteristics of Financial Information*, August 1990.

Australian Accounting Research Foundation. *Exposure Draft 42: Guide to Proposed Statement of Accounting Concepts*, December 1987.

Australian Accounting Standards Board and Public Sector Accounting Standards Board. *Statement of Accounting Concept No. 4: Definition and Recognition of the Elements of Financial Statements*, March 1995.

Financial Accounting Standards Board. *Statement of Financial Accounting Concepts No. 1: Objectives of Financial Reporting by Business Enterprises*, November 1978.

Hancock, P.J., 1990. *Financial Reporting by Financial Institutions and Accounting for Financial Instruments*, Discussion Paper No. 14, Australian Accounting Research Foundation, December.

Henderson, S., and Goodwin, J., 1990. 'The seeds of change', *Australian Accountant*, August, pp. 34–8.

Howieson, B., 1993. '*SAC 4*: A source of accounting change', *The Australian Accounting Review*, vol 3, no. 1, pp. 11–20.

Solomons, D., 1986. 'The FASB's Conceptual Framework: an evaluation', *Journal of Accountancy*, June, pp. 114–24.

Further reading

McGregor, W., 1990. 'The Conceptual Framework for general-purpose financial reporting', *Australian Accountant*, December, pp. 68–74.

Review questions

1 What is a conceptual framework of accounting?

2 Discuss the reasons why it is desirable to have a conceptual framework.

3 Why do you think any proposed changes to accounting practice arising out of the Conceptual Framework are likely to meet with strong resistance?

4 In your own words, define a reporting entity.

5 What is the importance of the reporting entity concept?

6 Discuss who uses general-purpose financial reports and why they require such reports.

7 Discuss the difference between control and ownership in terms of the definition of an asset.

8 Explain what is meant by the term 'contracts equally proportionately unperformed'. Give some examples. Should such contracts give rise to the recognition of assets and liabilities?

9 'The conceptual framework approach to setting accounting standards is not about defining ideal accounting practices but about legitimising current

practice, maintaining social and economic status and staving off attempts by the government to control standard-setting.' Discuss.

10   What is your understanding of the term 'conservatism'?

11   Give some examples, other than those in the text, of reliable and irrelevant financial information and of unreliable and relevant financial information.

Problems for discussion and analysis

1   You are asked to explain the following terms to a friend. In doing so, do not refer to the definition in your answer. Use your own words to express your understanding of the terms:
    a   an asset
    b   a liability
    c   equity
    d   an expense
    e   revenue.

2   Refer to the Woolworths financial report in Appendix 1.
    a   On what basis are the accounts prepared?
    b   What are the three main segments of the business? Which of the three provides the greatest revenue?

3   Give three examples of a liability. How do your examples meet the criteria listed in Key Concept 2.7? Do not use examples from the text.

4   Give three examples of an asset. How do your examples meet the criteria listed in Key Concept 2.6? Do not use examples from the text.

5   ABC Ltd is being sued by a client for $100 000. The company's legal advisers say there is only a 35 per cent chance of an unfavourable outcome. At the end of the financial year the case has still to go to court. Should the $100 000 be reported as a liability?

6   Refer to Case Study 2.1. Do you believe a soccer player should be recognised as an asset on Manchester United's statement of financial position? What about a player who plays for the local community soccer club?

7   With increased competition in the airline industry, most of the major airlines are offering 'frequent traveller' specials where travellers can receive upgrades from economy to first or business class, or free accommodation packages. Some airlines have been trying to gain more market share by giving double kilometres credit for each flight. How should the airlines account for upgrade and free accommodation packages that have been issued to travellers but have not as yet been redeemed? Are they a liability?

    (Adapted from R. Anthony and J. Reece, Accounting: Text and Cases, 8th edn, Richard D. Irwin Inc., 1988, Chapter 8, Case 8–5.)

Ethics case study

Tom has been employed at New Incentives Ltd for six months after recently graduating from university with a degree in accounting. It is his first job after trying to find employment for six months. Tom's boss has asked him for a favour in preparing the statement of financial performance for the year. She wants Tom to include in revenue cash received for services to be provided next year. She also wants him to record as an asset cash paid for advertisements which were screened on television two weeks before the end of the accounting period. Tom is aware that management is to be paid bonuses based on the net profit for the period.

Discuss:

a how the transactions should be reported according to your understanding of the Conceptual Framework

b what Tom should do.

Wealth and the Measurement of Profit

Learning objectives

At the end of this chapter you should be able to:

1 explain what is meant by the terms 'income', 'wealth' and 'profit'

2 explain the meaning of 'original cost' and 'historic cost'

3 explain the replacement cost and economic value methods

4 explain the net realisable value method of measurement.

NOTE TO INSTRUCTORS: Instructors may wish to defer consideration of this chapter until later in the course.

Introduction

In Chapter 1 we established that there are a number of different users of accounting information, each of whom requires different information for different purposes. However, there are some items of information that are required by most users. They want to know what an enterprise controls, what it owes, and how it is performing.

An asset was defined in Chapter 2 as an economic resource controlled—but not necessarily owned—by an entity. The information about what an enterprise controls and what it owes could be termed the worth of the enterprise or its wealth. This measure of wealth or worth relates to a point in time. The other information required concerns the way in which the enterprise performed over a period of time. This performance during a period can be measured as a change in wealth over time. If you increase your wealth you have performed better, in financial terms, than someone whose wealth has decreased over the same period of time. This measurement of changes in wealth over time is referred to in accounting terminology as *profit measurement*. Profit is sometimes referred to as income.

In this chapter we will look at the ways in which accountants can measure wealth and profit, and discuss the merits of the alternatives available. We also examine in some detail the way in which the choice of a measurement system affects the resultant profit and wealth measures. To do this we need to start by defining profit and wealth, because these two ideas are directly linked.

Income or profit, and wealth

A definition of profit that is widely accepted by accountants is based on the definition of an individual's income put forward by the economist Sir John Hicks (1946), who stated:

> Income [profit] is that amount which an individual can consume and still be as well off at the end of the period as he or she was at the start of the period.

This definition is shown in Figure 3.1.

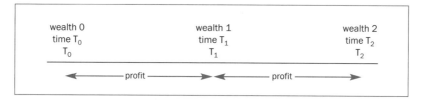

Figure 3.1 *Profit or loss is determined by measuring wealth at different points in time.*

By referring to the diagram we can arrive at the profit or loss for period 1 by measuring wealth at the start of the period, i.e. at a time T_0, and subtracting that figure from our measurement of wealth at the end of the period, i.e. T_1. Similarly, the profit or loss for the second period can be measured by subtracting the wealth at time T_1 from the wealth at time T_2.

It should also be clear from Figure 3.1 that wealth is static and represents a stock at a particular point in time. Thus, wealth 0 is the stock of wealth at time T_0, wealth 1 is the stock of wealth at time T_1 and wealth 2 is the stock of wealth at time T_2.

Key Concept 3.1

Income

A relationship exists between income, or profit, and wealth. Income can be derived by measuring wealth at two different points in time, and the difference between the two figures is the income or profit. An alternative view proposed by other economists suggests that if you first measure income then you can derive wealth. This implies that the relationship is circular, as depicted in Figure 3.2. The different views taken by various economists really relate to how you break into the circle.

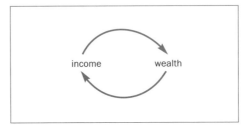

Figure 3.2 *The relationship between income and wealth is circular.*

Key Concept 3.2

Wealth

Wealth is a static measure and represents a stock at a particular point in time. This stock can change over time. Thus, the wealth measured at the start of a period will not necessarily be equal to the wealth measured at the end of the period. The difference between the two is the profit or loss for that period of time.

If we look at the way in which profit is depicted in Figure 3.1, it is apparent that profit is a flow over time. To measure the profit earned over a period of time, it is necessary to measure the stock of wealth at the start and end of that period.

Key Concept 3.3

Profit

Profit represents the difference between the wealth at the start and at the end of the period. Unlike wealth, which is essentially a static measure, profit is a measure of flow which summarises activity over a period.

To summarise, we have shown that we can express the profit for the first period, from time T_0 to time T_1, as:

$$\text{profit period}_1 = \text{wealth}_1 - \text{wealth}_0$$

Similarly we can express the profit for the second period, the period between time T_1 and time T_2, as:

$$\text{profit period}_2 = \text{wealth}_2 - \text{wealth}_1$$

We have also established that the profit or loss is derived by measuring the wealth of an individual, or an enterprise, at two points in time. This is straightforward, but let us look in more detail at what we are trying to measure and how we can measure it.

We will start by examining the case of an individual because this is simpler and more in line with your own experience. The underlying arguments and principles are just the same for an enterprise but the degree of complexity increases. Let us suppose that we asked an individual to measure his or her wealth, i.e. the sum of possessions less debts.

Example 3.1

Alex came up with the following list of assets and told us that he owed nothing.

At the start of the year: T_0	*At the end of the year:* T_1
A new Ford Laser	A one-year-old Ford Laser
One new suit	The same suit
Five shirts	The same five shirts
Four sweatshirts	Five sweatshirts
One surfboard	One surfboard
$400 cash	$500 cash

While the lists above might accurately reflect the assets Alex controls and what he owes, we cannot easily see whether he is better or worse off at the end of the year than he was at the start. We could perhaps say, with the benefit of our own knowledge of the world, that he must be worse off because everything is one year older; this, however, assumes that the value of his possessions decreases with time. In many cases that is a reasonable assumption but clearly there are some cases where their value increases: for example, would our attitudes change if the car was a 1957 FJ Holden? Leaving that question aside for a moment, you will have noticed that once we started to discuss the measurement of wealth we also started talking of the more abstract concept of value.

This raises two questions: one relates to the value, which we shall discuss in more detail later; the other relates to the way in which we assign value. In the case of the lists of possessions above, the easiest item to deal with in terms of value is the cash. This is because it has already had a value assigned to it with which we are all familiar, i.e. a monetary value. On the face of it, therefore, it seems that if we assigned a monetary value to each of the items in the list we would have solved part of our problem. In fact it is not as easy as that, as we all know that the value of money is not stable; we only have to listen to our grandparents or even our parents talking about what money used to buy to realise that the value of money has decreased over time.

If we leave the problem of the changing value of money aside and we use money as a measure of value, then we have no problem with the value of the cash in the bank, but what of the other items? What is the value of the car for example? Is it worth less because it is one year older, and if so how much less? The same line of argument can be applied to the suit, shirts and surfboard, but in the case of the sweatshirts we do not even know whether they are the same sweatshirts; clearly there must be at least one that has been acquired during the year, since he had five at the end of the year compared with four at the beginning. We also have yet to establish whether the age of the items is important for the purposes of arriving at a value. In order to decide on that question, we need first to look at the possibilities available to us.

Although numerous alternatives are put forward, many are combinations of those dealt with here. We shall limit our discussion to the most common possibilities. The terms are defined, where appropriate, later in this chapter. The important point to note at this time is the relationship between wealth and profit and the way in which a change in the measurement of one affects the other. This will be explored in more detail later, using our example of Alex.

Alternative systems of valuation

For convenience, we will first deal with those alternatives that relate to cost and then discuss those that are based on some concept of value. We start with original cost, then look at historic cost and finally discuss replacement cost.

Key Concept 3.4

Original cost

The cost of the item at the time of the transaction between a willing buyer and a willing seller.

Original cost

The original cost of an item is the cost at the time of the transaction between the buyer and the seller. We have made a number of assumptions about there being a willing buyer and willing seller which do not need to concern us at this point. Leaving those problems aside, on the face of it this seems to be a fairly easy figure to arrive at. It is in fact not so easy. Consider the case of this book. Is the original cost the price you paid in the bookshop? Or is it the price the bookshop paid to the publisher? Or do we go back even further to the cost to the publisher? Or further still to the cost to the authors? Each of these is a possible measure of the original cost, but the question is, which is the right cost? Cost is the amount paid by the individual or enterprise on which you are reporting. This cost is normally referred to as the historic cost.

Key Concept 3.5

Historic cost

The historic cost is the cost incurred by the individual or enterprise in acquiring an item measured at the time of the orginating transaction.

Historic cost

Historic cost is the cost incurred by the individual or enterprise in acquiring an item measured at the time of the originating transaction. It is extremely important because it underpins most current accounting practice. We can see that the historic cost of the book to you will be different from the historic cost to the bookshop. This difference is what keeps the bookshop in business. But let us take our example a stage further. Let us assume that at the end of the year you no longer need this book and decide to sell it. In this situation you will probably find that the book is no longer worth what you paid for it and therefore the historic cost is no longer a fair representation of the book's worth or of your wealth. In order to tackle this problem, when measuring your wealth at the end of the year you could write the historic cost down to some lower figure to represent the amount of use you have had from the book. Accounting follows a similar process and the resulting figure is known as the written-down cost. It can be described as the historic cost after an adjustment for use. The adjustment for use is commonly referred to as depreciation, and there are several ways to arrive at a depreciation figure. This concept will be discussed later.

The problem with historic cost and written-down historic cost is that, as the value of money and goods changes over time, they are likely to be only a fair representation of value at a particular point in time, i.e. at the point of the original transaction. At any other time the historic cost of an item is a fair representation of its worth only if the world is static, i.e. with no innovation, etc. Clearly this is not the case and so we should look for alternative measures. One such alternative to the original or historic cost of an item is its replacement cost. This is certainly more up to date and allows for the changes that take place in a non-static world.

Key Concept 3.6

Replacement cost

The replacement cost is the amount that would have to be paid at today's prices to purchase an item similar to the existing item.

Replacement cost

The replacement cost of an item is the amount that would have to be paid at today's prices to purchase a similar item. It is often very relevant, as those who have had cars written off will know. In those cases the amount that the insurance company pays you often bears no relationship to what it would cost to replace your car, perhaps because yours was better than average or had just had a new engine installed. The first problem that arises in using replacement cost is that you have to want to replace the item. You might not want to replace a textbook that you used at school because it is no longer of use to you. Even if you do want to replace the item, you may find that it is difficult to identify the replacement cost. Think of a unique item such as Leonardo da Vinci's *Mona Lisa*!

Even if you could replace an item with an exact replica, you might not wish to do so. You might wish to obtain a newer version or one with extra functions. The most obvious example of this kind is the replacement of computer equipment, which is constantly expanding in power while its size and its price are generally decreasing. This leads us to the same problem that we had with historic cost: the replacement cost of a computer does not take into account the age of the machine that we actually own. The solution is the same as for historic cost: estimate the effect of usage and arrive at a written-down replacement cost.

As we can see, there are distinct problems in using either historic cost or replacement cost. In a number of situations these are unlikely to be useful measures of value or wealth. Historic cost is unlikely to be useful when prices change, whatever the reason for that change. Replacement cost, while overcoming that problem by using up-to-date costs, is itself irrelevant if there is no intention of replacing the item.

Before reading the next section on measurement methods other than cost, it is worth spending a few minutes thinking of the situations in which historic cost and replacement cost are appropriate and those situations when they are unlikely to be suitable. Any measure is useful only if it is appropriate.

For example, while the acceleration of a car may be important in certain circumstances, it is irrelevant for an emergency stop. Similarly the historic cost or replacement cost of a motor car is unlikely to be useful if we wish to sell the car because the selling price will be governed by other factors. The alternatives to these cost-based measures are measures which are related to worth. However, as we will see, these measures also have their own set of problems.

Key Concept 3.7

Economic value

Economic value is, or would be, an ideal measure of value and wealth. Economic value is the value of the expected future earnings from using the item in question discounted at an appropriate rate to give a present-day value.

Economic value

The economic value of an item is the value of the expected earnings from using the item discounted at an appropriate rate to give a present-day value. For an example of what is meant by the terms 'present value' and 'discount rate', consider the following: a person deposits $100 in a bank at a fixed interest rate of 10 per cent compounded annually for five years. At the end of five years the $100 would have grown to $161.51 (assuming no taxes or charges). The present value of $161.51 discounted at 10 per cent per annum produces a figure of $100. Discounting is the opposite of compounding. Compounding asks: how much will I have after x periods at y interest rate? Discounting asks: what is the present value of a sum to be received in x periods given y interest rate? Chapter 16 has more detailed information on the time value of money and capital investment decisions.

The problem is not in defining the measure of economic value but in actually estimating future earnings. This implies a knowledge of what is going to happen; problems of foreseeing technological change, fashion changes and so on make the estimation of future earnings problematical. Even if we assume that we can make reliable forecasts, we are left with the question of finding an appropriate rate at which to discount the estimated future earnings. The problem here is that each individual might wish to use a different rate depending on his or her circumstances. For example, a millionaire might not worry very much if money is available in a year rather than immediately, but if you have no money to buy your next meal the situation is entirely different. We should not reject this measure because of these problems, since with the use of mathematical techniques relating to probability it is still a useful tool in decision making. In fact it is the underlying techniques such as net present value (see Chapter 16) which are often used in investment appraisal decisions.

Key Concept 3.8

Net realisable value

The net realisable value is an alternative measure of value to economic value. The net realisable value is defined as the estimated proceeds of sale, less (where applicable) all further costs to the stage of completion and less all costs to be incurred in marketing, selling and distribution to customers.

Net realisable value

The net realisable value is the estimated proceeds of sale less, where applicable, all further costs to the stage of completion and less all costs to be incurred in marketing, selling and distribution to customers. On the face of it, such a measure should be easily obtainable, but in practice the amount for which an item can be sold varies with the circumstances of the sale. These circumstances are not always connected with the item for sale but can depend on such things as the location of the property: for example, an ice works would have more value in the tropics than in Antarctica, all other things being equal. The problems of arriving at the net realisable value are apparent in the second-hand car market where there is a trade price and a range of retail prices. Another good example is the housing market, where independent valuations can differ by as much as $40 000 on a property worth between $110 000 and $150 000.

Besides the problem of arriving at a value, other factors affect the net realisable value. For example, if you are in financial difficulties you may be prepared to accept less than the market value in order to get a quick sale. The value in the latter situation is known as the forced sale value and is the most likely value where circumstances are unfavourable to the seller. Further, one is assuming that there is a buyer who is willing to buy, otherwise the property is valueless relative to converting it into cash. If, on the other hand, the market conditions are neutral between buyer and seller, then the net realisable value is likely to be the open market value.

It should be clear from the above that plenty of alternative measurement methods are available, each of which has its own problems. If you remember, the starting point for this discussion was that we wished to establish whether Alex was better off at the end of the period than he was at the start. Had he made a profit? The problem is not one of finding a concept of profit or income, as there are plenty in the economics literature besides the one that we have already referred to (Hicks, 1946): see, for example, the income concepts of Fischer (1930) and Friedman (1957). The problem is, in fact, one of measurement: most of these concepts rely either on a measurement of future income or on the measurement of wealth.

We have already pointed out that to measure future income is extremely difficult in the real world because of the effects of uncertainty. This leaves us with the alternative of measuring wealth and leads to the problem of finding the most appropriate measure. As we have seen, all the measures put forward so far have inherent difficulties, and it may be that the solution lies in combining two or more of these to obtain the best measure. For the purposes of this introductory text it is unnecessary to probe this area in greater depth but some references are given at the end of the chapter which provide further background for those interested in pursuing the topic. Before leaving this area, let us reconsider the example based on the wealth of Alex and assign some values to see what effect the choice of measure will have.

Description	Replacement cost	Year T_0 Historic cost	Net realisable value
	$	$	$
Ford Laser	13 500	13 500	10 500
Suit	200	210	30
Shirts	75	75	10
Surfboard	180	180	100
Sweatshirts	50	50	20
Cash	400	400	400

If you study the figures carefully you will notice that the only figure common to all three columns is the cash figure. Apart from the cost of the suit, the replacement cost and the historic cost for all the other items are also identical. In reality this will always be the case at the time when the goods are bought, but it is unlikely to be so at any other time. In this example, the fact that the replacement cost of the suit is different from the historic cost indicates that the suit was bought when the price of suits was higher than it was at the start of the year in question. In other words, the point in time at which we are measuring is different from the date of acquisition and, as we said, in these circumstances the replacement cost is likely to differ from the historic cost.

You will also notice that the net realisable value is lower than the historic cost and replacement cost, even though some of the items were clearly new at the start of the year. Once again, this is obviously the case in most situations because personal goods that are being resold are effectively secondhand goods even if they have not been used. The situation for a business enterprise is not necessarily the same because sometimes the goods are bought not for use but for resale, e.g. by a retailer or wholesaler. In these cases the net realisable value of the goods bought for resale should be higher than the cost—otherwise the retailer would not stay in business very long.

Let us now look at Alex's situation at the end of the year and assign some values to the items owned at that time. We will then be in a position to measure the increase in wealth, or profit, and to use this as a basis for discussion of some of the problems of measurement which we referred to earlier.

Description	Replacement cost	Year T$_1$ Historic cost	Net realisable value
	$	$	$
Ford Laser	10 000	13 500	8 000
Suit	270	210	27
Shirts	80	75	5
Surfboard	180	180	90
Sweatshirts	50	50	15
Cash	500	500	500

You will notice that (disregarding the cash) the figures have changed in all cases, except for historic cost where they are the same as at the start of the year. This highlights one of the problems with this measure: it tells us only what an item costs, not necessarily what it is worth today.

Let us look more closely at the car. As you can see, the replacement cost is lower than at the start of the year. This is because the car we are replacing at the end of the year is a one-year-old model rather than a new model. There is also a problem in using replacement cost for such items as the suit. It is unlikely that you would try or wish to purchase a year-old suit, whereas there is a ready market for secondhand cars. You will also see that the replacement cost is higher than the net realisable value. This is because costs would be incurred in selling the car, and the amount that you would receive would be reduced by these costs.

Let us now look at what we get in terms of our measures of wealth and profit, starting with historic cost.

Description	Year T$_0$	Year T$_1$
	$	$
Ford Laser	13 500	13 500
Suit	210	210
Shirts	75	75
Surfboard	180	180
Sweatshirts	50	50
Cash	400	500
	14 415	14 515

We can now measure the profit under historic cost as we have a figure for wealth at the start and end of the year. Thus, using the formula

$$\text{wealth at } T_1 - \text{wealth at } T_0 = \text{profit}$$

we get

$$\$14\,515 - \$14\,415 = \$100$$

The figures at T_1, and therefore the profit, would be different if we used written-down cost. Remember, written-down cost is the reduction in the cost of an asset to reflect the use of the asset.

Let us look at what would happen if we used replacement cost rather than historic cost.

Description	Year T_0 $	Year T_1 $
Ford Laser	13 500	10 000
Suit	200	270
Shirts	75	80
Surfboard	180	180
Sweatshirts	50	50
Cash	400	500
	14 405	11 080

We can now measure the profit under replacement cost as we have a figure for wealth at the start and end of the year. Thus, using the formula

$$\text{wealth at } T_1 - \text{wealth at } T_0 = \text{profit}$$

we get

$$\$11\,080 - \$14\,405 = \$3325 \text{ loss}$$

In other words, according to the replacement cost figures, Alex is $3325 worse off at the end of the year than he was at the start.

Finally, let us see what the situation would be if we were using the net realisable value to arrive at our measures of wealth.

Description	Year T_0 $	Year T_1 $
Ford Laser	10 500	8 000
Suit	30	27
Shirts	10	5
Surfboard	100	90
Sweatshirts	20	15
Cash	400	500
	11 060	8 637

We can now measure the profit under net realisable value as we have a figure for wealth at the start and end of the year. Thus, using the formula

$$\text{wealth at } T_1 - \text{wealth at } T_0 = \text{profit}$$

we get

$$\$8637 - \$11\,060 = \$2423 \text{ loss}$$

Once again using net realisable value as the basis of measuring wealth we find that Alex is worse off at the end of the year than he was at the start.

You might well be wondering at this point which is the correct answer. This takes us back to the question of who is to use the information and for what purpose it is to be used. Clearly this varies from case to case; however, it is more important, at the present time, that you understand that differences arise depending on the valuation method adopted. Alex is clearly worse off at the end of the year than he was at the start since he no longer has a brand-new car, so you may feel that replacement cost or net realisable value are the better alternatives. However, you must bear in mind that we are trying to measure the amount that can be spent while maintaining wealth; there is a hidden assumption that Alex wants to maintain the wealth he had at the start.

This might not, in fact, be the case. Alex might, for example, have been banned from driving, which could mean that he does not want to replace his car. The net realisable value would be more useful in this case, because he would probably want to sell the car. However, although he has lost his driving licence he will still need to go out—even if only to buy food—and will need to wear some clothes, so to value these on the assumption that they are going to be sold is not a defensible position.

Current accounting practice

The historical cost method is the common measurement method adopted in most countries. *AASB 1015: Accounting for the Acquisitions of Assets* requires assets to be initially recorded at the cost of acquisition. However, *AASB 1041: The Revaluation of Non-Current Assets* allows reporting entities to revalue certain non-current assets. Generally this will apply to property, plant and equipment. The revaluation allows reporting entities to report the changes in the value of non-current assets since the date of acquisition. The restated amount for these assets is in most cases an approximation of the asset's current value.

You should now read the Woolworths financial report in Appendix 1 and observe that Note 1(A) states that the company uses the historical cost model, except for certain assets which are at valuation.

CASE STUDY 3.1

Profits: profit measures that exceed the expected

by John Kavanagh

AFICIONADOS of corporate financial statements noticed something new in May when Westpac Banking Corporation added a line to the profit and loss statement in the reporting of its results for the six months ending March 31. Along with its earnings before interest and tax (Ebit) and operating profit after tax, it highlighted its 'economic profit', which is still a relatively new concept in Australian corporate finance circles.

(Economic profit measures a company's earnings after taking account of a notional cost of capital. This form of accounting is described by two other names: shareholder-value accounting and economic-value-added accounting.)

In conventional accounting, a company subtracts its operating costs, income tax, depreciation and interest on borrowings from its revenue to arrive at a profit figure. According to the proponents of economic-profit accounting, the conventional treatment leaves out one big cost item—the cost of capital. The argument is that investors who put capital into a company expect a minimum rate of return, and it is only when that minimum rate has been achieved that a company can be said to have added value for shareholders or made an economic profit.

The cost of capital can be worked out for any company using the risk-free rate of return (the 10-year government bond rate) as a base then adding a market-risk premium and a volatility ranking for the company. That rate is then applied to shareholders' funds. In Westpac's case the cost of capital was 12%. Twelve per cent of $9.6 billion of shareholders' funds is $1.2 billion. After some adjustments had been made, that $1.2 billion was subtracted from operating profit to arrive at an economic profit figure. Westpac reported an operating profit after tax of $818 million for the six months to March 31 and an economic profit of $493 million.

Richard Stewart, a partner in the financial advisory services group that operates at PricewaterhouseCoopers, says economic profit has been in common use in the United States for a decade and is finding wider acceptance in Australia. Westpac may be the only company to publish an economic profit figure but many other big companies are using it in their internal financial reporting. The funds management and broking communities are also taking it up. Stewart says investors should see more reference to it during this profit reporting season.

Despite increased usage, the concept of economic profit has its critics. The biggest problem is that there are no standards. The most commonly used formula is one developed by the US accounting firm Stern Stewart, but there are several variations. For investors, this means they may be unable to compare like with like.

Business Review Weekly, Business News,
18 August 2000

Commentary

The article refers to economic profit, which recognises that an entity does not add value for a shareholder until the cost of the shareholder's investment is covered. Underlying economic profit is the notion that shareholders are no better off until the company earns an amount sufficient to compensate them for the cost of their investment. It also confirms that the assessment of wealth and measurement of income is not a straightforward exercise.

Conclusion

We have seen that there are a number of alternative ways of measuring a person's wealth and that each has its own problems. One common objection to both replacement cost and net realisable value is that they are subjective, which is true in many cases. This is one reason why accounts are still prepared using historic costs or modified historic costs, even though, as we have seen in the simple example of Alex, this can lead to irrelevant information being produced and wrong decisions being taken. Another reason that is often cited for retaining historic cost in the accounts is that it is a system which is based on what was actually spent, and owners of enterprises need to know what the money has been spent on. But to what extent can the advantage of historic cost make up for its deficiencies as a measure of wealth and therefore as the basis of the profit measure? This question is and has been the subject of much debate which will continue for many years to come. For our purposes we need to be aware of the problems associated with using each of the alternatives, because they might well produce different decisions.

Summary

We have looked at a definition of wealth and of profit which is commonly used and indeed underpins current accounting practice, and we have found that there are problems in actually measuring wealth. We have looked at four alternative measures: historic cost, replacement cost, net realisable value and economic value. (There are other valuation systems that have found support, and discussion on some of these can be found in the references at the end of this chapter.) We have shown by way of a simple example that each of the first three produces a different answer, and we have pointed to some of the problems and assumptions underlying each alternative. At present there is no generally accepted right answer. The most commonly used system is that based primarily on historic cost. One other point of interest is that some industries in Australia, such as the superannuation industry, are required by law to use net market or net realisable value for the measurement of their assets. Change is likely to be slow in coming because the present system, based on historic cost, is familiar to all. It is said to have worked well in the past, although it is unclear what criteria are being used to back up this claim.

References

Fischer, I., 1930. *The Theory of Interest*, Macmillan.

Friedman, M., 1957. *A Theory of the Consumption Function*, Princeton University Press.

Hicks, Sir John, 1946. *Value and Capital*, Clarendon Press.

Further reading

Bell, P.W., 1982. *Accounting Theory Monograph 1: How Fundamental are the Differences?*, Australian Accounting Research Foundation, Melbourne.

Bierman, H. Jr., 1963. 'Measurement and accounting', *Accounting Review*, July, pp. 501–7.

Churchman, C. West, 1971. 'The facility, felicity, and morality of measuring social change', *Accounting Review*, January, pp. 30–5.

Review questions

1   Profit is normally seen as a flow over time, whereas wealth can be described as a stock at a point in time. Explain in your own words the difference between a stock and a flow.

2   There are a number of different ways in which we can measure wealth. List the alternatives discussed in the chapter, together with any drawbacks or problems that were identified with their use.

3   In certain situations we said that written-down costs could be used as an alternative measure. Explain in your own words the difference between cost and written-down cost and suggest when the latter would be more appropriate.

4   What effects, if any, do rapid changes in technology have on the appropriateness of each of the alternative ways of assigning a cost or a value to an item?

Problems for discussion and analysis

1   Refer to the Woolworths financial report in Appendix 1.
   a   What is the total revenue for the year?
   b   What is the total revenue from operating activities? What is meant by the term 'operating activities'?
   c   What is the operating profit before and after income tax?
   d   How are the assets measured? Why do you believe Woolworths does not use historic cost for all assets?

2   If $100 is deposited in a 5 per cent per annum account, and the interest compounded, what is the future value after three years? (show workings)

3   You are to receive a sum of $115.76 in three years, which has just been invested at 5% per annum compound. What is the present value? (show workings)

4   Make a list of all your possessions and all your debts (i.e. all your assets and liabilities) so that you can determine your own wealth. What values did you use for your possessions? Explain why you selected these values. You may also like to calculate your wealth one year ago. Did your wealth increase or decrease in the past year?

5   A Ford Laser was purchased by Totem Ford for $10 000 and later sold in new condition to Spike Buzley for $12 000. One year later, Spike crashed the car and was told by the Royal Automobile Club it would cost $4000 to repair. Spike was advised that his car would be worth $1000 if repairs were not made, and could be sold for $7000 if the repairs were made. Spike was alarmed to hear this, because Totem Ford were now selling new Ford Lasers for $13 000.

At the time Spike decides to have his car repaired, what would be:
   a   the historic cost
   b   the replacement cost
   c   the net realisable value?

6   Two sisters decided to go into business buying and selling beds. Details of their transactions are set out below.

They initially bought 400 beds at $200 each. At the end of six months they had sold 300 of the 400 beds for $300 each. Unfortunately, during that time the bed manufacturer, who was their only source of supply, had increased the price to $240 each. To make matters worse, a discount store had opened in the area and it was selling the same beds at $280 each. The sisters found that on average over the six months they had incurred costs for advertising, etc. which amounted to $20 for each bed sold.
   a   On the basis of the information above, calculate what the sisters' wealth was at the start and end of the six months and what profit had been made.
   b   Having calculated the profit for the first six months, discuss whether the profit figure is a useful benchmark for measuring the performance of the business, and also whether it is useful as a guide to future profitability.

7   Under certain circumstances only one of the alternative methods of valuation is appropriate. Giving brief reasons for your choice, suggest the most appropriate value to be placed on each item in the following.

Jean owns a shop which used to sell clothes but she has now decided that, given the location, she would make more money running a restaurant on the same premises. She has obtained planning permission for the change of use and has bought some of the equipment needed but has not yet started trading. She has made a list of the items that the business owns:

a   freehold shop
b   hanging display rail for clothes
c   a two-year-old car which is essential for the business
d   new restaurant tables and chairs
e   cash register
f   a quantity of fashion garments that were not sold in the closing down sale.

You may find that you need more information or have to make some assumptions. This is normal, but you should state any assumptions that you are making.

8   If the persons/things listed below were crucial to your enterprise and had to be insured, how would you value them?

a   An elite football player.
b   The *Mona Lisa*.
c   The Sydney Opera House.
d   The Prime Minister.

9   The KLT Company on 31 July 20X1 purchased a very specialised item of machinery. KLT is the only company in Australia producing a special instrument used in the medical industry and hence the new machinery has no resale value other than its scrap value. The following is a list of various values at 30 June 20X2 for the machine under different valuation methods discussed in this chapter.

	$
Historic cost	1 000 000
Net realisable value	10 000
Replacement cost	1 250 000

Required:

Discuss which value from those listed (or any other value you believe is relevant) the following users would consider as most relevant for their purposes.

a   A banker considering lending funds to KLT with the specialised machinery providing the security.
b   A shareholder in assessing the value of the company's shares.
c   Management in assessing the performance of the company.

10   Merlin's Magic Supply Company Ltd lists the following assets and liabilities at time periods T_0 and T_1.

	Historic cost		Replacement cost		Net realisable value	
	T_0	T_1	T_0	T_1	T_0	T_1
Cash	1 000	2 000	1 000	2 000	1 000	2 000
Land	10 000	10 000	12 000	14 000	12 000	14 000
Inventory	1 500	2 250	1 500	2 500	1 500	2 500
Trade creditors	1 000	1 500	1 000	1 500	1 000	1 500
Trade debtors	1 200	1 750	1 250	1 750	1 150	1 650

    a   Calculate the most appropriate change in net worth of the company, with supporting arguments for your decision, if it is:

        i   a small trading company

        ii   a superannuation plan.

    b   If you were liquidating this company at time T_1, what value would you place on it? Explain your assumptions.

11   In the example of Alex in the text, no allowance was made for the fact that an item had been in use for some time. While it is obvious that the utility of most things declines over time, it is more difficult to identify the extent of that decline over a given period. In addition, even if we could identify the decline in utility and the utility remaining, we still have to assign some monetary amount to both parts. We said in the chapter that this was done by arriving at a written-down cost or value. For each of the following examples suggest, with reasons, the best method for arriving at the written-down cost or value.

    a   A machine will produce 10 000 items and will then need to be replaced. Production each year is to be matched to sales, and estimates of sales are 1000 units in the first year, 4000 units in the second year. Sales in the years after that are uncertain and cannot be forecast with any accuracy.

    b   A leasehold property on a five-year non-renewable lease.

    c   A company car.

    d   A personal computer.

    e   Computer software.

12   One reads of large sums of money being exchanged between soccer clubs in Europe. How do you think a club arrives at a figure of, for example, $10 million for a player?

13   Michelle Computers Ltd has had a difficult year owing to increasing costs associated with keeping its hardware and software up to date in the face of rapidly improving technology. As company accountant, you are aware that the company is overstocked with out-of-date virus software which the board of directors wishes to have valued at cost. 'After all,' the managing director tells you, 'you accountants follow the historic cost convention.'

    a   Should the software be valued at cost? If not, what value should be placed on it?

    b   The directors are responsible for the final accounts. What action, if any, should you take?

    c   If historic cost is used, will it affect the statement of financial performance?

Ethics case study

Jane is the accountant for Salisbury Ltd and has received the following memo from her boss concerning a machine recently purchased from a competitor.

Dear Jane,

Due to the problems faced by our competitor I have negotiated to purchase their plant and equipment, which is only 12 months old, for $500 000. The plant and equipment is worth at least $1 000 000. Therefore, I want you to record the plant and equipment at $1 000 000 and the difference between this and the cash paid should be included in profit for the period.

Signed
Ted Johnson

Jane is aware that it has been a difficult year for Salisbury Ltd and it is likely to report a loss for the period. If the company reports a loss it will be in default of a contract with the bank and there is a risk the bank will stop the company's overdraft facility. Accounting Standards require that assets be initially recorded at cost. Salisbury Ltd intends to use the plant and equipment, and has no intention of selling it.

Discuss:

   a   the appropriate way to record the transaction
   b   what Jane should do.

The Statement of Financial Position

Learning objectives

At the end of this chapter you should be able to:

1   explain the meaning and purpose of a statement of financial position

2   define and explain the five main elements of a statement of financial position

3   explain the distinction between current and non-current assets

4   explain the distinction between current and non-current liabilities

5   explain the meaning of 'equity'

6   explain and apply the statement of financial position equation

7   understand the various factors which influence the format of the statement of financial position.

Introduction

In Chapter 1 we discussed the objectives of accounting reports and the influences of users on financial reporting. We also discussed the limitations of accounting information and the role of accounting in business, its effect on business and some of the factors influencing accounting. In Chapter 3 we examined some possible approaches to measuring income from the point of view of both the economist and the accountant. We now look more specifically at the ways in which accountants measure wealth and income.

We suggested that the problem facing accountants is that of finding an appropriate basis for the measurement of wealth. There is also the additional problem that, in the real world, a system that only measures wealth and derives income from it cannot cope with the complexity of present-day enterprises. Consider a large retailing group such as Woolworths: should they have to carry out a valuation of all their premises, vehicles, stocks, etc. on one day of the year? The costs of such an operation would make it prohibitively expensive, even if it were logistically possible. For companies such as BHP, where operations are carried out on a worldwide basis, these logistical problems would be even greater. Such a system would also make it very difficult for the managers or the owners to make decisions on a day-to-day basis because they would have information at hand only once a year. Because of these problems with annual valuation systems, we need to find separate ways of measuring wealth and income.

The measurement of income will be dealt with in detail in Chapter 5. In this chapter we concentrate on the problem of the measurement of wealth and the way in which accounting approaches it. We look in some detail at the use of the statement of financial position as the measurement of wealth, its component parts such as assets and liabilities, and finally the format in which this statement is presented and the way in which that is influenced by the type of organisation, regulations and the needs of the users.

The statement of financial position

NOTE: From 1 July 2001 in Australia, the balance sheet became known as the statement of financial position. The two terms refer to the same statement.

In the case of an individual, we have said the wealth can be measured by simply listing the economic resources you control—assuming, of course, that you do not owe anybody money. To some extent the same can be said for an enterprise, although the level of complexity is greater. The way in which this is achieved for an enterprise is similar to that for an individual, and the resulting statement is called a statement of financial position. You should note that the statement of financial position relates to a position at a point in time. It is because of this that the analogy with a snapshot is often found in accounting textbooks.

Key Concept 4.1

The statement of financial position

The statement of financial position is a statement, at one point in time, which shows all the resources controlled by the enterprise and all the obligations due by the enterprise.

This definition of a statement of financial position is not intended to be comprehensive—it merely provides us with an outline of what we are referring to. Although an enterprise does not exist in the same way as a person, for accounting and for some legal purposes an enterprise is presumed to exist in its own right and is treated as a separate entity from the person or persons who own or operate it. In broad terms it is possible to account for any unit which has a separate and distinct existence. It may be that this is a hotel, for example, or a group of hotels, or a more complex organisation such as Hilton International Hotels. This idea of a separate entity is often referred to in accounting literature as 'the business entity principle'. It applies equally to organisations that are not commonly referred to as businesses, such as charitable organisations, clubs and societies. The question of whether the entity should be accounted for separately relates not only to the legal situation but also to the question of whether it can be seen to have a separate existence.

Key Concept 4.2

The business entity principle

The business entity principle states that transactions, assets and liabilities that relate to the enterprise are accounted for separately. It applies to all types of enterprises, irrespective of the fact that the enterprise may not be recognised as a separate legal or taxable entity.

While the application of this principle and the reasons for it are self-evident when we are looking at large public companies such as ICI or Shell, they are less clear with smaller enterprises such as the corner newsagent or a secondhand-car business. If, for example, you decided to set yourself up as a car dealer, for accounting purposes the cars purchased by you as a car dealer and the money earned as a result of that activity would be treated separately from your own personal car and money. This allows the tax authority to tax you separately on the profits from your business and it also helps you to determine the value of your business should you wish to sell it or take in a partner. The important part to remember is that for each business entity it is possible to account separately and therefore to draw up a statement of financial position at a point in time. We will now examine the statement of financial position in more detail.

Purpose of statements of financial position

The purpose of a statement of financial position is to communicate information about the financial position of an enterprise at a particular point in time. It summarises information contained in the accounting records in a clear and intelligible form. If the items contained in it are summarised and classified in an appropriate manner it can give information about the financial strength of the enterprise and indicate the relative liquidity of the assets. It also gives information about the liabilities of the enterprise, i.e. what economic resources the entity is obliged to provide to other entities as a result of past transactions. The combination of this information can assist the user to evaluate the financial position of the enterprise. It should be remembered, however, that financial statements are only one part of the information needed by users and thus the importance of this accounting statement should not be overemphasised.

Key Concept 4.3

Liquidity

Liquidity refers to the ease with which assets can be converted to cash in the normal course of business.

In most enterprises, a statement of financial position is prepared at least once a year. It could be done more frequently, of course, or, indeed, less frequently. It is convention that dictates that a normal accounting period is a year, and tax laws and other legislation are set up on that basis. Because the statement of financial position represents the position at one point in time, its usefulness is limited: the situation may have changed since the last statement was prepared. For example, if you prepare a statement of financial position in December and consult it in October it will be ten months out of date. To extend our snapshot analogy, we can picture a business as a movie and a statement of financial position as a still from that movie. Clearly, in the case of a movie, the still does not give a complete picture, and the same can be said for the statement of financial position.

Elements of the statement of financial position

We need to know what statements of financial position contain. We have already said that they are similar to an individual's own measurement of wealth. If you think how you would measure your own wealth, you will realise that you need to make a list of the economic resources you control (assets) and take away the economic resources due to other entities (liabilities). For an enterprise this listing of assets and liabilities at a particular point in time is the enterprise's statement of financial position.

Given this information about the contents of a statement of financial position, let us look in more detail at what is meant by assets and liabilities. We consider assets by looking at what constitutes an asset and how they are classified into sub-categories. Definitions of assets and liabilities were given in Chapter 2. We restate these definitions and discuss each in turn.

Assets

Although we can find many definitions of assets, most of them refer to the legal ownership rights, and so do not accord with contemporary accounting thought. Most contain some of the vital elements of a useful description, but a clear working definition is needed. Assets are not defined in the Corporations Law; therefore we turn to that provided by paragraph 14 of *Statement of Accounting Concepts No. 4* (AARF 1995), already defined in Key Concept 2.6 and restated in Key Concept 4.4. This definition is in line with contemporary accounting thought. It is similar to that adopted by most of the professional accounting bodies and to the concepts statement issued by the International Accounting Standards Committee (*Framework for the Presentation and Preparation of Financial Statements*, IASC 1990).

Before an item can be considered as an asset for inclusion in the statement of financial position it must not only meet the definition of an asset, it must also pass certain recognition criteria. Firstly, it must be probable that the future economic benefits will eventuate and secondly, the asset must possess a cost or other value that can be measured reliably. Only when an item satisfies the definition and meets both recognition criteria will it qualify for inclusion on the statement of financial position.

Key Concept 4.4

Assets

Assets are future economic benefits controlled by the entity as a result of past transactions or other past events.

Future economic benefits

The clear implication in the term 'future economic benefits' is that, for an item to be an asset, there must be some clear expectation that some benefit will be derived from the item by the entity, either now or in the future, and that benefit does not depend on physical form. This implies that the item must have some specific usefulness to the entity. An item that has no specific usefulness for the entity is not an asset. This is particularly important in times of rapidly changing technology as it suggests that the question of what is and what is not an asset can only be decided on the basis of its usefulness to the entity. For example, it is fairly obvious that a gold mine full of unmined gold is an asset for a mining business. However, there will come a point when all the gold has been removed and all that is left is a hole in the ground. The hole in the ground is no longer useful to the mining entity and it ceases to be an asset. On the other hand, a hole in the ground could have future economic benefits for a different entity, for example, a rubbish disposal business.

Measurement

One of the recognition criteria is that an asset must be capable of reliable measurement. The normal measure that is used is the dollar (a monetary unit). The problem, as discussed earlier, is: on what basis do we measure? Some items which may give future economic benefits are extremely difficult to measure: for example, the Sarich orbital engine while still in the design stage was able to raise millions of dollars in funds from investors. Alternatively, consider the worth of a trade name such as 'Coca-Cola', which obviously has future economic value to the entity. The problem facing accountants, once they have decided that there is a future benefit, is how to measure that benefit in monetary terms. In these examples it would also be impossible to isolate the effect they have in monetary terms; therefore we do not include them in the statement of financial position as assets, even though the business is clearly getting a benefit from them. (As soon as the Sarich company had an orbital engine running which was able to demonstrate its potential, it was possible to assign a monetary figure to this asset.) Other examples of items which are clearly of benefit but which are not included for accounting purposes are a good location, a highly motivated workforce or a reputation for excellent service. You will remember from Chapter 1 that we discussed this problem in the context of the limitations of accounting information.

Legal ownership and control

Many definitions of assets imply that in order to be an asset something must be owned. In reality most assets are owned, but the assertion that ownership is a precondition for the recognition of an asset by an entity is not correct. The entity must have the capacity to control the future economic benefits. While control often arises from legally enforceable rights, the absence of legal ownership does not automatically deny the existence of control. For example, a rental agreement for a house that entitles you to occupy it at a rent of $20 a week obviously confers a benefit if the market rental is, say, $100 a week, and thus may be seen as an asset. On the other hand, the fact that an individual or entity owns an item does not necessarily mean that there is any future benefit to be obtained. For example an old motor car that has been ordered off the road by the police may cease to be an asset, and, in fact, unless it can be driven to the salvage yard it may become a liability.

Past transactions or other events

A decision to expand a business next year is not an asset and would not show up in the accounting records. However, if an irrevocable contract was signed which committed the entity to use economic resources which would give it future economic benefits, then the signing of that contract is the past event and the commitment could be seen as an asset.

Control by the entity

While it may seem patently obvious that the benefits should accrue to the entity, i.e. be received by the entity at some point in time, it is vital in many cases to be able to separate the assets of the entity from those of the owner, for reasons referred to earlier. For example, a factory building is likely to be an asset to an entity because the benefits from its use are likely to accrue to the entity. However, if the entity is a corner shop with residential accommodation, it is somewhat less clear which part of the building is an asset of the business and which is not. In practice it may well be that some of the goods held for resale are physically stored in part of the residential accommodation. There is unfortunately no general rule which can be applied and each case must be considered on its merits. The process of distinguishing between the assets of the owner and those of the business is merely an application of the business entity principle, referred to earlier, which states that the business should be viewed as separate from the owner and therefore accounted for separately.

Categories of assets

For accounting purposes assets are normally separated as far as possible into subcategories. The reasoning behind this is that accounting statements should provide information that is useful in making economic decisions. This is the objective of financial reporting, as stated in Key Concept 2.4. These decisions can be made more precisely if some indication is given regarding the nature of the assets of the entity. The categories used in Australia are current and non-current assets. In some countries the terms 'fixed assets' or 'long-term assets' are used instead of 'non-current assets'.

Current assets

Some accounting texts suggest that current assets are those which are part of the entity's operating cycle; they are also known as circulating assets. Other texts suggest that current assets are those which are converted into cash within an accounting period. Before continuing our discussion we need to know what is meant by the term 'operating cycle'.

The operating cycle

It is easier to understand the term 'operating cycle' if we look at one or two examples. In the case of a shop selling clothes, the operating cycle consists of buying garments and selling them for cash. In the case of an assembly business, the operating cycle involves more processes such as buying components, and then going through the process of assembly, selling and the collection of cash from a sale. Thus, the operating cycle has no fixed time period but depends on the nature of the business. It may, in fact, extend over a number of years. This is the case with property development, shipbuilding and heavy construction industries. The fact that the operating cycles are of different lengths is not vital, as in general terms those assets that are part of the operating cycle are similar and are likely to be items such as stock, cash in the bank, etc. This means that in general terms these assets are likely to be liquid (refer to Key Concept 4.3).

Key Concept 4.5

Operating cycle

Operating cycle is defined as the average time between the acquisition of materials entering into a process and their realisation in cash or an instrument that is readily convertible into cash. (*AASB 1040: Statement of Financial Position*, para. 9.1)

The realisation period

As mentioned earlier, other accounting texts suggest that what distinguishes current assets from other assets is whether or not they will be realised in the form of cash in the current accounting period. By convention, accounting periods are normally one year, though they can cover any period we care to use. If we applied this test strictly we would find that in certain cases, such as that of a shipbuilder, something that is part of the operating cycle will not in fact be realised in the form of cash within a year.

In Australia, the realisation period is normally one year, unless the operating cycle is longer, in which case the operating cycle is used.

Key Concept 4.6

Current assets

'Current asset' means an asset that
- is expected to be realised, or is held for sale or consumption, in the normal course of the entity's operating cycle; or
- is held primarily for trading purposes or for the short term and is expected to be realised within twelve months of the reporting date; or
- is cash or a cash-equivalent asset which is not restricted in its use beyond twelve months or the length of the operating cycle, whichever is greater. (*AASB 1040*, para. 9.1)

Examples of current assets include cash, accounts receivable, short-term investments, inventories and prepaid expenses. The assets should be classified according to either their nature (such as accounts receivable representing amounts owing from third parties) or their function (such as short-term investments representing assets being held for sale).

Non-current assets

Most texts refer to non-current assets as fixed assets. The term 'fixed assets' has been in use, in accounting literature, for decades and is still in use in a number of countries. Fixed assets generally included those assets which were acquired with the intention of retaining them for the purpose of generating income over a number of years. Items that met this classification included land and buildings, machinery, vehicles, plant and equipment.

The term 'non-current asset' is now finding favour in Australia. The change has mainly come about through changes to the Corporations Law and the updating of Accounting Standards to bring them into line with current thinking embodied in the Conceptual Framework. Though the term is not defined in the Corporations Law, it is required to be used as a heading in the statement of financial position to signify all assets other than current assets. The definition given as Key Concept 4.7, which fits intuitively with Corporations Law requirements, is used in Accounting Standards. As you can see, it is all-encompassing.

Key Concept 4.7

Non-current assets
Non-current assets are all assets other than current assets. (AASB 1040, para. 9.1)

Other items could be classed as either non-current or current assets depending on their nature. Examples are loans made to others over a period of years, a mortgage or a long-term investment in the shares of another entity. All these could be classed as current assets if they met the definition within the time constraint. For example, a long-term loan which had only 12 months left of its life would be reclassified from a non-current asset to a current asset.

Examples of non-current assets include plant and equipment, furniture and fixtures, motor vehicles, land and buildings, long-term receivables and intangibles. As with current assets, non-current assets are also classified according to their nature or function.

Having looked at what constitutes an asset and at the way in which assets are divided into the two classes on the statement of financial position, we can now turn to the other part of the statement—what economic resources are owed to other entities. In accounting terminology, these are the liabilities.

Liabilities

As with the general term 'assets' there are several definitions of liabilities, most of which refer to amounts owed by an entity. The term 'liabilities' is not defined in the Corporations Law. To be consistent with our approach to assets, we will use the definition already cited in Key Concept 2.7, provided by paragraph 48 of *Statement of Accounting Concepts No. 4* (AARF, 1995).

Key Concept 4.8

Liabilities
Liabilities are the future sacrifices of economic benefits that the entity is presently obliged to make to other entities as a result of past transactions or other past events.

As with assets, an item that meets the definition of a liability must satisfy the criteria for recognition before being recognised on the statement of financial position. It must be probable that settlement of the liability will be required, and the amount must be capable of being measured reliably.

From the definition given, we can see that there has to be an existence of a present obligation, in economic terms, and this obligation must result in the reporting entity having to sacrifice economic benefits at some future date. Further, these obligations must have arisen because of past events.

As is the case with assets, liabilities are divided into two classes: current and non-current.

Current liabilities

The definition of current liabilities is similar to that of current assets. That is, these liabilities become due in either the operating cycle or within an accounting period normally defined as one year. As with assets, we will follow the realisation concept and use the definition given in *AASB 1040: Statement of Finacial Position*. Although liabilities are defined in *SAC 4* and in *AASB 1014: Set-off and Extinguishment of Debt*, paragraph 16, a definition of current liability is found in *AASB 1034: Financial Report Presentation and Disclosures*, paragraph 15.1, and *AASB 1040*.

Key Concept 4.9

Current liability

A current liability is a liability that:
- arises and is expected to be settled in the normal course of the entity's operating cycle; or
- is at call or due or expected to be settled within twelve months of the reporting date.

Some examples of current liabilities are: amounts owed to creditors—entities from whom we have purchased items on credit; short-term loans such as bank overdrafts, which are normally repayable on demand; and other short-term loans, such as promissory notes which have a life of 90 to 180 days.

Non-current liabilities

Clearly there are other types of liabilities which do not have to be repaid in full in one year; an everyday example of this type of liability is a mortgage on a house. In the case of a business, this type of liability may take a number of forms such as a bank loan repayable in three years or five years. Liabilities of this sort are longer-term liabilities and are normally put under the heading of non-current liabilities. Some texts refer to non-current liabilities as long-term liabilities, though this term is being used less and less in Australia. Non-current liabilities, like non-current assets, are not defined, though the term is used, in the Corporations Law. The definition below is taken from approved Accounting Standard *AASB 1040*, paragraph 15.1.

Key Concept 4.10

Non-current liabilities

A non-current liability means a liability which is not a current liability.

Assets and liabilities

It can be seen that there is a thread which is common to both assets and liabilities: both are concerned with the accounting period (current) and a time span greater than the accounting period (non-current). The difference between the definitions of assets and liabilities, in general terms, centres on who controls the economic resources. Assets are resources controlled by the entity, and liabilities are economic resources owed to another entity, i.e. claims against those resources. It should be seen that if the claims against an entity exceed the resources controlled, then the entity will no longer be a going concern. Conversely, if assets exceed liabilities the excess will accrue to the owners of the entity.

Owners' equity

The owners' equity or share of the capital of the business can be viewed in a number of ways. In a sense it is a liability of the business in so far as it is a claim on the assets. However, it differs from other liabilities which have definite dates by which they are to be paid and are fixed in amount. The owners' equity is normally left in the business as long as it is required. Another way of viewing the owners' equity is as a residual claim on the assets of the business after all the other liabilities have been settled.

In general, the owners' equity is normally shown under two headings: that which is put into the business and that which is earned by and left in the business. The latter category we will refer to as retained profits. The total of the figures under these two headings, in the case of an individual, is analogous with wealth, whereas when the owner is in a business it is often referred to as capital. As we showed in Chapter 3, the amount of this wealth or capital is dependent on the measure used, i.e. replacement cost, net realisable value, etc. It is therefore better to view owners' equity as a residual claim rather than as capital or wealth because those expressions imply that an absolute measure of owners' equity is possible. Equity is not defined in the Corporations Law, though an acceptable definition is given in paragraph 78 of *Statement of Accounting Concepts No. 4* (AARF, 1995) and paragraph 15.1 of *AASB 1034*.

Key Concept 4.11

Equity
Equity is the residual interest in the assets of the entity after deduction of its liabilities. (SAC 4, para. 78)

The equity can be seen as the residual interest due to the owners of the entity; hence the often-used term 'owners' equity'. We will use this term until we come to Chapter 11, which discusses final accounts, partnerships and companies.

The statement of financial position equation

As we have already shown, the statement of financial position of an entity is a statement of assets and liabilities at a particular point in time. Because the business is an artificial entity, by definition all the benefits arising from its assets belong to someone else. This is summed up in the statement of financial position equation:

$$assets = liabilities$$

The equation describes the statement of financial position in its simplest form; it must always hold true. However, it uses a very loose definition of liabilities. It can be refined to highlight the differences between pure liabilities and owners' equity, as follows.

$$\text{assets} = \text{liabilities} + \text{owners' equity}$$

This form of the equation will be used in our worksheet in Chapter 6. The equation can be rewritten to highlight the fact that owners' equity is a residual claim on the assets.

$$\text{assets} - \text{liabilities} = \text{owners' equity}$$

Simple statements of financial position

To illustrate the equation, a simple statement of financial position can be constructed, using the information contained in Example 4.1.

Example 4.1: Keelsafe

Susan Keel had been made redundant and she decided to start up a small business making safety harnesses which she called Keelsafe Safety Harnesses. For this purpose she purchased:

	$
One industrial sewing machine	1 100
A quantity of heavy duty webbing material	600
A quantity of sewing materials	200
A secondhand typewriter	100
A supply of office stationery and letterheads	100
One cutting machine	800

The remaining $100 of her redundancy money was put into a business bank account. At this stage we could draw up a list of assets of the business as follows.

Assets	$
Sewing machine	1 100
Webbing	600
Sewing materials	200
Typewriter	100
Stationery	100
Cutting machine	800
Cash at bank	100
	3 000

We could also identify the owners' equity in the business as being $3000, i.e. the amount Susan Keel put in. Thus the other side of the statement of financial position—and, indeed, the accounting equation—would be:

Owners' equity	3 000
	$3 000

Before moving on, it is worth thinking about how we obtained the figure for the owners' equity; all we did was to list what economic resources Susan Keel's business controlled and then, as there were no outside claims against the business, we balanced the statement of financial position by recording the amount of residual interest in the assets to the owners' equity.

Let us take this example further.

Because she was just starting out, Susan decided that until the business got off the ground she would operate from home and use the garage to manufacture the safety harnesses and use the front room of her house as an office. The house had cost her $20 000 in 1979.

This additional information presents us with a problem: we do not know how much of the $20 000 relates to the garage and the front room. We know that the business uses some of the house and that the house is an asset. But is it an asset of Susan herself or of the business? If it is the latter, how should we record it and at what amount? To answer these questions we need to go back to our definition of an asset, which was:

> Future economic benefits controlled by the entity as a result of past transactions or other past events.

Bearing in mind the business entity principle, we can see from the definition that the garage is not an asset of the business where the business is viewed as a separate entity from the owner. It is Susan Keel herself who owns both the house and the garage, and she also retains the legal right to enjoy the benefits from their use. The garage is not an asset of the business because the business has no legal right to use the garage, and has no control over it. Therefore, it does not need to be included in the statement of financial position of the business. A similar argument can be applied to the front room which is being used as an office. However, suppose Susan entered into a long-term lease of the garage, whereby the business rented the garage from her, and this lease was secure even if Susan sold the business to another person. In this case the lease would be an asset of the business because the use of the garage would now come under the control of the business and not of Susan. If you are unsure of the argument, return to the discussion on the business entity and the definition of an asset.

When Susan starts to make the harnesses, she realises that she needs to buy some fasteners. She approaches her bank which agrees to give her a loan of $1000. She pays this sum into the business bank account and then buys the fasteners with a cheque for $600 drawn on that account.

We will look at this transaction and then draw up a new statement of financial position. A new one is needed because we are now at a different point in time: you will remember that a statement of financial position shows the position at one point in time only. The actual transaction on its own can be looked at in two stages.

Stage 1

The first stage occurred when Susan borrowed the money from the bank. This had two effects: it increased the business assets, because the business will get a future benefit from the use of that money; and it also increased the business liabilities, because the business now owes the bank $1000. This viewed on its own can be depicted as:

$$\text{assets} = \text{liabilities} + \text{owners' equity}$$
$$\text{cash in bank (\$1000)} = \text{loan (\$1000)} + 0$$

Stage 2

In the second stage, $600 of the money in the bank is used to buy the fasteners. We can extend Stage 1 and depict this as follows.

$$\text{assets} = \text{liabilities} + \text{owners' equity}$$

$$\text{cash in bank (\$1000)} = \text{loan (\$1000)}$$

$$\text{fasteners} + \$600 - \$600 \text{ cash in bank} = 0$$

All that has happened is that we have exchanged one asset for another, and the totals on either side of the equation remain the same.

Before going on to draw up a new statement of financial position, you should note the important principle that we have just illustrated: there are two sides to every transaction. In Stage 1, the two sides of the transaction were an increase in assets with a corresponding increase in liabilities; in Stage 2, there was a decrease in one asset with a corresponding increase in another asset. This is often referred to as the principle of duality, which is simply a grand-sounding title for the rule that all transactions have two sides.

Key Concept 4.12

The principle of duality

The principle of duality is the basis of the double-entry bookkeeping system on which accounting is based. It states that:
- Every transaction has two opposite and equal components.

Having established this principle, we can now draw up the new statement of financial position of Keelsafe Safety Harnesses. We use the following statement of financial position format:

$$\text{assets} - \text{liabilities} = \text{owners' equity}$$

The previous statement of financial position was a very simple one; this time we will classify the assets into current and non-current, and group them together to make the statement more informative.

Another way in which we can make the statement of financial position more informative is to list the assets in order of liquidity. Liquid assets are those which can readily be converted into cash: the more difficult the item is to turn into cash, the less liquid it is. (The liquidity concept was stated in Key Concept 4.3.) The sewing machine as a non-current asset is less liquid than the stocks of fasteners. Similarly these are shown as less liquid than the cash at the bank.

You will also note that each of the groups of assets is subtotalled and the subtotal is shown separately. The total of all the assets is then shown. It is conventional to use single underlining for subtotals and double underlining to denote final totals.

Having classified and listed the assets of Keelsafe, we then show the claims against the business, subclassified into current and non-current liabilities. The total liabilities are deducted from the total assets to give a figure for the residual assets (owners' equity). The residual assets amount is called the 'net assets'. This is the value of the business after all external liabilities have been met. It has double underlining to show that it is a final total. The amount of the owners' equity, which we have said comprises capital put into the business as well as residual profits, should balance against the net assets figure.

This is shown by our statement of financial position equation:

$$\text{assets} - \text{liabilities} = \text{owners' equity}$$

KEELSAFE SAFETY HARNESSES
STATEMENT OF FINANCIAL POSITION AT 31 MAY 20X2

Assets	$	$	$	$
Current Assets				
Cash at bank	500			
Fasteners	600			
Sewing material	200			
Webbing material	600			
Office stationery	100			
Total Current Assets		2 000		
Non-current Assets				
Typewriter	100			
One cutting machine	800			
One sewing machine	1 100			
Total Non-current Assets		2 000		
Total Assets			4 000	
Liabilities				
Current Liabilities				
Bank loan	1 000			
Total Liabilities			1 000	
Net Assets				3 000
Owners' Equity				3 000

The statement of financial position has been rearranged to emphasise the differences between the various types of assets and Susan Keel's residual claim on the assets after any liabilities have been paid. Note that the statement is headed with the name of the business and the date on which it was drawn up.

Before you proceed any further, re-examine the definitions of current and non-current assets and ensure that you understand why the items above have been classified as they have.

It is worth examining the statement of financial position for Woolworths. Note the classification of assets and liabilities into current and non-current categories. Also note that included in current assets are property, plant and equipment—items that we generally expect to see in non-current assets. The statement refers to Note 13, from which we can see that the assets involved are land and buildings held for development and sale. The company clearly intends to develop and sell the land and buildings within twelve months and therefore has properly classified them as current assets.

After studying the statement of financial position for Woolworths, you should be aware that it is not possible to obtain a complete understanding of all the elements on the statement without referring to the notes that follow. The financial statements are like the table of contents in a book: without reading the book, you cannot know the full story; similarly, without reading the notes accompanying the financial statements, it is not possible to understand an entity's position.

We can now proceed to examine the determinants of the formats of the statement of financial position and the ways in which they can be used, together with their limitations.

Determinants of the format of the statement of financial position

We now examine the purpose of the statement of financial position and its limitations. We also consider some influences that affect the way it is presented and the extent to which this is determined by the type of organisation and the users of the statements.

Purpose and limitations

The fact that a statement of financial position represents the position of an entity at one point in time is a limitation, because it is relevant only at that point in time. At any other time, as we have seen in the case of Keelsafe, a new statement of financial position has to be prepared. For the statement to be useful, it should be as up to date as possible; its utility diminishes as time passes. Similarly, for the statement of financial position to provide a relevant measure of the assets and liabilities, the values assigned to those assets and liabilities should be as recent as possible, and herein lies another limitation.

As we saw in Chapter 3, there are a number of ways in which assets can be valued, some of which are more subjective than others. The right value to choose depends on the purpose for which the statement of financial position is to be used. For example, if we want to know how much each item cost, then the original, or historic, cost would be appropriate. If, on the other hand, we wanted to know how much each item could be sold for, then the net realisable value would be appropriate. If we wanted to know how much the business as a whole was worth, it is likely that neither of these would be appropriate. Partly because of the difficulties involved in choosing an appropriate valuation and partly by convention, accountants have traditionally used the historical cost as the basis of the valuation of assets in the statement of financial position.

Clearly in certain cases this has led to assets being stated at a figure which bears little, if any, relation to their current value. Thus, in recent years, land and building values shown in published accounts are generally based on revaluations rather than historical costs.

Allied to the problem of fluctuations in the prices of specific assets is the fact that the unit of measurement, the dollar (or other unit of currency), does not itself represent a constant value over time. You cannot buy as many goods with a dollar today as you could ten years ago. This once again limits the usefulness of the information contained in the statement of financial position.

CASE STUDY 4.1

Accounting for the net: beyond the balance sheet

The new wave of technology threatens to overwhelm the old methods of accounting. But alternatives are already developing, according to David James.

WHEN two of the world's largest car makers, Ford and General Motors, moved their entire supply chains onto the internet, digital communications technology could no longer be regarded as peripheral to the main activities of commerce. The world's larger companies are being forced to rethink the entire structure of their business. Ford, for example, is pushing its US$80 billion components and materials purchasing on to the internet. Such developments require those who analyse and describe business to rethink their most basic assumptions.

For accountants, the implications are crucial. In particular, the balance sheet, the traditional snapshot of business value, is ill-suited to a commercial environment in which wealth creation is a function of intangibles: brand names, customer relationships, commercial history, knowledge, market positioning.

By heavily emphasising the importance of tangible indicators of wealth, the balance sheet has a heavy positivist bias: an assumption that was appropriate enough in the industrial period, when the ability to transform and move physical things with machinery was the key to commercial success. But in an environment where the key factors of wealth creation are not things but intangibles, and the transformation and movement of things is becoming a smaller part of a company's competitive strength, such an approach appears increasingly fragile.

Under pressure

Two things seem certain. One is a reduction in the perceived importance of the balance sheet. Or (far less likely, given the difficulties of changing the basic accounting structures when authorities are trying to normalise accounting internationally in order to adapt to globalisation) a change to the way the balance sheet is constructed. As John McMahon, vice president of Morgan Stanley Dean Witter comments, he has 'never heard of a Net analyst talking of a balance sheet'.

Soon, it will not just be analysts of internet companies who are ignoring the balance sheet. As the world's larger companies embrace the internet, hollowing out their physical operations and concentrating on their intangible strengths, one consequence is that they will be less well-depicted by a document that treats intangibles largely as an afterthought and imposes rigid treatment on their valuation (for example, forced depreciation of the goodwill of a brand name may be completely at divergence with the real impact in the market place).

Neither are the pressures that are encouraging the world's larger companies to emphasise the intangible likely to ease. Many conventional industrial companies are under severe stress in their conventional markets, mainly due to demographic changes. As populations in developed economies stabilise and contract, the key to market success becomes not the ability to produce goods cheaply, but the ability to attract customers to buy—and that usually means using intangibles.

Consider the business environment in which Ford and General Motors operate. It is estimated that all the automobile plants in North America could be closed down and there would still be a global oversupply. Kenneth Courtis, senior strategist for Deutsche Bank in Tokyo, says that the global financial crises of 1997 and 1998 were the symptoms of world-wide over-investment. He writes: 'We can today make, around the world, some 60 million cars annually, yet we are purchasing about 45 million. The result is that less than a third of the world's 40 largest car producers are cash flow positive.'

Economists can view such imbalances with a sanguine eye, asserting that the problem is simply one of incorrect pricing. But it is unlikely that the same applies to accountants. The speed of technological change suggests that this is not a transient issue: the ability to produce cheaply will no longer be the main or sole key to successful transacting. And if this is so in conventional industrial markets such as automobiles, it is even more the case in newer industries such as computing or service industries, where the physical, tangible aspects of the product are often of negligible importance.

Australian CPA, December 1999 (abridged)

Commentary

The article highlights the problems with the traditional balance sheet (statement of financial position) experienced by entities whose main assets are intangible. In the industrial revolution, the major assets were tangible and physical, but in the knowledge revolution, the major assets are intangible and non-physical. This problem challenges the accounting profession to establish a methodology for the reliable measurement of intangibles. If the accounting profession fails to do this, the statement of financial position will become less useful, and users will seek other means of obtaining the information they require to assist in their decision making.

Influences on the format of the statement of financial position

We will examine the various influences on the statement of financial position and then look at the needs of users; no discussion of financial statements would be complete without some reference to their needs.

Asset values

We have already shown that the activity in which the organisation is involved can determine the classification of an asset (remember the case of the car dealer compared with the manufacturing business). We have illustrated with the example of a gold mine that something which is a worthless asset for one business can be a valuable asset for another business undertaking a different activity. Those cases are reasonably clear cut, but consider, for example, the problems of a football club trying to account for star players, or of a high-technology business trying to decide whether the cost of the patent on a new product is going to yield any future benefit when technology is changing so rapidly.

There are also issues relating to the ways in which a business is perceived and the ways in which management wishes the business to be perceived. Research has shown that managers, especially the managers of smaller organisations, perceive that bankers are interested in the amount of assets available as security for a loan or overdraft. There is therefore a temptation to try to enhance the value of assets, perhaps by revaluing land and buildings, before applying for a loan. Similarly, in a number of cases where a business is in trouble, the assets have been revalued in order to bolster the image of the business and to promote the impression of a 'sound asset base'.

In Australia there are severe penalties for directors of public companies or other organisations who attempt fraudulently to inflate assets or decrease liabilities.

Types of business

One of the prime determinants of the content and format of the statement of financial position is the structure of the organisation. For example, an incorporated business, i.e. a company, is subject to certain rules and regulations imposed by the state, whereas a partnership or sole proprietorship has no such restrictions. A company has to produce annual accounts as laid out in the Corporations Law, and file a copy with the Australian Securities and Investments Commission (ASIC), whereas in the case of a partnership there is no such requirement. A business that is part of a larger organisation may have to comply with the rules and form of accounts that suit that organisation as a whole.

The need to comply with organisational requirements may also be affected by who owns the business. For example, an American-owned company operating in Australia would have to comply with Australian regulations, but would also report to the US parent company in a form that complies with US regulations. In contrast, there are no restrictions or rules imposed on a business that is owned by two partners, other than the Partnership Act; the partners can decide for themselves what form the statement of financial position should take. However, other bodies can affect the frequency and format of the statement of financial position. For example, the tax office needs to know how much income the partners have earned, and if the accounts are drawn up by a professional accountant then that person is required to follow the Accounting Standards and rules of the profession.

Another factor affecting the format of the statement of financial position is the size of the organisation. We have used a very small operation in our example, in which all the assets could be individually listed. In the case of a larger, more complex organisation, assets will need to be summarised under broad headings; otherwise the amount of detail would be so great that the user of the statement would find it impossible to get an overall picture.

(The financial statements for Woolworths show that some of the detail can be found in notes attached to the financial statements.)

Finally, we should mention the influence of organisational goals. Consider, for example, an organisation set up for charitable purposes (which may or may not be incorporated): of what relevance to that organisation is a classification such as 'owners' equity'? Similarly, if you looked at the accounts of your municipal council you would not expect to see a heading for owners' equity or retained profits.

Regulations

In this context the most pervasive influence on the form and content of the statement of financial position is the state, through the medium of legislation. Legislation is the reason that the format and content of statements of financial position, as well as the way in which they are prepared, is different in some respects between countries. Even within Australia there are different rules about the format and level of sophistication, depending on whether the organisation is a charity, a municipal council, or a company registered under the Corporations Law. Even within these categories there are different rules: for example a small company in certain circumstances is not required to produce annual accounts for filing with ASIC. A listed public company, on the other hand, also has to comply with the rules and regulations laid down by the stock exchange. While it is important to appreciate that these differences exist, the details of them are not relevant for the purposes of this text.

Users of accounts

As we discussed in Chapter 1, there are a number of different users who may have conflicting needs for information. To some extent the rules and regulations laid down by the state could be said to encompass some of these needs. However, these rules give only a minimum requirement. For example, while the Corporations Law requires that loans and overdrafts should be shown, research shows that bankers would like to see details of the repayment dates of those loans in the accounts. On the other hand, the owners of the company may not wish to have that information made public. A similar conflict arises between the needs of managers who wish to know what it will cost to replace an asset rather than what the asset cost when they bought it, and the needs of the owners who wish to know what the management has spent their money on and how much each item cost.

Conclusion

In this chapter we have defined the nature, purpose and content of statements of financial position and have highlighted some of the problems in such a statement. We have also introduced you to the wider context in which accounting reports can be viewed. It is important before proceeding further that you make sure that you understand the definitions involved and can apply them to real problems. As you have seen, a statement of financial position can take many forms and in a book of this nature there is no need to cover all of them. For simplicity, therefore, we will use one format throughout the book. A sample is given below, together with an explanation for the choice of this format. It is important that you understand the reasons for the choice of the suggested format because this will aid you in interpreting accounting information at a later stage.

Suggested format for a statement of financial position

SIMPLE LTD
STATEMENT OF FINANCIAL POSITION AT 31 DECEMBER 20X1

	$	$	$	$
Assets				
Current Assets				
Cash at bank	40			
Finished goods inventory	1 220			
Raw materials inventory	1 400			
Total Current Assets		2 660		
Non-current Assets				
Motor vehicles	10 100			
Machinery	5 000			
Land and buildings	100 000			
Total Non-current Assets		115 100		
Total Assets			117 760	
Liabilities				
Current Liabilities				
Bank overdraft	2 000			
Total Current Liabilities		2 000		
Non-current Liabilities				
Bank loan, due 1 January 20X6	50 000			
Total Non-current Liabilities		50 000		
Total Liabilities			52 000	
Net Assets				65 760
Owners' Equity				
Capital	50 000			
Retained earnings	15 760			
Total Owners' Equity				65 760

The format of the statement of financial position is determined by the needs of the organisation. We have chosen a format appropriate to an introductory text. Before following a different format, ensure that you understand the reasons behind it and consider whether the information is as clear as in the format given above (refer to Case Study 4.1).

Reasons for choosing this format

There are two reasons why we have chosen to present the statement of financial position in this format. Firstly, the statement of financial position lists all the assets in order of liquidity, within the two asset groups. For example, in the current assets group, cash at bank must be more liquid than either of the two inventories, and the finished goods would normally be easier to convert to cash than the raw materials. The same reasoning applies to the non-current assets.

The asset classification is followed by the liability classification, ranked in order of the dates when claims will become due. In our example a bank overdraft is normally due on demand, whereas the long-term loan has a definite repayment date. By deducting the liabilities from the assets we are left with a figure for the residual or net assets which accrue to the owners of the business.

Secondly, the format chosen is that which was previously required under the Corporations Law, and it appears that many companies still use this format.

The statement of financial position is headed with the name of the organisation and the date to which the statement relates. As has already been explained, a statement of financial position relates to one point in time and that date needs to be clearly stated in the heading.

Finally, we emphasise again that the statement of financial position format may differ due to the requirements of the users or owners. For example, it is unlikely that a corner store would be part of a public company: a more appropriate format, in this case, would be to list the current assets less the current liabilities. If the current assets were more than the current liabilities, this would indicate that the business should be able to meet short-term commitments when they became due.

Summary

In this chapter we have seen that a statement of financial position is an attempt to show the financial position at one point in time. We also introduced the idea that a business is viewed for accounting purposes as a separate entity from its owners (the business entity principle). From this starting point we have gone on to define assets, liabilities and owners' equity and to look at the statement of financial position equation. Before moving on to the next chapter you should ensure that you have understood what is contained in this chapter by working through the review questions and problems given below. As with previous chapters, the answers to the review questions are all within the text.

References

Australian Accounting Standards Board and Public Sector Accounting Standards Board. *Statement of Accounting Concept No. 4: Definition and Recognition of the Elements of Financial Statements*, March 1995.

The Corporations Law, CCH, Sydney, 1992.

International Accounting Standards Committee. *Framework for the Presentation and Preparation of Financial Statements*, London, 1991.

Review questions

1   What are the essential elements of a useful definition of an asset?

2   What are the deficiencies, if any, in the following definition of an asset? 'Assets are the things a business owns.'

3   Explain in your own words the difference between non-current assets and current assets and why it is important to classify assets into subgroups.

4   Explain in your own words what a liability is and the differences between liabilities and owners' equity.

5   What is the purpose of a statement of financial position and what information does it contain?

Problems for discussion and analysis

1   Refer to the Woolworths financial report in Appendix 1.
   a   What is the amount of total assets? Current assets? Non-current assets?
   b   Which class of non-current assets has the greatest value? How is this class of assets valued?
   c   Note 18 lists different provisions. What do you think the provisions represent?
   d   Are the provisions' liabilities in accordance with the definitions and recognition criteria in *SAC 4* and discussed in Chapter 2?

2   ABC Ltd, in 20X6, had total assets of $100 000 and owners' equity of $50 000. In 20X7 total liabilities were $50 000 more than in 20X6, and the owners' equity was $60 000.
   a   Calculate the total assets figure for 20X7, and
   b   the total liabilities figure for 20X6.

3   Prepare a statement of financial position from the following information and comment on the position of the business as shown by that statement of financial position.

	$
Stock of goods held for resale	13 000
Freehold land and building	64 000
Mortgage on land and building	58 000
Cash	1 000
Fixtures and fittings	15 200
Office furniture	4 600
Bank overdraft	20 700
Delivery van	3 200
Owners' Equity	?

4   Prepare a statement of financial position from the following information and comment on the financial position of the business.

	$
Cash	3 000
Inventory	8 000
Accounts payable	12 000
Salaries payable	?
Accounts receivable	16 000
Land and buildings	20 000
Plant and equipment	7 000
Furnishings and fittings	2 500
Owners' Equity	13 900
Bank loan	30 000

5   Ledger accounts of Mickey Ltd as at 30 June 20X1 are listed below. Prepare a statement of financial position in good form and insert the missing amounts.

	$		$
Total Owners' Equity	?	Other Current Assets	?
Total Non-current Assets	?	Total Assets	?
Tax payable	?	Loan payable (31/12/20X3)	?
Total Liabilities	?	Net Assets	27 400
Bank	10 000	Loan receivable (30/6/20X3)	100 000
Accounts receivable	15 700	Total Non-current Assets	?
Accounts payable	10 300	Debentures payable (30/6/20X9)	137 000
Inventory	27 200	Loan receivable (1/7/20X1)	10 000
Fixtures/fittings (net)	7 200	Plant and equipment (net)	3 600
Salaries payable	6 200	Other Current Liabilities	1 200
Land and buildings	120 000	Total Current Assets	63 600
Total Current Liabilities	30 000		

6   The final account balances, after all adjustments, of Debbie Ltd for the year ending 30 June 20X1 are listed below. From the information given, prepare a statement of financial position in good form and list the accounts, which would not be included in the statement of financial position.

	$
Bank overdraft	11 900
Salaries payable	1 000
Salaries expense	1 000
Sales	137 250
Inventory	13 100
Accounts receivable	17 300
Owners' Equity	?
Interest expense	330
Land and buildings (net)	110 000
Long-term loan (due 19/12/20X9)	100 000
Accounts payable	45 600
Plant and equipment (net)	22 000
Cost of goods sold	110 000

7   Below are the final account balances (after all adjustments) of ABC Ltd for the year ending 30 June 20X1. From these balances prepare a statement of financial position in good form, and list the accounts which would not be included in the statement of financial position.

	$
Cash	126 000
Sales discount	5 000
Accounts receivable	50 000
Inventory	88 000
Land	364 000
Plant and equipment	234 000
Accounts payable	26 000
Ninety-day bank bill payable	80 000
Long-term loan payable	45 000
Tax payable	10 000
Vehicle expenses	10 000
Cost of goods sold	40 000
Owners' Equity	701 000
Tax expense	10 000

8   The following items were extracted from the ledger of I. Dunno on 30 June 20X0. You are required to prepare a statement of financial position in good form and insert the missing amounts.

	$
Accounts receivable	20
Accounts payable	?
Cash	?
Debentures payable	160
Travelling expense	30
Other Current Assets	30
Inventories	210
Investments	
Three-month bank deposit	140
Loan to Y Ltd, due 30 August 20X0	70
Land and buildings	400
Loan payable, due 30 August 20X0	30
Loan payable, due 30 August 20X2	310
Net revenue	500
Net Assets	?
Plant and equipment	210
Prepaid expenses	160
Total Owners' Equity	560
Total Liabilities	?
Total Current Liabilities	230
Total Assets	1 260
Total Current Assets	?
Total Non-current Assets	610
Total Non-current Liabilities	?

9   The accounting department of the ABC Co. Ltd was struck by lightning and some of the accounting records destroyed. The senior accountant managed to salvage some records and requires you to prepare a statement of financial position, in good form from the information given below.

Debtors $10 000, bank overdraft $12 000, motor vehicles $20 000, net assets $115 000, total assets $217 000, inventory $20 000, land $50 000, capital $80 000, total non-current assets $185 000, plant and equipment $15 000, prepaid rent ? (note: the rent is paid monthly in advance), total current assets ?, buildings ? , creditors ? , total current liabilities ? , retained earnings ?, total owners' equity ?

10   In each of the following situations identify whether the item should be included in the statement of financial position of Transom Trading at 31 December 20X1, and if so at what amount and under which heading. Transom Trading is a retailer of motor parts and accessories. In all cases reasons for your decision must be given.

a   A freehold shop bought in August 20X1 for $176 000.

b   A mortgage of $60 000 taken out to buy the shop in August 20X1.

c   Goods on the shelves at the end of the day on 31 December 20X1. These goods had a resale value of $24 000 and had been purchased by Transom Trading for $16 000.

d   Delivery van, costing $12 000, which Transom Trading ordered on 20 December 20X1 but which was finally delivered and paid for on 2 January 20X2.

e   Shop fittings which were worth $6000 and had been bought at an auction by Transom Trading for only $3000 prior to opening the shop in August 20X1.

f   A Ford Falcon costing $7000 which the owner of Transom Trading had bought in November 20X1 for his wife to use. He had found that the Ford Escort which he had bought secondhand in September for $8000 was being used exclusively for collecting and delivering goods for Transom Trading and not as a family car as originally intended.

g   One cash register which was rented from Equipment Supplies at an annual rental of $400.

h   One cash register which Transom Trading had bought in November 20X1 for $1200.

i   A bank overdraft which amounted to $13 000 on 31 December 20X1.

j   A supply of seat belts which the owner of Transom Trading had bought for $12 000 in September from a market trader in good faith and which were subsequently found to be defective.

11   Using the information in Problem 10 above, calculate the owners' equity and draw up the statement of financial position of Transom Trading as at 31 December 20X1.

12   Fred owns a garage and has tried to get everything together ready for the business accounts to be prepared. He has drawn up the list of items below. You are required to identify, with reasons, the statement of financial position heading under which each item should be classified, and the amount which should be included.

a   A motor car bought for resale at a cost of $7000; the retail price was $10 000.

b   Various loose tools for car repairs which cost $1400.

c   Two hydraulic jacks which had each cost $240.

d   Freehold premises which had cost $80 000.

e   The cost of $1200 for digging and finishing a pit for repairs.

f   Spare parts held as general stock, originally costing $1580.

g   Spare parts bought from the previous owner when the garage was bought.

At that time the value was agreed at $12 000 but it was subsequently discovered that only $400 of these spares were of any use.

h   Breakdown truck which cost $6000 for the basic truck and $1200 to have the crane fitted.

i   A customer's car worth $3000 which was being held because the customer had not paid an outstanding bill of $600.

j   Fred's own car which cost $8000. This is used mainly for business but Fred also uses it in the evenings and at weekends for the family.

k   Customer goodwill which Fred reckons he has built up. He thinks this would be worth at least $14 000 if he sold the garage tomorrow.

l   A bank loan for $48 000 repayable within three months.

m   A 20-year mortgage on the property amounting to $48 000 which has not been fully repaid. The amount still outstanding is $36 000.

13   Month-end statement of financial position amounts for the dental practice of Dr Fang, a local dentist, for three consecutive months are presented below. The information is complete except for the balance in the owners' equity account.

	31 October	30 November	31 December
	$	$	$
Cash	9 100	3 900	3 000
Accounts receivable	16 100	16 500	8 050
Prepaid insurance	700	800	600
Surgery equipment	29 800	29 700	38 300
Building	81 000	80 800	80 600
Land	33 000	33 000	33 000
Accounts payable	10 100	3 100	3 000
Wages payable	5 100	4 100	4 800
Mortgage payable	34 700	34 300	33 900
Owners' Equity	?	?	?

a   Determine the balance in Dr Fang's equity account at the end of each month.

b   Assuming that Dr Fang made no additional investments, determine his drawings for the months of November and December.

c   Prepare a statement of financial position for the business at the end of December.

14   A dressmaker's statement of financial position exhibits an asset account titled 'uncharged receivables'. The owner says this represents work in progress valued at current rates for which customers will be charged. This will be the dressmaker's time. Why would the owner do this instead of valuing the work in progress at cost, as a manufacturing firm would do to its work in progress inventory? Will it make a difference in the dressmaker's statement of financial position to report such work in progress as receivables rather than inventory?

(Adapted from R. Anthony and J. Reece, *Accounting: Text and Cases*, 8th edn, Richard D. Irwin Inc., 1988, Chapter 5.)

15   ABC Company and XYZ Company conduct the same type of business. Both were recently formed; thus the statement of financial position figures for assets can be assumed to be at current market valuation. The statements of financial position of the two companies at 30 June 20X0 were as follows:

ABC COMPANY
STATEMENT OF FINANCIAL POSITION AT 30 JUNE 20X0

Assets	$	$	$	$
Current Assets				
Cash at bank	2 400			
Accounts receivable	4 800			
Total Current Assets		7 200		
Non-current Assets				
Office equipment	6 000			
Land	18 000			
Building	30 000			
Total Non-current Assets		54 000		
Total Assets		61 200		
Liabilities				
Current Liabilities				
Accounts payable	21 600			
Unsecured loan payable, due 30 September 20X0	31 200			
Total Current Liabilities		52 800		
Total Liabilities		52 800		
Net Assets				8 400
Owners' Equity				
T. Edwards Capital	8 400			
Total Owners' Equity				8 400

XYZ COMPANY
STATEMENT OF FINANCIAL POSITION AT 30 JUNE 20X0

Assets	$	$	$	$
Current Assets				
Cash at bank	12 000			
Accounts receivable	24 000			
Total Current Assets		36 000		
Non-current Assets				
Office equipment	600			
Land	3 600			
Building	6 000			
Total Non-current Assets		10 200		
Total Assets		46 200		
Liabilities				
Current Liabilities				
Accounts payable	4 800			
Unsecured loan payable, due 30 September 20X0	7 200			
Total Current Liabilities		12 000		

(continued next page)

Total Liabilities		<u>12 000</u>
Net Assets		<u>34 200</u>
Owners' Equity		
S. Allen Capital	34 200	
Total Owners' Equity		<u>34 200</u>

Required:

a   Assuming that you are a banker and that the owner of each business has applied for a short-term loan (repayable in six months) of $6000, which application would you select as being the more favourable? Why?

b   Assuming that you are a businessperson interested in buying one or both companies, and the owner of each has indicated her intention to sell, for which business would you be willing to pay the higher price, assuming you will be taking over the existing liabilities of the company? Explain.

c   If the existing owners agreed to be accountable for all the existing liabilities, how would this change your decision in (b) above, if at all?

(Adapted from B. Colditz and R. Gibbins, *Australian Accounting*, 3rd edn, McGraw-Hill, 1976.)

16   For a period of years, the Remote Shire Council controlled a very large rubbish site in the southern area of Western Australia. Unfortunately, the site was nearly full and the council had to search for a new location. One of the preferred locations was an area that had previously been an opencut coal mine. It was owned and controlled by the No More Coal Mining Venture, and the Remote Shire Council offered $4 per cubic metre to lease the quarry for a period of ten years. This amounted to a total lease payment of $8.8 million. Following this, the local paper reported the following:

> This has the appearance of something for nothing but, to some experts in private enterprise, it appeared more like nothing for something. One private company, Environmental Disposals, had previously tendered $5.00 per cubic metre for the same mine site for disposal purposes, a total of $11 million.

Using the above information, explain how an asset can consist of 'nothing' and, taking into account the amounts mentioned above, illustrate your understanding of the concept of asset valuation.

Using this information, discuss whether the No More Coal Mining Venture should recognise an asset for the abandoned coal mine.

17   Jill Wright, head of the Green Trees Playgroup, wanted to know how well the business was performing after six months of activity. To do this she needed to know what position the company was in at 30 June 20X1 and what the future outlook for the business was.

Mrs Wright founded the Green Trees Playgroup in January 20X1 to provide children of working parents with a specially supervised preschool education. Capital for the playgroup was raised by Mrs Wright who took out a personal loan for $26 250 of which she invested $22 500 in common shares of the company. A further $11 250 in cash was invested by local business and a one-year loan of $7455 was made to the company by the local shire council.

With this capital, Mrs Wright purchased, on behalf of the playgroup, premises for $42 000 of which $8400 was for land and $33 600 for a building on the land. This was financed in part by a $28 350 mortgage, the remainder being paid in cash. Interest on the mortgage was to be paid in three-monthly instalments though no repayment of the principal was required until the business had become established. Furniture and equipment were also purchased for $14 625 in cash.

During the first six months of operations, which ended June 20X1, the following additional amounts were paid by the business in cash.

	$
Salary to Mrs Wright	8 250
Salaries of part-time employees	5 526
Insurance (one-year policy)	1 650
Electricity	1 070
Food and supplies	4 590
Interest and miscellaneous	3 594
Total paid out	24 680

Other events which took place included the following.
- Student fees of $17 724 were received in cash. A further $690 for fees was owed to the playgroup by parents. This amount was received in the period ended 31 December 20X1.
- Mrs Wright estimated that $412 worth of supplies were still on hand at 30 June 20X1 and 31 December 20X1. The playgroup owed $712 to food suppliers at 30 June 20X1. This amount was paid in the period ended 31 December 20X1.
- Mrs Wright estimated that for the next six months, to 31 December 20X1, student fees received would total $26 880.
- She estimated for the next six months to 31 December 20X1 salaries of $13 768 would be paid by the playgroup, $1344 for the electricity bill, $5880 for additional food and supplies, and $2850 for interest and miscellaneous items. The loan from the council was also expected to be paid in this period.
- No depreciation was recorded on the company's assets (buildings, furniture or equipment) as Mrs Wright has been offered $58 875 in cash for these assets from someone wanting to buy the business and she had thought it would not be appropriate to record any.

Required:
a   Prepare a statement of financial position for the Green Trees Playgroup at 30 June 20X1. To minimise errors, treat each event separately. For events affecting owners' equity, other than the initial investment, record the transaction in the Retained Earnings account. Show negative amounts in parentheses. Show non-current assets at their original cost.
b   Prepare an estimated statement of financial position at 31 December 20X1.
c   Should the non-current assets be reported on the 30 June 20X1 statement of financial position at their cost, at $58 875, or at some other amount? (This amount need not be calculated.) If at some amount other than cost, how would the statement of financial position prepared in (a) change?

d   Does it appear likely that the Green Trees Playgroup will become a viable business, assuming that Mrs Wright's estimations prove correct?

(Adapted from R. Anthony and J. Reece, *Accounting: Text and Cases*, 8th edn, Richard D. Irwin Inc., 1988, Chapter 2, Case 2–4.)

Ethics case study

The manager of Centura Ltd has asked you to classify a $500 000 loan due for repayment in nine months as a non-current liability in the statement of financial position. The company's total assets are $2 million.

Discuss:

a   the impact of this classification

b   what the reasons might be for the request

c   whether any party is likely to suffer from this treatment

d   what you would do.

The Statement of Financial Performance

Learning objectives

At the end of this chapter you should be able to:

1 understand the importance of the statement of financial performance

2 define and explain the term 'revenue'

3 explain and apply the principles involved in the recognition of revenue

4 provide examples of revenue

5 define and explain the term 'expense'

6 explain and apply the expense recognition criteria

7 provide examples of expenses

8 understand the various factors which influence the format of the statement of financial performance.

Introduction

We have already seen that we can measure profit by comparing wealth at two points in time. We have also shown that the way in which wealth is measured in accounting terms can be roughly equated with statements of financial position, and we have looked at some of the issues arising from the choices in respect of assigning monetary values to wealth measurement.

In this chapter we consider an alternative way of measuring profit, using a statement of financial performance. We look at what a statement of financial performance is, why it is important, why it is produced and what it contains. We then consider what determines the content of a statement of financial performance and some of the issues that have to be dealt with when preparing one.

Importance of statements of financial performance

NOTE: From 1 July 2000 in Australia, the profit and loss statement became known as the statement of financial performance. The two terms refer to the same statement.

Unlike a statement of financial position which communicates information about a point in time, the statement of financial performance relates to a period of time. It summarises certain transactions taking place during that period. In terms of published reports the period is normally one year, although most businesses of any size produce statements of financial performance more regularly, usually quarterly and often monthly. The regular production of statements of financial performance allows managers to compare actual performance against the budget. This is important as it enables managers to identify any problem areas and implement remedial action. For example, if advertising expenses are too high, management may reduce future advertising expenditure or change advertising agents. These statements are normally for internal consumption only, although often banks request copies or make the production of such statements a condition of lending money. The reason that the banks require these statements on a regular basis is that they need to monitor the health of the business they are lending to. They want to be confident that the managers of the business are aware of what is happening and taking action to rectify the situation if the business is making losses.

For owners and managers, there is little point in finding out at the end of the year that the price at which goods or services were sold did not cover what it cost to buy those goods or provide those services. By that stage it is too late to do anything about it. However, if a problem is identified at the end of the first month, it can be dealt with immediately by raising prices, buying at a lower price or whatever is appropriate to the particular business.

Clearly the statement of financial performance is very important because it tells you whether a business is profitable or not. We have all heard the expression 'What is the bottom line?' The bottom line is the amount of profit made by a project or business. By comparing that profit with how much wealth is needed to produce it, you can decide whether to invest in a business. Other factors which also need to be taken into account are the risks involved and your own judgement of future prospects in order to decide whether the return as measured by the statement of financial performance is adequate. Therefore, it can be argued that the statement of financial performance provides some of the basic financial information for a rational decision to be made. However, although most of us think of business as being primarily motivated by profits, this is not always the case. Many small businesses make profits which are unsatisfactory from the point of view of a rational economic assessment, but the owners' motivation may not be solely for profit. They may simply hate working for any boss, or they may value leisure more than they do additional profits.

Having considered why a statement of financial performance is important, let us now look at what it is and what it contains. We have said that it is a statement covering a period of time, normally one year, and that its purpose is to measure profit, i.e. the increase in wealth. It does this by summarising the revenue for that period and deducting the expenses incurred in earning that revenue. The process is simple, but to be able to do it we need to look at the definitions of revenue and expenses.

Revenue

Paragraph 111 of *SAC 4* (AARF, 1995) defines revenues and we used this definition as Key Concept 2.9. It is given again as Key Concept 5.1. This definition is also in *AASB 1034: Financial Report Presentation and Disclosures*, paragraph 8.1.

Key Concept 5.1

Revenue

Revenues are inflows or other enhancements, or savings in outflows, of future economic benefits in the form of increases in assets or reductions in liabilities of the entity, other than those relating to contributions by owners, that result in an increase in equity during the reporting period.

This definition seems complex because it attempts to cover all possible outcomes. For our purposes we can substitute 'owners' equity' for 'equity' and 'accounting period' for 'reporting period'. As with the other elements, revenue is recognised in the financial statements only when it is probable that the inflow or other enhancement, or savings in outflows, of economic benefits has occurred and can be reliably measured.

From Key Concept 5.1 it can be seen that there are two main elements (besides contributions by owners) which result in increases in owners' equity. These are increases in assets and decreases in liabilities and we discuss each of them in turn.

Increases in assets

In most cases revenue recognition is fairly simple and does not need a detailed discussion. For example, we would all agree that a greengrocer's revenue is the amount that the fruit and vegetables were sold for, and in most cases that amount is in cash, which we know is a current asset. However, if we suppose that our greengrocer supplies fruit and vegetables to a couple of local restaurants who settle their bills every month, we find that in order to define revenue we have to include not only cash sales but also the other sales for which we have not been paid. The latter amounts are referred to as 'receivables' or as 'debtors'. Both these terms are used in Australia, although in large public companies debtors are often a subsection of receivables. (Other receivables, for example, are interest and short-term loans.) Debtors are shown in our statement of financial position as assets because they meet our definition of an asset. (If you are not certain of this point, check the definition contained in Key Concept 4.4.) We discuss the treatment of debtors in more detail in Chapter 8.

At this stage we should look at our accounting equation in the light of the two examples above. If the greengrocer has sold $100 worth of goods, either for cash or credit, and this we know has met our definition of an asset, then our accounting equation will be as follows:

$$\text{assets } (\$100) = \text{liabilities} + \text{owners' equity}$$

From our discussion of duality in Chapter 4, there must be another equal component to make the equation balance. (At this stage we are not discussing a reduction in an asset account through the goods being sold, but are only concerned with the cash received or the promise to pay.) It is obvious that another asset account has not decreased nor has a liability increased; therefore to balance the equation the owners' equity account must have increased. This has intuitive appeal because with the receipt of cash, for example, and with no other changes to the statement of financial position, our wealth must have increased.

$$\text{assets } (\$100) = \text{revenue } (\$100)$$

At this stage we might believe that we have a fair idea of what revenue is: it relates to goods and services sold. This view is not necessarily correct: revenue can come in various forms, as can be seen from our definition of revenue, which was fairly broad. However, we need to be careful to ensure that we include only sales that are part of our normal business activity in determining our trading profit and loss. These sales then are part of our trading revenue. To illustrate, let us assume that the greengrocer sells one of her two shops: should this be seen as revenue or is it different from selling fruit and vegetables? Clearly it is different, because the selling of the fruit and vegetables relates to the business of the entity while business profit relies on the success of the trading venture. The sale of the shop should be treated differently and shown separately in financial statements from the revenue earned through greengrocery sales. If, for example, the business was trading at a loss, a gain was made on the sale of the shop and the gain was greater than the trading loss, then this information would be lost if the two items were merged. Finally, before leaving the greengrocer illustration let us assume that, having sold one of the shops, the greengrocer decides to invest the money in some shares or in a building society until such time as a new shop can be found. In this situation the money invested, which is effectively surplus to immediate requirements, will generate additional revenue in the form of interest or dividends. This is a form of revenue which is different from our main source of revenue. It would, in this case, be shown separately but included in the total revenue for the period. In certain cases, however, the interest may be the major source of revenue—if, for example, the main activity of a business is lending money. Similarly, dividends may be the main source of revenue for an investment trust. Revenue which is derived from sources outside the normal activities of the business will be dealt with in more detail in later chapters.

From this discussion, we can see that, although broadly speaking trading revenue is synonymous in many cases with sales, the actual revenue of a business is dependent on the type of business and the particular activity giving rise to the revenue. In the example we have used, we saw that in its simplest form trading revenue was equal to cash sales. However, for some business activities the distinctions are not so clear and this leads to problems in deciding what revenue relates to a particular period. This, of course, would not be a problem if accounting periods were the same as the period of a business cycle. For example if a builder takes 18 months to build and sell a house there is no problem in finding the revenue for the 18 months. Unfortunately, the normal accounting period is 12 months and, as we have pointed out earlier, management and other users need information on a more frequent basis than that. What then is the revenue of the house builder for the first six months, or for the first year?

The definition of revenue requires that there be an increase in equity. The borrowing of money therefore increases an asset (cash), but the transaction also creates a liability of equivalent amount (loan payable). As we would expect, an entity does not create revenue by borrowing money.

Reductions in liabilities

The parts of the revenue definition which are applicable to this heading are '… savings in outflows, of future economic benefits in the form of … reductions in liabilities'. Though it is unlikely that a situation will arise where this part of the definition would apply at the level of this text, an example will be given.

Using the example of the greengrocer again, let us assume that a staff party is held at one of the restaurants supplied by the greengrocer, and that the cost of staff parties is always met by the business. After the function the restaurant sends an account for payment to the greengrocer. This account represents a liability incurred by the business. If it is agreed between the two parties that the greengrocer will supply vegetables up to the value of the debt, in settlement of the liability, then the extinguishment of the debt in effect represents an increase in owners' equity (remember our statement of financial position equation). This increase in equity represents revenue. Note that we have not yet addressed the cost of the transaction to the greengrocer, i.e. the cost of the goods supplied.

A more detailed explanation of this transaction will be found under the subheading 'increases in liabilities' (see page 99), under the main heading 'expenses', later in this chapter.

Contributions by owners

Certain increases in owners' equity do not qualify as revenue. For example, the owners of a business may invest more capital in the entity. This transaction does not meet our definition of revenue because the definition precludes contributions by owners that result in an increase of equity during the reporting period. This contribution of additional capital by the owners is an investment decision, possibly with a view to generating future revenue.

This leads us to the question of when revenue arises and when it should be recognised. To help us answer this question we follow what is known as the recognition principle.

Key Concept 5.2

The recognition principle

From our definition of revenue the recognition principle states that revenue should be recognised only:
- when the increases in assets or reduction of liabilities have probably resulted from inflows or savings of outflows of economic benefits, and
- these movements can be reliably measured.

This can be simplified to:
- when the earning process is substantially complete and measurable, and
- when the receipt of payment for the goods and services is reasonably certain.

(You should note that where something is simplified its meaning is often broadened and some precision is lost.)

The recognition principle

The recognition principle is defined in Key Concept 5.2. You may have noticed that, unlike our other definitions which are precise and all-inclusive, this simplified principle is carefully worded to avoid too much precision. It provides some basic criteria which can be applied to the particular circumstances. The final decision on whether revenue is recognised is in practice often a matter of judgement rather than fact. Before considering an example, look at the wording used in the simplified version of Key Concept 5.2. Firstly, you will see that it mentions process, which implies a period rather than a point in time. It also uses the term 'substantially complete', which raises the question of what is 'substantial': is it two-thirds or 90 per cent or what? The principle also says that payment should be reasonably certain. Once again this leaves room for the exercise of judgement and raises the question of what is 'reasonable certainty' in an uncertain world.

Obviously if we sell goods to a reputable customer of long standing we are reasonably certain that we will be paid. Rather than looking at numerous examples of this type, we will start by looking in general terms at a production and selling process and examine the possible points at which we could recognise revenue in accordance with the recognition principle.

- Point 1: inputs
- Point 2: production
- Point 3: finished goods
- Point 4: sale of goods — *recognise here not before .*
- Point 5: receipt of cash

Clearly, it is unlikely that revenue would ever be recognised at point 1 but, as we will see, all the other points could be appropriate in different circumstances. The end of the process, point 5, seems to be a safe place to recognise revenue, because the earnings process is likely to be complete and payment is certain because the cash has been received. In many cases point 5 is the appropriate point—as in the case of our greengrocer. However, she also had some other sales which were paid for monthly in arrears, so those may have to be recognised at point 4, as at that point the earning process is complete and payment is reasonably certain. On the other hand, if we take the example of the builder and use either of these points, we would have a situation where there was no revenue for the first 17 months but a lot in the 18th month. Of course, in practice, in the case of the builder, if there was a contract to build the house for someone, then some cash would have been paid in advance. The point we are making here is that points 4 and 5 are not necessarily appropriate in all cases.

One could argue that for a shipbuilder points 4 and 5 are inappropriate because cash is received throughout a contract and the point of sale is in fact before the production process starts. In this case, because a ship takes a number of years to build, it is also inappropriate to choose point 3 as this would lead to all the revenue arising in one year. Therefore it may be that point 2 is appropriate if the earning process is 'substantially' complete and it is likely that payments on account will have been received. A similar argument applies to the cases of a property developer and a building subcontractor.

Examples of revenue

From this discussion, each case obviously needs to be judged on its merits. Consider when the appropriate time for revenue recognition would be for the following businesses:

- a local newsagent
- a supplier of components to Ford Motors

- a gold mine where all output is bought by the government at a fixed price
- an aircraft manufacturer.

Applying the recognition principle, the first example is straightforward; the others are more problematic.

A local newsagent

The business is likely to be mainly cash so point 5 is probably most appropriate, although this will depend upon how many customers buy their newspapers, etc. on account.

Supplier of components

Clearly point 5 is too late because even at point 4 the earnings process is complete and payment is reasonably certain. However, it could be argued that if the component supplier has a fixed contract with Ford, an earlier point, such as the point at which the goods are ready to be delivered, might be appropriate. This will come closer to the norm if more large firms adopt just-in-time principles in which designated stocks are held by their suppliers rather than by them.

A gold mine

An argument similar to that for the component supplier could be applied here because the earnings process is substantially complete at the point of production and payment is certain because the government buys all output.

An aircraft manufacturer

Your answer here will depend on the assumptions you have made. If, for example, you assumed that the aircraft manufacturer was making to order, then your judgement of certainty of payment would be different from that made if you assumed that it produced aircraft and then tried to sell them. Similarly, if you thought of an aircraft producer which made Boeing 747s, you might have thought of the production process as spreading over a number of years, in which case point 2 might have been your choice. If, on the other hand, you thought of the manufacture of light aircraft such as Piper Cubs, you would have assumed a shorter production cycle, in which case point 2 would not be appropriate.

The problem of when to recognise revenue is very important because the statement of financial performance is based upon the revenue for a period and the expenses for that period.

CASE STUDY 5.1

BHP's $31m 'sale' profit questioned

by Tom Ravlic

THE increasingly common practice of selling and leasing back assets in order to move them off the balance sheet has come under fire from the corporate regulator, the Australian Securities and Investments Commission.

ASIC said yesterday it believed many deals were not true asset sales.

BHP was singled out for the structure of the sale and leaseback of its Mount Newman rolling stock, which, in the eyes of the commission, is a financing deal, not a sale.

The ASIC raised its concerns during the latest meeting of the accounting authority, the Urgent Issues Group, yesterday.

It asked the UIG to rule on the appropriate accounting for leasing renewal periods, sale-and-leaseback arrangements and corporate exploitation of the distinction between finance and operating leases.

Keith Alfredson, the chairman of both the UIG and the Australian Accounting Standards Board, told the meeting the issues were fundamental and 'that they should be brought to the next meeting of the UIG'.

The commission was particularly concerned about the accounting used by BHP relating to the sale and leaseback of rolling stock. It involved a $31 million profit from the transaction that was part of the Mount Newman Joint Venture in Western Australia, said the commission's chief accountant Jan McCahey.

She said ASIC disagreed with BHP's complex accounting treatment.

The main problem for the commission is the way it interpreted who held the risks and benefits of the leased assets.

While BHP's directors believe the accounting treatment is correct, the commission argues the deal represents a financing arrangement and not a sale. Therefore, it said, no profit from the sale-leaseback arrangement should have been recorded.

'Leases can only be accounted for as effectively transferring ownership of an asset if the lessor transfers substantially all of the risk, and substantially all of the benefits of ownership of the asset to the lessee,' Ms McCahey said.

The call for UIG to examine lease accounting practices follows widespread publicity over the past year of airport leasing arrangements and a Cable Wireless Optus–AAPT deal.

It also follows ASIC's warning that it will conduct a lease accounting blitz as part of its financial statement surveillance.

Ms McCahey said the commission was aware merchant banks were designing leasing arrangements they then marketed as getting a particular accounting outcome.

Age, 8 September 2000

Commentary

The article demonstrates that it is not always easy to determine when a sale is really a sale. *AASB 1008: Leases* deals with transactions described as sale and leaseback. These occur where an entity purports to sell an asset and then leases the same asset back from the new owner. You need to know if the entity has really sold the asset, or if the transaction was merely a loan arrangement, with the asset in question being the security for the loan. In this particular case, did BHP lose control of the economic benefits associated with the asset? Does BHP substantially retain all the risks and rewards incidental to the ownership of the asset? The article again demonstrates how transactions can be viewed in a number of ways, with each view having a different impact on the financial statements of the entity.

You should now study the Woolworths financial report. Accounting policy Note 1(C) discloses the revenue recognition policies for sales, interest, rents, dividends and proceeds from the sale of assets. The policy recognises revenue as such when (i) it is probable that the economic benefits will flow to the entity, and (ii) the flow can be reliably measured. While the recognition of revenue appears relatively straightforward for a retailer like Woolworths, this is not the case for many other industries, as the next case study illustrates.

Bougainville Copper Ltd Annual Report 1993

Extract from the Accounting Policies Statement

Net sales revenue

During normal operations, sales are recognised when the risk passes from the seller, which is at the time when the concentrate enters the ship's hold. The final sales value can only be determined from weights, assays, prices and treatment charges applying after a shipment has arrived at its destination. Estimates based on world metal prices ruling up to year end are used for those shipments not due for final valuation until the following year. In addition, the estimated results of forward contracts existing at year end in relation to concentrates shipped are reflected in sales revenue. Variations in revenue arising from final pricing and out-turn adjustments are recognised in the following year. Unrealised gains and losses on forward metal sales, not related to shipments, are included in earnings. There has been no sales revenue since 1990.

Commentary

This extract from the Accounting Policies Statement, issued three years after the company had ceased its mining operations, illustrates the problems which can face a supplier as to when to recognise revenue. The final sales price, and therefore the total revenue, is dependent on factors completely outside the control of the seller, for example, treatment charges after the ore has been delivered. The case study is a good example of the problems facing providers of accounting information and lends support to the concept that accounting is not an exact discipline: judgement and knowledge of the environment in which the entity is operating are very important.

Expenses

An expense, previously defined in Key Concept 2.8, is restated in Key Concept 5.3 which is taken from paragraph 117 of *SAC 4* (AARF, 1995) and paragraph 8.1 of *AASB 1034*. The definition is straightforward and similar to that for revenues in that it relates to changes in assets, liabilities and owners' equity. In this case assets are reduced or liabilities increased, with a resulting reduction in equity. You should note that the reduction in equity does not include dividends paid to, or withdrawals by, the owners of the business. Further, it must be probable that consumption or loss of economic benefits has occurred and that the amount can be reliably measured. Put simply, an expense means a money sacrifice or the incurring of a liability in pursuit of business objectives.

Key Concept 5.3

Expenses

Expenses are consumptions or losses of future economic benefits in the form of reductions in assets or increases in liabilities of the entity, other than those relating to distributions to owners, that result in a decrease in equity during the reporting period.

For our purposes we can substitute 'owners' equity' for 'equity'.

As with revenues, we will discuss each aspect of the definition in turn: assets, liabilities and owners' equity.

Reductions in assets

The definition notes that 'expenses are consumptions or losses of future economic benefits in the form of reductions in assets'. Using this part of the definition and applying it to the greengrocer mentioned earlier, we can see that when she sells goods for cash or credit, the cost of those goods is an expense. This expense results in a reduction of the asset account covering the greengrocery stock and the corresponding reduction in the equity account.

The stock of the greengrocery meets our asset definition: title to the goods passes to the purchaser, which results in an economic loss; the cost can be reliably measured; it is probable that the loss has occurred; the loss of this asset results in a reduction in wealth which reduces the equity balance. Note that the same reasoning applies whether the transaction was for cash or to a reliable debtor.

Turning to the second scenario, where the greengrocer sold one of her shops, whatever value was placed on the shop, and was disclosed in our statement of financial position, would meet the definition of an expense. For example, if the net value of the shop in the statement of financial position was $30 000 and the shop sold for $40 000, assuming no transactions costs, then there would be a net addition to equity of $10 000. If the reverse was true, shop value $40 000 and sale price $30 000, there would be a net reduction in equity of $10 000. As noted in the discussion on revenue, this information needs to be disclosed separately.

Increases in liabilities

As we can see from our definition, an increase in a liability due to the consumption or loss of economic benefits qualifies as an expense. Borrowing money creates a liability and an asset but not an expense as there has been no consumption of economic benefit at this stage. Using the same example as we did for revenues, the cost of goods supplied to the restaurant owner in settlement of the liability is an expense. To explain this in more detail: the original transaction, the staff party, gives rise to an expense, i.e. the increase of the liability results in the reduction of the wealth of the greengrocer. If the greengrocer paid cash to settle this liability we would have a reduction in an asset and liability account. The restaurant owner exchanges the debt for goods, which reduces the liability and increases the wealth of the greengrocer; this meets our revenue definition. The final part of the transaction, the supply of goods, results in a decrease in the asset account and a corresponding decrease in the equity account. Put simply, the cost of the goods supplied to the restaurant in settlement is the cost of the staff party. There were three parts to this transaction, two of which were expenses and one of which was a revenue:

- expenses of the staff party
- expenses of cost of goods supplied to the restaurant
- revenue of goods supplied to the restaurant.

Distributions to owners   — not expenses

When an owner withdraws goods, services or cash from the business, this is not an expense of the business but a withdrawal of capital by the owner. These withdrawals are often referred to in the accounting literature as drawings. We could provide numerous examples of these, some of which are less obvious than others. For example, is the tax and insurance on the car a business expense if the car is also used for family transportation? The guiding principle in making a judgement is whether or not the cost has been incurred in pursuit of the objectives of the business.

Owners who believe that they are entitled to be remunerated for the work they do should pay themselves a wage or salary which equates to the effort expended. This is a legitimate business expense.

The recognition principle

The criteria for the recognition of expenses are the same as for revenue. Therefore, an expense should be recognised in the current period when:

- it is probable that the consumption or loss of economic benefits has occurred; and
- the amount can be reliably measured.

The application of the recognition criteria should help preparers to decide when to recognise a cost incurred as an expense. However, while some costs such as rent payments are straightforward, others, such as research and development expenditure, present difficulties. The following examples illustrate some of the different types of costs incurred by organisations.

Examples of expenses

It is worthwhile to look at some examples of expenses, such as:

- payment of wages, which normally involves a monetary sacrifice
- use of electricity, which normally involves incurring a liability to pay at the end of a quarter
- purchase of a machine, which normally incurs a money sacrifice or a liability
- purchase of goods for resale, which normally incurs a money sacrifice or a liability.

Although all the examples can be seen to fit our definition of expenses, they are not necessarily expenses of the period. For example, the machinery is likely to last more than one period and so it cannot be seen as an expired cost. Similarly, the goods bought for resale may not be sold during the period and they therefore cannot be seen as an expense of the period: the benefit has not expired because we will be able to sell those goods at some time in the future. There are other situations where the point at which a cost is incurred and the point at which the benefit arises do not coincide. We will discuss this in more detail shortly.

Before we do that, it is worth emphasising once again that we are dealing with a separate business entity and only costs relating to the business objectives can ever become expenses. This is very important as in many cases, especially with small businesses, the owner and the business are to all intents and purposes the same, but we are preparing accounts for the business only. Thus, if we find that a bill has been paid to buy a new lounge suite for the owner of a newsagency, this cost is not an expense of the business because it relates to the owner personally, not the business. Such items often go through a business bank account but need to be separated and shown as withdrawals of the owner's capital rather than business expenses.

We will return to the discussion of drawings later, but let us now consider some possible situations in which we have to decide whether a cost which is clearly a business cost is an expense of the period. There are three possible situations that we need to discuss. These are where:

- costs of this year are expenses of this year
- costs of earlier years are expenses of this year
- costs of this year are expenses of subsequent years.

Costs of this year are expenses of this year

This is the usual situation and is also the simplest to deal with. It occurs when an item or service is acquired during a year and consumed during that same year. That is, costs of this accounting period are expenses of this accounting period. Where the accounting period is less than one year—for example, one month—then the discussion applies to this shorter accounting period.

No reference is made to whether the item acquired has been paid for. It may be that it has still not been paid for even though it has been acquired and used. A common example is telephone calls, which are only paid for at the end of the quarter. The question of the timing of payment is not relevant to the process of recognising an expense.

Costs of earlier years are expenses of this year

These can be divided into those that are wholly used up in the current period and those that are partly used up in the current period.

Wholly expenses of this year

The most obvious example of this is the stock of goods in a shop at the end of the year. The cost of buying those goods has been incurred in the year just ended, but the economic benefit has not expired; they are therefore assets at the year end. However, in the next year they will be sold and thus will become expenses of the next year. The process that has occurred can be illustrated as follows.

We buy goods in November 20X1 but do not sell them until January 20X2. If our accounting period coincides with the calendar year and ends in December 20X1, then the goods are an asset at that date, i.e. 31 December 20X1, because the economic benefit is not used up. The cost, however, has been incurred in that year. In 20X2 the goods are sold and therefore the benefit is used up and there is an expense for the year ended December 20X2, although the cost was incurred in the previous year. This can be seen in Figure 5.1.

Figure 5.1 *Expenses incurred this year, which are expenses of this year.*

A similar situation arises when services are paid for in advance and are not fully used up at the end of the accounting period. For example, if the rent is payable quarterly in advance on 31 March, 30 June, 30 September and 31 December and the enterprise ends its year on 31 December, then the cost will be incurred in year 1 for the quarter to 31 March, year 2. However, the economic benefit will be used up in the first quarter of year 2 and thus the expense belongs to year 2. The rent for the first quarter of year 1 would, of course, have been paid in the December preceding the commencement of year 1.

These expenses are normally referred to as 'prepaid expenses' and frequently arise in respect of rent and water rates. For an individual the most obvious example of this type of expense is annual subscriptions to clubs and societies, car insurance, driving licence, etc. For a business, other situations where a cost may relate to more than one period arise frequently. For example, if the car insurance of the business was payable on 1 July 20X1, then half of that cost would be used up and become an expense for 20X1 and half would be used up and be an expense of 20X2. The crucial test is whether the economic benefit has been used up at the year end. If not, there is a future economic benefit and we therefore have an asset.

All these examples refer to costs incurred in the past which are expenses of the current year. Another category that needs to be considered is where costs have been incurred in the past and only part of the benefit is used up in the current year.

Part expenses of current year

An everyday example of this is any consumer durable, e.g. a car, washing machine or television set. In all these cases the costs are incurred at a point in time but the economic benefits are expected to accrue over a number of years. In a business enterprise the equivalents of our consumer durables are non-current assets such as machinery and office equipment. The allocation of the cost of these items to subsequent accounting periods is called depreciation, and will be dealt with in more detail in Chapter 9.

Costs incurred this year which are expenses of later years

Just as some of the costs incurred in previous years are expenses of the current accounting period, costs incurred in the current period may be expenses of future periods.

Examples that spring to mind are car registration, insurance, rates, etc. The due date for payment of these is unlikely to coincide with the end of the accounting period, nor would we want it to because this would lead to an uneven cash flow. Other examples are goods held in stock at the year end and non-current assets bought during the year.

If we take the example of annual car insurance, we can see that, if we pay for that in the current year 20X2 on 1 July, then part of that cost will relate to next year 20X3, as shown in Figure 5.2.

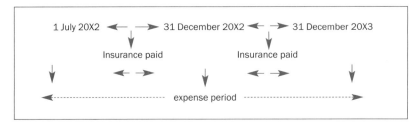

Figure 5.2 *Costs incurred this year, which are expenses of later years.*

Having looked at revenues and expenses, we now examine how these fit together in the statement of financial performance before looking at a simple numerical example.

The statement of financial performance

The purpose of this statement is to measure the profit or loss for the period. It does this by summarising the revenues for the period, and subtracting the expenses from the revenues to arrive at the profit or loss. This could be depicted as:

$$\text{revenue} - \text{expenses} = \text{profit}$$

Let us see how this fits with the measurement of wealth described in Chapter 3. We said that profit is the difference between wealth at the start and end of the year, i.e.

$$\text{wealth at } T_1 - \text{wealth at } T_0 = \text{profit at } T_1$$

The alternative way of measuring profit was to subtract expenses from revenue. We also said in Chapter 4 that wealth in accounting terms was measured by assets minus liabilities. The resultant figure, the residual, was referred to as the owners' equity. Thus, we said that at time T_0, the owners' equity is:

$$\text{assets at } T_0 - \text{liabilities at } T_0 = \text{owners' equity at } T_0$$

If we add to the owners' equity at T_0 the profit for the period T_0 to T_1, the resultant figure will be our wealth at T_1. This will equal our assets minus liabilities at T_1 (provided we have not changed our valuation method from one period to another). In other words:

$$\text{assets at } T_1 - \text{liabilities at } T_1 = \text{owners' equity at } T_0 + \text{profit at } T_1$$
$$= \text{owners' equity at } T_0 \pm (\text{revenue} - \text{expenses}) \text{ at } T_1$$

This shows us that there is a relationship between the statement of financial performance and the statement of financial position; the nature of that relationship will become clearer in Chapter 6. Let us now look at an example of a statement of financial performance and then consider what it is used for, its format and its limitations. In Example 5.1 we use the transactions of Blake's Enterprises, a paint shop, and see what should go into the statement of financial performance for the year to 31 December 20X1.

Example 5.1: Blake's Enterprises

Blake's Enterprises is a new retail paint outlet set up at the start of the year. Its transactions for 20X1, its first year, are summarised below.

Date	Description	$
1 Jan.	Purchase of freehold shop	120 000
1 Jan.	Rates for the year	4 000
1 Apr.	Van purchased	16 000
1 Apr.	Van registration and Insurance for a year	1 200
1 July	Purchase of washing machine	600
Various	Wages to shop assistant for year	12 000
Various	Goods bought and resold	36 000
Various	Goods bought but unsold	8 000
Various	Motor expenses and petrol	2 400
Various	Cash from sales	90 000
Various	Money withdrawn by Blake	12 000

Purchase of freehold shop

The economic benefit arising from this cost has clearly not expired during the period, although some part of the economic benefit may have been used up. At this stage we will not try to measure the part used up, but we should bear in mind that at a later stage we will need to make such allocations.

Rates for the year

This is clearly a cost and expense of the year in question and should be included in the statement of financial performance.

Purchase of van

As with the freehold shop, the economic benefit from the van is likely to be available over many periods and we should theoretically allocate to the statement of financial performance for the year, the amount of the benefit used up. The allocation is made by means of a depreciation charge, which we will discuss in Chapter 9. At this stage we will only note that an allocation should be made.

Van registration and insurance

This was paid for in advance on 1 April for a full year. At the end of our accounting period, i.e. 31 December, we have used nine months' insurance and registration, i.e. nine-twelfths of the total. The expense for the period, therefore, is $9/12 \times \$1200$, i.e. $900. The remaining $300 relates to the next year (next accounting period) and is an asset at the end of the year as the business will receive some future economic benefit. This and similar items are discussed in later chapters.

Purchase of washing machine

We know that Blake's Enterprises is a retail shop selling paint. It is highly unlikely that the washing machine was bought for use by the business, although it has been paid for out of the business bank account. Therefore, this is not an expense of the business, nor is it an asset of the business as the business will not get any future economic benefit from it. It is, in effect, a withdrawal of capital by the owner and should be treated as drawings.

Wages for year

This is clearly a business expense as the wages are paid to the shop assistant and the economic benefit has been used up. From the information we have, the whole $12 000 relates to the accounting period, and, therefore, the expense charged to the profit and loss should be $12 000.

Goods bought and resold

These goods have been sold to customers. The business no longer owns them and is not entitled to any future economic benefit. The whole of the $36 000 is an expired economic benefit and as such should be charged as an expense in the current year's statement of financial performance.

Goods bought but unsold

These goods are still held by the business at the end of the year. The economic benefit from the goods is still to come, in the form of cash or credit, when they are sold. Thus, goods held in stock are an asset rather than an expense of the period we are dealing with.

Motor expenses and petrol

Once again the economic benefit from these has expired. The whole of the $2400 should therefore be charged as an expense in this accounting period.

Cash from sales

This is the revenue of the business for the year, and, as far as we can tell, it is the only revenue. The full amount of $90 000 should be shown as sales revenue in the statement of financial performance.

Money withdrawn by Blake

Given the present information, we cannot categorically say whether this is a business expense or not. If it is, in effect, wages for Blake's work, then it could be argued that it is a genuine business expense. If, on the other hand, it has simply been withdrawn for personal use it is clearly drawings, and for the purposes of this example this is how we will classify it.

Preparing the statement of financial performance

We can now draw up the statement of financial performance of Blake's Enterprises for the year ended 31 December 20X1.

BLAKE'S ENTERPRISES
STATEMENT OF FINANCIAL PERFORMANCE FOR THE YEAR ENDED 31 DECEMBER 20X1

	$	$
Sales revenue		90 000
Less Cost of goods sold		36 000
Gross Profit		54 000
Rates	4 000	
Van registration and insurance	900	
Wages	12 000	
Motor expenses	2 400	
		19 300
Net Profit		34 700

You will notice that we have shown a gross profit and a net profit. Gross profit can be defined as sales less cost of goods sold. Net profit can be broadly defined as gross profit less operating and administrative expenses and other charges.

The reason for showing the gross profit is to enable Blake to see whether the business is doing as well as it should. Most retail businesses know what percentage of selling price is profit and what is cost. Blake, for example, has costs of 40 per cent of the selling price and would expect a gross profit margin of 60 per cent of the selling price. If these figures alter, Blake would need to know why, particularly if the gross profit figure was less than expected. This information would allow Blake to take corrective action, particularly if the accounting period was, for instance, one month.

The net profit figure can be affected by numerous expenses. It is the figure often referred to as the bottom line. Depending on the size of the business (usually for an owner-manager) you may deduct the drawings from this net profit figure to arrive at a figure of profit retained in the business. If the drawings were subtracted in the expense section of the statement of financial performance, this would distort the ratio of net profit to sales (because the drawings figure may bear no relationship to the sales of the business). As with the gross profit percentages, managers often try to keep costs within certain percentage points.

The format and uses of the statement of financial performance

Unlike the statement of financial position, which represents the position of a business at a point in time, the statement of financial performance represents a series of transactions over a period of time. We will look first at what determines the format of the statement of financial performance as this also, to some extent, determines its usefulness and its limitations.

Limitations of the statement of financial performance

To a limited extent the type of business activity will determine the presentation and context of the statement of financial performance. In the case of a retail business such as Blake's Enterprises, a gross profit figure may be useful, but in a service business such as a hotel, which is labour intensive, the revenue earned may bear little if any relationship to inputs of physical goods. Thus, the type of activity has an effect on what is being reported and how it should be reported. Similarly the objective of the preparers of information often has an effect on the statement of financial performance. If, for example, the accounts are being prepared for tax purposes the owner may wish to reduce profit, or defer it to the next year if at all possible. On the other hand, if the accounts are to be used to borrow money, then the owner may want to portray a healthy profit. While we should not give the impression that the profit can be manipulated at will, it is clear from our discussion that there are areas of judgement which allow slightly different results to be obtained from the same basic data. The extent to which management of profit is practised is often limited by the fact that there a number of conflicting requirements which mean that manipulation of the profit for one purpose is detrimental for another purpose. It should also be borne in mind that the statement of financial performance can only be as good as the information on which it is based. Thus, for a fish and chip shop whose owner records only every second sale through the till, the accounts will record only those transactions that go through the till.

Types of business

As with the statement of financial position, a prime determinant of the content and format of the statement of financial performance is the type of organisational structure involved. The content and format of the statement of financial performance for a company is influenced by the regulations imposed by the professional accounting bodies. The latter regulations are contained in Australian Accounting Standards. Another important determinant is ownership: a company may have to produce statements that comply with both Australian and US regulations, for example, if it is owned by a US parent.

You should now study Woolworths' statement of financial performance (profit and loss statement) in Appendix 1. The statement reports total revenue from operating activities and other sources in a few lines. Therefore, as with the statement of financial position, it is essential to study the notes following the statement while you look at the figures. Details of the revenue and expense items are disclosed in the notes. We explore Woolworths' statement of financial performance in more detail in Chapter 11.

For other types of organisations, such as sole proprietorships and partnerships, there are virtually no regulations covering format. Because the statement of financial performance is being prepared for owners who are also managers, it is normally the case that for these organisations the amount of detail in the statement of financial performance is greater. The reason for this is that the annual report, as well as being a report on performance, acts as a basis for management decisions about the organisation. The size and complexity of an organisation determines the level of detail contained in statements prepared for external consumption. These statements for external consumption are only one form of statement. As we have said, regular statements of financial performance are normally prepared for internal use by the managers of an organisation and these internal reports are generally more detailed than the reports produced for external users. Finally it is important to remind ourselves that the type of organisation and its goals can make a statement of financial performance less relevant and in some cases irrelevant. Should charitable organisations make profits, or is the prime interest how any surplus monies have been used to further the aims of the charity? Clearly, different statements are appropriate to the needs and aims of different organisations.

Regulations

As we stated in Chapter 4, there are a number of regulatory influences on the format and content of published financial statements, including the statement of financial performance. In some countries a particular influence that is more relevant to the statement of financial performance than the statement of financial position is the taxation legislation. In some European countries, such as Germany, unless an amount is in the statement of financial performance it is not allowable for tax purposes. (This is not the case in Australia, where accounting profit and taxable income are normally different amounts.) This can lead to charging in the current year 'expenses' from which there is still a future benefit to be obtained, in order to minimise the tax bill for the year.

Users of accounts

The users of accounts often have different requirements from each other. As we have said, owner-managers normally require detailed information. The tax authorities often require specific information to decide whether a particular expense is allowable for tax purposes. Apart from these influences, there is also confidentiality: a business does not necessarily want its competitors, or indeed its customers, to know how much profit it is making.

Summary

In this chapter we have identified what revenue is and explained the recognition principle in relation to revenue. We have also looked at the question of what constitutes a business expense and seen that:

- expenses are not necessarily the same as costs
- all costs must relate to the business before they can even be considered as expenses.

We have also pointed out that the definitions of both assets and expenses relate to economic benefits to the business. The important difference is that assets give future economic benefits whereas expenses relate to economic benefits used up in the accounting period. This leads us to a series of questions relating to assets and expenses which will help to classify items correctly. These questions are summarised in the form of a decision tree in Figure 5.3.

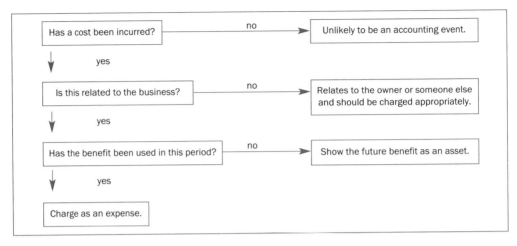

Figure 5.3 *Decision tree for classifying assets and expenses.*

Reference

Australian Accounting Standards Board and Public Sector Accounting Standards Board. *Statement of Accounting Concept No. 4: Definition and Recognition of the Elements of Financial Statements*, March 1995.

Review questions

1   In your own words define revenue.

2   At what point should revenue be recognised?

3   In your own words define an expense.

4   How does an expense differ from a cost?

5   'Expenses are always the same as costs for a period.' Discuss the truth of this statement, using examples to illustrate your argument.

6   What is the purpose of a statement of financial performance and who would use it?

7   Describe the difference between an expense and an asset.

8   In what circumstances would it be inappropriate to recognise a cost as either an expense or an asset?

Problems for discussion and analysis

1   Refer to the Woolworths financial report in Appendix 1.
   a   What is the revenue from operating activities for 1999?
   b   What is the operating profit before tax for 1999? For 1998? How much did this increase by?
   c   What is the amount for abnormal items for 1999? What do the abnormal items represent?
   d   What is the amount of earnings per share for Woolworths in 1999? In 1998?

2 Calculate the two missing amounts for each independent case below.

Case	Total Assets $	Total Liabilities $	Owners' Equity $	Total Revenue $	Total Expenses $	Net profit (loss) $
a	40 000	15 000	?	39 000	?	9 000
b	?	49 000	52 000	85 000	?	(15 000)
c	70 000	?	42 000	60 000	44 000	?
d	?	26 000	44 000	?	22 000	15 000
e	51 000	?	31 000	?	33 000	(14 000)

(Adapted from J. Hoggett and L. Edwards, *Financial Accounting in Australia*, John Wiley, 1990, p. 38.)

3 Data for K. Follet's business as at 31 December 20X0:

	$		$
Accounts receivable	12 000	Revenue earned	44 000
Accounts payable	8 000	K. Follet capital	?
Cash at bank	9 000	Mortgage payable	26 000
Building	42 000	Wage expense	14 000
Advertising expense	6 000	Land	15 000
Equipment	11 000	Bills payable	10 000
Electricity expense	4 000	Telephone expense	1 000

Prepare a statement of financial performance for the month of December, and a statement of financial position for K. Follet as at 31 December 20X0.

(Adapted from J. Hoggett and L. Edwards, *Financial Accounting in Australia*, John Wiley, 1990, p. 38.)

4 Study the figures below. Calculate the missing amounts for each independent case. Assume in case (f) that net profit is 25 per cent of revenue.

Case	Current Assets	Non-current Assets	Total Assets	Current Liabilities	Non-current Liabilities	Total Liabilities	Owners' Equity	Total Revenue	Total Expenses	Net Profit (Loss)
a	20 000	?	140 000	30 000	?	?	20 000	112 500	?	200
b	18 200	?	?	?	110 000	132 000	33 300	86 200	?	(7300)
c	?	86 300	103 700	12 800	80 000	?	?	17 350	17 300	?
d	21 270	?	86 350	3 200	?	43 580	?	158 600	?	3 200
e	?	110 200	?	?	98 300	110 260	23 400	?	33 000	7 800
f	?	36 400	377?	10 400	NIL	1040 0?	27 300	133 800	?	?

5 There are two partners in AB & Co., an electrical retailer. They have each withdrawn $10 000 in cash from the business during the year. B has also taken from the business for personal use a washing machine which cost $400 and which had a selling price of $560. A has been paid wages of $24 000 and B has been paid $12 000 in wages.

Discuss how each of the above should be dealt with in the accounts, giving reasons for your decisions.

6 Jimmy Jones received a $200 000 legacy from his great aunt. As he had some knowledge of the textile industry he decided to go into business manufacturing garments. He commenced trading on 1 July 20X1 and used all of the $200 000 as capital. Unfortunately, as he did not have an accounting background, he did not keep adequate records. At the end of the financial year he realised that he would have to prepare financial accounts so that he could ascertain whether or not he had made a profit, and whether he was liable for tax on any such profit.

From the information given below, prepare in good form a statement of financial performance for the year and a statement of financial position as at 30 June 20X2. Note: all figures given are for a full year and the owner, Jimmy Jones, withdrew an amount of $100 per week from the business to cover his expenses.

Debtors $50 000, inventory $100 000, bank loan (due 1 January 20X6) $80 000, machinery $80 000, total current assets $160 000, sales $127 800, rent $5000, motor vehicles $40 000, wages $42 100, motor vehicle expenses $8230, total non-current assets $132 500, electricity expense $2500, council rates $2500, total liabilities $117 600, advertising expense $2022, cost of goods sold $84 070, cash at bank ?, office equipment ?, selling expense ?, total assets ?, net assets ?, creditors ?, gross profit ?, capital ?, retained earnings ?, total owners' equity ?

7   In each of the following situations, discuss whether the item would be included in the statement of financial performance for the year to 31 December 20X1 and at what amount. The business is that of a builder and builder's trader.

a   Sales of general building materials by the builder's trader to third parties amounted to $52 000 of which $48 000 was received in cash by 31 December 20X1 and the remainder was received in January 20X2.

b   Three house conversions were started and completed during the year at a price of $48 000 each. These amounts were received in full by 31 December 20X1.

c   One office conversion which had been 60 per cent complete at the end of 20X0 was completed in 20X1 at a price of $80000. Invoices on account amounting to $48 000 had been sent out in 20X0.

d   The building materials sold to third parties during the year had cost $28 000 of which all but $2000 had been paid by December 20X1.

e   The building materials used on the three houses referred to in item (b) had cost $36 000 and had all been paid for by December 20X1.

f   Wages paid in respect of the houses mentioned in item (b) amounted to $40 000 for the year.

g   The costs relating to the office mentioned in item (c) were as follows.

	$
Wages paid in 20X0	16 000
Wages paid in 20X1	12 000
Materials used in 20X0	16 000
Materials used in 20X1	14 000

h   The storeworkers' wages in the yard amounted to $16 000 for the year.

i   The owner, who worked full time in the business, paid himself a salary of $18 000 and also withdrew $2000 cash from the business to pay a pressing personal debt.

j   The motor expenses paid in the year were broken down as follows (assume the owner uses his car 80 per cent for business).

		$
Annual registration on three vans paid	1 April 20X1	600*
Annual insurance on vans paid	1 April 20X1	960*
Repairs and petrol for vans		1 200
Annual registration on owner's car paid	1 June 20X1	200*
Annual registration on owner's wife's car paid	1 June 20X1	200*
Annual insurance on owner's car paid	1 June 20X1	240*

(continued next page)

| Annual insurance on owner's wife's car paid | 1 June 20X1 | 240* |
| Repairs and petrol for the two cars (50 per cent for each car) | | 1 600 |

* The charge for registration had gone up by $40 per vehicle and insurance premiums have risen by 20 per cent. All these charges are paid annually in advance.

k   The following bills were also paid during the year.

		$
Electricity (payable at end of each quarter)	1 February	108
	1 May	90
	1 August	90
	1 November	120
Rent for one year to 1 April 20X2	1 April 19X1	800*
TV rental to 1 April 20X2	1 April 19X1	120*

* The rent had remained the same as in 20X0 but the TV rental had gone up from $100 to $120.

8 Based on your decisions, draw up a statement of financial performance for 20X1 using the information above.

9 When a CitiPower customer uses electricity, the commission has earned revenue. It is impossible, however, to read all the customers' meters on the last day of its financial year. How does CitiPower determine its revenue for a given year?

10 The R & I Bank charges a 5 per cent service fee when issuing travellers' cheques to customers. Recently, a customer bought $1000 Diners Club International travellers' cheques, for which the bank received a fee of $50. How would the bank record this transaction, and how would the Diners Club International statement of financial position be affected?

11 During November 20X0, ABC Ltd sold goods for $50 000 to XYZ Ltd, who used them as security for a hire-purchase agreement and sent the $50 000 to ABC Ltd. ABC Ltd agreed to repurchase the merchandise on or before June 30 20X1 for $52 000, the difference being interest on the hire-purchase agreement and payment for XYZ Ltd's services. Will ABC Ltd have revenue in 20X0?

12 Swallow Ltd is a statewide real-estate brokerage company which is well known for selling small businesses through local real-estate brokers. A local broker joining the group pays Swallow Ltd an initial contract fee of $8000 plus 5 per cent of all future revenue as a service fee. In return, Swallow Ltd allows use of its well-known name, arranges various seminars throughout the year and provides a statewide referral system for the brokers. The initial contract fee currently accounts for 30 per cent of Swallow Ltd's revenues but it anticipates that the WA market will become flooded with competitors over the next two years, from which time the company will have to rely on the service fees and any new sources of revenue. Should each $8000 be recorded as revenue by Swallow Ltd in the year in which the contract agreement is signed? If so, what will be the effect on its profits after the market has become flooded with competitors?

13 A baby-food manufacturer enclosed a redeemable promotional coupon with every jar of baby food sold to supermarkets (at a wholesale price of $3.00). The coupon could be used by customers to receive $1.00 cash when they purchased a new product which the manufacturer was introducing at a wholesale price of $2.50. For every coupon returned, the manufacturer reimbursed the supermarket $1.20 (the extra $0.20 to cover the coupon handling costs incurred by the supermarket). In the past, similar promotions had seen approximately 30 per cent of the coupons redeemed; however, at the end of 20X0 only 15 per cent of the coupons issued at the beginning of the year had been redeemed. What allowance, if any, should the manufacturer make for these coupons in recording the 20X0 revenues? If an allowance should be made, should it apply to the sales revenue of the baby food or to the sales revenue of the new product?

(Case studies 10–13 adapted from R. Anthony and J. Reece, *Accounting: Text and Cases*, 8th edn, Richard D. Irwin Inc., 1988, Chapter 5, Case 5–4.)

14   B. Smart has asked for your advice. He is at present employed at an annual salary of $20 000. He is just 55 and, if he retired now, would receive a pension of half his salary until his 60th birthday. If he stays in his job until he is 60, he will be paid a lump sum of $50 000. Smart has invented a burglar alarm after spending $8000 developing his ideas. He has been offered $120 000 for the patent by Auto Company Ltd. However, he is proposing retiring from his present position to manufacture the alarms himself with the help of his wife, who could leave her present part-time job, which pays $6000 per annum. The two have estimated the following.

- Production and sale for each of the first five years would be 4000 alarms at $40 each.
- The cost of materials would be $19 per unit.
- Using their home garage as a workshop, the couple would do all the work themselves with the assistance of machinery costing $16 000.
- Packing and transport would cost $1 per unit.
- Other overheads, light, power, etc. would total $2000 per annum.

a   You are required to prepare figures to help Smart decide on the most favourable course of action in accordance with the above estimated data.
b   List any other factors that you consider should affect his decision.

(Adapted from I. Harrison, J. Horrocks and R. Newman, *Accounting: A Direct Approach*, Longman Cheshire, 1986, p. 32.)

15   You are the chief accountant of Elphick & Company, a firm of chartered accountants. Paul Cruit and his wife Debbie have asked for your advice in respect of the following business proposition.

At present, Paul earns $30 000 p.a. and Debbie has a part-time job in which she earns $7000 p.a. Their eldest son is a third-year apprentice and gives his mother $50 a week towards household expenses.

Paul has been left a legacy of $250 000 by his great aunt. This money can be invested in a bank deposit, earning 6 per cent per annum. However, Paul and Debbie favour buying a newsagency costing $370 000 (including stock, plant, equipment, a vehicle and goodwill).

The business broker selling the business states that Bankeast would be prepared to grant them a loan of $200 000 at 10 per cent per annum, repayable over 20 years.

At present, the business is operated by a husband and wife, plus one other staff member who earns $550 per week (this figure includes all employee outgoings such as payroll tax, insurance superannuation, etc.).

Additional information:

Sales for the previous 12 months:

	$
Newspapers and periodicals	780 000
Books	60 000
Stationery	87 500
Confectionery	27 600
Sundry sales	10 000

Gross profit on:

	%
Newspapers and periodicals	15
Books	40
Confectionery	50
Stationery	40
Sundry sales	30

The previous year's expenses were:

	$		$
Telephone	3 000	Wages and associated costs	28 820
Rent of premises	4 000	Rates	15 000
Insurance	12 750	Electricity and gas	7 300
Security	2 700	Advertising	3 450
Accountant's fees	3 620	Trade subscriptions	1 500
Vehicle expenses	2 300	Depreciation expense	3 820

Required:

a   What would your advice be?

b   It was suggested by the business broker that the son work in the business, at a reduced wage, instead of the present employee. This would increase profits. What points need to be considered if this course of action is to be taken?

c   What other factors should the Cruits consider before making a decision?

16   The Northshore Sailing Association (NSA) is a nonprofit association with 1875 members. The association represents the interests of its members through a management committee, which organises the publication of a quarterly newsletter, and holds an annual meeting; it has subcommittees which create various competitions and outings for the members, as well as getting involved in community-care programs.

Every June, the newly appointed management committee meets with the old committee to discuss whether the general policy of the NSA has been adhered to over the 12-month period. The financial policy of the association for each year focuses on matching expenses with revenues; in other words, the expenses of the year should approximately equal the revenues of the year.

At the annual meeting on 30 June 20X2, the executive secretary presented an estimated statement of financial performance for the past financial year to the new management committee. Even though some of the June transactions had been estimated, the executive secretary assured the committee that these figures were carefully arrived at and should approximate the actual totals for the month.

NSA
ESTIMATED STATEMENT OF FINANCIAL PERFORMANCE FOR THE PERIOD
1 JULY 20X1–30 JUNE 20X2

	$
Revenues	
Membership fees	76 680
Newsletter subscriptions	8 668
Publication sales	3 168
Government grant	14 400
Annual National Sailing	
Championship, 20X1 profit	908
Total Revenues	103 824
Expenses	
Printing and mailing publications	24 640
Committee meeting expense	13 120
Annual National Sailing	
Championship advance	2 880
IBM publishing system	7 200
Administrative salaries and expenses	45 724
Miscellaneous	6 680
Total Expenses	100 244
Excess of revenues over expenses	3 580

A question raised by one of the new committee members was whether a grant of $14 400 from the government should be included as revenue. If it was not, a deficit would show; this would mean that the association's reserves had been touched and therefore the 20X1–X2 board had not adhered to the general financial policy of the NSA.

This resulted in further questioning about items on the statement of financial performance, and led to the disclosure of the following information by the executive secretary.

- In March 20X2, the NSA received a $14 400 grant from the government to finance a clean-up and erosion prevention operation along the Swanlee River, to commence in August of the same year. Up to 30 June 20X2, $720 had been spent in preparations for the operation and was included in Committee Meeting Expenses. When asked to explain why the $14 400 had been recorded in the 20X1–X2 financial year instead of 20X2–X3, the executive secretary explained that the grant had been obtained as a result of the persuasiveness of the 20X1–X2 committee, and hence it should receive the credit for securing the grant.
- In early June 20X2, the association had fully installed and paid for an IBM publishing system which cost $7200. This system would dramatically reduce the hours involved in preparing membership lists, correspondence and manuscripts for publication. All of the other equipment in the association office was old.
- Members normally paid their fees during the first two months of the financial year. Due to the need to raise finance for the new IBM system, the association announced to members in April 20X2 that anyone paying their

fees before 20 June 20X2 would receive a free T-shirt which would be on sale when the Swanlee River clean-up and erosion prevention operation commenced later in the year. The approximate cost of producing this T-shirt was expected to be $7.20, and it was expected to sell for $15. As a result, $8640 of fees for 20X2–X3 were received by 20 June 20X2.

- In May 20X2, the association sent a membership directory to each member; such a directory was published and sent out to members once every two years. The preparation and printing costs totalled $5760. Of the 2000 copies printed, 1875 were posted to members while the remaining 125 were held until new members joined the NSA upon which time a directory would be sent to them free of charge.

- One of the entitlements of being an NSA member was the receipt of the association newsletter free of charge. The $8668 reported as subscription revenue was the cash received from non-members, such as libraries and interest groups, in the 20X1–X2 financial period, of which $2160 was for newsletters that would be delivered during the next financial period, 20X2–X3. Offsetting this was $1440 of subscription revenue received in 20X0–X1 for newsletters delivered in 20X1–X2.

- The association had advanced $2880 for preliminary expenses to the committee responsible for planning the 20X2 annual national sailing championship held in late May. Entrance fees at the competition were set at a price to cover all of the championship costs, so it was expected that the $2880, plus any profit, would be returned to the NSA after the committee had paid the championship bill. The 20X1 championship led to a $908 profit; the 20X2 results were not known, although the anticipated attendance was about the same.

Use generally accepted accounting principles to determine if the Northshore Sailing Association had an excess or deficit for 20X1–X2.

(Adapted from R. Anthony and J. Reece, *Accounting: Text and Cases*, 8th edn, Richard D. Irwin Inc., 1988, Chapter 3, Case 3–6.)

Ethics case study

The sales staff at Ellenmere are paid a bonus each year provided they sell a certain number of cars. One of your best friends, James, works as a salesperson and you work in the accounting department. In reviewing the sales records for James, you discover that his last sale for the period was large enough for him to qualify for the bonus. All that remained was for you to approve the sale. You tell James the good news and he is elated as he will now be able to pay for his daughter to receive special medical treatment for a rare disease she suffers from. Before the bonus can be paid, it is your job to check that the customer meets the company's credit rating requirements so that the sale can be approved. As it happens, you know the customer and you notice that his earnings, as stated on the company form, are about 30 per cent overstated. If you adjust the earnings, the customer does not meet the company's requirements and James will lose the sale and the bonus.

Discuss:

what you would do in this situation.

Introduction to the Worksheet

Learning objectives

At the end of this chapter you should be able to:

1 understand the format and purpose of the worksheet

2 explain single and double entry type errors

3 explain how to identify addition, subtraction and transposition errors

4 analyse and classify transactions onto a worksheet.

Introduction

In Chapter 4 we discussed the question of how we measure what a business is worth at a particular point in time by using the statement of financial position, while in Chapter 5 we discussed the measurement of the profit for a period of time through the use of the statement of financial performance. We also indicated that the profit could be measured either using the statement of financial performance or from the increase in wealth over a period of time. Because of the complexity of most business organisations and the number of transactions involved, we need to have a system from which the details for inclusion in the statements of financial position and financial performance can be drawn. This system also needs to have some built-in checks and balances to ensure, as far as possible, that no transactions are omitted and any errors are identified. To cope with these and other demands, a form of recording known as double-entry bookkeeping was developed. This system is based on a rule known as the *principle of duality* (see Key Concept 4.12). This principle was discussed in some detail in Chapter 4, and it was further exemplified in our discussion of the statement of financial position equation which we defined as:

$$\text{assets} = \text{liabilities} + \text{owners' equity}$$

We also showed that the owners' equity was increased by the profits made by the business, and we defined profit as:

$$\text{profit} = \text{revenue} - \text{expenses}$$

We can therefore see that, if the statement of financial position at the start of the period is stated as:

$$\text{assets at } T_0 = \text{liabilities at } T_0 + \text{owners' equity at } T_0$$

then the statement of financial position at the end of the period can be depicted as:

$$\text{assets at } T_1 = \text{liabilities at } T_1 + \text{owners' equity at } T_0$$
$$+ (\text{revenue} - \text{expenses}) \text{ at } T_1$$

From these equations it is clear that there is a relationship between assets, liabilities, owners' equity, revenue and expenses and that with every transaction recorded we must ensure that there are two sides in order that the equation remains true. This may seem complicated but it will become much clearer when you see how the double-entry system of recording works.

Key Concept 6.1

Application of the principle of duality

Applying the duality principle to our equation we find that, if we increase our assets, we must have either:

- increased our liabilities, or
- decreased another asset, or
- increased our owners' equity.

In other words, the principle of duality when applied to the statement of financial position equation holds that both sides of the equation must always be equal.

We deal with simple examples to illustrate the principles, which are the same no matter how complex the business. It is normally the number of transactions that is the problem rather than their complexity; most large businesses and some fairly small businesses require sophisticated recording systems to deal with the thousands of transactions that take place during the year. This is one of the major uses of computers in business today. Computers not only provide a vehicle for recording the accounting transactions but the more sophisticated systems also analyse the data and produce reports such as statements of financial position, statements of financial performance and other reports tailored to the particular needs of the users or managers of the business. For our purposes, however, we do not need to introduce a high level of sophistication to understand the principles involved. We can set up a perfectly adequate double-entry bookkeeping system using a spreadsheet. We refer to our manually produced spreadsheet as a worksheet and we use it to illustrate the basics of double-entry bookkeeping. The worksheet is set out in the form of the statement of financial position equation with the columns headed as appropriate. We use the following simple data to illustrate the worksheet.

Example 6.1: Beetle

Beetle started up a small business and the first transactions were as follows:

1 Open a business bank account and deposit $10 000 of Beetle's own money.
2 Buy a van for $4000 cash.
3 Buy some raw materials for $6000 cash.
4 Get a bank loan of $12 000 (for the purpose of this example we will assume the loan will be a current liability).
5 Buy some machinery for manufacturing for $8000 cash.

Each of these transactions has been entered on the worksheet (version 1) and you should look at that while reading the description of what has been done.

Before looking at the transactions in detail let us briefly discuss the way in which the worksheet has been set up. There is a column in which the transaction is identified and described. This identification and description in our case consists of the number of the transaction taking place. You could include a fuller description: the date, the invoice number, the name of the suppliers involved or whatever is appropriate.

After the column containing the description, there are columns for each asset purchased and these are followed by columns for the liabilities and owners' equity. Thus we have, in effect, across the top of our worksheet the statement of financial position equation:

$$\text{assets} = \text{liabilities} + \text{owners' equity (or equity)}$$

Having made that important point, let us examine each of the transactions in turn and see how they have been entered into our double-entry worksheet.

BEETLE WORKSHEET: VERSION 1

	Assets			=	Liabilities	+	Equity
Transaction	Cash	Cars	Raw materials	Machine	Loans		Equity
1	10 000						10 000
2	−4 000	4 000					
3	−6 000		6 000				
4	12 000				12 000		
5	−8 000			8 000			
Balance	4 000 +	4 000 +	6 000 +	8 000 =	12 000 +		10 000

Transaction 1

In the case of this transaction Beetle expects to get a future benefit; therefore we have an asset. So we have made a column for cash and entered the amount paid into the bank account. On the other side of our worksheet we have made a column entitled 'Owners' equity' and have entered in that column the amount that the owner has put into the business. It should be noted that if we were to total up our worksheet we would have the figures for the statement of financial position at that point in time, and this is true at every stage as long as all transactions up to the statement date have been recorded.

Transaction 2

For this transaction we have opened another column in which we have recorded the van as an asset because it will give a future benefit. We have also deducted the amount paid for the van from the cash column, i.e. Beetle has exchanged one asset (cash) for another (a van). The worksheet, if totalled now, would still balance and would correctly record that the business owns a van which cost $4000 and has $6000 in the bank.

Transaction 3

Next Beetle used some of his cash to purchase raw materials. We therefore need to record that the asset 'Cash' is reduced by $6000 and that there is a new asset, 'Raw materials', which cost $6000. We have classified the raw materials as an asset because we have assumed that Beetle will get a future benefit from them.

Transaction 4

In this transaction Beetle borrowed some money and put it in the bank. The amount in the bank is therefore increased by the amount of the loan ($12 000) and on the other side of the worksheet we open a column in which we record the fact that the business has a liability, i.e. it has an obligation to another entity to pay cash (in this case $12 000). Once again, if we were to total up our worksheet at this point we would find that it balanced.

Transaction 5

This transaction involves using one asset, our cash, to purchase another, machinery. Once again the machinery can be viewed as an asset of the business as the business is going to get some future benefit. All that is needed is to open a column for the new asset and show that it cost $8000 and reduce the amount Beetle has in the bank by the same amount.

From the worksheet it should be obvious that every transaction involves two entries. For example when the owner pays in the money an entry is made in the cash column and one is made in the owners' equity column. If all the columns are totalled, the worksheet will always balance. If either of these points is not clear to you it is important that you look again at what has been done so that you understand both these points before moving on. You might have noticed that in the worksheet all the transactions are ones that affect only the statement of financial position. In order to provide a clearer understanding of the way in which the worksheet is used and how statement of financial performance transactions are recorded we will extend our example by a few more transactions.

Further information

6 Beetle hired a machine operator who worked on the raw materials previously bought (see transaction 3) and who was paid $1000.

7 Beetle sold the finished goods for $10 000.

Dealing first with transaction 6, we can see that when Beetle paid the wages there was an expectation that there would be a future benefit because the cost of the goods held had increased by the amount spent on changing them from their original form to their final form. We could either record these wages as an asset in their own right or add them to the cost of the goods bought and call that finished goods. We will take the latter course in this example. Thus we need to open a column for 'Finished goods', and the entry we need to make will be to reduce the cash by $1000, and record the $1000 spent in the finished goods column.

However, we have said that the cost of the finished goods is the cost of the raw materials plus the wages and at present we have only dealt with the wages. To deal with the raw materials we need to reduce the raw materials column by $6000 and add that amount to the finished goods column.

Turning now to transaction 7, clearly we have some sales revenue so we can open a new column entitled 'Profit and loss' and in this we enter sales of $10 000. We also need to enter the increase in cash of $10 000 in the cash column.

If at this stage we were to draw up a statement of financial position, it balances and shows us that a profit of $10 000 has been made. However, that is incorrect because we have not shown any expenses incurred in producing the sales of $10 000. We can try to identify these expenses directly, as we know they consist of the cost of the raw materials and the wages, i.e. the amount in the finished goods column. An alternative is to look at each of our assets and ask ourselves the question: is there a future benefit to be obtained or has the benefit expired? If there is a future benefit, then we have an asset; if the benefit has been consumed, then we have an expense. If we did this, we would conclude that, as we had sold the goods represented by the figure of $7000 in the finished goods column and had received the benefit from selling them in the form of $10 000 in cash, then these are clearly not an asset any longer and should be charged as an expense of the period. We thus have to make a further adjustment to our worksheet which we will call transaction 7a. Our new worksheet will now be as follows.

BEETLE WORKSHEET: VERSION 2

	Assets					=	Liabilities	+	Equity	
Transaction	Cash	Van	Raw materials	Machine	Finished goods		Loans		Equity	Profit and loss
1	10 000								10 000	
2	−4 000	4 000								
3	−6 000		6 000							
4	12 000						12 000			
5	−8 000			8 000						
Balance	4 000	+ 4 000	+ 6 000	8 000			= 12 000	+	10 000	
6	−1 000				1 000					
6			−6 000		6 000					
7	10 000									10 000
7a					−7 000					−7 000
Balance	13 000 +	4 000 +	0 +	8 000 +	0		= 12 000 +		10 000 +	3 000

Before leaving this simple example let us extract from the worksheet a statement of financial position at the end of the period in question and a statement of financial performance for the period.

BEETLE
STATEMENT OF FINANCIAL POSITION AT THE END OF THE PERIOD

Assets	$	$	$	$
Current Assets				
Cash	13 000			
Total Current Assets		13 000		
Non-current Assets				
Van	4 000			
Machine	8 000			
Total Non-current Assets		12 000		
Total Assets			25 000	
Liabilities				
Current Liabilities				
Loan	12 000			
Total Current Liabilities		12 000		
Total Liabilities			12 000	
Net Assets				13 000
Owners' Equity				
Capital	10 000			
Profit	3 000			
Total Owners' Equity				13 000

You will notice that the statement of financial performance is simply a summary of the profit and loss column in the worksheet.

BEETLE
STATEMENT OF FINANCIAL PERFORMANCE FOR THE PERIOD

	$
Sales revenue	10 000
Less Cost of goods sold	7 000
Profit for the period	3 000

A careful study of the figures in the statement of financial position and a comparison with the last line of the worksheet will make it clear that the statement of financial position is in fact the bottom line of the worksheet after appropriate classifications have been made.

Common errors

The example shows that the system of double entry is a convenient way of recording transactions in a logical manner. The system is not complex—all it requires is an understanding of addition and subtraction, together with the knowledge that the equation must always be in balance. It also requires the application of our definitions to classify a particular transaction correctly, so if you have had problems in understanding why a transaction is dealt with in a particular way you should return to Chapters 3, 4 and 5 and reread the definitions of elements of financial statements. Before trying an example yourself, it is worth spending some time reflecting on the last example. If we look at any of the columns we can see that there is simply addition and subtraction taking place; a good example is the cash column where we make additions as money comes into the business and make deductions as money is spent. Another feature of the system is not so obvious: if we make mistakes there is an automatic check because in the end the worksheet will not balance. If this turns out to be the case, we have two ways of finding the error: we can either do a line-by-line check to ensure that each of our lines has balanced, or we can total the columns at various stages to see where the error is likely to be. For example, if we had an error in the worksheet we have just done, we could look at the totals after entering transaction 4 or transaction 5 or whatever. Quite often the error is reasonably obvious because the amount involved gives us a clue. The easy way to illustrate this is to put some deliberate errors into the context of the worksheet we have just completed.

Single-entry error

Let us assume that we forgot the basic rule that each transaction has two sides and when we paid the wages we simply deducted the $1000 from the cash column. Our worksheet would appear as follows.

BEETLE WORKSHEET: VERSION 3

Transaction	Cash	Van	Raw materials	Machine	Finished goods	=	Loans	Equity	Profit and loss
	4 000	4 000	6 000	8 000			12 000	10 000	
6	-1 000								
6			-6 000		6 000				
7	10 000								10 000
7a					-6 000				-6 000
Balance	13 000	+ 4 000	+ 0	+ 8 000	+ 0	= 12 000	+ 10 000	+ 4 000

You will notice that, because we did not record the other side of the wages transaction, the amount charged to the profit and loss column in respect of the goods sold is only $6000 and the profit is increased to $4000. If we now add up the two sides of our worksheet we find that the assets side totals $25 000, i.e. $13 000 + $4000 + $8000, whereas the liability and equity side totals $26 000, i.e. $12 000 + $10 000 + $4000. The difference between the two is $1000 which should direct us to the wages as the likely cause of the problem.

Double-entry error

Another common cause of errors is incorrect double entry. In this case two sides are recorded but they do not leave the equation in balance. Let us assume for example that we had got the entry for the wages correct but that we had incorrectly classified the $10 000 which Beetle obtained from selling the goods as an increase in cash and an increase in finished goods rather than as sales revenue. The resultant worksheet would then be as that on page 123.

You will notice from this worksheet that we no longer have a cost of goods sold which is logical because, as a result of our error, we no longer have any goods sold. What we have instead is a worksheet which shows assets which total $42 000 while the liability and equity totals $22 000. The difference in this case is $20 000, which is twice the amount involved in the error.

BEETLE WORKSHEET: VERSION 4

	Assets				=	Liabilities	+	Equity	
Transaction	Cash	Van	Raw materials	Machine	Finished goods	Loans	Equity	Profit and loss
	4 000	4 000	6 000	8 000		12 000	10 000	
6	-1 000				1 000			
6			-6 000		6 000			
7	10 000				10 000			
Balance	13 000 +	4 000 +	0 +	8 000 +	17 000 =	12 000 +	10 000	

Addition, subtraction and transposition errors

Another common cause of errors is that we have simply failed to add or subtract correctly. The only way to fix this problem is to recheck all our totals and the addition and subtraction. We can reduce the size of that task by balancing our worksheet on a regular basis so that we know where the error is likely to be. A similar problem is a transposition error where, for example, we recorded the total of our cash column as $10 300 instead of $13 000, i.e. we transposed the order of the 3 and the 0. This is a common error and happens to all of us. In this case we can identify that it may be a transposition error because the difference of $2700 is divisible by 9. This will always be the case if we simply transpose two figures, e.g. 45 as 54, 97 as 79 etc. Notice that the difference is divisible by 9 but it does not necessarily have the number 9 in the difference. The difference between 97 and 79 is 18 which is divisible by 9.

Before moving on, we suggest that you draw up your own worksheet for the following set of transactions and compare them with the answer. If your answer varies from the one given, try to identify what you have done, e.g. classified an item as the purchase of an asset. When you have done this, you can then compare your explanation with our explanation of that item. Your entries do not necessarily have to be identical with ours as there are many different ways of setting up the worksheet and arriving at the correct answer to show the position at the end of the month. We can illustrate this by reference to the example based on Mary's business which is set out below.

Example 6.2: Mary's Secondhand Cars

Mary decided to start a business selling secondhand cars. She had saved up some money of her own but this was not enough to start, and so she obtained an interest-free loan, to the business, from her parents. The transactions of the business for the first month were as follows. All transactions were cash.

Day 1   Opened a business bank account and paid in $1000 of her own money.

Day 2   Paid into the bank $4000 that she had borrowed from her parents for use by the business. (Note: as she will repay some of this loan within this trading month we will treat the loan as a current liability.)

Day 3   Found a suitable showroom and paid a fortnight's rent of $200.

Day 4   Went to a car auction and bought the following cars for cash:

- 1980 Ford Fiesta for $2000
- 1977 Ford Escort for $1000
- 1975 Volkswagen Beetle for $600.

Day 5   Bought some office furniture for $240.

Day 6	Employed a teenager who was on the dole to clean cars for her at the rate of $20 per car and paid out $60.

Day 6   Employed a teenager who was on the dole to clean cars for her at the rate of $20 per car and paid out $60.

Day 8   Placed advertisements for all three cars in the local paper. The cost of advertising was $40 per day for each car. She decided that all three should be advertised for two days, and so the total cost was $240.

Day 9   Sold the Ford Fiesta for $3000 cash.

Day 10   Sold the Ford Escort for $1400 cash.

Day 11   Returned to the car auction and bought a Gemini for $3000.

Day 12   Employed her teenage friend to clean the Gemini for $20.

Day 15   Re-advertised the Volkswagen for three days at $40 per day, total cost $120.

Day 17   Advertised the Gemini using a special block advertisement which cost $150 in total.

Day 18   Paid rent of showroom for the next fortnight amounting to $200.

Day 19   Was offered $800 for the Volkswagen.

Day 20   Accepted the offer for the Volkswagen and was paid $800.

Day 22   Sold the Gemini for $3600.

Day 23   Went to the car auction and bought a Datsun 270 for $4600.

Day 24   Had the Datsun professionally cleaned at a cost of $80.

Day 25   Advertised the Datsun using the special block advertisement at a cost of $150.

Day 26   Decided that as things were going so well she would repay her parents $400.

Day 27   Took the Datsun on a test drive with a customer, during which the engine seized.

Day 29   Had the Datsun repaired at a cost of $600.

Day 30   Sold the Datsun for $5400.

Day 31   Paid electricity bill of $80 for the month.

To illustrate the different treatments possible, let us consider the transaction on day 3 where Mary paid a fortnight's rent in advance. The question arises whether this is an expense or an asset. Let us consider the alternatives.

On day 3 it is reasonably clear that we have an asset in that we will get a future benefit in the form of the use of the showroom for two weeks. On the other hand, if we are recording the transaction for the first time at the end of the month we can then argue that the transaction is an expense because at that point in time the benefit has expired. Thus, we could record on day 3 the payment as an asset and then re-evaluate all our assets at the end of the month as we have done on our worksheet. Conversely, we could wait until the end of the month and just record an expense. We would recommend at this stage that you adopt the former treatment for two reasons: firstly it ensures that you re-evaluate all your assets at the end of the month, and secondly, shortcuts often cause more problems than they are worth if you are unfamiliar with the area.

Another transaction that should be mentioned is the advertisements on days 8, 15, 17 and 25. In these cases there exists a similar dilemma to that of the rent. However, there is another problem in that, although with the rent we knew that there was going to be a future benefit, with this advertising it is far from certain that there will be a future benefit. In other words, we do not know when we place the advertisement whether anyone will reply to it and, even if they do, whether they will buy the car. To answer this point we can look at our asset definition which includes the words 'that it is probable that the future economic benefits will eventuate'. In this case, as we are not certain that the advertisement will attract a buyer, we cannot classify this cost as an asset.

As you are probably beginning to recognise, accounting is not just about recording; it is also about exercising judgement within a framework of broad and often very general principles. The important factor to remember as you work through the example above is that you are making judgements and applying the definitions set out in the previous two chapters, and that you are aware of what you are doing and why you are doing it. You should now attempt to produce your own worksheet and extract statements of financial performance and financial position.

If your worksheet is correct, the balances on the bottom line of your worksheet should be those in the statement of financial position set out below. The statement of financial performance follows the statement of financial position and is merely a summary of the profit and loss column on the worksheet.

Even if you find that your answer is correct, before proceeding to the next chapter you should read the explanations for the treatment of the transactions on days 3, 6, 18, 19, 26, 27 and 29 as these are of particular interest and will assist you in the future. If your answer disagrees with ours, check the full worksheet and explanations which follow.

MARY'S SECONDHAND CARS
STATEMENT OF FINANCIAL POSITION

Assets	$	$	$	$
Current Assets				
Cash	5 460			
Total Current Assets		5 460		
Non-current Assets				
Furniture	240			
Total Non-current Assets		240		
Total Assets			5 700	
Liabilities				
Current Liabilities				
Loan	3 600			
Total Current Liabilities		3 600		
Total Liabilities			3 600	
Net Assets				2 100
Owners' Equity				
Capital	1 000			
Profit	1 100			
Total Owners' Equity				2 100

MARY'S SECONDHAND CARS
STATEMENT OF FINANCIAL PERFORMANCE

	$	$
Sales Revenue	14 200	
Less Cost of cars sold	11 200	
Gross Profit		3 000
Expenses		
Rent	400	
Cleaning	160	
Advertising	660	
Repairs	600	
Electricity	80	
		1 900
Net Profit		1 100

Prepare your own worksheet before you read on.

MARY'S SECONDHAND CARS
WORKSHEET

Day	Cash	Cars	Prepaid rent	Furniture	Loans	Equity	Profit and loss
		Assets			**= Liabilities +**	**Equity**	
1	1 000					1 000	
2	4 000				4 000		
3	-200		200				
4	-3 600	3 600					
5	-240			240			
6	-60						-60
8	-240						-240
9	3 000						3 000
9*		-2 000					-2 000
10	1 400						1 400
10*		-1 000					-1 000
11	-3 000	3 000					
12	-20						-20
15	-120						-120
17	-150						-150
18	-200		200				
20	800						800
20*		-600					-600
22	3 600						3 600
22*		-3 000					-3 000
23	-4 600	4 600					
24	-80						-80
25	-150						-150
26	-400				-400		
29	-600						-600
30	5 400						+5 400
30*		-4 600					-4 600
31	-80						-80
Balance	5 460	0	400	240	3 600	1 000	1 500
31†			-400				-400
Balance	5 460 +	0 +	0 +	240 =	3 600 +	1 000 +	1 100

* You will notice that every time we sold a car (on days 9, 10, 20, 22 and 30) we immediately transferred the cost of that car from our cars column to the profit and loss column as an expense. This transfer was carried out because, having sold the car, we no longer expected a future benefit and therefore we no longer had an asset. An alternative treatment would be to do this exercise at the end of the month.

† When we complete our worksheet it is important to review our assets and ask ourselves: are these still assets? If (as in this case) the answer is no, then we need to transfer their cost to the statement of financial performance as an expense of the period.

Transaction summary

We have set out the transactions that took place, together with the treatment of those transactions on the worksheet and, where appropriate, explanations of that treatment and acceptable alternatives. If there are any items that you still do not understand you should try to examine them in terms of basic definitions referred to in Chapters 4 and 5.

Day 1   Opened a business bank account and paid in $1000 of her own money.

Here we have created a business asset in the form of cash and have also opened an account to show the owner's stake in the business under the heading of owners' equity.

Day 2   Paid into the bank $4000 that she had borrowed from her parents for use by the business.

Once again the business has acquired an asset as it will get a future benefit from the cash. It has also acquired an obligation to pay somebody some money and thus has a liability for the amount borrowed.

Day 3   Found a suitable showroom and paid a fortnight's rent of $200.

We have already discussed this transaction. Our treatment has been to reduce our asset cash in the bank and to record an asset of the prepaid rent from which the business will derive a benefit in the future.

Day 4   Went to the car auction and bought the following cars for cash:
- 1980 Ford Fiesta for $2000
- 1977 Ford Escort for $1000
- 1975 Volkswagen Beetle for $600.

Clearly by paying out $3600 Mary has reduced cash at the bank and so that is one side of the entry. The other side is to record the cars as an asset because Mary will get a future benefit from them.

Day 5   Bought some office furniture for $240.

This is exactly the same as the previous transaction. Mary has merely exchanged one asset, cash, for another, furniture.

Day 6   Employed a teenager who was on the dole to clean cars for her at the rate of $20 per car and paid out $60.

In this case one side of the transaction is clear, in as much as the cash has clearly been reduced by $60. The question that then arises is whether there is an asset or an expense. We have shown the cost of the car cleaning as an expense because we are uncertain that any future benefit will arise from this particular expenditure. The fact that a car is cleaned does not add any intrinsic value and, in fact, it is probably necessary to clean all the cars in the showroom regularly because customers expect to buy clean cars.

Day 8   Placed advertisements for all three cars in the local paper. The cost of advertising was $40 per day for each car. She decided that all three should be advertised for two days, and so the total cost was $240.

Refer back for a detailed discussion of the reasons for our treatment of this item. What we have done is to assume there is no future benefit and treat the item as an expense and charged the item to the statment of financial performance at the same time as we reduced our cash by $240.

Day 9   Sold the Ford Fiesta for $3000 cash.

Clearly the business has another $3000 in our bank and so we increased the amount in the cash column. The sale accords with our definition of revenue, and so we bring that revenue into the profit and loss column.

Day 9*

Here Mary has reduced her assets by the cost of the car she sold; we have charged that cost, i.e. the cost of the expired benefit, to the profit and loss column.

Day 10 Sold the Ford Escort for $1400.

See the explanations for day 9 above. If you have got these wrong make sure you understand why, and then correct your worksheet for all similar items before reading on.

Day 11 Returned to the car auction and bought a Holden Gemini for $3000.

This is, in essence, the same as the transaction on day 4. If you have made an error, you should reread that explanation and check that your treatment of the transaction on day 23 is correct before moving on.

Day 12 Employed her teenage friend to clean the Gemini for $20.

This is, in essence, the same as the transaction on day 6. If you have made an error, you should reread that explanation and check that your treatment of the transaction on day 24 is correct before moving on.

Day 15 Re-advertised the Volkswagen for three days at $40 per day, total cost $120.

See the explanation for day 8 above.

Day 17 Advertised the Gemini using a special block advertisement which cost $150 in total.

See the explanation for day 8 above.

Day 18 Paid rent of showroom for the next fortnight amounting to $200.

This is, in essence, the same situation as day 3. The entry should therefore be the same. At this stage you could also reduce the amount in the rent column by the rent for the first two weeks and charge this to the profit and loss column as the benefit has now expired. We have not done this because we wished to illustrate the importance of the final review before a statement of financial position and statement of financial performance are finally drawn up.

Day 19 Was offered $800 for the Volkswagen. Was paid $800.

Now we have a sale and revenue can be recognised as for day 9.

Day 22 Sold the Gemini for $3600.

Once again we have a sale and revenue can be recognised.

Day 23 Went to the car auction and bought a Datsun 270 for $4600.

See day 4 for explanation of the treatment.

Day 24 Had the Datsun professionally cleaned at a cost of $80.

This is the same as the cleaning for day 6. The fact that it was done professionally does not alter the argument set out there.

Day 25 Advertised the Datsun using the special block advertisement at a cost of $150.

This should be treated in the same way as previous advertisements for the same reasons.

Day 26 Decided that as things were going so well she would repay her parents $400.

This is a different transaction from any of the ones we have dealt with so far. Those dealt with expenditure of cash for either a past or a future benefit. In this case we have reduced our cash in order to pay back an amount that the business owes, i.e. we have used some cash to reduce our liability. Thus, we reduce the amount shown as owing in the loan column by the $400 and we reduce the amount of cash by $400.

Day 27 Took the Datsun on a test drive with a customer, during which the engine seized.

Although an economic event has happened, we cannot account for it because at this stage the effect of that event cannot be adequately expressed in monetary terms.

Day 29 Had the Datsun repaired at a cost of $600.

We are now in a position to account for the event, because we know the effect in monetary terms. However, we are left with the question of whether the expenditure is going to provide a future benefit or whether it is an expense. We need to ask ourselves whether the expenditure increased the value of the asset. If it has, then there is no problem in recognising the transaction as one which creates an asset. If, however, the expenditure merely restores the asset to the state that it was in previously, then it is doubtful that it relates to an asset; we would be safer to charge it to the profit and loss column as an expense, which is what we have done. In essence this is a shorthand way of recording two events. The first is that the engine blew up, so reducing the future benefit we could expect from the asset. If we knew the extent of this reduction, we could have charged that as a past benefit. If we had done that, then the repairs could legitimately be viewed as enhancing the future benefit to be obtained in respect of the reduced asset. This whole process is in fact a shortcut because we do not know what the loss in value of future benefits was; we are therefore, in effect, using the cost of repairs as a surrogate for that loss in value.

Day 30 Sold Datsun for $5400.

See previous transactions of this type on days 9, 10 etc.

Day 31 Paid electricity bill of $80 for the month.

Here we have a reduction of the cash in respect of the use of electricity over the past month. The benefit has clearly expired and we therefore have an expense.

Day 31 The prepaid rent has been consumed and therefore the asset is reduced and an expense is recorded.

In this chapter we have demonstrated the use of a manual worksheet. In today's computerised world, spreadsheets in programs such as Excel or Lotus simplify the recording process. The principles are the same, but the software does have the capacity to store more data and eliminate errors in addition and subtraction. Of course, errors from incorrect recording remain.

Summary

This chapter has introduced you to the worksheet and recalled the concept of duality which states that for accounting purposes there are two sides to every transaction. We have also shown the importance of asking ourselves some basic questions: what exactly is an asset, an expense, etc.? We have also illustrated that, by referring to the definitions contained in Chapters 4 and 5, most of the problems you are likely to encounter can be solved.

We have also provided, by means of the worksheet, a simple vehicle for recording, checking and extracting statements of financial position and financial performance. We have shown that the basis of accounting is very simple as long as you follow the basic principles, and for those times when you do lapse, the system used on the worksheet provides a simple and effective check. Finally we have reiterated the idea that accounting is not a science and that it involves elements of judgement.

Review questions

1   Describe in your own words what is meant by the concept of duality.

2   In each of the following cases describe the two entries required on the worksheet.
   a   The owner pays $1000 into the business bank account.
   b   A desk is bought for $200 for the business, paid for from the bank account.
   c   The business buys goods for $400.
   d   The rent of the premises of $100 for the first week is paid.
   e   A potential customer makes an offer for the goods of $500.
   f   The wages of the employee, amounting to $120, are paid.
   g   The firm receives another offer of $700 for the goods, accepts this offer and is paid immediately.

3   In situations where doubt exists as to whether a transaction has resulted in an asset or expense, what questions should be posed?

4   If some doubt still remains, how should a choice be made? Explain any principles involved.

Problems for discussion and analysis

1   In each of the following situations discuss the potential effect on the business and suggest possible ways in which those effects could be reflected on the worksheet.
   a   The owner starts up a new business and pays $2000 into the business bank account. In addition it is decided that the owner's car will be used exclusively for the business. The car was purchased last year at a cost of $10 000 but a similar one-year-old car could be bought for $9000.
   b   Goods previously bought by the business for $1000 were sold to a customer who changed his mind and decided that he did not want the goods after all.
   c   Another batch of goods which had been bought for $800 and sold for $1200 was subsequently found to be faulty. The options available are as follows:

      • Give the customer a rebate on the purchase price of $200.
      • Refund the full selling price to the customer and reclaim the goods. If this course of action is followed, a further $280 will need to be spent to rectify the faults.

2   In each of the following cases, describe the two entries required on the worksheet.
   a   The owner pays $769 for a desk and chair.
   b   The insurance premium of $549 for one year is paid.

   c   The business checks the price of widgets from a supplier and is told the price is $650 per tonne.

   d   A computer was purchased for $4999 and payment made. It was subsequently found that the computer was faulty and the computer was returned to the supplier for a full refund. (Treat this as two separate transactions.)

   e   The owner withdrew $100 from the business for his personal use.

   f   The owner offers $5999 for a new computer.

   g   The purchase price of a Mazda De-Luxe is $48 999. A buyer offers $48 000 cash. The offer is accepted.

3   I. Cover decided to open Re-cover Upholstery Repairs on 1 March 20X0. She contributed office equipment valued at $10 000 and a commercial van valued at $12 000, and deposited $5000 cash in a business bank account. Transactions during March were:

March 4	Took a three-year lease on a shop and paid first month's rent $350.
4	Purchased office supplies for $260, and issued a cheque for $100 in part payment of same.
6	Cash received for minor repairs, $120.
6	Revenue earned for repair work for Shipshape Ltd on credit, $350.
7	Purchased an upholstery sewing machine for $1840, paying $400 cash and giving a promissory note for the balance.
8	Cash revenue earned $230.
11	Engaged an upholsterer at an agreed wage of $350 per week.
12	Paid petrol $20, postage $10, and electricity bill $30.
13	Cash of $200 received for over-the-counter repairs.
13	Revenue of $450 earned from sales to a customer on credit.
14	Paid for office supplies purchased on credit on 4 March.
15	Withdrew $100 for own use.
16	Office supplies purchased for $250 on credit.
17	Cash revenue received $365.
18	Paid weekly wages to the upholsterer.
21	Revenue earned for repairs: cash $80, on account $170.
23	Shipshape Ltd paid the bill for services rendered on 6 March.
24	Petrol expenses paid $20.
25	Paid weekly wages to the upholsterer.
28	Revenue earned for repair work $390, receiving $100 in cash and the remainder as a promissory note.
31	Office supplies used $200.

Required:

Complete a worksheet for the month of March using the above data and prepare a statement of financial performance for the period and a statement of financial position as at 31 March.

(Adapted from J. Hogget and I. Edwards, *Financial Accounting in Australia*, John Wiley, 1990, p. 97.)

4   Joe decided to start a business selling secondhand boats. He had some money of his own, but this was not enough so he borrowed money (on interest-free terms) from a rich uncle. The transactions of the business during March were all cash transactions as follows:

March 1   Opened a bank account for the business and deposited $10 000 of his own money.

        2   Deposited $20 000 borrowed from his rich uncle in the business bank account.

        3   Paid a fortnight's rent ($500) on a yard suitable for use as a boat sale yard.

        4   Went to an auction and was able to purchase the following boats (including trailers) for cash:
Thunderbird $4000
Chivers $2500
Swiftcraft $900

        5   Furnished the yard office with secondhand furniture costing $2900.

        6   Employed a young nephew to clean the boats.

        8   Advertising for all three boats in the local paper over two days cost $300, which included photos of the boats.

        9   Sold the Thunderbird for $5500 cash.

       10   Sold the Chivers for $3200 cash.

       11   Attended another auction and bought a Bertram for $15 000.

       12   Paid his nephew $20 to clean the new boat.

       15   Re-advertised the Swiftcraft for three days at a total cost of $300.

       17   Advertised the Bertram in a boating magazine at a cost of $800.

       18   Paid rent for the yard for the next fortnight ($500).

       19   Was offered $1200 for the Swiftcraft.

       20   Accepted the offer for the Swiftcraft and was paid $1200.

       22   Sold the Bertram for $19 000.

       23   Went to another auction and bought a Sports Fisherman for $8000.

       24   Had the Sports Fisherman professionally cleaned at a cost of $180.

       25   Advertised the Sports Fisherman in a fishing feature in the newspaper at a cost of $300.

       26   Decided things were going so well he would repay his rich uncle $3000.

       27   Took the Sports Fisherman on a test run with a customer and damaged the hull on a submerged reef.

       29   Had the Sports Fisherman repaired at a cost of $900.

       30   Sold the Sports Fisherman for $9300.

       31   Paid the electricity bill of $180 for the month.

Required:

  a   Complete a worksheet for the month using the above data.

  b   Prepare a statement of financial performance for the accounting period from the worksheet.

  c   Prepare a statement of financial position for the accounting period.

5   Mandy Plover has recently completed her professional accounting qualification and has registered as a tax agent. During the three years in which she was fulfilling the work requirement for her professional status she managed to save $30 000. As she had always wanted to run her own practice, she rented premises and opened for business. She decided the best time of year to commence her business was on 1 July, as this coincided with the beginning of the tax year.

During the month of July the following transactions took place.

July 1   Deposited $30 000 in a business bank account.
Paid three months' rent in advance on premises, $3000.
Placed an order with Quick Printers for stationery, business cards and letterheads. The stationery is expected to last for one year.
Paid Telstra a connection fee of $275 for the telephone and fax.
Paid the electricity company a meter rental fee of $50.
Signed a three-year lease with Office Supplies Pty Ltd at a rent of $475 per month, payable in advance, for office equipment, telephones and fax.

2   Paid Super Signs $1000 for a sign advertising her accounting services to be placed outside the premises.

3   Purchased a computer from Wizard Computers for $17 500, with payment due in 15 days.

4   Received the order from Quick Printers—payment of $1380 due on receipt of goods,

4–15   Completed a number of tax returns for clients with a total billing of $2750. Clients given 30 days credit.

15   Signed a contract with the Widget company for bookkeeping services. The terms of the contract were that Mandy would spend one day a week at the Widget factory and be paid a weekly fee of $300.

15   Paid herself a fortnightly salary of $750.

16   Received payment from one of the tax clients (listed above: 4–15 July) of $225.

16   Signed a three-year lease on a BMW at $2000 per month, payable in advance.

18   Paid for the computer.

22   Received $300 weekly fee from the Widget company.

23   The liquidator of Jimmy Jones Holdings has informed Mandy that one of her clients who took tax advice (period: 4–15 July) has no assets and will be unable to pay the credit account of $780.

29   Paid herself a fortnightly salary of $750.

29   Received $300 weekly fee from the Widget company.

16–31   Completed work for additional clients amounting to $3450. One of these clients paid $340 in cash; the rest were given 30 days credit.

Required:

a   Prepare a worksheet for the month of July.
b   From your worksheet prepare a statement of financial performance and a statement of financial position.
c   Comment on the financial position of the business.

6   Jill has recently gone into business selling office chairs. Details of her transactions for the first month are given below.

Day 1   Opened a bank account and paid in $10 000 of her own money. Transferred the ownership of her car to the business at an agreed price of $4000. Rented an office-showroom at a rental of $240 per month and paid one month's rent. Bought a desk, typewriter, answering-machine and sundry office equipment at a cost of $1600.

Day 2   Bought 100 chairs at a price of $70 per chair and paid for them immediately.

Day 3   Received delivery of the chairs.

Day 5 Placed an advertisement in a trade paper offering the chairs for sale on the following terms:
Single chairs, $100 per chair including delivery; ten or more chairs, $90 per chair including delivery. The advertisement cost $400 and was paid for immediately.

Day 8 Received separate orders for 12 chairs at $100 each, together with accompanying cheques.

Day 9 Paid the cheques into the bank and despatched the chairs. The delivery costs were $144 in total and were paid straight away.

Day 11 Received six orders for ten chairs each at a price of $90 per chair, together with six cheques for $900.
Banked the cheques and despatched the orders. The delivery charges were $100 for each order, making a total of $600 which was paid immediately.

Day 14 Jill paid herself two weeks' wages from the business, amounting to $300 in total.

Day 16 Bought another 20 chairs for $70 each and paid for them immediately.

Day 21 Paid $300 for car repairs.

Day 23 Received an order for 20 chairs at $90 each; banked the cheque and arranged delivery for $80 which was paid immediately.

Day 24 Placed a further advertisement in the trade paper at a cost of $400, which was paid immediately.

Day 27 Received one order for 15 chairs at a price of $90 each (this order totalled $1350) and another order for seven chairs at a price of $100 each (a total of $700). The cheques were banked and the chairs were despatched at a total cost of $200 which was paid immediately.

Day 28 Drew another $300 from the bank for her own wages.
Sold the remaining six chairs at a price of $500 for all six to a customer who walked into the showroom. The customer paid the $500 in cash and this money was banked. No delivery costs were incurred because the customer took the chairs away.
Paid the telephone bill of $60 and the electricity bill, $80.

a In each situation where there are two possible treatments, discuss the arguments in favour of and against each alternative.

b Based on the outcome of your discussions, draw up a worksheet and enter the above transactions.

c Extract a statement of financial position at the end of the month and a statement of financial performance for the month.

d Discuss the performance of the business for the period as revealed by the accounts you have prepared, paying particular attention to its cash position and its profitability.

Ethics case study

Sam is a junior clerk in the accounting department and his boss has asked him to copy the worksheet he has prepared for a meeting that afternoon in order to finalise the company's financial statements for the period. As Sam is copying the worksheet, he notices that a sale on account has not been correctly recorded. The amount has been transposed from the ledger—it was recorded as $54 000 instead of $45 000. Sam remembers the transaction as the sale was to one of his friends. If Sam says nothing, he will receive a higher bonus as the company pays a bonus to all its employees according to their total sales. The bonus will be very useful as Sam is leaving the company at the end of next week to go on an extended working holiday in Europe.

Discuss:

what you would do if you were Sam.

Inventories and Work in Progress

Learning objectives

At the end of this chapter you should be able to:

1. explain what is included in inventory

2. explain what is meant by raw materials, work in progress and finished goods

3. understand the importance of cost of goods sold, ending inventory and inventory management

4. explain the periodic and perpetual methods of recording inventories

5. explain the valuation rule for inventory

6. explain and apply how the cost of inventory is determined

7. explain and apply the first in, first out (FIFO), last in, first out (LIFO) and average cost methods of determining the cost of ending inventory and cost of goods sold.

7

Introduction

In all the examples so far, we have made some simplifying assumptions in relation to the goods purchased, i.e the inventory (or stock) of the business. The first assumption was that no inventories were held at the end of the period, so we had no problem in identifying what inventory had been sold or what it cost. This also avoided the question of whether the goods held in inventory at the end of the period were still worth what we had paid for them. Moreover, we dealt only with single-product businesses which had fairly straightforward processes for converting the goods purchased into saleable commodities. Finally, our examples dealt only with businesses in their first year, avoiding the question of how to deal with the inventory held at the beginning of the year.

Clearly the real world is more complex than this. Businesses have multiple processes or multiple inventory lines or both. In this chapter, we relax all these assumptions and discuss the effects on the statements of financial position and financial performance. We also consider:

- the nature of inventories in different types of business
- the determination of the cost of inventory sold during a period
- the accounting entries needed to record inventory on the worksheet
- the issue of valuation and how a change in the basis of valuation will affect the statement of financial position and statement of financial performance.

Inventory management

The points made above show how important inventory can be. There is often a high level of resources invested in the inventory of a business. Often businesses maintain large inventories in order to meet customer demand and to ensure that the production process is not held up. Many businesses have reappraised the way in which they operate and adopted techniques such as just-in-time management which can reduce the costs of holding high levels of inventories. Such costs are twofold: in order to hold inventory you need space and space costs money; and you have to borrow money or find some other form of finance to buy and maintain the inventory levels.

The adoption of just-in-time techniques requires a reappraisal of the production process and demand cycle in order to reduce inventories to a minimum. This has caused large manufacturing firms which have adopted the technique to assess their suppliers' capability to provide supplies regularly and on time. In some cases inventories previously held by the manufacturer are now being held by the components supplier, so shifting the cost of holding inventory.

If an entity holds too much inventory, it pays higher storage costs and risks possible loss in the value of inventory through changes in consumer demand. Alternatively, holding insufficient inventory may result in the potential loss of sales and thus profits. Given the significance of inventory management, some entities now outsource this function and pay other entities to specifically carry out this task.

Definitions

So far we have discussed inventory and work in progress without defining these terms. Rather than attempting to find one generic definition, we look at examples of inventory and work in progress as this will lead to a better understanding of the terms. Inventory can be said to comprise the following.

- Goods purchased for resale. For example, cans of baked beans are purchased by a supermarket to sell to their customers; cars are purchased by used-car dealers to resell to their customers.
- Raw materials purchased for incorporation into the product or products being manufactured or assembled for sale, e.g. wood purchased by a furniture manufacturer or steel purchased by a car manufacturer.
- Consumable goods, which are bought not for resale but for use within the business operation. These consist of such things as supplies of grease for machine maintenance, supplies of stationery and cleaning materials.

You might have noticed from the examples that the inventories are related to the type of business. For example, cars owned by a furniture manufacturer are not classified as inventory because they are held for use in the business and not for resale. The last category, consumable goods, is different from the others because it is not held for resale. It is, in fact, another form of current asset which is called inventory only because it is an inventory of items which are held by the business and we have no other suitable term.

Key Concept 7.1

Inventories

Inventories means goods, other property and services:
- held for sale in the ordinary course of operations;
- in the process of production for such sale; or
- to be used up in the production of goods, other property or services for sale including consumable stores, and supplies, but does not include depreciable assets as defined in *AASB 1019*.

Having looked at some examples of inventory, let us now look at work in progress and finished goods. These are both different types of inventory—the difference lies in the fact that they have normally gone through some production or assembly process.

In general, all these forms of inventory and work in progress fall within the definition of current assets which we adopted in Chapter 4.

Key Concept 7.2

Current assets

'Current assets' means an asset that
- is expected to be realised, or is held for sale or consumption, in the normal course of the entity's *operating cycle*; or
- is held primarily for trading purposes or for the short term and is expected to be realised within twelve months of the *reporting date*; or
- is cash or a cash-equivalent asset which is not restricted in its use beyond twelve months or the length of the operating cycle, whichever is greater. (*AASB 1040*, para. 9.1)

You will notice, if you consider the examples given, that it is expected that the goods will be realised within the year, as in the case of the baked beans for the supermarket, and the cars for the used-car dealer.

Key Concept 7.3

Work in progress

'Work in progress' is the term applied to products and services that are at an intermediate stage of completion; for example, if you envisage an assembly line for personal computers, at any point in time there will be some partly assembled machines somewhere on that production line. An even more obvious example, which we can observe by walking round any town centre, is partially completed buildings which are work in progress for some building contractor. A less obvious but equally valid example of work in progress is the time spent to date by an architect on a half-finished drawing.

Finished goods

Finished goods are goods that have been through the complete production or assembly cycle and are ready for resale to the customer. Examples are cars for Holden, computers for Apple or IBM, and videos for Philips.

The nature of the business is a major determinant of what is classified as inventory or work in progress. We will now explore this aspect of inventory and the question of inventory valuation in more detail.

The nature of the business and inventory valuation

We would expect the type of inventory held by a greengrocer to be different from that of a company like BHP. What might be less obvious is the way in which the nature of the business affects the question of inventory valuation. To illustrate this, let us first look at a retailer and a manufacturer, and then compare the latter with a provider of services, such as a firm of architects.

In the case of a retailing business, the inventories held are those goods purchased for resale; because of the nature of the business there is generally little, if any, change between the goods bought by the business and the goods it sells. Its operating cycle could be seen as

$$\text{purchases} \longrightarrow \text{inventory} \longrightarrow \text{sales}$$
$$\text{(input)} \qquad\qquad\qquad\qquad\qquad \text{(output)}$$

If we can establish what the goods cost, we can arrive at a valuation of inventory, because the operating cycle is very simple.

If we now examine the situation of a manufacturing company, we find that, in order to manufacture goods, we need inputs of raw materials, of labour and of other items such as the nuts and bolts needed to assemble a car and paint to protect and colour it. These inputs often occur at multiple points in the production process. For our purposes a simplified version of the manufacturing process, shown in Figure 7.1, illustrates the points being made.

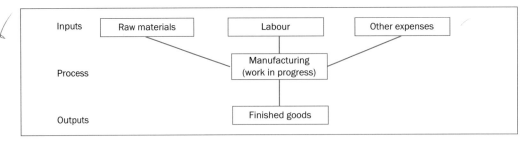

Figure 7.1 *The manufacturing process.*

A business with a process similar to that described is likely, at any point in time, to have an inventory of raw materials, an inventory of goods in the process of completion—its work in progress—and an inventory of finished goods. This is illustrated in Figure 7.2.

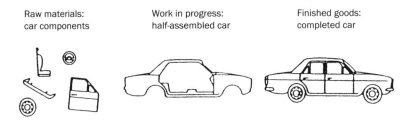

Figure 7.2 *Raw materials, work in progress, and finished goods.*

In the case of the raw materials, the question of inventory valuation is similar to that faced by a retailer. For the other categories, however, the question of valuation is often more complex. Do we include the cost of labour in the value of partially completed goods and, if so, which labour? One possible answer would be to include labour involved in the production process and exclude other labour. This is easy in theory, but in practice it is not so clear. For example, are the supervisor and production manager involved in the production process and, if so, what part of their labour cost is attributable to a particular product? The whole question of what should and should not be included is vital because it has a direct effect on profit. In some industries where pricing is on a 'cost plus' basis, it could be the difference between survival and bankruptcy. If, for example, we quote a selling price that does not cover all our costs we could enter into a contract which leads to the downfall of the business. Indeed, some commentators have suggested that the Compass Airlines collapse in 1991 was caused by their being tied into an unprofitable pricing war.

The discussion so far has emphasised the manufacturing sector, which we consider in more detail in the second part of this book when we look at accounting for internal users. What of the service sector? In this sector the question of inventory valuation can be straightforward, as in the case of a newspaper vendor, or more complex as in the case of a solicitor, architect and accountant. If we consider the case of a firm of architects, the inputs are not raw materials but are in the form of labour and expenses such as travelling expenses to see the client, to see local councils, etc.

However, it is quite likely that some proportion of the work handled by architects will take a considerable amount of time between inception and completion. Thus, for this particular service industry there will be a problem of valuing the work in progress every time that the annual accounts are prepared, as was the case for our manufacturing firm.

Determining the cost of goods sold

In previous chapters we assumed that all goods bought in the period were sold in the period and that we could clearly identify the actual goods we sold during the period. This is not the case in practice. Businesses that have been in existence for more than one year commence the year with some inventory on hand. During the year additional goods are purchased and some (we hope!) are sold. Therefore, at the end of the period it is necessary to determine:

- the cost of goods sold, which is the expense for the statement of financial performance
- the cost of goods unsold, which is the ending inventory figure and is an asset for the statement of financial position.

We can look at the problem in terms of Figure 7.3.

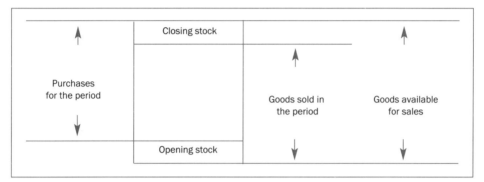

Figure 7.3 *Determining the cost of goods sold.*

In practice, even in simple businesses it is doubtful whether it would be possible to physically identify the goods actually sold: even if it were possible, we would need to consider whether doing so was cost-effective. Because of the difficulties of recording every item sold and the questionable cost-effectiveness of such an exercise, some smaller businesses have few if any formal inventory records. Instead they keep accurate records of purchases, and make an annual inventory count (or stocktake) to establish the cost of goods sold during a period. This annual inventory count is carried out at the statement of financial position date, and so the inventory figure in the statement of financial position represents a snapshot of the inventory level at that particular point in time. This is known as the *periodic method* of accounting for inventory. You will notice that in essence what happens here is what we described in Chapter 3, i.e. the wealth in the form of inventory is measured at two points in time to establish the change over the period. While at first sight this might seem to be an odd way to run a business, it is in fact quite sensible when you consider the impossible job a confectionery manufacturer would have in trying to keep track of every Mars Bar, KitKat, or Milky Way. If you talk to owners of small businesses you might be surprised at how accurately they can value their inventory simply by looking at what they have in the shop and on the shelves of their storerooms.

What we have just said should not be taken to imply that all retailers have poor inventory records. Some of the major retail chains have very sophisticated inventory record systems that operate at the point of sale: every time the cashier enters the sale of a tin of baked beans, the inventory records for that store are updated via a computer link from the tills to the inventory recording system. (Theft by staff, or 'shrinkage', can also be measured precisely.) This is known as the *perpetual method* of accounting for inventory.

In addition to entities with sophisticated computer systems, the perpetual method is also appropriate for certain types of businesses whose inventory is easy to keep track of, e.g. Boeing, which manufactures and sells planes, or a jewellery store which sells items with a large dollar value. Perhaps you can add other examples. However, while such a large investment for tracking inventory might be necessary and cost-effective for large entities and for certain types of businesses, it is, at present, outside the grasp of smaller retailers and is probably more sophisticated than they need.

Periodic method

Clearly, for a business that uses the perpetual method of recording inventories, it is reasonably simple to arrive at the value of inventory and the cost of goods sold. Therefore, let us look at the situation where detailed inventory movement records are not kept and see how we can arrive at the cost of the goods sold and the cost of those still in inventory at the end of the year. In this case we need to count the inventory at the start of the year and at the end of the year. From these two figures and the figure for goods purchased during the year we can derive the cost of the goods sold during the year. In other words, if we add the purchases to the inventory of goods we had at the start of the year, that will tell us the total of the goods we have held during the year. If we then subtract what we have left at the end of the year the resultant figure must be the cost of the goods we have sold during the year, assuming of course that we have allowed for any taken by the owner for personal use etc. Figure 7.3 will help you to understand the relationship, which can also be shown in the form of an equation.

opening inventory + purchases − closing inventory = cost of goods sold

The information to solve the equation can be derived as follows:

- opening inventory, from the statement of financial position at the start of the year
- purchases, from the supplier's invoices
- closing inventory, from a physical inventory count at the end of the year.

The importance of determining inventory level is examined in Key Concept 7.4.

Key Concept 7.4

The importance of determining inventory levels

Because with the periodic method the cost of goods sold is calculated by combining the purchases with the inventory figures, the opening and closing inventory levels are vital in determining the cost of goods sold. They therefore have a dual role, in the statement of financial position in determining wealth, and, through the cost of goods sold, in determining profit.

Let us look at a simple example to illustrate the process referred to in the equation above and see how it is entered on the worksheet.

Example 7.1: Leighroy

The summarised transactions of Leighroy during the year were as follows.

Sales	$20 000
Purchases	$12 000
Other expenses	$6 000

The inventories at the end of the period had been counted and were valued at $7000. The statement of financial position of Leighroy at the start of the period was as follows.

LEIGHROY
STATEMENT OF FINANCIAL POSITION AT START OF PERIOD

Current Assets	$	$	$	$
Inventories	5 000			
Cash	11 000			
Total Current Assets		16 000		
Non-current Assets				
Premises	20 000			
Total Non-current Assets		20 000		
Total Assets			36 000	
Net Assets				36 000
Owners' Equity				36 000

We start by entering the opening balances on our worksheet which now appears as follows.

LEIGHROY WORKSHEET: VERSION 1

	Assets			= Liabilities +	Equity
	Cash	Inventory	Premises		Equity
Balance	11 000	+ 5 000	+ 20 000 =		36 000

If we now enter the transactions for the year and draw up a preliminary total, our worksheet looks like this.

LEIGHROY WORKSHEET: VERSION 2

	Assets			= Liabilities +	Equity	
	Cash	Inventory	Premises		Equity	Profit and loss
Balance	11 000	5 000	20 000	36 000		
Purchases	-12 000	12 000				
Sales	20 000					20 000
Expenses	-6 000					-6 000
Balance	13 000	+ 17 000	+ 20 000 =		36 000	+ 14 000

The worksheet at this stage shows that we have an inventory of goods of $17 000, whereas we know from our inventory count that what we actually have is $7000. In other words, the asset at the end of the year, i.e. the part that will provide a future benefit, is only $7000. Using our equation we can establish that the cost of goods sold during the year was $10 000. This is of course an expense because the benefit is in the past.

The figure of $10 000 was arrived at as follows:

opening inventory	+	purchases	–	closing inventory	=	cost of goods sold
$5 000	+	$12 000	–	$7 000	=	$10 000

Having found that the cost of goods sold is $10 000, we can now enter this on our worksheet and draw up our balance at the end of the year. This is done as follows.

LEIGHROY WORKSHEET: VERSION 3

	Assets			= Liabilities +	Equity	
	Cash	Inventory	Premises		Equity	Profit and loss
Balance	11 000	5 000	20 000		36 000	
Purchases	-12 000	12 000				
Sales	20 000					20 000
Expenses	-6 000					-6 000
Subtotal	13 000	+ 17 000	+ 20 000	=	36 000	+ 14 000
Cost of sales		-10 000				-10 000
Balance	13 000	+ 7 000	+ 20 000	=	36 000	+ 4 000

Although the profit and loss column in the worksheet is part of equity, it is included to allow easier preparation of the statement of financial performance.

We show the calculations included in the worksheet above on a statement of financial performance as follows.

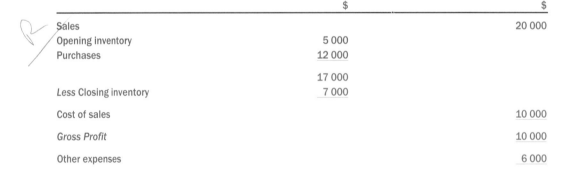

LEIGHROY
STATEMENT OF FINANCIAL PERFORMANCE FOR THE YEAR ENDED 30 JUNE 20X1

	$	$
Sales		20 000
Opening inventory	5 000	
Purchases	12 000	
	17 000	
Less Closing inventory	7 000	
Cost of sales		10 000
Gross Profit		10 000
Other expenses		6 000
Net Profit		4 000

A simplified presentation would be as follows.

LEIGHROY
STATEMENT OF FINANCIAL PERFORMANCE FOR THE YEAR ENDED 30 JUNE 20X1

	$
Sales	20 000
Cost of sales	10 000
Gross Profit	10 000
Other expenses	6 000
Net Profit	4 000

The latter format, which does not show how the cost of goods sold is calculated, is closer to what you are likely to see in the published accounts of listed companies. It should be noted that, because of the relationship between the statement of financial position and the statement of financial performance, an error in the opening inventory figure, the purchases figure or the closing inventory figure not only changes the profit but also changes the statement of financial position.

Valuing inventory

In general, if prices of goods stayed constant over time, tastes did not change and there were no changes in technology, then we would have no problem with inventory valuation. However, the real world fortunately is not like that; this has the advantage that civilisation can progress but it creates some problems for accountants. The question of how changes in prices can affect inventory valuation is wide ranging and is allied to the question of how the cost of inventory is arrived at. We therefore first consider the effects of changes in taste and technology; then we look at how cost is arrived at and finally consider the effects of price changes.

Changes in technology and taste

We have grouped technology and taste together because, although the causes are different, the effects on inventory valuation are the same. Let us consider the effect of changes in technology, of which there are hundreds of everyday examples such as the use of microcomputers instead of mainframe machines and the advances in microcomputer technology. An example of this effect was the introduction of the IBM personal computer, which made a number of other machines seem heavily over-priced. In turn, when other manufacturers had caught up with the technology, the IBM was over-priced and IBM had to reduce the retail price of its personal computers significantly. For the purposes of illustration, let us assume that a retailer has an inventory of ten IBM computers bought at a cost of $3000 each. Due to competition, IBM has since decreased the price to $2000. If the retailer values its closing inventory on the basis of cost, then the asset would be reported as $30 000.

However, we said in Chapter 4 that an asset is the right to a future benefit. In the retailer's situation the future benefit that can be obtained is only $2000 per machine, the new retail price. Thus, in this case the cost does not reflect the future benefit that the retailer is likely to get. A fairer reflection would be the amount the computers could be sold for. However, even the $2000 is probably overstating the benefit because there will undoubtedly be some costs incurred in selling the computers. If these costs were estimated to be $100 per machine, then the amount of the future benefit would in fact be $1900. This is referred to as the net realisable value of the goods.

Key Concept 7.5

lower cost

Net realisable value

Net realisable value is defined as the estimated proceeds of sale less, where applicable, all further costs to the stage of completion and less all costs to be incurred in marketing, selling and distribution to customers. (*AASB 1019*, para. 13.1)

A similar effect would have arisen if the goods could be sold only at a reduced price or for scrap because of changes in people's tastes. In each of these cases the cost paid for the goods is not relevant to the future benefit: a better valuation would be the net realisable value. This leads us to the idea that we should compare the cost of an item with what we can get for it and, if the latter figure is lower, use that figure to value our inventory. Expressed in more formal terms this is the valuation rule.

You might well wonder why, if the net realisable value is higher than the cost, that higher value is not used. The reason for this, it is argued, is that the attainment of the higher value is uncertain as tastes, etc. might change.

Key Concept 7.6

The valuation rule

The valuation rule states that inventory should be valued at the lower of cost and net realisable value.

Having established the general rule for inventory valuation and seen the reasons for the rule, the next question that we need to address is how to establish the cost that is referred to in the rule.

CASE STUDY 7.1

Ripple effect from Asia

Atmel expects a loss

ATMEL Corp. said it will report flat fourth-quarter revenues, take a $160 million charge for inventory write-downs and report a loss, mostly because of the inability of some of its Asian customers to get credit for purchases.

Atmel, a maker of programmable computer chips, did not specify the amount of the loss, but Wall Street had been expecting a profit from operations of 34 cents a share, according to a recent analyst survey by Zacks Investment Research.

The San Jose, California-based company is the latest technology concern to suffer from Asia's economics woes. Companies such as Oracle Corp., Netscape Communications Corp. and Micron Technology Inc. have said they expect weaker sales because of the region's troubles.

Atmel said it is taking the charge to write-down, or lower the value, of its inventory to reflect lower market prices. Some of its customers could not get 'letter or credit for orders previously scheduled for shipment in December,' the company said.

Atmel issued the warning after the market closed Tuesday.

The company said it will take steps to reduce costs—including the consolidation of operations in France—and will concentrate its resources on using newer, more efficient chip-making equipment.

'The outlook for 1998 is somewhat uncertain at the present time, but we believe we can grow faster than the industry average,' George Perlegos, Atmel chief executive, said in a statement.

Reuters, 6 January 1998

Commentary

The article demonstrates how the application of the lower of cost and net realisable value rule can have a significant impact on an entity's results. In this case, the decline in the market value of the inventory is related to the Asian financial problems of the late 1990s.

Establishing the cost of inventories

As we have already indicated, the more complex the process, the more difficult it is to establish the cost of the inventory. The problem is to decide what to include and what to leave out. The debate on this subject has been going on for some considerable time in the literature relating to management accounting and will be explored in more detail later in this book when we discuss the alternative methods that could be used to arrive at cost. Fortunately, we need only be aware in general terms what the alternative methods are, because the choice between the methods has to some extent been made for us through custom and practice and the rules laid down for entities in *AASB 1019: Inventories*. This deals with the question of inventories and work in progress. Before looking at that standard, let us briefly consider the alternatives by means of a simple example.

Example 7.2: Spanners

A business produces spanners. Each spanner requires $0.30 of steel, and takes 15 minutes' labour to produce. The business employs ten people to make spanners and they each produce 140 spanners per week and are paid $70 each per week. A supervisor oversees the workers and is paid $100 per week. At the end of the year we have one week's production, i.e. 1400 spanners, in inventory. The question that we have to answer is what the cost of the 1400 spanners we have in inventory is at the end of the year.

One solution is to establish how much it would cost to produce one extra spanner. Clearly one spanner would cost $0.30 for materials and we would need to pay a worker for 15 minutes to produce it. This would cost $0.50, i.e. $70 per week divided by the number of spanners produced, which was 140. Thus the marginal cost of producing one spanner is $0.80. If we then applied this cost to our inventory, we would value our inventory at 1400 × $0.80 = $1120. This would be the cost using a marginal cost basis.

On the other hand it could legitimately be argued that the cost of producing 1400 spanners, i.e. a week's production, is made up as follows.

	$
Steel (1400 @ $0.30)	420
Direct labour, ten staff at $70	700
Supervisor's wages	100
Total cost	1 220

This method of arriving at the cost is known as absorption costing.

You will note that the difference between the two is $100, i.e. the supervisor's wages are not included on a marginal cost basis.

As we have said, to some extent the choice between the two has been made for us by the requirements of *AASB 1019* which states (paragraph 13.1) that cost is:

* the cost of purchase
* the cost of conversion, and
* other costs

incurred in the normal course of operations in bringing the inventories to their present location and condition.

The costs of conversion referred to include direct labour and other production costs (such as the supervisor's wages) ascertained in accordance with the absorption costing method. An example of these would be the cost to Toyota of transporting engines from its production plant to the assembly line factory.

To summarise, we can say that costs will normally include:

- cost of purchase
- cost to transport goods to a location for sale or conversion
- cost of import duty or other taxes incurred prior to sale
- cost of conversion or repackaging to make goods ready for sale.

Example 7.3: Washing machines

A Perth appliance dealer orders ten washing machines from a manufacturer in Adelaide. The washing machines have a list price of $1000. The retailer buys on terms 2/10, N/30, which means they can deduct 2 per cent ($20) off the list price and pay only $980 if they pay within ten days. If they pay after ten days, they should pay $1000 within 30 days. Transport charges paid by the retailer are $50 per machine. Sales tax is 15 per cent of list price. The retailer incurs handling charges of $20 per unit to get the machines onto the showroom floor. The sales staff who sell the machines are paid a bonus of $50 per machine. What is the cost per machine, assuming the retailer pays in eight days?

	$
List price	1 000
Less Discount	20
	980
Plus	
Sales tax	150
Transport	50
Handling	20
	1 200

The sales staff's bonus is a selling expense and is not part of the cost. We deal with more complex examples on cost determination in the section on management accounting.

Effects of price changes

We have considered the effect of downward movements in price under the heading of changes in technology; we also need to consider the effect of increases in the input price of our inventories, i.e. increases in the prices we pay to our suppliers. As we have said, there would be no problem if all sales could be identified with the actual goods sold. In practice, however, a builder's merchant, for instance, has a pile of bricks and sells them in any order depending on the ease of access. We cannot therefore work out whether a particular brick sold was bought by the builder's merchant when the price of bricks was 30 cents or whether it was bought after the price had gone up to 33 cents. It is not cost-effective to trace each brick through the process. We have to find some system that will give a reasonable approximation of the cost of the goods we have sold and of the cost of the inventory remaining. There are many possible methods with various levels of complexity. For our purposes we will concentrate on three which exemplify the problem and show that solutions tend to be arbitrary.

In order to illustrate the differences between the methods, let us take some simple data.

Example 7.4: Jackie

Jackie started the year with some goods in inventory and bought ad
required during the year. The price of the goods she bought rose steadily
The summarised data for his transactions are as follows.

	Units	C
Goods in stock at the start of the year	400	
Purchases, quarter 1	500	$1
Purchases, quarter 2	400	$1.20
Purchases, quarter 3	400	$1.25
Purchases, quarter 4	300	$1.40

Goods sold during the year: 1800 units for a total of $2400.

Using these data and the periodic method, we illustrate how the adoption of different valuation rules affects not only the inventory value at the end of the year but also
affects the cost of sales and therefore the profit. We start by considering a method of
valuation called first in, first out (FIFO).

First in, first out   *(Australia method)*

The FIFO method is based on the assumption that the first goods bought are the first
sold. In effect, the inventory held at the end of the period is assumed to be that purchased most recently. There are many situations when it is the obvious choice, as for any
industry or business dealing in consumables. It should be pointed out that, surprisingly,
the choice of method for arriving at the cost of inventory generally has little if anything
to do with actual inventory movements.

With this method, all the opening inventory, together with that purchased in the first
three quarters, is assumed to have been sold, together with 100 units bought in the fourth
quarter. This leaves a closing inventory of 200 units which were bought in the fourth
quarter.

			$	$		$
Opening inventory	400	1.00	400.00	Sales	2 400.00
Quarter 1	500	1.10	550.00		
Quarter 2	400	1.20	480.00		
Quarter 3	400	1.25	500.00		
Quarter 4	100	1.40	140.00		
Cost of goods sold			2 070.00		2 070.00
Closing inventory	200	1.40	280.00	Profit	330.00

Last in, first out   *USA method*

Although this method is not legal in Australia, it is an allowable alternative in
International Accounting Standards (even though it is not permitted in many countries).

The last in, first out (LIFO) method is based on the assumption that the last goods
bought are the first sold. It therefore charges the latest price from suppliers against the
revenue, and leaves the closing inventory at a value based on outdated prices. In industries where prices are rising steadily this is more likely to give a profit figure that can
be maintained in the future. Its effect on the statement of financial performance is similar
to what would occur if we had used replacement cost.

purchased in the year, together with 200 units of
have been sold. This leaves a closing inventory
t the start of the year. These are included at the
of financial position value is deliberately under-

	$	$		$
	1.40	420.00	Sales	2 400.00
	1.25	500.00		
	1.20	480.00		
	1.10	550.00		
	1.00	200.00		
		2 150.00		2 150.00
	1.00	200.00	Profit	250.00

Weighted average cost

The weighted average cost method is a compromise between the two methods we have
already discussed. It makes no assumptions about the way in which goods flow through
the business.

For the purposes of arriving at the profit and loss charges, all that is needed is to work
out the weighted average cost per unit of inventory and multiply that by the number of
units sold. Similarly, the closing inventory is arrived at by taking the number of units
left in inventory and multiplying by the weighted average cost per unit. This leads to
profit and inventory figures which in our example are between the figures produced by
the FIFO and LIFO methods. It is calculated as shown below.

			$	$		$
Opening inventory	400	1.00	400.00		Sales	2 400.00
Quarter 1	500	1.10	550.00			
Quarter 2	400	1.20	480.00			
Quarter 3	400	1.25	500.00			
Quarter 4	300	1.40	420.00			
	2 000		2 350.00			
Weighted average cost	2 350 ÷ 2 000	= 1.18				
Cost of goods sold	1 800	1.18	2 115.00			2 115.00
Closing inventory	200	1.18	235.00		Profit	285.00

**You should now study the financial report of Woolworths. Note 1(G) states that
for short-life retail stock the company uses the lower of average cost and net realisable value. This is in compliance with *AASB 1019*. For long-life retail stock the
company uses what is described as the retail inventory method to arrive at an
estimate of cost. This involves estimating the cost of inventory based on the
mark-up that applies to the inventory. For example, if the value of stock is
$100 000 based on selling price, and the average mark-up is 25 per cent, then the
retail value of stock is 125 per cent and the cost is determined as:**

$$\frac{100}{125} \times \$100\ 000$$

This means the cost of the stock would be $80 000.

Accounting policies for inventories and implications for users

It is important when comparing the financial statements of entities to know how the financial statements were prepared. Did the companies use average cost or FIFO? We know, for example, that Woolworths uses average cost to determine the cost of its inventory. If we compare Woolworths' financial statements with Coles' financial statements, and Coles uses FIFO, then this fact must be allowed for when comparing the results of both companies. In times of rising prices, Coles' profits would generally be higher than Woolworths', based on the use of FIFO. Thus the difference in profits between the two companies is partly due to the accounting rules. This difference should be distinguished from differences in profits due to higher sales or lower operating costs.

Summary

In this chapter, the businesses considered have been trading for some time. We have shown how to establish both the cost of goods sold during a period and the closing inventory. We have also looked at what constitutes *cost* when dealing with inventory and have introduced the ideas of marginal and absorption costing. In the latter part of the chapter we have seen that changes in technology can lead to inventory being sold at less than cost, and that changes in prices affect the statements of financial position and financial performance. Finally, we have considered three possible methods for arriving at the cost of goods sold during a period and the closing inventory figure. Having arrived at a figure for the cost of inventory, we then compare this to the net realisable value figure. *AASB 1019* requires the lower of the cost or the net realisable value to be used for the closing inventory figure. It can be seen that some of the issues faced in accounting for inventory are a direct result of the management strategies adopted. For example, just-in-time management affects the amount of inventory held. Other factors at the organisational level that have an impact are the size of the organisation (Woolworths stocks a wider range of goods than the corner shop) and the organisational structure: a particular factory might manufacture just one component or a number of components. We have also discussed factors relating to changes in technology.

Reference

Australian Accounting Standards Board. *AASB 1019: Inventories*, March 1998.

Further reading

Wise, T.D., Needles, B.E. Jr., Anderson, H.R., and Caldwell, J.C., 1990. *Accounting in Australia*, 1st edn, Houghton Mifflin, Chapter 10.

Review questions

1   What main categories of inventory are likely to be held by a manufacturing business?

2   In arriving at a figure for inventory in a business that manufactures and assembles furniture, what questions would need to be considered?

3   What would be the effect on profit if goods costing $6000 were excluded from the opening stock figure?

4   What are the effects of omitting goods costing $500 from the year-end stock figure?

5   Why is it necessary to value inventory at the lower of cost and net realisable value?

6   Explain in your own words the difference between absorption costing and marginal costing.

7   Which of the following costs would be appropriate to include in a marginal costing system?
    a   director's salary
    b   supervisor's wages
    c   machine operators' wages
    d   cost of raw materials

8   Of the costs above, which would be appropriate to include in arriving at costs under an absorption costing system?

9   Name three methods of inventory valuation, and describe the differences between them and the effects of those differences.

10 Give examples of types of business where a particular method of inventory valuation is appropriate.

Problems for discussion and analysis

1   Refer to the Woolworths financial report in Appendix 1.
    a   Which method of inventory valuation is used for short-life retail stocks? What method is used for long-life retail stocks?
    b   Would you consider the explanations given for inventory valuation to be acceptable? If not, why not?

2   In your own words state what you understand by the phrase 'net realisable value'. Is this concept valid? Why?

3   To reduce expenses in preparing monthly financial statements, Pamic Company decided to estimate monthly inventories. Goods are sold at cost plus 25 per cent. Use the following data to estimate the inventory at the end of December.

Inventory 1 December	$50 650
Net purchases for December	$146 000
Net sales for December	$220 000

4   The Ready retail store prices its goods to sell at 150 per cent on cost. Records for one accounting period reveal the following information:

	Cost	Retail
Purchase returns	8 000	12 000
Purchases	100 000	150 000
Opening inventory	60 000	90 000
Sales (net)		198 000

What was the ending inventory for the accounting period?

5

MERCHANDISE ACCOUNT

Date		Purchase	Sold	Unit price $
May	3	200	–	2.00
	4	–	150	–
	5	300	–	2.20
	6	–	150	–
	6	50	–	2.30
	7	–	150	–

Using the data in the table, answer the following questions:

a   If inventory is based on FIFO periodic the closing inventory balance is:

A $200   C $225

B $230   D   None of the above.

b   If LIFO periodic was used the closing inventory balance is:

A $200   C $225

B $230   D   None of the above.

c   Assuming inflationary trends in the economy, the inventory amount shown in the statement of financial position, if based on LIFO, would be:

A   lower than FIFO value

B   equal to weighted average

C   equal to current market value

D   higher than FIFO value

E   higher than current market value

F   an extremely conservative value.

6   During 20X0, Rubber Balls Pty Ltd sold $42 400 worth of balls at $8 each. Beginning inventory on 1 January 20X0 amounted to 605 balls at a cost of $3600. Purchases during the year occurred as follows:

1596 units @ $4.00
2508 units @ $4.23
1748 units @ $4.40
730 units @ $4.55

Required:

a   Compute the 31 December 20X0 inventory using the following assumptions regarding the flow of costs:

i   FIFO, periodic method

ii   LIFO, periodic method

iii   Weighted average, periodic method.

b   Prepare statements of financial performance for each method to the gross profit stage.

7   Phijen are manufacturers of widgets which are on-sold to Mipam who use them in the manufacture of boat anchors. Phijen buys the raw materials on the world market, but during the past year prices have been erratic. Mipam has a firm contract price from Phijen for one year from 1 January 20X0. During the year ending 31 December 20X0, Phijen sold 160 000 widgets to Mipam at $1.90 each. Phijen's beginning inventory on 1 January 20X0 was 77 000 kg of raw materials at a cost of $7700. It takes 10 kg of raw material to make one widget.

Purchases of raw materials during the year ending 31 December 20X0 were as follows:

7 January	200 000 kg @ 9 cents per kg
2 February	180 000 kg @ 15 cents per kg
4 April	250 000 kg @ 6 cents per kg
26 May	250 000 kg @ 7 cents per kg
17 August	200 000 kg @ 9 cents per kg
19 September	350 000 kg @ 12 cents per kg
10 October	100 000 kg @ 17 cents per kg
11 December	175 000 kg @ 20 cents per kg

Required:

Calculate Phijen's closing inventory, periodic method, using the following cost methods. Then calculate the cost of raw materials sold for each method.
a   FIFO
b   LIFO
c   Weighted average.

8   The following information has been extracted from the records of Able Biscuits Co. Ltd.

Opening inventory: 750 tins of biscuits at $8 per tin. During the month, the company manufactured biscuits and placed them in inventory after calculating the cost of manufacture.

Date 20X1	Tins manufactured	Cost per tin ($)	Tins sold
May			
3	400	8.10	—
4	—	—	600
7	200	7.90	700
12	1000	8.05	—
14	—	—	600
16	300	8.20	—
18	—	—	700
20	800	8.00	—
23	—	—	600
25	300	8.50	—
27	—	—	450
30	100	8.00	—

Rounding to the nearest cent, calculate the closing inventory balance using
a   FIFO periodic and perpetual
b   LIFO periodic and perpetual
c   weighted average periodic and perpetual.

9   On 31 December 20X1, goods costing $1250 were received by Judy's Cake Shop and were included in the 31 December listing of all inventory items on hand. The invoice for these items, however, was not received until 7 January 20X2, whereupon the purchase was recorded for the first time in the accounts as a 20X2 purchase and as an account payable. The purchase should have been recorded in the 20X1 financial accounts. Assuming that the error was never discovered and that Judy's Cake Shop uses a periodic inventory system, indicate the effect (overstatement, understatement or none) on each of the following.

a Inventory, 31 December 20X1
b Inventory, 31 December 20X2
c Cost of goods sold, 20X1
d Cost of goods sold, 20X2
e Net profit, 20X1
f Net profit, 20X2
g Accounts payable, 20X1
h Accounts payable, 20X2
i Retained earnings, 20X2

10 For the following example discuss which costs, if any, should be included in the inventory valuation, and at what point in time they should be included.

Hank is in business manufacturing sails. The sail material is purchased in 100-metre lengths and these are delivered to the store-worker who sorts the materials according to quality and width. The material is then issued to the cutting room where five people are employed, one of whom is the cutting-room supervisor. After cutting, the material is passed through to the machining room where the sails are sewn up and the hanks, etc. are put on. The machining room has seven staff employed full time, including a supervisor. From the machining room the sails go to the packaging department and then the despatch department or are put into stock. The packaging department and the despatch department each employ one member of staff working on a part-time basis. The whole operation is under the control of a production manager who also has responsibility for quality control.

11 The perpetual inventory control system identifies the amount of inventory loss resulting from theft, damage and so forth, an amount which is not revealed by the periodic inventory system. How should this amount be recorded in the financial statements?

12 The LIFO method of inventory valuation assumes that the last goods purchased are the first sold. Since companies normally sell the oldest goods in their inventory first, the LIFO assumption is unrealistic. Comment on whether you think the LIFO method can be justified.

13 A motorbike dealer uses the original cost of each motorbike as the basis for setting the selling price. The original cost for a certain model can increase during a financial year as a result of increased assembly costs. Would it be appropriate for the motorbike dealer to use the LIFO method of inventory valuation? In contrast, a car-parts dealer changes the selling price of her goods to reflect changing wholesale prices. Would it be appropriate for the car-parts dealer to use the FIFO method of inventory valuation?

14 In times of rising inflation where the LIFO method of inventory valuation is used, ending inventory is usually well below current market prices. What are the supporting arguments, if any, for applying the lower of cost or net realisable value rule to LIFO inventories?

(Problems 12–15 adapted from R. Anthony and J. Reece, *Accounting: Text and Cases*, 8th edn, Richard D. Irwin Inc., 1988, Chapter 6, Case 6–6.)

15 Marx Pty Ltd has traditionally used the FIFO periodic method of inventory valuation. Information on transactions affecting Marx's accounts is provided below.

20X0		20X2	
Beginning balance	2 300 units @ $24.06	Beginning balance	1 300 units
Purchases	750 units @ $24.38	Purchases	1 250 units @ $26.56
	1 000 units @ $25.00		875 units @ $26.88
	500 units @ $25.31		875 units @ $26.88
	250 units @ $25.62		875 units @ $26.88
Sales	3 525 units @ $40.62	Sales	3 688 units @ $42.50
20X1			
Beginning balance	1 275 units		
Purchases	875 units @ $25.62		
	875 units @ $25.62		
	875 units @ $26.26		
	1 250 units @ $26.56		
Sales	3 850 units @ $42.50		

Required:

a   Calculate the cost of goods sold and ending inventory amounts for 20X0, 20X1, 20X2 using:
  i   FIFO
  ii LIFO
  iii weighted average cost.

b   Sales for 20X2 are expected to drop by an estimated 11 per cent as a worldwide recession is expected to continue for the next nine months. Total sales are estimated to be 3375 units. Marx Pty Ltd will be unable to increase its 20X1 selling price of $42.50, even though it is expected the costs will increase to $27.19 per unit for the entire year. As a result of these pressures, the company wishes to decrease its investment in inventory by keeping only 500 cartons of inventory on hand at any particular time during the year. What are the effects of LIFO and FIFO inventory valuation methods under these circumstances?

(Adapted from R. Anthony and J. Reece, *Accounting: Text and Cases*, 8th edn, Richard D. Irwin Inc., 1988, Chapter 6, Case 6–3.)

16 Joan Robbins, the owner of Joan's Fishing Tackle Shop, marks up the goods in her shop by 30 per cent. Figures for the past financial year, 20X0, are outlined below.

	$	$
Sales		1 550 000
Less Cost of goods sold		
Opening inventory	168 000	
Purchases	1 218 000	
	1 386 000	
Closing inventory	178 500	1 207 500
Gross Profit		342 500
Less Operating expenses		340 000
Net Profit		2 500

Joan has given no discounts during the 20X0 period and has kept turnover constant so her inventories have moved quickly. Nevertheless, she is unhappy with the year's results and asks you for your advice on the following.

a   Is it possible to determine from the figures whether there has been any theft by staff and/or customers?

b   On the assumption that theft has occurred, can it be determined from the figures whether it was cash or inventory that was taken?

c   A perpetual inventory control system could be established at a cost of $21 000 per year to monitor the more expensive goods in the shop. Would you recommend such a measure?

d   On the assumption that Joan is able to deter future theft, would you advise her to embark on a $21 000 advertising campaign if sales would rise by $210 000, leaving all other expenses unchanged?

(Adapted from B. Colditz and R. Gibbins, *Australian Accounting*, 3rd edn, McGraw-Hill, 1976.)

Ethics case study

Troy Harvey is the financial controller of Elsi Mate Ltd. In reviewing the operations of Elsi Mate Ltd, Troy has become concerned about the continued weak profit performance of the company. The chairman of the board stresses the need for the company to improve its profits if it is to maintain the confidence of its shareholders and the bankers. Troy is concerned that, with only two weeks of the year remaining, the company is destined to record another low profit. Therefore, it will have difficulty in refinancing some loans due next year and will be forced to pay higher interest rates.

While it is too late for operations to increase profits, Troy has developed the following plan. The company will purchase large amounts of inventory in the remaining two weeks of the year, which will result in increased reported profit for the following reasons:

• Prices of inventory have been falling in recent weeks.
• The company uses the LIFO method for inventories as permitted by international accounting standards.

Discuss:

a   whether Troy's plan will increase net profit for the year

b   what the positive and negative consequences of the proposed plan are for the company and the shareholders

c   whether, in your opinion, the plan is ethical.

Debtors, Creditors, Accruals and Prepayments

Learning objectives

At the end of this chapter you should be able to:

1 explain what is meant by the terms 'debtors' and 'prepayments'

2 appreciate the importance of the efficient management of debtors

3 explain what is meant by bad debts

4 understand the direct write-off and provision methods for handling bad debts

5 explain the nature of the provision for doubtful debts accounting

6 explain what is meant by the terms 'creditors' and 'accruals'

7 apply transactions involving debtors, prepayments, provision for doubtful debts, creditors and accruals to a worksheet.

Introduction

In our discussion so far, we have assumed that all transactions are on a cash basis. As we pointed out in Chapter 4, this is unlikely to be the case. Therefore, we need to consider how to deal with the situation in which a business buys goods from its suppliers on credit terms and also supplies goods to customers on credit terms. Similarly, we need to consider the situation in which a business has to pay for goods or services in advance, for example rent, or when it pays after receiving the goods or services, as is the case with most raw materials and with services such as electricity and telephones.

As these transactions directly affect both the statement of financial position and the statement of financial performance, we need a system that ensures that expenses and revenues are recognised in the appropriate period and that the statement of financial position reflects the position of the entity at the statement date. In other words, the system must ensure that the statement of financial position shows the assets held at the statement date and the amounts owed at that date. The statement of financial performance must also record the actual sales for the period and the expenses incurred in the period. If it did not, the accounts would reflect the timing of cash receipts and payments rather than the economic substance of the transactions that the business had engaged in during the period. Such a system of accounting is known as *accrual accounting*. In this chapter we examine situations in which the economic substance of the transaction does not occur at the same time as the cash flow and show how accrual accounting deals with these situations. In particular we look at debtors, prepayments, bad debts, creditors and accruals.

Debtors

Debtors are often referred to as 'accounts receivable'. You might find that this term is easier to remember as it is more descriptive than the term 'debtors'.

Key Concept 8.1

Debtors

Debtors arise when a business sells goods or services to a third party on credit terms, i.e. when the goods or services are sold on the understanding that payment will be received at a later date.

As we saw in Key Concept 8.1, debts are created when a business sells goods during the year for which payment is not received at the point of sale. We need to recognise the revenue from the sales even though the cash has not yet been received. We discussed the recognition of revenue in Chapter 5. However, if we simply entered the sales on the worksheet, the accounts would not balance because there would be only one side to the entry. This is in conflict with the principle of duality. We cannot use the cash account for the other side of the transaction because no cash has been received. However, we do have an asset: a right to a future benefit in the form of cash. The way in which accrual accounting solves the problem is to open a column, or account, for this asset which is called 'Debtors'. Normally debtors pay within a year (in fact in thirty days in many industries) so debtors are generally classified under current assets.

Management of debtors

In the previous chapter we discussed the importance of the efficient management of inventories for a business. Inventories and debtors represent a significant part of working capital, which is the current assets minus the current liabilities of a business. The management of debtors is also extremely important for a business. To allow no customers to purchase goods on credit would result in a loss of profitable sales opportunities. However, if a business allows all customers to purchase goods on credit it risks the problem of bad debts, for some customers will be unable to pay. Therefore, as with inventory management, a business must develop a policy on credit sales.

Entities want to benefit from selling goods on credit but at the same time ensure that losses from bad debts are kept within an acceptable range. Some bad debts are inevitable when an entity sells goods on credit. In fact, if the level of bad debts is very low, it may signal to management that its credit policy is too strict and it is losing potential profits by denying credit to low-risk customers. Conversely, it is important to extend credit to customers only where there are reasonable prospects of the debt being paid.

Incentives are often used by businesses to encourage debtors to pay the amount owing before the due date. When a business has a large number of debtors and significant amounts of inventories it has to have the capital to allow it to continue operating while it collects the amounts owing from debtors and attempts to sell its inventories. The higher the number of debtors and amount of inventories, the greater the working capital requirements. Working capital has to be financed by either equity or debt funds. This is discussed in more detail in Chapter 10.

Therefore, incentives are used to encourage early payment by debtors. These include discounts for early payment; for example, if the amount owing by a debtor is due to be paid in 30 days, the entity may offer a discount of 2 per cent if payment is made in ten days. If the debtor forgoes this offer, the debtor is electing to pay the extra 2 per cent for the right to another 20 days before paying the original amount. A rate of 2 per cent for 20 days is equivalent to approximately 36 per cent per annum, and this is a high cost for any business to pay for the use of credit. Hence, most businesses when presented with such an offer would do everything possible to take advantage of the 2 per cent discount.

CASE STUDY 8.1

Japanese lender orders debtors to sell their kidneys

from Robert Whymant in Tokyo

A FORMER employee of Nichiei Co., Japan's leading lender to small companies, was arrested yesterday after being accused of telling a borrower and his wife to sell their kidneys to repay their debt.

The case was the latest in a series of revelations about brutal debt-collection methods used by apparently respectable finance firms, including a threat to sell a debtor's daughter into prostitution. Thousands of other victims have complained to the regulatory authorities about harassment by money-lenders.

Police arrested Yukihiro Wada, 45, now employed by a Nichiei subsidiary, on suspicion of using intimidation to recover a 7.2 million yen (£40 400) loan. 'Make money by selling your kidneys. You can sell them for three million yen,' he was quoted by a police official as telling the borrower and his wife, who was the guarantor.

Yesterday police teams raided the firm's Kyoto headquarters and the home of Kazuo Matsuda, the president of Nichiei, along with 12 other locations, to investigate whether it was company policy to order strong-arm methods to collect loans.

They are piecing together a picture of systematic use of strong-arm tactics. Nichiei has drawn the most fire since the arrest last month of another former employee who is alleged to have pressured a loan guarantor to raise money by selling a kidney and an eye.

Mr Matsuda denies having encouraged employees to intimidate delinquent borrowers and their guarantors, and claims to be doing a public service by lending to high-risk clients shunned by traditional banks. Japan's loan sharks have a long history of unsavoury collection methods and there is nothing new in reports of debtors harassed to the point of suicide by consumer finance firms. But Nichiei Co. is no small-time loan-sharking business. With 2200 employees and 220 branches, it is listed on the First Section of the Tokyo Stock Exchange along with Japan's foremost companies. The firm has sought respectability by sponsoring prime-time television programmes and has obtained its funds from leading Japanese and foreign banks.

Japanese regulators have begun questioning 13 Japanese and foreign banks that provided funds to Nichiei, including Merrill Lynch and Citibank. Chase Manhattan has a 4.7 per cent shareholding.

The Nichiei scandal has also stirred much public anger because of a feeling that government policies are partly to blame, according to Kiyoshi Ueda, an opposition MP. 'Taxpayers' money is used by the Government to bail out the troubled banks. And these take the money and lend it to loan sharks,' said Mr Ueda, of the Democratic Party of Japan. 'Then ordinary citizens have to take out high-interest loans from loan sharks, and some of them hang themselves.' Money lenders such as Nichiei have prospered from financial woes caused by the collapse of the country's asset-inflated 'bubble' economy in the early Nineties. Banks hit by bad loans stopped lending to all but a favoured few, and small firms and individuals turned to usurers. The firms charge interest rates of up to 40 per cent. No collateral is required, but the guarantor becomes liable in case of default.

Nichiei is now facing a flurry of lawsuits from people who live in terror of its debt collectors. On Monday the 59-year-old owner of a small firm in Kyoto filed a criminal complaint accusing a Nichiei employee of threatening to kill him if he did not repay a loan for which he stood guarantor. According to the complaint, the Nichiei employee also threatened to sell the man's daughter into prostitution.

The Times, 27 November 1999

Commentary

The article highlights that it is not always incentives that are used to obtain outstanding amounts from debtors. It also demonstrates the significance of bad debts to a business and how the debts can ruin it.

Prepayments

Prepayments, as the name implies, are payments in advance. They often arise in respect of such services as insurance, rent, etc. The payments must relate to the use of such services by the business and not by the owner in a personal capacity, a distinction sometimes difficult to establish in the case of small businesses. The proportion of the payment that relates to benefits still unexpired at the end of the year is shown as a current asset in the statement of financial position of the business. Prepayments therefore differ from debtors in that they relate to payments made by the business rather than to sales. Also, the future benefit will be in a form other than cash receipts: for instance, prepaid rent entitles the enterprise to use the facilities for which the rent was paid.

Key Concept 8.2

Prepayments: assets or expenses?

When recording prepayments on a statement of financial position, the question that must be considered is whether the benefit has been consumed or whether there is still some future benefit to be obtained. If there is a future benefit accruing to the business we have an asset; if there is no future benefit we have an expense.

We can now look at an example of debtors and prepayments.

Example 8.1: Pamjen

A business, Pamjen, has the following transactions for the period from 1 January to 31 March 20X1.

	$
Sales for cash	6 000
Sales on credit	4 000
Cash received from credit sales	3 000
Rent for the quarter, paid 1 January	500
Insurance, year to 31 December 20X1, paid 1 January 20X1	1 200

We can see that the revenue consists of the sales for cash and the sales on credit. With reference to the latter we can see that there is still $1000 which has not been received, i.e. $4000 less the $3000 received. This $1000 should be shown as a debtor at 31 March. As far as the payments are concerned, the rent is clearly an expense of the quarter as all the benefit from using the premises for the quarter has expired. The insurance premiums paid are for the whole year and so we have to decide how much benefit has been used up and what is a future benefit. In this case we have used up three out of the 12 months' benefit and so we have an expense of $300 and a prepayment of $900.

Going back to our example, if we put this information onto a worksheet it appears as follows.

PAMJEN WORKSHEET: VERSION 1

	Assets			= Liabilities +	Equity
	Cash	Debtors	Prepaids		Profit and loss
Cash sales	6 000				6 000
Credit sales		4 000			4 000
Cash from sales	3 000	-3 000			
Rent	-500				-500
Insurance	-1 200		900		-300
Balance	7 300	+ 1 000	+ 900 =		9 200

Note that in our worksheet we have shown the credit sales in the profit and loss column which is part of equity and recorded at the same time an asset of $4000. This asset was subsequently reduced by the cash received of $3000. You can also see that we charged the rent immediately as an expense and split the insurance premium paid between the prepaids column and the expenses.

An alternative approach would have been to enter both the rent and the insurance as prepayments when they were paid on 1 January and then to consider at 31 March whether they were still assets. This we would do by answering the question: has the benefit been used up? If we had adopted that approach our worksheet would appear as follows.

PAMJEN WORKSHEET: VERSION 2

	Assets			= Liabilities +	Equity
	Cash	Debtors	Prepaids		Profit and loss
Cash sales	6 000				6 000
Credit sales		4 000			4 000
Cash from sales	3 000	-3 000			
Rent	-500		500		
Insurance	-1 200		1 200		
Balance	7 300 +	1 000 +	1 700 =		10 000
Rent expense			-500		-500
Insurance expense			-300		-300
Balance	7 300 +	1 000 +	900 =		9 200

As you can see, the result is the same. The advantage of the second presentation is that it shows clearly what we have done, which always helps when an error is made. The choice of which presentation to use is personal but we recommend that you use the latter and that you get into the habit of reviewing all the balances, to see whether they are still assets or liabilities, before finally extracting a statement of financial position and statement of financial performance. The advantages of this approach become more obvious as we proceed through this chapter and the next.

Bad debts

So far we have recorded all the credit sales as revenue for the period. If the business eventually collects all the amounts owing, this treatment would be correct. However, it is unlikely that the business will collect all monies owing because some debtors will not pay. This could be due to the debtor's bankruptcy, death, disappearance, etc. There are two ways in which we can account for this non-payment:

- direct write-off
- provision for doubtful debts.

We look at them each in turn.

Direct write-off

Under this approach the amount owing by the debtor is eliminated when it is determined that the debtor will not pay. We reduce the debtor's balance, and the other side of the transaction is the recognition of an expense: the loss of future economic benefits has caused a reduction in equity.

To return to our example: of the $1000 Pamjen is showing as debtors, it is likely to receive only $800 because a customer who owed $200 has left the country and is unlikely to pay. In this situation the $200 is not an asset because any future benefit expired when our customer left the country.

The first question that arises is whether it was a genuine sale. In other words, at the time of making the sale were we reasonably certain that we would receive payment? If the answer is yes, then we have correctly recognised the revenue and the debtor. If this is not the case, we should ask why the sale was made in the first place. It is now necessary to deal with the situation that has arisen as a result of later events. We need to reduce the amount shown as debtors by $200 and charge the $200 as an expense of the period. The worksheet now appears as follows. It should be noted that the last line now represents assets which have a future benefit at least equal to the amount shown.

PAMJEN WORKSHEET: VERSION 3

		Assets		= Liabilities +	Equity
	Cash	Debtors	Prepaids		Profit and loss
Cash sales	6 000				6 000
Credit sales		4 000			4 000
Cash from sales	3 000	−3 000			
Rent	−500		500		
Insurance	−1 200		1 200		
Balance	7 300 +	1 000 +	1 700 =		10 000
Rent expense			−500		−500
Insurance expense			−300		−300
Bad debts		−200			−200
Balance	7 300 +	800 +	900 =		9 000

Provision for doubtful debts

The business might not determine that a debtor is unable to pay until the next period following the credit sales. Therefore, if we use the direct write-off method the revenue (and therefore the profit) and assets will be overstated in the year of sale and understated the following year when it is determined the debtor will not pay. To overcome this problem, the common method of accounting for bad debts is to create a provision at balance date for the amount that we expect debtors will be unable to pay. The accountant has techniques for estimating the amount of expected uncollectable accounts, even though it is not possible to determine which debtors will not pay. For example the accountant might determine that of the debtors balance of $100 000, at balance date, an amount of $8000 should be allowed for expected uncollectable accounts. At balance date we do not know which debtors will not pay, but we are able to estimate the dollar amount we do not expect to receive.

Accountants use a number of methods to estimate the amount expected for bad debts:

- taking a percentage of credit sales based on previous years
- analysing all debtors at balance date according to the length of time amounts have been owing—allowances for bad debts increasing the longer the debt has been owing (this is known as an ageing of the debtors).

Returning to the example of Pamjen, we assume the accountant has determined that $200 of the debtors accounts at balance date will be uncollectable. As we do not know the identity of debtors who will not eventually pay, we cannot reduce individual debtors' balances as we did in the direct write-off method. To overcome this problem, accountants create another account generally referred to as the 'provision for doubtful debts'. The word 'doubtful' is more appropriate than 'bad' because at balance date no debtor has actually defaulted. The provision account does not represent a liability: it is not a future disposition of economic benefits the business is obliged to make. It is in fact a negative or contra asset because the amount of the provision for doubtful debts should be deducted from the debtors (just as we did in the direct write-off method) to provide us with the net amount of future economic benefits we expect to obtain from our debtors.

Key Concept 8.3

Provision for doubtful debts

The provision for doubtful debts is a contra debtors account and it shows the estimated total of future bad debts.

Let us now examine the worksheet for Pamjen which appears below. The provision for doubtful debts has a negative balance as it is a negative asset. The asset 'debtors' has a positive balance and, therefore, if the provision account is to be deducted from the debtors it must have a negative balance. The two accounts would be reported in the statement of financial position as follows:

	$
Debtors (Gross)	1000
Less Provision for doubtful debts	−200
Balance	800

PAMJEN WORKSHEET: VERSION 4

	Assets				= Liabilities +	Equity
	Cash	Debtors	Provision for doubtful debts	Prepaids		Profit and loss
Cash sales	6 000					6 000
Credit sales		4 000				4 000
Cash from sales	3 000	−3 000				
Rent	−500			500		
Insurance	−1 200			1 200		
Balance	7 300	+ 1 000		+ 1 700 =		10 000
Rent expense				−500	−500	
Insurance expense				−300	−300	
Doubtful debts expense			−200		−200	
Balance	7 300	+ 1 000	− 200	+ 900 =		9 000

The provision for doubtful debts account has allowed us to record our assets and profit in the year of the credit sales, at amounts which are not overstated, if our estimate is reliable. While the estimation of the provision for doubtful debts involves uncertainties, fortunately such estimates are normally reliable.

In the following year when we discover that certain debts are uncollectable, we reduce both the provision account and the debtors account by the same amount. Remember we recorded the expense in the previous year and this resulted in a better measure of profit in that year, together with a more reliable estimate of this amount expected to be collected from debtors.

For example, let us now assume that in the following period Pamjen determines that Bill Bear is not likely to pay the $100 he owes as he has been declared bankrupt. We would record a +$100 in the provision for doubtful debts column and a −$100 in the debtors column. With the total debtors and provision account change, the net amount remains the same, as shown below.

	$
Debtors (Gross)	900
Less Provision for doubtful debts	−100
Balance	800

PAMJEN WORKSHEET: VERSION 5

	Assets				= Liabilities +	Equity
	Cash	Debtors	Provision for doubtful debts.	Prepaids		Profit and loss
Cash sales	6 000					6 000
Credit sales		4 000				4 000
Cash from sales	3 000	−3 000				
Rent	−500			500		
Insurance	−1 200			1 200		
Balance	7 300	+ 1 000		+ 1 700 =		10 000
Rent expense				−500		−500
Insurance expense				−300		−300
Bad debts			−200			−200
Balance	7 300	+ 1 000	− 200 ·	+ 900 =		9 000
Next period Bill Bear unable to pay		−100	100			
Balance	7 300	+ 900	− 100	+ 900 =		9 000

Accounting policies for doubtful debts and implications for users

You should now study the financial report of Woolworths. Note 1(L) states that provision for doubtful debts is made when collection of the full nominal amount is no longer probable. Note 10 provides details of the amounts of provisions for trade receivables and other receivables. As is the case with inventories, it is important when comparing the financial statements of two entities to evaluate the provisioning for doubtful debts. If two entities are in the same industry and operating in similar locations, you would expect similar amounts of provisioning for doubtful debts. If this is not the case, and unless there is an explanation for the difference, some adjustment for this difference is necessary before a proper comparison can be made of the financial statements.

Creditors

When an established business buys goods it rarely pays cash. Only when a business is just starting, or in exceptional cases, is trade credit not given.

The question we have to address is how a business deals with goods supplied on credit which might have been used or sold before payment is made to the supplier.

However, before we deal with that question we need to explain the difference between creditors and accruals.

Creditors arise when goods or services are supplied to an enterprise for which an invoice is subsequently received and for which no payment has been made at the date of receipt of the goods or services. As we have already said, established businesses receive most of their raw materials and components on the basis that payment is due within a certain period after delivery. At the date at which we prepare a statement of financial position, therefore, we need to acknowledge that there are amounts owing (liabilities) in respect of these supplies. These are referred to as 'creditors' in Australia and the UK and as 'accounts payable' in the USA.

Accruals

Accruals are in some ways similar to creditors in that they relate to amounts due for goods or services already supplied to the enterprise. They differ not because of the nature of the transaction but because, at the time of preparing the statement of financial position, the amounts involved are not known with certainty. This is usually because the invoice for the goods *has not been received*. A common example of such a situation is telephone accounts, which are always issued in arrears; other examples are electricity and gas accounts. In these situations, all we can do is to estimate what we think is owed for the service which the business has used during the accounting period. This estimate is based on the last quarter of the previous year or on some other basis which the business considers more accurate. An example will clarify the treatment of creditors and accruals and the differences between the two.

Key Concept 8.4

Creditors and accruals

Creditors are amounts owing at a point in time, the amounts of which are *known*. Accruals are amounts owing at a point in time, the amounts of which are *not known with any certainty*.

Example 8.2: Mike & Co.

For the year to 31 December 20X1 Mike & Co. had the following transactions.

1 Paid $6000 of Mike's own money into a business bank account, together with $5000 borrowed from a friend for the business.
2 Bought 1000 items from a supplier at $12 per unit.
3 Paid the electricity accounts for lighting and heating for three quarters, amounting to $1500.
4 Paid a supplier $9000 for items purchased.

If we enter these transactions on a worksheet and explain how they are dealt with, we can then deal with the other transactions of Mike's business. Our worksheet for the first transactions looks like this:

MIKE & CO. WORKSHEET: VERSION 1

	Assets		= Liabilities +			Equity
Transaction	Bank	Inventory	Loan	Creditors	Profit and loss	Equity
1	6 000					6 000
1	5 000		5 000			
2		12 000		12 000		
3	−1 500				−1 500	
4	−9 000			−9 000		
Balance	500	+ 12 000	= 5 000	+ 3 000	− 1 500	+ 6 000

Let us examine each of the transactions in turn.

Transaction 1

By now we are familiar with transactions of this type which create an asset and a corresponding liability in the form of money owing either to the owner or to some other party.

Transaction 2

This is slightly different from the previous examples, which have dealt with the purchase of inventory. Up to now we have assumed that the inventory was paid for when we received it. In this case, however, we are only told that during the year Mike bought items for $12 000. We have no idea, at present, how much was actually paid out in respect of these items or how much is still owing. Therefore we show that Mike is owing money for all the items: we open a column for creditors and show $12 000 in that column.

Transaction 3

Once again this is a familiar item as we received an account which was paid for in cash. However, we have in fact paid for only three quarters whereas we have consumed a year's supply of electricity. We therefore need to make some provision for the other quarter. A reasonable estimate is that the fourth quarter's account will be the same as the other quarters, i.e. approximately $500. It might, of course, turn out to be more or less. We are not attempting 100 per cent accuracy: we just need to give a reasonable picture of the situation.

Transaction 4

We now know that, of the $12 000 which Mike owes to suppliers, $9000 was paid in the year. We therefore reduce our cash by that amount and reduce the creditors by the same amount.

Let us now return to the question of the electricity account. We said that we need to make an accrual which we estimated to be $500. Let us see how this affects our worksheet, using the balances from version 1 of the worksheet. As we can see in version 2, the worksheet still balances and it now gives a more accurate picture of the goods Mike controls and the amounts Mike owes.

MIKE & CO. WORKSHEET: VERSION 2

	Assets		=	Liabilities		+		Equity
Transaction	Bank	Inventory	Loan	Creditors	Accruals	Profit and loss		Equity
1	6 000							6 000
2	5 000		5 000					
2		12 000		12 000				
3	-1 500					-1 500		
4	-9 000			-9 000				
Balance	500	+ 12 000	= 5 000	+ 3 000		- 1 500		+ 6 000
Accrual					+ 500	- 500		
Balance	500	+ 12 000	= 5 000	+ 3 000	+ 500	- 2 000		+ 6 000

Further transactions

Before we leave the subject of debtors and creditors, here are some more transactions for Mike & Co. which you should try to work through yourself and then compare your answer with the answer shown below.

Mike & Co.'s other transactions in the year to 31 December 20X1 were as follows.

5 Paid loan interest of $300 in respect of the half year to 30 June 20X1.
6 Sold 900 items at $50 per item, all on credit.
7 Received $40 000 from customers in respect of sales.
8 On 1 January 20X1, paid $1000 rent for five quarters, covering the period 1 January 20X1–31 March 20X2.

These appear in the worksheet as shown below.

MIKE & CO. WORKSHEET: VERSION 3

	Assets				=	Liabilities		+		Equity
	Bank	Inventory	Debtors	Prepaids	Creditors	Accruals	Loans	Profit and loss	Equity	
Balance	500	12 000	0	0	3 000	500	5 000	-2 000	6 000	
5	-300							-300		
6			45 000					45 000		
7	40 000		-40 000							
8	-1 000			1 000						
Balance	39 200	+ 12 000	+ 5 000	+ 1 000	= 3 000	+ 500	+ 5 000	+ 42 700	+ 6 000	

If we review the position at the year end as shown on our worksheet, we find that the asset 'prepaids' no longer gives us a future benefit of $1000 because four quarters' rent relates to the year just gone and therefore the benefit has been used. We also find that the interest paid is only for the first half of the year and yet we have had the benefit of the loan for the full year; we therefore need to make a provision or accrual for a further $300. We should also realise that our inventory figure represents 1000 items at $12 each and that, of those, 900 items were sold; therefore our cost of sales should be $10 800. Our worksheet is now as shown in version 4.

We can now extract the statement of financial position and the statement of financial performance for the first year of Mike's business.

MIKE & CO. WORKSHEET: VERSION 4

	Assets				=	Liabilities		+		Equity
	Bank	Inventory	Debtors	Prepaids	Creditors	Accruals		Loans	Profit and loss	Equity
Balance	39 200	12 000	5 000	1 000	3 000	500		5 000	42 700	6 000
Rent				−800					−800	
Interest						300			−300	
Cost of sales		−10 800							−10 800	
Balance	39 200	+ 1 200	+ 5 000	+ 200	= 3 000	+ 800		+ 5 000	+ 30 800	+ 6 000

MIKE & CO.
STATEMENT OF FINANCIAL PERFORMANCE FOR THE YEAR ENDED 31 DECEMBER 20X1

	$	$
Sales		45 000
Cost of goods sold		10 800
Gross Profit		34 200
Electricity	2 000	
Loan interest	600	
Rent	800	
		3 400
Net Profit		30 800

MIKE & CO.
STATEMENT OF FINANCIAL POSITION AT 31 DECEMBER 20X1

Assets	$	$	$	$
Current Assets				
Stocks	1 200			
Debtors	5 000			
Prepayments	200			
Cash at bank	39 200			
Total Current Assets		45 600		
Non-current Assets				—
Total Assets			45 600	
Current Liabilities				
Creditors	3 000			
Accruals	800			
Loan	5 000			
Total Current Liabilities		8 800		
Non-current Liabilities	—			—
Total Liabilities			8 800	
Net Assets				36 800
Equity				
Capital	6 000			
Profit for 20X1	30 800			
Total Equity				36 800

Transactions in the second year

Having now established how to deal with debtors, creditors, accruals and prepayments, let us examine what happens in the second year of Mike's business.

For the year to 31 December 20X2 Mike & Co.'s transactions were as follows.

1 Bought 1000 items on credit at $12 per item.
2 Paid suppliers $14 000.
3 Paid electricity account of $2300 for the last quarter of 20X1 and three quarters of 20X2.
4 Paid loan interest of $600.
5 Sold 1000 items on credit terms at $50 per item.
6 Received $40 000 from customers.
7 Paid rent of $1000. This covered the period 1 April 20X2–31 March 20X3.
8 Made a provision for doubtful debts of $2000.

We will briefly discuss some of these items before we enter them on a worksheet.

Let us consider the payments to suppliers and the payment for electricity. In neither of these cases do we know exactly which parts of the payments relate to this year and which to last year. In the former case it does not really matter and in the latter case it is reasonable to assume that $500 relates to last year and $1800 to the first three quarters of this year. As with last year, we have to make an estimate of the amount due in respect of the last quarter. Based on the same quarter of the previous year we would estimate $500 but this is clearly too low as, based on the three quarters this year, electricity is now costing $600 a quarter. Therefore, a reasonable estimate would be $600.

The loan interest is similar to the situation just dealt with except that in this case there is more certainty that $300 relates to the previous year and $300 to this year. Therefore we need to make an adjustment in respect of the $300 which the business still owes for the current year.

As far as the cost of sales is concerned there is no problem as prices have remained constant and Mike has bought and sold 1000 items in the year.

The situation with debtors is the same as for creditors. We cannot identify the individual payments, but in this particular example it does not make any difference.

The annual rent is $1000, payable in advance. As the first quarter was paid for last year, this payment relates to three quarters of the current year and one quarter of next year. The rent has increased from $200 to $250 per quarter.

Finally we must make a provision for expected uncollectable accounts related to sales this year. We will not know which accounts will be uncollectable until next year. After we enter these transactions, the worksheet looks like the one shown in version 5. It is possible to take some shortcuts and get the same answer, but you should bear in mind that such shortcuts can lead to errors.

MIKE & CO. WORKSHEET: VERSION 5

| Transaction | Assets | | | | | = Liabilities | | + | | Equity |
	Bank	Inventory	Debtors	Provision for doubtful debts	Prepaids	Creditors	Accruals	Loans	Profit and loss	Equity
Balance	39 200	1 200	5 000	0	200	3 000	800	5 000		36 800
1		12 000				12 000				
2	-14 000					-14 000				
3	-2 300						-500		-1 800	
4	-600						-300		-300	

(continued over page)

	Assets					= Liabilities		+		Equity
Transaction	Bank	Inventory	Debtors	Provision for doubtful debts	Prepaids	Creditors	Accruals	Loans	Profit and loss	Equity
5			50 000						50 000	
6	40 000		−40 000							
7	−1 000				1 000					
Balance	61 300	+ 13 200	+ 15 000	0	+ 1 200	= 1 000	0	+ 5 000	+ 47 900	+ 36 800
Cost of sales		−12 000							−12 000	
Rent					−950				−950	
Electricity							+600		−600	
Interest							+300		−300	
Doubtful debts				−2 000					−2 000	
Balance	61 300	+ 1 200	+15 000	−2 000	+ 250	= 1 000	+ 900	+ 5 000	+32 050	+36 800

The statement of financial position at the end of 20X2 and the statement of financial performance for that year can now be extracted.

MIKE & CO.
STATEMENT OF FINANCIAL PERFORMANCE FOR
THE YEAR ENDED 31 DECEMBER 20X2

	$	$
Sales		50 000
Less Cost of goods sold		12 000
Gross Profit		38 000
Less Expenses		
Electricity	2 400	
Loan interest	600	
Rent	950	
Doubtful debts	2 000	5 950
Net Profit		32 050

MIKE & CO.
STATEMENT OF FINANCIAL POSITION AS AT 31 DECEMBER 20X2

	$	$	$	$	$
Assets					
Current Assets					
Cash at bank		61 300			
Debtors	15 000				
Less Provision for doubtful debts	(2 000)	13 000			
Prepayments		250			
Inventory		1 200			
Total Current Assets			75 750		
Non-current Assets		—			
Total Assets			75 750		

(continued next page)

Liabilities

Current Liabilities

Creditors	1 000		
Accruals	900		
Loan	5 000		
Total Current Liabilities		6 900	
Non-current Liabilities		—	
Total Liabilities		6 900	
Net Assets			68 850

Equity

Capital	6 000		
Accumulated profits*	62 850		
Total Equity			68 850

* *Includes profits for 20X1 and 20X2.*

You should now study the Woolworths financial report. Note 1(P) describes trade creditors and accruals. We are told the amounts are unsecured, which means that creditors do not have any claim on any specific assets of Woolworths if the amounts owing remain unpaid. The note also indicates that the amounts are normally paid in 45 days. The amounts owing for accounts payable and accruals can be obtained from the statement of financial position.

Summary

In this chapter we have considered how accrual accounting deals with the problem of accounts prepared on the basis of cash flows. The assets, liabilities, revenues and expenses arising in a cash flow system are often inconsistent with our definition and recognition principles for these items as outlined in the Conceptual Framework. We have shown how sales on credit are included as revenue, and how the amounts not received at the end of the year are dealt with as debtors and shown as current assets because they will provide the business with a future benefit. We have also examined the way in which payments in advance can be dealt with in order that expenses are recognised in the appropriate accounting period. In addition we have also looked at how to account for bad and doubtful debts. For goods supplied to the business, we have seen how creditors are dealt with and how accruals arise. The principle that is common to all these items is that assets, liabilities, revenues and expenses must be recognised only when they meet the appropriate definition and recognition criteria. Application of these criteria normally results in the recording of revenues and the relevant expenses in the same accounting period. The statement of financial position records the rights to future benefits and what the present obligations of the business are at a particular point in time.

Reference

Hoggett, J. and Edwards, L., 1996. *Accounting in Australia*, 3rd edn, John Wiley.

Review questions

1   In your own words describe what a creditor is and when creditors arise.

2   Explain the difference between creditors and accruals.

3   Why are debtors and prepayments classified as current assets?

4   When do prepayments arise and how do they differ from accruals?

5   Why is it necessary to identify debtors and creditors?

6   How do debtors affect the statement of financial performance?

7   Why is the accrual system of accounting a better guide to profitability?

8   What type of business could use a cash system of accounting? Give reasons.

Problems for discussion and analysis

1   Refer to the Woolworths financial report in Appendix 1.
   a   What is the value of current and non-current receivables?
   b   What is the value of employee loans?
   c   What is the normal period of time taken to settle trade creditors and accruals?

2   Accruals are sums owing at a point of time, the amounts of which are not known with certainty (see Key Concept 8.4). How would you estimate the following, and what points need to be considered?
   a   Electricity account
   b   Council rates
   c   Telephone account
   e   Water rates
   f   Income taxes

3   ABC Ltd makes all its sales on credit. For customers who pay within ten days of purchase, ABC gives a discount of 5 per cent. (Assume all sales are made evenly over the month and there are 30 working days every month.) ABC knows that, on average, 50 per cent of its customers pay within the discount period, 40 per cent pay within 30 days, and 8 per cent within 60 days. Two per cent are uncollectable.

Sales figures are:

Month 1	Month 2	Month 3	Month 4	Month 5
$1 200 000	$1 300 000	$880 000	$1 000 000	$1 250 000

How much cash did ABC collect in months 4 and 5?

4   In each of the following situations, describe the way that the transaction would be dealt with in the accounts of the business and identify, where appropriate, the effect on the statements of financial position and financial performance.
   a   Purchase of inventory of raw materials on credit terms.
   b   Purchase of production machines for cash.
   c   Receipts from customers in respect of credit sales.
   d   Repayment of a loan.
   e   Payment in respect of research expenditure.
   f   Sale of goods on credit.
   g   Payment to supplier in respect of goods already delivered.

h   Payment of wages to clerical workers.
i   Payment of wages to production workers.
j   Payment of loan interest.
k   Payment of an electricity bill from last year.
l   Payment of rent quarterly in advance.
m   Receipt of cash from the owner.
n   Withdrawal of inventory for personal use by the owner.
o   A customer going into liquidation owing money.

5   On 1 May 20X0 Barbara paid $3000 into a business bank account as capital for her new business, which she called Barbie's Bikes. The transactions during May were as follows:

May 3   Bought van for $800 cash.
    6   Bought goods on credit from Spokes for $700.
    8   Paid rent of $120 for the quarter.
    14   Bought goods on credit from Olympic for $300.
    16   Made cash sales of $200.
    18   Made credit sales of $400 to Bill's Bikes.
    21   Paid the garage account of $20 for petrol and oil.
    23   Sold more goods on credit to Wheels for $600.
    24   Paid Spokes $682.50 to take advantage of a 2.5 per cent discount for prompt payment.
    30   Received $360 from the liquidator of Bill's Bikes and was advised that no more would be forthcoming.
    31   Paid monthly salary to shop assistant of $400.
         Received back from Wheels goods, with an invoice price of $80, which they had not ordered.

Other information: No inventory count was done at the end of the month, but all goods were sold at a price based on the cost price plus one-third.

a   Discuss how each transaction should be treated.
b   Discuss what, if any, accruals and prepayments are involved or should be treated.
c   Draw up a worksheet, statement of financial position and statement of financial performance. (Take all figures to the nearest dollar.)

6   The Philjet company makes all its sales on 30 days credit. For the year ending 31 December 31 20X9, cash collections from customers amounted to $1 078 333. Net credit sales in 20X9 totalled $1 022 111 and the balance of debtors on 31 December 20X9 was $187 000. What was the balance of debtors on 31 December 20X8?

7   Ace Silver runs a music school for young pianists. Beginners pay in advance for the first 52 weekly lessons at a rate of $5 per lesson, while more advanced students pay $7.50 per lesson in advance. Ace's financial year runs from 1 July to 30 June. On 30 June 20X8 Ace had 20 beginners with an average of 20 lessons each paid in advance, plus a further 30 advanced students with an average of ten lessons paid in advance. Cash receipts for the year ended 30 June 20X9 amounted to $25 650. At 30 June 20X9, Ace had received advance payments for 500 lessons for beginners and 250 lessons for advanced students.

Given the above information, what is the revenue earned by Ace from piano lessons for the year ending June 30 20X9?

8   Alister Bondy runs a school for aspiring entrepreneurs who wish to become millionaires. All students pay their fees in advance. The fees are $100 per session (two-hour sessions) for beginners, $200 per session for intermediate students and $400 per session for advanced students. The school has a limit of 20 students for each class. The school's financial year follows the taxation year—from 1 July to 30 June each year.

Cash receipts from students for the year ended 30 June 20X8 came to $2 631 819 and unearned fees as at 30 June 20X8 amounted to $480 636. The school (Make-a-Million Pty Ltd) showed fees earned in the statement of financial performance for the year ended 30 June 20X8 as being $2 500 000.

What was the *total* of unearned fees reported in the statement of financial position as at 30 June 20X7?

9   A lawyer received $20 000 from a client on 1 August 20X0 as a retainer; in return, the lawyer agreed to give legal advice whenever required by the client for a year. Neither the lawyer nor the client knew at this stage when such advice would be sought, if indeed it would be sought at all. Of the $20 000, how much should be recorded in 20X0?

10 On 31 December 20X1 the accountant for Zeebug Corporation reviewed certain transactions affecting the accounts receivable and provision for doubtful debts accounts, before preparing the yearly financial statements. The accountant first reviewed the 31 December 20X0 statement of financial position.

ZEEBUG CORPORATION
STATEMENT OF FINANCIAL POSITION AT 31 DECEMBER 20X0

	$	$
Assets		
Current Assets		
Cash		335 672
Accounts receivable	494 128	
Less Provision for doubtful debts	14 824	479 304
Government bonds		137 030
Inventories		867 202
Total Current Assets		1 819 209
Non-current Assets		
Investments		206 147
Land		93 282
Buildings	1 202 630	
Less Accumulated depreciation	331 690	870 940
Machinery	1 712 792	
Less Accumulated depreciation	821 179	891 613
Office equipment	28 242	
Less Accumulated depreciation	20 200	8 042
Manufacturing equipment	29 149	
Less Accumulated depreciation	18 578	10 571
Motor vehicles	21 267	
Less Accumulated depreciation	14 002	7 265

(continued next page)

Tools	30 647
Patent	28 125
Bank securities	50 095
Total Non-current Assets	2 196 727
Total Assets	4 015 936
Liabilities	
Current Liabilities	
Accounts payable	255 000
Taxation payable	354 677
Accrued interest	70 739
Accrued salaries	34 650
Total Current Liabilities	715 066
Non-current Liabilities	
Long-term debt	623 684
Total Liabilities	1 338 750
Net Assets	2 677 186
Shareholders' Equity	
Paid-up capital	1 251 638
Retained earnings	1 425 548
Total Shareholders' Equity	2 677 186

The accountant then analysed the year's transactions applicable to the accounts receivable listed as follows:

i   Sales during 20X1 totalled $4 936 286.

ii   Payments received on accounts receivable during 20X1 amounted to $4 747 367.

iii   During the year accounts receivable deemed uncollectable totalled $12 509 and were written off.

iv   Two accounts previously written off in 20X0 were collected in 20X1. One account for $958 was paid in full, the other for $1130 was partially paid and the accountant was reasonably sure that the remainder of $426 would be paid in full in the near future.

v   The provision for doubtful debts was adjusted to equal 3 per cent of the year-end balance of the accounts receivable.

Required:

a   Examine the effect of each of these transactions in terms of their effect on accounts receivable, provision for doubtful debts and any other account that might be involved.

b   After making any adjustments to the accounts resulting from the transactions above, determine the right totals for accounts receivable and the provision for doubtful debts at 31 December 20X1.

(Adapted from R. Anthony and J. Reece, *Accounting: Text and Cases*, 8th edn, Richard D. Irwin Inc., 1988, Chapter 5, Case 5–1.)

11   Fun Travel Agency chartered an aeroplane to tour the Kimberley region for the week commencing 14 February 20X1, at a cost of $150 000. The plane's owner

agreed to finance the fuel and staffing costs of the tour. During December 20X0, the travel agency sold all of the seats on the plane (to passengers) for $180 000 in cash. As an advance payment, the Fun Travel Agency paid $30 000 to the plane's owner. Of the $180 000 received by the travel agency, how much, if any, should be recorded as revenue by the firm in 20X0? Would your answer change if passengers were entitled to a refund in 20X1 if they cancelled their reservations?

12   Examine the data on loans and delinquent loans (bad debts) for the credit unions and answer the following questions:

ASSET QUALITY
Delinquent loans/total loans

Credit Union size	20X1	20X2	20X3	20X4	20X5	20X6
Less than $5m	4.79%	3.97%	3.73%	3.76%	3.58%	3.74%
$5m to <$10m	3.27%	3.01%	3.70%	3.45%	3.29%	2.80%
$10m to <$50m	2.36%	2.15%	2.16%	2.12%	2.07%	2.32%
$50m to <$100m	2.14%	2.24%	2.63%	2.26%	2.32%	2.26%
$100m to <$200m	1.81%	1.91%	1.94%	2.12%	2.04%	2.04%
Over $200m	1.31%	1.42%	1.44%	1.48%	1.56%	1.34%
All Credit Unions	1.75%	1.79%	1.89%	1.88%	1.89%	1.80%

a   Which category of credit unions performs best in terms of loan delinquency rates?
b   What reasons do you think may explain this performance?
c   Is information on doubtful debts more important for financial institutions than other types of commercial entities? Explain your answer.

13   Ultra Conservative Ltd is a small credit union with total assets of $50 million, most of which is made up of loans to members amounting to $46 million. The following selected data relates to the credit union's first three years.

SELECTED ACCOUNTS

	31 December 20X1	31 December 20X2	31 December 20X3
	$	$	$
Loans to members	40 000 000	43 000 000	46 000 000
Provision for doubtful debts	400 000	430 000	460 000
Doubtful debts expense	400 000	110 000	116 000

The credit union commenced operations on 1 November 20X1 and by 31 December 20X1 had established loans worth $40 million, and had incurred no bad debts. However, the board of directors wanted to be conservative and, based on other credit unions' experience with delinquent loans, decided on establishing a provision amount of 1 per cent of loans outstanding as at each balance date. Hence, the figure of $400 000 at 31 December 20X1. All loans regarded as uncollectable are written off against the provision for doubtful debts account. In the time since it commenced operations there have been no cases where a loan previously written off has had to be reinstated.

Required:

a   Determine the amount of loans written off against the provision account in 20X2 and 20X3.

b Given your answer to (a) above, evaluate the directors' policy of providing for doubtful debts at 1 per cent of loans outstanding at balance date. Evaluate the impact of this policy on the statement of financial position and statement of financial performance.

c Would you recommend any changes to the policy? If so, would adjustments be required to the provision for doubtful debts account? What would be the worksheet entries?

Ethics case study

John Jerkins is the Chief Executive Officer of a chain of retail stores which trade as Bains Ltd in Australia and New Zealand. The company has been very successful in its 50 years of operations—until the past three years. The entry of new competition from overseas, plus a downturn in the economy, has made trading very difficult.

In reviewing the year's performance to date, John is concerned that the company's profit is down again from last year. The predicted result, if the current trends continue, will bring added pressure on the company from its bankers and the financial press.

To alleviate the problem John develops the following plan.

i He will instruct all stores to reduce the level of income required for customers to qualify for credit. This, he reasons, will allow more families to purchase appliances such as television sets and video recorders.

ii He proposes to amend the method of providing for doubtful debts according to the following schedule.

Age category	Amount in the age category uncollectable $	Original percentage expected to be uncollectable %	Proposed percentage for expected uncollectable %
Not yet due	10 000 000	2	1.5
1–30 days past due	5 000 000	6	4
31–60 days past due	2 500 000	20	18
61–90 days past due	1 000 000	35	30
Over 90 days past due	600 000	80	60
Totals	19 100 000		

Required:

a Determine whether the amount of increase in profit is a result of the revised schedule for determining doubtful debts expense.

b Discuss the effects of the revised credit policy on the company's profitability.

c Discuss the ethical issues associated with John's plan.

Non-current Assets and Depreciation

Learning objectives

At the end of this chapter you should be able to:

1   explain and apply the criteria for determining what items constitute the cost of a non-current asset

2   explain the concept of depreciation

3   discuss the variables involved in the determination of the amount of depreciation

4   understand why non-current assets are depreciated

5   understand that the process of depreciation does not involve the setting aside of cash funds for asset replacement

6   explain and apply the straight-line and reducing-balance methods of depreciation

7   explain what is meant by the term 'intangible assets'

8   discuss the difference between identifiable and unidentifiable intangible assets.

Introduction

In Chapter 4 we defined assets, and discussed non-current and current assets. The definition of an asset is restated as Key Concept 9.1.

Key Concept 9.1

Assets
Assets are future economic benefits controlled by the entity as a result of past transactions or other past events. (SAC 4, para. 14)

The distinction that we made in earlier chapters between assets and expenses is that an asset relates to present or future benefits whereas an expense relates to past or expired benefits. Thus, inventories of goods held at the end of the year are shown as an asset, and the cost of the inventories sold during the year is charged as an expense. Some assets change form during a period, or from one period to the next. For example, debtors become cash, or they become expenses when a debt becomes uncollectable. This applies to all assets in the long run, but in the case of non-current assets it takes longer to use up the future benefits than it does with current assets. We defined non-current assets in Chapter 4, and repeat the definition here.

Key Concept 9.2

Non-current assets
Non-current assets are all assets other than current assets.

The fact that these assets neither change form nor get used up in a short period poses some problems for accountants. These problems are in some ways similar to those we identified when discussing inventory valuation. We found that there was a problem in allocating costs such as the wages of the supervisor and in deciding which part of that cost should be allocated to the costs of the goods sold during the period, i.e. the expired benefit. There was also the question of how much should be allocated to the inventory held at the end of the period. (This was shown as an asset because there was a future benefit to be derived.)

The problem can be looked at in a more general way. For the statement of financial position (which tells us what we control at a particular point in time) we have to try to identify the amount of the future benefit left at the end of each year. On the other hand, for the statement of financial performance, we need to measure the amount of the future benefit used up during the year so that we can show it as an expense, together with the revenue earned in that period. Whichever way we look at the problem, we are left with the issue of how to measure the future benefit to be derived from the use of the asset. This is because the statement of financial position and statement of financial performance are linked.

It was argued in Chapter 3 that accounting generally adopts a definition of profit based on Sir John Hicks' definition of income.

Key Concept 9.3

Income

Income is that amount which an individual can consume and still be as well off at the end of the period as he or she was at the start of the period.

This we said could be illustrated as in Figure 9.1.

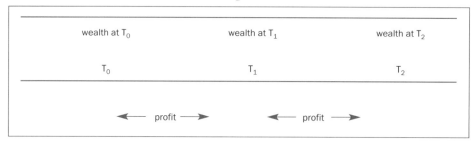

Figure 9.1 *Profit or loss is determined by measuring wealth at different points in time.*

We can see from the diagram that wealth at T_0 plus the profit for the period will give us wealth at T_1. Thus, we can either measure the wealth in the form of future benefits at the end of each period, which brings with it the problems of valuation (as discussed in Chapter 3), or we can try to measure the profit by deducting from revenue the benefits used up during the period, which brings its own attendant problems (as we found with inventory and cost allocation in Chapter 7).

We look first at the idea of measuring future benefits with specific regard to non-current assets. Theoretically this might be possible. For example, we could measure the benefits to be derived from selling the products which our non-current assets help us to produce. However, in an uncertain world this process is far from straightforward. For example, what effects do technological advances have on the market for our products? How does that affect the future benefits to be derived from the use of our asset? What is the effect of competition? It might affect our market share. What is the effect of a change in production technology? It might allow competitors with newer equipment to produce the same product at a cheaper price.

In fact, it is extremely difficult to measure the future benefit in the long term because we do not know what changes the future will bring, and therefore we cannot estimate their effects. Traditionally accounting has solved this conundrum by the simple expedient of valuing assets at cost unless there is reasonable certainty that this value is incorrect—either because it is lower, as would be the case if changes in technology made the non-current assets obsolete, or because it is clearly considerably higher. This situation generally applies only to land and buildings (although some would argue against the latter). It is difficult to measure profit by valuing assets in terms of future benefits, which leaves us with the alternative approach, i.e. measuring expired benefits and deducting these from revenues. The problem with this system is that if you were able to tell how much benefit had expired you would then be able to work out what the unexpired or future benefit was. This, we have just argued, is extremely difficult to do in reality because of the problems of uncertainty.

Accountants handle the difficulty by trying to take some cognisance of the fall in value of the non-current assets. This is done by means of a *depreciation charge*, which is a way of spreading the original cost of a non-current asset over its useful life and thereby charging the statement of financial performance with some amount relating to the use of the asset. This approach does not, in itself, solve the problem of how to deal with uncertainty because the useful life of a non-current asset is itself uncertain. Other issues also arise.

- How does a non-current asset differ from a current asset?
- What is the cost of a non-current asset?
- How should we spread the cost over the useful life?

We need to examine each of these issues if we are to understand what the figures in the statements of financial performance and financial position mean.

Difference between non-current and current assets

We have already defined non-current and current assets in Chapter 4 and again at the beginning of this chapter. If you look at the definitions you will see that the difference is, in the main, related to the intention and the nature of the business. In simple terms a car is not a non-current asset for a motor dealer because it is not the intention of the dealer to use it within the business for a considerable period of time. The problem with a definition that relies on the intentions of the business is that these change from time to time as the nature of the business changes or the product changes. An asset that was classified as a current asset might be reclassified and become subject to depreciation. As these problems rarely arise, we can ignore them in this book.

The cost of a non-current asset

The question of what an asset costs should present few difficulties, but in some cases the answer is not clear. To illustrate the point, let us look at the situation in which an individual buys a house. The legal contract between the seller and the buyer states an agreed price. We could argue that the cost is that agreed price, but were you to talk to someone who has recently purchased a house you would find that there were other costs associated with the purchase, such as solicitors' and agents' fees, and stamp duty. The question is whether these should be treated as part of the cost of the asset or whether they are expenses. In this situation an accountant might argue that the amounts involved are not material compared with the cost of the house. This is not a satisfactory solution because it avoids the question instead of answering it. Accounting does not, in fact, provide an answer to the problem. However, there are some broad guidelines which accountants use. In Chapter 7 we observed that the cost of inventories includes all costs incurred in the normal course of operations in bringing the inventories to their present location and condition. This same principle is applied in the determination of the cost of non-current assets, i.e. the cost of a non-current asset includes all costs necessarily incurred in order to have the non-current asset ready for its intended use in the business. We will examine some examples and identify the basis of the decision.

Key Concept 9.4

Cost of a non-current asset

The cost of a non-current asset includes all reasonable and necessary costs incurred to place the asset in a position and condition ready for use.

Materiality

Before doing that, however, we need to explain the idea of materiality.

Key Concept 9.5

Materiality

Broadly, an item can be said to be material if its non-disclosure would lead to the accounts being misleading in some way.

Materiality is a concept often used in accounting literature and, like a number of other concepts, it provides a rule of thumb to assist in making judgements. For example, the cost of a car is likely to be material in the case of a small retailer, but in the case of BHP the effect on the non-current assets would be negligible because they are measured in millions of dollars. Thus, materiality is a relative measure and all aspects of the situation need to be looked at before a decision is made. Having introduced the idea of materiality, we can try to establish the guidelines we referred to above through a series of examples.

Example 9.1

A delivery van is purchased by a retailer of electrical goods for $40 000. The price includes number-plates and one year's registration.

Discussion

It is clear that in this example we have a non-current asset. The question is how much the non-current asset cost. Included in the $40 000 is the cost of number-plates and one year's registration. The registration can hardly be described as a non-current asset since it lasts for only one year, whereas the number-plates are clearly part of the cost of the non-current asset since they will remain with the van over its useful life.

Example 9.2

Let us now assume that, as the retailer did not have the cash to buy the van outright, it was purchased on hire purchase. The hire-purchase contract allowed the retailer to put down a deposit of $10 000 and then make 36 monthly payments of $1000. Thus, the total cost of buying the van is $46 000, compared with the cash price of $40 000.

Discussion

The fact that the retailer has decided to finance the purchase in a different way has, on the face of it, added to the cost of purchasing the van.

However, this is somewhat misleading because the cost of the van is in fact the same. What has happened in this case is that the retailer has incurred an additional cost which does not relate to the van itself. This additional cost is the cost of borrowing money, which is effectively what hire purchase is. If the retailer had borrowed money through a bank loan and then paid cash for the van, the cost of the van would have been the cash price and the interest on the loan would be dealt with separately. Thus, in the case of hire purchase all that needs to be done is to identify the part of the payments that is interest and deal with it in the same way as we would deal with interest on loans. In this particular example the interest is $6000. The $6000 interest would of course be charged to the statement of financial performance as an expense over the 36 months it takes to pay the hire-purchase company.

Example 9.3

A manufacturer bought a secondhand machine for $10 000, which had cost $15 000 new. The cost of transporting the machine to the factory was $500 and the costs of installation were $400. When it was installed it was found that it was not working properly and it had to be repaired, which cost $300. At the same time a modification was carried out at a cost of $500 to improve the output of the machine. After two months' production the machine broke down again and was repaired at a cost of $200.

Discussion

The starting point is the basic cost of the machine, which was $10 000. The fact that it had cost $15 000 when it was new is not relevant. What we need to bring into the accounts of our manufacturer is the cost to that business, not the original cost to the seller. With the other costs, though, the decisions are less clear. For example, should the cost of transport be included? If we apply the principle outlined in Key Concept 9.4 the answer is yes, because the cost is necessary to get the machine to its place ready for use. In other words, in order to obtain the future benefits from the asset we needed to incur this cost and so this is in fact a payment for those future benefits. If we followed this line of argument we would then include the costs of installation, the initial repairs and the modifications.

You will have noticed that we referred specifically to the initial repairs rather than all the repairs. Let us compare them. For the initial repairs, it could be argued that the reason the business was able to buy the machine cheaply was because it was not working properly. For the later repairs, however, the argument is less clear: the repairs might be due to normal wear and tear and should therefore be judged as part of the cost of running the machine, in the same way as the cost of car repairs is regarded as a part of the costs of running a car. If a business incurs costs which significantly improve a non-current asset so that its ability to generate future economic benefits is enhanced, then the cost might qualify for inclusion as part of the cost of the asset.

For example, an expenditure of $2000 is incurred to install a new engine in a car which has a written-down cost of $3000. This extends the life of the car by another four years. This cost is properly treated as an addition to the cost of an asset rather than being treated as an expense.

We can now improve the definition of the cost of a non current asset (previously given in Key Concept 9.4).

Key Concept 9.6

Cost of a non-current asset

The cost of a non-current asset includes:
- all reasonable and necessary costs incurred to place the asset in a position and condition ready for use
- all costs incurred which enhance the future economic benefits of the asset beyond those initially expected at acquisition.

We can see from these examples that there is no easy solution to the problem of what should and should not be included in the cost of non-current assets. Each case is judged upon its merits and a decision is made about whether the cost should be included in the expenses for the year or added to the cost of the asset. The rule of thumb that can be used to assist in these decisions is: has there been an enhancement of the potential future economic benefits? If there has, then the cost should be added to the asset. If, however, the effect is simply to restore the status quo, as is the case with car repairs, then it is more reasonable to treat those costs as expenses of the period in which they arise.

The useful life of non-current assets

In our introduction we mentioned the useful life of the asset and how we spread the cost over the useful life. This raises a number of issues.

- How do we judge the useful life?
- What cost do we spread over the useful life?
- How do we spread it?

The last point will be dealt with below in our discussion of depreciation, but it is worth examining the other two first.

The first point is how we judge the useful life. The answer is that all we can hope for is an approximation, because of uncertainty in respect of the future. In determining the cost that we wish to spread over the useful life, we should take into account the sum that we will get for selling our asset when it is no longer viable to use in our business, and this amount, the residual value, is only a guess because of the uncertainty involved. In reality such issues are sidestepped and assets are classified into broad groups, which are then assumed to have a useful life based upon either past practice or the norm for the industry. All too often one can visit factories where a vital machine in the production process has no book value in the accounts because the estimate of its useful life was incorrect. Having made it clear that there is no magic formula for arriving at either the cost or the useful life, let us now examine the way in which we spread the cost over the useful life. This is done by means of depreciation.

Depreciation

We have suggested some reasons for charging depreciation which we will discuss further in a moment. What we have not done is to define depreciation precisely; instead, we have tried to give a flavour of what depreciation is. No discussion of depreciation is complete without looking at the definition provided in the Accounting Standard on the subject, *AASB 1021: Depreciation*.

Key Concept 9.7

Depreciation expense

An expense recognised systematically for the purpose of allocating the depreciable amount of a depreciable asset over its useful life. (*AASB 1021*)

The definition refers to a 'systematic charge' which means that it is not an ad hoc process but should be done on a consistent basis each year. It is also clear from the definition that depreciation is a process of allocation, not valuation. In other words, the depreciation amount is not meant to represent the decline in the value of the asset. It is meant to represent the allocation of the depreciable amount of the asset over its useful life. Therefore the depreciable amount of the asset less the depreciation represents the unallocated amount, and not necessarily the asset's value at any point in time. We could spend some time analysing the definition, but it is more important to consider the question of why we depreciate assets and what depreciation can and cannot achieve.

Why depreciate?

The definition of depreciation refers to a depreciable asset. A depreciable asset is one that has a finite life extending over several accounting periods. Machinery is a depreciable asset, while land is not. Depreciation is intended to show the consumption of economic benefits during an accounting period. The economic benefits associated with all depreciable assets are eventually consumed, and depreciation shows the consumption of these benefits as an expense in the statement of financial performance.

A second and more contentious reason for providing for depreciation is in order for a business to maintain the capacity to continue its production. Clearly if a machine comes to the end of its useful life the business will need another machine if it is to carry on producing the goods. This, of course, assumes that it wishes to replace the machine, which itself has underlying assumptions about the product still being produced, the technology in terms of production processes being the same, etc. This question is directly related to our original problem in Chapter 3 of measuring wealth or the state of being well off. Such a measure depends on how you define wealth and whether that changes. For example, a car might be seen as an asset until such time as the world runs out of petrol reserves; at that stage we might not want to include a car in our measurement of wealth. Therefore, to have retained profits in order to ensure we always had a car would not have been appropriate.

This second reason for providing for depreciation is also contentious because in fact all accounting depreciation does is to spread the original cost and maintain the original capital. In fact, operating capacity is not maintained through depreciation, as no account is taken of changes in prices, in technology, or in consumer demand. Neither is any account taken of changes in the size of the business. This might have implications in terms of economies of scale. We cannot guarantee that we will have enough funds left in the business as a result of our depreciation charges to replace an existing machine with one of equal capacity should we wish to.

Having made the point that there is no guarantee that the charges will equal the requirements for replacement because of changes in those requirements and the commercial environment, let us look at how depreciation would maintain capital if the requirements and the commercial environment did not change. We will start by looking at an example to see what happens if we ignore depreciation and then how it is dealt with in terms of the accounts.

Example 9.4

Toni buys a van for $4000 and sets up in business as an ice-cream seller. In addition to the van, she puts $1000 cash into the business, which is subsequently used to buy inventories of ice cream.

At the end of the first year the sales have been $6000 and the total expenses, including the cost of ice creams, van repairs and running costs, were $3000; all the inventory has been sold and so all the money is in cash. Thus, the business has $4000 in cash—the original $1000 plus the money from sales of $6000 less the expenses paid of $3000.

Toni therefore withdraws $3000 on the assumption that the business is still as well off as it was at the start. That is, the business had at the start of the year a van plus $1000 in cash; it still has the van so there needs to be only $1000 left in for the status quo to be maintained. Let us assume that the situation is repeated for the next three years.

Under these assumptions the statements of financial performance and statements of financial position of the business are as follows.

TONI'S BUSINESS
STATEMENTS OF FINANCIAL PERFORMANCE

	Year 1	Year 2	Year 3	Year 4
	$	$	$	$
Sales revenue	6 000	6 000	6 000	6 000
Cost of sales	3 000	3 000	3 000	3 000
Profit	3 000	3 000	3 000	3 000
Withdrawal	3 000	3 000	3 000	3 000
Retained Profit	0	0	0	0

TONI'S BUSINESS
STATEMENTS OF FINANCIAL POSITION

	Year 1	Year 2	Year 3	Year 4
	$	$	$	$
Current Assets				
Cash	1 000	1 000	1 000	1 000
Non-current Assets				
Van	4 000	4 000	4 000	4 000
Total Assets	5 000	5 000	5 000	5 000
Owners' Equity	5 000	5 000	5 000	5 000

If we assume that the van will last four years and have no further useful life, we can see that in fact the statement of financial position at the end of year 4, assuming it reflects future benefits, should be as follows.

TONI'S BUSINESS
STATEMENT OF FINANCIAL POSITION AT THE END OF YEAR 4

	$
Current Assets	
Cash	1 000
Non-current Assets	
Van	—
Total Assets	1 000
Owners' Equity	1 000

As we can see, there is not enough cash left in the business to replace the van and in this situation the business cannot continue. If we compare results with our definition of profit in Chapter 3, it is clear that our profit measure must have been wrong, because Toni is not as well off at the end of year 4 as at the beginning of year 1.

The problem is that the profit has been overstated because no allowance has been made for the fact that the van has a finite useful life which is being consumed each year. If we assume that the cost should be spread evenly over the four years and call this expense depreciation, then the statements of financial performance appear as follows.

TONI'S BUSINESS
REVISED STATEMENTS OF FINANCIAL PERFORMANCE

	Year 1	Year 2	Year 3	Year 4
	$	$	$	$
Sales revenue	6 000	6 000	6 000	6 000
Cost of sales	3 000	3 000	3 000	3 000
Gross Profit	3 000	3 000	3 000	3 000
Depreciation	1 000	1 000	1 000	1 000
Net Profit	2 000	2 000	2 000	2 000
Withdrawal	2 000	2 000	2 000	2 000
Retained Profit	0	0	0	0

As can be seen, the net profit has been reduced by $1000 for the depreciation each year and Toni has withdrawn only $2000 each year. The statements of financial position would now be as follows.

TONI'S BUSINESS
REVISED STATEMENTS OF FINANCIAL POSITION

	Year 1	Year 2	Year 3	Year 4
	$	$	$	$
Current Assets				
Cash	2 000	3 000	4 000	5 000
Non-current Assets				
Van	4 000	4 000	4 000	4 000
Less Accumulated depreciation	(1 000)	(2 000)	(3 000)	(4 000)
	3 000	2 000	1 000	0
Total Assets	5 000	5 000	5 000	5 000
Owners' Equity	5 000	5 000	5 000	5 000

As we have seen, the effect of charging depreciation in the statement of financial performance was to reduce the net profit, which in turn led to a reduction in the amount withdrawn each year. The reduced withdrawal has led to the cash balance increasing each year by $1000 until at the end of year 4 there is $5000 in the bank and Toni is in a position to replace the van, assuming of course that the price of vans has not changed. If you compare the two sets of statements of financial position there is another change— the non-current asset reduces each year by the amount of the depreciation charge. The accumulated depreciation is a contra or negative asset account. It is similar in a way to the provision for doubtful debts account which we discussed in Chapter 8. It is shown as part of the assets on the worksheet with a negative balance as it is a negative asset, i.e. the accumulated depreciation is deducted from the asset in the statement of financial position. These two effects should not be mixed up. The increase in cash is a result of Toni withdrawing less cash and not a result of providing for depreciation. The latter does not in itself affect the cash balance, as is obvious if we work through year 1 of this example on a worksheet.

WORKSHEET SHOWING YEAR 1 OF TONI'S BUSINESS

	Assets			=		Liabilities + Equity	
	Cash	Van	(Accumulated depreciation)			Equity	Profit and loss
Balance	1 000	4 000				5 000	
Sales	6 000						6 000
Expenses	−3 000						−3 000
Depreciation			−1 000				−1 000
Withdrawal	−2 000					−2 000	
Balance	2 000	+ 4 000	−1 000	=		3 000	+ 2 000

An alternative way of dealing with depreciation on a worksheet is to reduce the assets column by the amount of depreciation. If we do this, our worksheet appears as shown below. However, we recommend that, wherever possible, the worksheet should include a separate column for accumulated depreciation because this adds to the clarity and allows us to identify roughly how far through its useful life the asset is at the end of the year. In our example we can see that the van cost $4000 and $1000 depreciation has been charged, and so we know that it is one-quarter of the way through its estimated useful life.

TONI'S BUSINESS: ALTERNATIVE WORKSHEET FOR YEAR 1

	Assets		= Liabilities +		Equity		
	Cash	Van				Equity	Profit and loss
Balance	1 000	4 000				5 000	
Sales	6 000						6 000
Expenses	−3 000						−3 000
Depreciation		−1 000					−1 000
Withdrawal	−2 000					−2 000	
Balance	2 000	+ 3 000	=			3 000	+ 2 000

In this example we have assumed that the cost should be spread evenly over the life of the asset. This is known as straight-line depreciation and is one of a number of alternative methods that can be used as the basis for providing depreciation. Each of these alternatives gives a different figure for depreciation each year and as a result the 'written-down value', also referred to as the 'net book value', differs. This is illustrated in more detail after our discussion of the most common methods of depreciation. Before going on to that discussion you need to understand what 'written-down value' means.

Key Concept 9.8

Written-down value

The written-down value is normally t
depreciation to date. In certain cas
might be revalued. In these cases t
depreciation to date.

Methods of depre

As we have said, there are sever
appropriate method, at least the
depreciated. In practice, howeve
method and the reducing-bala
because it is simple to calculate
accounting policies statement in publisncu ..
lying the choice of depreciation method. As we will see ...
can be made for using different methods for different assets or classes oi a...
it might be the fact that assets are put into broad categories that leads to the predomi-
nance of straight-line depreciation, which we now discuss more fully.

The straight-line method

We have already seen that this is a simple method, which explains why so many companies use it. The assumption concerning asset life that underlies this method is that the asset
is equally useful for all periods of its life. The depreciation charge is calculated by taking
the cost of the asset, subtracting the estimate of any residual value at the end of its life,
and dividing the resulting amount by the useful life of the asset. Thus a machine which
cost $100 000 and which has an estimated life of four years and an estimated residual
value of $20 000 is depreciated by $20 000 per year. This was arrived at by using the
formula:

$$\frac{\text{cost} - \text{residual value}}{\text{useful life}}$$

In our case this works out as follows.

$$\frac{100\ 000 - 20\ 000}{4} = \$20\ 000 \text{ per annum}$$

Reducing-balance method

The reducing-balance method assumes that the future benefits associated with the asset
decline more in the earlier years of the asset's life than in the later years. In fact, in most
cases the cost of repairs rises as the asset becomes older, and so this method, when the
cost of repairs is added, produces a more even cost of using an asset over its total life.
It is less frequently used than the straight-line method because it is slightly more difficult
to calculate, although with the increasing use of computers this should not cause any
problems. The method applies a pre-calculated percentage to the written-down value, or
net book value, to ascertain the charge for the year. In order to arrive at the percentage we use the following formula.

$$\text{useful life} \sqrt{\dfrac{\text{residual value}}{\text{cost of asset}}}$$

...e above example:

$$\text{...n} = 1 - \sqrt[4]{\dfrac{20\,000}{100\,000}}$$

two times (handwritten)

$$= 1 - \sqrt[4]{0.2}$$

$$= 1 - 0.6688$$
$$= 0.3312 \text{ (approximately)}$$
$$= 33.12\%$$

Depreciation, year 1	$= 33.12\%$ of 100 000
	$= \$33\ 120$
Depreciation, year 2	$= 33.12\%$ of (100 000 – 33 120)
	$= \$22\ 151$
Depreciation, year 3	$= 33.12\%$ of (100 000 – 33 120 – 22 151)
	$= \$14\ 814$
Depreciation, year 4	$= 33.12\%$ of (100 000 – 33 120 – 22 151 – 14 814)
	$= \$9\ 908$
Total depreciation	$= 33\ 120 + 22\ 151 + 14\ 814 + 9908$
	$= \$79\ 993$

The $7 difference between the total depreciation after four years under the two methods is because 33.12 per cent has been taken to two decimal places. We call the $7 difference a rounding error.

In practice, it is common to use a simpler approach to determine the percentage rate under the reducing-balance method. Often a rate of one-and-a-half times or double the straight-line rate is used. In our example the straight-line rate is 25 per cent as the life is four years. Therefore, a reducing-balance method which used one and a half times the straight-line rate would result in a percentage of 37.5 per cent (25 × 1.5). Thus, returning to our example, we could replace 33.12 per cent with 37.5 per cent and obtain $37 500 for the depreciation charge for year 1.

As can be seen in the following table, the charge to the statement of financial performance in each year and the accumulated depreciation in the statement of financial position are quite different with the two methods, although they both charge, in total, the same amount and come to the same residual value (except for the rounding error).

Comparison of the two methods

COMPARISON OF TWO METHODS OF DEPRECIATION
Straight-line method

	Statement of financial position		Statement of financial performance	
Year 1	Cost	100 000	Depreciation expense	20 000
	(Accumulated depreciation)	(20 000)		
	Book value	80 000		
Year 2	Cost	100 000	Depreciation expense	20 000
	(Accumulated depreciation)	(40 000)		
	Book value	60 000		

(continued next page)

Year 3	Cost	100
	(Accumulated depreciation)	(6(
	Book value	4
Year 4	Cost	1/
	(Accumulated depreciation)	(
	Book value	

Rec

Statement of financial position		
Year 1	Cost	
	(Accumulated depreciation)	
	Book value	
Year 2	Cost	
	(Accumulated depreciation)	
	Book value	44 729
Year 3	Cost	100 000	Depreciation expense	
	(Accumulated depreciation)	(70 085)		
	Book value	29 915		
Year 4	Cost	100 000	Depreciation expense	9 908
	(Accumulated depreciation)	(79 993)		
	Book value	20 007		

The reducing-balance method alternative to a direct measure early years, as would be the the number of hours a ma is not worthwhile from of hours a machine is machine is subject asset relates to ti asset is used up the reducing in a period You that t fro f

- Under the straight-line method, the charge to the statement of financial performance is $20 000 each year and so the accumulated depreciation rises at a rate of $20 000 a year.
- Under the reducing-balance method, the charge to the statement of financial performance is based on 33.12 per cent of the balance at the end of the previous year.

As we have said, both methods achieve the same result in the end, because in both the asset is written down to its residual value at the end of year 4. It is the incidence of the charge to the statement of financial performance which varies, not the total charged.

While in theory the choice of depreciation method should be governed by the nature of the asset and the way in which the benefit is used up, in practice little, if any, attention is paid to this. However, it is worth spending some time understanding when each method is appropriate.

We have said that the straight-line method implies that the benefit from the use of the non-current asset is used up in an even pattern over its useful life. This suggests that it is time which is the determining factor governing the life of the asset, rather than the amount of use to which it is put. In the case of a building, it is unlikely that the amount of use it gets will materially affect its lifespan and so straight-line depreciation is appropriate. On the other hand, the way in which a car engine, for example, wears out is likely to relate to usage, i.e. the more miles the car does, the more wear and tear on the engine. In such a case the straight-line method is unlikely to be the appropriate method. In these cases it is possible to use a method referred to as the *units-of-output method*. This involves calculating the depreciation charge based on the kilometres travelled in each accounting period as a percentage of the total kilometres the car is expected to travel during its useful life.

however, has characteristics that make it a possible
related to usage: it charges the most benefit used to the
ase if the asset were used up by the kilometres alone or by
chine was run, etc. It is, of course, only an approximation. It
cost-benefit point of view, however, to measure the number
run for and calculate a precise figure, because the total life of the
estimation errors. We can therefore argue that where the life of the
he, the straight-line method is likely to be appropriate; but where the
through hours run, or kilometres, or any other measure relating to usage,
balance method will give a better approximation if the benefit is used up

nould now refer to the financial report of Woolworths. Note 1(J) reveals
he company uses the straight-line method for all assets. The lives used range
n 3 to 40 years for some assets. Details of the amounts of depreciation can be
bund at Notes 3 and 13.

Sale of non-current assets

Before leaving the discussion of non-current assets and depreciation, we should examine
the situation that arises when we sell a non-current asset. It should be obvious from our
discussion above that the net book value of the asset, i.e. the cost less depreciation to
date, is unlikely to bear any resemblance to the market price of that asset. When an asset
is sold, the selling price will be either less than or more than the net book value. If, for
example, we sold the asset used in our previous example at the end of year 2 for $50 000,
then under the straight-line method there would be a difference of minus $10 000: the
net book value of $60 000 compared with the $50 000 we sold it for. However, under the
reducing-balance method the difference would be plus $5271: the net book value of
$44 729 compared with the sale proceeds of $50 000. These differences arise because
of the difference between our estimate of the future benefit being used up and the actual
benefit used up. In other words, they are a measure of the error in our estimates. We
now look at the way in which the sale of an asset is recorded, using a worksheet.

Example 9.5

Using the above data, let us assume we used the straight-line depreciation method and
we sold the asset at the end of year 2 for $50 000.

WORKSHEET: DEPRECIATION

	Assets			= Liabilities +		Equity
	Cash	Machine	(Accumulated depreciation)		Equity	Profit and loss
Balance		100 000	−40 000		60 000	
Sale proceeds	50 000					50 000
Asset removal		−100 000	40 000			−60 000
Balance	50 000	+ 0	+ 0 =		60 000 − 10 000

In the worksheet we record the proceeds from sale as an increase in the profit and
loss column because it represents revenue to the business. (If you are unsure about this
you should look back at Chapter 5.) We have also recorded the reduction in the book

value of the asset as a negative amount in the profit and loss column because it represents an expense to the business. (Again, if you are unsure about this you should look back at Chapter 5.) Notice that the machine column and the accumulated depreciation column both have zero balances which, of course, is essential as the business no longer controls the asset.

Accounting policies for depreciation and implications for users

It is important when comparing the financial statements of entities to be aware of how the financial statements were prepared. Did the companies both use straight-line or reducing-balance methods of depreciation? For example, we know that Woolworths uses the straight-line method for all non-current assets. If we are comparing Woolworths with Coles, and Coles uses a reducing-balance method of depreciation, then Coles will record higher levels of depreciation when the assets are new. Users of financial statements must adjust for this when comparing the results of both companies. Thus, as with accounting for inventories and bad debts, a component of the difference in profits between the two companies is due to the accounting rules. This difference should be distinguished from differences in profits due to higher sales or lower operating costs.

Another complication for users is the impact of different accounting rules on cash flows. If a company records a higher depreciation expense than another company, then, all other things being equal, the company with the higher depreciation expense will initially report a lower profit. However, we know depreciation is a non-cash-flow adjustment and over time the differences between the two companies will average to zero. Therefore, differences in profit due only to different depreciation policies should not result in a different valuation of either company.

However, what if the companies use the same depreciation method for both the report to shareholders and the calculation of taxable income? The company with the higher initial amount of depreciation will have greater tax deductions in earlier years than the other company. Given the value of $1 today is greater than $1 in one year's time, the company with the higher initial amount of depreciation should have a higher value than the other company, for it pays less tax in the earlier years of the life of the asset.

CASE STUDY 9.1

New recipe for managing the books

by Tom Ravlic

RECENT changes to accounting standards will alter the way profit is calculated and put investment analysts, fund managers and shareholders on a steep learning curve if they are to understand companies' reported results, according to a Merrill Lynch report.

The changes will alter the way analysts break down company results, Merrill claims. In particular, the abolition of abnormal items from the profit-and-loss statement means consensus forecasts could become meaningless.

Companies have been criticised in the past for using abnormal items as a way of lessening the blow of a bad year on profits by highlighting profits without abnormals.

Mr Andrew Perks, an equity analyst with Merrill Lynch, said the significant changes would affect company results and analysts would find it hard to keep track of the way companies implemented the new accounting rules.

'We're looking at the impact of the standards on companies, but some entities are yet to decide how they will adopt the new accounting standards,' Mr Perks said.

The Merrill Lynch report says the changes will bring domestic accounting rules into line with those of international standard-setting authorities.

An advantage of the international harmonisation of accounting standards is analysts will probably use the profit–equity ratio more often than other analytical tools because accounting rules used in determining the profit figures will generally be the same.

The report also notes some top companies might use new accounting rules on asset revaluation to devalue assets, thereby enabling them to reduce depreciation and report higher profits.

A standard on self-generating and regenerating assets may result in some companies being pressured to boost dividend payments because it requires them to book as revenue gains in the value of biological assets such as vines, forests and animals.

The Merrill report says analysts and shareholders will be able to understand a company's financial position better because of improved disclosures relating to segment reporting and cost of goods sold.

Colin Parker, director, accounting and audit, at CPA Australia, said there were other new rules to enable better understanding of company financial statements, including a recent standard on discontinuing operations.

Mr Parker said the standard covers an area, previously unregulated, in a single accounting standard.

Age, 14 September 2000

Commentary

The article highlights a number of issues, one of which is the possible use by some companies of the new accounting rules to devalue their assets and thus reduce depreciation. This would in turn increase reported profit. The important question is whether such a strategy would mislead investors and analysts. In Chapter 14 we discuss the efficient market hypothesis. In an efficient market, investors would not be fooled by such a change in profit.

Intangible assets

Many organisations have non-current assets which lack physical substance and are not held for investment purposes. Yet these items still provide future economic benefits similar to plant, machinery, and buildings. Such assets are described as intangible assets. Examples include trademarks, patents, intellectual property, franchises and goodwill. Assets such as accounts receivable and prepaid expenses also lack physical substance and are not investments. However, such assets are classified as current assets and not intangible assets.

Intangible assets are either identifiable or unidentifiable. Identifiable intangible assets include those intangibles that have a separate existence, such as patents, trademarks, franchises and brand names. Unidentifiable intangible assets are the benefits that flow to an organisation from such things as good location, outstanding image in the market place or excellent customer relations. Goodwill is the name used to describe the future economic benefits which flow from the collection of all these unidentifiable assets.

Cost of intangible assets

The determination of the cost of intangible assets is relatively straightforward for those purchased externally but far more complicated for those developed internally. For example, if Delta Company pays $200 million to acquire the patent for a new product, then the acquisition cost of the patent in Delta's accounts is $200 million. The cost of an identifiable intangible asset is the purchase price paid. Goodwill is normally purchased when one organisation acquires all or a significant portion of the net assets of another organisation. Goodwill is the excess of the amount paid for the fair value of the net assets acquired.

Many companies develop their own intangible assets, and establishing a cost for these assets is far more difficult. In the case of identifiable intangibles, the cost could include items such as legal fees to develop documents, e.g. patents and copyrights, registration costs of such documents and possibly any legal costs incurred in successfully defending the ownership of the asset. In the case of goodwill, the Accounting Standards prohibit the recognition of internally developed goodwill.

Companies that develop intangible assets internally are keen to recognise such assets on their statements of financial position. Such companies are then not at a disadvantage when users compare their company to another which has purchased similar types of intangible assets. However, it is important that only those expenditures which provide economic benefits beyond the current period are recorded as an asset. Those expenditures where all the benefits are consumed in the current period should be recorded as an expense. Expenditures wrongly recorded as an asset will overstate current profit and understate future profits.

Research and development

Many companies spend large sums of money in the area of research and development (R&D). They may be hoping to discover a new product or process or to improve an existing product or process.

The accounting question is whether such expenditures should be recorded as assets or expenses. In theory, the answer should be determined by applying the definition and recognition criteria for assets and expenses. Is it probable that future economic benefits will arise from the R&D expenditures? Does the company control such benefits and can the benefits be reliably measured? In practice R&D expenditures are generally expensed as incurred. This is largely due to the uncertainty about the probability of future economic benefits from R&D expenditures.

If all R&D expenditures are expensed, does this mean that no future economic benefits will flow to the organisation? Of course the answer is no, but in theory the expensing of all R&D expenditures is essentially conveying this message to users of financial statements.

Patents

This is a legal right granted to one person or company for the exclusive use of a certain product or manufacturing process. When a company develops a new product (through research and development) it will register a patent. The legal life of a patent is 16 years, but of course its useful life may be shorter as new products are developed to compete against it. A company with a patent can then sell the right to manufacture and sell the product to others. Thus, the patent can be a valuable asset. How would you have liked to have been the owner of the patent on products like the television, the camera or the electric shaver?

Copyright

Copyright provides protection to the creators of original work, which could be a book like this one, films, songs, music or computer games. For a small fee a copyright can be registered. Other parties are then not permitted to copy such original work without paying a royalty to the creator. Elvis Presley's estate continues to earn millions of dollars in royalties for his music, despite Elvis having been dead for over 20 years.

Trademarks or brand names

The costs of creating a trademark or brand name may be relatively small and would include costs paid to an artist, or advertising agency, and a small registration cost. However, the values of such trademarks and brand names can be huge. How much would you pay for the use of the name 'Coca-Cola'?

Franchises

A franchise provides the franchisee with the exclusive right to sell or distribute a certain product. For example, McDonald's and Hungry Jack's are conducted through franchise arrangements. A manager of a McDonald's store pays a franchise fee. This would be recognised on the statement of financial position as an asset for the amount paid.

Amortisation of intangible assets

The treatment of intangible assets once they are recognised on the statement of financial position is quite a controversial issue. Some argue that intangible assets are no different from tangible assets in that they have a finite life during which the economic benefits are consumed. This consumption of economic benefits should be recognised as an expense in a similar fashion to the depreciation of tangible non-current assets. Others argue that the life of some intangible assets such as brand names is extremely long, and amortisation (write-off) is not appropriate.

Accounting Standards require that purchased goodwill be amortised over a period not exceeding 20 years. There is no specific Accounting Standard in Australia dealing with identifiable intangible assets. The IASC issued *IAS38: Intangible Assets* in 1998, which covers identifiable intangible assets, but the Australian Standard setters have yet to issue a standard on the topic. However, the general requirements for the depreciation of non-current assets would indicate that the cost of identifiable intangibles should also be written off over their expected useful life.

The methods available to amortise intangible assets are the same as those used for tangible non-current assets such as property, plant and equipment. The term 'amortisation' has essentially the same meaning as depreciation, i.e. the systematic allocation of the cost of the intangible asset over its expected useful life. The straight-line method of amortisation is now required for goodwill in Australia and the formula is:

$$\text{Amortisation amount} = \frac{\text{cost of intangible asset} - \text{residual value}}{\text{useful life in years}}$$

The amortisation amount is recorded as an expense in the statement of financial performance and as a reduction in the cost of the asset. An accumulated amortisation account is generally not used for intangible assets. These assets are generally not replaced at the end of their useful life and information about the estimated useful lives of intangibles is included in the notes to the accounts.

Rules switch to 'cost' billions

by Mark Fenton-Jones

NEW international accounting rules on the valuation of intangible assets could wipe billions of dollars off the balance sheets of some of Australia's leading companies.

The new rules, approved by the London-based International Accounting Standards last July, are likely to be adopted by the Australian Accounting Standards Board (AASB) as part of its harmonisation of international accounting standards program, although implementation could still be some time off.

The Australian Securities and Investments Commission wants the new rules introduced as soon as possible, but is facing strong opposition from the accounting profession.

The new international rule assumes a straight-line depreciation of an intangible asset over 20 years. It also requires companies to revalue intangible assets if there is an active market, but this is not always the case with intangible assets. Intangible assets predominantly fall into 3 broad categories: trademarks and brand names; patents and mastheads; and media (television and radio) licences. It also covers program rights, liquor licences and telecommunication licences.

The most popular treatment is to measure trademarks and brand names at cost and to amortise on a straight-line basis over the period of expected benefits.

The new rule would mean 2 major accounting policy adjustments for many large Australian companies—the reversal of previous revaluations of intangible assets where no active market exists for the exchange of those intangible assets; and the need to amortise all intangible assets over their useful life, with a 20-year rebuttable presumption.

'If you can justify the useful life is longer than 20 years, then you can depreciate it over a longer period,' said Mr Stig Enevoldsen, chairman of the International Accounting Standards Committee, the group that is leading the global harmonisation process of financial reporting.

Australian companies with significant identifiable intangible assets (excluding goodwill) as at 30 June, 1998, include News Corporation ($24.9 billion or 45.72% of total assets), Publishing and Broadcasting ($2.6 billion or 70% of total assets) and John Fairfax ($1.2 billion, or 60% of total assets).

New research by Deloittes shows that the new valuation rules would have shaved a total of $1.3 billion off last year's financial reports of News Corporation, John Fairfax, Publishing and Broadcasting, Seven Network, Fosters, Cable & Wireless, Optus, BHP, CSR and Pacific Dunlop.

Use of the standard would have cut $1 billion off News Corporation's operating profit alone for the year ended 30 June 1998.

Australian Financial Review, 2 June 1999

Commentary

The article highlights the impact on reported profits if new rules on accounting for intangible assets are adopted. The issue, then, is whether such changes will impact on a company's share price. One argument holds that, because it is only the way profit is reported and not the actual profit that has changed, there should be no effect on share prices. This is consistent with an efficient market (discussed in Chapter 14). The alternative argument is that share prices will fall owing to the fall in profits. The impact this may have on certain contractual arrangements of a company is discussed in Chapter 1. Research would favour the efficient market argument, but there may be some companies whose share prices will fall.

Summary

In this chapter we have reintroduced the definitions of assets and of non-current assets and have examined some of the problems associated with arriving at the cost of a non-current asset and estimating the useful life and the residual value. We have also considered the nature of depreciation, why it is charged to the statement of financial performance, and the way in which it is treated in the statement of financial position. We have seen that there are two methods of depreciation in common use and we have examined the differences between them and the effects on the statements of financial performance and financial position. We have discussed and illustrated the way in which a sale of a non-current asset is dealt with in a worksheet. Finally, the notion of intangible assets was discussed and examples provided.

References

Australian Accounting Standards Board and Public Sector Accounting Standards Board. *Statement of Accounting Concept No. 4: Definition and Recognition of the Elements of Financial Statements*, March 1995.

Australian Accounting Standards Board. *AASB 1021: Depreciation*, August 1997.

Hicks, Sir John, 1946. *Value and Capital*, Clarendon Press.

International Accounting Standards Committee. *IAS 38: Intangible Assets*, October 1998.

Further reading

Colditz, B.T., Gibbons, R.W., and Noller, G.C., 1988–89. *Australian Accounting*, 4th edn, McGraw-Hill, Chapter 14.

Review questions

1   What is the purpose of depreciation?

2   Why is it unlikely that depreciation will provide for replacement of a non-current asset?

3   What factors need to be taken into account in determining the useful life of an asset?

4   On what basis do we decide what should and should not be included in the cost of a non-current asset?

5   Describe what is meant by the net book value and the written-down value of an asset.

6   What are the assumptions underlying the two main methods of depreciation?

7   An expense has been defined as a past or expired benefit. In what way does depreciation differ from other expenses?

8   What is the difference between identifiable and unidentifiable intangible assets? Give examples.

Problems for discussion and analysis

Poge 526

1 Refer to the Woolworths financial report in Appendix 1.
  a What is the accumulated depreciation/amortisation at June 1999 on
    i land and buildings   *Page*
    ii leasehold improvements   *518*
    iii plant and equipment?
  b What is the expected useful life of
    i buildings
    ii fixtures, fittings and plant?
  c What method of depreciation does the company use?
  d What is the amount of depreciation expense on plant and equipment for 1999?

2 A widget machine is purchased and expected to have a residual value of $20 000 at the end of its eight-year useful life. If the machine were depreciated on a straight-line basis and sold at the end of four years for $88 000, giving a gain of $4000 over book value, what was the cost of the machine?

3 The following data relates to plant owned and operated by the Bazmic Company.

	$,000
Accumulated depreciation, 31 December 20X8	750
Accumulated depreciation, 31 December 20X9	1 025
New plant acquired on 31 December 20X9	500
Gain on disposal of old plant, 31 December 20X9	50
Depreciation on plant for year ended 31 December 20X9	500
Balance in plant account 31 December 20X8	2 000
Balance in plant account 31 December 20X9	2 100

How much was the old plant sold for?

4 Anwar (Perth) Ltd purchased a machine from a company in Sydney. The machine cost $30 000; transport to Perth cost $1000; site works for the machine cost $2000; and insurance to cover damage on the trip was $500. While the machine was being installed it was damaged through careless handling. The machine cost $4000 to repair. The machine was expected to have a useful life of ten years, with a salvage value of $1000.
  a Calculate depreciation expense for the first two years using
    i the straight-line method, and
    ii the declining-balance method.
  b Which method would you expect to have the greatest impact on the company's profit/loss?

5 Using a worksheet, draw up the statement of financial position and statement of financial performance for the business whose transactions are set out below.
  Month 1 Bert put in $9000 of his own money and transferred his own car into the name of the business. At the time of the transfer it would have cost $6000 to buy a new model of the same car, but as the car was one year old its secondhand value was only $4000. The business then bought a machine for $4000, paying cash, and at the same time bought a second machine on credit terms. The credit terms were a deposit of $1000 which was paid in cash and two equal instalments of $900 payable at the start of months 4 and 7 respectively. The cash price of the machine was $2500.

Month 2 Bought raw materials for $3000 and paid cash and made cash sales of $3000.

Month 3 Paid rent in arrears for the three months, amounting to $600 in cash. Paid wages of $1500 for the three months to date. Made cash sales of $4000 and purchased more raw materials, again for cash, amounting to $8000.

Month 4 Paid instalment on machine of $900 in cash and made cash sales of $4000.

Months 5–7 Bought raw materials for cash for $2000 and made cash sales of $5000, paid wages for three months of $1500, the rent for three months ($600) and the second and final instalment on the machine of $900.

Months 8–12 Made cash sales of $14 000, bought raw materials for cash for $6000, paid wages for six months of $3000, and paid rent for three months of $600.

At the end of the year Bert has raw materials in inventory which cost $2000. He calculates that the car will last two more years, after which he will be able to sell it for $400. The machines have useful lives estimated at three years and will then be sold for $100 each. Since Bert is not very good with figures, he opts for straight-line depreciation on all the non-current assets.

6   A company purchased four machines during 20X5 and 20X6 and it used different methods of allocating depreciation on each. The following information is available:

Machine number	Date acquired	Cost $	Estimated life	Residual value $	Depreciation method
1	29 June 20X5	8 600	8 years	400	Straight-line
2	30 Oct. 20X5	7 800	4 years	300	Declining balance
3	15 Jan. 20X6	8 500	20 000 units	700	Units of production
4	30 Sept. 20X6	?	8 years	680	Declining balance

Machine Number 3 produced 3000 units in 20X6 and 5000 units in 20X7. Machine Number 4 had a $5880 invoice price. Freight charges on Machine Number 4 were $200 and were paid by the buyer. Machine Number 4 had to be placed on a special base which cost $380. The company's own employees installed Machine Number 4 and their wages during the installation period were $140.

Required:

Prepare and complete a table with the following headings, using twice the straight-line rate in depreciating Machine Numbers 2 and 4 (assume a 31 December balance date).

Machine number	20X5 depreciation	20X6 depreciation	20X7 depreciation

(Adapted from B. Colditz and R. Gibbins, *Australian Accounting*, 3rd edn, McGraw-Hill, 1976.)

7   The Fairhead Company, owned by Gordon Fairhead, is a manufacturer of electrical equipment. At 31 December 20X7, the non-current assets of the business were as follows:

	Date acquired	Cost $	Residual value $	Useful life years	Accumulated depreciation $
Building A	1 Jul. 20X3	252 000	12 000	20	54 000
Machinery	1 Jan. 20X4	29 000	1 000	7	16 000
Office equipment	1 Jul. 20X5	14 000	1 500	5	6 250
Delivery equipment	1 Apr. 20X4	40 000	4 000	4	33 750
Land	1 Jul. 20X5	68 000			

During 20X8, the following transactions took place:

1 Jan. Purchased for $160 000 a tract of land and three buildings. An independent appraiser's report on this property showed a total valuation of $200 000, broken down as follows: land, $100 000; building B, $40 000; building C, $50 000; and building D, $10 000. The appraisal indicated a useful life of 20 years for buildings B and C, and five years for building D, with no residual value for any of the three.

2 Jan. Building D was demolished to make room for construction of a new storage building. The necessity of this move had been taken into consideration by management when purchasing the property. The expense was nominal.

1 Apr. Purchased new delivery equipment with a list price of $27 000. Paid nothing initially, but signed an agreement for $28 620. This amount was payable in 12 equal monthly instalments of $2385 each. Useful life of this equipment was estimated at four years, residual value at $1800. The old delivery equipment was retained for emergency use.

1 Jul. Construction of a new storage building, E, was completed at a contract price of $28 000. The building was erected by the Fairhead Construction Company owned by Robert Fairhead, brother of Gordon Fairhead. Gordon Fairhead stated that other contractors had bid $50 000 or more to do the job. Payment was made by delivery of marketable securities acquired five years previously at a cost of $20 000. Stock market quotations indicated a present value of $28 000. The life of building E was estimated as 20 years, with no residual value.

1 Oct. Purchased additional office equipment for $7500 cash. Estimated useful life, five years; residual value, $500.

Required:

Prepare a depreciation schedule to compute the 20X8 depreciation expense. Use the following headings.

Type of asset	Date of acquisition	Cost	Residual value	Amount to be depreciated	Useful life	Accumulated depreciation 31 Dec. 20X7	Depreciation expense 20X8

In this schedule, use a separate line for each of the four depreciable items owned at 31 December 20X7, and a separate line for each unit of plant and equipment acquired during 20X8. For assets acquired during the year, compute depreciation for an appropriate fraction of the year, including the month in which the acquisition occurred.

8   In each of the following situations discuss the most appropriate method of depreciation, giving reasons for your choice.

   a   *Land and buildings*: The land was purchased for $300 000, and $400 000 was spent on the erection of the factory and office accommodation.

   b   *Motor vehicles*: The business owns a fleet of cars and delivery vans, all of which were bought new. The owners have decided to trade-in the vehicles for new models after four years or 60 000 kilometres, whichever is sooner. The anticipated kilometre figures are 12 000 kilometres per annum for the cars and 20 000 kilometres per annum for the vans.

   c   *Plant and machinery*: The plant and machinery owned by the business can be broadly classified into three types as follows.

   • Type 1: Highly specialised machinery used for supplying roller bearings to Manicmotors Ltd. The contract for supply is for five years, after which it might be renewed at the option of Manicmotors. The renewal would be on an annual basis. The machinery is so specialised that it cannot be used for any other purpose. It has an expected useful life of ten years and the residual value is likely to be negligible.

   • Type 2: Semi-specialised machinery which is expected to be productive for ten years and have a residual value of 10 per cent of its original cost. However, other firms operating similar machines have found that after the first three years it becomes increasingly costly in terms of repairs and maintenance to keep them productive.

   • Type 3: General-purpose machinery which has an estimated useful life of 80 000 running hours. At present levels of production the usage is 6000 hours a year, but as from next year this is expected to rise to 8000 hours a year if the sales forecasts are correct.

9   Multiplex Ltd used its own construction crew to extend its existing factories. What would be the correct accounting treatment for the following?

   a   Architects' fees.

   b   Cost of debris removed during construction, due to a storm. *yes*

   c   Cash discounts received for payment of materials purchased for *reduce ym cost* construction before the invoiced due date.

   d   Cost of building a workshop that will be demolished once the extensions have been completed. *– include*

   e   Interest on money borrowed to finance construction. *yes*

   f   Government land taxes on the portion of land to be occupied by the new extensions for the period of construction. *yes include*

   g   The cost of errors made during construction. *. no*

   h   Overhead costs of the construction department, including supervision, *yes* depreciation on buildings and equipment of construction department, electricity, water, and allocation costs for the cafeteria, medical office and personnel department.

   i   Cost of workers' compensation insurance during construction and the cost of damages on any injuries not covered by insurance. *no*

10 Kent Pty Ltd purchased a new machine for its manufacturing plant. While it was clear that both the invoice price of the machine and the transport costs of bringing the machine to the manufacturing plant should be brought to account, there was some uncertainty surrounding the treatment of the following items.

a Installation costs of reinforced steel to support the new machine, which is heavier than the machine it is replacing. Should this cost be charged to the building, added to the cost of the machine, or treated as an expense?

b An outside fitter was called in to assist with the installation of the machine because the regular maintenance crew were unable to do it. Costs of the fitter included his fee, transport, accommodation and meals. The supervisor of the maintenance crew and a senior engineer both spent a considerable amount of time assisting the fitter. Before the new machine was working properly, a large quantity of materials had been ruined during trial runs. How should all of these costs be treated?

c A state sales tax was paid when the machine was purchased. Should this be included in the machine's cost?

d Part of the finance agreement between Kent Pty Ltd and the machine manufacturer was a trade-in on the old machine as part payment. The amount given for the trade-in exceeded the depreciated value of the old machine in the books of Kent Pty Ltd. Should the difference be treated as a reduction in the cost of the new machine or a gain on disposal of the old one?

11 A firm which manufactured office equipment sold approximately 30 per cent of its products (in dollar volume) and leased the rest. On average, the equipment was leased for five years; the initial cost of the leased equipment was recorded as an asset and was depreciated over the five years. The company assisted its customers in installing the office equipment and provided a regular maintenance service; both these services were provided free of charge and recorded as a service expense. Service costs averaged about 7 per cent of the sales value of a piece of office equipment, but about 25 per cent of the first-year rental revenue of a leased piece of equipment. Over the past year, the company's installation of office equipment grew rapidly, but because the service cost was such a high percentage of lease revenue, reported income showed no increase at all. Research and development costs were treated as expense as incurred. Should the same principle apply to service costs, or could these costs be added to the asset value of leased office equipment and amortised over the lease period? If so, should other service costs relating to leased office equipment be treated in the same manner?

(Problems 9–11 adapted from R. Anthony and J. Reece, *Accounting: Text and Cases*, 8th edn, Richard D. Irwin Inc., 1988, Chapter 7, Case 7–2.)

12 George Swain is interested in buying a computer-manufacturing business and has found two viable businesses for sale. Both businesses began operations three years ago, each with an invested capital of $450 000. A significant portion of the assets of each company comprises a building with an original cost of $150 000 and an estimated useful life of 60 years, and machinery with an original cost of $150 000 and an estimated useful life of 30 years. There is nil residual value.

The first business (A Ltd) uses straight-line depreciation while the second business (B Ltd) uses the reducing-balance method. The nature of products, other characteristics of operation and accounting policies of the two businesses are the same.

Figures from the financial statements for the three years show the following net income results.

Year	A Ltd	B Ltd
	$	$
1	31 500	30 000
2	34 650	33 150
3	38 100	36 450

George asks your advice as to which business he should buy. He is inclined to choose A Ltd because of its higher net income earnings, but he is impressed with B Ltd's higher cash supply and stronger working-capital position. Both businesses are on the market for the same price. B Ltd uses double the straight-line depreciation rate in applying the reducing-balancing rate.

Required:

a   Calculate the depreciation recorded by each business in the first three years. Round off depreciation expense to the nearest dollar.

b   Prepare a report for George outlining which business in your opinion is the most viable and why.

(Adapted from B. Colditz and R. Gibbins, *Australian Accounting*, 3rd edn, McGraw-Hill, 1976.)

13   Two brothers are planning to start a bakery in Melbourne and Sydney. They are contemplating the purchase of two stores currently owned by the same company and used as retail outlets for shoes. For this reason, the buildings and fixtures for both shops have the same cost, residual value and useful lives. They also plan to purchase the same type of equipment. The following schedule provides details of the assets.

	Cost of each	Residual value of each	Useful life of each
	$	$	$
Building	408 000	8 000	40 years
Fixtures	40 000	5 000	5 years
Equipment	34 000	2 000	8 years

In addition each building will need to be renovated at a cost of $40 000. The estimated statements of financial performance for the first year for the two shops have been separately determined by each brother and are shown in the schedule below.

SYDNEY

Projected statement of financial performance for year ended 31 December 20X1

	$	$
Sales		380 000
Cost of goods sold		200 000
Gross profit on sales		180 000
Operating expenses:		
Salaries expense	60 000	
Depreciation expense:		
Building	20 400	
Fixtures	16 000	
Equipment	8 500	
Building renovation	40 000	
Other expenses	8 000	
Total expenses		152 900
Net profit		27 100

MELBOURNE

Projected statement of financial performance for year ended 31 December 20X1

	$	$
Sales		380 000
Cost of goods sold		200 000
Gross profit on sales		180 000
Operating expenses:		
Salaries expenses	60 000	
Depreciation expense:		
Building	11 000	
Fixtures	7 000	
Equipment	4 000	
Other expenses	8 000	
Total expenses		90 000
Net profit		90 000

The brother who plans to open a store in Sydney does not understand how his projected profits can be so much lower than his brother's when they are projected to make the same sales, employ the same number of people, and spend about the same amount for other necessary operating items.

Required:

a Which depreciation method has each elected to use for their buildings, fixtures and equipment? Show the calculation of depreciation for each of the assets.

b How did each account for the $40 000 cost of renovation? Which is correct?

c Based on the projected statements of financial performance, which shop would you invest in? Lend money to?

Ethics case study

Bazley Manufacturing Company has two operating divisions, each producing different products. Company policy requires that capital expenditures of each division be approved by the company's budget committee if an expenditure exceeds $100 000. The manager of Excel Division, Adam Lake, received a memo from the budget committee in mid-April which stated that no more requests for capital expenditures above $100 000 would be considered for the remainder of that year because of the company's overall financial situation. Adam was very upset at the contents of the memo because he was about to request an approval to purchase a new machine for $200 000. He rang the chairman of the budget committee to see if an exemption could be made to allow the purchase of the new machine. The chairman said there would be no exemptions. Adam was upset because without the new machine his division would not be able to complete a large order for an important customer and the Excel Division would not meet its profit projections.

After giving some thought to the situation, Adam called in the division controller, Kylie Hansen, to find a solution. During their discussion, Adam came up with what he thought was a great idea. He told Kylie to order the new machine for delivery and installation by 1 May. Kylie would insist that the machine manufacturer charge the division for three separate components of the machine by means of three separate invoices, which should be written as if each invoice were for a different machine. He suggested that Kylie tell the machine manufacturer that Excel Division would take their business elsewhere if the manufacturer was not willing to charge with three separate invoices for the amounts of $69 000, $87 500 and $43 500. Under this plan, no one invoice would exceed $100 000, so the policy stated in the budget committee's memo would not be violated.

However, Kylie indicated some reluctance in carrying out this plan, pointing out that both she and Adam would have some serious explaining to do if the intentional deviation from company policy were discovered. As Excel Division controller, Kylie reported to Adam, the division manager, and the company controller. She realised that she could be in a difficult position if she did what Adam asked and it was later discovered that she did not inform the company controller about the situation. Despite Kylie's concerns, Adam insisted that his plan was the only solution to the Division's dilemma. He told Kylie to call in the order the next day and request the separate invoices for the three components of the machine. Kylie left Adam's office very worried and uncertain what to do.

Discuss:

a   who Kylie ultimately reports to

b   whether Kylie should agree, because if Excel does not purchase the machine the customer may go elsewhere and the company could lose a substantial profit

c   what Kylie should do.

Financing and Business Structures

Learning objectives

After completing this chapter you should be able to:

1 appreciate the importance of working capital to a business

2 discuss short-term sources of finance such as bank overdraft, trade credit and factoring

3 discuss medium-term sources of finance such as loans, hire purchase and leases

4 discuss long-term sources of debt finance such as long-term loans and debentures

5 explain what is meant by equity finance and how it varies according to the type of business organisation

6 understand that the costs of different sources of finance vary and depend on factors such as length of the time period involved, risk of the turnover and security available

7 understand what is meant by gearing, and the effect this can have on returns to shareholders in a company.

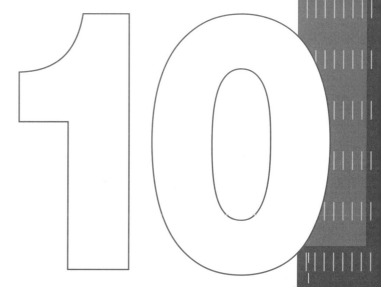

Introduction

So far the chapters have been mainly concerned with what an organisation does with an asset once it has been acquired. In this chapter we turn our attention to how the business raises the money to acquire its assets. The various types of finance available to different types of organisations are discussed, as are the effects of the finance mix on the returns to the owners.

We consider the different forms of finance used by a business and the effects of the organisational structure upon the sources of finance available. We also consider the financing structure of an organisation and its effect on financial risk. For these purposes, it is necessary to differentiate between business risk and financial risk.

Broadly speaking, business risk applies equally to all firms in an industry, with some variations according to size and diversity—i.e. it is industry-specific rather than firm-specific. Financial risk is more firm-specific; it relates to the financial structure of a business, i.e. the way in which it finances its assets.

Before commencing our discussion of the different types of finance, it is important to appreciate that the choice of appropriate finance can be vital to the long-term success of a business. Ideally, the type of finance should match the purpose for which it is to be used. For example, using what is essentially short-term finance for the purchase of a building merely creates problems when the financier has to be repaid. The building is still needed, and so replacement finance has to be found. Similarly, taking out a loan repayable over 20 years to buy an asset that is only going to be needed for a few years would leave the business in the position of having to pay interest on money it no longer needs. These are, of course, extreme examples, but they do serve to illustrate the point that the finance must be matched with the purpose for which it is to be used.

Key Concept 10.1

Type of finance

The finance used and the period of that finance should be matched to the period for which it is required and the purpose for which it is to be used.

Although any attempt to classify different types of finance is problematic, it is useful to look at some broad categories, and a division based on the period of finance is the one we have chosen to use. In considering the various forms of finance we shall endeavour to follow a pattern that provides a general description of the source of finance as well as a discussion of its uses, limitations, costs and availability.

Working capital

Working capital is represented by the current assets of a business minus its current liabilities. The management and funding of working capital is an important issue for all businesses. A business that fails to properly plan for its working capital requirements is likely to experience difficulties and could ultimately fail because of it. As discussed in Chapters 7 and 8, entities need to hold certain levels of inventories and debtors. Having the appropriate amount of inventories and the appropriate number of debtors is an important management concern. In order to be able to hold inventories and debtors, entities must be able to finance such assets. Remember, the statement of financial position tells us that assets equals liabilities and equity. In other words, to hold assets an entity must have equity or debt to finance such assets. In this chapter we examine the various sources of finance that can be used to fund working capital in addition to other assets, such as property, plant and equipment.

Short-term finance

Conventionally, short-term finance is seen as finance for a period of less than a year. It should be used to finance short-term capital requirements, such as working capital requirements, i.e. the financing of stock and debtors. A number of sources of finance are available, the most common being trade credit, bank overdraft and factoring.

Trade credit

We have already come across trade credit in Chapter 8, which dealt with debtors and creditors. Normally a supplier will allow business customers a period of time after goods have been delivered before requiring payment. The period of time and the amount of credit a business gets from its suppliers is dependent on a number of factors. These include the 'normal' terms of trade of that industry, the creditworthiness of the business and its importance to the supplier. Thus, for example, a small clothing retailer is likely to get less favourable terms than a major group such as Woolworths.

In general, trade credit, which is widely used as a source of finance, provides short-term finance. This is normally used to finance, or partially finance, debtors and stock. As such, its importance varies from industry to industry. For example, manufacturing industries, where there is greater investment in stock and work in progress, are more likely to rely on trade credit than are service industries. There may also be variations within an industry. For example, a restaurant is less likely to rely on trade credit than is a hotel, where a lot of money is tied up in stocks. In fact, within the licensed trade many hoteliers rely quite heavily on trade credit and this reliance makes them vulnerable if that credit is not managed effectively. Effective management in a small business setting requires a balance to be struck between taking advantage of trade credit and not being perceived as a slow payer. If too long a period is taken to pay, the supplier may subsequently impose less favourable terms. The temptation to extend the repayment date can lead to the withdrawal of any period of credit, which means that all supplies have either to be paid for in advance or on a cash on delivery basis. Ultimately, too heavy a reliance on trade credit can leave a business vulnerable to the supplier petitioning for bankruptcy or liquidation. Although suppliers are generally reluctant to take such steps, they will do so if they believe that they are more likely to recover their money by such a course of action.

Trade credit is often thought of as cost-free credit, which is not strictly true, as quite often suppliers allow a small discount for early payment. Therefore, using the full period to pay has an opportunity cost in the form of the discount foregone. This cost can be significant. For example, assume a supplier offers terms of 2/10 Net/30. This means that a 2 per cent discount is given if payment is received within ten days of receipt of the invoice; otherwise the net amount due is payable in 30 days. To forego the discount means a cost of 2 per cent is paid for a further 20 days' use of the money. This equates to an approximate cost of 36 per cent per annum, which is expensive. This opportunity cost has to be weighed against the availability of funds within the business, or the cost of raising additional funds. Unlike other forms of short-term finance, there is generally no requirement for security.

Key Concept 10.2

Trade credit

Trade credit is a form of short-term finance provided to a business by suppliers. It has few costs and security is not required.

Factoring

If a business makes sales on credit, it will have to collect payment from its debtors at some stage. Until that point, it will have to finance those debtors, either through trade credit, an overdraft, or its own capital. The costs of this finance can be very high and many small businesses will be hard up against their limits in terms of their overdraft and the amount and period of trade credit taken.

In Chapter 8 we discussed the importance of the management of debtors. Entities offer discounts for early payment as one strategy to manage the amounts owing by debtors. Another strategy used by some entities to reduce the money tied up in debtors is to approach a factoring company. A factoring company is a finance company which specialises in providing a service for the collection of payments from debtors.

Essentially, the way the system works is that the factoring organisation assesses the firm's debtors, in terms of risk and collectability. It then agrees to collect the money due on behalf of the business concerned. Once an agreement has been reached, the factoring company pays the business in respect of the invoices for the month virtually straight away. It is then the factoring organisation's responsibility to collect from the debtors as soon as possible. In this form of finance, the security provided by the business is in the form of the debts being collected. The factoring company charges for the service in the form of interest that is based on the finance provided, and by a fee for managing the collection of the debts. This form of finance is therefore more expensive than trade credit, but can be useful as it allows the business to concentrate on production and sales, and it improves the cash flow. Factoring, however, is not available to all industries. In some cases this is because it is inappropriate—as is the case in most retailing operations—while in others the factoring companies are reluctant to be involved because of a lack of clear legal definitions.

Key Concept 10.3

Factoring

Factoring provides short-term finance. Costs include an interest charge and a debt management charge. Finance is secured on the debtors and is provided by a finance company specialising in factoring. The finance company collects payment from the debtors.

Bank overdrafts

Banks provide short-term finance for working capital, either in the form of short-term loans or, more commonly, in the form of an overdraft. The difference is that a loan is for a fixed period of time and interest is charged on the full amount of the loan, less any agreed repayments, for that period. An overdraft, by contrast, is a facility that can be used as and when required and interest is only charged when it is used. Thus, if a business knows that it needs money for a fixed period of time then a bank loan may be appropriate. On the other hand, if the finance is only required to meet occasional short-term cash flow needs, then an overdraft would be more suitable. We discuss loans in more detail under the heading of medium-term finance.

Although many businesses use overdrafts as a semi-permanent source of finance this is not how the banks would like to see this form of finance used. Bank managers like to see a business bank account, on which an overdraft facility has been provided, 'swinging' between having money in the bank account and using the overdraft. They do not see an overdraft as a form of permanent working capital.

A bank overdraft carries with it a charge in the form of interest and often a fee for setting up the facility. The bank may also charge an annual fee for the overdraft facility. As far as the interest is concerned, the rate charged is related to the risk involved and the market rates of interest for that size of business. In general, the more risk involved, the higher the rate of interest. Because they operate in a volatile market, small firms tend to be charged higher rates of interest than large firms.

In addition, banks normally require security, which can take various forms. In the case of a small business the security could be a charge on the assets of the business. In many cases, however, the property is already subject to a charge as it is mortgaged. In these situations the bank may take a second charge on the property, or on the owner's home or homes if more than one person is involved. Alternatively, or in addition, the bank may require personal guarantees from the owner or, in the case of a limited company, the directors.

For larger companies, the security may be a fixed charge on certain assets, or a floating charge on all the assets. In the case of very large companies the risk involved is lower and the competition between the providers of finance is greater. Because of this competition, overdrafts tend to be cheaper and more accessible for large companies; and security is less of a factor.

Key Concept 10.4

Bank overdrafts

Bank overdrafts provide finance when it is needed to meet short-term cash flow needs. Costs include interest and often a set-up charge. In general, some form of security will be required—usually a fixed charge on certain assets or a floating charge on all assets.

Medium-term finance

There are a number of sources of medium-term finance for a business. We limit our discussion to medium-term loans, leases and hire purchase.

Loans

As we pointed out, bank loans are an alternative to overdraft finance for short-term finance requirements. In general, loans should only be used when finance is required for a known period of time. Ideally, that period should relate to the life of the asset or the purpose for which the finance is to be used. Loans can be obtained for short-term, medium-term or long-term finance. Compared to an overdraft facility, which can be used as and when needed, a loan is more permanent. Repayment of the loan is negotiated at the time the loan is taken out, and is generally at fixed intervals. Loans are often secured in the same way as overdrafts and, if the repayment conditions are not met, the lender will take action to recover the outstanding amount.

Bank loans are often granted for a specified purpose and limitations may be imposed regarding the use of the loan and the raising of other finance while the loan is outstanding. Unlike an overdraft, the cost of this form of finance is known in advance as interest accrues from the time the business borrows the money—irrespective of the fact that it may not use it straight away. In common with other forms of finance discussed so far, the rate of interest charged and the availability of this source of finance is dependent upon the size of the business and the lender's assessment of the risk involved. Thus, in general, the larger and more diversified a business, the easier will be its access to this form of finance.

Key Concept 10.5

Loans

Loans are generally made for a fixed purpose and a fixed period of time. They have set repayment dates and costs include interest and set-up fees. They are normally secured on assets.

Hire purchase

An alternative way of financing the acquisition of an asset is through the use of hire purchase. Under a hire-purchase agreement a finance company buys the asset and hires it to the business. Thus, a business can acquire the asset and use it, even though it has not yet paid for it in full. The finance company owns the asset during the period of the hire-purchase agreement.

The hirer has the right to use the asset and carries all the risks associated with using that asset. Thus, for example, if a car is purchased on hire purchase, the hirer would be responsible for all the repairs and costs associated with the use of the car in the same way as if they had bought the car directly. The ownership of the asset is transferred to the hirer at the end of the period of the hire-purchase agreement. A normal hire-purchase agreement consists of a deposit and a set number of payments over a number of years.

This type of finance can only be used when a specific asset is purchased, i.e. the finance is for a specified asset purchase and the amount borrowed is therefore limited by the price of the asset. Hire-purchase finance, therefore, cannot be directly used for financing working capital requirements or for any other purpose. The hire-purchase company actually pays the supplier of the asset directly and the asset belongs to the hire-purchase company. If repayments are not made in accordance with the hire-purchase agreement, the hire-purchase company has the right to repossess its property. The money borrowed is repaid by monthly instalments which include both a repayment of the capital borrowed and a charge for interest. The rate of interest charged will be dependent upon the market rate of interest, but is likely to be higher than the interest on a bank loan.

Key Concept 10.6

Hire purchase

Hire purchase is for a fixed period of time. Costs are in the form of interest charges. Ownership of the asset remains with the provider of the finance until all instalments are paid.

Hire purchase is available to all businesses and individuals, subject, of course, to the hire-purchase company being satisfied as to the creditworthiness of the person or business.

Leasing

A lease is an agreement between a lessor, the person who owns the asset, and a lessee, the person who uses the asset. It conveys the right to use that asset for a stated period of time in exchange for payment, but does not normally transfer ownership at the end of the lease period. The leases can vary from very short to very long periods. In common with hire purchase, this form of finance is tied to a specific asset. Thus, its use as a source of finance is limited to the purchase of capital items. Leasing companies often provide leases tailored to the needs of an industry. For example, in the hospitality industry it is possible to obtain lease finance for the internal telephone system or even the complete furnishing of a hotel.

In general the cost of leasing is similar to that of hire purchase. The major difference between the two types of finance is that, in general, leases tend to be for longer periods of time and are frequently used as sources of finance for specialised assets. In essence there are two distinct types of leases—operating leases and finance leases. An operating lease is the same in reality as renting the equipment, and usually applies to items such as photocopiers, computers, cars, etc.

Key Concept 10.7

Leasing

Leases are for a fixed period of time; the costs are in the form of interest charges. Security is related to the asset in question.

The underlying economic substance of a finance lease, on the other hand, is equivalent to borrowing money from a finance company and using that money to buy an asset. These differences are reflected in the definitions given in Key Concept 10.8.

Key Concept 10.8

Types of lease

An operating lease

A lease where the underlying substance of the transaction is a rental agreement.

A finance lease

A lease where the underlying substance of the transaction is a financing arrangement.

The reason for emphasising the difference between the two types of lease is that they are accorded different treatment in the accounts.

Operating leases present few accounting problems. The lessee records a lease payment as a decrease in cash and an increase in expenses. No asset or liability other than accrual at year end for the amount of the yearly lease payment owing as at balance date is recorded.

The most contentious issue has been whether certain leases which are non-cancellable should result in the recognition of an asset and a liability on the statement of financial position of the lessee. This is illustrated in Case Study 10.1.

CASE STUDY 10.1

	Company A $	Company B $
Assets		
Current Assets	100 000	100 000
Non-current Assets	1 900 000	1 400 000
Total Assets	2 000 000	1 500 000
Liabilities		
Current Liabilities	500 000	500 000
Non-current Liabilities	500 000	—
Total Liabilities	1 000 000	500 000
Net Assets	1 000 000	1 000 000
Shareholders' equity		
Paid up capital	500 000	500 000
Retained profits	500 000	500 000
	1 000 000	1 000 000

Commentary

The only difference between the statements of financial position of A and B is $500 000 in non-current assets and $500 000 in non-current liabilities. A has just borrowed $500 000 from the bank over a period of ten years. It has purchased an item of plant which has an estimated life of ten years with a zero residual value. B has just signed a lease agreement to acquire the use of an identical item of plant to that purchased by A. The lease agreement is for ten years and is non-cancellable by either party. Given these facts, should the statements of financial position of A and B be any different? In the statement of financial position, A shows total liabilities to shareholders' equity of 100 per cent. However, for B this ratio is only 50 per cent. This suggests that B is less risky than A, but is this a fair conclusion?

Case Study 10.1 demonstrates that the absence of information about the lease arrangements in the case of B could lead to an incorrect assessment of the relative risk positions of A and B. The fact that lease arrangements were traditionally not captured on the lessee's statement of financial position was pushed by leasing companies as a major advantage of leasing. This advantage is normally referred to as off-balance-sheet financing. As the name implies, it refers to a method whereby an entity obtains funds but the method used does not result in the recognition of a liability on the statement of financial position. Prior to the release of *AASB 1008*, entities could acquire the use of an asset via a finance lease, but were not required to recognise the liability to pay the lessor.

In response to the problem of leases, the accounting profession in Australia released *AASB 1008: Accounting for Leases*. This Standard requires a lessee to record a finance lease as an asset and a liability, which is the present value of the minimum lease payments. The present value of the lease payments, when the residual value is guaranteed by the lessee, equates with the fair value of the asset at the inception of the lease. A finance lease is defined (in paragraph 5) as one which:

> **effectively transfers from the lessor to the lessee substantially all the risks and benefits incident to ownership of leased property.**

The Accounting Standard also provides criteria to assist in the classification of a lease. A lease will normally be a finance lease when the lease is non-cancellable and:

a   the term of the lease is equal to 75 per cent or more of the expected useful life of the asset being leased; or

b   the present value of the minimum lease payments is equal to 90 per cent or more of the fair value of the lease asset at inception of the lease.

The asset recorded in the lessee's accounts is then amortised or depreciated to the statement of financial performance over a period equal to either the lease period or the asset's useful life. Each lease payment incorporates a principal and interest component; the interest component is treated as an expense. The liability is systematically reduced in each period by the principal component of each lease payment. Therefore, each lease payment is similar to the loan repayment that A would be required to make to the bank in Case Study 10.1.

Long-term finance

The number of alternative sources of long-term finance available is, to some extent, dependent on the type of organisation involved. We start our discussion with debt finance, such as long-term loans, which are more generally available, and then discuss equity finance. The latter discussion will be subdivided in terms of organisation types, i.e. sole proprietorships, partnerships and companies, as these affect the type of equity finance available.

Debt finance

This is the term given to any source of long-term finance that is not equity finance. Often, debt finance is seen exclusively as long-term interest-bearing finance. This is, in fact, a misconception, as all the finance we have discussed so far has been debt finance. We look at two broad categories of long-term debt finance, i.e. long-term loans, which are available to all organisations, and debentures and loan stock, which tend to be used by incorporated businesses.

Long-term loans

As we have said, loans can be used for short-term, medium-term or long-term finance. Interest rates are likely to be different for different loan periods as these will need to be adjusted to take into account the higher risk associated with lending money for a longer period of time. Long-term loans are often for a specific purpose, e.g. the purchase of property, and the time period is affected by the life of the asset, the repayments required and the willingness of the lender to lend money. For many small businesses these loans often take the form of a commercial mortgage on property. As is the case with all the other types of finance we have discussed, the availability of this source of finance is also heavily dependent upon the lender's assessment of the creditworthiness of the prospective borrower.

In the case of large companies, international groups and, in particular, multi-nationals, there is also the opportunity to raise funds from other markets around the world, as is evident from Case Study 10.2.

CASE STUDY 10.2

EXTRACT FROM WESTPAC BANKING CORPORATION ANNUAL REPORT 1999

Note 20. Debt issues

WESTPAC DEBT PROGRAMS

Access in a timely and flexible manner to a diverse range of debt markets and investors is provided by the following programs and issuing shelves:

Program/issuing shelf	Outstanding	Program/issuing shelf type
AUSTRALIA		
No limit	AUD 300 million	Debt issuance program
No limit	AUD 650 million	Subordinated debt issuance program
EURO MARKET		
AUD 2 billion	AUD 707 million	Asian debt program
USD 1 billion	USD 75 million	Euro certificate of deposit program
USD 3 billion	USD 560 million	Euro commercial paper program[1]
USD 7.5 billion	USD 6066 million	Euro medium term note[1]
JAPAN		
JPY 100 billion	Nil	Samurai shelf
JPY 100 billion	JPY 54 billion	Uridashi shelf
New Zealand		
NZD 750 million	NZD 210 million	Medium term note program[2]
NZD 500 million	NZD 100 million	Subordinated note program
UNITED STATES		
USD 4 billion	USD 2100 million	Commercial paper program
USD 2 billion	USD 466 million	Commercial paper program[2]
USD 4 billion	USD 2495 million	Medium term deposit program
USD 1.2 billion	USD 323 million	SEC registered shelf

[1] Westpac Trust Securities NZ Limited is also an issuer under this program.
[2] Sole issuer is Westpac Trust Securities NZ Limited.

Source: Westpac 1999 Annual Report

Commentary

This note shows that most of Westpac's loans are in US dollars. However, they do have other loans in Japanese yen, New Zealand dollars and Australian dollars.

Debentures

These terms refer to particular types of long-term loans to limited companies. They basically mean the same thing and are essentially long-term loan finance. The main difference between these and long-term loans is that interest tends to be at a fixed rate and repayment tends to be at a fixed point in time, rather than over the period of the loan as would be the case for a commercial mortgage or other long-term loan. Debentures are issued by the company raising the finance and can usually be traded on what are known as secondary markets. The price at which they can be sold and bought on the secondary market will not be the same as the price at which they were issued. This variation is related to changes in interest rates over time. In virtually all debenture deeds there is a right to repayment or appointment of a receiver if interest is not paid when due. The cost of this type of finance is similar to that for long-term loans and is affected by the market rate of interest, the security available, and the risk involved. For this reason, they are more commonly seen in the accounts of larger companies.

Key Concept 10.9

Debt finance—long-term

Long-term debt finance is generally for a fixed period of time and interest rates can be higher than for short- or medium-term.

Equity finance

The other major source of long-term finance is equity finance, and here we need to look at organisational types, as this can have a major effect on both the type and the amount of equity finance available.

Sole proprietorships

In the case of a sole proprietorship, as we have seen, the only sources of equity finance are those supplied by the owner, and the retained profits. In many small businesses, the amount of funds that the owner has available to put into the business is limited. This means that the only source of equity finance is retained profits. In a fast-growing business it is unlikely that there will be sufficient retained profits to finance expansion. As such, sole proprietorships, in common with many small businesses, become very reliant on debt finance and, as we see, this exposes them to more risk, as a downturn in the market, or an increase in interest rates, could have a dramatic impact on their ability to service the debt. Unlike debt finance, equity finance has no limitations in terms of the use to which it is put.

Partnerships

Partnerships, as the name implies, are organisations that are owned, and often managed, by a number of individuals. They are most common among professionals, and so we see doctors, dentists, lawyers, architects and, of course, accountants working in partnerships. In essence, the sources of equity finance for partnerships are the same as for sole proprietorships, i.e. money contributed by the owners and retained profits. There are, of course, more people involved, so more equity can be raised through contributions by the owners.

Partnerships are governed by the legislation contained in Partnership Acts and by case law. In general the main difference between partnerships and sole proprietorships is that, in a partnership, the partners are jointly and severally liable. This means that if a partner cannot pay his or her share of the debts, the other partners must pay. The other important difference is related to the division of profits, which must be divided amongst the partners in accordance with the partnership agreement.

We look at the subject of partnerships in more detail in Chapter 11. For our purposes here, we can view partnerships as having the same sources of equity finance as sole proprietorships. The only difference is that they are likely to have access to a greater supply of funds. In addition there may be differences in relation to the availability of retained profits as some partners may leave more profits in the business than others. This will, of course, depend upon the individual partner's requirements for funds.

Limited companies

Limited companies have the advantage, from an investor's point of view, that the liability of the owners is limited to the amount they have invested in the company. As with partnerships and sole proprietorships, the major source of equity comes from the owners. However, in the case of limited companies this is through the issue of ordinary shares.

Ordinary shares

In the case of companies, the amounts in shareholders' equity represent the shareholders' interest in the company. Some amounts have been directly contributed by the shareholders when they subscribe to shares issued by the company. This is described as issued and paid-up capital. The other amounts represent retained or undistributed profits and various reserves. Reserves can be created in a number of ways; however, one element common to all reserves is that there is no cash in them. Cash is an asset and appears in the current assets section of the statement of financial position.

You should now study Woolworths' financial statements. Look at the statement of financial position and then turn to Notes 19 and 20. Note 19 discloses that the company has issued 1 152 827 897 shares, with a collective value of $721.4 million. This is the book value of the share capital and does not represent the market value. The market value is obtained from the price of the shares on the stock exchange.

Note 20 provides details of the reserves, none of which represents cash. Capital profits reserve is an amount transferred from the asset revaluation reserve. The asset revaluation reserve is created when the value of an item of property, plant or equipment is increased to reflect an increase in value above cost. This is easily achieved by increasing both accounts by the same amount. The general reserve is also created by transferring an amount from the retained profits account. These entries are what accountants call a book entry. The share premium reserve has been reduced to zero and will no longer appear in statements of financial position from the year 2000 onwards. The foreign currency translation reserve arises from the translation of a foreign subsidiary's statement of financial position into Australian dollars.

The following article illustrates how the issuing of shares is one way that small businesses can raise much needed capital to finance expansion.

CASE STUDY 10.3

BinCom will bring forward expansion

BINCOM Satellite Systems said yesterday it planned to accelerate the expansion of its satellite communications network following a $4.5 million initial public offering.

The Perth company will issue up to 17 867 600 shares at 25 cents, with a free attaching option on the basis of one option for every two shares, to raise up to $4.5 million.

Another $1 million can be raised through oversubscriptions.

After the issue, BinCom will have 54 977 160 shares on issue (excluding oversubscriptions), giving it a market capitalisation of about $13.7 million.

BinCom began commercial services through a voice-and-data gateway from its first network control centre in Perth last June.

A second metropolitan centre is being deployed in Darwin to supply voice-and-data services to mining company clients in the Northern Territory.

It plans to launch a second gateway in Perth in the fourth quarter of 2000 to deliver high-speed broadband services such as interactive multimedia and online tele-education services.

BinCom said a third gateway for delivery of multipoint video-conferencing and tele-health services was planned.

Its high-speed voice-and-data satellite services, which have been deployed to four WA clients in the resource sector so far, use very small aperture technology (VSAT).

This provides a platform to carry both narrow band and broadband services to metropolitan and rural Australia.

Managing director Brenton Woods said VSAT technology was a low-cost flexible solution to the 'bandwidth gap' between metropolitan and regional Australia.

'The demand for new high-speed services is not being met in rural and remote regions of the country,' Mr Woods said.

AAP/Age, 15 September 2000

As with any other form of organisation, the other main source of equity capital is retained profits. Unlike a sole proprietorship or partnership, a company distributes its profits by way of dividends. The directors decide on the amount of dividend to be paid and the timing of the dividends, and until a dividend is declared by the directors, the shareholders have no *prima facie* right to a dividend. Dividends can be paid during the year and/or at the end of the year. If they are paid during the year they are referred to as interim dividends and the dividend at the end of the year is referred to as the final dividend. Dividends are treated differently from drawings which, as we have seen, are normally deducted from the owner's equity. These differences will be looked at in more detail in Chapter 11.

A company has the advantage over a sole proprietorship or a partnership in that it can issue shares to whoever it wishes in whatever proportions it wishes. The shareholders do not have to take part in the management of the company, and in most large companies the vast majority of shareholders play virtually no part in the management of the company. They merely invest their money and take the risk that they will get better returns, in the form of their share of the profits, than they would by investing in fixed interest investments. Ultimately, all the profits belong to the shareholders, so if they do not get their share of the profits in the form of dividends, i.e. the profits are retained in the company, their share of the profits and the future profits is reflected in the price at which they could sell their shares.

Preference shares

Apart from ordinary shares, a company can also issue preference shares. Unlike ordinary shares a preference share normally has a fixed dividend and even if more profits are made, the preference dividend remains the same. In addition they normally carry a right to preference in the order of payment in the event of the company going into liquidation. They are therefore less risky than ordinary shares and appeal to a different sort of investor. Whether these shares should be classified as equity or debt would depend on the particular type of preference shares in question and the rights attaching to them. Preference shares may be redeemable or non-redeemable. A redeemable preference share with a fixed redemption date is classified as debt in the statement of financial position. A non-redeemable preference share is classified as equity. They may carry a right to dividends on a cumulative basis, i.e. if the directors do not pay any dividends in a year the preference shareholders will have a right to be paid that year's dividend and any others that have not been paid, before the ordinary shareholders can be paid any dividend. Some preference shares are participating preference shares, whereby they get a share of profits if the profit is over a certain figure.

Key Concept 10.10

Equity finance

This is long-term permanent finance and comes from two main sources, i.e. contributed capital and retained profits.

Financing structures and financial risk

The mix of debt finance and equity finance is known as gearing, or leverage, and it affects the financial risk of an enterprise. Basically, the more reliant a business is on debt finance, i.e. the more highly geared, the greater the risk. The risk we are referring to here is that if interest rates go up or the profit margin comes down, the enterprise would not be able to pay the interest or repayments due on its debt finance. There are, of course, advantages to being highly geared as well as disadvantages, as Example 10.1 illustrates.

Example 10.1

Ellenmere has equity capital consisting of 20 000 ordinary shares of $1 each. It has retained profits of $10 000 and has $40 000 in loans on which interest at 3 per cent above bank base rate, which currently stands at 12 per cent, is due.

Roseview has equity capital consisting of 40 000 ordinary shares of $1 each. It has retained profits of $10 000 and has $20 000 in loans on which interest at 3 per cent above bank base rate, i.e. 15 per cent, is due.

Situation 1

Both companies make sales of $100 000 and their net profit before interest is 10 per cent on sales.

The statements of financial performance for the two companies would be as shown below.

	Ellenmere $	Roseview $
Sales	100 000	100 000
Costs	90 000	90 000
Net profit	10 000	10 000
Interest	6 000	3 000
Available for equity shares	4 000	7 000
Profit per share	0.20	0.17

The profit per share, which is normally referred to as earnings per share, is arrived at by dividing the profit by the number of shares in issue. Thus, for Ellenmere the profit of $4000 is divided by 20 000 shares to arrive at the profit per share of 20 cents. The ordinary shareholders of Ellenmere are getting a better return than the shareholders of Roseview—20 cents per share, as compared to 17 cents per share in Roseview. This is despite the fact that both companies have the same sales, costs and net profit. The differences arise as a result of the financing structure, its effect on the interest charges and the remaining profit after interest.

Situation 2—Increased costs

In this situation, instead of making a net profit before interest of 10 per cent of sales, the companies find that they can only make 8 per cent.

In this case the statements of financial performance of the two companies would be as follows.

	Ellenmere $	Roseview $
Sales	100 000	100 000
Costs	92 000	92 000
Net profit	8 000	8 000
Interest	6 000	3 000
Available for equity shares	2 000	5 000
Profit per share	0.10	0.13

The profit margin of both businesses has fallen by the same amount. As a result, the profit available for the equity shares has dropped in both cases. However, the effect on the profit per share is more dramatic in the case of Ellenmere than it is in the case of Roseview, due once again to the effects of the financing structure. Thus, although in Situation 1 it looked as though Ellenmere had the better financing structure, we find from a shareholder's point of view that it is more vulnerable to a reduction in the profit margin than Roseview.

Situation 3—Increased interest rates

In this situation the facts are the same as in Situation 2 above, i.e. the net profit before interest is 8 per cent on the sales. However, in addition, the bank base rate moves to 13 per cent and the interest on the loans therefore moves up to 16 per cent.

In this case the statements of financial performance of the two companies would be as follows.

	Ellenmere	Roseview
	$	$
Sales	100 000	100 000
Costs	92 000	92 000
Net profit	8 000	8 000
Interest	6 400	3 200
Available for equity shares	1 600	4 800
Profit per share	0.08	0.12

Once again both businesses are affected by the change in circumstances. However, the effect of the rise in interest rates is greater, in terms of the return to the shareholders, in Ellenmere than it is in Roseview.

These examples illustrate the effects of high gearing, which are to increase the returns to shareholders but at the same time make them more vulnerable to decreases in the profit margin. In addition, their returns are also affected more by increases in interest rates than are those of a low geared company.

On the other hand, a fall in interest rates is more beneficial to the shareholders of a highly geared company. There is therefore a trade-off between risk and return.

It is worth mentioning that the lower the share of the business that is financed by equity, the more difficult it is to raise debt finance. Banks will often include clauses in debt contracts which impose penalties on borrowers if the proportion of debt to equity increases beyond a specified level. Such clauses mean that decisions on how much profit to retain, whether to revalue land and buildings etc. can have a dramatic effect on a company's ability to raise finance.

Summary

In this chapter we have considered the main types of short-term, medium-term, and long-term finance that are available to all organisations. We have also looked at equity finance in the form of contributed capital and retained profits. The effects of different organisational forms on the sources of equity finance have been discussed, while the effects of the mix of debt to equity finance on the returns to equity shareholders have been discussed and illustrated. One vital point raised in this chapter was that the type of finance used should relate to the purpose for which that finance will be used.

Further reading

Arnold, J., Hope, T., Southworth, A., and Kirkham, L., 1994. *Financial Accounting*, 2nd edn, Chapter 8, Prentice Hall.

Berry, I., 1993. *Financial Accounting: An Introduction*, Chapter 11, Chapman & Hall Ltd.

Review questions

1   Why is it important to match the type of finance with the purpose of raising that finance?

2   What are the forms of short-term finance discussed in this chapter?

3   What are the main differences between equity finance and debt finance?

4   What are the differences between drawings and dividends?

5   What does the term 'highly geared' refer to?

6   What are the advantages and disadvantages of being highly geared?

7   Which types of short-term finance require a business to provide some form of security?

8   What form of security is required for each of the forms of short-term finance discussed in this chapter?

9   What is a lease? Give an example.

10 What are the diifferences between an operating and a finance lease?

Problems for discussion and analysis

1   Refer to the Woolworths financial report in Appendix 1.
    a   What are the net financing costs of the company in 1999?
    b   What are the minimum lease payments on leased equipment and premises for 1999?
    c   What is the value of goodwill and the accumulated amortisation? How much goodwill was expensed in 1999?
    d   What is considered by the company to be the useful life of a liquor licence? What method of amortisation is used?

2   ABC Ltd wishes to acquire a new widget machine. The machine costs $30 000 and is expected to have a useful life of five years and no residual value. As it is short of liquid funds, the company has approached a finance broker for help. It is offered two alternatives:
    i   a loan of $30 000 with an annual reducing-interest component of 20 per cent, the principal of the loan to be paid in equal annual instalments over five years at the same time the annual interest payments are made
    ii a hire-purchase agreement that requires the company to pay a monthly instalment of $799 over five years.

    Given there are no other options available to the company, which proposition should it accept?

3   A friend has been to see the bank manager about borrowing some money to finance the acquisition of a new van and a new machine. The bank manager has said that, in view of the current financial structure of the company, the bank would not be prepared to provide funds unsecured. The latest statement of financial position of the company is given below.

STATEMENT OF FINANCIAL POSITION

	$	$	$	$
Current assets				
Stock		36 000		
Cash		15 000		
Total Current Assets			51 000	
Non-current assets				
Equipment	60 000			
Less Accumulated depreciation	(15 000)	45 000		
Vehicles	36 000			
Less Accumulated depreciation	(12 000)	24 000		
Total Non-current Assets			69 000	
Total Assets				120 000
Current liabilities				
Trade creditors		7 500		
Taxation		10 800		
Bank overdraft		12 900		
Total Current Liabilities			31 200	
Non-current liabilities				
Bank loan		25 000		
Total Non-current Liabilities			25 000	
Total Liabilities				56 200
Shareholders' equity				
Ordinary shares ($1)		60 900		
Retained profits		2 900		
Total Shareholders' Equity				63 800
Total Liabilities and Shareholders' Equity				120 000

a   Advise your friend what alternative sources of finance are available and which would be appropriate for the purpose of buying a van and a new machine.

b   Explain why, in your opinion, the bank manager was not prepared to lend unsecured.

4   Ben was planning to open a fish and chip shop. He has produced the following projections for the first year, based on his experience of the area and some careful research.

	$
Sales	36 000
Cost of ten-year lease	30 000
Refurbishment	3 000
Equipment	20 000
Rent	2 000
Electricity	900
Wages	8 000
Personal drawings	5 000

Ben estimates that the costs of fish, etc. required to make the sales target of $36 000 will be $12 000. He says that the equipment will last for five years and have no residual value. He has $40 000 in savings but is reluctant to invest the whole of that. He has been offered a loan of $20 000 to help buy the lease, at an interest rate of 10 per cent per annum for the first year, with no repayments required during that year. After the first year the rate will be 4 per cent above base rate. Base rate currently stands at 12 per cent. Alternatively, he can borrow money, using a bank overdraft at a rate of 17 per cent per annum.

a   Calculate what Ben's profit would be if he were to put in all his own money and borrow anything else he needs. Hint: The receipts and payments have to be looked at in terms of their regularity and their timing.

b   Calculate what Ben's profit would be in the first year, assuming he takes the loan.

c   Calculate what Ben's profit would be in the second year, assuming he does not take the loan and sales and costs are the same as the first year.

d   Calculate Ben's profit in the second year, assuming he takes the loan.

Ben has asked you to advise him on the choice between the two alternatives. How would you advise him, and what reasons would you give?

5   In each of the cases below, decide whether the leases described are finance or operating leases for a lessee. Give reasons.

A

Motor vehicle leased for	3 years
Fair value (cost)	$10 000
Lease rental	$230 per month
Total lease payments	$8280
Estimated residual value	$6000 (60%)
Implicit interest rate	18%
Present value of minimum lease payments (no guaranteed residual)	$6500
Useful life	6 years
Useful life	50%
Present value of minimum lease payments	65%

B   Same particulars as above, except that this is the first time a motor vehicle has been leased. All previous vehicles have been purchased and sold three years later (there is a Union agreement that motor vehicles operated by employees must be no older than three years).

Useful life	50% or 100%
Present value of minimum lease payments	65%

C   Same particulars as in A above, but there is a guaranteed residual value of $6000. The present value of minimum lease payements therefore is $10 000.

Useful life	50%
Present value of minimum lease payments	100%

D   Same particulars as in A above, but the lessee guarantees the lessor that he will make up any deficiency of the residual amount between $4000 and $6000. The maximum present value of minimum lease payments is $7700.

Useful life	50%
Present value of minimum lease payments	77%

E   As in D above, except that there is no guaranteed residual and the lessee can cancel (subject to conditions) at any time.

Useful life	50%
Present value of minimum lease payments	65%

6   Ladner Pty Ltd (Leasing Brokers) is a small company with 24 employees which negotiates leasing arrangements with lessors. Its clients are small- to medium-sized businesses.

The managing director of Ladner, L. Murrish, had recently overheard, at a cocktail party, a discussion of the future prospects of leasing following the introduction of a statutory-approved accounting standard which requires increased disclosures of lease commitments by lessees. Concerned at what he heard at the party, Murrish invited the company accountant, A. Hill, and marketing manager, C. Raby, into the conference room to discuss the issue. The following dialogue occurred between these three.

Murrish: This approved accounting standard I hear of requiring additional disclosures has me a little concerned about the industry's future prospects. How will leasing be affected by these mandatory requirements?

Raby: Well, I am glad you have asked me that question. I am really concerned about the implications of the new requirements but I did not wish to worry you about them due to your recent poor health.

Murrish: Forget that talk! Just level with me for once.

Raby: All right! Look, our business is mainly in arranging finance leases. In the past, the lease costs associated with such leases were commonly left off the statement of financial position. This is why leasing has become so popular over the last 20 years. In fact, I would go so far as to argue that this is the only reason why leasing has been a growth industry.

Murrish: But surely there are other reasons, such as tax advantages, flexibility and lower costs in many cases, compared with alternative forms of finance.

Raby: Oh yes! There are other advantages, but I believe that most of our clients leased in the past because they could keep large assets off their statements of financial position, thus ensuring the apparent rate of return was higher. Of course, the commitments themselves were also not included among the liabilities, ensuring the apparent leverage level was lower. Lower leverage means ...

Murrish: That's enough! For a marketing manager, you are sounding a bit too pessimistic for my liking. I think finance leasing should continue to run at the same level because it's easy, quick, the price is usually right, the term of amortisation is generally the actual life of the equipment, and, very importantly, there's no other security required. We will just have to push these advantages much harder to generate the same volume of business.

Hill: Just a moment! I think both of you have missed a very important point concerning the new disclosures. The accounting standard does not require those leases considered to be of an operating nature to be capitalised in the statement of financial position. In other words, costs associated with operating leases may remain off the statement of financial position.

Murrish: Go on, please. This sounds interesting.

Hill: Well, I think the company should seek out those lessors which package leases as operating leases. Operating leases are defined as those where substantially all of the risks and benefits incident to ownership of the asset

> remain with the lessor. I believe a number of lessors are restructuring their leasing packages to get around the guidelines provided in the accounting standard. In fact, I saw an advertisement in this morning's newspaper which promoted a lease as being outside the capitalisation guidelines. We have conducted business with this lessor before and found it to be most satisfactory.

Murrish: I am so pleased someone in the office remains up to date with trends in the industry. Now that we have a clear understanding of the issues, I want our marketing department to send out a letter to all our clients outlining the following: 'The benefits associated with operating leases as opposed to a finance lease are now being recognised by firms as a way of assisting their statement of financial position presentation due to their leverage and rate of return implications.'

Raby: Do you wish to add anything about those other advantages of leasing you mentioned earlier?

Murrish: Do you still want to be a marketing manager?

Required:

a   Outline the advantages and disadvantages of leasing.
b   In your view, has Raby's argument been rightfully rejected by Murrish? Justify your opinion.
c   Is Hill's perception of changes in lease packaging by lessors supported by any available evidence?
d   How do you believe clients of Leasing Brokers would react upon receiving the letter referred to from the marketing department?
e   If a client of Leasing Brokers was a listed company with significant finance leases, how would you have expected the market to react to the company upon the day the accounting requirements of the standard on leasing became known?

(Adapted from G. Carnegie, J. Gavens and R. Gibson, *Cases in Financial Accounting*, revised edn, Harcourt Brace & Company, 1991, Case 86.)

Ethics case study

Jack is finance director for the New Horizons Company. The company has had declining profits for the past two years, and is in serious trouble in the current year. With just two weeks before year end, the company is set to report a loss. If this occurs, it will be in default of a loan contract with its major bank, which will result in the bank appointing an official manager to begin winding up the company. At the end of the previous year the bank had been persuaded to allow the company another year to trade out of its difficulties after reporting a small loss. This is not likely to happen this year if the company reports a larger loss. Jack has developed the following plan: New Horizons will sell $1 million worth of goods for $2 million to Close Encounters Ltd, which is a company run by his brother-in-law. The $1 million profit on the sale will allow New Horizons to report a modest profit for the year. At the same time a put option will be given to Close Encounters, giving that company the right to sell the goods back to New Horizons in three months for $2 100 000. The goods will actually remain in New Horizons' warehouse for the three months.

Discuss:

a   how the transaction with Close Encounters should be recorded

b   whether the bank would still be able to appoint an official manager if New Horizons records the transaction as a sale and thus reports a profit

c   whether Jack's plan is ethical.

Final Accounts, Partnerships and Companies

Learning objectives

At the end of this chapter you should be able to:

1 understand the role of debits and credits

2 understand the relationship between the worksheet approach and the use of debits and credits

3 explain the role of journals, ledgers and a trial balance

4 explain the difference between a sole proprietorship, a partnership and a company

5 explain the advantages and disadvantages of a partnership and a company form of organisation

6 understand the major differences between the financial statements of a sole proprietor, partnership and company

7 understand the meaning of extraordinary items.

Introduction

The first section of this chapter has been included to assist readers who wish to continue with their studies using other textbooks, which are likely to use a more traditional approach for explaining accounting and its mechanics. It will also be helpful to readers who are familiar with that traditional approach as an aid to understanding how the exposition in this book relates to that in other texts. In the next part of the chapter we move on to look at the trial balance and the final adjustments required before final accounts are extracted from the worksheet. In the remainder of the chapter we consider alternative formats of final accounts and how they relate to different forms of organisation. We consider the advantages and disadvantages of the different organisational forms available, and examine the ways in which the presentation of accounting information differs. Before these new areas are discussed, however, we examine the traditional approach to accounting found in other textbooks and compare it with the worksheet approach.

The traditional approach

In this approach, instead of using columns to portray the individual accounts in an organisation's accounting system, these are represented by T accounts. In many basic bookkeeping courses these T accounts form a major part of the course and students are required to spend a lot of time practising entries to these accounts. Often this is done on the basis of rote learning. It is further complicated by the terminology used: 'debits' and 'credits'.

For people studying accounting for the first time, the worksheet approach has been shown to be superior. Moreover, it is more in line with the increasing use of electronic spreadsheets. However, experience has shown that those who already know something of accounting often experience initial problems in converting from one representation of an accounting system to another. In this chapter we work through a simple example to illustrate that the difference between the two methods is superficial and does not in any way change the principles involved.

Example 11.1

Phil started a business and during the first year the following transactions took place.

1   Opened a business account and paid in $10 000 of his own money.
2   Bought a van for $5000 and paid cash.
3   Bought goods for $35 000 on credit, of which $33 000 has been paid for at year end.
4   Sold goods for $45 000, all for cash.
5   Had goods in inventory at the end of the year which cost $4000.
6   Paid expenses on the van of $1000.
7   Paid rent on his premises of $1500.

Let us see what the worksheet looks like for Phil's business and we will then see how the same transactions are represented under the traditional method.

PHIL'S BUSINESS WORKSHEET: VERSION 1

| Transaction | Assets | | | | = Liabilities + | Equity | |
	Cash	Prepaids	Van	Inventory	Creditors	Profit and loss	Equity
1	10 000						10 000
2	–5 000		5 000				
3				35 000	35 000		
	–33 000				–33 000		
4	45 000					45 000	
5				–31 000		–31 000	
6	–1 000					–1 000	
7	–1 500	1 500					
Balance	14 500	+ 1 500	+ 5 000	+ 4 000	= 2 000	+ 13 000	+ 10 000

You should make sure that you understand the entries on the worksheet before moving on. If you do have problems, refer back to the appropriate chapters.

Now we record the same transactions using the traditional T accounts.

Cash

Transaction 1	10 000	Transaction 2	5 000
Transaction 4	45 000	Transaction 3	33 000
		Transaction 6	1 000
		Transaction 7	1 500
		Balance c/d	14 500
	55 000		55 000
Balance b/d	14 500		

Inventory

Transaction 3	35 000	Transaction 5	31 000
		Balance c/d	4 000
	35 000		35 000
Balance b/d	4 000		

Prepaids

Transaction 7	1 500		

Van

Transaction 2	5 000		

Equity

		Transaction 1	10 000

Creditors

Transaction 3	33 000	Transaction 3	35 000
Balance c/d	2 000		
	35 000		35 000
		Balance b/d	2 000

Profit and Loss			
Transaction 5	31 000	Transaction 4	45 000
Transaction 6	1 000		
Balance c/d	13 000		
	45 000		45 000
		Balance b/d	13 000

c/d, carried down; b/d, brought down

If we examine the two systems carefully, we can see that they have recorded the same transactions. All that has changed is the way in which the recording is shown. This will be clearer if we explain some of the transactions and the ways in which they have been treated.

For example, in the worksheet, to deal with transaction 1 where Phil puts some money into the business, we opened columns entitled 'Cash' and 'Equity'. We then entered the amount involved, $10 000, in each of these columns. By contrast, under the traditional approach we opened two T accounts, one for cash and the other for equity. We then entered the amount involved, $10 000, in these two accounts. All that is happening is that, in contrast with the use of T accounts to represent accounts, the worksheet uses columns.

Using T accounts, it is perhaps less clear which side of the account the entry should go on. However, we can apply some simple rules to make the transposition of entries from the worksheet to debits and credits relatively straightforward. All pluses on the left side of the worksheet are recorded as debits and all minuses are recorded as credits. Debits are placed on the left-hand side of the T account and a credit on the right-hand side. The reverse situation applies on the right side of the worksheet, where all pluses are recorded as credits and all minuses as debits. Therefore transaction 1 is a debit for cash and a credit for equity.

Key Concept 11.1

Debits and credits

Under the traditional approach, assets are shown as debit balances and liabilities are shown as credit balances.

We now consider the way in which transaction 2, the purchase of the non-current asset, is dealt with. In the worksheet, a new column is opened for the asset and the cash column is reduced by the amount paid for the new asset, i.e. $5000. The traditional approach starts in the same way by opening a new account for the new asset, and puts the cost of $5000 on the left side because it is an asset. So far, the methods are essentially similar. The other half of the transaction is perhaps slightly more difficult to follow because we have to reduce the cash balance. This is done by putting the $5000 on the right-hand side of the cash account. This is called crediting an account—in this case we are crediting a cash account.

Even at this stage it is obvious that the worksheet is easier to follow beause it relies less on jargon and rote learning than the traditonal approach. Another advantage of the worksheet is that we know at the end of the exercise that the accounts are balanced; if they do not balance, the error can be found by working back through the worksheet as described in Chapter 6. In the case of the traditional approach we do not yet know if our accounts balance, so we have to extract what is commonly known as a trial balance. If, having extracted this trial balance, we found that it did not balance we would have to check through the entries in our accounts to find the error. It is to be hoped that that will not be the case with the trial balance for Phil's business, which is as follows.

PHIL'S BUSINESS
TRIAL BALANCE

	Debit	Credit
	$	$
Cash	14 500	
Prepaids	1 500	
Equity		10 000
Creditors		2 000
Van	5 000	
Inventory	4 000	
Profit and loss		13 000
	25 000	25 000

We can see that the accounts do balance. You may have noticed that the columns are headed 'Debit' and 'Credit'. All the accounts from the left side of our worksheet, the asset accounts, are in the debit column and all the accounts from the right side of the worksheet, those that relate to what the business owes, are in the credit column. The accounts with a negative balance would have the opposite title to the one they would have if they had a positive balance. For example, an asset account with a negative balance would be a credit. The negative asset accounts, like provision for doubtful debts and accumulated depreciation, have a credit balance. An entity overdrawing on its bank account would have a negative (credit) balance. If an entity pays more than the amount owing to creditors, the account will have a negative (debit) balance. In this case we assume we have not made an error in our double entries because the trial balance balances, but remember, in Chapter 6 we pointed out that a trial balance can balance and still be incorrect, e.g. $1000 may be recorded as $10 000 on both sides of the worksheet as a debit and a credit.

Key Concept 11.2

Rules for debits and credits

For asset accounts, increases are recorded as debits and decreases as credits.
For liability and equity accounts, increases are recorded as credits and decreases as debits.

Ledgers

Up until now we have used T accounts to demonstrate the traditional approach to accounting. In practice, the T accounts are called ledger accounts and are a means for a business to accumulate information to assist decision making. A typical ledger account is shown below.

TITLE OF ACCOUNT								
							Account No. ( )	
Date	Explanation	Ref.	Amount		Date	Explanation	Ref.	Amount

As can be seen, there are two sides to this ledger, the left-hand side for debit entries and the right-hand side for credit entries. These sides are separated by the middle space between the amount and date.

The columns show the following data:

- Date: The date of the transaction.
- Explanation: Only recorded for unusual items and therefore seldom used.
- Ref.: The page or folio number of the journal where the transaction is recorded.
- Amount: The amount of the entry.

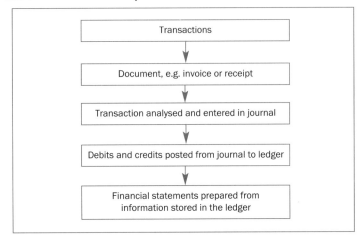

Figure 11.1 *The role of the journal.*

The journal

Transactions are normally not entered directly into a ledger account. Most businesses use a journal to initially enter a transaction into the accounting records. The journal is often called the book of original entry. It is a chronological record showing the debits and credits from transactions. At convenient intervals these transactions are transferred (posted) from the journal to the relevant ledger accounts.

Example 11.1 (continued)

We will now record the transactions from Example 11.1 into a journal. The journal we use is called a general journal. Many businesses use a number of journals for different items. Some examples are the cash receipts journal, the cash payments journal and the purchases journal. We record all the transactions in the general journal.

General Journal				Page ...
Date (transaction)	Account titles and explanation	LP	Debit	Credit
1	Cash		10 000	
	Equity			10 000
	Invested cash in the business			
2	Van		5 000	
	Cash			5 000
	Bought a van for cash			
3	Inventory (or purchases)		35 000	

(continued next page)

	Creditors			35 000
	Bought goods on credit			
	Creditors	33 000		
	Cash			33 000
	Paid creditors (in practice these occur throughout the year)			
4	Cash	45 000		
	Profit and loss (or sales)			45 000
	Sold goods for cash			
5	Profit and loss (or cost of goods sold)	31 000		
	Inventory			31 000
	Cost of goods sold for the period			
6	Profit and loss (or van expenses)	1 000		
	Cash			1 000
	Paid van expenses			
7	Prepaids	1 500		
	Cash			1 500
	Paid rent for the period			

The column LP is used to record the ledger account number when the entry is posted from the journal to the ledger. Until the entry is posted, no number is entered into the LP column. The number assists cross-referencing and can help to locate errors.

All transactions which involve entries to the profit and loss account have an alternative account name in brackets. What happens in practice is that information is accumulated in various revenue and expense accounts throughout the period. At the end of the period a closing entry is recorded in the journal, and these closing entries transfer the totals of the revenue and expense accounts to the profit and loss account. We have recorded these amounts direct to the profit and loss account in this example.

We will move on to the next stage, where final adjustments are made for accruals, depreciation, etc. These adjustments are often referred to as end-of-period or end-of-year adjustments.

End-of-period adjustments

End-of-period adjustments are required to provide for depreciation, bad debts, accruals, prepayments, etc. These have all been covered in Chapters 7–9 and you should be familiar with the way in which they are dealt with in the worksheet. For the purposes of comparison we will show again how they are dealt with in the worksheet and then look at how they are dealt with in the traditional approach.

We continue with the example of Phil's business. At the end of the year Phil decides that the van will have no scrap value and should be depreciated at $1000 a year for five years, and he also tells you that the rent is payable quarterly in advance, so that only $1200 relates to this year.

PHIL'S BUSINESS WORKSHEET: VERSION 2

	Assets					= Liabilities +	Equity	
Transaction	Cash	Van	(Accum. dep.)	Inventory	Prepaids	Creditors	Profit and loss	Equity
1	10 000							10 000
2	–5 000	5 000						
3				35 000		35 000		

(continued over page)

| | Assets | | | | | = Liabilities + | Equity | |
Transaction	Cash	Van	(Accum. dep.)	Inventory	Prepaids	Creditors	Profit and loss	Equity
	−33 000					−33 000		
4	45 000						45 000	
5				−31 000			−31 000	
6	−1 000						−1 000	
7	−1 500				1 500			
Balance	14 500	+ 5 000		+ 4 000	+ 1 500	= 2 000	+ 13 000	+ 10 000
Adjustment			−1 000				−1 000	
Adjustment					−1 200		−1 200	
Balance	14 500	+ 5 000	−1 000	+ 4 000	+ 300	= 2 000	+ 10 800	+ 10 000

Entering these adjustments on the worksheet results in the worksheet above. You will notice that we have had to open two new accounts or columns to deal with the changes and then arrive at a new balance.

In the traditional approach we also have to create the new accounts and then extract another trial balance. However, there is a shortcut which is often shown in textbooks which involves making adjustments on what is effectively a type of worksheet. The difference between that worksheet and the one we use is that the rows become columns and *vice versa*. This worksheet is shown below and, as you can see, it merely extends our earlier trial balance to the new trial balance. This type of worksheet is often referred to as the extended trial balance. The main difference between the two approaches in this respect is that when using our worksheet approach the final adjustments are automatically part of the double-entry system. Under the traditional approach they can be and often are outside the double-entry system. This can, of course, lead to errors and omissions which might be difficult to trace. Let us look at the extended trial balance of Phil's business.

PHIL'S BUSINESS
EXTENDED TRIAL BALANCE

			Adjustments			
	Debit $	Credit $	Debit $	Credit $	Debit $	Credit $
Cash	14 500				14 500	
Equity		10 000				10 000
Creditors		2 000				2 000
Van	5 000				5 000	
Inventory	4 000				4 000	
Profit and loss		13 000	2 200			10 800
Accum. dep.				1 000		1 000
Prepaids	1 500			1 200	300	
	25 000	25 000	2 200	2 200	23 800	23 800

As can be seen, the extended trial balance has also resulted in the need to open two new accounts and to make some adjustments to our existing statement of financial performance. If these adjustments were done through double-entry in the journal and T accounts they would be shown as follows.

General Journal				(Page ...)
Date	Account title and explanation	LP	Debit	Credit
Adjustment	Profit and loss (depreciation expense)		1 000	
	Accumulated depreciation			1 000
	To record depreciation for the period			
Adjustment	Profit and loss (rent expense)		1 200	
	Prepaids			1 200
	To recognise rent expense for the year			

These entries are called adjusting journal entries. Like all journal entries they are posted to the relevant ledger accounts.

Prepaids

Balance	1 500	Adjustment		1 200
		Balance c/d		300
	1 500			1 500
Balance b/d	300			

Profit and loss

Transaction 5	31 000	Transaction 4		45 000
Transaction 6	1 000			
Balance c/d	13 000			
	45 000			45 000
Adjust	1 000	Balance b/d		13 000
Adjust	1 200			
Balance c/d	10 800			
	13 000			13 000
		Balance b/d		10 800

Accumulated depreciation

		Adjustment		1 000

We have seen that the differences between the two approaches are not differences of principle. Rather, the two methods are alternative ways of depicting the same entries in the books of account of a firm. In the authors' opinion the advantages of the work-sheet-based approach outweigh the advantages of the alternative approach and make it easier for those coming to the subject for the first time to assimilate the main principles involved in a double-entry bookkeeping system. We now consider the way in which final accounts are produced, and the rules and regulations governing their format.

Final accounts

Before we look at the regulations and the effects of different organisational forms, we should remind ourselves of the way in which the final accounts, i.e. the statement of financial position and the statements of financial performance are derived from the worksheet. This is readily understood if we consider the example of Phil's business. We will extract the final accounts from the worksheet above.

PHIL'S BUSINESS
STATEMENT OF FINANCIAL PERFORMANCE FOR THE YEAR ENDING 30 JUNE 20X9

	$	$
Sales		45 000
Cost of goods sold		31 000
Gross Profit		14 000
Rent	1 200	
Van expenses	1 000	
Van depreciation	1 000	3 200
Net Profit		10 800

You will notice that the formal statement of financial performance merely summarises what is contained in that column of the worksheet. You will also notice that it is called the statement of financial performance for the period ended on a certain date. This emphasises that the statement of financial performance is a period statement. If we contrast its heading with the heading of the statement of financial position below, we can see that the latter refers to a particular point in time; it is a snapshot of one moment in time.

PHIL'S BUSINESS
STATEMENT OF FINANCIAL POSITION AT 30 JUNE 20X9

	$	$	$	$
Assets				
Current Assets				
Cash	14 500			
Prepaids	300			
Inventory	4 000			
Total Current Assets		18 800		
Non-current Assets				
Van (at cost)	5 000			
Less Accumulated depreciation	(1 000)			
Total Non-current Assets		4 000		
Total Assets			22 800	
Liabilities				
Current Liabilities				
Creditors	2 000			
Total Current Liabilities		2 000		
Non-current Liabilities	NIL	NIL		
Total Liabilities			2 000	
Net Assets				20 800
Equity				
Capital	10 000			
Profit and loss	10 800			
Total Equity				20 800

Notice that the statement of financial position merely takes the final line of the worksheet and classifies it under appropriate headings to enable the reader to interpret the information more readily. We deal with the subject of analysis in more detail in Chapter

14. At this point, we need to consider the effect of different forms of organisational structure on the presentation of final accounts.

Computerised accounting systems

These days most business organisations use a computerised accounting system rather than a manual one to prepare financial statements. There are a large number of computerised systems (e.g. Quicken, MYOB, AcPac, Quick Books Attaché and Microsoft Money) and the software an entity chooses depends on the size, type and complexity of its business. In all cases, however, the bookkeeping process is simplified.

Forms of organisation

As stated in Chapter 1 there are many forms of business organisation, from a sole trader, through partnerships, companies and groups of companies to multinational conglomerates. In addition there are other less common forms such as co-operatives, friendly societies and provident societies. Each of these organisational forms requires slightly different accounts. This is because the needs of the users are slightly different or because of other factors such as the requirements of legislation or other regulations, e.g. those imposed by the stock exchange. Rather than attempting to deal with all the different forms of organisations we concentrate our discussion on simple forms of organisation: the sole trader, the partnership and the limited company.

There are distinct differences in the presentation of final accounts, which are related to the structure, size, patterns of ownership and goals of an organisation. These influences operate at the organisational level which was explained at the start of this book. Other influences which operate in the commercial context are legal requirements such as the reporting requirements of the Corporations Law, the Partnership Act and case law. These will be discussed in some detail here. Other influences, such as the stock exchange requirements, are beyond the scope of an introductory text. We commence by discussing the smallest and most common form of business organisation: the sole trader.

The sole trader

The statements of financial position and financial performance in this case are straightforward because the business is the most simple form of organisation in accounting terms. A one-owner business is a common form of business organisation, and is simple to set up. All that is required is a business bank account. Because it is so simple and because it has little recognition in law, there are no formal guidelines for the format of the accounts, except in the situation where the sole trader is a reporting entity (refer to Chapter 2). The fact that the business and the owner are not seen as separate legal entities can be a problem if the business gets into difficulties: the owner is liable for all the debts of the business and might have to sell personal possessions such as the family home to meet them. In addition, this form of organisation relies heavily on the owner for finance and this can cause problems if the business expands. Owners tend to have limited funds at their disposal. These problems can be alleviated or solved by, for example, introducing a partner to the business. Alternatively, the owner may set up a company which limits his or her liability.

Partnerships

A partnership is a relationship existing between two or more people to carry on a business in common with a view to profit. The partnership form of organisation offers certain advantages and disadvantages compared to the sole trader. A partnership is not regarded as a legal entity separate from the partners who comprise it.

Advantages

- *Ease of formation:* A partnership can be easily formed between two or more persons: all they have to do is agree to form a partnership. The partnership agreement is usually written, although a verbal agreement can be sufficient to constitute a partnership.
- *Limited rules and regulations:* Unlike a company, a partnership is not subject to the requirements of the Corporations Law. The partners are not required to prepare financial statements which comply with Accounting Standards unless the partnership is a reporting entity as defined in *SAC 1* and discussed in Chapter 2.
- *Provision of capital and expertise:* A partnership is often formed to raise more capital than is possible for a sole trader. It may also be formed to bring together different skills of the partners, e.g. an accountant and an engineer.
- *Income tax:* There may be income tax advantages in forming a partnership since it is not a separate legal entity. A partnership is not taxed as is the case for a company. However, the individual partners pay income tax on their share of partnership profits.

Disadvantages

- *Limited life:* A partnership can end at any time through, for example, the death of a partner, withdrawal of a partner, bankruptcy of a partner, incapacity of a partner, or admission of a new partner. However, the end of the partnership does not signify the end of the partnership business: it may continue under a new partnership for many years.
- *Unlimited liability:* As each partner is personally liable for all debts of the partnership, there is unlimited liability with all partnerships. Partners in accounting firms normally purchase professional indemnity insurance because of this risk.
- *Mutual agency:* As each partner is an agent of the partnership, he or she has the authority to enter contracts on behalf of the partnership provided such contracts are within the scope of normal operations.

As we have already stated, unless a partnership is a reporting entity as defined in *SAC 1* (see Chapter 2), it is not required to prepare general-purpose financial reports which must comply with all Accounting Standards. As most partnerships are not reporting entities, they have a great deal of flexibility in how they prepare financial statements. Let us now look at a set of partnership financial statements.

Financial statements

PRICE WATERSHED PARTNERSHIP
STATEMENT OF FINANCIAL PERFORMANCE FOR THE YEAR ENDED 30 JUNE 20X1

	$	$
Sales		100 000
Cost of goods sold		60 000
Gross Profit		40 000
Expenses		20 000
Net Profit		20 000

(continued next page)

Distributions

Salary

Price	6 000	
Watershed	4 000	10 000
		10 000

Profit Share

Price	5 000	
Watershed	5 000	10 000

A comparison of the statement of financial performance of the sole trader, Phil, with that of the partnership reveals that the main difference is the distribution statements for the partnership. This statement shows that Price and Watershed were each paid a salary for services provided to the partnership and then the remaining profit was shared equally.

PRICE WATERSHED PARTNERSHIP
STATEMENT OF FINANCIAL POSITION AT 30 JUNE 20X1

	$	$	$	$
Assets				
Current Assets				
Cash	10 000			
Inventory	10 000			
Total Current Assets		20 000		
Non-current Assets				
Land and building	100 000			
Total Non-current Assets		100 000		
Total Assets			120 000	
Liabilities				
Current Liabilities				
Creditors	20 000			
Total Current Liabilities		20 000		
Non-current Liabilities	NIL	NIL		
Total Liabilities			20 000	
Net Assets				100 000
Partners' Equity				
Capital Accounts				
Price	40 000			
Watershed	40 000			
Total Capital Accounts		80 000		
Current Accounts				
Price	11 000			
Watershed	9 000			
Total Current Accounts		20 000		
Total Partners' Equity				100 000

A comparison of the statement of financial position of Phil the sole trader with that of Price Watershed reveals that the difference arises in the equity part of the statements. The statement of financial position for the partnership shows a balance for each partner under the headings of capital and current accounts. The current account reveals the partners' entitlement to profit, salary, interest, drawings and other, more short-term, transactions. The capital account records the capital contributed by the partners. As current and capital items might be treated differently for legal purposes, it is useful to record them separately in the accounts.

Companies

Unlike the partnership and the sole trader, a company is recognised as a separate legal entity quite distinct from its owners. The debts incurred in the normal course of business are those of the company. In the case of a default in payment, it is the company which is sued rather than the owner. The fact that the owners might also be the managers and the only employees is irrelevant: in the eyes of the law all these roles are different.

The Corporations Law identifies the following types of companies under its administration.

- Limited liability companies
    Proprietary companies: small or large
    Public companies
    Companies limited by guarantee
- Unlimited liability companies
- No-liability companies
- Special companies
    Investment companies
    Banking companies
    Life insurance companies
- Chief entity, controlled entity and related entity
- Borrowing and guarantor companies.

Limited liability companies

This class of company restricts the liability of members (shareholders) to a specified amount. For a limited company, the shareholders' liability is restricted to the amount paid for the share.

- *Proprietary companies or private companies:* These must have a minimum of two members and normally have a maximum of 50 members. A proprietary company must have the word 'Proprietary' or 'Pty' before the word 'Limited' or 'Ltd' as part of its name. These companies are often family companies and have fewer legal formalities than public companies, but they are unable to approach the general public to raise monies.
- *Small or large proprietary companies:* A small company is one that meets at least two of the following criteria:
    —sales less than $10 million
    —assets less than $5 million
    —fewer than 50 employees.
    A small proprietary company does not generally have to prepare audited financial statements. All other proprietary companies are large and are required to lodge audited financial statements with the ASIC unless granted an exemption.
- *Public companies:* A public company must have at least five members and there is no maximum number. Usually ownership of these companies is widespread. A public company can invite the public to subscribe to its shares or debentures. A public company can be listed, which means that its shares are traded on the stock exchange, or unlisted. A public company must have the word 'Limited' or 'Ltd' as part of its

name. A public company is subject to many more rules and restrictions under the Corporations Law than are proprietary companies.

- *Companies limited by guarantee:* These are public companies whose members undertake to provide a guaranteed amount of money in the event of the company being liquidated. This form of company is often used for sporting clubs and non-profit charitable organisations.

Unlimited liability companies

Members of an unlimited liability company are liable for all the debts of the company. For this reason such companies are not common in Australia, although some mutual funds are organised in this way. An advantage of this type of company is that there are no restrictions on the return of capital to shareholders.

No-liability companies

This category is restricted to mining companies. The words 'No Liability' or 'NL' must be part of the company's name. Shareholders in these companies are not required to contribute the unpaid value of shares if the company is liquidated.

Special companies

Investment companies deal primarily in marketable securities with a view to making profit rather than gaining control. There are certain restrictions for investment companies in relation to borrowing, investing, underwriting and speculating in commodities.

Banking companies are governed by the *Banking Act 1959* and are given certain privileges in relation to prospectuses and the presentation of their financial statements.

Life insurance companies are registered under the *Life Insurance Act 1945* and also have special requirements concerning their financial statements and other matters.

Chief entity, controlled entity and related entities

There are special requirements for these types of companies concerning the presentation of consolidated accounts and the disclosure of additional information.

Borrowing and guarantor companies

A borrowing corporation is one that borrows money from the public via an issue of debentures. A guarantor corporation is one that guarantees the repayment of such monies received by a borrowing corporation. These companies are subject to additional disclosure requirements.

Advantages

- *Separate legal entity:* Unlike a sole trader and a partnership, a company is a separate legal entity. Therefore it can buy or sell property, sue or be sued, enter into contracts, hire and dismiss employees, be responsible for its debts and pay tax.
- *Limited liability:* Shareholders are liable only for the value of their shares.
- *More capital:* A company has the potential to raise substantial amounts of capital, which is not possible for sole traders or partnerships.
- *Ease of transfer of ownership:* Shareholders can buy and sell shares without affecting the operations of the company.
- *No mutual agency:* Shareholders cannot enter contracts which would bind the company.
- *Professional management:* A company is managed by a board of directors and a managing director, while the shareholders maintain ownership. It is therefore possible to hire the best managerial talent available.

- *Continuous existence:* A company has an indefinite life and does not cease each time a shareholder sells shares, dies, or goes bankrupt.

CASE STUDY 11.1

Professional ingredient in recipe for success

by Hui Yuk-min

THE key for the long-term survival of Chinese family businesses is to respect and appreciate the role of professional management by outsiders.

That is the advice for longevity from the head of 121-year-old Chinese-medicine maker Eu Yan Sang International Holdings.

'The most important thing is you have to separate the ownership and the management,' said Richard Eu Yee-ming, managing director of the company formed in 1879 by Eu Kong, his flamboyant tin-miner tycoon great-grandfather.

'You have got to decide whether you want to grow the business or you just want a rice bowl for the family,' Mr Eu said.

'If you want to grow the business, you have got to look for professional management.'

He is not in favour of a family-controlled business being run by people with family ties.

His views mirrored a report issued yesterday by the Economist Intelligence Unit in co-operation with management consultancy Andersen Consulting.

It said the traditional rigid hierarchies and emphasis on personal relationships of Chinese family businesses were ill-equipped to deal with an environment of accelerating competition and increasing complexity in post-crisis Asia.

Eu Yan Sang has long been a small-size business of the Eu family, selling flagship Bak Foong pills for women and its Chinese herbs.

It is one of the few traditional Chinese businesses to last four generations.

It was operated in a traditional way until Richard Eu took over 10 years ago and started a process of modernisation.

'At that time, I think the business was not realising its full potential,' Mr Eu said. 'If we did not do something at that time the business would probably have eventually conked out.'

He brought about a major change in the organisational structure, which resulted in retirement for old people and hiring professional-trained newcomers as managers.

The company also introduced extensive staff training on product management, sales and marketing services to improve its standards—something Mr Eu believed was essential to enhance its competitiveness.

Richard Eu and his executive director cousin, Clifford Eu Yee-fong, are the only two Eu family members involved in the company's management. The rest of the staff at managerial level are professional employees.

'If you do want the right person to stay, you have to give them a career path. You cannot give them career path if you do not grow the business,' Mr Eu said.

Mr Eu said his vision was to transform the company into a major regional and global player in the traditional Chinese-medicine business.

It seems he has succeeded, transforming the firm into a modern health-care products provider with a wider range of clients than the middle-aged women who were its staple for nearly 100 years.

Sales have risen from about S$500 000 (about HK$2.27 million) to an estimated S$70 million plus this year.

South China Morning Post, Business Post, 30 August 2000

Commentary

The article discusses the importance of professional management to the success of a business. Perhaps more than any other, this is the greatest advantage of a public company structure.

Disadvantages

- *Taxation:* A company is a separate legal entity and is required to pay company tax, which is not the case for a sole trader or partnership. However, provided shareholders receive their profits as franked dividends, the taxing of companies might not be a significant disadvantage, and, in fact, depending on income levels, may be an advantage.
- *Regulation:* A company is subject to more government intervention in the form of rules and regulations. This is particularly true for public companies. For example, they are required to produce accounts annually and to have them audited by a recognised firm of auditors, which can be expensive. A copy of the audited accounts must be lodged with the Australian Securities and Investments Commission, where it is available for inspection by the public. The form of these accounts is also subject to the requirements of the Corporations Law which require that a company's accounts should consist of: the company's statement of financial position; the company's statement of financial performance; the directors' report; the auditors' report; and a directors' statement. In addition to these general requirements, there are detailed requirements, particularly in Accounting Standards, covering the content of the actual accounts. Such requirements are more onerous for companies which are reporting entities. (Refer to Chapter 2 for a discussion of reporting entities.)
- *Limited liability:* While limited liability is generally an advantage, it may be a disadvantage for a small company if its ability to borrow money is restricted by the fact its members have limited liability.
- *Separation of ownership and control:* This can also act as an advantage or a disadvantage. Managers might have incentives to make decisions which are not in the best interests of all shareholders. The Corporations Law contains certain provisions intended to discourage managers from behaving in this manner.

Clearly, to go through these requirements in great detail is outside the scope of an introductory text. Instead we have included below a set of accounts for a private company. The following text highlights areas of difference between the accounts of the limited company and those of the other forms of organisation considered. We consider first the statement of financial performance.

Example 11.2

JACK PTY LTD
STATEMENT OF FINANCIAL PERFORMANCE FOR THE YEARS ENDING 30 JUNE

	Notes		This year		Last year
		$	$	$	$
Sales	1		60 000		45 000
Cost of sales			40 000		30 000
Gross Profit			20 000		15 000
Distribution costs	2	3 000		2 500	
Administration costs	2	11 000	14 000	9 000	11 500
Profit before taxation			6 000		3 500
Taxation	3		2 600		1 400
Profit after taxation			3 400		2 100
Dividends					
Interim	4	1 000	—		—
Final	4	1 600	2 600		1 100
Transfer to reserves			800		1 000

The first difference is in the title of the statement of financial performance: the fact that Jack is a proprietary limited company must be stated, and the new title does this. In addition, the statement of financial performance contains comparative figures for the previous year, as well as references to a number of notes. These notes contain greater detail than can be shown on the face of the statement, and as such are an integral part of the analysis of the accounts of a company. This will be discussed in more detail in Chapter 14. We can see that down to 'Gross Profit' the format is familiar. However, we then find that 'Expenses' are classified into broad categories. These categories are laid down in *AASB 1018: Statement of Financial Performance.*

It is from the point at which the net profit is shown that the real differences arise. The most striking of these is that taxation is included in the statement of financial performance. This is because the company is recognised as a separate entity for legal and tax purposes and its profits are liable to corporation tax. In contrast the sole trader and the partnership are not separate legal or taxable entities: their profits are not taxed as such, but only as they form part of the income of the owner.

Moving on to 'Profit after taxation', we find that some of this is distributed by way of 'dividend' and some is transferred to 'reserves'. This part of the statement of financial performance can be seen as analogous with the distribution statement in the partnership statements which we have just considered. The dividends themselves are in fact a form of distribution to the owners (the shareholders) and are paid according to the number of shares held. There might be an interim and final dividend in one year but not in the next. This is not unusual: the declaration of any dividend depends upon the needs of the business and the availability of both profits and liquid funds to pay it. An interim dividend is in fact a payment made part way through the year and is also dependent on both profitability and the availability of liquid funds. The final line of the statement of financial performance is the sum transferred to reserves: this is the residual balance being transferred to the profit and loss reserves, and is a profit in this case.

We now look at the statement of financial position of a proprietary limited liability company and the differences that arise therein.

The format uses the current/non-current classification. *AASB 1040* allows companies to choose an alternative format in which assets and liabilities are listed in order of liquidity. Most banks list assets and liabilities in order of liquidity and do not use the current/non-current classification.

JACK PTY LTD
STATEMENT OF FINANCIAL POSITION AT 30 JUNE

	Notes $	This year $	Last year $
Assets			
Current Assets			
Cash at bank		3 500	2 000
Debtors		10 000	4 000
Inventory	7	10 000	7 000
Total Current Assets		23 500	13 000
Non-current Assets			
Equipment	5	10 000	11 000
Land and buildings	6	50 000	56 000
Total Non-current Assets		60 000	67 000
Total Assets		83 500	80 000

(continued next page)

Liabilities

Current Liabilities

Creditors		4 000		3 000
Taxation	3	2 600		1 400
Dividends	4	1 600		1 100
Total Current Liabilities			8 200	5 500
Non-current Liabilities			–	–
Total Liabilities			8 200	5 500
Net Assets			75 300	74 500
Capital and Reserves				
Share capital	8	70 000		70 000
Retained profits	9	5 300		4 500
Total Capital and Reserves			75 300	74 500

As you can see, the top part of the statement of financial position is similar to those we have encountered before, apart from the inclusion of dividends and taxation and the fact that a lot of the detail is left to the notes to the statements. For example, note 6 would contain details of non-current assets bought and sold during the year, as well as the depreciation to date and that charged during the year.

The lower part of the statement of financial position is somewhat different: the owners' equity is referred to as share capital. This might consist of different types, each carrying different voting rights, etc. This would only be apparent if we looked at the detail contained in the notes. Similarly, there may be a number of different types of reserves, such as a 'revaluation reserve' for revalued assets such as land and buildings. However, in this case the only reserve is the retained profits, which is similar to the statement for that purpose in the case of a sole trader.

The above statements are for a private company and are simpler than those for a public company. Woolworths is a public company and its financial statements illustrate the usual format of each statement. Refer to the Woolworths financial report in Appendix 1. Many of the items in these statements should now be familiar. The names of the statements have of course changed since 1999. From 1 July 2000, the profit and loss statement became known as the statement of financial performance, and the balance sheet became known as the statement of financial position. The statement of cash flows was not renamed. (This statement is discussed in Chapter 12.) Other changes were also introduced on 1 July 2000 which would have resulted in further alterations to financial statements. We make reference to such changes where relevant in the discussion below.

Note that the accounts have four columns; the first two are labelled 'consolidated' and the second two 'Woolworths Limited'. Consolidated statements are prepared for an economic entity and will be briefly discussed in Chapter 12. The information in the 'consolidated' columns is for the economic entity which includes Woolworths and other entities controlled by Woolworths. The information in the 'Woolworths Limited' columns refers only to Woolworths.

The profit and loss statement refers to abnormal items. These were defined in AASB 1018: Profit and Loss or Other Operating Statements as:

items of revenue and expense included in the operating result/profit or loss after income tax for the reporting period, which are considered abnormal by reason of their size and effect on the operating result/profit or loss after income tax for the reporting period.

Abnormal items are not included in a revised *AASB 1018*, which applied from 30 June 2000. However, *AASB 1018* does require the separate disclosure of any revenue or expense items from ordinary activities that are unusual because of their size or nature.

One other item which is often separately disclosed in the profit and loss state-ment (statement of financial performance) is an extraordinary item, defined in *AASB 1018* as:

items of revenue and expense which are attributable to transactions or events of a type that are outside the ordinary operations of the entity and are not of a recurring nature.

The intention in Australia is that the statement of financial performance should include all the entity's revenue and expense items for the period. This is sometimes described as the 'all-inclusive concept of income'. To allow entities to exclude items too easily from the statement of financial performance detracts from the usefulness of this statement according to those who support reporting all revenues and expenses through this state-ment. Others argue that the statement of financial performance should include revenues and expenses relating only to the entity's normal operations. The statements of finan-cial performance and financial position also refer to outside equity interest. This term is discussed in Chapter 12.

The notes attached to the statements provide valuable information about some of the line items in the statements. As we mentioned in Chapters 4 and 5, the statements and the notes must be read together.

Summary

In this chapter we briefly discussed the traditional approach to recording transactions in the accounting records. The roles of the journal, ledger and trial balances were explained. The rules for debits and credits were presented and related to the worksheet format used in this book. We then reiterated the idea that different organisations require statements in different forms and the reasons for these differences. For example, in the case of a partnership, there is a need to differentiate between the amounts belonging to each partner and to distinguish between amounts that are permanent in nature and those that are temporary. In the case of companies, the information disclosed in finan-cial statements depends on the type of company. Public companies provide financial statements which are accompanied by detailed notes and can be difficult for the unin-formed user to read. We also looked at the advantages and disadvantages of three forms of organisation: the sole trader, the partnership and the company.

References

Australian Accounting Standards Board, *AASB 1018: Statement of Financial Performance*, October 1999.

Australian Accounting Standards Board, *AASB 1040: Statement of Financial Position*, October 1999.

Review questions

1   Explain in your own words the meaning of the terms 'trial balance' and 'extended trial balance'.

2   Explain the meaning of the term 'final adjustments'.

3   Explain the difference between a sole proprietorship and a partnership.

4   Why it is advantageous to set up a business as a limited company?

5   What are the differences between a sole proprietorship and a limited liability company?

6   Describe how the choice of organisational form determines the format of the final accounts.

7   Explain the difference between a limited liability, an unlimited liability and a no-liability company.

8   Discuss the advantages and disadvantages of a partnership.

9   What do you think the phrase 'it's only a $2 company' means?

Problems for discussion and analysis

1   Refer to the Woolworths financial report in Appendix 1.
    a   How are earnings per share calculated?
    b   How much was the final dividend per share?
    c   How many of the dividends—paid, final and interim—were converted into shares?
    d   How many shares were issued under the dividend reinvestment plan?
    e   How many fully paid ordinary shares were issued as at 27 June 1999?

2   Prepare general journal entries for the following independent transactions. You can also prepare a worksheet for the same data. *Note:* Some of the terms used need to be looked up in the glossary or an accounting dictionary.
    i   Issued 5000 fully paid $1-shares for cash.
    ii   Exchanged a piece of equipment with a fair value of $10 000 for 5000 fully paid $2-shares.
    iii The profit for the year was $12 500. The directors decided to pay a total dividend of $5000 on issued shares, the balance transferred to retained earnings.
    iv   Transferred $6000 from retained earnings to general reserve.
    v   Repaid $100 000 of debentures, together with accumulated interest of $4000 from cash.

3   Prepare a statement of financial position from the following information.

	$
Creditors	7 500
Debtors	10 000
Equipment	137 000
Land and buildings	270 000
Inventory	7 300
Dividends	6000
Debentures payable	250 000
Cash	6 500
Taxation	10 000
Retained profits	24 500
Paid-up capital	?

4   Return to problem 6 in Chapter 6 and prepare a trial balance from your worksheet.

5   Record the following transactions, using a worksheet, and then translate each transaction into debits and credits and show them in the form of T accounts.

Jan. 2	J. Smith paid capital into bank account	$20 000
2	Bought goods from Hall; paid cash	3 400
3	Purchased shop fittings on credit, from Alco	1 450
3	Returned faulty shop fittings to Alco	450
3	Sold goods to Jones on credit	200
5	Paid account due to Alco	1 000
6	Received payment from Jones	
	Less the allowed discount	190
8	Paid wages	200
9	Paid a fee to have the telephone connected	50
10	Paid the rent for January	100

6   Galactic Pty Limited commenced business on 1 January 20X3 as a manufacturer of toy spaceships. Transactions for 20X3 were:
i   Issued shares for $400 000 cash.
ii   Manufactured 32 000 spaceships at a cost of $10 each.
iii All costs were paid in cash.
iv   Sold 18 000 spaceships for $20 each. Costs of delivery were $2 per unit.
v   Collected cash on 10 000 spaceships sold.

Prepare a statement of financial performance and statement of financial position for 20X3, assuming that revenue was recognised at the point of sale.

(Adapted from C. Martin, *An Introduction to Accounting*, McGraw-Hill, 1988, p. 353.)

7   Partners Mike and Phil share profits and losses in proportion to their fixed capital balances. The following balances were taken from the partnership's books as at 30 June 20X9.

	$
Cash	3 000
Debtors	12 500
Inventory	8 400
Plant	100 000
Accumulated depreciation	3 000
Creditors	8 600
Capital: Mike	36 320
Phil	54 480
Sales	210 000
Cost of goods sold	163 000
Selling expenses	7 316
Depreciation expense	4 322
Financial expenses	1 827
General expenses	12 035

On the basis of the figures above:
i   Calculate the profit for the period.
ii   What was the amount of profit/loss allocated to each partner?

8   Prepare the trial balance at the end of the period, after recording the following opening balances and transactions completed in the appropriate accounts.

	Debit $	Credit $
Cash at bank		4 000
Accounts payable		5 600
Mortgage		10 000
Capital		20 000
Accounts receivable	9 600	
Inventory	13 200	
Delivery vehicles	2 400	
Premises	14 400	
	39 600	39 600

The transactions were:
i   Purchases (on credit) amount to $2800.
ii   Sales bring in $1600 cash, $800 credit.
iii   Capital is increased by $8000.
iv $2000 bill for rates and taxes is received, not yet paid.
v   Creditors are paid $2800.
vi   Wages are paid, $800.

9   For an enterprise which balances annually on 30 June, record, in general journal form, the adjustments necessitated by the following:
i   The firm holds 12 per cent government bonds of $1200 face value. Interest on these bonds is payable on 15 March and 15 September.
ii   Rent is paid quarterly in advance. $2100 rent was paid on 1 June.
iii   Amounts owing as at 30 June are:
      Drivers' wages $4 500
      Office salaries $2 000
      Delivery expenses $1 800
iv   Estimated doubtful debts are $3500. The balance in the provision for doubtful debts account is $2800, and $2350 of bad debts written off during the period have not yet been offset against the provision.
v   Commission earned by selling goods as agent for another firm but not yet received amounts to $800.

(Adapted from J. Harrison, J. Horrocks and R. Newman, *Accounting: A Direct Approach*, Longman Cheshire, 1986, p. 87.)

10   Prepare general journal entries to record the following transactions:
i   A building worth $100 000 is acquired and financed by paying $20 000 in cash and negotiating a mortgage for the remaining $80 000.
ii   Depreciation on factory machines is estimated to be $2000.
iii   100 shares in Ravan Publishing are acquired as a long-term investment for $1350 cash.
iv   A partner introduces a new truck valued at $3000 as part of his partnership capital.
v   Henry Smith opens a business bank account with his own personal cheque for $4000.
vi   Provide $1000 for depreciation on the factory building for this period.
vii   A ten-year $100 000 debenture secured by the company's real estate is issued at a discount of 5 per cent with the balance of $95 000 received in cash.
viii   A two-hectare vacant block at Welshpool is acquired for a cash payment of $50 000 to provide for future expansion.

ix Faulty goods which had cost $25 are returned to the supplier for credit to our account.

x   Harold Black, a partner in Black, Brown, Green and White, withdraws $200 cash to meet his own personal expenses.

xi A cheque for $6000 is received for six months' interest to 30 June, on debentures held as an investment.

11 The trial balance of the Hourglass Organisation presented below does not balance. On examining the records you discover the following information:

i   The purchase of supplies with a cheque for $210 was erroneously recorded as a purchase on credit.

ii The debits and credits of debtors totalled $9400 and $6900 respectively.

iii The balance in the mortgage payable account is $2300.

iv A $790 payment for salaries was not posted to the cash at bank account.

v   The debit to record a withdrawal of $500 in cash by the owner was not posted.

THE HOURGLASS ORGANISATION
TRIAL BALANCE AT 30 JUNE 20X3

Account title	Debit $	Credit $
Cash at bank	2 400	
Debtors		2 480
Supplies inventory	390	
Equipment	6 700	
Creditors		2 610
Salaries payable	310	
Mortgage payable		3 200
G. Hourglass Capital		7 200
G. Hourglass Drawings	3 920	
Service revenues		13 800
Salary expense	5 100	
Rent expense	3 200	
Other expenses	2 300	
Totals	24 320	29 290

Prepare a corrected trial balance.

(Adapted from J. Hoggett and L. Edwards, *Financial Accounting in Australia*, John Wiley, 1990, p. 90.)

12 The following trial balance has been extracted from the books of the Tiger Partnership.

THE TIGER PARTNERSHIP
TRIAL BALANCE AT 30 JUNE 20X7

	Debit $	Credit $
J. Lion Capital (1 July 20X6)		25 000
K. Jaguar Capital (1 July 20X6)		31 000
Commission received		1 250
Petty cash advance	250	
Cash at bank	3 400	
J. Lion drawings	3 700	
K. Jaguar drawings	2 100	

(continued next page)

Rent	3 300	
General office expenses	1 750	
Travelling expenses	3 600	
Cartage on sales	850	
Accounts payable		19 800
Purchases	124 500	
Provision for doubtful debts		1 300
Inventories (1 July 20X6)	22 400	
Sales		135 750
Insurance	600	
Bad debt expense	850	
Discount allowed	2 900	
Loss on sale of van	1 000	
Accounts receivable	20 000	
Motor vehicles (cost)	16 000	
Accumulated depreciation: motor vehicles		6 400
Furniture (cost)	4 400	
Accumulated depreciation: furniture		600
Salaries	9 500	
Totals	**221 100**	**221 100**

The following additional information is available:

i   Inventories at 30 June 20X7 are $14 500.

ii   Depreciation is to be charged at the following rates:
    Motor vehicles: 20 per cent per annum on cost
    Furniture: 5 per cent per annum on cost.

iii   Rent for June 20X7 ($300) is unpaid.

iv   Insurance ($150) is paid in advance.

v   The provision for doubtful debts is to be increased to $1500.

Prepare a statement of financial performance for the partnership for the year ended 30 June 20X7, and a statement of financial position at that date. Use a worksheet to determine the figures for the financial statements.

(Adapted from J. Harrison, J. Horrocks and R. Newman, *Accounting: A Direct Approach*, Longman Cheshire, 1986, p. 90.)

13   Bev and Daniel want to buy a business of their own. Bev is a school teacher and Daniel has worked in the public service and has a degree in commerce. They decide to buy a delicatessen, and choose one close to their home. The shop has been there for several years, but has not been a great success. Bev and Daniel will have to borrow a large amount of money to finance the purchase.

Required:

You have been asked to advise the following:
    a   What form of organisation should they adopt for the business, a partnership or a company?
    b   Will the choice of organisation affect the availability of finance for their business? Explain.
    c   What skills will Bev and Daniel need to manage the business?
    d   How can they raise the required finance? What security do you think they will need to provide?

(Adapted from R. Craven, I. Urquhart and R. Woolley, *Case Studies in Accounting*, 3rd edn, VCTA Publishing, 1985, Case 3–3.)

14 Norma and Christopher Rhyme have recently decided to start a business of
their own. Christopher has for a number of years been the manager of a chain
of retail food outlets, and Norma has been employed as a bookkeeper in a
local building business. They decide to acquire a restaurant. The one they
choose has been in existence for a number of years but has not enjoyed much
success in recent times. Norma and Christopher will have to borrow a
substantial sum of money in order to finance their business venture.

Required:

 a What factors should they consider in choosing a form of ownership for
their business?
 b What form of ownership do you think would be appropriate for their
business? Explain fully.
 c Do you think the choice of the form of ownership will affect the availability
of finance for their business? Explain.
 d What type of skills do you believe they will need in order to manage their
business?
 e What are some possible sources of finance available? What security does
each alternative require?

(Adapted from R. Craven, I. Urquhart and R. Woolley, *Case Studies in
Accounting*, 3rd edn, VCTA Publishing, 1985, p. 36.)

15 John Upton and Julia Townshend have been working separately for two
different firms in the fashion industry. They decide that they should get
together to do their own fashion designing under the Uptown label, and
establish either a company or a partnership to do so.

If they form a partnership, each individual would contribute $45 000 in cash.
Townshend would also contribute a laptop computer valued at $4400. Neither
Upton nor Townshend knows much about forming a partnership and so have
come to you for advice. They asked the following questions over a business
lunch:
 a What are the advantages and the disadvantages of forming a partnership?
 b What documentation is necessary, and what should it contain?
 c Both Upton and Townshend would work full time in the partnership, and
would share profits and losses equally. However, Townshend wonders how
she would be compensated for her additional investment of the laptop
computer. What would you suggest?
 d The talents of Upton and Townshend complement each other, and if one
dies, the partnership would have to be wound up. Furthermore, it would
be difficult for the surviving partner to pay out in cash the deceased
partner's estate for the partnership interest. What should they do?

Required:

Prepare a report with response to each of the above questions.

(Adapted from J. Hoggett and L. Edwards, *Financial Accounting in Australia*,
John Wiley, 1990, p. 675.)

16 The Magic Lawn Corporation is a family-owned company that produces and
sells lawn care products. The company has recently developed a new product
which enhances the water retention properties of all types of lawn. The
potential for this product is unlimited, but, in order to capitalise on its potential,
the company needs a substantial injection of cash into the business. At present

the family owns all the 10 000 shares of $1 value which have been issued. The shareholder's section of the most recent statement of financial position is reproduced below.

	$
10 000 $1 value shares fully paid	10 000
Retained earnings	2 990 000
	3 000 000

The following are the options which are being considered by the family in order to raise the additional cash.

a   five-year bank loan for $3 million—interest rate 10 per cent, payable annually in arrears; principal to be repaid at the end of five years.

b   converting to a public company and issuing 600 000 shares at an estimated market price of $5. Family members will have priority in the purchase of shares.

c   the issue of 600 000, 6 per cent, $5 cumulative preference shares to an investment company. The shares will be redeemable at the discretion of the Magic Lawn Company.

There are two important issues for the company:

i   The company has always been family owned and they are concerned about losing control of the company.

ii   The company has always had cash flow problems. Alternatives (a) and (c) both involve regular cash payments for interest or dividends.

Required:

Write a report to the family outlining the advantages and disadvantages of each option. The tax rate for companies is 36 per cent. Interest is tax-deductible but dividends are not.

17   Bob and Phil Partnership

Bob Strongarm and Phil Hannock are partners in a consulting business. In the last three years Bob's share of partnership profits has been $15 000, $20 000 and $30 000. He has been offered $80 000 for his share of the partnership. Bob decides that if his total share of profits over the next three years is less than $100 000 he will sell. The following schedule sets out some estimates of profits for the next three years.

Schedule

TOTAL PARTNERSHIP PROFITS

	Year 1	Year 2	Year 3
Optimistic estimate	75 000	85 000	95 000
Most probable estimate	55 000	65 000	75 000
Pessimistic estimate	45 000	55 000	65 000

Bob and Phil currently share profits as follows: Bob receives a salary of $20 000, Phil's salary is $15 000, and the remainder is split in a 60 per cent/40 per cent ratio, with Bob getting the 60 per cent.

Required:

a   Calculate Bob's share of the profits over the next three years if his optimistic estimate is correct.

b   Calculate Bob's share of the profits over the next three years if his most probable estimate is correct.

c   Calculate Bob's share of the profits over the next three years if his pessimistic estimate is correct.

d   If the probabilities are 20 per cent that the optimistic estimate will be correct, 60 per cent that the most probable estimate will be correct, and 20 per cent that the pessimistic estimate will be correct, should Bob sell for $80 000?

e   Discuss the other factors Bob should consider when deciding whether or not to sell.

Ethics case study

Jan Skully was the founder and chairperson of Extraordinary Products Ltd. The company had performed very well in the past, but over the last year the share price of Extraordinary had steadily declined. As Skully owned a majority of the shares, she decided to do something to protect her investment. She secretly channelled $200 million from other companies she owned into the purchase of additional shares in Extraordinary. These new shares were used by the other companies as security for the loans taken out to raise the necessary cash to purchase the shares in Extraordinary Ltd. After her death a year later the transactions were uncovered and revealed in the press, and the price of Extraordinary's shares plummeted.

Discuss:

a   whether the transactions were unethical

b   how the scheme could have been prevented.

Cash Flow Statements and Other Issues

Learning objectives

At the end of this chapter you should be able to:

1   explain what is included in the term 'cash' according to *AASB 1026*

2   understand what is meant by cash flows of operating, investing and financing activities

3   understand the purpose of cash flow statements

4   understand the difference between cash flows and net profit

5   explain what is meant by the term 'consolidated accounts'

6   understand the purpose of consolidated statements

7   understand why it is necessary to eliminate the investment in subsidiary accounts and inter-entity transactions

8   understand the difference between the taxes payable and tax-effect accounting methods of accounting for income tax

9   Explain the meaning of 'provision for deferred tax'.

Introduction

In this chapter we briefly discuss some issues which will provide a greater understanding of financial statements. We first examine the content and use of cash flow statements and then turn our attention to two other important issues: consolidated accounts and accounting for income tax.

Cash flow statements

In addition to the statement of financial position and statement of financial performance, reporting entities are now required to prepare a statement of cash flows following the release of *AASB 1026: Statement of Cash Flows*. In this section we examine the objective of cash flow statements and the relationship between the cash flow and the statement of financial performance; we then look at an example of a cash flow statement and how it is to be interpreted.

Purpose

The main purpose of the cash flow statement is to provide information about the cash receipts and cash payments for an entity during its accounting period. It is cash and not profits that an entity must use to pay its bills. It is possible for a profitable firm to have insufficient cash to meet its debts and be insolvent.

The statement of financial position shows the assets an entity has at a particular point in time and how these assets are financed. The statement of financial performance shows how much profit the entity has earned during the accounting period. These statements cannot be used to answer the following types of questions.

- Did the entity's operations produce sufficient cash to meet dividend payments?
- Did the entity issue shares or increase liabilities during the year and, if so, what happened to the proceeds?
- Did the entity purchase any new assets during the year? How did the entity pay for these new assets?

The statement of cash flows is intended to provide answers to these and other questions.

What is cash?

The statement of cash flows shows the net increase or decrease in cash during the accounting period. *AASB 1026* defines cash as 'cash on hand and cash equivalents'. Cash equivalents are highly liquid investments such as money-market accounts and government treasury bills. They can be readily converted to cash on hand by the entity, and their use is part of a cash management function. Cash equivalents also include borrowings, such as bank overdraft; again this is used by the entity as part of its cash management function. For the purposes of the cash flow statement, any transfers of cash between cash equivalents and cash on hand do not need to be reported as cash receipts or payments.

What does a cash flow statement show?

Having established the need for a statement of cash flows we need to look in more detail at what the statement shows. In broad terms, as we have pointed out, it tells us where we got money from, and how it was used. The money coming in is referred to as cash inflows, while money going out is referred to as cash outflows. The difference between the cash inflows and the cash outflows is known as the net cash flow, which can be either a net cash inflow or a net cash outflow, depending on the magnitude of the two components. Typical cash inflows would be monies generated from trading, commonly referred to as cash flows from operations, monies from new share issues or other forms of long-term finance, and any monies received from the sale of fixed assets. Typical outflows would be monies used to buy new fixed assets, to pay tax and dividends and to repay debenture holders or other providers of long-term capital. As we shall see, the cash flow statement separates these cash flows into various categories. The format we shall follow is the one recommended in the Accounting Standard *Statement of Cash Flows* (*AASB 1026*). We shall use the example of a cash flow statement shown in Example 12.1.

Example 12.1

SAMPLE CASH FLOW STATEMENT

	$000s	This year $000s	Last year $000s
Cash flow from operating activities		1 800	1 400
1 400			
Cash flow from investing activities			
Payments to acquire fixed assets	(900)		(200)
Payments to acquire investments	—		(100)
Receipts from disposal of fixed assets	50	(850)	—
Cash flow from financing activities			
Dividends paid	(2 500)	—	(1 200)
Issue of ordinary share capital	300		
Repayment of loan	(150)	(2 350)	
Increase/decrease in cash in period		(1 400)	(100)

Example 12.1 shows that the cash flow statement not only provides the detail of the change in cash as the last figure, $1.4 million this year and $100 000 last year, but also divides the cash flows into the business and out of the business under a number of separate headings. These headings or subdivisions are intended to provide information about the source and nature of the cash flow. For example, cash flow from operating activities tells us that the cash comes from the normal continuing operations of the business and these operations and their related cash flows are likely to continue each year. The cash flows under 'Cash flows from investing activities', on the other hand, are different as they are not likely to recur each year. If we think of our own lives you may equate these differences with the cash flows related to running a car, where expenditure on petrol, insurance, etc. will recur each year but we will not make the capital investment of buying another car each year. Before we move on to looking at the subheadings and what they mean in more detail, we first need to define cash flows.

Key Concept 12.1

Cash flows

Cash inflows are defined as increases in cash.
Cash outflows are decreases in cash.
Net cash flow consists of the net effect of cash inflows and cash outflows.

Cash flow from operating activities

The first subheading in the cash flow statement is cash flow from operating activities. If we had kept our business as the simple cash-based model we used up to Chapter 7 (before we introduced year-end stock, debtors, creditors, non-current assets, etc.), the cash flow from operating activities would have been the same as profit. However, as we have pointed out from Chapter 7 onwards, this may reflect how the cash has been spent but not the economic activity. This, if you remember, is because some of the spending relates to future years and some to past years, etc. This presents us with a problem because what we have done in effect from Chapter 7 onwards is to adjust the cash figure to arrive at a figure for profit based upon the principles of accrual accounting. Therefore, if we start with the profit figure, we have to reverse all those adjustments in order to arrive at the cash flow from operations.

It is very important to your understanding of the cash flow statement and its inter-relationship with the statement of financial performance and statement of financial position that you understand this process and the reasons for it.

Example 12.2

Valerie's business had the following balances at the start of the year.

	$
Debtors	350
Creditors	760
Bank and cash	580

At the end of the year the balances were:

	$
Debtors	210
Creditors	530
Bank and cash	1 640

If we look first at the creditors, we can see that we have used our cash to reduce the amount we owe from $760 to $530. Thus, we have used up $230. So we would expect our cash balance to be reduced by $230, but in fact it has increased by $1060, so clearly there are other factors involved. One of these is that we sell goods for more than we buy them and so we get more cash in than we pay out. Some of that cash is used to buy more stock, some is put in the bank and some is used to finance debtors.

Clearly in order to proceed we need more information. This is given on the following page.

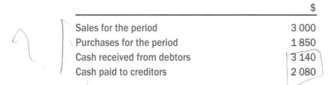

	$
Sales for the period	3 000
Purchases for the period	1 850
Cash received from debtors	3 140
Cash paid to creditors	2 080

From the information we have we could produce the cash flow statement very easily as we have the cash flows in—from debtors—of $3140 and the cash flows out —to creditors—of $2080, so we have a net cash flow of $1060 ($3140 – $2080) which is the difference between the opening and closing bank balance. However, as pointed out in Chapter 1, users also want to know how much profit has been made. Once again from the information we could produce a statement of financial performance as follows:

STATEMENT OF FINANCIAL PERFORMANCE
FOR VALERIE'S BUSINESS: VERSION 1

	$	$
Sales		3 000
Opening stock	0	
Purchases	1 850	
Closing stock	0	
Cost of sales		1 850
Profit for the year		1 150

The worksheet for Valerie's transactions is shown below.

VALERIE'S WORKSHEET: VERSION 1

	Assets		= Liabilities +			Equity
	Bank	Stock	Debtors	Creditors	Equity	Profit and loss
Description						
Balances	580	0	350	760	170	
Sales			3 000			3 000
Purchases		1 850		1 850		
Cash in	3 140		-3 140			
Cash paid	-2 080			-2 080		
Cost of goods sold		-1 850				-1 850
Balances	1 640	0	210	= 530	170	1 150

The difficulty we have now is that we have told the users that the cash that came in was $1060 ($3140 – $2080) more than the cash going out and we have also told them that we have made a profit of $1150. Given this information, they might justifiably ask, why are these figures different?

Of course, by now we know that the answer is because one system is based on cash measures and the other is based on accrual accounting, which takes into account sales made that we have not yet received money for, purchases that are not yet paid for and changes in the levels of stock held, etc.

So how can we reconcile the two figures? We can start by thinking about the effect changes in the level of debtors would have on the cash figure. If we decrease the level of debtors we get more cash in than is shown by our sales figure. Conversely if we increase the level of debtors we will get less cash in than is shown by the sales figure. In the case of Valerie's business, the cash coming in was $3140 and the sales for the period were $3000. The difference between the cash received and the sales of $140 was due to the fact that at the start of the year we had $350 due to be received from our debtors and at the end of the year we only had $210 due from our debtors, a difference of $140. The general rule we have just derived is given as Key Concept 12.2.

Key Concept 12.2

Sales, debtors and cash received

An *increase* in the debtors due over the period must be *subtracted* from the sales to arrive at the cash received.
A *decrease* in debtors due over the period must be *added* to sales to arrive at the cash received.

This is useful to help us on our way but is not the whole story, because our starting point is profit, not sales, and what we are trying to reconcile is net cash flow from operating activities, not cash received.

Profit is derived by subtracting the cost of goods sold figure from the sales figure, so it is also a net figure like the cash flow from operating activities. Thus, we are dealing with two net figures. This is a useful starting point. We now need to look at the effect an increase in the gross figures, i.e. sales and cash received, has upon the net figures we are dealing with. In the case of sales there is a direct relationship between sales and profit, i.e. an increase in sales leads to an increase in profit and a decrease in sales leads to a decrease in profit.

Similarly, in the case of cash received, an increase in cash received leads to an increase in the net cash flow from operating activities and a decrease in cash received leads to a decrease in net cash flow. Thus, the gross figures and net figures follow the same pattern as a result of increases or decreases: the effect on the net figures is the same as the effect on the gross figures. So we can simply restate Key Concept 12.2 in terms of profit rather than sales, as shown in Key Concept 12.3.

Key Concept 12.3

Profit, debtors and net cash flow from operating activity

An *increase* in the debtors due over the period must be *subtracted* from the profit to arrive at the net cash flow from operating activity.
A *decrease* in debtors due over the period must be *added* to profit to arrive at the net cash flow from operating activity.

If we now think about creditors, we have a similar situation to that for debtors. If we increase the amount that we owe at the end of the year it means that our cash payments will be less than our purchases. If we reduce the amount that we owe, then our cash payments will be more than our purchases. In the case of Valerie's business the cash paid and the purchases were $2080 and $1850 respectively, a difference of $230. This difference was due to the fact that at the start of the year we had $760 owing to our creditors and at the end of the year we only had $530 owing, a reduction of $230. The general rule we have just derived is given as Key Concept 12.4.

Key Concept 12.4

Purchases, creditors and cash paid

An *increase* in the creditors over the period must be *subtracted* from the purchases to arrive at the cash paid.

A *decrease* in creditors over this period must be *added* to purchases to arrive at the cash paid.

At this point we need to acknowledge an important distinction between differences in debtors and their effect on sales and profits and the differences in creditors and their effect on profits. The important point here is that, as we stated above, the relationship between an increase in sales and an increase in cash received on the net figures is the same, i.e. an increase in sales results in an increase in profit and an increase in cash received results in an increase in the net cash flow from operating activity. Thus, the relationships are direct and in the same direction.

In the case of cash paid, the relationship between increases in cash paid and the net cash flow is an inverse relationship, i.e. an increase in cash paid will have the effect of decreasing the net cash flow. Conversely, a decrease in cash paid will increase the net cash flow. Similarly, the relationship between an increase or decrease in purchases and the effect on profit is an inverse relationship. If we leave aside the effect of holding stock for the moment, as Valerie has no opening or closing stock, we can see that an increase in purchases would have the effect of increasing the costs and therefore reducing the profit. A decrease in purchases, on the other hand, would reduce costs and increase profits.

So, in order to adjust profit to take account of the differences between purchases and cash payments in respect of those purchases, we need to reverse the effects set out in Key Concept 12.4. Key Concept 12.5 sets out the relationship between profits, increases and decreases in creditors, and profits and net cash flows from operating activities.

Key Concept 12.5

Profit, creditors and net cash flow from operating activity

An *increase* in the creditors over the period must be *added* to the profit to arrive at the net cash flow from operating activity.

A *decrease* in creditors over the period must be *subtracted* from the profit to arrive at the net cash flow from operating activity.

So far, so good, hopefully! Let us see how what we have done to date works.

RECONCILIATION OF OPERATING PROFIT AND CASH FLOW FROM OPERATING ACTIVITY

Version 1	
	$
Profit for the year	1 150
Less Decrease in creditors	(230)
Add Decrease in debtors	140
Increase in cash	1 060

NOTE: Brackets are commonly used in published accounts to denote negatives.

As you can see, we have been successful in reconciling the profit to the cash flow from operating activity.

Unfortunately, the debtors and creditors are only one part of the adjustments we made when using accrual accounting. The most common of these relate to the effect of holding stocks and the effects of having non-current assets. In general terms these have an effect on the statement of financial performance but not on the cash flows arising out of the operating activity. In the case of non-current assets, as we illustrated earlier using the example of a car, there may be an effect on cash flows in respect of capital expenditure but no effect on operating cash flows.

To understand the effects of stock and depreciation, let us extend our Valerie example a bit further by adding some stock figures and some figures for non-current assets and depreciation.

	$
Opening stock	420
Closing stock	480
Non-current asset – cost	1 000
Depreciation at start	400
Depreciation for year	200
Depreciation at end	600

The new worksheet for Valerie would be as shown below.

VALERIE'S WORKSHEET: VERSION 2

	Assets				= Liabilities	+ Equity		
	Bank	Non-current assets	Accumulated depreciation	Stock	Debtors	Creditors	Equity	Profit and loss
Description								
Balances	580	1 000	−400	420	350	760	1 190	
Sales					3 000			3 000
Purchases				1 850		1 850		
Cash in	3 140				−3 140			
Cash paid	−2 080					−2 080		
Cost of sales		—		−1 790				−1 790
Depreciation			−200					−200
Balances	1 640	1 000	−600	480	210	= 530	1 190	1 010

STATEMENT OF FINANCIAL PERFORMANCE FOR VALERIE'S BUSINESS: VERSION 2

	$	$
Sales		3 000
Opening stock	420	
Purchases	1 850	
	2 270	
Closing stock	480	
Cost of sales		1 790
Gross profit for the year		1 210
Depreciation		200
Operating profit for the year		1 010

If we look at the difference between the profit under version 1 and version 2 we can see that there are two reasons for the difference. The first is that the cost of goods sold figure has changed, due to the presence of opening and closing stock. The second is that the resultant profit has also been reduced by the depreciation charge for the year. However, it is obvious from a quick glance at the cash column of version 2 of the worksheet that there has been no change in the cash received or paid. The double entry for both these items is between the statement of financial performance and the item concerned, and the cash column is not affected.

Looking first at the depreciation we can see that if we charge depreciation we reduce the profit but do not affect the net cash flow. Therefore, we need to add back the depreciation charge for the year to the operating profit to arrive at the cash flow. We state this as a general rule in Key Concept 12.6.

Key Concept 12.6

Profit, depreciation and net cash flow from operating activity

Charges for *depreciation* and *amortisation* of non-current assets charged to the statement of financial performance for the period must be added back to the operating profit to arrive at the net cash flow from operating activities.

If we now turn to decreases and increases in the stock held over the period, we can see from the Valerie example that, because we held more stock at the end than at the start, this led to a decrease in cost of goods sold and an increase in profit. Similarly, a decrease in stock would lead to an increase in cost of goods sold and a decrease in profit. Thus we can state a general rule for stock as shown in Key Concept 12.7.

Key Concept 12.7

Profit, stock and net cash flow from operating activity.

An *increase* in the stock held over the period must be *subtracted* from the profit to arrive at the net cash flow from operating activity.
A *decrease* in the stock held over the period must be *added* to the profit to arrive at the net cash flow from operating activity.

It is important to note that, although the effects of an increase in stock are the same as an increase in debtors, the relationship is different. In the case of debtors the relationship is direct, whereas in the case of stocks it is indirect and can be thought of as two inversions which cancel each other out.

Let us now see if we can reconcile the new profit from version 2 of Valerie's statement of financial performance with the net cash flow from operating activity.

We already have some of the figures in respect of debtors and creditors, and now need to deal with stock and depreciation. For stock we have an increase of $60; as this is an increase it has to be taken off the profit to arrive at cash flow from operations. In the case of depreciation we need to add back the charge for the year, $200, to profit.

RECONCILIATION OF OPERATING PROFIT AND CASH FLOW FROM OPERATING ACTIVITY

	$
Profit for the year	1 010
Less Decrease in creditors	(230)
Add Decrease in debtors	140
Less Increase in stock	(60)
Add Depreciation charge	200
Increase in cash from operations	1 060

As a by-product of the explanation of how the figure for net cash flow from operating activity is arrived at and reconciled with the operating profit, we have produced the reconciliation statement that the Accounting Standard *AASB 1026* requires to be produced in published accounts. Having done that, let us now return to our example of a sample cash flow statement and look at the other headings. To remind ourselves of the format of the cash flow statement, the sample is reproduced below.

SAMPLE CASH FLOW STATEMENT

	$000s	This year $000s	Last year $000s
Cash flow from operating activities		1 800	1 400
Cash flow from investing activities			
Payments to acquire fixed assets	(900)		(200)
Payments to acquire investments	—		(100)
Receipts from disposal of fixed assets	50	(850)	—
Cash flow from financing activities			
Dividends paid	(2 500)	—	(1 200)
Issue of ordinary share capital	300		
Repayment of loan	(150)	(2350)	
Increase/(decrease) in cash in period		(1 400)	(100)

CASE STUDY 12.1

Cash: burning a hole in the pocket

by Gayle Bryant

THE latest quarterly cashflow statements lodged with the Australian Stock Exchange by July 31 indicated that life was likely to be short for many dot-com companies. Based on these statements, stockbroker Ord Minnett released a report on the cash position of dot-com companies. The report claimed that 15 will run out of cash within 12 months if recent burn rates continue.

Many of the companies have limited cash reserves to fund marketing campaigns to attract and retain customers. Companies such as the online education group Isis Communications, ecorp and Bourse Data were in the best position; Isis has almost 12 years until it runs out of cash.

The struggling online music retailer ChaosMusic lifted its revenue from $2 million to $2.2 million during the three months to June 30, 2000, and had an operating cashflow of $1.6 million. To reduce costs, ChaosMusic cut its advertising expenditure: from $2.1 million for the previous quarter to $484 000 for the June quarter.

The online education service Worldschool had no revenue in the June quarter, and it spent $8.7 million on staff, advertising, and research and development. The company had only $4 million at the start of the June quarter, but it raised $25.5 million from the market in May.

The property portal realestate.com.au confirmed that it would not survive the year based on its current quarterly cash-burn rate of $1.2 million. Realestate.com.au had revenue of just $783 000 in its latest quarter. Like many dot-coms, the company said that as a result of reviewing its strategic direction, it would be reducing its monthly operating expenditure. It now expects to become cashflow positive by January 2001.

Business Review Weekly, 25 August 2000

Commentary

The article identifies dot-com companies' cash flow problems and illustrates how cash flow problems can ruin a company, even if future prospects seem reasonable. The article highlights the need for cash flow statements to enable users to properly assess all aspects of a business.

Cash flow from investing activities

These are broadly of two types: the first relates to non-current assets and the second to purchase of shares in other companies and similar investments. As far as non-current assets are concerned, this would involve cash outflows in respect of purchase of non-current assets and cash inflows from the sale of non-current assets (see Figure 12.1 on page 270). Clearly such cash flows are different from those we have discussed so far. They tend to be non-recurrent, as an individual non-current asset or investment can only be replaced or sold once. The second type is when a business sells off a complete part of the business, or buys an existing business. The intention here is to differentiate the cash flows that relate to these one-off activities from the recurring cash flows.

Cash flow from financing activities

The final heading involves the cash flows relating to the financing of the business. These include amounts received from share issues, new loans or debentures—in other words, from long-term financing. It would also show amounts paid out in respect of loans or debentures that have been repaid during the year, and in respect of any shares redeemed and dividends paid. Figure 12.1 summarises the classification of cash flows according to *AASB 1026*.

Increase/(decrease) in cash in the period

The final figure shown on the cash flow statement is the increase or decrease in cash. This can be reconciled fairly easily with the information in the statement of financial position.

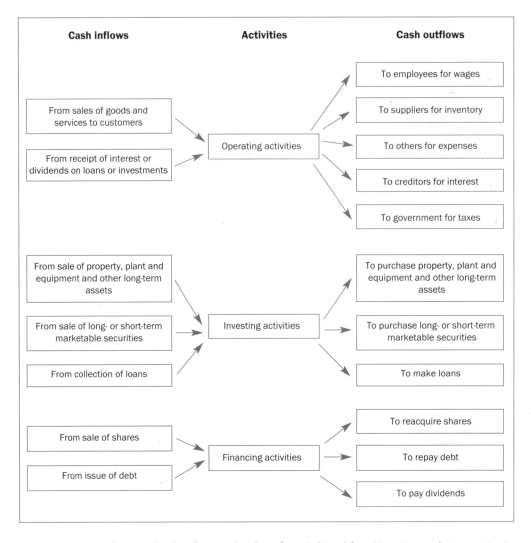

Figure 12.1 *Classification of cash inflows and cash outflows (adapted from T.D. Wise et al.,* Accounting in Australia, *Houghton Mifflin, 1990, p. 714).*

Non-cash investing and financing activities

Sometimes an entity is involved in transactions such as acquiring land and buildings by issuing shares which do not involve cash. Such transactions, where significant, must be disclosed in a note to the cash flow statement, so that the user has a complete picture of the entity's investing and financing activities.

You should now study Woolworths' statements of cash flows in Appendix 1. Note that the company has presented the cash flows from operating, investing and financing activities as required by the Accounting Standard. It also reports a reconciliation of net cash flows from operations and operating profit after income tax. This reconciliation reinforces the lesson that profit does not equal cash in an accrual accounting system.

We now make a number of observations based on Woolworths' statements of cash flows. The comments relate to the figures in the consolidated columns.

Cash flows from operating activities

Net cash flows from the operations increased by $65 million in 1999. The $574 million provided by operating activities more than covered the $154.1 million paid in dividends in 1999. This is a positive position for the company. The cash receipts from customers increased by $1636.5 million, which is a very healthy sign for the company, provided it represents an increase in sales and not merely a reduction in amounts owing from debtors (which of course also represents receipts from customers). Our knowledge of Woolworths would suggest that most of its sales are for cash and few are on credit. This is confirmed by the fact that:

a the revenue from operating activities for 1999 from the profit and loss statement (statement of financial performance) is $18 765.5 million and the collections from customers is $18 446.2 million; and

b the total for receivables in the balance sheet (statement of financial position) is only $181.6 million.

Also, the reconciliation statement of cash flows from operations and operating profit shows that, in fact, debtors increased by $22.8 million.

The cash payments to suppliers also increased by $1543.7 million. The increase in interest costs is consistent with the increase in borrowings disclosed in the section on financing activities. This increase in borrowings needs to be assessed to determine whether the company is taking on too much debt. We say more on this in Chapter 14.

Cash flows from investing activities

The major item in this section is the acquisition of $695.6 million worth of property, plant and equipment. This is consistent with the previous year and clearly demonstrates that the company is expanding and growing.

Cash flows from financing activities

This section shows that the company has retired $1155.1 million of debt and borrowed an additional $1440.9 million. Therefore, we can conclude that Woolworths has used cash flows from operations and an increase in debt to finance the acquisition of the property, plant and equipment, and the payment of dividends. This represents sound financial management provided

a the debt is long term and thus matches the source of funds with the use of such funds; and

b the company's debt ratios are still within acceptable limits.

Net increase in cash

The cash on hand increased by $82.3 million for the period.

Non-cash financing and investing activities

This reveals that the company reinvested 21 per cent of the dividends paid in shares. The implication of this is that the number of shares upon which dividends will be paid in the future has increased.

Financing facilities

Note 16 discloses that the company has generous sums of standby lending facilities available, should the need for finance arise.

Consolidated accounts

Most major companies such as BHP, CSR and CRA operate in a parent–subsidiary (or controlled entity) relationship for a variety of reasons. In fact, these large companies often control 100 or more companies. Note 28 in the Woolworths report discloses that there are 52 entities either directly or indirectly controlled by Woolworths Limited.Since users of financial reports need to examine the performance and financial position of the parent entity on its own, and of the combination of the parent entity and the other entities it controls, group accounts are prepared. The preparation of these group accounts is called consolidation, and the terms 'group' and 'consolidated' accounts are interchangeable. In these accounts, the parent entity and its controlled entities are grouped to constitute an economic entity. It does not have the status of being a legal entity; it does not have the legal rights and obligations of a company, which were discussed in Chapter 11.

Consolidated financial statements are useful to the management and shareholders of the parent entity in judging how well the parent has achieved its goals. Other users such as creditors and employees find this information useful in their decision making.

Preparation of consolidated accounts

Consolidated accounts are prepared in accordance with *AASB 1024: Consolidated Accounts*. This standard requires consolidated financial statements to be prepared for a parent entity and all other entities which it controls. Control is defined (in paragraph 9) as:

> the capacity of an entity to dominate decision-making, directly or indirectly, in relation to the financial and operating policies of another entity so as to enable that other entity to operate with it in pursuing the objectives of the controlling entity.

The concept of control is consistent with the approach taken in the definition of assets in *SAC 4* and discussed in Chapter 2.

CASE STUDY 12.2

The diagrams below are examples of different organisational structures which would meet the definition of an economic entity for the purpose of *AASB 1024*.

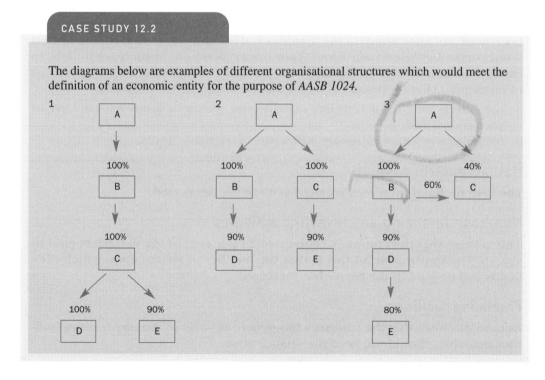

Commentary

In all three cases, we have assumed that the percentage of ownership also equals the voting entitlements. Therefore, in Case 1, the economic entity consists of A, B, C, D and E, and A is the parent entity or chief entity. In Case 2, A obtains control of D indirectly through its control of B. Therefore, the economic entity in Case 2 is still A, B, C, D and E, with A still the parent or chief entity. In Case 3, A achieves control of C both through its own interest in C and through B's interest in C. Therefore, the economic entity is still A, B, C, D and E, and A is again the parent or chief entity.

In all three cases, A controls entities B, C, D and E because of the voting rights attached to its ownership interest.

The purpose of consolidated financial statements is to give a view of the parent entity and its controlled entities as if they were one entity, i.e. the economic entity, so that on the statement of financial position the debtors represent the debtors of the parent entity and all its controlled entities. Similarly, the consolidated statement of financial performance shows total revenue from sales made by the parent entity and all its controlled entities. In preparing consolidated financial statements, similar accounts from the individual statements of the parent entity and its controlled entities are combined. However, some accounts result from transactions between the parent entity and a controlled entity. If consolidated financial statements are to represent the position and results of an economic entity as a whole, then any transactions between members within the economic entity must be eliminated.

If we look at Figure 12.2, we can see why it is necessary to eliminate inter-entity transactions.

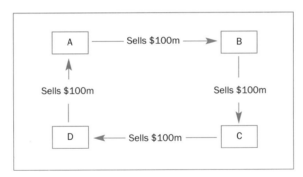

Figure 12.2 *Transactions between members of an economic entity.*

If A, B, C and D are all members of the same economic entity, then adding sales figures together would produce $400 million of sales. However, the economic entity A, B, C and D has not sold any of this to parties external to the group. Therefore, the sales for the economic entity in relation to the transactions shown in Figure 12.2 should be zero. In preparing consolidated financial statements for A, B, C and D, it is necessary to eliminate each of the sales of $100 million which appear in each of the individual financial statements for entities A, B, C and D. This also applies to the expenses and to the profits or losses made from these sales.

It is also necessary to eliminate any amounts owing to or due from members within the economic entity. If A in Figure 12.2 was owed $100 million by B, in the consolidated financial statements it would be necessary to reduce debtors and creditors by $100 million. If this was not done, the consolidated statement of financial position for the economic entity would show $100 million as owing from itself and payable to itself. Obviously this is inappropriate.

Another item which must be eliminated in the consolidated statement of financial position is Investment in the Subsidiary account which appears in the parent entity's statement of financial position.

The Investment in the Subsidiary account is replaced in the consolidation process with the assets and liabilities of the controlled entity. Thus, the Investment account and the shareholders' equity section of the controlled entity must be eliminated. The following example demonstrates this process.

Accounts	Company A	Company B	Elimination	Consolidation
	$	$	$	$
Assets	50 000	30 000		80 000
Investment in B				
(100% of shares in B)	10 000			–10 000
	60 000	30 000		80 000
Liabilities	20 000	20 000		40 000
Paid-up capital	20 000	10 000	–10 000	20 000
Retained profits	20 000			20 000
	60 000	30 000		80 000

In this example, A owns all the shares of B. Therefore the Investment in B account represents A's ownership and control of the total shareholders' equity of B. The shareholders' equity section of B represents the ownership of the net assets of B, i.e. $30 000 – $20 000. Therefore, A owns and controls the net assets of B. Thus, the elimination of the Investment in B account and the shareholders' equity section of B allows the net assets of B to be added to the net assets of A. This produces the net assets of the economic entity of A + B.

The consolidated financial statements are prepared by combining similar accounts from the separate statements of the parent entity and its controlled entities after elimination of all transactions between members of the economic entity.

An examination of Woolworths' financial report shows that Woolworths Limited is registered in New South Wales. Therefore, the columns in the financial statements for Woolworths Limited relate only to the activities in New South Wales. The consolidated columns show the results for Woolworths in all parts of Australia and for all the entities listed in Note 28 that are controlled by the board of Woolworths Limited. Without consolidated statements, it would not be possible to properly assess the financial performance of the board.

Taxation

A company's tax liability is determined by the taxable income of the company in Australia. In Chapter 1 we mentioned that accounting profit and taxable income may not be the same. This is because accounting rules used to determine accounting profit sometimes differ from the tax rules used to determine taxable income. The example used in Chapter 1 was income that is exempt from tax but still included as revenue in the determination of accounting profit. Another example is the differences that arise from the different depreciation rates used for accounting and tax purposes. These differences

between taxable income and accounting profit result in the recognition of a current liability for taxes payable and possibly a non-current liability for deferred taxes payable.
It is also possible for companies to have deferred tax assets. In this section we attempt
to explain deferred tax assets and liabilities.

Temporary differences

The use of different rules for tax and accounting leads to temporary differences between
the carrying value of an asset or liability in the statement of financial position in a
company's books and the balances for the same asset and liability for taxation. This is
best explained with some examples.

Rent receivable

Assume Company A recognises revenue of $10 000 at 30 June 20X1 for rent it is owed
but has not yet received in cash. This results in the recognition of an asset rent receivable of $10 000. For accounting purposes, the rent revenue increases accounting profit
by $10 000. However, the company uses the cash basis for tax purposes and is there-
fore not required to pay tax until the rent is received in cash. When the rent is received,
the company will have to pay tax. This means the company will pay more tax in future
periods; this meets the definition of a liability.

The future tax consequence for the company of receiving the rent and reducing the
asset rent receivable to a zero balance is a tax liability of $10 000 × the tax rate. If we
assume a tax rate of 40 per cent, this results in future tax of $4000. This will be recog-
nised in the current year as a deferred tax liability. If we assume the accounting profit
is $100 000 for 20X1 and taxable income is $90 000, the worksheet entries involved in
the current period are as follows.

WORKSHEET: COMPANY A, 20X1

Assets	= Liabilities		+ Profit and loss
	Tax payable	Deferred tax payable	Tax expense
	36 000	4 000	– 40 000
	(40% × $90 000)	(40% × $1000)	($36 000 + $4000)

Tax expense is determined by taking the tax payable and adding (subtracting)
increases (decreases) in the deferred tax payable.

In the following year, if we assume the rent was paid to Company A and the taxable
income is $100 000 and accounting profit $90 000, the worksheet would be as shown
below.

WORKSHEET: COMPANY A, 20X2

Assets	= Liabilities		+ Profit and loss
	Tax payable	Deferred tax payable	Tax expense
	40 000	– 4 000	– 36 000
	(40% × $10 000)	(40% × $10 000)	($40 000 – $4000)

The tax payable the following year is $4000 higher than the previous year and this,
in effect, represents settlement of the deferred tax amount from the previous period.

The deferred tax payable arises because of the temporary difference in the balance
of the asset rent receivable in the books of Company A ($10 000) and the value of the
asset for tax purposes (zero).

Provision for warranty costs

Companies who provide warranties on products they sell estimate the expected costs to be incurred in future periods as a result of sales in the current period. This is based on their experience in previous years and is similar to the estimation of doubtful debts discussed in Chapter 8. This results in the recognition of an expense and a liability in the current period. However, for tax purposes, there is no deduction for any warranty costs until the actual repairs have been made and the costs incurred.

Assume Company B has estimated the liability for warranty costs at $20 000 and has created the liability provision for warranty costs and recorded the expense. This results in an accounting profit of $80 000 and taxable income of $100 000 in 20X1.

The future tax consequence of creating this liability is that the liability will be reduced when the warranty repairs are provided and the company will pay less tax in future periods. The payment of less tax in the future meets the definition of an asset. Therefore, Company B must recognise a deferred tax asset of $20 000 × 40 per cent, or $8000.

This will result in lower tax expense for the period as illustrated in the worksheet below.

WORKSHEET: COMPANY B, 20X1

Assets	= Liabilities	+ Profit and loss
Deferred tax asset	Tax payable	Tax expense
8 000	40 000	– 32 000
(40% × $20 000)	(40% × $100 000)	($40 000 – $8000)

The deferred tax asset arises because of a temporary difference in the balance of the provision for warranty costs in the books of Company B ($20 000) and the value of the liability for tax purposes (zero). If in 20X2 the actual warranty costs incurred total $20 000 and the taxable income is $80 000, and accounting profit is $100 000, then the accounting entries would be as follows.

WORKSHEET: COMPANY B, 20X2

Assets	= Liabilities	+ Profit and loss
Deferred tax asset	Tax payable	Tax expense
–8 000	32 000	– 40 000
(40% × $20 000)	(40% × $80 000)	($32 000 – $8000)

The amount of tax payable in 20X2 is $8000 less than in 20X1. This in effect represents the consumption of the deferred tax asset.

Tax expense is determined by taking the tax payable and subtracting (adding) increases (decreases) in the deferred tax asset.

Tax losses

When a company incurs a loss for tax purposes it potentially has a deferred tax asset which it can recognise on the statement of financial position. This is because the tax laws allow losses to be carried forward and used to reduce taxable income in future periods. Therefore, if a company decides it is probable it will earn taxable income in future periods, it can recognise a deferred tax asset in the current period.

Assume that Company C incurs a tax loss of $100 000 in the current period. The loss resulted from an unusually long and protracted strike, but the company expects to return to profitability next year. If the tax rate is 40 per cent, the company can recognise a deferred tax asset of $100 000 × 40 per cent, or $40 000. This represents future tax savings of $40 000.

Summary

In this chapter we have looked at the structure and use of cash flow statements. The cash flow statement replaces the funds statement in general-purpose financial reports. We also discussed two other accounting issues which will further help you understand financial statements. The first was consolidated financial statements. Most company annual reports disclose results for a parent or holding company and the group. The group is an economic entity and not a legal entity. The concept of control is used to determine the members of the group. Finally, we saw that accounting profit and taxable income are normally different amounts. This results in the recognition of deferred tax assets and liabilities.

References

Australian Accounting Standards Board. *AASB 1020: Accounting for Income Tax*, December 1999.

Australian Accounting Standards Board. *AASB 1024: Consolidated Accounts*, May 1992.

Australian Accounting Standards Board. *AASB 1026: Statement of Cash Flows*, October 1997.

Graham, K.M., et al., 1992. *Graham, Jager and Taylor's Company Accounting Procedures*, 5th edn, Butterworths.

Leo, K.J., and Hoggett, J.M., 1998. *Company Accounting in Australia*, 4th edn, John Wiley.

Wise, T.D., et al., 1990. *Accounting in Australia*, Houghton Mifflin.

Review questions

1 What are the reasons for requiring a statement of cash flows?

2 What information can be obtained from a statement of cash flows?

3 What are consolidated financial statements? What is their purpose?

4 Describe what is meant by the concept of control.

5 What are the three basic types of elimination that need to be made when preparing consolidated financial statements?

6 What are deferred tax assets and liabilities?

7 Why might accounting profit and taxable income differ?

Problems for discussion and analysis

Page - 515

1 Refer to the Woolworths financial report in Appendix 1.
   a   What kinds of services did Woolworths provide for its subsidiaries?
   b   Did Woolworths have a 100 per cent beneficial interest in all its subsidiaries?
   c   From your general knowledge, can you identify any subsidiary that could be said to not be part of the main business of Woolworths, i.e. not be a food-oriented company?
   d   Did cash increase over the 52 weeks ended 27 June 1999? If so, by how much?

e   How much tax was paid in the year? By how much did external borrowings exceed repayments of external borrowings?

f   What amounts are reported for Future Income Tax Benefit and Deferred Income Tax Liability?

2   Explain how it is that a business which is making profits can have difficulties in meeting its debts. Perhaps you can bring to class some examples of businesses in this situation.

3   Discuss the impact of each of the items below on the statement of financial position, statement of financial performance and cash flow statement, giving reasons for your answer where appropriate.

a   During the year the company sold a fixed asset with a net book value of $5000 for $3000.

b   The company also revalued its land from its original cost of $130 000 to $200 000.

c   The building, which had cost $90 000 and on which depreciation of $30 000 had been provided, was revalued to $100 000.

d   The company has also made an issue of 100 000 8 per cent $1 preference shares at a price of $1.20 per share.

e   The company had paid back a long-term loan to the bank of $80 000.

4   Each of the transactions listed below will affect one of the four categories on the statement of cash flows: cash flows from operating activities, cash flows from investing activities, cash flows from financing activities, or non-cash investing and financing activities. Analyse each transaction and state which category will be affected.

a   Machinery to the value of $80 000 was acquired for cash.

b   Copyright was sold for $30 000 that had a book value of $20 000.

c   Office supplies on hand valued at $2000 were exchanged for a secondhand car.

d   Used machinery having a book value of $50 000 was traded for 500 shares of another company. The shares are intended to be a long-term investment.

e   Dividends to the amount of $5000 were paid.

f   Long-term debenture notes payable for the amount of $20 000 were paid in cash.

g   Interest was paid on the amount of $5000.

5   ABC Company engaged in the following transactions. Classify each as: (a) an operating activity, (b) an investing activity, (c) a financing activity, (d) a non-cash transaction, or (e) none of the above.

Paid employees for wages.

Purchased a 90-day Treasury bill.

Purchased land and buildings.

Exchanged issued shares for amounts owed to convertible debt holders.

Signed a four-year lease agreement for a motor vehicle.

Declared and issued a bonus share dividend.

Issued ordinary shares.

Received cash from customers.

Purchased an investment.

Paid interest.

Sold equipment for a gain.

Received dividends on investments owned.

Issued long-term debentures for long-term assets.

Declared and paid a cash dividend.

(Adapted from T.D. Wise et al., *Accounting in Australia*, Houghton Mifflin, 1990, Chapter 19, Exercise 19.1.)

6 The Royal Park Company statement of financial performance for 20X1 appears below:

ROYAL PARK COMPANY
STATEMENT OF FINANCIAL PERFORMANCE FOR
THE YEAR ENDED 31 DECEMBER 20X1

	$000
Sales	160 000
Cost of goods sold	(96 000)
Gross profit on sales	64 000
Operating expenses:	
Rent expense	20 000
Depreciation expense	15 000
Other operating expenses	18 000
Total operating expenses	(53 000)
Net income	11 000

The following information from Royal Park's statement of financial position is available.

Account title	Balance January 1 $	Balance December 31 $
Accounts receivable	10 000	12 000
Inventory	3 000	10 000
Prepaid rent	5 000	8 000
Accounts payable	26 000	28 000

Determine the cash flow from operating activities for Royal Park.

7 Given a simplified statement of financial position of Bazz & Lee Ltd, prepare a worksheet for the consolidation of the accounts of the parent company (Bazz Ltd) and its subsidiary (Lee Ltd). From your worksheet prepare the consolidated statement of financial position.

The following need to be taken into consideration.

i Bazz Ltd acquired all the shares of Lee Ltd for $320 000 on the morning of 30 June 20X1.

ii All assets and liabilities are stated at their fair values.

iii Lee Ltd owed Bazz Ltd $10 000 for goods purchased on 15 June 20X1.

BAZZ & LEE LTD
STATEMENT OF FINANCIAL POSITION AT 30 JUNE 20X1

	Bazz Ltd $	Lee Ltd $
Assets		
Current Assets		
Bank	180 000	50 000
Accounts receivable	100 000	150 000
Total Current Assets	280 000	200 000
Non-current Assets		
Plant and equipment (net of depreciation)	300 000	300 000
Investment in Lee Ltd	320 000	—
Total Non-current Assets	620 000	300 000
Total Assets	900 000	500 000
Liabilities		
Current Liabilities		
Accounts payable	400 000	180 000
Total Liabilities	400 000	180 000
Net Assets	500 000	320 000
Equity		
Paid-up capital	400 000	300 000
Retained earnings	100 000	20 000
Total Equity	500 000	320 000

8   Given the statements of financial position for Phil and Jan Ltd below, prepare a worksheet for the consolidation of the accounts of the parent company Jan Ltd. Then, from your worksheet, prepare a consolidated statement of financial position.

    i   Jan acquired all the issued capital of Phil Ltd on 30 June 20X1 for $200 000.

    ii All assets and liabilities are stated at their fair values.

    iii Of the debentures issued by Jan Ltd, $100 000 worth are held by Phil.

    iv Jan owed Phil $13 000 for goods purchased in June 20X1.

PHIL & JAN LTD
STATEMENTS OF FINANCIAL POSITION AT 30 JUNE 20X1

	Jan Ltd $		Phil Ltd $	
Assets				
Bank		2 000		1 000
Debtors		33 000		27 000
Inventory		12 000		63 000
Total Current Assets		47 000		91 000
Non-current Assets				
Plant and equipment	120 000		63 000	
CBS accumulated DEPN	73 000	47 000	6 000	57 000
Debentures investment in Phil		200 000		100 000

(continued next page)

Total Non-current Assets		247 000		157 000
Total Assets		294 000		248 000
Liabilities				
Current Liabilities				
Creditors		36 000		53 000
Taxation		10 000		60 000
Total Current Liabilities		46 000		113 000
Non-current Liabilities				
Debentures	150 000		–	
Total Non-current Liabilities		150 000		–
Total Liabilities		196 000		113 000
Net Assets		98 000		135 000
Equity				
Paid-up capital	80 000		100 000	
Retained earnings	18 000		35 000	
Total Equity		98 000		135 000

9   During its first year of operations ending 30 June 20X6, Liquid Amber
Ltd earned an operating profit of $100 000. Included in this figure
were:

Depreciation (straight-line) on equipment	$12 000
Depreciation of buildings	$6 000
Provision for doubtful debts	$5 000
(Tax rate is 33%)	

The company also incurred research and development expenditure of $15 000
which it had treated as an asset.

In order to calculate its estimated taxable income for the year, accelerated
depreciation on equipment of $18 000 was charged. There were no deductions
allowable for depreciation of buildings, and no bad debts were written off.
Furthermore, the company claimed its total expenditure on research and
development as a tax deduction.

Calculate:

a   taxable income
b   income tax expense
c   payable income tax
d   payable deferred tax.

(Adapted from J. Hoggett and L. Edwards, *Financial Accounting in Australia*,
John Wiley, 1990, p. 803.)

10   On 1 January 20X4 the Widget Company acquires a piece of equipment which
costs $40 000 and has an estimated life of four years with no residual value.
The equipment is to be written off at 25 per cent per annum, straight-line.
Assume the operating profit for the next four years is $100 000 per annum
(before the deduction of depreciation and tax). For tax purposes the company
is allowed to write off the asset over two years at 50 per cent per annum,
straight-line. The tax rate is 50 per cent.

Set up a table with the following headings and fill in the blank spaces.

Year ending 31 December	Profit before depreciation and tax	Taxable profit after tax depreciation	Tax payable	Taxable profit after accounting depreciation	Tax expense	Differences between tax payable and tax expense
20X4						
20X5						
20X6						
20X7						
Total						

11   The following cash flow statement is available for the Bee Pee Company.

	2000 $m	2001 $m
Cash flows from operating activities		
Receipts from customers	3 000	3 000
Payments to suppliers and employees	(2 500)	(2 600)
Interest received	60	35
Interest paid	(75)	(150)
Taxation paid	(2)	(8)
Payments from provisions	(15)	(5)
Net cash from operating activities	468	272
Cash flows from investing activities		
Acquisition of property, plant and equipment	(250)	(1 800)
Proceeds from sale of non-current assets	50	200
Net cash from investing activities	(200)	(1 600)
Cash flows from financing activities		
Short-term borrowing—increase (decrease)		1 450
Long-term borrowing—increase (decrease)	40	
Dividends paid	(200)	(200)
Net cash from financing activities	(160)	(1 250)
Net increase (decrease) in cash held	108	(78)
Add opening cash brought forward	(50)	58
Closing cash carried forward	58	(20)

Required:

Analyse the cash flow statement for Bee Pee. What changes to the cash management policies would you recommend to the company? Should the company continue to pay a dividend?

12   The directors of Kowloon Enterprises Ltd are concerned at the results of trading activities reported for the year ended 30 June 20X6, and failure to keep within the limit of the bank overdraft ($12 000).

KOWLOON ENTERPRISES LTD
STATEMENTS OF FINANCIAL PERFORMANCE FOR THE YEARS ENDED 30 JUNE

	20X4		20X5		20X6	
	$	$	$	$	$	$
Sales		200 000		180 000		165 000
Less Cost of sales						
Opening stock	36 000		41 000		44 000	
Purchases	95 000		87 000		80 000	
	131 000		128 000		124 000	
Less Closing stock	41 000	90 000	44 000	84 000	49 000	75 000
Gross profit		110 000		96 000		90 000
Less:						
Selling and distribution expenses	40 000		40 000		46 000	
General and administrative expenses	20 000		20 000		18 000	
Financial expenses	15 000	75 000	16 000	76 000	20 000	84 000
Net operating profit before tax		35 000		20 000		6 000
Less Provision for taxation		15 000		9 000		2 500
Net operating profit after tax		20 000		11 000		3 500
Less Loss on sale of investment						1 000
Net profit for year		20 000		11 000		2 500
Add:						
Balance of unappropriated profits b/f		10 000		7 000		1 000
Transfer from reserve				10 000		
Amount available for distribution		30 000		28 000		3 500
Less Dividends paid and proposed						
Preference—final	3 000		3 000		3 000	
Ordinary—interim	10 000		12 000			
Ordinary—final	10 000	23 000	12 000	27 000		3 000
Unappropriated profits c/f		7 000		1 000		500

KOWLOON ENTERPRISES LTD
STATEMENTS OF FINANCIAL POSITION AT 30 JUNE

	20X4		20X5		20X6	
	$	$	$	$	$	$
Assets						
Current Assets						
Bank	1 000					
Inventory	41 000		44 000		49 000	
Trade debtors	26 000		31 000		37 000	
Less Provision for doubtful debts	(1 000)		(1 000)		(2 000)	
Prepayments	2 000		3 000		3 000	
Total Current Assets		69 000		77 000		87 000
Non-current Assets						
Plant and equipment	10 000		10 000		21 000	
Less Depreciation						
(1 000 in X3)	(2 000)		(4 000)		(7 000)	
Vehicles	80 000		80 000		114 000	
Less Depreciation						
(4 000 in X3)	(16 000)		(32 000)		(54 000)	
Land (at valuation)	60 000		70 000		70 000	
Buildings (at cost)	40 000		56 000		56 000	
Investments (at cost)	25 000		25 000			
Total Non-current Assets		197 000		205 000		200 000
Total Assets		266 000		282 000		287 000
Liabilities						
Current Liabilities						
Bank overdraft			8 500		12 500	
Trade creditors	12 000		8 000		14 000	
Accrued wages and interest	1 000		1 500		2 000	
Provision for taxation	15 000		9 000		2 500	
Provision for dividend	13 000		15 000		3 000	
Total Current Liabilities		41 000		42 000		34 000
Non-current Liabilities						
Mortgage on land (due 30.6.X9)			21 000		34 500	
Term loan (due 20Y2)	75 000		75 000		75 000	
Total Non-current Liabilities		75 000		96 000		109 500
Total Liabilities		116 000		138 000		143 500
Net Assets		150 000		144 000		143 500
Owners' Equity						
50 000 6% $1 preference shares		50 000		50 000		50 000
100 000 $1 ordinary shares						
paid to 75c		75 000		75 000		75 000
Asset revaluation reserve				10 000		10 000
General reserve		18 000		8 000		8 000
Unappropriated profits		7 000		1 000		500
Total Owners' Equity		150 000		144 000		143 500

Required:

a   What factors have contributed to this cash problem?

b   What steps would you recommend for Kowloon Enterprises Ltd to overcome the current cash problem?

Ethics case study

Jane Golly is the Chief Financial Officer for Woppet Enterprises Ltd. She has decided to add a new ratio to the financial statements based on *cash flow per share*. The ratio will be reported on the cash flow statement and she believes it will provide useful information to readers of the financial statements. The *cash flow per share* this year will show a 25 per cent increase from last year. This will contrast with the 5 per cent decline in *earnings per share*.

Discuss whether there is anything unethical about Jane Golly's decision.

Accounting Regulation and Audit

Learning objectives

At the end of this chapter you should be able to:

1   explain the current arrangements for standard setting in Australia

2   understand the roles of the AASB, the UIG and ASIC in relation to accounting standards

3   understand what is meant by the term 'due process'

4   explain the influence of Accounting Standards, the Corporations Law and the stock exchange on financial reporting requirements

5   understand the role of the audit and the auditor in financial reporting

6   explain what is meant by the term 'expectation gap' and what its impact has been on the auditor's report.

Introduction

General-purpose financial reports prepared in Australia for external users are subject to various influences and rules, dependent on the type of business organisation involved.

The most extensive regulations exist for companies, in particular for listed public companies. Their financial reports must comply with various professional, statutory and stock exchange requirements. Other types of business organisations—such as small private companies, partnerships or sole proprietorships—are subject to much less regulation. In this chapter we examine the regulation of external financial reporting in Australia. Major emphasis is placed on the establishment of Accounting Standards and the parties involved in the standard-setting process, the regulation of financial reports prepared by companies, and their audit.

The framework for setting standards

On 1 January 2000, new arrangements for the setting of accounting standards in Australia came into existence. The Australian Accounting Standards Board (AASB) sets accounting standards for both the private and public sectors. Prior to 2000, Australian Accounting Standards (AAS) were set by the Public Sector Accounting Standards Board (PSASB) and AASB standards were set by the AASB. The AAS applied to public-sector reporting entities and private-sector reporting entities other than companies, while the AASB standards applied only to companies that were reporting entities. The AAS are still applicable to reporting entities, but no new AAS will be issued.

The new arrangements came about as part of the Corporate Law Economic Reform Program initiated by the Howard government. The new arrangements also involve a Financial Reporting Council (FRC) which has oversight responsibility for the AASB.

Membership of the FRC comprises key stakeholders from professional accounting bodies, the business community, government, and regulatory agencies like the Australian Securities and Investments Commission. Members are appointed by the Treasurer.

The FRC is responsible for the priorities, business plan, budget and staffing arrangements of the AASB but is not able to influence the AASB's technical deliberations. In theory, this means the FRC cannot determine the content of Accounting Standards. However, given its control of the budget and priorities of the AASB, it has the potential, in practice, to influence the setting of Accounting Standards. The FRC is also responsible for advising the government on the process of setting Accounting Standards and on the development of International Accounting Standards.

The new AASB held its first meeting on 29 May 2000. There are ten members, including a full-time chairperson. At the first meeting, the board agreed to continue with due process (as depicted in Figure 13.2) in the development of Accounting Standards. This included a commitment, for the first time, to holding public meetings on all technical matters. This is in line with a new approach of openness and transparency in the standard-setting process.

The AASB has its own dedicated technical staff. It is also proposed to establish Project Advisory Panels with members appointed by the FRC. These panels would assist AASB technical staff in the preparation of various papers for the AASB to consider as it develops Accounting Standards.

The Urgent Issues Group (UIG) continues to operate, but it is now a committee of the AASB and the chairperson of the AASB also chairs the UIG. The role of the UIG is to review problems in the interpretation of Accounting Standards and to issue a consensus view if deemed appropriate. The UIG is able to respond in a more timely fashion than the AASB, but it is not empowered to issue Accounting Standards and the AASB maintains a right of veto over the UIG consensus views which are issued as Abstracts. The standard-setting structure is represented in Figure 13.1.

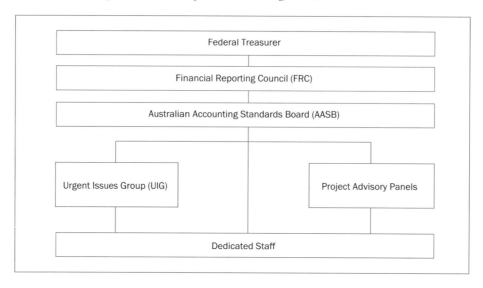

Figure 13.1 *Administrative structure for the setting of Australian Accounting Standards (adapted from C. Parker and B. Porter, 2001 Australian GAAP, Parker Publishing, 2001, p. 30).*

In accordance with the Corporations Law, compliance with the Accounting Standards issued by the AASB is mandatory for all companies that are reporting entities. Other jurisdictions such as state governments may also adopt AASB standards and make compliance with such standards mandatory. The Australian Securities and Investments Commission (ASIC) is responsible for enforcing compliance with the Corporations Law.

Compliance with previously issued Australian Accounting Standards and UIG Abstracts is required by the professional accounting bodies in Australia, including the Institute of Chartered Accountants in Australia, CPA Australia and the National Institute of Accountants. Members of these bodies are obliged to comply with all AAS and UIG Abstracts. Now that the UIG is a committee of the AASB, it is possible that the Abstracts will have the legal status of AASB standards, but this remains unclear.

Due process

This process is designed to allow all interested parties maximum opportunity to comment on proposed Accounting Standards. The process is depicted in Figure 13.2.

Selection of topics

Projects are selected by the AASB, presumably in response to emerging issues, although some would argue that the topics are selected following particular problems or crises in financial reporting.

Discussion paper or theory monograph

A contractor is appointed initially to investigate all relevant aspects of a topic and prepare a discussion paper or an accounting theory monograph which is designed to inform readers in an unbiased manner. The contractor can be a staff member from the AASB or can be from industry, the profession, academia, the public sector or elsewhere. The contractor is assisted by a project advisory panel, which consists of people with expertise in the area under consideration. The panel acts as a resource for the contractor, in addition to reviewing draft copies of the paper.

Key decisions questionnaire

This document identifies the main issues to be resolved in relation to the topic, and is based on the discussion paper or accounting theory monograph. The boards discuss the issues raised in the questionnaire and make tentative decisions. These decisions form the basis for a draft exposure draft which is prepared by staff from the AASB.

Draft exposure draft

The draft exposure draft is circulated to parties with an interest and knowledge in the area. Their comments are used by the boards to refine the exposure draft before it is released.

Exposure draft

The exposure draft is distributed to all registrants on the AASB mailing list and to any other interested parties, with an invitation to comment on the proposed Accounting Standard. Following the review period, additional opportunities, such as a public hearing, are provided if the boards deem it appropriate.

Draft standard

A draft Statement of Accounting Standard is prepared after comments have been received on the exposure draft. The draft may be given additional public exposure or it may be forwarded direct to ASIC and to the Commonwealth Treasurer. These parties then have 30 days in which to comment.

Final standard

Comments received from ASIC or the Commonwealth Treasurer are incorporated into a final standard which is then issued by the AASB. The Federal Parliament has a 15-day veto period.

This completes the due process. Once the veto period has passed, the standards are issued for application from a specified date.

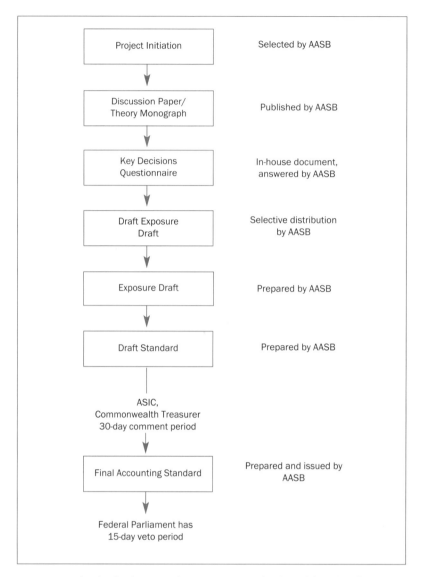

Figure 13.2 *Due process for the development of Accounting Standards and the roles of the participants.*

The political nature of accounting standard setting

In Chapter 1 we discussed the choice of accounting policies and their economic consequences. The standard-setting body selects accounting standards based on the objective of providing useful information to the users of financial statements. Managers, however, may choose accounting policies based on the economic consequences to themselves and their firms.

The due process employed by the standard setters provides an opportunity for managers to lobby the standard setters. They attempt to influence their deliberations, particularly with reference to standards relevant to their company. The Group of 100 is an association of the chief financial managers of the 100 largest companies in Australia. The group is very active in making submissions to the standard setters.

The managers' agenda for lobbying the standard setters may be to ensure that financial statements provide useful information. Alternatively, their reasons may well be more in their own self-interest, and that of the companies for which they work.

In any event, the impact of this interest in the standard-setting process is that it is recognised as a political process. Therefore, the standard-setting bodies have to contend with trying to achieve their stated objective within a process which is quite political.

CASE STUDY 13.1

Queries raised on MYOB's accounts

by Tom Ravlic

THE Federal Opposition has called on the Australian Securities and Investments Commission and the Australian Stock Exchange to investigate the accounting practices of software developer MYOB.

Senator Stephen Conroy, the shadow minister for financial services and regulation, branded MYOB's accounts as non-compliant and urged both the ASIC and the ASX in separate letters to take steps to ensure MYOB complied with an accounting standard, known as AASB 1015, that was amended by the Senator earlier this year.

He also attacked accounting firm Ernst Young, the auditors of MYOB, for not indicating there was controversy related to the accounts and notifying shareholders of the reporting issues in its independent review attached to the financial statements.

He urged the company to take legal action against Ernst Young over the alleged misleading advice.

MYOB's half-year accounts, lodged with the ASX last week, reported a $20.6 million profit after tax, but a disclosure note revealed that the profit would have been slashed by more than half had it complied with the accounting rules finalised by Federal Parliament.

The accounting software player based its accounts on a book value exemption that was a part of the accounting standard when it was created by the Australian Accounting Standards Board. However, the Senate decision to disallow the book value method meant all companies had to account for reconstructions within corporate groups at fair value.

Fair value accounting gives rise to goodwill, which must be written off over a period not exceeding 20 years, resulting in lower stated profits.

Senator Conroy said it was 'ludicrous' for MYOB to rely on the short period between the accounting standard being made and February's parliamentary disallowance as a basis for not complying with the fair value accounting rules.

ASIC allowed MYOB's accounts to incorporate the book value method because they were completed before the disallowance, but requested that MYOB change its accounting earlier this year to reflect the effect of the disallowance. The company told the ASX in June it did not intend to change its accounting method.

'The MYOB accounts do not provide accurate information and information which is comparable with other companies,' Senator Conroy said.

Age, 8 September 2000

Commentary

The article reports on the accounts of MYOB not complying with an Accounting Standard which was revised after the federal parliament voted to change a certain clause in *AASB 1015: Acquisition of Assets*. The article clearly illustrates the political nature of Accounting Standards and the preparing of financial statements.

Statements of Accounting Concepts

The project of developing the Conceptual Framework which is discussed in Chapter 2 has resulted in the publication of Statements of Accounting Concepts. These are developed by the same due process used for the development of Accounting Standards.

Accounting Concepts provide general guidance on issues, such as definitions of assets, liabilities, revenues, expenses and equity, to help accountants resolve particular problems as they arise.

Accounting Standards establish procedures on how to account for certain transactions and events, as well as providing detailed disclosure requirements. For example, cash flow statements must be prepared in accordance with *AASB 1026: Statement of Cash Flows*.

The Accounting Standards must be complied with by members of the accounting profession, under *APS 1: Conformity with Statements of Accounting Standards. APS 1* states that Statements of Accounting Concepts should be used by members as guidance. In addition, members are also required to comply with UIG abstracts.

The reporting entity

The concept of the reporting entity, which is detailed in *SAC 1: Definition of the Reporting Entity* and discussed in Chapter 2, effectively means that Statements of Accounting Standards are mandatory only for reporting entities. Thus, while the Accounting Standards issued by the AASB are relevant to all companies, application of the reporting entity concept means that a company which is not a reporting entity is not required to comply with these standards. Small family-owned companies are generally not reporting entities and are therefore not required to prepare general-purpose financial reports.

International Accounting Standards

The International Accounting Standards Committee (IASC) issues International Accounting Standards (IASs) on various topics. Although such standards do not override national standards, the IASC hopes that its activities will result in more uniform worldwide Accounting Standards. Where a country does not have a standard-setting authority, it can adopt the IASs.

A survey on the use and application of International Accounting Standards by Hancock (1998) shows that IASs are only directly applied in seven countries. A further 12 countries apply IASs with some slight modifications. While it is unlikely in the short term that there will be a single set of accounting standards which are applied worldwide, there is a view that international harmonisation of accounting standards will facilitate the flow of capital across country borders. This has potential benefits to investors and for companies wishing to list their shares in other countries.

In April 1996, *Policy Statement No 6, International Harmonisation* was issued by the AASB. In essence, what this statement does is indicate that accounting standards in Australia are to be harmonised with the International Accounting Standards. To this end Australian Standards are being reissued so that they conform more closely with the IASs. This has resulted in the redrafting of many Accounting Standards to bring them into line with the IASs. However, this does not mean that an Australian Standard will be changed in circumstances where the AASB disagrees with the IAS approach. Instead, the board will work to influence the IASC to review their standards.

The AASB at its first meeting in May resolved to continue to work closely with the IASC. Under the new standard-setting arrangements, the Treasurer may give the AASB a direction on the role of International Accounting Standards in the setting of Accounting Standards in Australia. This will be based on advice from the FRC. At one stage in the development of the new standard-setting structure, it was proposed that Australia would simply adopt IASs from a certain date. The final structure is a retreat from this position, but Australia continues to revise existing Accounting Standards so that they comply more closely with IASs.

Corporations Law

It is not our intention in this section to cover the requirements of the Corporations Law in detail. They are dealt with in courses on company law and company accounting.

Most companies are required to prepare a statement of financial position and statement of financial performance in accordance with applicable Accounting Standards so as to show a true and fair view of the company's financial position and results for the period. Compliance with applicable Accounting Standards issued by the AASB is mandatory for all companies which are reporting entities under Section 298 of the Corporations Law.

The Corporations Law also requires the following to be included with a company's financial statements:

* the directors' report
* the directors' statement
* the auditor's report.

The directors' report

The directors' report is required to give certain information, including directors' names, activities of the company, profit or loss for the year, amount of dividends, review of operation and many other matters in relation to the company.

The directors' statement

The directors' statement states whether, in their opinion, the statement of financial performance and the statement of financial position present a true and fair view, whether the company will be able to pay its debts as they fall due, and whether the financial statements comply with Accounting Standards.

You should now read the Directors' Declaration in the Woolworths financial report and note that it complies with the law. The reference to the ability of the company to pay its debts is an important statement about the solvency of the company and is clearly intended to reassure users such as employees, shareholders, creditors and lenders. There have been cases where directors of companies have been found guilty of making this statement when the company could not in fact pay its debts.

The auditor's report

The auditor's report is prepared by an external auditor and is meant to reassure the shareholders that they can rely on the financial statements prepared by the company. The auditor is required to form an opinion about the financial statements. The auditor's report must state whether the financial statements comply with the requirements of the Corporations Law, whether they provide a true and fair view of the state of affairs of the company, and whether they are in accordance with applicable Accounting Standards. This is discussed in more detail later in the chapter.

Annual, half-yearly and concise financial reports

In December 1998, the AASB issued *AASB 1039: Concise Financial Reports*. A concise financial report contains:

- a statement of financial performance
- a statement of financial position
- a statement of cash flows
- a discussion and analysis of the operations.

A concise financial report does not contain the detailed notes that are included in the annual report and are intended for users who do not want, and do not use, the more detailed annual report. Of course, users must understand that the same detailed information cannot be extracted from a concise report that can be extracted from an annual report. Companies give shareholders the choice of receiving the full annual report or a concise financial report. The concise financial report must include a statement by the auditor that the financial report has been audited and whether, in the auditor's opinion, the financial report complies with relevant Accounting Standards.

Until 1994, companies in Australia, other than those listed on a stock exchange, were required to prepare financial statements on an annual basis. However, the Corporate Law Reform Act 1994 also requires disclosing entities to prepare half-yearly reports. The requirements for the half-yearly reports are specified in *AASB 1029: Half Year Accounts and Consolidated Accounts*. Generally, a disclosing entity is an entity which issues securities that are listed or traded on a stock market, or those for which a prospectus has been lodged, or those offered under a takeover offer. A disclosing entity could be a non-corporate entity but is still required to comply with these requirements.

Essentially, the half-year accounts required by disclosing entities provide information to users on a more timely basis. This is despite the fact that the half-year accounts need not be as detailed as the annual accounts.

The half-year accounts consist of:

- a statement of financial performance
- a statement of financial position
- a cash flow statement
- a directors' statement
- a modified directors' report
- either an audit report or an audit review, in which the auditor states whether he or she is aware of anything to indicate that the financial statements do not comply with the law.

Stock exchange influence on financial reporting

Public companies in Australia which have their shares listed on a stock exchange must comply with the listing requirements of the Australian Stock Exchange Limited (ASX).

The listing rules impose additional requirements on listed companies. These rules require companies to provide:

- half-yearly reports
- a preliminary final statement
- additional details to the annual report
- additional details for mining exploration companies.

If companies do not comply with the listing rules, they are likely to be delisted, so that their shares can no longer be traded on the stock exchange.

Audit

Users of general-purpose financial reports wish to be assured that the information contained in these reports represents a true and fair assessment of the economic activities of the entity. The person who audits these general-purpose financial reports, the auditor, is seen as an independent external observer who is called upon, in the case of a company, to express an opinion that the reports provide a 'true and fair' representation of the company's financial status. It is important to stress here that it is the directors of public companies, not the auditor, who are responsible for the preparation and presentation of the general-purpose financial reports of the company. The purpose of an audit is to add credibility to these reports.

All companies, except small private companies and some large private companies, must have their accounts audited as required by the Corporations Law. Other entities, such as banks, insurance companies, credit unions, building societies, and some unions, are also required to be audited under separate legislation. In fact, besides those bodies for which there is a statutory requirement, many other organisations present audited accounts to show users that their accounts can be relied upon: for example, sporting organisations, clubs and societies.

The auditor, as noted above, does not prepare the general-purpose financial reports: this is the responsibility of the company's directors. The auditor's task is to review the accounting systems used to prepare the reports, to check on the accuracy of certain transactions, particularly those involving large dollar amounts, and to state that the accounts have been prepared in accordance with the Corporations Law and applicable Accounting Standards and that they provide a true and fair view.

You should now read the independent audit report prepared by BDO Nelson Parkhill for Woolworths' 1999 financial report.

From the audit report, we can observe several important points:

1 **The auditors express an opinion, they do not state that the accounts are accurate.**
2 **The report states that the accounts present a 'true and fair' view of the company and the consolidated entity's financial position. This term is very broad and it is obvious that there are different interpretations of what is true and what is fair. This part of the report has been debated over a number of years as being impracticable. Because of the looseness of this phrase, there is a body of opinion that wants to replace it with the phrase 'presents fairly' as is required in the USA.**
3 **The report states that the requirements of the Corporations Law have been followed and that the accounts are in accordance with Accounting Standards and other mandatory professional reporting requirements. These would include UIG Abstracts. This is to show that all the statutory and professional obligations have been met.**
4 **The audit report of Woolworths is an unqualified one. This means that the auditors have found nothing within the accounts which did not follow the**

statutory and professional requirements. If the auditors are of the opinion that the accounts are not true or fair then they have to state why, in their opinion, this is so. Under these circumstances the report is said to be qualified.

The auditor

A person who is appointed as a company auditor is required, under the Corporations Law, to meet certain requirements. Briefly, the auditor must:

- be a fit and proper person
- be a member of the Institute of Chartered Accountants, CPA Australia or any other prescribed body
- hold a recognised tertiary qualification majoring in accounting, with an auditing component
- be registered with the Australian Securities and Investments Commission
- have had practical experience in auditing.

The auditor is appointed by the shareholders at an annual general meeting, though in practice management usually provides the name of an auditor for approval by the shareholders.

The auditor is required to form an opinion on the general-purpose financial reports of a company, to determine whether proper records have been kept, and to report to shareholders. The auditor must also inform the commission of any suspected wrongdoing by management or any non-compliance with applicable Accounting Standards.

The auditor can be removed only by special notice, given at the annual general meeting, and the commission must be informed. The commission has the power to stop an auditor from resigning or being removed from office.

Beside the statutory requirements, noted above, the auditor is bound by professional obligations, which cover:

- independence, integrity, confidentiality and ethical considerations
- conformity with accounting and auditing standards, auditing guidelines and statements of auditing practice.

The expectation gap

As discussed previously, the directors of a company are responsible for preparing the accounts, and the auditors are responsible for seeing that those accounts have been prepared according to statutory and professional requirements. Are auditors responsible for detecting fraud and/or illegal acts? The law requires auditors to exercise due care when forming their opinion; it does not require them to detect fraud, though if a suspicion is aroused it must be followed.

During the past decade the auditing profession has been criticised for not fulfilling what is seen as its role. This criticism has arisen, in part at least, because a number of companies have failed after being given an unqualified opinion by an auditor. The difference between what an auditor is required to do and what is expected by users is known as the expectation gap.

Guy and Sullivan (1988) note that users of financial statements believe that auditors should:

1   assume more responsibility for the detection and reporting of fraud and illegal acts
2   improve audit effectiveness, that is, improve detection of material misstatements
3   communicate to the user of the financial statement more useful information about the nature and results of the audit process.

The reporting of fraud and illegal acts, whether actual or suspected, is a requirement of company law. The problem the auditor faces is that it is often extremely difficult to detect a well-organised fraud, particularly where more than one party is involved. The cost of the additional audit time might outweigh the benefits, and this cost has to be met by the shareholder. At the end of the chapter there is a list of articles and references discussing some landmark cases. The audit profession continues to grapple with the problem of fraud and illegal acts and professional pronouncements continue to be updated.

The reading in Case Study 13.2 illustrates some of the issues involved in the detection of fraud and the problems faced by the auditor.

CASE STUDY 13.2

Still Pussyfooting

IT used to be that when auditors caught their corporate clients lying, Form 8-K protected both parties from an embarrassing public row. Form 8-K? That's the document that management must file with the Securities and Exchange Commission explaining why it has changed auditors. Generally, the departing auditor must also comment on management's explanation.

These filings used to be as dull and unrevealing as minutes from a Romanian agricultural committee meeting. But they're getting a lot less so. A rule implemented by the SEC last year, but only now showing up in filings, requires outside auditors to be much more specific as to why they resign from an account. And if you miss the 8-K, don't worry. The substance of the auditor/client disagreements must now also be reported in a company's annual proxy statement.

This makes for some spicy reading. Consider this passage from the 8-K filed in May 1989 by New York's Bombay Palace Restaurants, Inc.: 'On 18 April 1988, Peat Marwick advised the company that it could no longer rely on the representations of management and thus resigned as the company's auditors.' And in an extraordinarily blunt follow-up letter to the SEC, the auditors said that they had discovered 'invoice documentation prepared by the company to be false and inaccurate'.

What Peat Marwick Main and Co. was really saying was that they had dropped Bombay Palace because management had lied. The SEC's enforcement division began an investigation of Bombay Palace.

'We're not making a legal judgment', said Peat Marwick's Associate General Counsel John Shutkin. 'We came to a conclusion about the integrity of management.' In other words, they didn't trust them.

Are accountants finally becoming what many people have long thought them to be: corporate policemen, responsible for digging out managerial wrongdoing? The answer here is definitely no. Independent auditors don't—can't—check every transaction and every invoice. The cost of doing so would be prohibitive.

What that means, of course, is that the auditor's letter certifying a company's books merely signifies that the auditors came across no specific instances of wrongdoing and found no reasons for distrusting management's words. It doesn't guarantee that everything is right; only that the auditor found nothing that wasn't all right. 'What the reader [of financial statements] infers is that the opinion letter is a Good Housekeeping Seal of Approval [of the accuracy of the financial statements]' says John Shank, Noble Professor of Management Accounting at the Tuck School of Business at Dartmouth. 'But what the opinion really says is vacuous and innocuous: "We did what auditors do, and nothing came to our attention that would suggest that things are not okay."'

For an example of how pussyfooting the auditor's opinion can sometimes be, look at Convenient Food Mart. Inc., a Rosemont, Illinois-based chain of retail convenience stores. In an 8-K, management reported that the company's auditors, Laventhol and Horwath, had conducted a study of the company's internal controls back in the spring of 1988. That study had concluded that the Convenient Food Mart's internal accounting system was such a mess that Laventhol couldn't be sure of the accuracy of the company's financial statements. Nevertheless, Laventhol issued an unqualified opinion in the company's 1987 results. Then, three months later, after management began an investigation of its books, Laventhol withdrew that opinion. The company later restated its results to reflect numerous accounting errors. In January 1989 Laventhol quit the account altogether. In other words, Laventhol's certification was meaningless. Both Laventhol and the company are being sued.

Should accountants take the responsibility for rooting out managerial messes and evildoings? Peat Marwick's Shutkin says this is not practical, given current auditing standards. 'You can perform an audit entirely consistent with Generally Accepted Auditing Standards and not detect a fraud that exists', says Shutkin. 'That's simply the way life is.'

Adapted from Subrata N. Chakravarty, in *Forbes*, 21 August 1989, p. 51.

The second and third points raised by Guy and Sullivan are being addressed by the profession. With the advent of computers and the ability to use sophisticated statistical techniques, the quality of audits is improving. One of the objectives of the Conceptual Framework, through the Statement of Accounting Concepts, is to identify the users and the information needed by them. This is an ongoing process and was discussed in detail in Chapter 2.

The one area that still remains to be dealt with is the detection of fraud and illegal acts. Users of accounting information wish to be assured that the information can be relied upon. One of the problems is the subjective nature of that information. The question must be asked, whether the users of accounting information are prepared to meet the cost of additional audit investigation; if so, are they prepared to accept that, irrespective of the level of surveillance, someone, at some time, will successfully circumvent the system?

CASE STUDY 13.3

Auditors critical of CarLovers Carwash

by Neville DeCruz

MELBOURNE—The annual report of the Berjaya-owned CarLovers Carwash Ltd explicitly criticised the dire state of the company's financial records, the *Australian Financial Review* reported today.

While noting limitations on the scope of their work, the auditors, Grant Thornton, cast doubt [on] whether the company, which is suspended from trading, can continue as a going concern.

According to the auditors, the company's status depended on the support of its Malaysian-based parent, the Berjaya Group

(which provided a letter of comfort to CarLovers' directors), and on the company's ability to continue profitable operations.

The auditors note that the company's financial controls deteriorated in the 10 months to April 30, 2000, as it was faced with several destabilising influences including a move to new premises, changes in its accounting and warehouse personnel and an update of its computerised accounting systems to make them Y2K compliant.

The auditors said the company failed to monitor franchise and branch operations, did not maintain perpetual inventory records, conducted an inadequate stock-take and did not adequately maintain its accounts payable and cash management systems.

The report also reveals that CarLovers is likely to encounter trouble at the tax office [for irregularities under the] Assessment Act or the Superannuation Guarantee Charge Act during the period, when it reported operating profit before tax and abnormal items of A$175 000.

This is up from a loss of A$1.5 million last year and A$11.9 million the year before.

While admitting it was a difficult year, the directors' report said CarLovers intended to 'rectify these difficulties' by using the computer, human and financial resources of its subsidiary, Video Ezy Australasia Pty Ltd.

CarLovers intends to expand by joint venturing with oil companies to provide carwashes at petrol stations and by increasing the number of franchises.

Financial Times Information Limited,
21 November 2000

Commentary

The article deals with the issue of going concern and highlights the importance of problems between an auditor and a company. Investors clearly dislike uncertainty and would penalise the company's share price accordingly.

Summary

In this chapter we examined the regulation of external financial reporting in Australia. As the financial reports of companies are the most regulated, most of the discussion related to issues affecting companies.

The government-appointed AASB produces Accounting Standards which under the Corporations Law are mandatory for all companies which are reporting entities.

Prior to July 2000, the accounting-profession-appointed Public Sector Accounting Standards Board also produced Accounting Standards, primarily for the public sector and certain non-corporate private-sector reporting entities. The AASB now sets Accounting Standards for all entities in both the private and public sectors. The AASB has a full-time chair and employs a number of technical staff.

In addition to Statements of Accounting Standards there are also UIG Abstracts, Statements of Accounting Concepts and Accounting Guidance Releases which influence the preparation of external financial reports.

The external financial reports prepared by companies are also influenced by certain requirements in the Corporations Law. In particular the requirements of AASB Standards, the directors' report, the directors' statement and the auditor's report influence the external financial reports prepared by companies.

For listed public companies, the listing rules of the Australian Stock Exchange require companies to present half-yearly reports, preliminary final statements, and additional details in their annual report.

Under *The Corporate Law Reform Act 1994*, disclosing entities are required to prepare yearly and half-yearly accounts and to comply with continuous disclosure requirements.

Most companies are required to have their accounts audited. The purpose of the audit is to add credibility to the accounts. Over time, the gap has widened between what an auditor is required to do and what the users expect from the auditor.

References

Australian Securities and Investments Commission Act 1989.

Campbell, R.J., 1996. *Psychiatric Dictionary*, 7th edn, Oxford University Press.

Guy, D.M., and Sullivan, J.D., 1988. 'The expectation gap: auditing standards', *Journal of Accountancy*, April, pp. 36–46.

Delbridge, A., 2000. *The Macquarie Dictionary*, Federation Edition, Macquarie Library.

Reese, W.L., 1980. *Dictionary of Philosophy and Religion*, Humanities Press.

Statsky, W.P., 1985. *West's Legal Thesaurus/Dictionary: A Resource for the Writer and the Computer Researcher*, West Publishing Company.

Further reading

Baxt, R., 1990. 'A swing of the pendulum', *Charter*, June, pp. 16–18.

Davison, A.G., and Khan, A.N., 1981. 'Should auditors be independent and neutral?', *The Chartered Accountant in Australia*, March, pp. 33–5.

Flint, D., 1971. 'The role of the auditor in modern society', *Accounting and Business Research*, Autumn, pp. 287–93.

Hancock, P.J., 1998. 'Use and application of International Accounting Standards', unpublished report prepared for the International Accounting Standards Committee.

Review questions

1   Discuss the arrangements in Australia for setting standards for the accounting profession.

2   What is meant by the term 'due process' in relation to the setting of Accounting Standards?

3   Discuss the various influences on external financial reporting for companies in Australia.

4   What is the purpose of an audit?

5   What is meant by the 'expectation gap' in relation to auditing?

6   Do you think that public financial statements would present a 'true and fair' view if they were not audited?

7   Are the auditors required to check the accuracy of the financial statements? Should they be?

8   You are considering investing in two similar types of private companies. One has an unqualified audit report and the other has no audit report. How important is this to you in making your decision?

Problems for discussion and analysis

1   Refer to the Woolworths financial report in Appendix 1.
    a   Were the accounts qualified or unqualified by the auditor?
    b   How much were the auditors paid for audit work and for other services?

2   Refer to Case Study 13.3. What would be your reaction if you held shares in the company IPC? Why?

3   Why do you think companies take an active interest in the standard-setting process of the accounting profession?

4   What information would a new auditor require before accepting the position of auditor for a public company?

5   There are a number of stakeholders with an interest in the performance and activities of public companies. Who are the different stakeholders? Should the auditor be responsible to all these stakeholders or only to the shareholders of the company?

6   Given that general-purpose financial reports are aimed at providing 'information useful to users for making and evaluating decisions about the allocation of scarce resources', discuss to what extent these users are represented in the due process.

7   Discuss and explain the different reporting requirements for public and private companies. Why do you think some private companies are exempted from regulatory standards?

8   The due process has been criticised for its lack of 'transparency' to parties outside the regulatory process. Do you think a more overt standard-setting mechanism would enhance the credibility of financial reports and/or help to reduce the expectations gap?

9   **Braithwaite, Carter and Co.—History**

The partnership was formed in 1980, to carry on the business of secondhand-car dealers, including a petrol station and car repair workshop. There were, until 1991, two partners, Braithwaite and Carter. Braithwaite looked after the office and accounting records, as well as obtaining and dealing with customers. Carter was a good motor mechanic and spent most of his time supervising the workshop. There was no partnership agreement. Braithwaite was getting 10 per cent of net profit, and Carter 5 per cent of work done by the repair workshop (as management salary). The office staff in 1991 numbered two.

Allan and Simons joined the partnership in 1991. The basis of the agreement was the partnership accounts for the previous three years. Capital introduced by the new partners was employed to buy a shop selling newspapers and confectionery and a real-estate agent's business. It was considered that the two businesses would make valuable new contacts.

A partnership agreement was not drawn up. Allan was to run the real-estate agency and get 10 per cent of any increased business. Simons was to manage the other business, and get 10 per cent of any increase in gross profit. The balance of the new profit of the combined business was to be shared as follows: Braithwaite and Carter, 30 per cent each, Allan and Simons, 20 per cent each. There was no agreement on partners' drawings. The three businesses were within half a kilometre of each other.

Accounts and audit

The accounting date is 30 June. The accounts are prepared annually by Anderson and Wilkinson, a local firm of chartered accountants, who were invited to act for the partnership by Braithwaite. The annual accounts consisted until 1991 of a trading account, a profit and loss statement (statement of financial performance) and a balance sheet (statement of financial position). They were typed in the office of Anderson and Wilkinson, whose report was at the bottom of the profit and loss statement (see Schedule 1). One copy was sent to the Taxation Department and each partner was also given a copy.

On the admission of Allan and Simons it was agreed to have:
- a separate balance sheet for each business
- two trading accounts, one for the car business and the other for the newsagent, tobacconist and confectionery shop
- a combined profit and loss statement for the three businesses.

Anderson and Wilkinson continued to act as before.

Accounting records of the car business and the newsagent, tobacconist and confectionery shop were kept in Braithwaite's office. There were three full-time employees in Braithwaite's office in 1993 and 1994. Braithwaite dealt with all the clerical and accounting matters, and the accountants referred all the queries to him. Allan, assisted by his wife, kept the records of the real-estate business.

Written partnership agreement

The annual accounts to 30 June 1993 were disputed by Carter, who refused to sign them. He insisted that Braithwaite was entitled to 10 per cent of the net profit of the car business only, and not of the combined business. Carter accused the accountants of favouring Braithwaite. He said, 'They never come to see me, never consult me, just tell me to sign the accounts each year. When we were small it was different. I frequently thought it strange not to have a written partnership agreement, but it suits Braithwaite and his accountants. The accountants are supposed to serve the partnership, not one partner only.'

After more arguments and a threat of legal action against the accountants, Carter agreed with the other partners to instruct the accountants to draw up a partnership agreement. The agreement was duly prepared, and signed by the partners.

Legal action against the auditors

Carter refused to sign the accounts for the year to 30 June 1994, on learning, for what he said was the first time, that the assets disclosed on the balance sheet had not been verified. 'What good is it to employ a firm of accountants to prepare the accounts if they do not audit them? One can rely on such accounts, but how can anybody rely on accounts when neither assets nor liabilities have been both properly verified and valued?'

It was found, in August 1994, that the bank balance of the real-estate agency account did not equal the amount of the deposits and rents received on behalf of the clients, the shortage appearing to be $15 000. Allan could not explain this.

Carter wrote to the senior partner of Anderson and Wilkinson as follows: 'I am consulting my solicitors on the right legal steps to be taken against your firm for negligence in discharging your professional duties as the auditors of the partnership.' It was also understood that a client of the real-estate agency was consulting his solicitors, intending to bring a legal action against both the partnership and the auditors.

Simons also thought now that he had probably paid too much for his share of the business.

Auditors' defence

The senior partner replied to Carter's letter, and sent a copy to the other partners, part of which read:

> My firm has never acted in the capacity of auditors of the partnership, consequently we have not conducted a full audit. There is no mention of the balance sheet [statement of financial position] in our report to you (see Schedule 1), and our fee notes make the extent of our duties quite clear (see Schedule 2). We were appointed, primarily, to prepare your accounts for the purpose of settling the partnership taxation matters, and the full audit of the balance sheet items is not necessary for this purpose. The placing of our report at the bottom of the profit and loss statement [statement of financial performance] is a further indication that the verification of assets is excluded from our work. There has never been any doubt in my mind that you and the other partners understood the precise nature of our appointment. If asked, we would be pleased to act as your auditors. I should add that our fee would then be approximately double the present figure.

Schedule 1

> REPORT TO THE PARTNERS OF BRAITHWAITE, CARTER AND CO.
>
> We have prepared the above Profit and Loss Statement [statement of financial performance] for the year ended 30 June 1994 from the books written up by your staff and partners, invoices and information made available to us. We confirm the statement in accordance therewith. We have found no material mistakes or likely omissions and are of the opinion that the amount of profit is true and fair.
>
> 101 Walter Street   Anderson and Wilkinson
> West Perth   Chartered Accountants
> 5 September 1994

Schedule 2

> BRAITHWAITE, CARTER AND CO.   15 September 1994
> 1201 Long Lane
> West Perth
> Anderson and Wilkinson
>
> For professional services rendered in connection with:
>
> Balancing the books and preparing two trading accounts, and one Profit and Loss Statement for the year ended 30 June 1994. Preparing three balance sheets as at 30 June 1994.
>
> Checking the items transferred from the accounts to the trading and Profit and Loss Statement, for the same period, in order to satisfy ourselves that they were the proper items to be charged or credited to these accounts.
>
> Correspondence with the Deputy Commissioner for Taxation to agree the amount of assessable profit and tax liability of each partner.
>
> FEE $5575.00
>
> With Compliments.

Required:

1   Can you blame Anderson and Wilkinson for not insisting on the partnership having a written agreement on
    a   legal grounds?
    b   professional grounds?
    c   business grounds?

2   Is there enough information in the case to decide whether or not the accountants are likely to be held liable?

3   If you were asked, as accountant or auditor, to prepare a partnership agreement for this firm:
    a   Would you agree to do it?
    b   What should be the main provisions of the agreement?

(Adapted from J. Santocki, *Case Studies in Auditing*, Macdonald & Evans (Handbook Series), 1976, Case 28.)

Ethics case study

Michael P. Cockley is a young accountant who has just commenced practice in the Perth suburb of Murdoch. He is at present trying to build up his practice, specialising in giving taxation advice and preparing clients' taxation returns.

One of Michael's clients is Leslie Raby, a rather testy ex-navy officer. Captain Raby has only just come to Michael, as a result of his falling out with another accountant. Amanda Trefrey, the former accountant, merely mentioned that there had been 'personality clashes and communication problems'.

Michael, in perusing Raby's taxation assessment, noticed that it differed materially from the estimate and was very much in favour of his client. In checking Raby's file, it became clear to Michael that the Taxation Office had made an error. Further, there was a strong likelihood that this error would result in a permanent advantage to his client. Raby's tax return had been a full and proper disclosure and had been correctly prepared. An error had been made by the Taxation Office and it was unlikely that the error would ever be discovered. In discussions with his client, it became apparent to Michael that Raby was aware of the error and the monetary gains that would accrue to him if this error was over-looked.

Discuss:

a   what Michael should do under the circumstances.
b   whether it is any different from stealing if nothing is said about Captain Raby standing to benefit from the error made by a government department and he keeps the money.
c   what responsibility Michael has. Should he act independently of the captain's wishes?

(Adapted from Paul H. Northcott, *Ethics and the Practising Accountant: Case Studies*, Australian Society of Certified Practising Accountants, 1993.)

Financial Statement Analysis

Learning objectives

At the end of this chapter you should be able to:

1 discuss the information needs of the various users in respect of the analysis of financial statements

2 understand in broad terms the process of financial analysis

3 explain the relevance of sources external and internal to the business in the analysis of financial statements

4 explain the significance of profitability and risk in the analysis of financial statements

5 understand and explain the importance of comparability of financial statements through time and with other firms

6 explain and apply the techniques of trend analysis and common-size statements

7 explain and apply the various ratios that can be used in financial statement analysis

8 understand that the importance of ratios relates to the interpretation of the ratios

9 explain the limitations involved in the analysis of financial statements

10 understand the implications of the efficient market hypothesis for financial statement analysis.

14

Introduction

In the previous chapters we considered the way in which accounting information is produced and what the components of financial statements mean. In this chapter we consider the statements themselves and more specifically the ways in which they can be analysed. This chapter is not intended to be comprehensive in its approach on the subject of financial analysis but to offer some guidelines on the subject and to provide the reader with some basic tools of analysis. We consider the needs of the person for whom the analysis is being undertaken or, in other words, the 'user group'. Using this approach it is possible to establish the form of analysis most appropriate to these needs. The 'user groups' were discussed in Chapter 1.

Users' information needs

Investor group

Among the resource providers are the investors, who were discussed previously as if they were a homogeneous group with similar needs, but there are in fact different types of investors. For sole traders and partnerships the investor is the owner or partner. The equivalent of this type of investor in a company is the ordinary shareholder. All these investors will be referred to from now on as equity investors. We need to establish what this group has in common, and what distinguishes the equity investor in a large company from the equivalent in a sole trader.

In general, equity investors take on all the risks associated with ownership and are entitled to any rewards after other prior claims have been met. For a sole trader the equity investor, i.e. the owner, is also likely to be heavily involved in the management and day-to-day running of the business. Where there is direct involvement, the owner's information needs are the same as those of managers (discussed below). In the case of larger organisations, such as large private companies and all public companies, there is likely to be a separation of ownership and management. For large businesses the final accounts meet the information needs of the shareholders, who are in the main properly characterised by the term 'absentee owners'. In general, the smaller the organisation and the greater the direct involvement of the owners in the day-to-day running of the business, the more detail required in the accounts. However, the information required to meet the needs of equity investors is broadly the same, irrespective of the type of ownership involved. The needs of this group of users can be met with information about the following.

- profitability, especially future profitability
- management efficiency; for example, are assets being utilised efficiently?
- return on their investment
  —within the firm
  —compared with alternatives
- risk being taken
  —financial risk
  —business risk
- returns to owners
  —dividends
  —drawings, etc.

Preference shareholders

Investors in some companies are able to purchase shares known as preference shares, which were discussed in Chapter 10. These shares are generally seen as less risky than ordinary shares and therefore normally earn a smaller return. Although it is difficult to generalise the differences between these shares and ordinary shares (this varies from share to share), normally preference shareholders are entitled to a fixed rate of dividend and to repayment before ordinary shareholders in the event of the business being 'wound up'. Because of the nature of the shares these users are likely to be interested in:

- profitability, mainly future profitability
- the net realisable value of the assets
- the extent to which their dividends are covered by profit.

If we compare the needs of these two groups of investors, we see that preference shareholders are more likely to be interested in the extent to which income is safe, rather than in the growth of the business. This is because in most cases only ordinary shareholders benefit from such growth. The preference shareholders' return is in the form of a dividend at a fixed rate, irrespective of the profits made.

Preference shares can either be equity or debt depending on their characteristics. Redeemable preference shares which have a fixed redemption date are regarded as debt, and dividends paid on such shares are classified as interest. Therefore this type of preference share is similar to a long-term loan. Non-redeemable preference shares are repaid only if the business ceases to exist and sufficient funds are available. Therefore, such shares are similar to ordinary shares and are classified as equity.

We can now move on to look at other resource providers who are also users of accounting information.

Lenders

Lenders can be conveniently subdivided into three subgroups: short-term creditors, medium-term lenders and long-term lenders. These types of debt finance were discussed in Chapter 10.

Short-term creditors are normally trade creditors, i.e. those who supply the business with goods on credit. Their areas of interest are:

- short-term liquidity or solvency
- net realisable value of the assets
- profitability and future growth
- risk (financial and business).

Medium-term lenders are usually banks and other financial institutions. Their areas of interest are:

- profitability (future profits providing cash for repayment of loans)
- security and the nature of the security
- financial stability.

Long-term lenders have the same needs as medium-term lenders, unless they are 'secured' lenders. A secured lender is someone who has a legal charge over the assets of the business and can claim those assets if the business does not repay or service the loan in accordance with the lending agreement. The charge may be a fixed charge over a specific asset, e.g. land, or it may be a floating charge over all the assets in general but none specifically. A fixed charge gives the holder the right to seize that asset if the business defaults on its loan payments. The lender can then sell the asset to recoup the amount owed. A floating charge gives the holder a higher priority in liquidation than an unsecured creditor, but not the right to seize any specific asset. In the case of secured lenders, the areas of interest are as follows:

- risk, especially financial risk
- security: net realisable value of specific assets
- interest cover: how well their interest is covered by the profits being made.

These different types of lenders have broadly the same needs for information. It is the emphasis that changes, depending on whether the loan is short-term or long-term.

Employees

Employees are interested in judging job security and in assessing whether their wages are relatively fair. Their areas of interest are:

- profitability: average profits per employee for the purposes of productivity bargaining
- liquidity: future trends in profit.

There has been considerable debate over the extent to which these needs are met by conventional accounts and whether a value-added statement would meet these needs better.

Auditors

Auditors are not normally seen as users of accounting information. However, in order to carry out an audit efficiently, an analysis of accounts is frequently carried out. The audit function was discussed in Chapter 13. For the purposes of planning and carrying out their audit, the auditors are interested in:

- trends in sales, profit, costs, etc.
- variations from the norm
- accounting policies.

Management

It is difficult to describe the needs of managers because they vary greatly from situation to situation. They require all of the above information, because they are likely to be judged on their performance by outside investors or lenders. In addition, they require detailed information on the performance of the business as a whole and on its parts to enable them to manage the business on a day-to-day basis. This information includes such items as profitability by major product, costs per product, changes in sales or component mix. The information needs of management are discussed in the last seven chapters of this book.

The needs of users listed above are not intended to be comprehensive. We have tried to give the reader a flavour of the differing information required by the various groups, and to indicate that some of this will not be provided by the annual accounts. At this stage we need to establish what, if any, are common information needs and what other factors need to be considered.

Some common information needs which can be readily identified are profitability, liquidity and risk. The problem is how these are measured and how to judge good or bad performance. Before going on to discuss these issues in detail, let us first examine the common information needs in more detail and look at the context in which the financial analysis is to be carried out.

Common information needs

The most obvious information that all these groups want is information about the profitability of the business. This can be divided into two components: past profitability and future profitability. Another factor that is common to several groups is the requirement for information about financial risk and 'liquidity'. Another theme that emerges is the return on the investment in the business. This has associated measures such as the riskiness of the return (dividend cover or interest cover). There are also information needs that are specific to particular user groups. A good example of these is the security measures used by lenders. We examine how the common needs can be analysed in some detail after we have established the context in which the analysis should take place.

Context for financial statement analysis

Key Concept 14.1

Financial analysis

Good financial analysis requires that the person for whom the analysis is being done is clearly identified, together with the purpose of the analysis. It is unlikely to be useful if it does not take into account as many relevant factors as possible.

In doing an analysis, you must view it in a wide context; it is not merely a mechanical exercise using various techniques. We outline some of the factors that are directly relevant to an analysis of business performance.

The size of the business

The fact that a business is the size of BHP makes it less vulnerable to the decisions of people outside the organisation. For example, a banker might lend money to a small business at a rate of 3 or 4 per cent above base rate, whereas for BHP or CSR the rate would be much lower. Similarly, the banker is likely to ask for security from the small business whereas with BHP the name itself is enough security.

The riskiness of the business

Besides size, the nature of the business needs to be taken into account: gold prospecting has a different level of risk (and return) from a bank. Other factors which affect the risk, known as business risk, are reliance on a small number of products, degree of technological innovation, and vulnerability to competition.

The economic, social and political environment

Examples of the way in which the economic, social and political environment affects industry can be found in virtually any daily newspaper. For example, if the Australian dollar declines relative to the American dollar, imports and exports will be affected and firms will gain or suffer accordingly. Changes in interest rates often have sharp effects on firms that are financed by a large amount of borrowing (loans or overdrafts). We have only to look at the problems experienced by some of the high-flying entrepreneurs in the 1980s, such as Bond and Skase, who managed companies with a very high proportion of debt.

The effects of the social environment tend to be more subtle. A study of recent Australian history shows a movement towards acceptance of profit as the prime motivation for business, whereas in some countries this is balanced with regard for the natural environment or for ensuring full employment. These social changes frequently coincide with political changes, although the natural environment is a good example of a social concern which is likely to transcend political changes. This was apparent in the 1990 federal election in Australia.

Industry trends, effects of changes in technology

In order to make any judgements about the performance of a business, and more especially about the future, it is vital to understand the way the industry is headed. For example, in the late 1980s and early 1990s many firms in the textile, clothing and footwear industries went bankrupt.

Effect of price changes

While we have mentioned high rates of inflation, the effect of price changes might be more specific. For example, the price of property in the mid-1980s rose faster than the general change in prices. Over the last 20 or more years, several methods have been proposed for taking account of price changes in corporate reports, none of which has gained general acceptance. Although the perfect solution has not been found, the problem cannot be ignored: even with a low rate of inflation of 5 per cent, what appears to be a gentle growth of sales is in fact a decline. It should be pointed out that, although we normally think of price changes in terms of increases, there are many examples where the effects of new technology, competition and economies of scale have led to *reductions* in price. The most obvious examples are in the electronics industries and the computer industry. For example, a calculator cost approximately $25 for the most basic model at the start of the 1970s; an equivalent today costs less than $5.

Projections and predictions

While we can all take a guess at the future, clearly there is a case for taking into account the opinions of those closely involved in the business and those who have expertise in the industry and in analysing likely economic trends. Financial analysis must, after all, relate not only to what has happened but also to what is going to happen.

Having looked at some of the factors which need to be taken into account, it should be clear that, although a set of accounts contains some of the required information, a lot more information will have to be obtained from other sources. These other sources of information can be conveniently subdivided into sources external to the business and those internal to the business. Some examples are discussed below.

Sources external to the business

- *Government statistics:* These are available from the Australian Bureau of Statistics.
- *Trade journals:* These include journals specific to the trade and more general professional or business journals such as *Business Review Weekly.*
- *Financial press:* A lot of information can be gleaned from the financial pages of quality newspapers, from the *Australian Financial Review* and from specialist publications such as the *Professional Administrator.*
- *Databases:* There are now a number of on-line databases, such as Statex, which contain information about companies, industry statistics, and economic indicators.
- *Specialist agencies:* These can provide an industry-wide analysis, general financial reports, credit-scoring services and many other services, e.g. Moody's Rating Agency.

The first three of these sources are readily accessible in good libraries. The others are more specialist and access is more difficult and much more expensive.

Sources internal to the business

Chairman's statement

In the case of public companies, a chairman's statement is included with the annual accounts. It contains summarised information for the year, as well as some predictions for the future. The information should not be taken at face value because it is likely to reflect one point of view which may be biased. The statement often highlights the positive side. As a leading banker commented, 'It is as important to ascertain what is left out as it is to ascertain what has been included'.

Directors' report

This is a statutory requirement for all companies and the information to be contained in it is laid down in the Corporations Law. The statutes, however, lay down a *minimum* and that is therefore normally *all* the information that is given.

The statement of financial position

This gives information about the position at a point in time. The information is only valid at that point in time; given that the median time for publication by large companies is over three months after the statement of financial position date, and for small companies it is thought to be at least ten months, the information might have little bearing on the current position. This question of how timely the information is has a major bearing on what can be concluded from an analysis of the accounting information contained in the published accounts.

The statement of financial performance

As with the statement of financial position, the information in the statement of financial performance is quite old by the time it is published. A further problem is that the information is summarised: this may disguise the weak performance of parts of the business because it is offset by the strong performance of others.

The accounting policies statement

As we have seen, there are a number of different ways of dealing with items such as stocks. Is FIFO or average cost being used? For depreciation, is reducing-balance or straight-line being used? Many other items are subject to similar preconditions, and so it is vital to understand the basis which has been adopted. This is stated in the statement of accounting policies. Unfortunately, all too often, these statements are of such generality that they mean little. It is not uncommon to find a statement on depreciation which says, 'depreciation is charged on the straight-line method over the useful life of the assets'. The problem with such a statement is that different assets have different lives and residual values. In fact it is quite likely that similar businesses have different estimates for the *same* asset. This makes it difficult to compare one company with another, because the basis adopted affects the profits, statement of financial position values, etc. The problem of comparability is explained in Key Concept 14.2.

Key Concept 14.2

Comparability

It is not sufficient that financial information is relevant and reliable at a particular time, in a particular circumstance or for a particular reporting entity. The users of general-purpose financial reports need to be able to compare aspects of an entity at one time and over time, and compare entities at one time and over time.
An important implication of this concept of comparability is that users need to be informed of the policies employed in the preparation of the general-purpose financial reports, changes in those policies and the effects of those changes. (*SAC 3, paras 31, 33*)

Key Concept 14.3

Consistency

Consistency implies that the measurement and display of transactions and events need to be carried out in a consistent manner throughout an entity, and over time for that entity, and that there is consistency between entities in this regard. (*SAC 3, para. 32*)

Within the one business, the problem of comparability is to some extent alleviated by the requirement to follow the basic accounting concept of consistency, defined in Key Concept 14.3.

Notes to the accounts

These are vital to any financial analysis because they contain the detailed information. Without this information the level of analysis is likely to be superficial, especially in complex business organisations. However, users often find that the level of detail in the notes, their complexity and their technical language make it difficult to understand the treatment of various items in the accounts. The first note to the accounts is the accounting policies statement discussed above.

Observe the large number of notes attached to the financial statements in Woolworths' 1999 financial report. Imagine trying to understand the statements of financial performance and financial position without the notes. It would also be impossible to compare the results of Woolworths and Coles if details of accounting policies were not provided.

Statement of cash flows

Since 30 June 1992 all reporting entities in Australia have been required to prepare
statement of cash flows based on *AASB 1024*. The cash flow statement shows the gross
cash inflows and outflows of the business. It normally shows cash flows associated with
operating, financing and investing activities.

It is argued this statement will allow users to assess an organisation's ability to meet
its obligations and continue to operate as a going concern. Chapter 12 gives some further
information on cash flow statements, and we have studied the cash flow statement for
Woolworths.

Auditors' report

Every company which is a reporting entity is subject to an annual audit of its accounts.
Included in the accounts is a report from the auditors stating whether, in their opinion,
the accounts show a 'true and fair' view. As far as financial analysis is concerned, this
report is best treated as an exception report: that is, unless it is qualified in some way no
account needs to be taken of it.

It is worth mentioning that for most bankers an auditors' report does add credibility
to the figures. It does not, however, mean that the accounts are correct in their details:
quite often the report contains a number of disclaimers in respect of certain figures. The
auditors' report was discussed in Chapter 13.

The common needs explained

We have identified common needs for information about profitability, liquidity, financial
risk, etc., but before we can carry out any analysis we need to know what is meant by
these terms. We therefore discuss what each term means and identify what we are trying
to highlight in our analysis. For this purpose we will use the example of Jack Pty Ltd,
which was introduced in Chapter 11, and is reproduced below.

JACK PTY LTD
STATEMENT OF FINANCIAL PERFORMANCE AT 30 JUNE

	Notes	$	This year $	$	Last year $
Sales	1		60 000		45 000
Cost of sales			40 000		30 000
Gross Profit			20 000		15 000
Distribution costs	2	3 000		2 500	
Administration costs	2	11 000	14 000	9 000	11 500
Profit before taxation			6 000		3 500
Taxation	3		2 600		1 400
Profit after taxation			3 400		2 100
Dividends					
interim	4	1 000	—		—
final	4	1 600	2 600		1 100
Transfer to reserves			800		1 000

, it is obvious that the starting point is the statement of financial
ooking at the information provided by the statement of financial
to establish what information is required.
of comparison. Is the business more profitable than it was last
ble than a similar business, or even a dissimilar business? Each
...uons requires us to measure the profit *relative* to something else. The last
question cannot be answered by looking at one set of statements. We need to compare
a number of different businesses, and to do this we have to make sure that the accounts
are comparable. Are assets being depreciated over the same time period? The shorter the
life of the asset, the greater the charge, and the smaller the final profit figure. It is for
these comparisons that the accounting policies statement is required.

We will look at comparisons over time within Jack Pty Ltd. The business made more
profits this year, when it earned $6000 profit before taxation, than last year when the
figure was only $3500. The question is whether it is more profitable because it is selling
more, i.e. $60 000 this year compared with $45 000 last year, or whether it is more
efficient, or whether it is a combination of the two.

We can go some way to answering this by working out what the increase in sales
was and what the increase in profit was. In this case the sales increased by 33 per cent
as follows:

$$\text{sales increase} \quad = \quad \$60\ 000 \quad - \quad \$45\ 000$$

$$\text{percentage increase} \quad = \quad \frac{\$15\ 000}{\$45\ 000} \quad \times \quad 100 = 33\%$$

The profit, however, increased by over 70 per cent:

$$\text{profit increase} \quad = \quad \$6\ 000 \quad - \quad \$3\ 500$$

$$\text{percentage increase} \quad = \quad \frac{\$2\ 500}{\$3\ 500} \quad \times \quad 100 = 71\%$$

Thus we have discovered that not only is Jack making more profit by selling more
items but it is also making a greater profit on each sale. However, we do not know
whether this seemingly favourable change is because this year was a good year or last
year was a bad year, nor do we know whether Jack has had to invest a lot of money in
order to increase the profitability. The former question can only be satisfactorily
answered by comparisons over a longer period than two years, and then by comparing
Jack Pty Ltd with a similar business in the same industry. The question about investment perhaps can be answered, in the case of a small company, by determining the
return on investment, as represented by the profit. This then requires us to ask what is
the amount invested: often in a small business the major investment made by the owner
is the time spent in the business. However, for a public company, there is normally very
little relationship between the amount of equity shown in the accounts and the amount
you would have to pay to buy the company.

While not ignoring those problems, we can, for the present, look at the statement of
financial position, reproduced on the next page, as a rough guide in the absence of
any other information. We can see that in this case the investment in the form of capital
and reserves has hardly changed—it was $74 500 last year and is $75 300 this year.
Therefore, we can be reasonably certain that there is a real increase in efficiency from
last year.

JACK PTY LTD
STATEMENT OF FINANCIAL POSITION AT 30 JUNE

	Notes	$	This year $	Last ye. $
Assets				
Current Assets				
Cash at bank		3 500		2 000
Debtors		10 000		4 000
Inventory	7	10 000		7 000
Total Current Assets			23 500	13 000
Non-current Assets				
Equipment	5	10 000		11 000
Land and buildings	6	50 000		56 000
Total Non-current Assets			60 000	67 000
Total Assets			83 500	80 000
Liabilities				
Current Liabilities				
Creditors		4 000		3 000
Taxation	3	2 600		1 400
Dividends	4	1 600		1 100
Total Current Liabilities			8 200	5 500
Non-current Liabilities			—	—
Total Liabilities			8 200	5 500
Net Assets			75 300	74 500
Capital and Reserves				
Share Capital	8	70 000		70 000
Retained Profits	9	5 300		4 500
Total Capital and Reserves			75 300	74 500

Before leaving the question of profitability, we need to discuss the future profitability of the business because this was identified as a common need for many users. The fact that a company has been profitable is comforting, but if you want to make a decision about whether to buy or sell a business you need information about the future, not the past. This information is not contained in the statement of financial performance, although it could be argued that information about the past is the best guide to the future. In practical terms the only way you can form an opinion about the future is by using a combination of information, including past profits, knowledge of the industry, predictions about the economy and many other factors.

Summary
Profitability requires comparisons:

- over time
- with other businesses.

Profitability relates to:

- the past for evaluation
- the future for prediction.

sk

il risk or solvency was discussed in Chapter 10. It is of vital impor-
y cases where a business has gone bankrupt because of cash flow
gh it was profitable. There are also cases where two companies in
iness produce dramatically different results purely because of the
d. For example, if a business makes a return of 15 per cent on every
uunar invested and it can borrow money at 10 per cent, it is worthwhile for the business
to borrow money because the excess return goes to the owners. However, there is some
risk involved in such a course of action because the business will lose if the interest rate
rises to, say, 17 per cent and it is still making only 15 per cent. This caused problems
for many businesses in the late 1980s and early 1990s. A way of measuring the financial risk is to look at the statement of financial position of a business and identify the
amount of debt finance, i.e. loans, debentures, bank overdrafts and other borrowings,
and compare this with the amount of equity finance, i.e. owners' capital, retained
earnings and reserves. The term 'leverage' is used to describe the amount of debt in a
statement of financial position.

In Australia, debt finance does not normally exceed equity finance, although the extent
to which this generalisation holds true is dependent on the size and nature of the
business. There were some notable exceptions in the late 1980s, particularly the companies of the high-flying entrepreneurs mentioned earlier. This is largely as a result of
the banks' policy of lending on a dollar-for-dollar basis, i.e. for each dollar of your money
that you invest in the business the bank lends a dollar. While this is not a hard-and-fast
rule, it is used as the benchmark by bank managers in Australia. It is interesting that other
countries adopt different benchmarks. For example, banks in Germany and Japan tend
to lend well above the one-for-one norm.

In the case of Jack Pty Ltd there is no long-term borrowing, nor is there even a bank
overdraft. This might be a good thing as the company is making only $6000 on the capital
invested of over $75 000. This is less than 10 per cent, but it should be compared with
the rate at which money could be borrowed.

Turning now to short-term solvency: a company has to maintain sufficient assets to
meet its commitments as they fall due. The major area for concern is the short term,
which is generally taken to be one year. This is convenient as it fits the definition used
for current assets and current liabilities, and so we have a suitable measure which is
apparent in the statement of financial posiiton. For example, Jack Pty Ltd has current
assets of $23 500 and current liabilities of only $8200. It has to reserve enough funds in
the next year to meet its commitments in that year.

One of the problems that arises with this measure is that 'current' can mean due
tomorrow or due in twelve months. In the case of some current assets, for example
inventory, the asset first has to be sold and then the money has to be collected. Another
problem is the question of what is the correct level of current assets for the business.
If, for example, there is a lot of cash, this is hardly an efficient use of resources. In the
case of Jack, the amount of $3500 in the bank may be far in excess of its true needs.
There is also the question of whether $10 000 tied up in debtors is excessive on sales
of $60 000, especially if we compare this to last year where the debtors were $4000 on
sales of $45 000.

Other problems with interpreting the information about short-term solvency arise if
we try to compare different businesses. For example, an aircraft manufacturer has different requirements from a food wholesaler. Even within the same industrial sector, the
needs differ. For example, a whisky distiller has different needs from a brewer: whisky
has to be matured over years, whereas beer is produced in a few months and has a
limited shelf life.

Summary
- Financial risk involves long-term and short-term solvency.
- Requirements and norms differ widely from industry to industry.

The general conclusion to be drawn is: analysis of the financial statements is only a small part of the story; that analysis needs to be put into a wider context of knowledge of the industry and the environment. The maxim that a little learning is a dangerous thing applies as much to business analysis as it does elsewhere. With this point in mind, we can now look at some of the techniques that are used to analyse financial information.

Techniques of analysis

Many techniques are used in financial analysis: they range from simple techniques, such as studying the financial statements (as we have just done) and forming a rough opinion of what is happening, to sophisticated statistical techniques. It should be pointed out that this rough analysis based on 'eyeballing' the accounts is vital: it forms the base on which the more sophisticated techniques are built. If, for example, we fail to notice that a business has made a loss for the past few years, the application of the most sophisticated techniques will not help, because we have failed to grasp an essential point.

We examine some of the simpler techniques. The choice of technique is once again a function of what you are trying to do and the purpose of your analysis. For example, managers and auditors might be interested in establishing any variations from past norms and explaining these and, where necessary, taking appropriate action. For a shareholder in a large company, such an analysis, even if it were possible, would be inappropriate as no action could be taken and the level of detail is too specific.

Comparison of financial statements over time

A simple comparison of the rate and direction of change over time can be very useful. This can be done both in terms of absolute amount and in percentage terms. Both are normally required in order to reach any conclusions. For example, a 50 per cent change on $1000 is less significant than a 50 per cent change on $50 000. If you have only $1000 to start with, a change of $500 is significant. It is not only the absolute amount but also the amount relative to other figures that is important.

The period of time chosen is also worth considering. Too short a period will not be informative. This was the case with Jack where we could only say that the profit had increased but had no idea whether that was part of a trend or whether it was because last year was a particularly bad year. Consider the results of companies in the mid-1980s compared to the early 1990s; the economy in Australia changed dramatically in this period from strong growth to recession. Finally, it must be borne in mind that other changes might have affected the figures; for example, the business might have decided to depreciate its vehicles over three years instead of four. Having taken account of these warnings, let us now look at how we can make the comparisons.

Trend analysis

Trend analysis is normally used for periods of more than two or three years in order to make the results easier to understand and interpret. It involves choosing a base year and then plotting the trend in sales, profits, or whatever from then on.

Key Concept 14.4

Trend analysis

In trend analysis the choice of an appropriate base year is vital. If the base year chosen is not typical the resultant analysis will be at best extremely difficult and at worst actually misleading.

Example 14.1: ABC Ltd

ABC LTD
PROFIT AND LOSS SUMMARY

	20X1 $000	20X2 $000	20X3 $000	20X4 $000	20X5 $000
Sales	12 371	13 209	16 843	14 441	13 226
Cost of sales	11 276	11 896	14 818	12 595	13 017
Operating profit	1 095	1 313	2 025	1 846	209
Interest charges	215	252	460	768	676
Pre-tax profit	880	1 061	1 565	1 078	-467
Taxation	464	529	875	579	-2
After-tax profit	416	532	690	499	-465
Extraordinary items	-18	132	-263	426	-11
Net Profit after tax and extraordinary items	398	664	427	925	-476
Dividends	164	185	336	337	112
Retained Profit	234	479	91	588	-588

If we take the cost of sales, it is clear from a casual examination of the figures that it rises in 20X1 and 20X2 to a peak in 20X3, after which it falls in 20X4. This is shown as a graph in Figure 14.1. As you can see, the information in the graph is limited; it reflects what we have already found. To make any sensible comment we need to see how these costs are behaving in relation to something else. This could be in relation to another item in the statement of financial performance such as sales, or in relation to the costs in a comparable company. To make the latter comparison, however, we first have to find some common means of expression because the companies being compared are unlikely to be exactly the same size. One way of doing this is to use index numbers to express the figures we are looking at and the way in which they change from year to year.

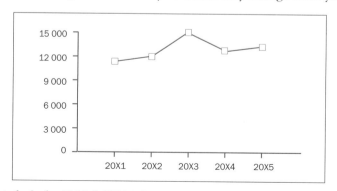

Figure 14.1 *Cost of sales for ABC Ltd, 20X1–X5.*

Index number trends

As with other forms of trend analysis, this technique is normally used for periods of more than two or three years. It is intended to make the results easier to understand and interpret. An index number is determined by choosing a base year, setting that base year at 100 and expressing figures for all other years in terms of that index.

Using the example of the sales of ABC Ltd, if we took 20X1 as the base year and set that at 100, we would calculate the index for 20X2 as follows.

$$\frac{20\text{X2 sales}}{20\text{X1 sales}} \times 100 = \frac{13\,209}{12\,371} \times 100 = 107$$

For 20X3 the calculation would be:

$$\frac{20\text{X3 sales}}{20\text{X1 sales}} \times 100 = \frac{16\,843}{12\,371} \times 100 = 136$$

Using the same formula we can find the index for each of the other years and then study the sales trend. In this case the figures are:

20X1, 100; 20X2, 107; 20X3, 136; 20X4, 117; 20X5, 107

We can do the same with the figures for the cost of sales and the profit and then analyse these trends. In the case of sales, we can see that they peaked in 20X3 and then declined to the same level as in 20X2. This can be seen more easily in Figure 14.2, which shows the sales in the left-hand blocks and the cost of sales in the right-hand blocks for each year.

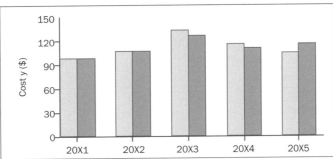

Figure 14.2 *Sales and cost of sales for ABC Ltd, 20X1–X5.*

Figure 14.2 is more informative than Figure 14.1 because it relates sales to cost of sales; in addition the use of index numbers allows us to compare this company with another, irrespective of size. The graph in this case shows that both sales and cost of sales peak in 20X3. After that, although sales fall in both 20X4 and 20X5, the cost of sales rises again in 20X5, producing a loss.

Percentage changes

Another technique used in trend analysis is to identify the percentage change from year to year and then examine the trends in it. For example, if we look at the sales we find that the change from 20X1 to 20X2 was 7 per cent, while that from 20X2 to 20X3 was 27 per cent. These figures are calculated as follows.

$$\frac{\text{this year's sales}}{\text{last year's sales}} \times 100 = \frac{13\,209}{12\,371} \times 100 = 107\%$$

i.e. an increase of 7 per cent.

Once again it should be pointed out that these trends are of most use if they are compared with other trends, either in the business itself or in the industry. You should also bear in mind that percentage increases are often illusory because they merely reflect the increase that would be expected as a result of the prevailing rate of inflation.

Common-size statements

In examining accounts, we often encounter large numbers; these are more digestible if they are presented as 'common-size statements'. This technique, as the name implies, deals with the problem of comparing companies of different sizes. It involves expressing the items in the statement of financial position, for example, as percentages of the statement of financial position total.

This is illustrated by looking again at ABC Ltd, the statements of financial position of which are reproduced below. We can derive some information by examining the statements of financial position, but it is not easy to identify exactly what is happening. For example, why has the land and building account gone up in 20X3 by a greater amount than the other non-current assets? Where did the intangibles come from, and what are they? These questions can often be answered, in part at least, by using the detailed information contained in the notes to the accounts.

ABC LTD
SUMMARY STATEMENTS OF FINANCIAL POSITION

	20X1 $000	20X2 $000	20X3 $000	20X4 $000	20X5 $000
Assets					
Current Assets					
Cash	400	464	183	15	41
Debtors	2 259	2 389	3 012	2 776	2 508
Inventory	3 645	3 952	3 903	3 289	3 255
Total Current Assets	6 304	6 805	7 098	6 080	5 804
Non-current Assets					
Plant and equipment	875	849	959	863	767
Land and buildings	639	660	682	1 070	1 103
Other non-current assets	450	554	486	663	683
Intangibles	0	0	470	451	460
Total Non-current Assets	1 964	2 063	2 597	3 047	3 013
Total Assets	8 268	8 868	9 695	9 127	8 817
Liabilities					
Current Liabilities					
Bank overdraft	0	3	86	427	663
Creditors	3 701	3 706	4 842	3 311	4 277
Taxation	110	415	196	44	48
Dividends	121	137	224	225	1
Total Current Liabilities	3 932	4 261	5 348	4 007	4 989
Non-current Liabilities					
Deferred tax	922	843	620	369	0
Loans	297	148	0	427	92

(continued next page)

Total Non-current Liabilities	1 219	991	620	796	92
Total Liabilities	5 151	5 252	5 968	4 803	5 081
Net Assets	3 117	3 616	3 727	4 324	3 736
Shareholders' Equity					
Share capital	1 447	1 459	1 471	1 476	1 476
Share premium	137	145	153	157	157
Retained profits	1 533	2 012	2 103	2 691	2 103
Total Shareholders' Equity	3 117	3 616	3 727	4 324	3 736

The problem when looking at standard statements of financial position is that the figures often disguise what is really happening. If we convert the statements to some common measure, the underlying trends become clearer. We could take, for example, the share capital for 20X1 and express it as a percentage of the total net assets. We find that it is 46 per cent in that year compared with 40 per cent in 20X2. To calculate this we divided the share capital figure by the net assets and then multiplied the result by 100. Thus for 20X3 we have:

$$\frac{\text{share capital}}{\text{net assets}} \times 100 = \frac{1471}{3727} \times 100 = 39\%$$

Following this procedure for all items in the statements of financial position produces common-size statements as follows.

ABC LTD
COMMON-SIZE STATEMENTS

	20X1 %	20X2 %	20X3 %	20X4 %	20X5 %
Assets					
Current Assets					
Cash	13	13	5	0	1
Debtors	72	66	80	64	68
Inventory	117	109	105	76	86
Total Current Assets	202	188	190	140	155
Non-current Assets					
Plant and equipment	28	24	26	20	21
Land and buildings	21	18	18	25	30
Other non-current assets	14	15	13	15	18
Intangibles			13	11	12
Total Non-current Assets	63	57	70	71	81
Total Assets	265	245	260	211	236
Liabilities					
Current Liabilities					
Bank overdraft	0	0	2	10	18
Creditors	118	102	130	76	114
Taxation	4	11	5	1	1
Dividends	4	4	6	5	0
Total Current Liabilities	126	117	143	92	133

(continued over page)

	20X1	20X2	20X3	20X4	20X5
	%	%	%	%	%
Non-current Liabilities					
Deferred tax	30	23	17	8	0
Loans	10	5	0	10	2
Total Non-current Liabilities	40	28	17	18	2
Total Liabilities	165	145	160	111	136
Net Assets	100	100	100	100	100
Shareholders' Equity					
Share capital	46	40	39	34	40
Share premium	4	4	4	4	4
Retained profits	50	56	57	62	56
Total Shareholders' Equity	100	100	100	100	100

One of the many things that we can see from an analysis of these statements is that the current assets have shown a marked decline over the period, from 202 per cent of net assets total in 20X1 to only 155 per cent in 20X5. We can also see that 20X4 was in many ways an atypical year: the levels of inventory, debtors and creditors were out of line with other years. By 20X5 the bank overdraft had risen to its highest level ever and inventories, debtors and creditors had gone back to the levels of 20X3. It should be noted that with this technique the choice of the base year is just as important as it was with trend analysis.

Common-size statements can be applied as easily to the statement of financial performance as to the statement of financial position. In the case of the statement of financial performance it is usual to express all items as a percentage of sales, as illustrated below.

ABC LTD
COMMON-SIZE STATEMENTS OF FINANCIAL PERFORMANCE

	20X1	20X2	20X3	20X4	20X5
	%	%	%	%	%
Sales	100	100	100	100	100
Cost of sales	91	90	88	87	98
Operating profit	9	10	12	13	2
Interest charges	2	2	3	5	5
Pre-tax profit	7	8	9	8	-3
Taxation	4	4	5	4	0
After-tax profit	3	4	4	4	-3
Extraordinary items	0	1	-2	3	0
Dividends	1	1	2	2	1
Retained profit	2	4	0	5	-4

This statement is self-explanatory. Note the obvious rounding errors which occur when working in whole numbers. An item that is worth highlighting is that the cost of sales in 20X5 had squeezed the operating profit down to only 2 per cent return on sales in a year when the interest charges were in excess of 5 per cent of sales. This illustrates the risk of high gearing which we referred to earlier in the chapter. There could be several reasons why the cost of sales as a percentage of sales has increased. Recessionary con-

ditions in the economy could have squeezed margins;
war could have reduced selling prices. Consider the imp
caused by the development of the Apple-Macintosh com
consider the results for ABC together with other information.

Common-size statements and the other techniques that we have c
largely ignored the relationship between any two components of the fir
of a business. Other techniques of analysis are available which look at th
between items in the statement of financial position and items in the statemen
cial performance. The most common of these techniques is known as ratio analy
this is explored more fully below.

Ratio analysis

Ratio analysis is explained in virtually every accounting textbook, and most students have
little difficulty in calculating ratios. However, many students find extreme difficulty in
understanding what the ratios mean once they have been calculated. Because of this
we will not deal extensively with all the possible ratios that can be calculated; instead
we will concentrate on the relationships that the ratios express. This approach will
increase your understanding of the reasons for calculating these ratios and enable you
to interpret the results from a knowledgeable basis.

Table 14.1 (pp. 324–5) gives a list of ratios often used in analysis, together with an
indication of their significance. We compute the ratios for ABC Ltd to illustrate the calculations involved. We have used 20X4 figures from ABC to illustrate the calculations
involved as 20X5 results show a loss. The ratios can still be calculated for 20X5 but are
not appropriate for our purposes here.

We now discuss some ratios which express relationships between items in statements
of financial position, and then ratios based upon items in statements of financial performance. Finally, we examine ratios which combine information from the two types of
statement.

Firstly, we need to understand exactly what a ratio is. A ratio compares two quan-t-
ities. The common mathematical notation used is A:B. For example, a ratio 3:2 ('three
to two') means that for every 3 units of A, there are 2 units of B. Ratios are often written
as simply as possible, e.g. 10:4 = 5:2. It is convenient if one of the numbers in the ratio
is a 'one'. For example, if A:B = 10:4, dividing by B gives

$$\frac{A}{B} : 1 = \frac{10}{4} : 1 = 2.5 : 1$$

This clearly shows that A is two-and-a-half times B.

Ratio, as used in accounting, is defined in Key Concept 14.5.

Key Concept 14.5

Ratio

In accounting, when comparing quantity A with quantity B, the ratio R is defined by
R = A ÷ B. This means that A is R times B, and may be written R:1. In essence a ratio
is merely a shorthand notation for the relationship between two or more things. It is
the relationship which must be understood. Without that understanding, the ratio,
no matter how precisely calculated or sophisticated, is meaningless.

new competitors or a price-cutting
...act on the price of computers
...puter. Again we need to

...examined so far have
...ancial statements
...e relationship
...of finan-
...sis and

TABLE 14.1
Analysis ratios

Ratio	Components		ABC Ltd (20X4)			
SHORT-TERM SOLVENCY ratios						
1 Current ratio	current assets / current liabilities		$\dfrac{6080}{4007}$	= 1.52		
2 Quick ratio	quick assets / current liabilities	$\dfrac{CA-I}{CL}$	$\dfrac{2791}{4007}$	= 0.70		
EFFICIENCY RATIOS						
1 Debtors' turnover	net credit sales / average debtors		$\dfrac{14\,441}{(3012+2776)\div 2}$	=	$\dfrac{14\,44}{28¢}$	
2 Average days sales uncollected	days in year / debtors' turnover		$\dfrac{365}{5}$	= 73 days		
3 Inventory turnover	cost of goods sold / average inventory		$\dfrac{12\,595}{(3903+3289)\div 2}$	=	$\dfrac{12\,595}{3596}$	= 3.5
4 Inventory turnover in days	days in year / inventory turnover		$\dfrac{365}{3.5}$	= 104.3 days		
PROFITABILITY RATIOS						
1 Net profit margin	net profit (before extraordinary items) / sales		$\dfrac{499}{14\,441}$	= 3.5%		
2 Gross profit margin	net sales − cost of goods sold / net sales		$\dfrac{14\,441-12\,595}{14\,441}$	= 12.8%		
3 Asset turnover	sales / average total assets		$\dfrac{14\,441}{(9695+9127)\div 2}$	=	$\dfrac{14\,441}{9411}$	= 1.53
4 Return on assets	net profit (before extraordinary items) + income tax + interest / average total assets		$\dfrac{499+579+768}{9411}$	=	$\dfrac{1846}{9411}$	= 19.6%

investments ...

Shows the number of days to
convert inventory into sales.

Profit produced by each dollar of
sales.

Indicates the efficiency of
management in turning over the
company's goods at a profit.

Shows how efficiently assets are
used to generate sales.

Shows the overall earning power
of total assets irrespective of
capital structure.

Ratio	Formula	Calculation	Result	Description
5 Return of ordinary shareholders' equity	net profit − preference dividend / average ordinary shareholders' equity	$\frac{499}{(3727 + 4324) \div 2} = \frac{499}{4026}$	= 12.4%	Shows the profitability of ordinary shareholders' equity.
6 Earnings per share	net profit (before extraordinary items) − preference dividend / weighted average number of ordinary shares issued	$\frac{499}{1476}$ (assume shares are $1)	= 33.8 cents	To facilitate comparisons of earnings between companies.
LEVERAGE				
1 Debt to equity	total liabilities / total shareholders' equity	$\frac{4803}{4324}$	= 1.11	Shows the relationship between debt financing and equity financing.
2 Debt to total assets	total liabilities / total assets	$\frac{4803}{9127}$	= 0.53	Shows the proportion of total assets financed by debt.
3 Equity ratio	total shareholders' equity / total assets	$\frac{4324}{9217}$	= 0.47	Shows the proportion of total assets financed by equity.
4 Interest coverage	net profit (before extraordinary items) + income tax + interest / interest expense	$\frac{499 + 579 + 768}{768} = \frac{1846}{768}$	= 2.40	Shows the protection of lenders from a default on interest payments.
MARKET-BASED RATIOS				
1 Price/Earnings (P/E)	market price per ordinary share / earnings per share	$\frac{\$3.30^*}{0.338}$ *Assume market price is $3.30	= 9.76	Shows the amount the market will pay for $1 of profit.
2 Earnings yield	earnings per share / market price per ordinary share	$\frac{0.338}{\$3.30}$	= 10.2%	Shows the earnings yield based on the current market price.
3 Dividend yield	dividends per ordinary share / market price per ordinary share	$\frac{337 \div 1476}{\$3.30} = \frac{0.2283}{3.30}$	= 6.9%	Shows current yield on dividends.
OTHER RATIOS				
Net tangible asset backing	net tangible assets / number of ordinary shares issued	$\frac{4324 - 451}{1476}$	= $2.62	Shows the value per ordinary share based on net tangible assets at book values.

For example, if we want to know how many police are needed to maintain order at a football match, we could work out a ratio of police officers to spectators. If we found that we needed 200 police for a crowd of 40 000 spectators, the ratio would be one to 200 or 1:200.

As well as understanding the relationship expressed by the ratio, we also need to examine ratios in a wider context. The above ratio is meaningless on its own: it does not give us any idea whether we are using the right number of police. To decide this we would need to establish whether there were problems of violence or, if not, whether we could achieve the same result with fewer police. To answer the first question we require additional information while the latter could be answered, in part at least, by looking at other football clubs and what ratio of police to spectators they use. This simple example serves to illustrate the fact that the ratio on its own cannot tell us very much. It needs to be looked at in the context of other information and experience.

Ratios based on the statement of financial position

As we have already said, the important point to bear in mind is what the ratio is attempting to illustrate. For example, we could look at the statement of financial position of ABC Ltd and calculate the ratio of plant and equipment to other fixed assets, but this would be of little use unless we knew what the relationship meant and what we expected. The calculation of ratios is not an end in itself.

There are some relationships that are significant. For example, earlier in this chapter we discussed the need to find out about short-term solvency and financial risk. We said that financial risk was related to the amount of debt finance compared with equity finance. To express this as a ratio, using ABC Ltd for example, we take the loans in 20X1 and compare them with the equity in that year. The figure for loans for that year was $297 000 and the equity figure was $3 117 000. The ratio is calculated by dividing the equity figure by the loans figure as follows.

$$\frac{\$3\ 117\ 000}{\$297\ 000} = 10.5 \text{ or } 10.5{:}1$$

This tells us that for every $1 of loan finance there is $10.5 of equity finance, or that there is 10.5 times more equity than loans. If we compare this with 20X4 we find that the ratio in that year is:

$$\frac{\$4\ 324\ 000}{\$427\ 000} = 10.1 \text{ or } 10.1{:}1$$

If we had calculated this ratio for all years we would find that it goes up and down, which is something we could have established by looking at the common-size statements. We still do not know whether this is good or bad or why it is going up and down. To answer those questions we need to look at the commercial environment, industry norms, and what else is happening in the particular business we are analysing.

To illustrate the latter point we can look in more detail at the statements of financial positions for the two years in question. We find that, apparently, the ratio we have just calculated suggests that the business is almost as reliant on debt in 20X4 as it was in 20X1. In fact this is not the case as the short-term debt, in the form of the bank overdraft, has increased from nil in 20X1 to $427 000 in 20X4. Thus, the ratio we calculated tells us only part of the story, because ABC is now relying on short-term as well as long-term borrowing.

One way to overcome this problem is to calculate more than one ratio to establish the relationship between debt and equity. For example we could also calculate the ratio of

total debt to equity, or the ratio of the total long-t
less cash balances to equity. All these ratios attemp
cial risk involved.

Other statement of financial position ratios th
ship between current assets and current liabiliti
monetary assets, such as debtors and cash, and
used to express what is happening in relation
solvency'. They are calculated by dividing, fo
current liabilities figure. Once again, on its
necessarily tell us very much. We need to loc
of the business. For example, we expect a giv
be different to that of, say, a car manufacturer. This is be
tory, being perishable goods, has a limited shelf life. Besides the na
we also need to take into account the industry norms and the size of the bus

Turning now to the trends in ABC's short-term solvency ratios, we can see whethei
they give us any idea of what is happening.

$$\text{current ratio} = \frac{\text{current assets}}{\text{current liabilities}}$$

$$\text{current ratio for 20X1} = \frac{\$6\ 304\ 000}{\$3\ 932\ 000} = 1.6 \text{ or } 1.6{:}1$$

The ratios for the other years are as follows:

20X2, 1.6:1; 20X3, 1.3:1; 20X4, 1.5:1; 20X5, 1.2:1

These show that the ratio is declining, but what does this mean? To answer that, we
need to think about the relationship being expressed, i.e. the relationship between those
assets that will be converted into cash in the short term and the amounts we potentially
have to pay out in the short term. If the ratio is going down, it means that we have less
cover and therefore there is more risk.

With more risk we might wish to use a more sensitive measure. One such measure
simply excludes the inventory from the current assets and compares the remaining
current assets with the current liabilities. The reasoning behind the exclusion of inventory is that it will take time to turn it into cash: it first has to be sold and then the debtors
have to pay before we can use the cash to pay our creditors.

This ratio, i.e. the ratio of current assets, excluding inventory, to current liabilities, is
often referred to as the *acid test* or *quick ratio* and is defined as follows:

$$\text{acid test or quick ratio} = \frac{\text{current assets} - \text{inventory}}{\text{current liabilities}}$$

A modification of this ratio is to deduct prepayments from the current assets, because
prepayments are not normally available to pay debts.

Calculating this ratio for ABC Ltd for 20X1 we obtain:

$$\frac{\$6\ 304\ 000 - \$3\ 645\ 000}{\$3\ 932\ 000} = 0.67 \text{ or } 0.67{:}1$$

The fact that the ratio is less than one-to-one tells us that we could not pay our current
debts if we were called upon to do so. To put it another way, the ratio tells us that we
have 67c to pay each $1 of current liabilities. The question is: does this matter? ABC did,
after all, stay in business well after 20X1. In reality, the business on which ABC is based
carried on for a further five years.

328 CONTEMPORARY ACCOUNTIN

The interpretatio
the other ratios,
is not as straigh
depending o
based on a
be exerci
isons
with

...n of the information obtained from calculating this ratio, as with all ...an make sense only if it is compared to a set of industry norms. This ...forward as it sounds: there are often different norms within an industry, ... the size and relative power of the firms in that sector. Moreover, any norm ...number of firms will be the average rather than the best, and so care has to ...sed when applying it to a particular firm. This all seems to imply that compar-...ith norms are not informative. This is certainly true if the comparison is made ...ut adequate attention to what the norms really represent.

...he question of the usefulness or otherwise of an industry norm does not apply in the ...ase of ABC Ltd as we do not have that information. However, we do have the information to calculate trends and the trend in the quick ratio for ABC is shown below.

20X2, 0.67:1; 20X3, 0.6:1; 20X4, 0.7:1; 20X5, 0.5:1

Once again the trend shows an overall decline, with 20X4 being the odd year out. As before, we can conclude that the risk is increasing but we cannot say whether this is in line with what is happening generally because we are looking at the company in isolation. In reality our knowledge of what was happening in the economy generally would tell us whether credit was getting tight or easing off, and this information would help us in our interpretation of the trend shown above.

Having looked at some of the statement of financial position ratios for measuring financial risk, let us now turn our attention to the statement of financial performance.

Ratios based on the statement of financial performance

Most ratios that relate solely to the statement of financial performance are expressions of costs as a percentage of sales, e.g. the gross profit or net profit expressed as a percentage of sales. These relationships are also made apparent with common-size statements, which we have already examined. Therefore, they will not be discussed any further. Instead we will consider some of the relationships between the statement of financial performance and the statement of financial position.

Ratios between statements of financial performance and financial position

Suppose we have an increase in sales: we would expect our debtors to increase; we would probably have to buy more goods to sell, and so our creditors might rise; and in all probability our level of inventories would have to rise to cope with the increased demand. In the case of ABC Ltd, the sales have risen as have the debtors. At this stage we are not sure whether the increase in debtors is solely due to the increase in sales or whether it is in part caused by the debtors taking longer to pay. The use of a ratio that compares sales and debtors would provide the answers.

When calculating ratios that relate statement of financial position items to statement of financial performance items we have to bear in mind that if prices are changing, the relationship can be distorted. This is because the statement of financial position represents prices at one point in time, whereas the statement of financial performance represents the results of operations for a period. This can be shown diagrammatically.

T_0 —————————— statement of financial performance —————————— T_1

opening statement
of financial position

closing statement
of financial position

Thus, the opening inventory figure or debtors figure is expressed in beginning-of-the-year prices, the profit and loss figures in average prices, and the closing figures in end-of-year prices. In addition to the problem of changing price levels is the problem that the volume will also change. For example, as sales increase we need to hold more units of inventory in order to provide the same service. Thus, we have two problems, i.e. changes in prices and in volumes. One way to compensate for this is to use the average of the opening and closing statement of financial position figures and compare that average figure for inventories, debtors, etc. with the figure from the statement of financial performance which is already expressed in average prices. Thus, to calculate the relationship between sales for 20X5 and the debtors we take the debtors at 20X4 and at 20X5 and average the two figures. This gives us a better approximation of the true level of debtors required to sustain that volume of sales. In fact, an average based on monthly balances of debtors might be even more appropriate. However, this information is not available in annual reports.

The relationship thus calculated can be expressed either as the turnover of the statement of financial position figure, e.g. debtors' turnover, or as the number of days debtors take to repay. We use the latter for purposes of illustration, because experience shows it is more readily understood.

To calculate this ratio the formula we require is:

$$\text{debtor collection period (days)} = \frac{\text{average debtors}}{\text{sales}} \times 365$$

Thus, for 20X5 for ABC the debtor collection period is:

$$\frac{1/2\ (2776 + 2508)}{13\ 226} \times 365 = 73 \text{ days}$$

Once again we cannot comment on whether this is good or bad without some reference point and some more information. For example, if the sales mix had changed and ABC had moved into overseas markets, this might be taking longer to collect money due.

Several other ratios of this type can be calculated, e.g. the number of days inventories are held or the period taken to pay creditors, using cost of sales and purchases respectively. We will not deal with these other ratios in depth; instead we encourage you to identify the relationships which will aid your understanding, and derive your own ratios. Table 14.1 provides some for you to consider.

Efficient market hypothesis (EMH)

The semi-strong form of the EMH states that share prices on average reflect all publicly available information. As a consequence of this, it is not possible to consistently use publicly available information to generate above-average profits from trading.

There is a substantial amount of evidence which supports the notion that share prices adjust very quickly to the release of accounting information. Figure 14.3 shows the results of a study by Brown and Hancock which looked at the release of the annual net profit figures by Australian companies. The graph shows that a large adjustment to share prices occurred during the announcement period. The study supports the notion that the market was efficient and that the release of the annual net profit figures provided information.

While there exists a large body of evidence supporting market efficiency there are also some anomalies. For example, in Figure 14.3 there appears to be a continued drift downwards of share prices for the decreases in net profit. This post-announcement drift has been observed in other studies. It may be possible to use this information to generate a trading strategy which could yield abnormal profits. However, any such profit is likely to be less than the transaction costs.

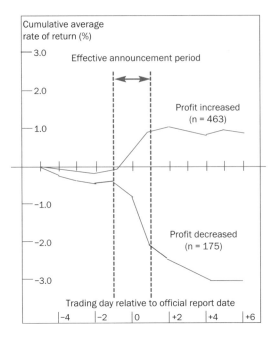

Figure 14.3 *Cumulative average share price reactions to 638 Australian profit reports when the dividend payment was unchanged.*

Implications of the EMH

If one subscribes to the EMH, then there are some interesting implications for managers and investors.

For managers, the EMH would mean that any attempt to influence share prices by choosing accounting policies which increase reported net profit will not succeed. The share market will see through the cosmetic change in reported profit and thus share prices will not change. Of course, if managers do not subscribe to the EMH, or if they are concerned about compensation plans and debt contracts as discussed in Chapter 1, then incentives still exist for the selection of income-increasing accounting policies.

For investors, the EMH would suggest there is little point in spending time analysing publicly available information. Instead, they would be better served in investing in a diversified portfolio. In fact, it might seem the annual reports and financial statements have very little information for investors. However, without financial statements and published annual reports the share market would be less efficient. Financial statements are used by analysts who diligently analyse the information as soon as it is publicly available. This ensures that share prices are efficient and this enhances the efficiency of the allocation of resources.

Furthermore, the EMH applies on average and therefore it is possible that at any time there will be individual stocks which are under- or overpriced. Some investors may see this as a worthwhile challenge.

Another important implication of the EMH for investors concerns the role of market-based ratios. Market-based ratios shown in Table 14.1 include the price earnings ratio and the earnings yield. In an efficient market the price of any stock should represent the intrinsic value of the stock, i.e. what it is worth. Therefore, a company's price earnings ratio can be compared to other firms in the industry. A higher than normal P/E ratio could mean either the price is too high or the EPS is too low. For example, ABC has a P/E ratio of 30/2 or 15 and the average in the industry is 10. If the EMH is valid then the price on average will not be too high as this would mean the share is overpriced.

In our example, the price of $30 for ABC is what the shares are worth. Therefore, the share market believes the current EPS of $2 is lower than what it expects the future level of EPS to be. In our example, if we assume a P/E ratio of 10 is appropriate for ABC then the market is expecting future EPS of ABC to be $3.

The other explanation for the difference in P/E ratios between companies could be different accounting policies. For example, a company that uses reducing balance depreciation methods should, other things being equal, report a lower P/E ratio than a comparable company that uses straight-line depreciation. Therefore, before comparing P/E ratios between different companies, adjustments should be made to the EPS to compensate for differences in accounting policies.

CASE STUDY 14.1

NRMA in breakdown lane despite profit increase

by Jim Hanna

SHARES in NRMA Insurance Group have dived below their $2.75 facility price for the first time, despite the insurer posting a better than expected annual net profit yesterday.

NIGL reported a net profit of $346.31 million for the year to June 30, a result boosted by a $51.02 million abnormal tax gain.

An extraordinary charge of $49.92 million for demutualisation and listing costs brought the bottom-line profit figure to $296.39 million, still above analysts' forecasts and 17 per cent better than the previous year.

However, the share price fall—down 10 cents to $2.71, a new low—indicated that the market wanted to see evidence of a growth strategy.

Managing director Eric Dodd said yesterday he would return $500 million in excess capital to shareholders if no acquisition was made within 12 months.

However, NIGL had several potential acquisitions 'under the microscope at the moment', he said.

These were in general insurance, domestically and regionally, and funds under management, which he said he wanted to quadruple.

'We will certainly need to have some acquisition/alliance help getting to that target,' he said.

Parts of Queensland-based Suncorp-Metway 'are very attractive to us', he said, although he stressed that no talks had begun, nor would NIGL undertake anything other than a friendly acquisition.

Market observers believe Suncorp would be an ideal fit for the New South Wales-based insurer; Suncorp has 56 per cent of Queensland's compulsory third party insurance market, 28 per cent of its home insurance market and 28 per cent of the motor insurance market.

It also has 20 per cent of the state's retail deposits and a significant chunk of the Queensland lending business, giving NIGL an established banking platform and expertise it could roll out nationally.

Shareholders must wait until April at the earliest for a dividend; yesterday's result relates to the period before NIGL was demutualised and floated on the stock market.

AAP/Age, 8 September 2000

Commentary

Despite the profit increase, the share price of NRMA declined by 10 cents, or about 4 per cent. The article suggests that this was due to the fact that the market wanted to see evidence of a growth strategy. The share price reflects future expectations and it appears that the market is not optimistic about the future prospects of NRMA. This reaction is consistent with an efficient market: the share price has not simply reacted to the profit announcement (which we are told was above analysts' expectations) by increasing.

Before leaving the subject of financial analysis and in particular ratio analysis, it is worthwhile reviewing some of the points made in this chapter about putting the analysis into context and also reiterating the limitations of this sort of analysis.

Summary of major issues

There is no point in using sophisticated techniques for analysis without understanding the following.

- What are the economic, social and political pressures? What type of industry is involved and where is the industry as a whole going?
- What type of organisation are we dealing with? Is it a charity? Does it have an American parent company? How do these factors affect the information that is presented and the way in which it is presented, and how should they affect our analysis? What business is the organisation in? How big is the organisation? These are all relevant questions that have to be answered if the analysis is to be carried out properly.
- Who is the analysis prepared for? Different users have different needs in terms of analysis and, even when their needs appear to overlap, the emphasis is frequently different from group to group.
- Any analysis is only as good as its base data. So far our analysis has been based on historic cost accounts, which assume that prices do not change, when in practice this is not the case. Even if we overcome that problem, there is the question of how up-to-date or out-of-date the information is. There are also issues of comparability because different accounting policies are adopted and because the size of the organisation affects norms. And what do norms actually mean?

Finally we need to be clear about the purpose of the analysis. Are we providing accounting information on which a user will base a decision, and, if so, what alternative decisions is that user facing? Having identified in our example that ABC seems to have some problems, who will determine what, if any, action can be taken to solve some of those problems? In general, the role of outside users is limited to identifying problems: there is little they can do to solve them. This is a task that should be carried out by the management of the company.

In order for managers to be able to carry out this task, as we have already said, they need more detailed information and often they also require different forms of information. For example, the fact that the costs are rising is not sufficient: they need to know *which* costs are rising. Perhaps the problem is caused by a lower level of sales which loses the economies of scale. Then they need to know the level of sales and costs they expect in 20X6 and thereafter, so that they can take appropriate actions to improve the performance of the business. In the next chapters we consider these additional needs of managers and how they are met through the analysis of past information, whether in the form we have already seen or in a different form. We also consider what other information is needed for planning, decision making and control, where this is obtained, and how it is used.

Before moving on to that discussion, we will briefly summarise the key features and limitations of financial statement analysis.

Key features

- Financial analysis has to be looked at in the wider context of the industry, the political and social environment, etc.
- Financial analysis has to be targeted to meet the needs of the user of the analysis.
- Financial analysis is only as good as the base information that is being analysed.
- Financial analysis involves comparisons both over time and between firms, and this imposes limitations.

These key features point to some limitations that have to be borne in mind when discussing financial analysis. These can be usefully summarised under three headings as follows.

Key limitations

Information problems

- The base information is often out of date; i.e. timeliness of information leads to problems of interpretation.
- Historic cost information might not be the most appropriate information on which to base the decision for which the analysis is being undertaken.
- Information in published accounts is generally summarised; detailed information might be needed.
- Analysis of accounting information identifies only symptoms, not causes, and thus is of limited use.

Comparison problems: over time

- Effects of price changes make comparisons difficult unless adjustments are made.
- Changes in technology affect the price of assets, the likely return and the future markets.
- A changing commercial environment affects the results and this is reflected in the accounting information.
- Changes in accounting policies may affect the reported results.
- There are problems in establishing a normal base year with which other years can be compared.

Comparison problems: between firms

- The selection of industry norms and the usefulness of norms based on averages are problematic.
- It is difficult to compare the distribution of ratios for each firm with industry averages.
- The financial risks and business risks of firms differ, and this affects the analysis.

- Firms use different accounting policies.
- The size of the business and its comparators affects risk, structure and returns.
- Environments affect results, e.g. different countries, or home-based versus multi-national firms.

These are the issues that you need to bear in mind when carrying out your analysis and interpreting and reporting the results. They should not, however, be used as a reason not to attempt the analysis.

References

Brown, P. and Hancock, P.J., 1977. 'Profit reports and the share market' in Tilley, I. and Jubb, P. (eds), *Capital, Income and Decision Making*, New York, Holt, Rinehart and Winston.

Public Sector Accounting Standards Board and the Accounting Standards Review Board. *Statement of Accounting Concept No. 3: Qualitative Characteristics of Financial Information*, August 1990.

Review questions

1 Identify the main user groups and their common needs in terms of financial analysis.

2 How do the needs of long-term lenders differ from those of equity investors?

3 What factors do we need to take into account in order to put a financial analysis in context?

4 What sources of information outside the business are available to you and how would you use this information in your analysis?

5 What information would you derive from reading the chairman's statement?

6 What other parts of the annual report would you use in your analysis?

7 Explain briefly the difference between financial risk and business or commercial risk.

8 How would you measure financial risk in the short and long term?

9 What are the limitations to analysis which are inherent in the accounting data we are using?

Problems for discussion and analysis

1 Refer to the Woolworths financial report in Appendix 1.
   a What were the two major sources of finance used by the company? What were the amounts from each of these sources?
   b What was the value of shares issued under the dividend re-investment plan?
   c How much was paid for goodwill on acquisition of businesses?
   d Calculate the following ratios for Woolworths:
      i   current ratio
      ii   quick ratio
      iii gross profit margin
      iv   asset turnover
      v   return on assets
      vi   debt to equity

  vii debt to total assets
  viii equity ratio
  ix earnings per share.
e Determine the share price of Woolworths at 30 June 1999. What was the
   dividend yield?

2 The following information is available concerning Wuffalot Pet Foods Ltd.

Current ratio	1.5:1
Non-current liabilities to equity ratio	0.5:1
Issued capital	$150 000
Retained earnings	$50 000
Total assets	$400 000

What is the value of Wuffalot's current assets?

3 Homer and Bart Ltd reported the following information for a five-year period.

	20X1	20X2	20X3	20X4	20X5
	$	$	$	$	$
Sales	400 000	425 000	450 000	525 000	650 000
Gross profit	200 000	220 000	230 000	265 000	330 000
Net profit	40 000	41 000	42 000	38 000	45 000

From the above data, prepare a trend analysis and comment on the results.

4 Below is a simplified statement of financial position of XYZ Ltd.

XYZ LTD
STATEMENT OF FINANCIAL POSITION AT 30/06/20X1

	$
Current Assets	
Bank	12 000
Inventory	7 500
Debtors	5 000
Total Current Assets	24 500
Non-current Assets	
Land and buildings	100 000
Total Non-current Assets	100 000
Total Assets	124 500
Liabilities	
Current Liabilities	
Creditors	20 000
Total Liabilities	20 000
Net Assets	104 500
Equity	
Share capital	100 000
Retained earnings	4 500
Total Equity	104 500

The present current ratio is: 1.25:1.

The company has been told by its bank to increase its current ratio to 1.5:1.
Given the statement of financial position above, what simple step does the
company have to take to achieve the required current ratio?

5   As an analyst you have extracted the following information from the accounts
    of Romeo Construction Co. Ltd.

ROMEO CONSTRUCTION CO. LTD
STATEMENTS OF FINANCIAL PERFORMANCE FOR
THE YEARS ENDED 30 JUNE

	20X4	20X5	20X6
	$	$	$
Sales	60 000	54 000	75 000
Less Expenses			
Material	22 500	21 000	35 813
Labour	15 000	13 500	18 000
Production expenses	7 500	6 000	6 750
Administrative expenses	7 500	7 500	8 250
Finance expenses	1 500	1 500	1 500
	54 000	49 500	70 313
Net Profit	6 000	4 500	4 687

ROMEO CONSTRUCTION CO. LTD
STATEMENTS OF FINANCIAL POSITION AT 30 JUNE

	20X4	20X5	20X6
	$	$	$
Work in progress	60 000	52 500	67 500
Non-current Assets	30 000	37 500	37 500
	90 000	90 000	105 000
Bank overdraft	15 000	18 000	12 000
Other Current Liabilities	15 000	12 000	18 000
Shareholder funds	60 000	60 000	75 000
	90 000	90 000	105 000

Required:

a   Comment on the profitability of the business.
b   Comment on the financial situation of the business.
c   What action do you suggest for the forthcoming year?

6   The statements of financial position and selected information are given below
    for Katrina Ltd and Catherine Ltd for the year ended 30 June 20X2.

	Katrina		Catherine	
	$	$	$	$
Assets				
Current Assets				
Cash at bank	80 000		220 000	
Marketable securities	8 000		190 000	
Accounts receivable (net)	100 000		130 000	
Merchandise inventory	560 000		300 000	
Total Current Assets		748 000		840 000
Non-Current Assets				
Property, plant and equipment (net)	1 200 000		1 280 000	
Intangibles	6 000		—	
Total Non-current Assets		1 206 000		1 280 000
Total Assets		1 954 000		2 120 000

(*continued next page*)

Liabilities and Shareholders' Equity

Current Liabilities	180 000	310 000
Non-current Liabilities	340 000	330 000
Paid-up capital ($10 value)	1 300 000	1 300 000
Retained earnings	134 000	180 000
Total Liabilities and Shareholders' Equity	1 954 000	2 120 000

Other information:

Accounts Receivable, 1 July 20X1	130 000		110 000
Merchandise inventory, 1 July 20X1	520 000		420 000
20X1/X2 Sales:			
Cash	852 000		400 000
Credit	1 100 000		1 500 000
20X1/X2 cost of goods sold	1 200 000		1 100 000
20X1/X2 Net Profit	310 000		400 000
20X1/X2 interest expense	60 000		40 000
Total Shareholders' Equity, 1 July 20X1	1 334 000		1 380 000
Total Assets, 1 July 20X1	1 854 000		2 020 000

Required:

a   Calculate the current ratio, quick ratio, inventory turnover, accounts receivable turnover and average age of receivables for each company.

b   Which company do you think has a better liquid position? Why?

c   Calculate for each company the rate of return on total assets and the rate of return on ordinary shareholders' equity.

d   Which company is using leverage more effectively to increase the rate of return to ordinary shareholders? Explain.

e   What do accountants mean by 'window dressing'? Show how Katrina Ltd and Catherine Ltd could improve their liquid ratios by window dressing.

7   Given below are the summarised accounts of Apple Ltd for the past five years. These form the basis for the questions which follow.

APPLE LTD
SUMMARISED STATEMENTS OF FINANCIAL POSITION OF APPLE LTD

	20X1 $000	20X2 $000	20X3 $000	20X4 $000	20X5 $000
Non-current Assets					
Intangible Non-current Assets	5 247	5 220	7 305	9 969	10 674
Tangible Assets	20 175	23 130	43 920	43 740	69 225
	25 422	28 350	51 225	53 709	79 929
Current Assets					
Stock	20 031	23 034	53 091	74 823	99 606
Debtors	17 589	24 693	60 270	48 987	66 768
Bank and cash	4 698	6 801	7 839	3 273	9 747
	42 318	54 528	121 200	127 083	176 121
Current Liabilities					
Creditors	16 197	24 588	55 659	41 130	72 831
Taxation	459	768	4 302	2 712	3 444
Dividends	801	1 812	3 339	3 738	3 672
Bank loans and overdraft	10 581	4 026	18 180	29 316	37 638
	28 038	31 194	81 480	76 896	117 585
Net Current Assets	14 280	23 334	39 720	50 187	58 536

(continued over page)

	20X1	20X2	20X3	20X4	20X5
	$000	$000	$000	$000	$000
Total Assets *less*					
Current Liabilities	39 702	51 684	90 945	103 896	138 465
Non-current Liabilities					
Loans	14 793	15 477	35 241	35 430	67 844
	24 909	36 207	55 704	68 466	70 621
Represented by					
Ordinary share capital	5 160	10 359	17 994	18 039	19 464
Retained profits	19 749	25 848	30 975	43 692	41 734
Revaluation reserve			6 735	6 735	9 423
	24 909	36 207	55 704	68 466	70 621

Notes

i   During 20X5 some of the freehold properties were revalued.

ii   Loans amounting to $22 million were repaid during 20X5.

iii   No non-current assets were disposed of during the year.

SUMMARISED STATEMENTS OF FINANCIAL PERFORMANCE OF APPLE LTD

	20X1	20X2	20X3	20X4	20X5
	$000	$000	$000	$000	$000
Sales	93 930	116 232	259 470	278 340	372 753
Cost of goods sold	65 751	82 525	197 197	208 775	294 475
Gross Profit	28 179	33 707	62 273	69 585	78 278
Operating expenses	17 022	21 398	36 830	35 130	59 881
Net Profit before					
interest and tax	11 157	12 309	25 443	34 455	18 397
Interest	2 727	2 652	7 707	10 167	14 082
Net Profit after					
interest and tax	8 430	9 657	17 736	24 288	4 315
Taxation	2 517	1 746	9 270	7 833	2 601
Net Profit after tax	5 913	7 911	8 466	16 455	1 714
Dividends	801	1 812	3 339	3 738	3 672
Retained profits	5 112	6 099	5 127	12 717	(1 958)

a   Complete the common-size statements of financial performance for the five
years and analyse these statements with particular reference to the
profitability of Apple.

COMMON-SIZE STATEMENTS OF FINANCIAL PERFORMANCE OF APPLE LTD

	19X1	20X2	20X3	20X4	20X5
	$000	$000	$000	$000	$000
Sales	100	100	100	100	100
Cost of goods sold	70	71	76		
Gross Profit	30	29	24		
Operating expenses	18	18	14		
Net Profit before					
interest and tax	12	11	10		
	3	2	3		

(continued next page)

Net Profit after			
interest and tax	9	8	7
Taxation	3	2	4
Net Profit after tax	6	7	3
Dividends	1	2	1
Retained profits	5	5	2

b   Using whatever form of analysis you consider appropriate, analyse and comment on the financial performance and financial position of Apple Ltd.

c   What are the limitations of your analysis?

8

JAYCO LTD
STATEMENTS OF FINANCIAL POSITION AT 30 JUNE

	20X4	20X5	20X6
	$	$	$
Assets			
Current Assets			
Cash	364 700	292 720	123 790
Inventories			
Finished products	600 000	700 000	800 000
Work in progress	245 500	258 000	342 000
Raw materials and supplies	483 050	450 000	550 000
Accounts receivable	521 000	669 280	1 184 210
Total Current Assets	2 214 250	2 370 000	3 000 000
Non-current Assets			
Land (at cost)	600 000	816 300	1 334 104
Buildings (at cost)	1 215 500	1 323 000	2 400 000
Machinery (at cost)	1 538 980	1 500 370	3 505 640
Goodwill (at cost)	2 000 000	2 000 000	2 000 000
Total Non-current Assets	5 354 480	5 639 670	9 239 744
Total Assets	7 568 730	8 009 670	12 239 744
Liabilities			
Current Liabilities			
Accounts payable	355 700	360 000	544 620
Provision for tax	500 000	500 000	800 000
Provision for dividend	130 000	430 000	672 000
Total Current Liabilities	985 700	1 290 000	2 016 620
Non-current Liabilities			
Debentures	683 030	903 370	2 999 020
Mortgages	500 000	400 000	1 000 000
Total Non-current Liabilities	1 183 030	1 303 370	3 999 020
Total Liabilities	2 168 730	2 593 370	6 015 640
Net Assets	5 400 000	5 416 300	6 224 104
Owners' Equity			
8% preference shares	500 000	500 000	1 200 000
Ordinary shares ($1 par)	4 000 000	4 000 000	4 000 000
Profit and loss appropriation	900 000	916 300	1 024 104
Total Owners' Equity	5 400 000	5 416 300	6 244 104

ADDITIONAL INFORMATION FROM JAYCO LTD'S FINANCIAL STATEMENTS

		20X4	20X5	20X6
		$	$	$
i	Annual sales			
	Credit (terms 2/10 net 45)	2 605 000	3 011 760	4 500 000
	Cash	120 000	142 600	1 500 000
ii	Cost of goods sold	1 662 250	1 861 070	3 720 000
iii	Net Profit (after tax at 50%)	463 250	473 150	789 902
iv	Interest expense	94 642	104 269	399 902
v	Share price	$1.50	$1.52	$2.08
vi	Balances as at 30 June 20X3			$
	Accounts receivable			450 000
	Total Tangible Assets			5 000 000
	Inventory			1 441 870
vii	Selected Financial Ratios			Industry
				20X6
				$
	Current ratio			2.25
	Quick ratio			1.10
	Receivable turnover			6 x
	Inventory turnover			4 x
	Debt/Total Assets			33%
	Debt/Net Tangible Assets			0.6
	Equity ratio			72%
	Rate of return on ordinary shareholders' funds			16%
	Gross profit margin			40%
	Net profit margin			16%
	Net operating profit rate of return			26%
	Overall interest coverage			11 x

Required:

Evaluate the position of Jayco Ltd. Cite specific ratio levels and trends as evidence.

9   The information below relates to Orange Ltd.

ORANGE LTD
STATEMENTS OF FINANCIAL PERFORMANCE OF ORANGE LTD
FOR THE YEAR ENDED 30 APRIL 20X2

	Notes	20X1	20X2
		$000	$000
Sales		5 614	4 814
Cost of goods sold	1	5 039	4 299
Operating profit		575	515
Interest charges		53	156
Profit before tax		522	359
Taxation	2	292	193
Profit after tax		230	166

STATEMENT OF FINANCIAL POSITION OF ORANGE LTD
AT 30 APRIL 20X2

	Notes	20X1 $000	20X2 $000
Current Assets			
Stocks	4	1 194	1 763
Debtors		1 004	1 259
Cash		61	5
		2 259	3 027
Non-current Assets			
Land and Buildings	3	227	360
Fittings	3	320	285
Motor Vehicles	3	162	221
		709	866
Total Assets		2 968	3 893
Current Liabilities			
Creditors		1 147	1 370
Taxation	2	332	215
Bank Overdraft		255	676
		1 734	2 261
Non-current Liabilities			
Loans	5	130	200
Total Liabilities		1 864	2 461
Net Assets		1 104	1 432
Represented by			
Share Capital	6	483	545
Retained Profit	6	621	787
Asset Revaluation Reserve	6	0	100
Total Equity		1 104	1 432

Extracts from the notes to the accounts

1   Included in the costs of goods sold are the following charges:

	$ 000
Depreciation	123
Auditors' remuneration	55
Director's remuneration	240
Hire of plant	30
Profit on sale of fittings	20

3   Non-current Assets

	Land $000	Buildings $000	Fittings $000	Motor vehicles $000
Balance at 1 May 20X1	120	140	600	440
Additions			100	140
Revaluations	60	40		
	180	180	700	580
Disposals			90	
Balance at 30 April 20X2	180	180	610	580
Depreciation				
Balance at 1 May 20X1		33	280	278
Charge for year		(33)	75	81
		0	355	359
Disposals			30	
Balance at 30 April 20X2		0	325	359
Net Book Value 20X2	180	180	285	221
Net Book Value 20X1	120	107	320	162

5   A long-term loan amounting to $70 000 was repaid during the year. This was replaced with a new loan of $140 000 repayable in ten years.

6   Share Capital and Reserves

(*continued over page*)

	Share capital $000	Retained profit $000	Other reserves $000
Balance at 1 May 20X1	483	621	
Share issue	62		
Movements in year		166	100
	545	787	100

CASH FLOW STATEMENT OF ORANGE LTD
FOR THE YEAR ENDED 30 APRIL 20X2

		$000
Net cash inflow from operating activities		(449)
Cash flow from investing activities		
Payment to acquire tangible non-current assets	(240)	
Receipts from sales of non-current assets	80	
Net cash outflow from investing activities		(160)
Cash flow from financing activities		
Issue of ordinary share capital	62	
Issue of new loan	140	
Repayment of loan	(70)	
Net cash inflow from financing activities		132
Decrease in cash in period		(477)

Notes to the cash flow statement

1 Reconciliation of operating profit to net cash flow from operating activities:

	$000
Operating profit	166
Depreciation charges	123
Profit on sale of non-current asset	(20)
Increase in stocks	(569)
Increase in debtors	(255)
Increase in creditors	223
Decrease in tax payable	(117)
	(449)

2 Analysis of changes in cash and bank balances:

	20X1 $000	20X2 $000	Change $000
Cash in hand	61	5	(56)
Bank overdraft	(255)	(676)	(421)
	(194)	(671)	(477)

a   Produce a common-size statement of financial position and statement of financial performance for Orange Ltd and comment on each of these statements.

b   Calculate the percentage changes in the statement of financial position and the statement of financial performance from 20X1 to 20X2 and comment on what this analysis reveals.

c   Using all the information and techniques available to you, comment on the performance of Orange Ltd as reflected in the accounts and the cash flow statement.

10   The directors of Efficient Distributors Ltd are concerned at the results of trading activities reported for the year ended 30 June 20X6, and failure to keep within the limit of the bank overdraft ($12 000).

They request that a comprehensive survey be made of the financial state of the company, and provide the following information.

STATEMENTS OF FINANCIAL PERFORMANCE FOR THE YEARS ENDED 30 JUNE

	20X4		20X5		20X6	
	$	$	$	$	$	$
Sales		200 000		180 000		165 000
Less Cost of sales						
Opening stock		36 000		41 000		44 000
Purchases		95 000		87 000		80 000
		131 000		128 000		124 000
Less Closing stock	41 000	90 000	44 000	84 000	49 000	75 000
Gross profit		110 000		96 000		90 000
Less:						
Selling and distribution expenses	40 000		40 000		46 000	
General and admin. expenses	20 000		20 000		18 000	
Financial expenses	15 000	75 000	16 000	76 000	20 000	84 000
Net operating profit before tax		35 000		20 000		6 000
Less Provision for taxation		15 000		9 000		2 500
Net operating profit after tax		20 000		11 000		3 500
Less Loss on sale of investment						1 000
Net profit for year		20 000		11 000		2 500
Add:						
Balance of unappropriated profits b/f		10 000		7 000		1 000
Transfer from reserve				10 000		
Amount available for distribution		30 000		28 000		3 500
Less Dividends paid and proposed						
Preference—final	3 000		3 000		3 000	
Ordinary—interim	10 000		12 000			
Ordinary—final	10 000	23 000	12 000	27 000		3 000
Unappropriated profits c/f		7 000		1 000		500

STATEMENTS OF FINANCIAL POSITION AT 30 JUNE

	20X4		20X5		20X6	
	$	$	$	$	$	$
Assets						
Current Assets						
Bank	1 000					
Inventory	41 000		44 000		49 000	
Trade debtors	26 000		31 000		37 000	
Less Provision for doubtful debts	(1 000)		(1 000)		(2 000)	
Prepayments	2 000		3 000		3 000	
Total Current Assets		69 000		77 000		87 000
Non-current Assets						
Plant and equipment	10 000		10 000		21 000	
Less Depreciation (1 000 in X3)	(2 000)		(4 000)		(7 000)	
Vehicles	80 000		80 000		114 000	
Less Depreciation (4 000 in X3)	(16 000)		(32 000)		(54 000)	

(continued over page)

	20X4		20X5		20X6	
	$	$	$	$	$	$
Land (at valuation)	60 000		70 000		70 000	
Buildings (at cost)	40 000		56 000		56 000	
Investments (at cost)	25 000		25 000		—	
Total Non-current Assets		197 000		205 000		200 000
Total Assets		266 000		282 000		287 000
Liabilities						
Current Liabilities						
Bank overdraft			8 500		12 500	
Trade creditors	12 000		8 000		14 000	
Accrued wages and interest	1 000		1 500		2 000	
Provision for taxation	15 000		9 000		2 500	
Provision for dividend	13 000		15 000		3 000	
Total Current Liabilities		41 000		42 000		34 000
Non-current Liabilities						
Mortgage on land (due 30.6.X9)			21 000		34 500	
Term loan (due 20Y2)	75 000		75 000		75 000	
Total Non-current Liabilities		75 000		96 000		109 500
Total Liabilities		116 000		138 000		143 500
Net Assets		150 000		144 000		143 500
Owners' Equity						
50 000 6% $1 preference shares		50 000		50 000		50 000
100 000 ordinary shares						
paid to 75c		75 000		75 000		75 000
Asset revaluation reserve				10 000		10 000
General reserve		18 000		8 000		8 000
Unappropriated profits		7 000		1 000		500
Total Owners' Equity		150 000		144 000		143 500

Required:

a Analyse the company's financial position, indicating the causes of the present situation and recommending future policy. What are the implications of the continuation of the company's present practices?

b Indicate any limitations of your analysis.

c What additional information (if any) would you like to assist your analysis?

Ethics case study

Allandale Ltd is a company which builds small luxury boats and employs 500 people. The company has been operating for ten years. Two years ago the company underwent a major expansion of its boat-building facilities because of increased demand for its boats from overseas buyers. To do this it borrowed $20 million through a mortgage loan with a major bank.

The loan agreement contains the following clauses:

i Allendale is to maintain a current ratio of at least 2:1; and

ii after-tax return on assets must be at least 10 per cent.

If the company fails to meet either ratio in any year, the $20 million is immediately repayable.

Last year the government removed a 10 per cent tariff on small luxury boats and the company has had difficulty competing in overseas markets. Consequently, the company has had to reduce its profit margin in order to compete against suppliers from other countries.

Tom Lyons is the accountant of Allandale Ltd, and he has completed the preliminary financial results for the current year. Based on these results, the current ratio is 2.1:1 and the return on assets is 11 per cent. However, Tom has some concerns about the following items:

i   One boat unsold at year end is recorded in the statement of financial position at $500 000. However, Tom is certain that the most it could be sold for is $350 000.

ii An overseas customer who owes the company $1 million has recently informed Allandale Ltd that they are in severe financial trouble and will only be able to pay half the amount owing. The balance in the provision for doubtful debts is only $300 000.

If Tom recognises the decline in the net realisable value of $150 000 and the $200 000 uncollectable account in excess of the provision, the company's current ratio will fall to 1.6:1 and the return on assets to 2 per cent. This would result in a call for immediate repayment of the $20 million loan. In turn, this would force the company into bankruptcy and Tom and his best friends will lose their jobs.

Discuss:

a   the ethical problems faced by Tom

b   what Tom should do.

Internal Users, Internal Information, Planning and Control

Learning objectives

At the end of this chapter you should be able to:

1 explain why management's information needs are not met solely by general-purpose financial reports

2 explain which external users are likely to be able to gain access to internal company information not published in annual reports

3 explain why the size and structure of a company influences the need for management to have access to more complex internal information

4 explain what the planning and control processes are in relation to company objectives

5 understand the problems in establishing company objectives and the concept of goal congruence

6 explain what is meant by strategic and operating decisions

7 explain the concept of responsibility accounting and how it helps management to monitor and control performance within the company

8 explain the problems companies have in contending with, establishing and implementing control systems

9 explain the potential costs and benefits of developing accounting information systems to implement monitoring and control of performance.

15

Introduction

In Chapter 14 we discussed external users of information, their information needs and the ways in which they use the accounting information available. This information is derived from the financial reports via the annual accounts of the enterprises which are being analysed. The underlying information for these financial reports comes from the organisation's accounting system. This accounting system might be very simple or extremely sophisticated, depending on the size of the business and the needs of the users of the accounting information. One of these users is management, who need not only more detailed information than that normally contained in the financial accounts, but more up-to-date information and indeed some different types of information. This does not mean that the information which management needs is not useful to other users external to the enterprise; it might in fact be very useful to them if they had it. One reason it is not used by the external user groups discussed in Chapter 14 is that in some cases they do not have the power to demand access, as for example in the case of the larger public companies such as BHP Ltd. In other cases, the enterprises are too small and their internal accounting system too unsophisticated to produce any information other than that required for the annual accounts; this would be the case with, for example, your local fish-and-chip shop.

To be able to make decisions wisely, individuals and organisations need to have some vision about the future. A decision made without any thought to the future could well result in undesirable consequences. This is particularly so in the business context: small businesses often fail despite the fact that they trade profitably. One of the main reasons for this is the lack of planning for future cash requirements. As well as the need to make plans, actual performance has to be monitored to ensure that the plans are being attained. The latter activity is an essential part of the control exercised by organisations to help secure their survival and efficiency.

In this chapter we examine the needs of management in terms of the information it requires in order to make decisions between alternative opportunities, to plan the enterprise's activities and to ensure that the plans are carried out. This information is primarily prepared for internal users; it would be available to external users only if they had sufficient power to obtain access.

We then examine the planning and control process, using a framework which not only explains the process itself but also provides an essential foundation for analysis and discussion in subsequent chapters. It is important to recognise that the planning and control process cannot be examined in isolation. There are a number of factors that influence its design and application. In this chapter we discuss some of the more significant factors, such as technology, which influence the design of accounting information systems in the context of the planning and control process, and consider some of the main limitations on the application of these processes.

Management's information needs

As a starting point we examine the situation of an existing business where management has already decided on the course of action to follow. In this situation management is interested in the outcomes of those past decisions. The managers can obtain certain information from the annual accounts, but often this is insufficient for their purpose because, for one thing, the annual accounts contain summarised and simplified information. This summarised information might alert management to the fact that profit is lower than anticipated, but it is unlikely to be sufficiently detailed to identify the cause of this variation. Managers almost always need more detailed information about the results of their past decisions and actions than that which is contained in the annual accounts.

As the name implies, annual accounts are drawn up only once a year, and this is another reason why they are unlikely to be sufficient to meet the needs of managers, who need more regular and up-to-date information. The fact that annual accounts are produced only at the year's end means that, even if they are able to establish why the results have varied from those anticipated, it might be too late to take appropriate action. For example, if an enterprise has a January year-end for accounting purposes, its accounts will normally not be available until some time after the end of January. Thus, any corrective action is correspondingly delayed. Although management has access to the year's results before they are published, there might still be considerable delays. These delays will not be as great as for the published accounting information: the time span between the year's end and the actual production of the annual accounts varies from about three to four months for listed companies to periods of more than ten months for smaller enterprises.

Key Concept 15.1

Management information needs

Managers generally need detailed information.
They need up-to-date information.
They need frequent information.
They need information suited to the decisions they are required to take.

We have established some needs of management that are not satisfied by the production of annual accounts. The reason that managers are likely to require information more frequently is so that they can monitor the results of their actions and decisions and fine-tune the business as required. This is not to imply that none of the needs of managers are met by the financial information system on which the annual accounts are based. For example, although the annual accounts show only one figure for debtors, the accounting records contain much more information about the individual debts making up that debtors figure. This includes information about when the sales took place and the customer's past payment record. This detailed information allows management to collect the money more quickly and to chase the slow payers. By doing this, management will be able to ensure that business does not face more problems, because of poor cash flow, than are absolutely necessary.

There are, of course, other examples of information contained within the accounting system that, if presented and used in different ways from that required for drawing up annual accounts, meet management needs better. For example, as we indicated in Chapter 7, the basic information required for both marginal and absorption costs is available from the accounting system. In that chapter we also discussed the impact of the Accounting Standard *AASB 1019* on the choice between absorption and marginal costing for reporting purposes. Chapter 18 contains a fuller explanation of these alternative systems and the problems associated with their use in practice. This provides the basis for an understanding of the relative merits and limitations of these alternatives from the point of view of management. From that discussion you will see that, depending on the decision faced by management, it might need information presented in different ways. For example, to decide whether to continue making a particular product or not, managers require forward-looking information in the form of forecasts. They might, for example, wish to know the point at which the revenue is going to be equal to the cost, i.e. the breakeven point, and how likely it is that such a point will be reached. Whether sales are likely to be sufficient to break even is a question for the sales and marketing department; the cost of the product at different levels of output is a question that accountants will be called upon to answer.

A full discussion of the way in which costs behave and how to establish the breakeven position is contained in Chapter 17. An understanding of these principles is vital if appropriate decisions are to be made by management, whatever industry is being considered. For example, it can be argued that in the airline industry you need to know a breakeven position that covers costs, a breakeven position that covers costs plus the interest charges incurred in buying planes, and a third position at which the airline is profitable. In that case the breakeven positions could be expressed in terms of seat occupancy. This knowledge, of course, is only a portion of that which is required by managers in the airline industry.

Having said that management needs other information, possibly in different forms, it is important to understand that the base information used to produce the annual accounts is also used as the source for many different reports that are provided to meet the specific needs of management. As with the other users referred to in Chapter 14, for management purposes financial information is only one of a number of types of information needed in order to make decisions about the future direction and actions of the business. These other types of information are outside the scope of this text, but they include marketing information, employment legislation, etc. We will continue our discussion of management's information needs within the relatively narrow confines of financial information.

We have said that management needs frequent and detailed information, in a different format from that contained in the annual accounts; this information is used to monitor progress and take appropriate actions to fine-tune the business. Implicit in this process of monitoring is that the results are judged against some expectations. These expectations might be rough plans carried in the head of the owner of a small business or detailed plans and budgets in the case of a larger enterprise.

The process of planning and control and the ways in which the information is derived and used are discussed in detail later in this chapter, where we look at the process of setting objectives and the problems of goal congruence. The budgeting process is discussed in Chapter 21, which contains a detailed analysis of the ways in which budgets can be used within an organisation to help planning, both as a control mechanism and as a motivator of people.

As we have said, most if not all of this information is also useful to users other than managers. However, some of it is commercially sensitive and achievement of the goals of an enterprise might be dependent on its plans being kept secret from its competitors. Not all external users will be able to obtain access to the information: it depends not only on who they are but also upon their importance to the enterprise. We now consider what these external users' needs might be, who they are, and the factors—such as relative power, competition and confidentiality—that determine their access or lack of access to internal information. The information required to implement budgets and restructuring is confidential to the company and, if made generally available, would be of value to its competitors.

External users' information needs

One group of external users who can demand access to internal accounting information is the taxation authorities. The nature of the information they require varies but is normally either more detailed breakdowns of particular expense headings or details of the timing of purchases and sale of non-current assets. The reason for this is that the taxation system is based upon a set of rules for arriving at the taxable profit which are different from those used to arrive at the accounting profit. The taxation authorities, which include the Australian Taxation Office, the Customs and Excise Department and state governments, have a statutory right of access to information.

Another group of external users which is often in a sufficiently powerful position to obtain further information is the enterprise's bankers. The information they demand will of course depend on the circumstances. If the enterprise is doing well, the information demanded would be quite different from that required if the enterprise had problems. We will discuss at a general level some of the additional information which bankers might require and why, before going on to examine what determines whether or not this information is available to these external users.

In general, the information demanded by an enterprise's bankers can be divided into two categories: that required for routine monitoring and that required to arrive at judgements about the future needs of the enterprise. The former category includes regular management accounts such as monthly profit statements, an analysis of debts in terms of how old they are (this is known as an 'aged debtors analysis') and other up-to-date information such as the amount owed by the enterprise, i.e. the monthly creditors' balance. All this information is required to monitor the health of their customer's business on a more regular basis than would be possible if they had to rely on the information provided by annual accounts which, as we have said, are likely to be a few months out of date when they are produced.

Bankers also require other information to make judgements about the future needs and prospects of the enterprise in order to ascertain whether to lend money, when it is likely to be repaid and the risk involved. The information on future prospects is normally required in the form of projected cash flow statements and statements of financial performance, but also includes information about any other loans that the enterprise has and their due dates for repayment. The financial information is only part of the information that the banker requires; this could also include future orders, plans, analysis of competitors etc.

As we have already indicated, there are circumstances where, like other external users such as shareholders and competitors, the banker cannot get access to this additional information. We examine those circumstances in our discussion of the impact of organisational size and structure on the information produced for management purposes, which is one factor that determines what these external users have access to.

Effects of organisational size

We have discussed the needs of management in terms of information to make decisions about the future, to plan future actions and to control the business on a day-to-day basis. The more complex and sophisticated the business, the more likely that it will require additional information. For example, the local garage owner might be able to carry in his head all the information needed to enable the business to be run effectively on a day-to-day basis. This is because the business is sufficiently small and the proprietor, who is also the manager, is directly involved in the running of the business and is available to take whatever action is necessary.

In a large and complex business there is a need for a more formalised system for a number of reasons. Firstly, the amount of information required in, for example, a multi-product firm is such that it is unlikely that the management would be able to carry in their heads all the detail necessary to run the business effectively. (A fuller discussion of the problems faced by multi-product firms and the techniques available to solve them is contained in Chapters 19 and 20, where we look at the effects of resource constraints and at make or buy decisions.) Secondly, the larger the business, the more distant the senior managers are from the day-to-day operations. Not only do they require information of a strategic type, but they also require additional information to control the activities and actions of those below them.

Thus, the size of the organisation influences the information needs of its managers and the way in which these needs are met. More formal systems are needed as the size of the business increases. The nature of the business also has an effect on the information needs: a multi-product business requires more sophisticated information systems than a single-product business. Consider for example the information required to run a restaurant, where the only product is food, compared with that required to run a hotel. In the latter case, not only do you need information about the food operation, but information is also required on bed occupancy rates, the bar profit, etc.

In discussing the information needs of managers it has to be borne in mind that information is not free. In general, the more sophisticated the information system, the more it costs to set up and run. The need for better and more up-to-date information always has to be balanced against the costs and benefits of obtaining that information. However, as we point out later in this chapter, although there is considerable literature on cost-benefit analysis, the practical implementation of such an approach is fraught with difficulties. We should also remember that more up-to-date information is not in itself better: it also needs to be relevant to the use to which it is to be put. A fuller discussion of what constitutes relevant information in relation to costs and benefits and how these relate to short-term decisions is contained in Chapter 19. The need to obtain relevant information at a reasonable cost partly explains why many small businesses produce little in the way of formal management information. In many of these cases the information, if it exists at all, is held in the owner-manager's head in a form that is not readily accessible to others. In these situations bankers are often able to exercise considerable influence as a major provider of finance; however, no matter how much pressure they exert, they cannot access information that does not exist. They therefore have to rely on the annual accounts and such other information as is available.

We have shown that the information available is influenced not only by the needs of managers but also by the size and complexity of the organisation's products. We have also suggested that the nature of the product or products can influence the information systems. There are, of course, many other factors which will have an influence on what is required and what is produced. Consider several examples: the needs of high-technology industries, the effects of flexible manufacturing systems and of management techniques such as 'just-in-time'. These, like the nature of the industry, produce specific needs. In subsequent chapters we will look at different industries in both the manufacturing and service sectors. We now consider a more general influence upon the information needs of managers, i.e. the structure of the organisation.

Effects of organisational structure

It is clear that different organisations have different structures and this means that their information needs also differ. If we consider retailing, it is obvious that a business such as Woolworths that operates both within Australia and overseas needs information about its New Zealand branches that differs from that about its Sydney branches, if for no other reason than the effect of different currencies. Thus, in general, an organisation that has a multinational operation has different information requirements to one which operates solely in the domestic market.

Similarly, department stores such as Myer are organised on departments as profit centres and the departments' profits are identified separately. This implies that both the cost records and the takings from sales have to be identified and recorded by the department. In such organisations the managers may be rewarded on the basis of schemes such as profit sharing, or by comparing profits achieved against predetermined targets. In such circumstances the information system has to be designed to meet the structural requirements of the organisation. These and similar matters are touched on in the discussion of department and divisional accounting in Chapter 19 and the impact and uses of budgets in Chapter 21. We could, of course, find many more examples of different structures apart from those referred to above. Other structures depend on and to some extent are determined by the product, the market in which the business operates and the competitive environment, as well as more mundane factors such as geography and location of its branches or outlets. In general terms, the more decentralised an organisation is, the more complex its information systems are.

The planning and control process

Key Concept 15.2

Planning and control

Planning involves the determination of objectives and expressing how they are to be attained. The control process is the means of ensuring that the plans will be achieved.

A number of stages have been identified in the planning and control process.

- *Stage 1:* setting objectives
- *Stage 2:* making strategic decisions
- *Stage 3:* making operating decisions
- *Stage 4:* monitoring and possible corrective action.

We begin by considering the four stages in the planning and control process before turning to the technical aspects of this process and factors that might influence the design of the accounting system within it.

Objectives

From both a practical and a theoretical perspective, the determination and setting of objectives is probably the most complex stage of the planning and control process in a business organisation. In the absence of any explicit objectives, there is no basis for management to evaluate whether the business is succeeding, nor any criterion for choosing between alternative business opportunities.

Organisations themselves do not have objectives; the objectives of the organisation are those of the people involved in it. These individuals each have their personal goals, and it is likely that some will conflict with other participants. A sales manager's objective might be the maximisation of sales, in volume terms, without any strong consideration of profitability. This might conflict with the objectives of the financial management of the firm whose primary concern could be to maximise profits through the introduction of higher prices with lower volumes of sales. This conflict in objectives is commonly referred to as a lack of goal congruence. The problem of goal congruence is more acute in large business organisations because of the number of participants and their varying vested interests. In the case of a company, it is likely that employees would desire an increase in remuneration and this could be one of their personal goals. However, this might conflict with the interest of shareholders if it reduces the amount available to them for payment of dividends.

Key Concept 15.3

Goal congruence

Goal congruence is the alignment of organisational goals with personal and group goals of the individuals within an organisation.

From a wider social perspective, there is a growing awareness of the need to recognise the interests of parties external to the organisation itself when it sets its objectives. In particular, customers, government and the local community all have an interest in the survival and the activities of the organisation. For example, in recent years there has been a growing public concern about environmental issues. As a result of public pressure, a number of firms have changed policies regarding their production activities. A good illustration of this is the change in policy of petrol companies to produce unleaded petrol.

If a business organisation's objectives are to be effective, there must be a congruence of goals. Horngren et al. (1997) state that:

Goal congruence exists, for example, when managers working in their own best interests also act in harmony with the goals of the organisation as a whole.

When an organisation sets its objectives, the interests of all the participants need to be recognised and common goals identified.

A number of academics maintain that it is not important to consider the goals of each individual, since their major interests tend to converge to form group objectives. For example, it is likely that more pay will be a common goal for all employees. However, for an organisation, there still remains the problem of identifying and setting objectives that satisfy all interest groups. Lowe and Chua (1983) suggest that by looking at the common ground shared by the participants, it is possible to establish organisational goals. They start by designating the possibilities open to organisations as 'activity spaces', which are defined by the interests of the varying groups involved with the organisation. For example, the activity space for shareholders of a company might be to reduce labour costs, whereas that of employees (and possibly of governments) would be to maintain jobs and wage levels. Figure 15.1 shows the activity space for each interested group.

Where the boundaries of the activity space for each group overlap in Figure 15.1 the acceptable activity is common to more than one group. The area where the activity spaces for all groups overlap is described as the 'feasible region'. Lowe and Chua argue that it is the task of management of an organisation to confine its activities within this feasible region.

The most obvious activity in the feasible region for a business organisation in a capitalist economy is the making of profit. Where markets are, by and large, unregulated and competitive, profit-making is an essential element in ensuring a firm's survival. Profits are by nature quantifiable and targets can readily be set in terms of formulating objectives.

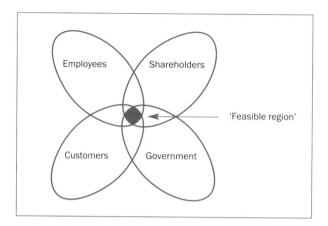

Figure 15.1 *The activity spaces of interest groups determine what is feasible for an organisation.*

The quantifiable nature of profits also means that they are measurable. This attribute is very attractive to managers, as deviations from the set objectives during an accounting period can easily be identified. This feature is particularly important in the control process, which will be discussed later in the chapter. It is common, in practice, to find the profit objective stated more precisely in terms of maximisation of profits.

Qualitative objectives, in contrast with those of a quantitative nature, suffer from the problems associated with measurement. The quality of a product (in meeting its purpose and customer requirements) is far more difficult to define in measurable terms, and difficulties also arise when comparing the objective with the actual performance in the control process. Although product or service quality is often cited as a prime objective of a business, in reality it is often disregarded or assessed inappropriately through movements in sales revenue.

Due to the difficulty of setting unquantifiable goals, such as a quality definition or social responsibilities, most firms tend to compromise and take the easier option of profit setting as the major (or sole) criterion for expressing their objectives. Although this gives a simple version of the firm's objectives, it has the disadvantage of disregarding the interactions which take place with various other interests. This can effectively undermine the firm's performance and even, paradoxically, threaten the profit which the company has put in esteem.

These problems with regard to unquantifiable goals are particularly pertinent to nonprofit-making organisations, e.g. municipal councils and charities. Frequently the objective of such organisations is expressed in terms of the amount of the service rendered and the quality of that service. These objectives are inherently difficult or impossible to express in quantitative terms. A considerable amount of research has been carried out over recent years in an attempt to overcome these problems associated with non-profit organisations. A detailed discussion of the potential ways in which qualitative objectives can be effectively employed in such organisations can be found in Henley et al. (1992) and Jones and Pendlebury (1996).

Making strategic decisions

Strategic decisions in a business organisation relate to policy changes in respect of the products or services that are currently being offered and the markets where they are sold.

Key Concept 15.4

Strategic decisions

Strategic decisions are those that determine the long-term policies of the firm and that are necessary if the firm is to meet its objectives.

The nature of the commercial environment in which businesses operate is uncertain and outside the control of management. Some examples of the variables that can confront an organisation are changes in taste, high inflation, recession and competitiveness. If organisations remain static and do not consider alternative policies in such an environment, it is likely that their objectives will not be met, which could threaten their survival in the long term. There have been many examples of companies making strategic decisions primarily to meet their objectives. Often these decisions have been made to maintain their long-term profitability by diversifying, making them less dependent on their traditional markets. For example, Rothmans, who primarily concentrated on the tobacco market, have in recent years started to invest in the confectionery industry.

Drury (1996) suggests that, to make effective strategic decisions, management should be proactive in:

identifying potential opportunities and threats in its current environment and take specific steps immediately so that the organisation will not be taken by surprise by any developments which might occur in the future.

He argues that firms should be constantly searching for alternative courses and developing:

* new products for sale in existing and new markets
* new markets for existing products.

Because of the importance of strategic decisions, they tend to be taken at the higher levels of management of organisations. These decisions are of a long-term nature, and this is one of the features that differentiates them from operating decisions.

CASE STUDY 15.1

Telstra's initiatives

TELSTRA seems to be coping well, even in a fiercely competitive deregulated market. With sales revenues of A$18.6 billion (RM43 billion), Telstra announced a profit of A$4 billion for its year ending June 30.

'These results indicate Telstra's successful operations in an intensely competitive market where we have been subjected to fierce competition from the many multinational telcos and in a less-than-conducive local regulatory environment,' declares a top Telstra official.

The telco has implemented several initiatives in the past year, including a new organisation structure, new networks and products, business alliances and a high internal focus on costs.

Several new services in the areas of the Code Division Multiple Access network (CDMA) and mobile data have also been rolled out. There was also the launch of asymmetric digital subscriber line (ADSL) and e-commerce initiatives—including the organisation evolving into a Web-enabled company.

Telstra's alliance with Pacific Century Cyberworks will also propel the telco's ambitions in the Asia-Pacific. Telstra's growth plans revolve around a four-pronged strategy to pump up its future revenue streams.

First is the strategy to optimise returns from local, traditional telecoms products and services. Several programmes are being implemented to better utilise its extensive distribution networks and to improve the delivery of traditional telephony services.

The second strategy focuses on key growth opportunities in the mobile, data, broadband and the Internet spaces.

Plans for the mobile communications market include further expansion of the GSM coverage and the introduction of new information services such as the general packet radio service for higher speed data packets, and GSM WAP applications. Extension of Telstra's new CDMA network would provide for additional digital coverage to rural and regional parts of Australia.

In the data, Internet, e-commerce and content-based space, Telstra intends to:

- Complete the data mode of operation (DMO) project to ensure appropriate conditioning of Telstra's networks and systems for the impending telecoms era where data traffic far exceeds voice.

- Rollout of ADSL service to allow fast, 'online always' Internet service over ordinary phone lines.
- Embark on strategic partnerships, investments, acquisitions and internal product/platform development to enhance the ability to offer an expanded range of data, Internet, e-commerce and content-based products and services.
- Utilise the existing broadband capabilities to develop and market additional broadband applications.

Third is the exploration of areas out of its existing business territory.

Telstra may reshape its wholesale business to provide offerings with commercially attractive terms and conditions, and value-added wholesale services—such as managed network services on a global network.

And lastly, Telstra seeks to transform its corporate culture to improve productivity, achieve cost savings and provide better customer service.

New Straits Times, 4 October 2000

Commentary

The article discusses how Telstra has responded to the challenges of operating in a competitive deregulated market when it previously operated in almost a monopoly position. The company developed a three-pronged strategy with the objectives of improving productivity, achieving cost savings and providing better customer value. It is essential that companies continue to address their strategic plans if they are to survive and be successful.

Key Concept 15.5

Operating decisions

Operating decisions are decisions that focus on the efficient use of the resources available to the firm in the short term.

Making operating decisions

The majority of operating decisions in an organisation are concerned with pricing and output, e.g. price setting and the determination of production volumes and stock levels.

To be effective, the decisions must conform with the objectives and strategic policies of the organisation. As these decisions are taken in an economic environment, often there are constraints on the levels of sales and production which prevent an organisation, in the short term, from meeting its objectives. For example, a firm might experience short-ages of skilled labour which effectively constrain the level of output in the short term. If the maximisation of profits is an objective of the firm, the constraint effectively limits the extent to which the objective can be met in the short term. In the long term these constraints can usually be relieved—more skilled labour, for example, can be trained or recruited. In circumstances where resource constraints exist, although the long term objectives cannot be satisfied, it is still important to allocate scarce resources ef-ficiently. Management accounting techniques have been developed to allocate scarce resources efficiently in these circumstances and they will be considered in detail in a later chapter.

The long-term plans of an organisation, as previously mentioned, are formulated through the making of strategic decisions with reference to overall objectives. In cases where, in the short term, the targets embodied within the long-term plans cannot be met, there is a need to amend or revise these plans in the light of the current economic situation. The process of re-examining long-term plans in such circumstances is an impor-tant feature of the effective management of organisations in a dynamic economic environment.

Operating decisions are translated into a short-term plan which is referred to as a budget. Budgets are simply plans of action expressed in monetary terms. The process of aggregating operating decisions into a plan compels managers to look ahead and co-ordinate their activities. For example, from this aggregation process the required level of stocks for production activities over the planning period can be identified. Without forward plans that co-ordinate production activities, the business might drift along and encounter undesirable situations—such as not having enough stocks to meet production requirements—that should have been anticipated and avoided. The budget also provides a basis for judging performance, through comparison of actual and budgeted figures. This comparison can highlight strengths and weaknesses within the organisation. It is impor-tant that budgets should be communicated to personnel in an organisation so that they are aware of the planned (budgeted) targets. This enables them to act in accordance with the plan.

The degree of sophistication and detail of budgets depends on the size of the organ-isation and the needs of the internal users. Often the budgets cover a period of one year and are broken down in monthly intervals. Monthly budgets provide control, and enable a comparison of budget and actual activity at regular intervals so that timely monitor-ing of the plan is facilitated.

The process of preparing budgets and the types of budgets that are commonly employed will be examined in detail in Chapter 21.

Monitoring and corrective action

Monitoring and corrective action are the major parts of the control activities of any organ-isation. The first element is the monitoring of actual performance against budget. From this comparison, differences (commonly referred to as 'variances') are identified—it is unlikely that the actual performance will be exactly the same as the budget. The reason for this is that the operating decisions embodied in the budget are normally determined well in advance of actual performance, and the process of forecasting costs and revenues in a dynamic economic environment is surrounded by uncertainty.

Key Concept 15.6

Monitoring and corrective action

Monitoring is the process of comparing actual performance with a predetermined target (plan). It provides the basis from which corrective action can be planned and taken.

To monitor performance effectively, personnel in an organisation who incur expenditure and generate revenues are identified and made responsible for these costs and revenues. The approach adopted is known as 'responsibility accounting'. It recognises various decision centres throughout an organisation and traces costs and revenues to individual managers who are primarily responsible for making decisions and controlling the cost and revenues of their centres. Managers' knowledge of their centres places them in an advantageous position within the organisation to ensure that budget targets are achieved. These responsibility centres are normally departments, branches or divisions of a company.

In effect, in responsibility accounting systems, managers to some extent participate in the preparation of their own budgets. Evidence from research suggests that participation by responsible managers in the setting of budgets enhances the probability of effective planning and control within an organisation.

To support a system of responsibility accounting, the reporting system of the organisation needs to communicate relevant information. The reports should show the actual performance, the budget and the deviations (variances) from budget. The mode in which budgeted and actual costs and revenues are collected and then reported, e.g. by product, labour or material input costs, is determined by management. The major factors which influence management in deciding the extent and sophistication of the reporting system are the costs of installing and operating such a system compared with the benefits which it generates. A more detailed discussion of the costs and benefits of information systems will be covered in a later chapter.

When variances have been identified, it is necessary to determine the reason for them in order for corrective action to be taken. If deviations from budget—assuming the budget reflects realistic targets—are not corrected it could be harmful to the company in the long run. For example, the use of materials in a production process might exceed the budget in a particular control period, which could result in losses and consequently threaten profitability if action is not taken. While the methods for identification of variances and their causes are outside the scope of this text, you should have some insight into the general nature of the causes of variances. Traditionally, textbooks have tended to concentrate on variances that are caused by operating problems, e.g. the prices of raw materials are greater than anticipated in the budget, perhaps because of inefficient buying practices by buyers. A few academics, in particular Demski (1982) and Bromwich (1980), have argued that there are other causes of variance that have been overlooked in the control process. They identify three causes of variances.

- Operating variances are related to human or mechanical factors that result in the budget targets not being achieved.
- Random variances are caused by divergences between actual and planned costs that arise at random: i.e. they occur by chance and there is no means of controlling them. For example, in some chemical processing the output can vary per unit of input because of evaporation; this variation is inherent in the process.
- Planning variances occur if plans are not realistic at the time of actual performance, even if operations have been efficiently carried out. Put simply, the plans might be out of date. For example, during the planning stage, material costs might have been

set with due care, but, because of rapid inflation, these costs become out of date during the control period and therefore do not represent realistic budget targets. Case Study 15.2 illustrates variances from budget.

CASE STUDY 15.2

Variances

ABC employs a budgeting system to control costs. The original budget for 20X1 included material A, which was estimated to cost $5 per kilogram. It was anticipated that 1000 kg would be used during the year. Therefore, the budget in total cost terms was $5000. During the year, however, although 1000 kg was used, the cost was $6000.

Commentary

Traditionally, the analysis of the variance between actual and budget would be presented as follows.

	Actual	Budget	Variance
	$	$	$
Material A 1 000 kg	6 000	5 000	(1 000)

The negative variance of $1000 (often indicated by brackets) indicates that it is 'unfavourable', i.e. actual costs exceed budget (plan).

This analysis does not give any indication as to the cause of the variance. For example, it could be because of inefficient buying practices by the purchaser of the materials or because prices have increased through inflation during the year. In the former case the variance is due to operating problems, so action might be taken in the future to ensure that more efficient buying practices are used. In contrast, if the variance is caused by inflation after the price was set in the original budget, the variance arises because the plan is out of date. In this case it is unlikely that the firm can take any action to prevent such variances occurring again.

Let us now assume that the firm has information at the end of the year 20X1 indicating that a realistic planned price, taking account of inflation during the year, would be $5.50 per kilogram. The variances could then be analysed as follows.

	Actual	Budget	Variance
	$	$	$
Variance caused through inefficient operations	6 000	5 500	(500)

	Original budget	Updated budget	Variance
	$	$	$
Variance caused by the plan being out of date	5 000	5 500	(500)

In this analysis the causes of the variance are clearly identified, i.e. $500 relates to operating problems and $500 is because the original budget was out of date. The information presented in this way is more informative and useful for management purposes.

Although the analysis of operating, random and planning variances is theoretically sound, there are a number of practical problems which limit its use in practice. For example, in Case Study 15.2 the up-to-date budget of $5500 was established at the end of the year. In other words this budget was established in hindsight after the purchase of the material. To establish a realistic budget reflecting recent operating conditions, these budgets, by their nature, must be determined after the event. While such budgets are useful for variance analysis purposes, they do not give any targets for management to work towards during the actual production period. This is a major deficiency in the use of these types of budgets. There are a number of other major criticisms, the most critical commentator being Lloyd Amey (1973).

It is not necessary for us to delve too deeply into the causes of variances nor to examine the criticisms in detail. The work of Demski and Bromwich highlights the limitations of traditional variance analysis, which restrict the effectiveness of the planning and control process in its practical application.

Another effective limitation is the cost of investigating the cause of variances. The activity of investigation can be costly. It might not be worth the time and money to carry out an investigation for the benefits derived, particularly for variances which are seen as insignificant.

The control system

The accountant's control system, the monitoring and corrective action, is often compared with that of an engineer, using the analogy of a central heating system. Figure 15.2 is a diagram of a central heating system. In this system the desired temperature is set and a comparator compares this with the actual room temperature. If there is any deviation, action is automatically taken by the system to fuel the boiler to enable it to compensate. This system thus involves the process of monitoring actual output against a desired output, and, when a variance is identified, corrective action is taken automatically.

Earlier, when we were examining the planning and control process, similar stages were identified and described. However, there are several interesting differences between the two systems which give us a greater insight into the limitations of the planning and control process.

An important difference is that the central heating model is a physical system where there are *automatic* responses to outputs. That is, corrective action is taken to obtain the desired temperature automatically and without any reference to operatives. In contrast, the control model, within the planning and control process, normally depends on humans. In this system the response to deviations from the budget is not taken automatically. Time lags are experienced in all accounting reporting systems and people have to be motivated to respond to variances and take corrective action if it is perceived to be necessary.

The extent of these time lags in reporting depends on the sophistication of the accounting information system. Some large companies monitor performance every week and, with computerisation helping to speed up the reporting process, have the capacity to take corrective action relatively quickly. However, in most organisations control reports are produced on a monthly basis. The main restriction on implementing more timely systems is the installation and running cost, which relates to costs and benefits: an information system should be installed only if the benefits generated from the system exceed the cost of installing and running it. The variances that are reported in an accounting information system can, of course, be used only as a guide for future operations. An organisation cannot remedy past mistakes.

It is only in recent years that the accounting function and its interaction with human behaviour has been brought to the forefront of accounting research and literature. It is now recognised that the effectiveness of accounting information systems is very much dependent upon the internal and external attitudes of individuals associated with the organisation. (For a detailed explanation of accounting and its relationship with human behaviour, refer to Hopwood, 1976.) Attention is now correctly given to the influence of individuals on accounting information systems, but there is still considerable scope for further research into how human behaviour distorts the effectiveness of accounting systems.

In the context of the control systems, the process of setting targets is influenced and affected by the behaviour of individuals. A sales manager might respond negatively if she is set a target that, in her opinion, is impossible. Another example is the action required to correct further undesirable variances: this action will very much depend upon the motivation of the responsible managers and their subordinates. Managers who perceive that targets are unrealistic are unlikely to be motivated to take corrective action to ensure that they are met in the future. The accountant's control system is therefore limited in its application by the motivation of individuals in setting budgets and taking action on variances that have been identified.

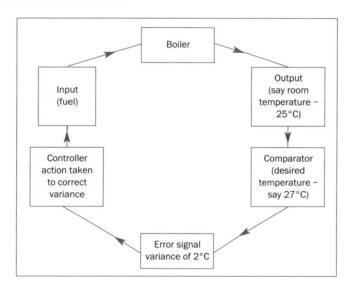

Figure 15.2 *A central heating system demonstrates automatic monitoring and controls.*

Costs and benefits of accounting information systems

An accounting information system is a commodity in much the same way as household goods such as detergents, soap and food. That is, there is a cost, often considerable, in installing and running the system. The benefits from employing the system should exceed the cost; otherwise it should not be installed.

The best system for an organisation is the system that generates the greatest amount of benefits net of costs. Horngren et al. (1997) contrast this approach with choosing a system because it is more accurate or a truer approximation of economic reality. The cost-benefit approach does not use accuracy as a criterion but focuses on the net benefits derived from alternative systems, giving preference to the system that generates the greater net benefits. The practical implementation of the cost-benefit approach, however, is rather complex. While it might be feasible to determine the cost of alternative systems, the benefits (the quality of information) are difficult to measure because they are qualitative. Although this is a problem, the cost-benefit approach is relevant in the choice of systems and is particularly relevant to the systems within the planning and control process described earlier.

The commercial context

A number of writers and researchers argue that the installation of effective planning and control processes in businesses requires consideration of individual and organisational factors. We have briefly examined individual behaviour with reference to the setting of budgets and the motivation required to take corrective action to maintain control of costs and revenues within an organisation. We will now briefly consider other organisational and environmental issues.

Businesses are affected by, and dependent on, the commercial environment. Emmanuel, Otley and Merchant (1990) stress that a firm's 'ultimate survival is determined by the degree to which it adapts and accommodates itself to environmental contingencies (uncertain events)'. Therefore, the design of a planning and control system must be carefully tailored to match the environment and the organisational context in which it will be employed. This approach is not new; it has been implicitly recognised by accountants for a number of years.

Traditionally, writers of textbooks have suggested that there is one best way in which a particular task can be carried out, regardless of the environment in which the organisation operates, e.g. the nature of the market and the production process. Accounting information systems as illustrated in textbooks have adopted this approach, and have not differentiated among the needs of accounting for different organisations. This approach follows classical management and scientific management theories. (See, for example, F.W. Taylor, 1947.) The *contingency theory* of organisations, in contrast, accepts that different types of organisation require differing types of accounting information to enable them to function effectively.

Emmanuel, Otley and Merchant identify three major classes of contingent factors:

- *technological:* e.g. whether the production process is labour-intensive
- *environmental:* e.g. the degree of competition and the degree of predictability
- *structural:* e.g. the size and type of the organisation.

These contingent factors affect accounting information systems, and in particular the effectiveness of the planning and control process. For example, in the context of planning, businesses that are in a relatively risky market tend to invest more in planning in an attempt to predict outcomes and analyse alternative opportunities to reduce their risk. The design of planning and control systems should take account of these wider issues if a firm is to survive.

Needs of small business

So far we have made little reference to small businesses in the context of employing planning and control systems. Clearly, there are constraints for small businesses in their use and choice of such systems. One of the major constraints relates to the cost and benefits of installing these systems, as described earlier. Nevertheless, there is increasing evidence to suggest that there is a greater chance of survival if small firms use budgets to plan their future and employ control mechanisms to ensure that these plans are met. The reason often cited for the high failure rate in Australia of small firms is the lack of planning and control of cash resources. Much of what has been said so far regarding the need for planning and control is relevant to small businesses.

Summary

In this chapter we have looked at the information needs of internal users. We have shown that the broad term 'management' covers a wide range of people in the organisation who each have differing information needs. These vary from the detailed information needs of the manager of a department within a store to the more strategic needs of the general manager of the whole store. This analysis can, of course, be applied to other organisations where there are multiple layers of management, ranging from those involved in the day-to-day running up to the board of directors. We have also indicated that the size and complexity of the organisation, as well as its structure, affect both the information requirements of those within the organisation and the relative availability of this information to those external users who have the power to access it. The common thread that runs throughout is that management needs detailed up-to-date information for the purposes of planning, decision making and control of organisations.

For organisations to operate efficiently in a dynamic and uncertain environment, they need to plan and control their activities. Four important stages of the planning and control process were identified and examined in this chapter.

The setting of objectives is clearly critical to the process. The other stages are dependent upon clear objectives being set and communicated to personnel within an organisation. In the uncertain environment that confronts business organisations it is important that they constantly make and review strategic decisions to maintain their position in the marketplace and to exploit opportunities for growth. In the short term, organisations must manage their resources efficiently in their day-to-day operating decisions; these are embodied within short-term plans known as budgets. If an organisation is to ensure that it is meeting its objectives in the long and short term it is necessary to monitor results and take corrective action when needed. This was examined in the last stage of the process. A number of problems were also identified relating to these four stages in the planning and control process. Potentially, these problems can limit the effectiveness of the process. However, there is growing evidence that successful companies invest heavily in planning and control information systems.

References

Bromwich, M., 1980. 'Standard cost for planning and control', *Topics in Management Accounting* (ed. J. Arnold, B. Carsberg and K. Scapens), Philip Allen.

Demski, J.S., 1982. 'Analysing the effectiveness of traditional standard cost variance model', *Information for Decision-making*, 3rd edn (ed. A. Rappaport), Prentice-Hall.

Drury, J.C., 1996. *Management and Cost Accounting*, International Thomson Business Press.

Emmanuel, C.R., Otley, D.T., and Merchant, K., 1990. *Accounting for Management Control*, Chapman and Hall.

Horngren, C., Foster, G., and Datar, S., 1997. *Cost Accounting: A Managerial Emphasis*, 9th edn, Prentice-Hall.

Jones, R. and Pendlebury, M., 1996. *Public Sector Accounting*, 4th edn, Pitman Publishing.

Lowe, E.A., and Chua, W.F., 1983. 'Organisational effectiveness and management control', *New Perspectives in Management Control* (ed. E.A. Lowe and J.L.F. Macklin), Macmillan.

Further reading

Amey, Lloyd, 1973. 'Hindsight vs expectations in performance measurement', *Readings in Management Decisions* (ed. L. Amey), Longman.

Anthony, R.N., and Young, D.W., 1984. *Management Control in Non-profit Organisations*, Richard Irwin.

Gray, D.H., 1986. 'Uses and misuses of strategic planning', *Harvard Business Review*, January–February.

Henley, D., Holtham, C., Likierman, A., and Perrin, J., 1992. *Public Sector Accounting and Financial Control*, 4th edn, Chapman and Hall.

Hopwood, A., 1976. *Accounting and Human Behaviour*, Prentice-Hall.

Siegel, G., and Ramanauskas-Marconi, H., 1989. *Behavioural Accounting*, South-Western Publishing Co.

Taylor, F.W., 1947. *Scientific Management*, Harper & Row.

Thompson, A.A., and Strickland, A.J., 2000. *Strategic Management: Concepts and Cases*, 10th International Edition, Irwin/McGraw-Hill.

Review questions

1   What are the main reasons management requires more information than is given in the annual reports?

2   One of the major improvements that bankers wish to see in respect of financial information is more timely information. Explain what this means and why it is important to bankers. How might this differ for managers?

3   What is likely to be the major impact of organisational size on the information needs of managers?

4   What useful management information is available from the accounting records from which the annual reports are produced?

5   What additional information would bankers wish to have and for what purposes would they use this?

6   There are several stages in the planning and control process. Identify these and give a brief description of each stage.

7   In recent years, more external users of accounting information have required internal management accounting information. Explain why such information is useful to these users.

8   Define responsibility accounting with reference to the planning and control process.

Problems for discussion and analysis

1 Refer to the Woolworths financial report in Appendix 1.
   a Do you think there is more information in the accounts than is required by the average investor?
   b Who do you consider would most likely benefit from reading the detailed accounts?
   c What is meant by the term 'contingent liability'?
   d Were there any contingent liabilities listed in the accounts? Why are they not included in the statement of financial position? What is the total amount of this liability?

2 With regard to the information which you identified in your answer to question 1 above: would managers' use of this information differ from the way it is used by bankers, and if so, how would it differ?

3 In each of the situations below, identify what you believe your information needs would be.
   a You are the manager of a local branch of a national retail organisation. All buying is done centrally and prices are fixed. You are in charge of the day-to-day management and hiring and firing of staff. Your annual remuneration is fixed.
   b The situation is the same as above, except that in addition to your annual salary you receive a bonus of $2 for each $200 profit made above that expected by your employer.
   c As in (b) above, except that you are able to decide on selling prices yourself.
   d You have been so successful as a branch manager that the company has promoted you to the position of regional manager in charge of 20 shops. The managers of these shops work under the conditions outlined in (c) above.

4 Discuss the main differences between the control models of accountants and engineers. Give details of any limits on the planning and control process that can be identified through this comparison.

5 Give illustrations of ways in which the behaviour of individuals can affect the planning and control process.

6 'For plans to be effective, management should consider the wider environmental factors that relate to the firm.' Discuss.

7 Describe why it is important to set objectives in a firm, and comment on the problems of setting objectives.

8 You work for an organisation primarily involved in health care, which runs a number of nursing homes for the elderly and has a head-office staff consisting of yourself and two owner-directors. Each of the nursing homes has a sister-in-charge who looks after the day-to-day running of the nursing home, but the advertising of the service, etc., is carried out by one of the directors, while the other director looks after the billing of the patients and collection of monies due. The overall profitability of your organisation has fallen drastically in the last year and you have been asked to investigate the situation.

   Identify what information you would need and what level of detail is required in order for you to start your investigation.

9   Giggling Brothers, wholesalers of fine wines, have been trading profitably for a number of years using a manual accounting system. However, they have experienced, every six months or so, severe cash-flow problems which appear to have been caused by a number of factors. These include the excessive purchase of 'special price' stock from vineyards, inappropriate timing of stock purchases relative to sales, inadequate control of debtors and mistimed marketing drives. Gigglings believe that many of these problems are caused by inadequate and untimely feedback from the Accounting Department. Purchasing Department staff maintain that they are given inadequate financial information by the Accounting Department, and that the Sales Department consistently misrepresents expected sales. Sales Department staff consider that management's expectations of their performance are unrealistic and that the Accounting Department does not keep them sufficiently informed about the payment performance of customers. Additionally, Accounting Department staff maintain that they are not consulted with regard to expenditure on purchases, or given sufficient information about the credit history of customers. Management believes that the implementation of a computerised accounting and reporting system will obviate most of these problems.

Required:

a   What type of accounting and reporting information system should be designed for Giggling Brothers?

b   What benefits would such a system offer to the firm and how might the information produced be incorporated into the planning process?

c   Suggest how Gigglings might best evaluate the cost against the benefit of implementing a new system.

d   Who do you think should be involved in the design and specification for the new system?

e   Do you think that an examination and evaluation of the approaches used by their competitors would be of benefit to Giggling Brothers?

Ethics case study

John Kellog is the financial controller for Energisers Ltd. He is preparing a report for a proposed plant expansion at two possible locations—Mandurah or Rockingham. He is of the opinion that Mandurah is the better location for the new plant and he therefore intentionally excludes any reference to the fact that property taxes are 100 per cent higher in Mandurah than they are in Rockingham. Kellog owns some properties in Mandurah and if the plant is built there, property values should significantly increase.

Discuss:

whether John is behaving in an ethical manner.

Capital Investment Decisions

Learning objectives

At the end of this chapter you should be able to:

1   explain and apply the concept of accounting rate of return

2   explain and apply the concept of payback

3   explain and apply the concept of internal rate of return (IRR)

4   explain and apply the concept of net present value (NPV)

5   explain and apply the rule for dealing with IRR and NPV when projects have unequal lives.

Introduction

In this chapter we examine decisions which involve the commitment of substantial sums of money over significant periods. This is an important decision-making area for management. Capital investment decisions are difficult because they involve cash flows over time, and the time value of money must be incorporated into the decision. There is also the problem of determining the relevant future cash flows associated with an asset that may have an expected life of a number of years.

Management must make decisions such as whether to purchase machine X or Y, or whether to invest money in project A or B, and there are techniques to assist these decisions. Examples of these techniques are presented in this chapter.

NOTE: Before we can examine methods of evaluating capital investment decisions, it is necessary to understand some basic financial mathematics. If you are not familiar with financial mathematics, you should study the material in Appendix 2.

Traditional methods of project evaluation

We begin the analysis of capital investment decisions by examining the traditional methods used to evaluate capital projects. These methods are based on accounting numbers and do not consider the impact of cash flows occurring in different years. They were popular because they were simple and easily understood and used familiar terms such as 'net profit'.

Accounting rate of return (ARR)

This method was widely used by businesses before the development of the discounted cash flow techniques discussed in the next section. The appeal of the ARR was its simplicity and the use of the familiar terms 'net profit' and 'book value of investment'. The ARR can be calculated in two ways: by using either the average value of investment or the total book value of investment in the denominator. Key Concept 16.1 illustrates the two formulas for the ARR.

Key Concept 16.1

Accounting rate of return

Formula 1

$$\text{ARR(\%)} = \frac{\text{average net profit}}{\text{average book value of investment}} \times 100$$

Formula 2

$$\text{ARR(\%)} = \frac{\text{average net profit}}{\text{total initial investment value}} \times 100$$

The ARR using formula 1 will be higher than that under formula 2. Provided the same formula is used to evaluate competing projects, a consistent approach is achieved. The net profit in the formula is after depreciation and tax expenses.

Example 16.1

The following details relate to projects Alpha and Beta. The combined initial book value for both projects is $15 000:

		Year 1 $	Year 2 $	Year 3 $	Average $
Alpha Net Profit (after depreciation & tax)		4 000	6 000	8 000	6 000
Beta Net Profit (after depreciation & tax)		8 000	6 000	4 000	6 000
Book Values	1 January	15 000	10 000	5 000	–
	31 December	10 000	5 000	0	–
	Average	12 500	7 500	2 500	7 500

Using formula 1, the ARR for each project is:

$$\text{ARR (Alpha)} = \frac{6000}{7500} \times 100 = 80\%$$

$$\text{ARR (Beta)} = \frac{6000}{7500} \times 100 = 80\%$$

Using formula 2, the ARR for each project is:

$$\text{ARR (Alpha)} = \frac{6000}{15\ 000} \times 100 = 40\%$$

$$\text{ARR (Beta)} = \frac{6000}{15\ 000} \times 100 = 40\%$$

The decision criterion for ARR is to accept projects with a rate of return higher than some minimum desired rate of return. If the projects are competing or mutually exclusive, we accept the project with the highest rate of return provided it is above the minimum desired rate of return.

From Example 16.1, projects Alpha and Beta appear equally desirable. However, Beta returns more profit in the earlier year. Would you prefer $100 today or $100 in one year's time? Of course we would all choose $100 today as the money could be invested, and in one year's time we would have $100 plus interest (this is often referred to as the time value of money). Consequently, we would value Beta more than Alpha. However, this is not the result of the application of the ARR. A major weakness of the ARR is that it ignores the time value of money.

Advantages of ARR

- It is simple to calculate and easy to understand.
- Profit and returns on assets are used by investors as a ratio to assess the performance of management. This was discussed in Chapter 14. The ratio is familiar to managers and investors.

Disadvantages of ARR

- It applies the same weighting to profits in all years and ignores the time value of money.

- It uses accounting measures and not cash flows. While accounting measures are important in assessing managerial performance, cash flows are important in investment evaluations, for it is the cash flows that are used to pay wages, pay for supplies, etc.
- The two different formulas for ARR can result in different decisions.

Payback period

Another traditional method used to assist in decisions about capital investments is the payback period. An important issue when considering any long-term investment is how long it will take for the initial investment to be recouped. Investments are made with a view to profit, but an important component of this view to profit is the desire to avoid a loss. The payback period is the period of time within which recovery of the initial investment is expected. Other things being equal, if two competing investments offered similar expected benefits, the one with the shorter payback period would be preferred.

The payback period is used as a measure of risk: the longer the payback period, the higher the risk of the project. This is a crude measure of risk and there are certainly more sophisticated techniques available, such as sensitivity analysis, to assess risk. Nevertheless, it continues to be used in conjunction with other techniques of investment analysis, including discounted cash flow methods.

To determine the payback period for a project, the after-tax cash inflows are added together until the sum equals the initial investment, as shown in Example 16.2.

Key Concept 16.2

Payback period for equal cash inflows

The payback period is calculated by dividing the initial investment by the net cash inflow.

Example 16.2

Project Z costs $15 000 and will return a net cash flow of $5000 per annum for four years.

$$\text{payback} = \frac{\text{initial investment}}{\text{net cash inflow}}$$

$$\text{payback} = \frac{15\,000}{5\,000}$$

$$= 3 \text{ years}$$

To determine payback when the net cash flows are uneven, we sum each year's cash inflows, until the sum equals the initial investment.

Project Y offers the following cash flows for an investment of $15 000.

	Net cash flow $	Cumulated cash flow $	$
Year 1	2 000	2 000	
Year 2	4 000	6 000	
Year 3	6 000	12 000	15 000
Year 4	6 000	18 000	
Year 5	20 000	38 000	

The payback period for project Y is three and a half years, assuming cash inflows are evenly spread over the year.

The decision criterion for the payback method would be to set a minimum period and accept only projects with a payback below this minimum. For mutually exclusive investments where only one project is required, the one with the lowest payback period would be selected, provided this was less than the minimum period.

For projects Z and Y, the payback method would favour project Z. Project Y does offer significantly higher cash flows, but these occur after the payback period. Hence, a significant deficiency with the payback method is that it ignores cash flows after the payback period.

Advantages of the payback period

- It is easy to understand.
- It provides some assessment of risk.
- It is a simple and well understood method. Managers are well aware that the payback period means the time required to recoup the initial investment.
- It is used as a means of assessing the risk associated with a project—even though it is a crude measure of risk.

Disadvantages of the payback period

- It does not take into consideration a project's cash flows after the payback period and can therefore result in the selection of less profitable investments if used in isolation.
- It ignores the time value of money and treats all cash flows as equal, irrespective of the year in which they occur. This problem can be overcome by using the discounted payback period, in which cash flows are discounted to reflect the time value of money. However, cash flows after the discounted payback period are still ignored and so the first disadvantage of payback remains.

Discounted cash-flow techniques

The most common methods for evaluating capital investment proposals involve the use of discounted cash-flow techniques. The two main methods are: the *internal rate of return* and *net present value*. Both methods focus on cash flows, rather than accounting income, and utilise the fact that the use of money has a cost. The alternative to buying a productive asset would be investing the money, which will then be compounded. With capital investments, cash is invested now with the hope of receiving a greater amount in the future.

In this section, we will again use the present value of $1 per period. It will be useful to represent this by PVP(r,n) where r is the interest rate and n is the number of years.

Remember, the concepts of financial mathematics are explained in Appendix 2. The present and future value factor tables are located in Appendix 3 and are used in the examples that follow.

Internal rate of return (IRR)

To overcome the problems associated with the traditional methods of project evaluation, the IRR method was developed and is now widely used in business. We have already discussed various rates of return in Chapter 14, and in the previous section we examined the accounting rate of return.

The internal rate of return (IRR) differs from the ARR in that it uses cash flows and adjusts for the fact that $1 today is worth more than $1 in one year's time. The IRR is that rate of return which equates the present value of the expected cash inflows with the present value of the expected cash outflows. It is therefore not the same as the ARR and is regarded a superior method.

Key Concept 16.3

Internal rate of return

The internal rate of return (IRR) is the rate of return which discounts the cash flows of a project so that the present value of cash inflows equals the present value of cash outflows.

To calculate the IRR, the following formula is used. We have to solve for R in the formula:

$$OC = \frac{NCF_1}{(1+R)^1} + \frac{NCF_2}{(1+R)^2} + \dots + \frac{NCF_n}{(1+R)^n} +$$

where

OC = original cost
NCF_a = net cash flow in year a
R = IRR $\div$ 100
n = number of periods

When the net cash flow remains the same each year, the formula becomes:

$$OC = NCF \times [\frac{1}{(1+R)^1} + \frac{1}{(1+R)^2} + \dots + \frac{1}{(1+R)^n}]$$

$$OC = NCF \times PVF(IRR,n)$$

Example 16.3

$17 946 was outlaid on a machine which is expected to return cash inflows of $6000 per year for five years. At that time the machine is expected to be worthless. Calculate the internal rate of return on the machine.

The investment of $17 946 produces a benefit of $6000 a year for five years. Therefore OC = 17 946, NCF = 6000 and n = 5. R is unknown.

$$OC = NCF \times PVF(IRR,n)$$
$$17\,946 = 6000 \times PVF(IRR,5)$$
$$PVF(IRR,5) = 17\,946 \div 6\,000$$
$$= 2.991$$

In Table 4 in Appendix 3, we can look along the n = 5 row until we find the PVF closest to 2.991. This is 2.9906, in the 20 per cent column. Hence the IRR is 20 per cent.

This approach is possible only when the cash inflows each year ⬛
this is not likely to be the case. Determining the IRR when net ⬛
year to year is more complicated. Consider the following data:

	Net cash flow			
Year 0	Year 1	Year 2	Year 3	Year 4
-5 000	1 000	1 500	2 300	2 800

In this case, OC = 5000, NCF_1 = 1000, NCF_2 = 1500, etc. We want to find the value
of R which will make OC equal to 5000, i.e.:

$$OC = 5000 = \frac{1000}{(1+R)^1} + \frac{1500}{(1+R)^2} + \frac{2300}{(1+R)^3} + \frac{2800}{(1+R)^4}$$

Solving such an equation algebraically would be too difficult for most people! An alternative approach is to use trial and error. We pick a value for R and substitute into the
right-hand side of the above equation.

Let IRR = 20 per cent, so R = 0.2.

$$OC = \frac{1000}{(1.2)^1} + \frac{1500}{(1.2)^2} + \frac{2300}{(1.2)^3} + \frac{2800}{(1.2)^4}$$

$$= 833 + 1042 + 1331 + 1350$$
$$= 4556$$

This is too small since we want OC to equal 5000.
Try IRR = 10 per cent, i.e. R = 0.1.

$$OC = \frac{1000}{(1.1)^1} + \frac{1500}{(1.1)^2} + \frac{2300}{(1.1)^3} + \frac{2800}{(1.1)^4}$$

$$= 909 + 1240 + 1728 + 1912$$
$$= 5789$$

This is too large since we want OC to equal 5000.
Our next try would be a value of IRR between 10 and 20 per cent.
Try 16 per cent.

$$OC = \frac{1000}{(1.16)^1} + \frac{1500}{(1.16)^2} + \frac{2300}{(1.16)^3} + \frac{2800}{(1.16)^4}$$

$$= 862 + 1114 + 1473 + 1546$$
$$= 4995$$

Therefore, IRR is approximately 16 per cent.
You can see how much time this trial-and-error approach could take. Fortunately,
computers and certain calculators make the task of determining IRR a matter of pressing
a few buttons.

The decision criterion for IRR is to accept projects which offer an IRR above a certain
minimum desired rate of return. For mutually exclusive investments, the project with the
highest IRR is accepted, provided the IRR is above the minimum.

Advantages of IRR

- It uses the concept of a rate of return and this concept is familiar to many managers.
  Managers will often prefer to make decisions using concepts with which they are
  familiar. (Remember, this is one of the advantages of the ARR.)
- It does not treat cash received in different years as equal and thus incorporates the
  time value of money. It is essential that cash flows received or paid in different
  periods are not treated equally.

uses cash flows and not profit figures. It is the cash inflows from a project which will be required to pay the cash outflows.

Disadvantages of IRR

- Some types of investment can have more than one IRR, and in some cases no IRR. These types of investment are often described as non-conventional. A conventional investment is one in which there is a cash outflow in year 1 and then a series of cash inflows during the years that follow. A non-conventional investment is one in which further cash outflows occur during the life of the investment. It is these investments that can have more than one IRR, and this complicates the decision-making process for managers. We say more about this problem later in the chapter.
- For competing investments, where the selection of one means the rejection of the others, the IRR can provide a ranking of investments different from the net present value (discussed next). In effect, this means that the project that will not maximise firm value may be ranked first using IRR.
- It is dependent on the accuracy of the estimates of future cash flows. Consequently, the less reliable the estimates, the less reliable the IRR.

Net present value (NPV)

The second discounted cash flow technique is the net present value method. Unlike the IRR, which expresses a result in a percentage, the NPV expresses a result in dollars. The NPV is determined by calculating the present value of all cash inflows and outflows at a certain rate and then adding the two together to arrive at either a positive or a negative result. A positive NPV suggests that the project should be accepted, while a negative NPV that the project should be rejected.

Example 16.4

An investment of $100 000 is expected to yield a company $60 000 net cash inflows at the end of each year for two years, after which time it will be worthless. The company requires a rate of return of 10 per cent on such investments. To determine the NPV, we must calculate the present value at 10 per cent of a cash inflow of $60 000 each year for the next two years.

The outflow occurs immediately, and so the value in today's dollars is $100 000.

The inflows occur at the end of each of the next two years and the present value is calculated by using Table 2 in Appendix 3 as:

Year 1 $60 000 x 0.90909 = $54 594
Year 2 $60 000 x 0.82645 = $49 587
Total $104 181

The NPV is:

−$100 000 + $104 181 = $4181

As the NPV is positive, the decision would be to accept the project, even though the amount is only small and management would have to consider other factors, like the risk associated with the investment. How certain are the cash inflows? Are there alternative uses for the money? What is the opportunity cost of investing in this project?

How did we arrive at the figure of 10 per cent as the discount rate? This is often called the minimum required rate of return, the hurdle rate or the cost of capital. It is beyond the scope of this book to discuss how this rate is determined. However, the rate should be such that acceptance of all projects with a positive NPV will result in an increase in the overall value of the firm.

Key Concept 16.4

Net present value

The NPV is the figure that results from discounting all cash flows of a project at the minimum rate of return and summing the resultant present values.

We can develop formulas for the calculation of NPV as follows:

$$\text{NPV} = -\text{OC} \frac{\text{NCF}_1}{(1+K)^1} + \frac{\text{NCF}_2}{(1+K)^2} + ... + \frac{\text{NCF}_n}{(1+K)^n}$$

where
$$\begin{aligned}
\text{OC} &= \text{original cost} \\
\text{NCFa} &= \text{net cash flow in year } a \\
\text{K} &= \text{minimum desired rate of return per annum} \div 100 \\
\text{n} &= \text{number of periods} \\
\text{NPV} &= \text{net present value}
\end{aligned}$$

For example, assuming a minimum rate of 10 per cent and the following cash flows:

Year 0	Year 1	Year 2
-10 000	12 000	5 000

$$\begin{aligned}
\text{NPV} &= -10\,000 + \frac{7000}{(1.1)^1} + \frac{5000}{(1.1)^2} \\
&= -10\,000 + 6364 + 4132 \\
&= \$496
\end{aligned}$$

When the net cash flow is the same each year, this formula becomes:

$$\text{NPV} = -\text{OC} + \text{NCF} \frac{1}{(1+K)^1} + \frac{1}{(1+K)^2} + ... + \frac{1}{(1+K)^n}$$

or
$$\text{NPV} = -\text{OC} + \text{NCF} \times \text{PVF}(K,n)$$

Using the data from Example 16.3 and assuming a minimum desired rate of return of 10 per cent, we now calculate the NPV as follows.

$$\begin{aligned}
\text{NPV} &= -\text{OC} + \text{NCF} \times \text{PVF}(K,n) \\
&= -17\,946 + 6000 \times \text{PVF}(10,5) \\
&= -17\,946 + 6000 \times 3.7907 \text{ (from Table 4 in Appendix 3)} \\
&= -17\,946 + 22\,744 \\
&= \$4798
\end{aligned}$$

The IRR for this investment was 20 per cent, and, as it is a conventional type investment, the NPV should be positive—as indeed it is. This means that by using both the IRR and NPV methods we arrive at the same 'accept' decision for this particular project. However, as stated earlier, the two methods can give conflicting results for projects with non-conventional cash flows and in the ranking of mutually exclusive projects. Therefore, the decision rule for NPV is to accept all projects with a positive NPV except mutually exclusive projects; for mutually exclusive projects, choose the project with the highest positive NPV.

Advantages of NPV

- It incorporates the time value of money into calculations and so does not treat as equal cash flows received or paid in different years.
- Once the cash flows have been discounted at the minimum rate of return, they can be added together to arrive at an amount in present-day dollars.
- For mutually exclusive projects, it gives a ranking superior to IRR (this is explained in the next section).
- It uses cash flows, not profit numbers, and is a more sophisticated and less arbitrary approach to investment evaluation.

Disadvantages of NPV

- If the calculation of the minimum rate of return is not accurate, then the NPV will be less reliable.
- As it is dependent on the accuracy of the estimates of future cash flows, the less reliable the estimates, the less reliable the NPV.

Comparison of IRR and NPV

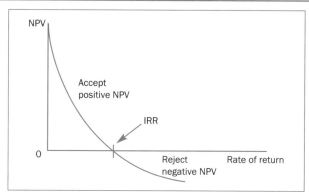

Figure 16.1   *Decision making with IRR and NPV.*

The graph in Figure 16.1 shows the relationship between NPV and IRR. Remember that:

$$NPV = -OC + \frac{NCF_1}{(1+R)^1} + \frac{NCF_2}{(1+R)^2} + \ldots + \frac{NCF_n}{(1+R)^n}$$

This value will be at a maximum when the rate of return, R, is zero. This is the intercept on the vertical axis and will be a positive value if the sum of the net cash flows exceeds the original cost.

As R becomes larger, each term $\frac{NCF_1}{(1+R)^1}$, $\frac{NCF_2}{(1+R)^2}$, etc. becomes smaller.

Hence the NPV decreases, as R increases, in a curve as shown. At some stage, the NPV becomes zero. At this point:

$$NPV = -OC + \frac{NCF_1}{(1+R)^1} + \frac{NCF_2}{(1+R)^2} + \ldots + \frac{NCF_n}{(1+R)^n} = 0$$

so $$OC = \frac{NCF_1}{(1+R)^1} + \frac{NCF_2}{(1+R)^2} + \ldots + \frac{NCF_n}{(1+R)^n}$$

But this is the formula we use to find the IRR. Hence the intercept on the horizontal axis is the IRR.

Do the IRR and NPV methods give the same answer for decision-making purposes? Unfortunately they do not! The answer will depend on whether the investments are *independent*, i.e. the acceptance or rejection of one project has no effect on the other; or *mutually exclusive*, i.e. if one project is selected, the other is automatically rejected. It will also depend on whether the cash flows associated with the project are what are described as conventional, i.e. cash outflow, followed by cash inflows; or not conventional, i.e. cash outflow, cash inflow, cash inflow, cash outflow.

Conventional cash-flow projects

Independent projects are ranked the same using both the NPV and IRR methods.

For mutually exclusive projects, the IRR and NPV methods can give different rankings and hence lead to different decisions as illustrated in Example 16.5.

In the following examples, note that the net cash flow for year 0 is the negative of the original cost. For example, if the year 0 net cash flow is –10 000, the original cost is +10 000.

Example 16.5

The cash flows for two mutually exclusive projects are as follows:

NET CASH FLOW (NCF)

	Year 0	Year 1	Year 2	Year 3	Year 4	Year 5
Project A	-4 500	1 350	1 350	1 350	1 350	1 350
Project B	-3 000	915	915	915	915	915

Which project should be chosen? Assuming a minimum rate of 10 per cent per annum, the NPV and IRR for both projects can be calculated. The answers are summarised and ranked in the table below.

IRR

$$OC = NVF \times PVF(IRR,n)$$

Project A

$$4500 = 1350 \times PVF(IRR,5)$$
$$3.333 = PVF(IRR,5)$$

Looking across the row n = 5 in Table 4 in Appendix 3, you will see that the PVF for 15 per cent is 3.3521. Hence the IRR is slightly more than 15 per cent. Using a computer program gives a more accurate answer of 15.2 per cent.

Project B

$$3000 = 915 \times PVF(IRR,5)$$
$$3.2787 = PVF(IRR,5)$$

Looking once again across row n = 5, you will see that the PVF for 20 per cent is 2.9906. Therefore, the tables only tell us that the IRR is closer to 15 per cent than to 20 per cent. A sensible guess would be about 16 per cent; a computer program confirms this answer.

NPV

$$NPV = -OC + NCF \times PVF(10,5)$$

Project A

$$NPV = -4500 + 1350 \times 3.7907$$
$$= \$617.45$$

Project B

$$NPV = -3000 + 915 \times 3.7907$$
$$= \$468.49$$

Using these results, we can rank the projects:

	IRR	Rank	NPV	Rank
Project A	15.2%	2	$617	1
Project B	16%	1	$468	2

The above table shows that the IRR method ranks B the best while the NPV method ranks A the best. Which project should be chosen? We could answer the question by looking at the return on the extra dollars invested in project A.

Differences in net cash flow for projects A and B

	Year 0	Year 1	Year 2	Year 3	Year 4	Year 5
A − B	-1 500	435	435	435	435	435

$$OC = NCF \times PVF(IRR,n)$$
$$1500 = 435 \times PVF(IRR,5)$$

$$PVF(IRR,5) = \frac{1500}{435} = 3.448$$

From Table 4, the IRR is between 12 per cent and 15 per cent. Using a computer,

$$IRR (A - B) = 13.8\%$$

Therefore, the extra investment in A (the incremental IRR) provides a rate of return higher than the minimum rate of return, and therefore should be accepted. If we apply the NPV method, then project A should be chosen because it returns more dollars to the company and therefore increases the firm's overall value.

Comparison of IRR and NPV rankings

The difference in the ranking of projects under the IRR and NPV methods arises because of the assumption on the reinvestment rates for intermediate cash flows from projects. IRR assumes reinvestment of intermediate cash flows at the IRR of the project, while NPV assumes reinvestment at the minimum rate of return. This is illustrated in this example.

Example 16.6

Net cash flows

	Year 0	Year 1	Year 2	IRR	NPV
Project A	-20 000	2 000	36 400	40%	$1 190
Project B	-20 000	20 000	15 000	50%	$1 059

Note that a minimum rate of return of 10 per cent was assumed. The IRRs were calculated using the trial-and-error method. The NPVs were calculated using:

$$NPV = -OC + \frac{NCF_1}{(1.1)} + \frac{NCF_2}{(1.1)^2}$$

As an exercise, you might like to check that the values in the table are correct.

Analysis of reinvestment assumptions

		Project A		Project B	
IRR	Proceeds year 1 reinvested at IRR year 2	$2 000 × 1.4 =	2 800	$20 000 × 1.5 =	30 000
			36 400		15 000
			$39 200		$45 000
NPV	Proceeds year 1 reinvested at 10% year 2	$2 000 × 1.1 =	2 200	$20 000 × 1.1 =	22 000
			36 400		15 000
			$38 600		$37 000

The above analysis illustrates the IRR reinvestment assumption results in project B ranking above project A. The NPV assumption results in the ranking being reversed.

If we wish to evaluate the two projects, then reinvestment should be considered at the minimum rate of return; otherwise, we are prejudging the use of available funds for other projects. A business should be able to reinvest funds at a return at least equal to its minimum rate of return for all projects.

The recommended rule to use is the NPV rule, although supporters of the IRR method argue that using the incremental IRR overcomes all the problems with mutually exclusive projects.

Key Concept 16.5

Decision rule

The net present value (NPV) method is the recommended method for evaluating capital investment decisions.

Multiple rates of return

Earlier in this chapter we mentioned projects with conventional and non-conventional cash flows. Projects with conventional cash flows typically have cash outflows at the start which are then followed by a series of cash inflows. Projects with non-conventional cash flows occur when there is at least one year after commencement in which the cash outflows exceed the cash inflows. An example of this type of project would be a mining site where significant cash outflows are required at the end of the mine's life to restore the site to its original condition. Example 16.7 illustrates a project with non-conventional cash flows.

Example 16.7

A project has the following cash flows:

Year 0	−$4 000
Year 1	+$25 000
Year 2	−$25 000

Using a minimum rate of return of 10 per cent,

$$NPV = -4000 + \frac{25\ 000}{(1.1)} + \frac{-25\ 000}{(1.1)^2} = -\$1934$$

To calculate the IRR we must solve the equation:

$$OC = -4000 + \frac{25\ 000}{(1+R)} + \frac{-25\ 000}{(1+R)^2}$$

The rates which make this true are 25 per cent and 400 per cent. (To confirm this, substitute R = 0.25 into the equation. Repeat for R = 4.) These values can be found by trial and error, or by using a computer or programmable calculator. If you are expert at quadratic equations, you could proceed as follows:

Multiplying both sides by $(1+R)^2$ gives

$$4000(1+R)^2 = 25\ 000(1+R) - 25\ 000$$
$$4000(1+2R+R^2) = 25\ 000 + 25\ 000R - 25\ 000 = 25\ 000R$$
$$4 + 8R + 4R^2 = 25R$$
$$4R^2 - 17R + 4 = 0$$
$$(4R - 1)(R - 4) = 0$$
$$R = 1/4\ or\ 4$$

One example of such a project is bauxite mining, since once mining is completed, a large outlay is required to re-establish the environment. The graph in Figure 16.2 shows the relationship between NPV and the IRRs in Example 16.7. The horizontal intercepts are given by the IRR values. The NPV is positive between these two values. Hence,

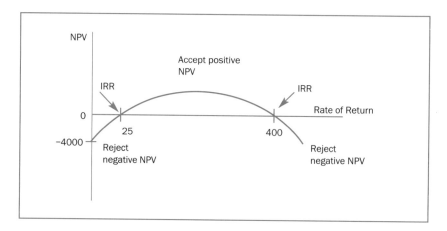

Figure 16.2 *The graph shows a situation with multiple IRRs.*

The previous project should only be accepted based on a positive NPV which would require a rate of return of between 25 per cent and 400 per cent. At any other minimum rate of return, the project should be rejected.

While the existence of negative cash flows in a later year of a project is a necessary factor to have multiple rates of return, this is not automatic, i.e. multiple IRRs may not necessarily occur. This additional weakness of IRR is another argument in favour of NPV as the preferred decision rule.

Comparing projects with unequal lives

What do we do when trying to compare projects with unequal lives? We could proceed on one of three assumptions.

- *Assumption 1:* Assume at the end of each project's life that the company will invest funds to earn the minimum rate of return. In this case, we can ignore the fact that the projects have unequal lives and simply compare their NPVs.
- *Assumption 2:* Assume that funds are reinvested in projects identical to the original projects. This is called the constant chain of replacement. There are several possible methods for comparing projects under this assumption. They are detailed in the next section.
- *Assumption 3:* Make specific assumptions about future investment opportunities.

While the third assumption is conceptually more appealing, the first two are more practical. These assumptions are illustrated in the following examples.

Example 16.8

The firm is considering investing in either project A or B, which have the following net cash flows.

	Year 0	Year 1	Year 2	Year 3
Project A	−20 000	24 000		
Project B	−20 000	10 000	10 000	10 000

$$\text{NPV} = -\text{OC} + \text{NCF} \times \text{PVF}(r,n)$$

Assuming $r = 10\%$

$$
\begin{aligned}
\text{NPV(A)} &= -20\ 000 + 24\ 000 \times \text{PVF}(10,1) \\
&= -20\ 000 + 24\ 000 \times 0.9091 \text{ (from Table 4 in Appendix 3)} \\
&= -20\ 000 + 21\ 818 = \$1818 \\
\text{NPV(B)} &= -20\ 000 + 10\ 000 \times \text{PVF}(10,3) \\
&= -20\ 000 + 10\ 000 \times 2.4868 \text{ (from Table 4)} \\
&= -20\ 000 + 24\ 868 = \$4868
\end{aligned}
$$

Under assumption 1, we simply compare the NPVs of projects irrespective of their lives. Therefore project B is selected.

Under assumption 2, we could compare projects A and B by assuming that project A was repeated until project B had ended. The figures for repeating project A three times are as follows:

	Year 0	Year 1	Year 2	Year 3
	-20 000	-20 000	-20 000	
		+24 000	+24 000	+24 000
Net cash flow	-20 000	4 000	4 000	24 000

Using the formula:

$$NPV = -OC + \frac{NCF_1}{(1+K)} + \frac{NCF_2}{(1+K)^2} + \frac{NCF_3}{(1+K)^3}$$

$$NPV(A) = -20\ 000 + \frac{4000}{1.1} + \frac{4000}{(1.1)^2} + \frac{24\ 000}{(1.1)^3}$$

$$= -20\ 000 + 3636 + 3306 + 18\ 032 = \$4974$$

Based on assumption 2, investment in project A is recommended because $4974 is greater than the $4868 NPV in project B.

While it is possible to use assumption 3, this is not commonly done. With mutually exclusive projects it is preferable to assume reinvestment in identical assets.

Key Concept 16.6

Unequal lives

To evaluate investment projects with unequal lives, the constant chain of replacement assumption is used.

Constant chain of replacement

It is possible to use any of the following three approaches under the constant chain of replacement assumption.

- NPV for a common life, using the lowest common multiple approach (LCM).
- Calculate the equivalent annual value for each project.
- Calculate NPV into perpetuity for each project.

As each of these three approaches yields the same decision, we will illustrate only the LCM approach. This method involves finding the LCM for the lives of the projects under consideration. For instance, if two projects with lives of two and three years are being compared, the LCM is six years. We then calculate the NPV for the two projects over six years. During this time the project with a life of two years would be invested in three times, while the project with a life of three years would be invested in twice. Example 16.9 illustrates the LCM approach.

Example 16.9

Compare the NPVs of projects A and B, using the LCM approach.

	Life	Original cost	Annual cash inflow
Project A	3 years	$20 000	$8 000
Project B	2 years	$10 000	$6 000

Minimum rate of return = 10 per cent.

	Year 0	Year 1	Year 2	Year 3	Year 4	Year 5	Year 6
Project A	-20 000			-20 000			
		8 000	8 000	8 000	8 000	8 000	8 000
Net cash flow	-20 000	8 000	8 000	-12 000	8 000	8 000	8 000
Project B	-10 000		-10 000		-10 000		
		6 000	6 000	6 000	6 000	6 000	6 000
Net cash flow	-10 000	6 000	-4 000	-6 000	-4 000	6 000	6 000

$$NPV = -OC + \frac{NCF_1}{(1+R)^1} + \frac{NCF_2}{(1+R)^2} + \ldots + \frac{NCF_n}{(1+R)^n}$$

$$NPV(A) = -20\,000 + \frac{8000}{(1.1)^1} + \frac{8000}{(1.1)^2} + \frac{-12\,000}{(1.1)^3} + \frac{8000}{(1.1)^4} + \frac{8000}{(1.1)^5} + \frac{8000}{(1.1)^6}$$

$$= -20\,000 + 7273 + 6612 - 9016 + 5464 + 4967 + 4516$$

$$= -\$184$$

By performing similar calculations, we find that NPV(B) = $3769.

The solution has assumed there has been investment in two project As and three project Bs. Project B has the highest NPV and is selected based solely on financial considerations.

Qualitative factors and capital investment decisions

The techniques outlined in this chapter provide important quantitative information for managers to assist in their very significant and important capital investment decisions. However, it is the role of managers to take the quantitative information provided by the accountant and consider this with qualitative factors before arriving at a final decision.

Qualitative factors include considering the impact of the decision on:

- employees
- other parts of the business
- the environment
- future opportunities
- the image of the company.

Finally, managers must decide, even if there is a positive NPV, if the risk is too high. In short, the financial details are only part of the puzzle; managers must bring together all pieces of the puzzle and make the final decision.

Retailers rebound on Woolies' whopper

by Leonie Wood

A BUMPER profit from supermarket group Woolworths and expectation of higher dividends from other retailers helped spur a 2.3 per cent jump in the retail sector yesterday as market heavyweights regained favour among investors.

Woolworths surprised the market with a better-than-expected 14 per cent increase in full-year net profit before abnormals to $355.6 million, and rewarded shareholders by lifting fully franked, final dividends three cents to 13 cents a share.

Woolworths' shares closed on a record high of $6.75, up 30 cents, after peaking at $6.77, as the retailer suggested the GST had not impinged on its business.

At the same time, rumours abound that Coles Myer in October will unveil a special dividend of up to 35 cents, or launch an off-market buyback, as it moves to discharge as much as $400 million of accrued franking credits.

After opening five cents above their previous close, Coles Myer shares ran as high as $7.55 and ended the day up 24 cents, or 3.3 per cent, at $7.49.

Even David Jones, which despite launching a shareholder discount card earlier this year, has struggled to find favour with investors, rose three cents, or 2.2 per cent, to $1.39 amid hopes that stronger sales across the retail sector have translated into higher profits for the department stores group.

Woolworths' solid result followed a volatile trading year for retailers, who endured hot and cold consumer sentiment, spent heavily on systems adjustments associated with the Y2K rollover for computers early in the year, and ended the financial year with massive reticketing and systems changes related to the GST.

Woolworths heralded steady trading ahead, and executives noted revenues from the Big W, Dick Smith Electronics and Powerhouse stores were already 9 per cent ahead of 1999 levels.

'We anticipate ongoing sales growth in the high single digits and profit growth in the low double digits,' said Woolworths chief executive Roger Corbett.

This year, Mr Corbett has slashed Woolworths' capital expenditure budget to $420 million from $764 million, with spending on new stores, major refurbishments and store updates all cut.

Gross abnormal charges totalled $93.9 million, including $53.2 million related to GST implementation and $68.1 million on Woolworths' long-term project to cut costs and improve its supply chain.

Woolworths expects the tighter management system will help trim annual costs by as much as $134 million within three years.

Chairman John Dahlsen said the result reflected a renewed focus on Woolworths' core stores as it improved its capital management strategies. It sold the Rockmanns fashion chain in February. The 585 Woolworths and Safeway supermarkets generated 16.8 per cent higher profit before interest and tax of $601 million as sales rose 8.3 per cent to $16.67 billion.

Profit before tax, and before paying dividends to holders of income securities, rose 20 per cent to $593.8 million, and Woolworths' underlying earnings per share climbed 18.8 per cent to 32.4 cents (before abnormals). In total, Woolworths lifted shareholder payments by five cents in 1999–2000, from 18 cents to 23 cents. It will pay final dividends on October 5 to shareholders registered by September 14.

Age, 29 August 2000

Commentary

The article describes how Woolworths has a new capital management strategy with a focus on its core stores. This has resulted in a reduction in its capital expenditure budget of some $344 million and a 20 per cent increase in profit for the year. The decision to focus on core activities is based not only on financial data but also important qualitative considerations.

Summary

In this chapter we provided an introduction to capital investment decisions. Capital investment decisions are significant because they generally involve the commitment of large sums of money for long periods. (Appendix 2 covered some basic financial mathematics involving the effects of compounding of interest. Examples presented showed how tables and formulas are used to find the present value and future value of $1, and the present value and future value of $1 per period.)

The techniques for evaluating capital investment decisions were then explained. The traditional techniques of accounting rate of return and payback are not widely used because they fail to recognise the time value of money. However, payback is sometimes used in addition to discounted cash-flow techniques. The discounted cash-flow techniques of internal rate of return and net present value were then presented. The net present value is the preferred method of investment evaluation. With IRR, incorrect rankings of mutually exclusive investments can occur and it is also possible to get multiple IRRs with non-conventional cash-flow investments. Finally, methods for assessing projects with unequal lives were presented. The constant chain of replacement or lowest common multiple approach to unequal lives is the preferred option.

Finally, we briefly mentioned the role of qualitative factors in capital investment decisions.

Further reading

Peirson, G., Bird, R., Brown, R. and Howard, P., 1997. *Business Finance*, 8th edn, McGraw-Hill.

Review questions

1 Find the simple interest on $900 at 4.5 per cent per annum from 1 April to 16 May.

2 If the following amounts are invested at compound interest, what will they amount to at the end of the following periods:
    a $1000 invested at 5 per cent for five years
    b $200 invested at 10 per cent for 15 years?

3 If cost of funds is 10 per cent, what is the present value of:
    a $1000 to be received in three years' time
    b $1500 to be received in ten years' time?

4 A machine costing $100 000 has a life of ten years and no salvage value. It will require annual maintenance expenditure of $10 000 but will save labour costs totalling $25 000 per annum. What rate of return can be expected from this machine?

5 How long will it take $100 to accumulate to $200 at 6 per cent per annum?

6 An investment costs $75 and pays $100 ten years later. What is the effective annual compound interest rate?

7 At a given annual compound rate of interest, $1000 amounts to $1500 in ten years. What will it amount to after six years?

8 A family buys a house for $12 000. It sells its old house for $7000 and uses this as a deposit. It borrows the balance at 7 per cent per annum compound interest. What amount, payable at the end of each year, would pay off the loan over ten years?

9 What is the purchase price of a house which can be bought for $4000 cash plus $400 at the end of each year for 20 years? (Interest 6 per cent per annum compound.)

10 If I deposit $100 in the bank now; $100 regularly at 12-month intervals for the next five years and $200 regularly at 12-month intervals for the following ten years, what is
   a the accumulated value at the end of the 15 years
   b the present value of the payments?

   (Assume 5 per cent per annum compound interest.)

11 What annual rate of interest must be earned for deposits of $500 at the start of each year to accumulate to $10 000 in 15 years?

12 A company pays $1000 each year into a bank sinking fund earning 6 per cent per annum compound interest. After five payments, the rate of interest granted by the bank on the fund is reduced to 4 per cent. The company therefore decides to increase its future deposits to $1200. What amount is in the fund after 15 payments altogether have been made?

13 A loan of $81 000 is to be repaid by ten equal annual instalments of principal and interest which is at the rate of 5 per cent per annum.
   a What is the annual instalment?
   b Draw up a schedule showing the amount of principal and the amount of interest contained in each instalment, and the principal still outstanding after each payment.
   c As a check, calculate independently the amount outstanding after the fourth and seventh payments.

14 What amount payable in ten years' time would be equivalent to $500 payable in five years' time plus $1000 payable in 15 years' time? (Assume 6 per cent per annum compound interest.)

15 A person owes $1000 payable in three years' time and $1000 payable in 13 years' time, and would like to settle the debt by making a $2000 payment. If interest is 5 per cent per annum compound, when should the payment be made?

16 A $200 refrigerator is sold 'on easy terms'. These terms are:
   i   No deposit.
   ii   Simple interest of 10 per cent.
   iii Monthly repayments over two years.

   Given such terms, what is the true rate of compound interest which the customer is paying?

Problems for discussion and analysis

1   What is the present value of an annuity with payments of $1000 per year for five years if money is worth 12 per cent per annum compounded quarterly?

2   A car is priced at $27 000 cash, or $6000 deposit and six two-monthly payments of $4200. What is the implied interest rate in the hire-purchase option?

3   A car yard is offering special terms of no repayments for two years. A down payment of $5000 is required, followed by six half-yearly payments of $2000 starting at the end of two years. If the cash value of the car is $11 000, what is the implied interest rate? (Note, interest is calculated from date of purchase.)

4   Bloggs Ltd has to replace its widget-making machine in five years. The company estimates the machine will cost $30 000. It wishes to provide for this machine by putting aside a regular annual amount in a reserve. Natbank has offered the company two options:
    i   deposit five equal amounts at the beginning of each year to earn 5 per cent compound interest
    ii   deposit five equal amounts at the beginning of each year to earn an increasing compound interest rate of 2.5 per cent for the first year and increasing by 1 per cent each year after that.

   Which option allows the company to put the least annual amount into a reserve, and what is that annual amount?

5   The Waugh Electronics Company Ltd is thinking of buying, at a cost of $25 093, some new quality control equipment that is expected to save $5000 in cash operating costs. Its estimated useful life is ten years, and it will have a zero disposal value. Calculate:
    a   the internal rate of return
    b   the net present value if the cost of capital is 10 per cent
    c   the payback period.

6   Dr Oliver has $1000 which he will decide to invest if he can be reasonably confident that his investment will earn at least 10 per cent per annum. He is considering three projects, each of which would cost $1000 to begin:
    a   Project A would earn $1090 at the end of the first year.
    b   Project B would earn $1250 at the end of the second year.
    c   Project C would earn $655 at the end of the first year, and another $655 at the end of the second year.
   Advise Dr Oliver.

7 Sarah Talbot invested a total of $50 000 in the ordinary shares of a number companies in January. In December the market price of all her shares amounted to $60 000. She received no dividends during the year. Assuming a monthly compounding rate of 2 per cent is appropriate, is she economically 'better off' at the end of the year than at the beginning of the year?

   (Adapted from J. Godfrey, et al., *Accounting Theory*, 2nd edn, Jacaranda Wiley, 1994, p. 457.)

8   Using the following data, calculate:
    a   the accounting rate of return
    b   the payback period
    c   the internal rate of return
    d   the net present value.

Project cost	$20 000
Estimated life	5 years
Estimated salvage value	$2 000
Annual net cash inflow	$6 000
Required rate of return	10%

e   How would your answers differ if the net cash inflows were as follows?

	$
Year 1	6 000
Year 2	7 000
Year 3	12 000
Year 4	3 000
Year 5	10 000

9   The following details are available about three projects:

CASH FLOW ($)

Project	Year 0	Year 1	Year 2	Year 3	Year 4	Year 5
1	-5 000	500	500	500	500	5 500
2	-5 000	1 319	1 319	1 319	1 319	1 319
3	-5 000	—	—	—	—	8 053

a   Calculate the net present value of each of these projects, then rank them. Use discount rates of 5, 10 and 15 per cent.
b   Calculate the internal rate of return for each of the projects and then rank them.

10   The following investment proposals are independent. Given a required rate of return of 10 per cent, which proposals are acceptable?

CASH FLOW ($)

Project	Year 0	Year 1	Year 2
ICON	-10 000	2 000	12 000
EDN	-10 000	11 000	—
ZON	-10 000	-12 000	—

(Problems 8–10 adapted from G. Peirson, R. Bird, R. Brown and P. Howard, *Business Finance*, 5th edn, McGraw-Hill, 1990, Chapter 4.)

11   The following details are available for two mutually exclusive projects.

	Tom	Huck
Cost of investment	$8 000	$20 000
Life expected	5 years	8 years
Payback period	3 years	5 years
Internal rate of return	13.5%	16%

Required:

a   If the company has a cost of capital of 12 per cent would you recommend Tom or Huck?
b   Discuss the problems in making the decision.

12 Silver Corporation is evaluating five investment opportunities. The company's cost of capital is 15 per cent. No investment is accepted if the payback period is greater than three years. The company will only accept a maximum of two investment projects. The following investments are being considered.

Investment	Initial cost	Expected returns
A	130 000	40 000 per year for five years
B	60 000	30 000 per year for six years
C	40 000	12 000 per year for ten years
D	25 000	9 000 per year for six years
E	15 000	4 500 per year for three years

Required:

   a Which projects would be accepted using the NPV and payback methods to screen investments?
   b Discuss the benefits of using the payback method together with NPV or IRR.

13 Reflex Ltd is considering the purchase of a new punch machine to produce coins. The machine would cost $11 000 cash. A service maintenance contract on the machine is essential and would cost an extra $100 per month. Expected life of the machine is four years and expected salvage value $200. The new machine will save $350 per month in labour costs and $40 per month in materials costs. The old machine would be sold for its book value of $500. The cost of capital for Reflex is 15 per cent. The tax rate is 40 per cent, which means depreciation tax savings of $1080 each year.

Required:

   a Calculate:
      i the payback period
      ii the net present value.
   b Should the company buy the new machine?

14 The management of New World Airlines is considering the replacement of its present fleet of ten piston-engine planes with five turboprops. A survey has revealed the following estimates:

Piston engine	Estimates	Turboprop	Estimates
Remaining life	5 years	Life	5 years
Salvage value		Cost	$3 430 000
at the present time	$10 000	Annual net cash inflows	$1 000 000
in two years' time	$5 000	Salvage value	
in five years' time	nil	after two years' operation	30% of purchase price
Annual net cash inflows	$100 000	after five years' operation	5% of purchase price

   a Should replacement be undertaken now, or in five years' time?

Immediately after the decision has been reached, management is informed of a superjet which will become available in two years' time. The estimates for the new plane are:

Superjet	Estimates
Cost	$4 500 000
Annual net cash inflows	$1 200 000
Life	five years
Salvage value after five years' operation	3% of purchase price

It is considered that four of the new superjets will be adequate to cover the estimated passenger load.

Other available information is as follows:

   i   Management cannot foresee any further developments beyond the superjet.

   ii   Annual net cash inflows are assumed to be received at the end of each year.

   iii   The required rate of return is 10 per cent per annum.

   iv   Taxes may be ignored.

b   Should management:

   i   Retain the piston-engine planes for five years and then replace them with superjets?

   ii   Replace immediately with turboprops, operate them for five years and then replace with superjets?

   iii   Replace now with turboprops, operate them for two years and then replace with superjets?

   iv   Retain the piston-engine planes for two years and then replace with superjets?

(Adapted from G. Peirson, R. Bird, R. Brown and P. Howard, *Business Finance*, 5th edn, McGraw-Hill, 1991, Chapter 5.)

Ethics case study

Newark Ltd is planning to build a new manufacturing plant. Jenny Frame is the person appointed to head the task force responsible for preparing an analysis of the alternatives available to Newark. Frame's team completes a detailed analysis of three alternative types of manufacturing facilities.

Alternative 1: This is the lowest cost alternative but it has a higher risk of employee injuries and a greater risk of environmental damage from toxic gases arising from poor venting.

Alternative 2: Has a higher cost than alternative 1 but reduces the risk of injury to employees. Still has a potential for environmental damage.

Alternative 3: This is the highest cost alternative but provides the greatest safety to workers and offers the least danger to the environment.

Jenny submits the results of the analysis to her boss and he thanks her for the fantastic job that she and her team have done. He will make special mention of her efforts in her job evaluation report this year.

Jenny is pleased with her boss' response, but a week later she is disturbed after coming across a copy of a report from her boss to the board. The report focuses on the costs with each alternative and does not mention the risks to the workers and the environment.

Jenny is unsure of what she should do. She could speak to her boss and risk losing the favourable job evaluation or even her job. Alternatively she could pretend she never saw the report. She is uncertain as to where her responsibilities end. She is, however, also worried about how she would feel if someone were to be hurt as a result of the company selecting Alternative 1.

Discuss:

Jenny's responsibilities, after you have identified them. Suggest a possible course of action.

Cost Behaviour and Cost-volume-profit Analysis

Learning objectives

At the end of this chapter you should be able to:

1   explain the difference between variable and fixed costs

2   understand the relationship between fixed costs and variable costs of production

3   explain what is meant by a linear cost function

4   explain and apply cost estimation using a linear cost assumption

5   explain and apply a cost-volume-profit analysis based on a linear cost assumption

6   understand what is meant by 'breakeven'

7   explain and apply the contribution margin approach to measuring breakeven sales levels and other sales levels for required profits

8   discuss the limitations of using a linear cost assumption in the CVP analysis.

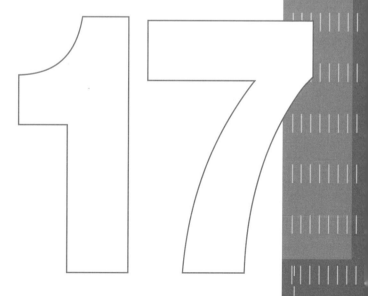

Introduction

For managers to be able to choose among alternative business opportunities they need information regarding future costs and revenues and the way in which these vary at different levels of activity. In order to use this information effectively, managers also need to understand how costs are determined.

In this chapter we begin by examining cost behaviour and the ways in which costs are predicted, and then we consider the application of this information to decision making, using cost-volume-profit (CVP) analysis. This technique, examining the interrelationships between cost, volume and profits at differing activity levels, aids managers in their decision making. We also critically appraise the traditional methods and models that are used and their underlying assumptions.

Fixed and variable costs

To understand how costs behave, it is first necessary to recognise the different types of costs. Some costs are essentially fixed in nature, e.g. the service and equipment charge for the domestic telephone service. Others vary with usage or activity, e.g. the cost of calls made. The latter are known as variable costs. Unfortunately, not all costs fall neatly within these categories and therefore it is necessary to make some simplifying assumptions for the purpose of decision making.

Before examining fixed and variable costs it is worthwhile to define these.

Key Concept 17.1

Fixed costs

A cost is fixed if it does not change in response to changes in the level of activity. (The activity level may be measured in terms of either production output or sales output. The choice will depend upon what is being measured.)

Key Concept 17.2

Variable costs

A cost is variable if it changes in response to changes in the level of activity. For the sake of simplicity, it is assumed that the unit activity cost does not change. Therefore, total variable costs will increase or decrease in direct proportion to the increase or decrease in the activity level.

Cost functions

A basic notion of science is the idea that one thing may depend on another according to some mathematical relation. It is likely that in your study of economics you have also come across mathematical relations. For example, to show that the total spending (c) of a nation depends on the total income (y) of all persons in the nation, economists use the following equation.

$$c = \mathrm{f}(y)$$

This states that consumption is a function of the level of income.

Mathematical formulas are also used in accounting to show relationships between costs and activity levels.

There are two important variables involved in the construction of cost functions. We will use the example of the cost of travelling to illustrate the nature of these variables and their interrelationship.

- The dependent variable, expressed as variable y, is the cost to be predicted—the total cost for an activity, e.g. the cost of petrol for a journey.
- The independent variable x is the level of activity, e.g. the number of kilometres to be travelled on the journey.

The dependent variable is expressed as a function of the independent variable.

$$y = f(x)$$

In our example, this relationship can be expressed as: 'The total cost of petrol for a journey is a function of (depends upon) the number of kilometres travelled.'

The relationship between the dependent and independent variables is illustrated in Figure 17.1, where the vertical axis shows the dependent variable, the total cost of petrol, and the horizontal axis shows the independent variable, the activity, i.e. the kilometres travelled.

A cost function may be linear or non-linear. Traditionally accountants assume cost functions to be linear, which is not necessarily a realistic assumption.

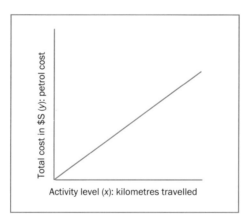

Figure 17.1 *The relationship between a directly dependent variable (petrol cost) and an independent variable (kilometres travelled).*

The choice of the independent variable

Often, there is more than one independent variable that affects the total cost of an activity. The speed at which the vehicle travels, as well as the distance travelled, are variables that affect the amount of petrol consumed and thus the total cost of a journey. However, it is usually too complex to take account of all variables that affect total costs. The independent variable chosen should be the most influential variable in relation to the cost. In the case of petrol for a journey, this is obviously the distance travelled rather than the speed.

In some cases the selection of the most influential variable is obvious. When it is not, past costs should be examined to establish which of the independent variables are most influential.

Variable costs

The cost of raw material is a good example of a cost that varies directly with the level of production output. For example, if one unit of output requires 2 kilograms of material which costs $3.00 per kilogram, then the material cost for 50 units of output will be:

$$2 \text{ kilograms} \times \$3.00 \text{ per kilogram} \times 50 \text{ units} = \$300$$

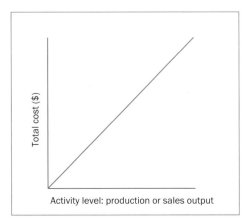

Figure 17.2 *A linear cost function.*

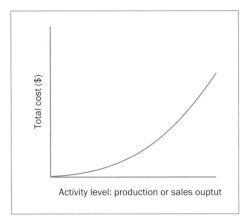

Figure 17.3 *A curvilinear cost function.*

Figure 17.4 *A fixed cost is not affected by increases in activity levels.*

Sales commission normally varies with sales output. For example, if a salesperson receives 10 per cent commission on every unit that is sold, and the selling price per unit is $40, the commission received will be $4 per unit. If the salesperson sold 3000 units during the year, the total commission received would be 4 × 3000 units = $12 000.

Labour paid on a hourly basis is conventionally classified as a cost that varies with production output. In reality, however, workers are paid a fixed wage which bears no direct relationship to output levels. There might be some output-linked incentive bonus included in the pay structure, but most of the remuneration is fixed for a set working week. Nevertheless, for decision-making purposes it is assumed that this category of labour is variable because, physically, production levels are a function of the labour input.

Figure 17.2 illustrates a cost which varies directly with activity levels. Note that the graph goes through the origin, i.e. when the activity is zero, the costs are zero. As activity increases, the variable cost increases. This can later be compared with Figure 17.6 where fixed costs are also included.

In reality it is unlikely that costs which are traditionally classified as variable will behave strictly in a linear fashion. The variable cost function often tends to be curvilinear, or made up of several straight lines. The following examples illustrate some of the reasons why variable costs are not strictly linear.

- Manufacturers are likely to benefit from bulk discounts for the purchase of raw materials.
- Prices of resources tend to increase as a scarcity arises, due to increased demand.
- Increased activity may lead to diminishing returns: for example, attempts to sell more units may entail transporting the extra units over longer distances to reach more distant markets, and therefore distribution costs may increase at a faster rate than activity. Assuming that selling prices are constant, these greater distribution costs will result in diminishing profit margins.

Figure 17.3 shows a variable cost function with diminishing returns.

Fixed costs

Examples of costs that are normally classified as fixed are rent, rates, salaries of administrators, and the service and equipment charge for a telephone service referred to earlier. Fixed costs of this type are normally also classified as overhead costs, which are described in Chapter 18. Figure 17.4 shows a fixed cost function.

However, the concept that fixed costs are constant over all levels of activity is often unrealistic. In reality, a fixed cost is fixed only over a limited range of output. For example, in the case of the telephone bill, the service and equipment charge is theoretically fixed. However, if the telephone company increases its charges, or if an extension is required, the service and equipment charge increases. Similarly, a factory has a limited capacity; if production were to exceed that capacity another factory would be required, and thus costs would increase. Therefore, these types of costs tend to behave in a stepped fashion. Figure 17.5 illustrates a stepped cost function in the case of renting a factory. The rent is $2000 for one factory which has a capacity in output terms of 1000 units. Another factory will be required for output levels exceeding 1000 units, and the total rent will increase to $4000 (assuming that the rental and the capacity are the same). This cost will remain at $4000 up to 2000 units, when another factory will be required and costs will increase in the same fashion and so on.

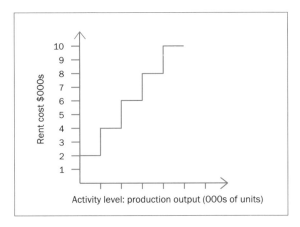

Figure 17.5 *A stepped cost function: renting factory space.*

Linear cost functions

In reality, many cost functions are made up of two parts—a fixed cost and a variable cost.

Key Concept 17.3

Linear cost functions

In general, we can express a linear cost function as
$$y = a + bx$$
where y is the total cost to be predicted; x is the level of activity measured in units of output; a is the 'fixed cost'; and b is the 'variable cost'.

Let us again consider a telephone bill, since this is a good example of a linear cost function. Look at the graph in Figure 17.6. Point a represents the fixed costs, which remain the same for any level of activity—the service and equipment charge. The line illustrates the variable cost (the cost of calls), rising in proportion to increases in activity x (the number of call units).

We can determine the total telephone bill (y) using the above equation if we know the service and equipment charge (a), the cost per unit call (b) and the number of units registered (x).

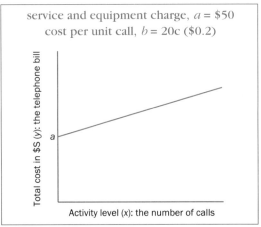

Figure 17.6 *A linear cost function of a telephone bill.*

The number of unit calls made, x, is 1500. The total cost of the bill, y, can be calculated thus:

$$y = \$50 + (\$0.2 \times 1500) = \$350$$

If the number of unit calls increased to 1800 the total cost of the bill would be:

$$y = \$50 + (\$0.2 \times 1800) = \$410$$

To help you to understand this equation and its use, examine a recent telephone bill for your household and calculate the total cost of the bill if the number of unit calls made increased by, say, 50 per cent. This exercise might also result in your spending less time on the telephone!

The relevant range of activity

Assuming that the intention is to operate in the relevant range of activity, we can be reasonably confident about predicting the pattern of cost behaviour. This confidence is important to managers because the information regarding the way in which costs behave is the basis for decision making about the future. If the costs do not behave as predicted, decisions could be taken that will jeopardise the organisation's future.

Outside the relevant range, we cannot be confident that the relationship between the variables will hold. Figure 17.7 shows a cost function in the relevant range of activity and other cost functions outside this range, which are not of a similar pattern.

Key Concept 17.4

The relevant range of activity

The relevant range of activity relates to the levels of activity that the firm has experienced in past periods. It is assumed that in this range the relationship between the independent and dependent variables will be similar to that previously experienced.

If an organisation is intending to operate at an activity level not experienced before, it must be extremely cautious in the prediction of future costs, relying more on forecasting methods than on predicting costs on the basis of past behaviour. The examination of forecasting methods is outside the scope of this text; you can find references to the methods in advanced management accounting texts.

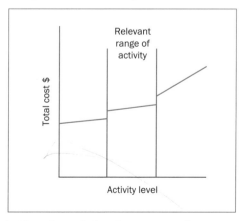

Figure 17.7 *Cost functions inside and outside the relevant range of activity.*

Conventionally, for convenience, graphical representations of the relations between costs and volumes show cost functions that are the same for all levels of activity, i.e. the same pattern of costs is shown inside and outside the relevant range of activity. This is the case in all the graphical representations showing cost functions illustrated in Figures 17.1 to 17.6.

Cost behaviour: assumptions and limitations

As we have already mentioned, accountants conventionally employ linear cost functions for use in making operating decisions. This practice is based on a number of assumptions and we have discussed most of them. For clarity, they are summarised below.

- All costs can be divided into either fixed or variable costs.
- Fixed costs remain constant over different activity levels.
- Variable costs vary with activity but are constant per unit of output.
- Efficiency and productivity remain constant over all activity levels.
- Cost behaviour can be explained sufficiently by one independent variable.

From our earlier analysis it will be recognised that these assumptions are simplistic and tend to be approximations of reality. Therefore the question arises: are the cost functions used by accountants justified? The answer is often difficult to establish with much confidence. Primarily this is a cost-benefit question (this approach was generally considered in Chapter 15): are the net benefits greater when accountants' linear cost functions are used compared with more sophisticated cost functions such as curvilinear functions? The non-linear functions are more costly to establish but developments in information technology have tended to reduce the cost of using these more sophisticated models.

Arnold and Turley (1996) argue that the use of a linear cost function:

is not unreasonable as statistical studies have presented evidence which suggests that within specified output limits [the relevant range of activity], organisations do have cost functions which are approximately linear.

Figure 17.8 shows a curvilinear cost function. Look closely at the curve in the relevant range of activity. In fact, it is very close to a straight line. You might like to use a ruler to mark in such a line. Note that the curve on either side of the relevant range could be approximated with two different straight lines.

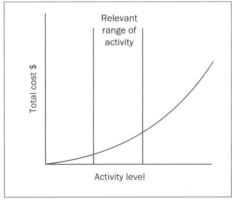

Figure 17.8 *A curvilinear cost function approximates to a linear cost function within the relevant range of activity.*

Estimating costs

Key Concept 17.5

Cost estimation

Cost estimation relates to methods that are used to measure past (historical) costs at varying activity levels. These costs are then employed as the basis for predictions of future costs that will be used in decision making.

There are many methods of cost estimation. Detailed knowledge of each of these methods is not necessary at this stage of your studies. However, it is important that you appreciate the basic principles and limitations of cost estimation. For a detailed examination of the methods see Horngren et al. (1997).

Methods of cost estimation range from simple to mathematically complex. The essential factor is to choose the estimation technique that generates the greatest benefits net of the costs of deriving the information. This to a great extent depends on the size of the organisation. The smaller the organisation, the less likely it is that a sophisticated method will be employed, because the costs will be relatively high compared to the benefits that will be generated from the use of such a method.

Cost estimates are based on historical cost accounting data, i.e. on the costs of past production, service and sales activity. One of the simplest methods is the account classification method, which involves simply observing how costs behaved in a previous period and classifying these costs as fixed or variable. The method relies on subjective judgement and thus is limited in its ability to predict the future behaviour of costs accurately.

A more sophisticated method of cost estimation is regression analysis. The linear regression model involves making a number of observations from past cost behaviour and statistically analysing the data to produce a line of best fit. Figure 17.9 shows graphically a number of points (past costs at varying levels of activity), and the line of best fit established using the mathematical technique of regression analysis.

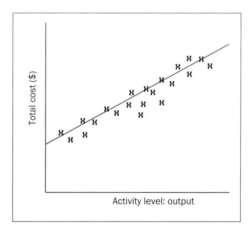

Figure 17.9 *Regression analysis of past cost behaviour.*

A clear pattern of behaviour, i.e. where the points lie close to the line of best fit over the activity range, indicates a high correlation between cost and output (activity), while a more widely dispersed arrangement of points indicates a lower correlation. (For further explanation see a text on quantitative methods, such as Curwin and Slater, 1996, *Quantitative Methods for Business Decisions.*) In the example illustrated in Figure 17.9 there is a fairly clear pattern and thus we can conclude that there is a relatively high correlation between cost and output.

There are more sophisticated regression analysis techniques. These include multiple regression, which takes account of more than one independent variable, and curvilinear regression.

The use of past data to determine future costs and the way in which they behave is problematic. The following briefly summarises some of the problems.

- *Relevant range of activity:* As previously mentioned, little confidence can be placed in cost estimates beyond the range of activity from which the data have been derived. It is dangerous to extrapolate cost trends well beyond the levels of output previously experienced.
- *The number of observations:* It is important in statistical analysis to derive many observations of output and cost levels in order to be able to make accurate predictions about future behaviour. The greater the number of observations, the higher the accuracy of the estimate and therefore the better the prediction.
- *Changes in prices:* Past costs may not reflect current price levels and they will bias the estimates downwards. There is thus a need to adjust these prices to current levels.
- *Changes in technology:* Only observations made under current production procedures should be included in the analysis. Costs of work practices using, for example, machinery that is no longer used, are irrelevant to future decisions.
- *Incorporating past inefficiencies:* If operations were performed in an inefficient manner in the past and cost estimates are derived from this past period, they will incorporate inefficiencies.

With the development of more sophisticated techniques, there is increasing use of industrial engineering methods to predict future costs. Using time and motion studies, input and output analysis, and production control productivity surveys it is possible to specify relatively accurately the relationship between labour time, machine time, materials and physical output. These techniques look to the future physical levels of resources and then convert them into money values instead of using past costs as the basis of estimating future costs.

Cost-volume-profit analysis

Organisations are constantly faced with decisions relating to the products and services they sell, such as the following.

- Should we change the selling price, and if so what would be the effect on profit?
- How many units must be sold to break even?
- How many units must be sold to make a specified target profit?
- Should more money be spent on advertising?

The cost data used in CVP analysis are derived from the prediction of future costs discussed earlier in this chapter.

Key Concept 17.6

Cost-volume-profit (CVP) analysis

CVP analysis is a tool used by organisations to help them make decisions by examining the interrelationships between cost, volume and profits.

Sales revenue

It is normally assumed in CVP analysis that sales revenues, like costs, behave in a linear fashion for varying output levels. That is, the sales price per unit sold is the same for all levels of output. Figure 17.10 illustrates a sales revenue function; the vertical axis represents the total sales revenue and the horizontal axis is the sales output levels.

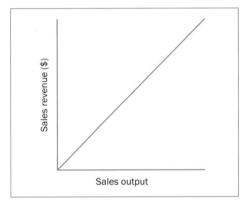

Figure 17.10   *The sales revenue increases in direct proportion to sales output.*

It can be seen that the sales revenue function increases in direct proportion to sales output. This is because the selling price is the same for every unit sold.

The assumption that the selling price remains constant for all levels of sales is often unrealistic. For example, often you will find quantity discounts being offered for consumable goods at supermarkets: if you buy one tablet of soap the price is 60c, whereas if you buy two tablets the price is $1.00, or 50c each. This limitation on the application of CVP analysis will be considered in more detail later.

CVP equation

CVP analysis is based on the relationship expressed by the following equation.

$$P = Sx - (FC + VCx)$$

where
S = selling price per unit
x = number of units sold
FC = fixed cost
VC = variable cost
P = expected profit.

This expression can be rearranged as follows.

$$Sx = VCx + FC + P$$

This equation is similar to the cost functions considered earlier. Only one independent variable is being considered, i.e. the sales activity. The fixed and variable costs together are equal to total cost. The only additional variables are sales price, and profit, which is the difference between sales revenue and total costs.

To illustrate the application of CVP analysis in decision making, we consider the example of Boycott Industries.

Example 17.1: Boycott Industries

Boycott Industries produce only one product. The following revenues and costs have been estimated for the forthcoming month.

- selling price, $70 per unit (S)
- variable costs, $40 per unit (VC)
- fixed cost, $2400 (FC).

The managers of the firm wish to know the following.

1. How many units must be sold to break even (i.e. to make neither a profit nor a loss)?
2. How many units must be sold to make a profit of $600?
3. Would it be worthwhile to introduce advertising at a cost of $1200 if this increases sales from 520 to 600 units?
4. What should the selling price be to make a profit of $8640 on sales of 120 units?

Solution

Question 1

S = 70, VC = 40, FC = 2400. At the breakeven point, P = 0. Use the sales version of the CVP equation.

$$
\begin{aligned}
Sx &= VCx + FC + P \\
70x &= 40x + 2400 + 0 \\
30x &= 2400 \\
x &= 80 \text{ units}
\end{aligned}
$$

We can check this in the following manner.

	$	$
Sales (80 units @ $70)		5 600
Less Costs		
Variable cost (80 units @ $40)	3 200	
Fixed costs	2 400	5 600
Profit		0

Question 2

For this question, P = 600.

$$
\begin{aligned}
Sx &= VCx + FC + P \\
70x &= 40x + 2400 + 600 \\
30x &= 3000 \\
x &= 100 \text{ units}
\end{aligned}
$$

Question 3

First determine the profit for x = 520 units. Use the profit version of the CVP equation.

$$
\begin{aligned}
P &= Sx - (VCx + FC) \\
P &= 70 \times 520 - (40 \times 520 + 2400) \\
P &= \$13\,200
\end{aligned}
$$

Advertising costs will increase fixed costs by $1200 (FC = 3600). The profit for x = 600 units will be as follows:

$$P = 70 \times 600 - (40 \times 600 + 3600)$$
$$P = \$14\,400$$

Therefore, the profit with advertising is \$14 400 compared to \$13 200. Pre firm will go ahead and advertise the product because it will generate great However, management must decide on matters such as the probability of selling t units if the \$1200 is paid for advertising.

Question 4

$P = 8640$, $x = 120$. Use the sales version CVP equation.

$$Sx = VCx + FC + P$$
$$S \times 120 = 40 \times 120 + 2400 + 8640$$
$$120 \times S = 15\,840$$
$$S = 132$$

The breakeven chart

A useful method of illustrating the relationships between cost, volume and profits is a breakeven chart. The relationship between these variables is plotted on a graph. The cost functions and the sales revenue function, which in previous illustrations have been shown separately, are now included together in the breakeven chart.

Figure 17.11 shows the breakeven chart for Boycott Industries, using the data given earlier. You will notice that in the construction of this chart the variable costs are plotted above the fixed costs, resulting in a total cost function that rises from the intercept at \$2400 and increases at the rate of \$40 per unit. (Another way of constructing the total cost function in breakeven charts will be illustrated later.) The main advantage of the chart for management is that the breakeven point and the areas of loss and profit can be clearly and quickly identified. This enables management to establish the effect of varying output levels that it wishes to consider. For example, the profit at an output level of 90 units can be read from the chart without the need to solve the CVP equation.

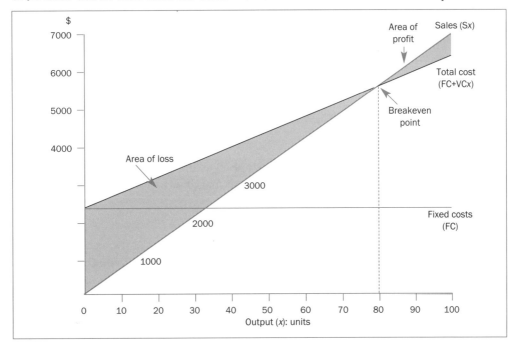

Figure 17.11 *The breakeven chart for Boycott Industries.*

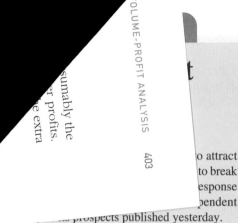

...sumably the
...r profits.
...e extra

...o attract
to break
...esponse
...pendent
...prospects published yesterday.

Bad publicity about the Dome's contents, queues and cost mean that the £758 million exhibition will probably sell just over 10 million tickets this year, nearly 2 million short of its target, the report by Volterra Consulting found.

The results add to growing fears that the Dome will not prove to be popular enough to cover its costs, even though the organisers insist that tickets are selling better than expected. It must attract an average of 33 000 visitors a day, but is operating at a reduced capacity of 20 000.

Volterra's figures were compiled using an advanced computer modelling process known as complex systems analysis.

The New Millennium Experience Company said: 'Ticket sales are ahead of expectations at this stage, and well on track for what we need. Any computer model of how we are doing would need to take all sorts of things into account to be accurate—such as higher demand in the summer and even the weather.'

Better news for the Dome came from an opinion poll of 505 visitors carried out since its opening. It found that 80 per cent had enjoyed their day out.

The Times, 14 January 2000

Commentary

The article discusses how the Millennium Dome in London was not expected to attract the 12 million visitors it needed to break even. Given the cost of the dome was £758 million (about $2 billion), the failure to achieve the attendance needed to break even would have been a major concern to shareholders. The article does not indicate the expected loss if only 10 million people paid to visit the Dome. The management of the Dome could have considered increasing the admission charge to reduce the numbers required to break even, but this might have discouraged even more people from visiting the Dome.

The contribution margin method

The contribution margin is equal to the sales price per unit, less the variable cost per unit, i.e.

$$C = S - VC$$

The contribution margin is commonly described as the contribution per unit. Using the data from Boycott Industries the contribution margin is as follows.

$$
\begin{aligned}
C &= S - VC \\
&= 70 - 40 \\
&= \$30
\end{aligned}
$$

This means that each unit sold makes a contribution of $30. The contribution initially reduces the loss incurred by fixed costs by $30 per unit. When fixed costs have been covered at the output level of 80 units (i.e. at the breakeven point) every unit sold thereafter contributes $30 to profits.

Figure 17.12 is another version of the breakeven chart, once again using the data relating to Boycott Industries.

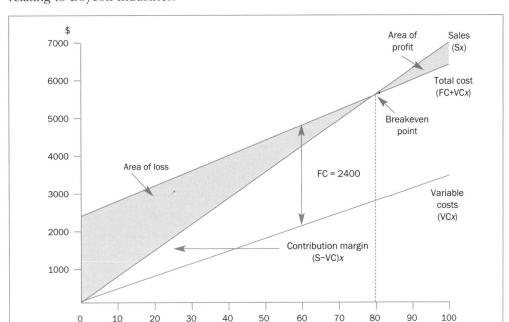

Figure 17.12 *The breakeven chart for Boycott Industries, showing the contribution margin.*

Here, the total cost function is constructed by first plotting the variable costs and then adding the fixed costs. By constructing the total cost function in this way we can identify the contribution margin, i.e. the difference between the sales and variable cost functions, as shown on the chart.

Note that at the origin (i.e. no sales) a loss is made of $2400, which is the sum of the fixed costs. When one unit is sold it contributes $30, thereby reducing the loss to $2370. As sales output increases, the loss is reduced by $30 per unit to the breakeven point where the fixed costs are totally covered. After the breakeven point, each unit sold increases profit by $30 per unit; thus if 81 units are sold a profit of $30 would be made.

The contribution margin is an important concept and is used widely in accounting to aid managers in making decisions. We examine the concept in more detail in Chapters 19 and 20.

Using the contribution margin approach, we can answer the problems posed earlier. First we need to rearrange the CVP equation:

$$Sx = VCx + FC + P$$
$$Sx - VCx = FC + P$$
$$(S - VC)x = FC + P$$
$$\text{since } C = S - VC$$
$$Cx = FC + P$$

To find the breakeven point, we put $P = 0$

$$Cx = FC$$
$$x = FC \div C$$

Using the data for Boycott Industries:

$$x = 2400 \div 30$$
$$= 80 \text{ units}$$

CASE STUDY 17.2

Amex Sounds Ltd

Amex Sounds Ltd is a company which specialises in the sale of domestic electronic sound equipment. The company purchases goods from manufacturers and sells them to the retail trade. A high proportion of the goods they sell is manufactured abroad and imported. Since starting five years ago they have been very successful, in terms of sales and profit growth. The managing director has recently been offered an exclusive contract to sell a cassette recorder that is manufactured in South Korea. Although this recorder has been sold successfully in the USA, it has yet to be sold in the Australian market.

The company is currently assessing whether or not to enter into the contract. The following information relates to the estimated costs and revenues of the contract.

- A market survey has been completed with the help of a market consultant. At a price of $40 per recorder the estimated sales in the first year would be 9500 recorders. This is considered to be the most realistic price and volume level in the forthcoming year, taking account of competition.
- The price paid for each recorder will be $19.50. This includes the cost of packaging and shipment. The contract specifies that this price will be fixed for one year from the contract date.
- Variable costs, other than the cost of the recorder, are estimated to be $3.00 per recorder sold.
- The company is currently trading from a rented warehouse in Sydney. However, there is very little space for further expansion. After due consideration of location and costs it is decided that, if the contract is accepted, a warehouse in Parramatta will be rented and used exclusively for the sale of these recorders. Parramatta has been chosen primarily because of the relatively lower cost of renting premises and the better employment situation. The rent

of this warehouse will be $46 000 per year and it is estimated that salaries will be $65 000 per year.

- Other fixed costs are anticipated to be $15 000.

The following summarises the costs per unit that will be incurred in selling the recorder.

	$ Costs per unit
Variable costs	
Purchase price of recorders	19.50
Other variable costs	3.00
	22.50
Fixed Costs (per year)	
Rent of warehouse	46 000
Salaries	65 000
Other fixed costs	15 000
	126 000

In the decision whether or not to accept this contract, CVP analysis will be a useful aid. We begin by determining the profit for the estimated sales of 9500, first rearranging the equation used earlier:

$$Sx = VCx + FC + P$$
$$P = x(S - VC) - FC$$
$$P = 9500(40 - 22.50) - 126\,000$$
$$= \$40\,250$$

To determine the number of units which need to be sold to break even, we find that putting P = 0 gives:

$$x = FC \div C$$
$$\text{where } C = S - VC$$
$$= 40 - 22.50$$
$$= 17.50$$
$$\text{so} \quad x = 126\,000 \div 17.50$$
$$= 7200 \text{ units}$$

The difference between the breakeven point and the estimated sales in terms of units is 9500 − 7200 = 2300 units; this would give the company a margin of safety in percentage terms of 2300 ÷ 9500 × 100 = 24 per cent approximately.

Clearly the information derived from our analysis is useful in the assessment of this contract. In particular, the determination of the breakeven point gives the management of the company a basis to evaluate an element of the risk associated with the contract. Knowledge that there is a margin of safety of 2300 units will be useful in this assessment.

We now extend our analysis to consider advertising. It will be assumed that costs and revenues above remain constant with the exception of any effect associated with advertising.

The company consults an advertising firm regarding the sales of the recorder. Two separate strategies are proposed:

1 Expenditure on advertising of $16 000 will increase the sales volume in the year to 10 300 units.
2 Expenditure of $30 000 will increase the sales volume in the year to 11 500 units.

These two strategies will be considered separately and compared with the original analysis above, taking into account the profit and breakeven levels.

1 Advertising costs $16 000, sales volume 10 300 units

The advertising costs would be classified as fixed costs; therefore fixed costs will now be $126 000 + $16 000 = $142 000. Using the equation we can determine the profit:

$$P = x(S - VC) - FC$$
$$P = 10\ 300 \times 17.50 - 142\ 000$$
$$= \$38\ 250$$

The breakeven point is given by:

$$x = FC \div C$$
$$= 142\ 000 \div 17.50$$
$$= 8114 \text{ units (to the nearest whole number).}$$

This proposal, we can safely say, will not be attractive to the company because profits are $40 250 – $38 250 = $2000 lower than the original proposal, and the risk is greater because the breakeven point is higher by 8114 – 7200 = 914 units.

2 Advertising costs $30 000, sales volume 11 500 units

Fixed costs increase to $126 000 + $30 000 = $156 000.

$$P = x(S - VC) - FC$$
$$P = 11\ 500 \times 17.50 - 156\ 000$$
$$= \$45\ 250$$

The breakeven point is:

$$x = FC \div C$$
$$= 156\ 000 \div 17.50$$
$$= 8914 \text{ units (to the nearest whole number).}$$

In this case the decision whether to use advertising is somewhat more complex. Firstly, the profit will increase by $45 250 – $40 250 = $5000, which presumably will be attractive to the company. However, the risk measured in terms of breakeven analysis is greater, because the breakeven point has risen from 7200 to 8914 units.

The analysis of these advertising strategies, in terms of profit and breakeven points, is clearly useful in determining whether the company should use advertising. However, it is important to appreciate that this is only a part of the total information necessary to evaluate such a proposal. For example, it is also necessary to consider the effect on cash flow. It is likely that the company will require additional funds to support an advertising campaign and this should be taken into account.

CVP analysis: assumptions and limitations

The cost-volume-profit model that has been examined and illustrated in this chapter has been assumed to be linear. The assumptions and limitations of a linear cost function were described earlier in the section relating to cost behaviour, and these are relevant to the CVP model.

The sales function, as previously discussed, is also linear as it is assumed that the sales price will remain constant for all levels of activity. Empirical evidence suggests that this is unlikely for the majority of goods and services. A more realistic sales function would be represented by a curvilinear pattern. However, although the assumption of a linear function seems to be too simplistic, there is evidence that within the relevant range of activity the sales function, like cost, does approximate to a linear pattern.

The choice of employing a linear or a non-linear function to represent sales in the analysis once again depends on the costs and benefits of the information.

In the examples of the application of CVP analysis we examined a one-product firm, Boycott Industries. In reality, most firms produce more than one type of product. There are particular problems associated with the application of CVP analysis in multi-product firms.

In many cases, there are interdependencies between the production and demand of two or more of the firm's products. For example, the demand for one product, such as butter, might be affected by the demand for another product, such as margarine. In these cases it is necessary to examine the CVP relationships together. This will not cause a problem if the sales mix (the proportion of sales volumes of the interdependent products) and the profit margins are the same. If the mix changes, the overall volume targets might be achieved but the effects on profits will depend on whether the product of higher or lower margin predominates in the mix.

Not all costs are fixed or variable. Some costs are mixed costs, having both a fixed and a variable component. For example, a computer salesperson might be paid $1000 a month, plus $100 for each computer sold.

Fixed costs represent another problem in the application of CVP analysis in multi-product firms. If the fixed cost can be identified with particular products, there is no cause for concern. But if fixed costs are of a general nature, e.g. head office expenses, they will have to be apportioned or allocated on some fairly arbitrary basis. This could be misleading and lead to inaccurate decisions.

If one or more of the resources available to a firm is scarce, there will be a constraint on the potential total sales output. The problem is how the resources should be allocated among the products. This depends on how effectively each product uses the resource. We will be examining this problem in more detail in Chapters 19 and 20.

Summary

In this chapter we have examined the nature of fixed and variable costs and the way in which these costs behave over activity levels. We explained the way in which these costs are used in predicting future costs. In practice, important decisions are made by organisations based on past cost behaviour and the prediction of future costs. However, it was stressed that simplistic assumptions were made in deriving this information. While the adoption of these assumptions reduces the accuracy of the information, we can derive reasonable approximations of the real world by using methods that are not wholly realistic. CVP analysis was examined. This is an extremely useful technique in the decisionmaking process of organisations, although it is also limited by the simplistic assumptions underlying the determination of future costs and revenues over varying activity levels.

References

Arnold, J., and Turley, S., 1996. *Accounting for Management Decisions*, 3rd edn, Prentice-Hall.

Curwin, J., and Slater, R., 1996. *Quantitative Methods for Business Decisions*, 4th edn, International Thomson Business Press.

Horngren, C., Foster, G., and Datar, S., 1997. *Cost Accounting: A Managerial Emphasis*, 9th edn, Prentice-Hall.

Further reading

Hilton, R., 1997. *Managerial Accounting*, 3rd edn, McGraw-Hill.

Hirsch, M.L., Louderback, J.G., and Smith, E., 1989. *Cost Accounting: Accumulation, Analysis and Use*, Thomas Nelson.

Review questions

1   It is often assumed that there is only one independent variable in cost behaviour. Explain the nature of independent variables and why this assumption is made.

2   Explain what is meant by the relevant range of activity and its significance in CVP analysis.

3   Variable and fixed costs are traditionally assumed to be linear. Explain why this assumption is unrealistic.

4   What are the problems associated with CVP analysis in a multi-product firm?

Problems for discussion and analysis

1   In the table below fill in the blank spaces.

Sales $	Variable costs $	Fixed costs $	Total costs $	Profit $	Contribution $
2 000	1 400	6 00	2 000	0	6 00
3 000	1 4 00	600	2 0 00	1 000	16 n
1 000	1 000	6 00	1 600	2 400	3 00
4 000	3 000	600	3 6 00	400	1 000

2   With a sales figure of $500 000, Fidget Ltd achieves breakeven for widget sales. Fixed costs are $200 000.
    a   What is the contribution margin?
    b   If variable costs are $6 per widget, what is the selling price?
    c   If 55 000 widgets are sold, calculate the profit/loss.

3   Clean-it P/L makes washing machines, and with its existing plant capacity the maximum production possible is 1000 units per year. Fixed costs are estimated at $36 000 per annum and the selling price of each machine is $240. Sales for the next year are expected to drop to 800 units. The cost of each washing machine is calculated as follows.

   •   direct material cost $40
   •   direct labour cost 10 hours at $8 per hour.

a   Calculate (i) the breakeven point, (ii) the maximum profit, and (iii) the profit at an estimated sales level of 800 units.

b   Costs alter by the following proportions:

- direct materials increase by 20 per cent
- fixed costs come down by $12 000
- direct labour costs increase by $2 per hour.

What will be (i) the new breakeven point and (ii) the new profit at the estimated sales level of 800 units?

4   Cords P/L manufactures a style of corduroy jeans that it sold last year at $36 a pair. The cost specifications for these jeans were as follows.

Variable cost per pair of jeans	$
Materials	13
Labour	7
Fixed overheads per month	52 800

Cords P/L made a profit of $22 080 each month.

a   How many pairs of jeans did Cords P/L sell each month?

b   Cords P/L is now planning next year's operations. The sales director is proposing to boost sales by reducing the selling price to $34 and spending an additional $6000 per month on advertising. She estimates that these actions will enable the company to sell 5800 pairs of jeans each month.

Evaluate the sales director's proposals, taking into account the expected impact on profits and on the breakeven point. State any assumptions you need to make.

c   If the managing director of Cords P/L were to require that next year's profit show a 15 per cent increase over last year's performance, how many pairs of jeans would have to be sold each month, (i) assuming that the sales director's policies were adopted, and (ii) assuming that they were not?

5   The Incr-Edible Pie Company Ltd has the following revenue and cost functions for 20X3.

$$\text{Total revenues} = \$30x$$
$$\text{Total costs} = \$150\,000 + 20x$$
$$\text{where } x = \text{number of units}$$

Required:

a   Prepare a cost-volume-profit graph for the Incr-Edible Pie Company. Label the vertical axis in $50 000 increments and the horizontal axis in 5000 unit increments.

b   Prepare a profit-volume graph for the Incr-Edible Pie Company Ltd.

c   What is the breakeven point in units and dollars? Prove your answer by calculating profits at the breakeven level.

(Adapted from W.J. Morse and P.H. Roth, *Cost Accounting*, 3rd edn, Addison-Wesley, 1986, p. 323.)

6   The Thredbare Clothing Company has to decide whether to produce trousers or skirts. The manager knows that the demand for trousers is 1200 per month at a selling price of $45 each and the demand for skirts is 800 at $60 each. Costs of production are as follows:

	Trousers	
Monthly rent	$550.00	
Material per unit	$15.00	
Labour hours per unit	1.25	
Selling costs per unit	$0.25	
Administration costs	$1 000.00	$1
Labour rate per hour	$8.50	
Depreciation on plant	$120.00	$

Required:

Advise the management whether it is more profitable to produce trousers or skirts, giving the breakeven points (in both dollars and units) for each product, and the level of profits or losses in either event.

7 ABC Ltd produces stereos and sells these for $250 each. The company can produce a maximum of 5000 units per year. Variable costs are $185 per unit and fixed costs are $250 000 per year, regardless of production.
  a Calculate the breakeven point.
  b What is the profit for the company if it sells 5000 units?
  c The company believes it can sell more units if it leases additional equipment. The lease costs are $200 000 a year and the company has to give one year's notice to cancel the lease. Because of the increased production, variable costs are reduced to $175 per unit. If the maximum number of units the company can produce and sell with the new equipment is 8100, should the company lease the new equipment?
  d What if there is a recession in the audio industry and the company can now sell only 4000 units at $240? Should the company keep producing or not? Give reasons for your answer.

8 You are in charge of organising a conference for a group of accounting academics. You have obtained the following details:

	$
Rental of conference venue	300
Speakers' costs	500
Note books and pens	100
Cost of lunch and morning and afternoon teas (per person)	30

The cost for the 45 academics is $50 per person.

Required:

  a How many academics would have to attend at $50 per person for the conference to break even?
  b If 60 academics attend at a cost of $50, what is the expected profit?
  c The committee believes that $250 spent on promotion would attract a total of 80 academics. Should they spend this if they want to keep the cost at $50 per person?

9 Two competing food firms are located side by side at a fair. Each occupies equal space at the same rent of $1250, and charges similar prices for food. Firm A employs three times as many employees as B. Other information is:

	A	B
Sales	$8 000	$4 500
Cost of goods sold	50% of sales	50% of sales
Wages	$2 250	$750

Explain (showing detailed figures) why A is more profitable than B.

b   By how much would B's sales have to increase in order to justify doubling the number of its employees (at the same rate of pay) if the desired net profit is $350?

(Adapted from J. Harrison, J. Horrocks and R. Newman, *Accounting: A Direct Approach*, Longman Cheshire, 1986, p. 440.)

10   Bilge and Sludge Ltd is planning the introduction of a new product and estimates the demand at various selling prices as follows.

Price	Estimated unit sales
	$
2.00	200 000
2.25	180 000
2.50	160 000
3.00	130 000

The estimated costs are:

Fixed manufacturing costs	$30 000
Variable overhead costs	10 cents per unit
Direct materials	80 cents per unit
Direct labour	40 cents per unit
Selling expenses (variable)	10% of sales
Administration expenses (fixed)	$15 000

Prepare a schedule showing the selling price that Bilge and Sludge Ltd should charge in order to maximise its profit on the figures supplied.

(Adapted from J. Harrison, J. Horrocks and R. Newman, *Accounting: A Direct Approach*, Longman Cheshire, 1986, p. 440.)

11   The Fireside Bookshop sells books from the Adventure Series, Mystery Series and Classics Series. Unit selling prices and variable costs per series are as follows.

	Adventure Series	Mystery Series	Classics Series
	$	$	$
Selling price	50	35	100
Variable cost	30	25	50

Fireside incurs fixed costs of $90 000 per year and is subject to an income tax rate of 40 per cent. The company would like to earn after-tax profits of $27 000 per year. The current unit sales mix is as follows:

	Percentage of total
Adventure Series	40
Mystery Series	50
Classics Series	10

Required:

Determine each of the following for the current sales mix:
a   the range of breakeven points in units
b   the average unit contribution margin

c the breakeven unit sales volume

d the unit sales volume needed to attain the desired after-tax profits.

(Adapted from W.J. Morse and P.H. Roth, *Cost Accounting,* 3rd edn, Addison-Wesley, 1986, p. 324.)

12 In 20X1 Ashfield Ltd sold 8000 car alarms at $90 each. The following details are available.

Variable Costs:		Fixed Costs:	
Production	$50 per unit	Production	$100 000
Selling	$10 per unit	Selling	$80 000
	$60 per unit		$180 000

Ashfield can reduce its variable production costs by $10 per unit if it invests $100 000 in new equipment.

Required:

a Calculate the breakeven in units for the original and revised set of figures.

b Calculate the profit using the original and revised set of figures for sales of 8000 units.

c What is the sales in units when the profit is the same for both the original and revised set of figures?

d If the company reduced its selling price by $10 per unit, expected sales would increase to 15 000 units. Should the company reduce its selling price under either alternative?

Ethics case study

Dave Johnston is analysing a request from a special customer for an order of 1000 electric kettles. The customer has proposed that he will pay an amount per unit based on the contribution margin plus 20 per cent. The customer is in Hong Kong and he wants the goods before Christmas and the date is 12 December.

The other details of the proposal are:

i The customer is to pay all freight costs.

ii Dave's company is to make a $5000 payment to a friend of the customer who works in the customs area in Hong Kong so that the kettles can be cleared through customs before Christmas.

The relevant data for the kettles are as follows:

Variable unit manufacturing costs	$25
Variable unit selling and administrative costs	$12
Selling price	$50

Dave's boss has explained that the customer is a very important one and, as the order will lead to the plant operating at full capacity, workers will be able to earn a little extra for Christmas by working overtime.

Discuss:

a the accounting and ethical issues in this case

b whether Dave should accept the terms proposed for the special order.

Accounting for Overheads and Product Costs

Learning objectives

At the end of this chapter you should be able to:

1 understand that attaching costs to a product is a problem for multi-product firms

2 explain the difference between direct and indirect costs

3 explain what is meant by full costing

4 explain what is meant by product and period costs

5 explain the stages involved in determining the allocation of overheads to products for full costing purposes

6 explain what is meant by predetermined overhead absorption rates

7 understand what is meant by activity-based costing

8 explain what is meant by the marginal-costing approach

9 discuss the relevance and the impact of both costing methods for the valuation of inventory and the determination of net profit.

Introduction

The statement of financial performance summarises all the costs and revenues of an organisation over a defined period. While this information is extremely useful in determining the overall profitability of the organisation, there is also a need to determine the costs and the profitability of individual products. This issue is examined in this chapter. We look at the use of full costing and marginal costing as the two main approaches to allocating overhead costs to products in a multi-product organisation. Activity-based costing is also briefly discussed.

Management's need for information about costs

To control costs

Actual product costs will be compared with planned costs. If the actual costs deviate from the plan, management may need to take corrective action so that their predetermined targets are met in the future.

To aid planning

Past product costs are a useful base for estimating future product costs in the planning process. But when using past costs for this purpose, management must be careful to take account of any potential changes in the level of costs in the future, due to inflation, scarcity and so on.

To value inventories

Product costs need to be determined so that the value of products that are complete (finished goods) and products that are partially complete (work in progress) can be established at the end of each accounting period for inclusion in the statement of financial position and statement of financial performance.

To aid the setting of selling prices

The cost of products influences the setting of prices. From a marketing viewpoint it can be argued that the price is determined through market forces, i.e. from consideration of what the market can bear. However, in a number of situations, particularly where there is little or no competition, prices are often set with reference to the cost.

To ascertain the relative profitability of products

In times of scarce resources when a firm is constrained as to its level of output, it is likely that management will favour selling only its most profitable products. In these circumstances, knowledge of product costs is essential.

Costing in multi-product firms

When firms manufacture only one product, the process of product costing is relatively straightforward. All the costs of the business are directly attributable to the single product that is produced. The complexity of product costing occurs when an organisation produces more than one product. In multi-product firms, management is confronted with two main problems. Firstly, it is necessary to set up a system to account for costs that can be directly attributed to individual products. These costs are known as direct costs. For example, the amounts of raw materials used to produce individual products can normally be identified and a system is required to account for this direct cost. The second problem, which is more complicated, is to account for costs that are not directly attributed to any one product. There are two terms in accounting terminology for these types of costs— indirect or overhead costs. An example of an indirect cost is the cost of renting a factory in a multi-product firm, where it is impossible to attribute the cost directly to individual products.

Key Concept 18.1

Direct and indirect costs

A direct cost is one that is traceable, and thus attributable, to a product. Indirect costs (also known as overhead costs) are those that cannot be easily and conveniently identified with a particular product.

In this chapter we focus on two main approaches used in the determination of product costs in multi-product firms: marginal costing and full costing. Under the marginal-costing approach, only direct costs are included in the cost of the product. Costs that are not directly identifiable with products (indirect costs) are excluded from the cost of individual products. In contrast, the full-costing approach includes not only direct costs but also indirect costs. It is argued by those who favour the full-costing approach that, in order to facilitate the fair and equitable computation of product costs, overheads must be included.

Before we examine these two approaches it should be stressed that the need to identify the costs and revenues is not restricted to manufactured products but extends to services provided and to organisations that are purely service-oriented. An insurance broker, for instance, needs to identify costs of selling different types of policy, for example car insurance and life assurance, in order to determine the profitability of the varying policies that are sold. This information will influence what policies are sold and the mix of policies. For the purposes of our analysis we will focus on manufacturing organisations.

We begin our analysis by examining the full-costing approach for determining the cost of products.

Before we begin, however, study Note 9 in Woolworths' financial report (see Appendix 1). This note reports the results of the three segments of Woolworths. The supermarkets segment is by far the largest. Its revenue increased by $1220.8 million from 1998 to 1999 and yet profit for the segment increased by only $700 000. The general merchandise segment increased revenue by $221.9 million and profit by $10.7 million, and the wholesale segment increased revenue by $182.5 million and its loss decreased by $6.7 million.

The wholesale segment probably operates to break even and the general merchandise segment has performed satisfactorily for the year. Management should be concerned with the increase in supermarkets' revenue yielding very little increase in profit. It is important that you appreciate the usefulness of collecting costs and revenues by segments so that management can initiate policy reviews and implement strategies to control costs. This is, in fact, what management of Woolworths have indicated in the article in Case Study 16.1 (see p. 384).

Full costing

Definition

In a manufacturing organisation the costs incurred in producing and selling a product consist of production costs and other business expenses such as administration, selling and distribution expenses. The costs to be included in the full-costing approach might include all these costs or just some, e.g. the production costs. The definition of full costing adopted will depend upon the purpose for which products are being costed, and the preferences of management. For management purposes, accounting information, as has already been emphasised, is not regulated by any external forces, such as the law or accounting standards set by the professional accounting bodies. Management may adopt definitions and use accounting data at its discretion to meet the organisation's requirements. For external financial reporting purposes in Australia, entities must comply with *AASB 1019: Inventories* as discussed in Chapter 7. This Standard requires companies to use the absorption (full) costing method for inventories for external financial reports.

For purposes of our analysis we will adopt the definition of full costing that includes only production costs. This is the definition of full costing conventionally used for the purpose of valuing finished inventories and work in progress, which was discussed in Chapter 7. In the context of inventory valuations, it is argued that it is only appropriate to include those costs that are incurred prior to sale of the inventory. Normally, these costs will consist of only those related to production.

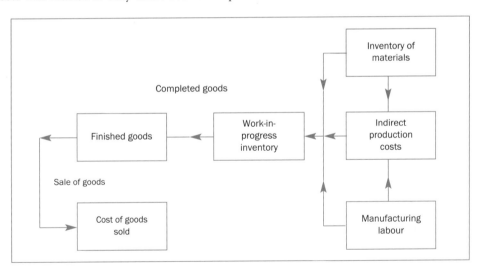

Figure 18.1 *The flow of costs in a manufacturing organisation under the full-costing approach.*

Figure 18.1 shows the flow of costs associated with a manufacturing organisation when the full-costing approach is adopted, where 'full cost' represents only those costs associated with production, whether they are direct or indirect costs. Materials and labour are classified here as both direct and indirect costs. For example, in the case of manufacturing labour the arrows are directed both to work in progress (i.e. directly into the production process, thereby indicating that they are a direct cost) and to indirect production costs (i.e. indicating they are an indirect cost). The classification of these costs into direct and indirect, not surprisingly, will depend upon whether the cost can be identified directly with products or not.

Key Concept 18.2

Full costing

The full cost of a product consists of the direct and indirect costs of production.

Sometimes it is more convenient to classify a cost as indirect even though it is possible to identify it directly with a product. Consider, for example, the labour costs of a supervisor who is responsible for a group of employees working on various products. An elaborate system would have to be set up to record the time supervising each employee and then to relate this time (and thus costs) to particular products. In this case it may be considered more cost-effective and convenient simply to classify supervision costs as indirect.

An example of indirect material cost is the cost of machine lubricant. Indirect costs, other than materials and labour, are typically costs related to heating, lighting, training and the depreciation of machinery and premises (if owned). All direct production costs are 'absorbed' into the products being produced, so that at any point in time the value of work in progress and finished goods consists of materials, labour and indirect costs. The cost of goods sold is matched with the revenue from the sales of these goods in the statement of financial performance. When full costing is applied, as in our definition, the cost of goods sold consists of both direct and indirect production costs, as shown in Figure 18.1.

Product and period costs

Before examining the procedures that are used to absorb indirect costs into product costs, it is appropriate to consider another classification of costs, namely period costs. Any costs not categorised as product costs are normally classified as period costs.

Product costs, as we have already mentioned, are recognised in the statement of financial performance only when the product is sold. Prior to the sale, the cost of products is shown as an asset (either as work in progress or finished goods) in the statement of financial position, thereby indicating that these items have some future benefit to the business. The principle adopted here is the concept of accruals. Period costs, in contrast, are seen as costs that relate to the current period in question. They are therefore viewed as costs that cannot justifiably be carried forward to future periods because they do not represent future benefits or because the future benefits are so uncertain as to defy measurement. Thus, period costs are recognised in the statement of financial performance in the accounting period when they are incurred. The distinction between product and period is important in the valuation of inventory and the determination of income. We examine the effect of this categorisation of costs in further detail later in this chapter, when we analyse the differences between marginal costing and full costing.

Absorbing overheads

We have already mentioned that a system has to be devised to trace costs to individual products. This process is relatively straightforward for direct costs since they can be identified precisely with a particular product. For example, when materials are obtained from inventory, their cost is recorded against the product and accounted for as a cost to the product. The complexity arises when we have to share out indirect costs to products. The objective is to share them out equitably. The method adopted should therefore take into account the amount of indirect services used to support the manufacture of products. The term used for the process of sharing out indirect costs to products is 'absorption of overheads'.

Production overhead costs are incurred by cost centres that support the production activity. A 'goods inwards' department, whose function it is to ensure that goods and materials received from suppliers are of the standard and quantity ordered, is a typical example of a service cost centre in a manufacturing organisation. The overhead costs of both the production and service cost centres must be absorbed into the product to establish the full cost of products.

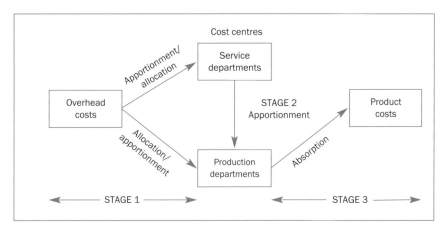

Figure 18.2 *Stages in the absorption of overheads.*

At this stage it is appropriate to summarise the stages in the absorption of overheads. Figure 18.2 shows the three stages in this process, which we go on to examine in detail.

Stage 1

The first stage in the absorption of overhead costs is to identify and collect overhead costs associated with both the production and service cost centres. Some of these costs can be relatively easily allocated to particular cost centres. The word 'allocated', in the context of product costing, means that the cost can be directly traced to a cost centre. For example, in a drawing office, classified as a service cost centre because it provides a service to a number of production cost centres, the salaries of draughtsmen and women can be identified with the centre by recording the salary payment from the payroll against the cost centre. In contrast, the cost of heating and lighting consumed by the drawing office may not be so easy to establish. The cost of heating and lighting is probably billed for the whole building, in which the drawing office is only one of many occupant cost centres. In such cases, because the cost is difficult, if not impossible, to identify accurately with any one cost centre, a method of apportioning these costs on a fair and equitable basis must be adopted. The term 'apportioning' describes the sharing out of overhead costs that cannot be directly traced to a cost centre. A reasonable method of apportioning heat and lighting costs that relate to the benefits (i.e. heating and lighting) enjoyed by the drawing office is on the basis of the area that the office occupies. For example, if the total cost of heating and lighting is $15 000 and the area used by the drawing office, measured in square metres, is 6000 out of a total area of the building of 30 000 square metres, the cost apportioned to the drawing office would be $15 000 × 6000 ÷ 30 000 = $3000.

Stage 2

When all the overhead costs, allocated and apportioned, have been established for each service cost centre, it is then necessary to charge these costs to the production cost centres. Once again some method of apportionment has to be used. The reason for this is that the service cost centres normally service several production cost centres and the costs of the service are unlikely to be easily identified with any one of them. Using the example of the drawing office again, it is likely that the service supplied by this office spreads over a number of production cost centres and it will be impractical to identify accurately the cost of this service with production departments. In these circumstances, a method of apportionment has to be adopted that fairly charges the service cost to the production cost centres. Before we move to stage 3 of the process of absorbing overhead costs into products, we will consider an example that illustrates the allocation and apportionment of costs to production cost centres.

Example 18.1

This example demonstrates the allocation and apportionment of overhead costs to production cost centres, as shown in Table 18.1 (see p. 421). Costs for various overhead 'items' are first identified and shown under 'total amount'. The costs are then allocated or apportioned to production and service cost centres. In the case of indirect labour and materials, the costs are allocated to these cost centres because they can be directly identified with them. With reference to the table, of the total amount of indirect materials consumed ($20 000), $8000 has been directly identified with production cost centre A. In contrast, the costs related to power, rent and rates, and insurance cannot be directly identified with the cost centres. Therefore, they are apportioned to the centres, using some equitable basis reflecting the benefits the centres have enjoyed. In the case of the cost of power, for example, the number of machine hours consumed by the cost centres is considered an equitable basis for apportionment. If you refer to the information relating to the use of machine hours in the example, you will notice that machinery was used only in the two production cost centres. Of the total of 110 000 machine hours, 50 000 were consumed by production cost centre A and 60 000 hours by cost centre B. The cost of electricity for each of these centres is then calculated with reference to the consumption by the two departments as shown below.

	$
Production cost centre	
A 50 000 hours ÷ 110 000 hours × $22 000 =	10 000
B 60 000 hours ÷ 110 000 hours × $22 000 =	12 000
Total cost of electricity	22 000

Therefore the apportioned charge to production cost centre A is $10 000 and to B is $12 000.

Similar calculations using different assumptions are made to establish the apportioned charge to the cost centres for rent and rates, and insurance.

After allocating and apportioning the overheads to the production and service cost centres, the next stage is to apportion the service centre costs to the production cost centres. The basis of apportionment chosen, in the case of service cost centre X, is the

TABLE 18.1
ALLOCATION AND APPORTIONMENT OF THE COSTS OF ONE YEAR

Item	Basis	Total amount	Production cost centres		Service cost centres	
			A	B	X	Y
		$000	$000	$000	$000	$000
Indirect materials	Allocated	20	8	4	5	3
Indirect labour	Allocated	30	14	6	4	6
Electricity	Machine hours	22	10	12	–	–
Rent and rates	Area	10	2	5	2	1
Insurance	Book value	8	3	2	3	–
Total overheads		90	37	29	14	10
Service X to production	Number of employees		5	9	(14)	
Service Y to production	Direct labour hours		8	2		(10)
Total overheads		90	50	40	–	–

Data used for apportioning overheads

Item	Quantity					
Machine hours	110 000		50 000	60 000	–	–
Area	3 000 sq. m		600	1 500	600	300
Book value of fixed assets	$96 000		$36	$24	$36	–
No. of employees	7 000		2 500	4 500		
Direct labour hours	20 000		16 000	4 000	–	–

number of employees in each production cost centre. The number of direct labour hours worked by the employees in the production cost centres is the basis of apportionment used for service centre Y. As previously mentioned, the basis of apportionment should reflect the benefits enjoyed by the consuming production cost centres. For example, it might be that service cost centre X is the works canteen. If so, the number of employees in each production cost centre might be a reasonable basis for calculating the amount of use made of this facility by each of the two production cost centres. The calculation of the apportioned charge to the production cost centres is very similar to the calculation described above for apportioning electricity costs. Thus, in the case of service cost centre X the calculation will be as follows.

	$
Production cost centre	
A (2500 ÷ 7000) × $14 000 =	5 000
B (4500 ÷ 7000) × $14 000 =	9 000
Total cost of service cost centre X	14 000

It can be seen that the whole of the costs of service centre X are now apportioned to the two production cost centres. Similar calculations will be made to apportion the cost of service cost centre Y to the two production cost centres. Finally, the overhead costs are aggregated for each of the two production cost centres, as can be seen in the final line in the example.

Stage 3

As has been mentioned, the production cost centres are where the manufacturing activity takes place. Units of products physically pass through these cost centres in the course of the manufacturing cycle. As the products pass through the centre, a proportion of the overhead cost is charged to the product (or absorbed into the product). The objective here is to charge overheads to units of production on some equitable basis. Normally an absorption rate is used for this purpose. The absorption rate is determined by the following formula.

$$\frac{\text{total overheads of a production cost centre}}{\text{level of activity}}$$

We discussed how the numerator in this formula is determined in stage 2 above. The denominator, the activity level, is chosen with reference to the types of products passing through the production cost centres and the main activities of these centres. If, for example, the particular products passing through the centre are homogeneous, i.e. similar in construction, the appropriate activity to be chosen is likely to be the number of units worked on in the production centre. In these circumstances the activity, units of production, should represent an equitable basis for absorbing the overheads because the benefits enjoyed by each unit from the expenditure of overheads should be equal or very similar. In Example 18.1, if it was estimated that 10 000 units were to be worked on in the year by production cost centre A, and assuming the products were homogeneous, the absorption rate would be $50 000 ÷ 10 000 units = $5 per unit. This rate would then be applied to each unit of production worked on in the cost centre and would represent a reasonable share of the overhead cost appropriate to each product.

In contrast, if the products are not homogeneous it is necessary to choose an activity measure that corresponds more closely with the overhead expenditure of each production cost centre. If, for example, overhead expenditure of a production cost centre is mainly incurred in supporting the direct labour function, the measure chosen should be based on this activity. In these circumstances the number of direct hours would be a suitable measure.

In practice, the most common activity measures used to absorb overheads into product costs are the following:

- direct labour hours
- direct labour costs
- machine hours
- cost of materials.

The following shows the calculation of the absorption rate with reference to the data given in Example 18.1 for production cost centre A, assuming that the number of machine hours is the appropriate activity measure.

$$\frac{\text{total overheads of cost centre A}}{\text{level of activity}} = \frac{\$50\,000}{50\,000\text{ machine hours}}$$

Therefore the absorption rate is $1 per machine hour. This rate is applied to units of product passing through cost centre A. For example, if one of the products passing through cost centre A uses up 40 machine hours in the manufacturing process, the charge to the product will be

$$40\text{ hours} \times \$1\text{ per machine hour} = \$40$$

Predetermined overhead absorption rates

In practice, overhead absorption rates are normally determined once a year, before the actual cost is incurred. Thus, the two elements of the above formula will be estimates. That is, the total overheads of each production cost centre and the level of activity chosen are based on estimates rather than on actual costs.

There are two main reasons why estimates are used rather than actual costs. Firstly, some overhead costs are not known until some months after they have been incurred. For example, electricity costs are normally billed to consumers at the end of each three months. Therefore, an organisation would have to wait three months before it could determine this overhead cost, and only then could it charge the cost to products that had already been manufactured and sold. Clearly, such a delay in determining costs would mean that management received out-of-date information. Secondly, some overhead costs, such as heating costs, are seasonal. Seasonal variations can distort the costing of products. For example, if a product is manufactured in summer, the cost of heating absorbed into the product cost is likely to be zero, whereas if the product was manufactured in winter, the cost would include a charge for heating. Thus, the cost of a product can depend upon when it was produced. It can be argued that such circumstances distort the costing of products, and a firm would have to set up complex costing systems to reflect seasonal variations.

The use of estimates in determining the overhead absorption rate creates problems. Often the actual overheads incurred during a period are not equal to the overheads that have been absorbed into product costs because the absorption rate is based on estimates. The amount of overheads absorbed during a period will be the same as the cost actually incurred only if the actual overhead cost of the production cost centre is equal to the estimated cost (the numerator in the formula) and the actual level of activity is equal to the estimated activity level (the denominator in the formula). Normally, any difference between the total overheads absorbed and the actual overheads incurred during a period is directly charged to the statement of financial performance for that period. These differences in costs are not allocated or apportioned to products, but are classified as a period cost. It is generally seen as impractical and too costly to identify these differences for individual products, but large differences might need to be investigated.

Example 18.2 illustrates the process of absorbing overheads into units of production where the actual overhead cost is different from the original estimates on which the absorption rate was based.

Example 18.2

The following are estimates relating to the manufacture of a number of similar products for the forthcoming year 20X1.

Estimated units to be produced during the year	100 000
Estimated overhead cost during the year	$150 000

Therefore the overhead absorption rate is calculated thus:

$$\frac{\$150\,000}{100\,000 \text{ units}} = \$1.50 \text{ per unit}$$

The actual number of units produced in 20X1 was 110 000; thus, the charge to products passing through the cost centre is 110 000 units × $1.50 (the absorption rate) = $165 000.

However, the overheads actually incurred during 20X1 were $176 000. Thus, the difference between actual overhead costs and what was absorbed during the year is $176 000 − $165 000 = $11 000. This $11 000 is charged to the statement of financial performance as 'under-recovery of overhead' during the year; it is classified as a period cost because it is not identified with any of the units of production produced during the year.

In this example, the cost and the activity level were underestimated during the year. Differences between estimates and actual costs and activity levels often occur in practice, because it is very difficult to make accurate estimates.

Case Study 18.1 illustrates a number of the procedures and principles regarding the absorption of overheads that we have discussed.

CASE STUDY 18.1

Sarick Machines Ltd

Sarick Machines Ltd has organised its production cost centres by the types of machines it uses to manufacture its products. There are four production cost centres which are known by the machine type—101, 201, 301 and 401. The company wishes to establish an overhead absorption rate for each of these cost centres, based on machine hours. The company also wishes to determine the cost per unit of one of its products, Aztec.

The management of the company has made the following estimates for the forthcoming year 20X3.

	$	$
Indirect materials		
Machine type 101	300	
Machine type 201	600	
Machine type 301	700	
Machine type 401	400	2 000
Maintenance costs		
Machine type 101	700	
Machine type 201	800	
Machine type 301	1 200	
Machine type 401	900	3 600
Other overhead expenses		
Electricity		1 400
Rent and rates		3 200
Heat and lighting		800
Insurance of buildings		800
Insurance of machinery		1 000
Depreciation of machinery		10 000
Supervision		4 800
Total overheads		27 600

Management provides the following relevant information, based on estimates.

Machine type	Effective horsepower	Area occupied sq. m	Book value of machinery $	Working hours
101	10	400	5 000	2 000
201	15	300	7 500	1 000
301	45	800	22 500	3 000
401	30	500	15 000	2 000
	100	2 000	50 000	8 000

To determine the machine hour rate, we must first allocate costs that can be directly identified with the four cost centres, i.e. the indirect materials and the maintenance costs. We then need to apportion those overheads that cannot be directly identified with a cost centre, i.e. those described in our example as 'other overhead expenses'. This is done by sharing out these overheads to the cost centres based on some equitable method that reflects the use made of these resources. The following sets out the apportioning of costs to the four cost centres. The basis of apportionment is indicated in parentheses.

Machine type	101	201	301	401
	$	$	$	$
Costs allocated				
Indirect materials	300	600	700	400
Maintenance costs	700	800	1 200	900
Costs apportioned				
Electricity (effective horsepower)	140	210	630	420
Rent and rates (area)	640	480	1 280	800
Light and heating (area)	160	120	320	200
Insurance on building (area)	160	120	320	200
Insurance on machines				
(book value of machine)	100	150	450	300
Depreciation of machines				
(book value of machine)	1 000	1 500	4 500	3 000
Supervision (working hours)	1 200	600	1 800	1 200
Total overheads	4 400	4 580	11 200	7 420

The calculation of the apportioned costs to the cost centres in this Case Study is similar to that in Example 18.1. To illustrate it further, the calculation of the apportioned costs of rent and rates to cost centres is shown below.

Machine type	Calculation	Cost
		$
101	(400 sq. m ÷ 2 000 sq. m) × $3 200 =	640
201	(300 sq. m ÷ 2 000 sq. m) × $3 200 =	480
301	(800 sq. m ÷ 2 000 sq. m) × $3 200 =	1 280
401	(500 sq. m ÷ 2 000 sq. m) × $3 200 =	800
Total cost of rent and rates apportioned		3 200

The basis of apportionment for each type of overhead cost, we can assume, has been chosen because it represents a reasonable method for sharing out the cost and reflects the benefits enjoyed by the cost centre from the resource. For example, the supervision cost has been apportioned on the basis of working hours and it is likely that this basis reasonably reflects the benefits enjoyed from this resource by each cost centre.

Now that the total overheads have been collected for each of the four cost centres, we can divide these costs by the estimated working hours of each machine to obtain the absorption rate.

Machine type	Calculation	Cost
		$
101	$4 400 ÷ 2 000 hours =	2.20
201	$4 580 ÷ 1 000 hours =	4.58
301	$11 200 ÷ 3 000 hours =	3.73
101	$7 420 ÷ 2 000 hours =	3.71

An alternative system that could be adopted by the company would be to absorb the total overhead cost by the total estimated machine hours. In this case it would not be necessary to allocate and apportion costs to individual cost centres because the same rate would be applied to all cost centres. The overhead absorption rate would therefore be

$$\text{total costs} \div \text{total hours} = \$27\,600 \div 8\,000 \text{ hours}$$
$$= \$3.45 \text{ per machine hour}$$

This rate is then charged to all items of production passing through all cost centres. Although this method is appealing, because far less time is spent in calculating the overhead absorption rate, it does not take account of the resources consumed by the individual cost centres in the production process. It is therefore likely that such a system would distort the costing of individual products.

Turning now to the product costs of Aztec, the following information is given. A total of 2000 units were produced in the year. The direct costs incurred were:
- direct material, $870
- direct labour, $940.

The machine hours actually worked in the year, producing 2000 units of Aztec, were as follows:

Machine type	Hours
101	400
201	400
401	200

To determine the cost per unit, we first need to determine the total cost associated with the manufacture of the product. The direct costs are given above. The overhead costs to be absorbed into the product are based on the overhead absorption rate, the machine hour rate and the actual hours worked in these cost centres on the product. The total cost of product Aztec is as follows.

	$
Direct material	870
Direct labour	940
Machine type 101: 400 hours × $2.20 =	880
Machine type 201: 400 hours × $4.58 =	1 832
Machine type 401: 200 hours × $3.71 =	742
Total cost	5 264

It is now necessary to divide the total cost by the number of units produced to determine the cost per unit.

$$\$5264 \div 2000 \text{ units} = \$2.63 \text{ per unit}$$

Activity-based costing

In the use of absorption costing, as shown in Case Study 18.1, an overhead absorption rate is determined. This rate is calculated by dividing the overhead cost of a production department by a selected volume of activity. In Case Study 18.1, the activity chosen was machine hours, and the rationale for this choice was that the overhead costs have been incurred supporting one particular activity. With advanced manufacturing technology, overhead costs tend to be predominant, and direct cost tends to be a very small proportion of cost. The majority of today's overhead costs are not necessarily incurred in direct manufacturing activities but rather as a result of transactions in the service departments where the overhead is incurred. Activity-based costing (ABC) tries to capture this change in technology by apportioning overheads into product costs on a more realistic basis that takes account of the activity and transactions that drive the cost. Thus, costs are grouped according to what drives them or causes them to increase. These cost drivers are then used as the bases upon which overhead costs are absorbed into the product. The following example illustrates the way in which ABC is used, and contrasts this method of full costing with absorption costing.

Example 18.3

Onyx Ltd manufactures two products, X and Y. The manufacturing process for the two products is very similar. The following details the product data for these two products for 20X4:

	X	Y
Units produced	5 000	7 000
Direct labour hours per unit	1	2
Number of set-ups	10	40
Number of orders	15	60
Machine hours	3	1
		$

Overhead costs:	
Cost of setting up	20 000
Cost of handling orders	45 000
Costs relating to machine activity	220 000
Total overhead costs	285 000

The company wishes to determine the cost per unit in respect of overhead costs, using:

a absorption costing, absorbing costs on the basis of direct labour hours and machine hours, and

b ABC using suitable cost drivers to trace overheads to cost.

a Absorption costing

Direct labour hour basis		Total direct labour hours
Product:		
X	(5 000 x 1 h)	5 000
Y	(7 000 x 2 h)	14 000
Total		19 000

Total overhead costs: $285 000.

Therefore the overhead absorption rate is

$$\frac{\$285\ 000}{19\ 000\ \text{hours}} = \$15 \text{ per direct labour hour}$$

The overhead is absorbed into each unit of:

$$X \quad 1\ h \times \$15 = \$15 \text{ per unit}$$
$$Y \quad 2\ h \times \$15 = \$30 \text{ per unit}$$

Machine hour basis		Total machine hours
Product:		
X	(5 000 units x 3 h)	15 000
Y	(7 000 units x 1 h)	7 000
Total		22 000

Total overhead costs: $285 000.

Therefore, the overhead absorption rate is

$$\frac{\$285\ 000}{22\ 000\ \text{hours}} = \$12.95 \text{ per machine hour}$$

The overhead absorbed into each unit is as follows:

X	3 hours × $12.95 = $38.85
Y	1 hour × $12.95 = $12.95

b Activity-based costing

The appropriate cost drivers in this example are those which relate to the way in which overhead costs are incurred. Overhead costs are those relating to machine activity, product run set-ups and the number of orders handled.

The overhead costs, based on the following cost drivers, will be absorbed into products:

Machining costs	$220 000/22 000 h	=	$10 per machine hour
Set-up driven costs	$20 000/50 set-ups	=	$400 per set-up
Order driven costs	$45 000/75 orders	=	$600 per order

Product costs:

X			$
Machine costs	(15 000 h x $10)	=	150 000
Set-up costs	(10 x $400)	=	4 000
Order costs	(15 x $600)	=	9 000
Total		=	163 000
Unit cost	$163 0Q0/5 000	=	$32.60

Y			$
Machine costs	(7 000 h x $10)	=	70 000
Set-up costs	(40 x $400)	=	16 000
Order costs	(60 x $600)	=	36 000
Total		=	122 000
Unit cost	$122 000/7 000	=	$17.43

Commentary

i   *Direct labour hour basis:* None or very little of the overhead costs appears to be incurred in support of the direct labour activity. That is, overhead costs are not driven by the direct labour activity. Using direct labour hours as the basis for apportioning overhead costs in these circumstances could distort the costs apportioned to individual products. From the example it can be seen that product Y, relatively under the direct labour hour basis, absorbs an unrealistic amount of overhead costs. This is simply because more direct labour hours are worked on Y than on X.

ii *Machine hour basis:* Although this basis for absorbing overheads clearly takes account of the main cost driver—machine-related costs—it does ignore other cost drivers associated with overhead costs, namely handling and set-up costs.

iii *Activity-based costings:* A more realistic basis for absorbing costs because it takes account of all the significant cost drivers. The following steps are taken when employing ABC as shown in the example:

Step 1: Identify major activities, e.g. machining, production runs and orders.

Step 2: Collect the overhead costs in a cost pool for each major activity.

Step 3: Determine the cost drivers for each activity.

Machining—cost per machine hour

Production runs—cost per set-up

Number of orders—cost per order

Step 4: Trace the cost of the activities to the product, using the cost drivers as a measure of demand.

CASE STUDY 18.2

COMPANY PRESS RELEASE

Energy companies turn to activity-based costing to identify profitable customers in deregulated markets

ATLANTA—When two energy customers buy the same products and services at the same price and at the same time, are those customers equally profitable?

In today's high competitive energy arena, all customers are not created equal. In fact, for energy companies to win under deregulation they will have to distinguish between profitable customers and 'losers', according to an exclusive report in the current issue of Energy Competition Strategy Report.

Smart energy executives are turning to activity-based cost management (ABC/M), financial experts say, to help identify desirable customers and, at the same time, track and cut costs.

In a revealing look at the power of ABC/M to help companies understand where they make and lose money, the director of industry relations at the nation's leading supplier of activity-based management software shares the three steps energy companies must take to make their customers more profitable. And executives at two energy companies—Duke Energy and Tampa Electric Company (TECO)—reveal why they chose ABC/M to track costs and better manage business processes.

'This is a great opportunity for companies looking for ways to increase profitability to find out how to better align their cost structure with their business strategies,' says David Schwartz, president of NHI publications, publisher of ECSR. 'Duke is using ABC to identify activity costs at its three nuclear power stations. And TECO has improved cash flow by more than $2 million since it implemented activity-based cost management with a five-step process that TECO executives reveal in this issue.'

The report includes ABC-related cost-saving opportunities in meter department processes, contributions in aid of construction, meeting costs, and other key areas.

NHI Publications, 26 July 2000 (abridged)

Commentary

This extract reveals that energy companies are making use of activity-based costing to identify profitable customers from 'losers' and thus allow them to control costs and increase profits. Activity-based costing is a powerful tool which more and more companies are using to properly allocate and control costs and to set more appropriate prices for products.

Types of production process

In the examination of full costing, we discussed the general principles of costing systems that take into account direct and indirect costs. In practice there are a number of different types of costing systems that are contingent on the type of technology used in the production process and the type of product being produced. Traditionally, the systems are classified into two categories: job costing and process costing.

At this stage of your studies it is not necessary to examine these two systems in detail, but a brief description will be useful. Job-costing systems are used when the costs of each unit of production, or a batch of units, can be identified at any time in the manufacturing cycle. The examples we have looked at mirror the job-costing system. In contrast, in a system of process costing, individual products cannot be identified until the manufacturing process is complete. A number of similar products are manufactured at the same time within the process. Costs are accumulated on a process or departmental basis and are then divided by the number of units produced to obtain an average unit cost. In such cases, product costs represent the average unit costs of production.

Marginal costing

In this chapter so far, no reference has been made to fixed and variable costs. Variable costs, as previously defined, vary in proportion to production. The term 'marginal cost' refers to the change in total costs resulting from the production of one more (or less) unit of production. The marginal cost is synonymous with the variable cost of a product, and in the context of product costing we assume that these two terms have the same meaning.

The classifications of costs that we have concentrated on in this chapter are direct and indirect costs. We have defined a direct cost as one that is traceable, and thus attributable, to a given cost objective—in our case, a product. For a multi-product firm, the only direct costs that can be identified with a product are those costs that change when production increases or decreases.

Key Concept 18.3

Marginal costing
Only direct production costs are included in marginal costing.

When we defined product costs, in the case of full costing we said that both direct and indirect costs of production should be included in the cost. It follows that product costs, in this case, will include both fixed and variable costs of production. The process of absorbing overheads, and in particular the apportionment of costs, although based on clearly identified criteria, is relatively arbitrary. Often several equally fair bases for apportioning overhead costs are available. However, the use of these different bases will result in differing amounts of costs being apportioned to products. The cost of a product often depends on the choice of the basis used to apportion costs. It is part of the job of a management accountant to examine the basis of apportioning costs.

In the following chapters relating to decision making it will be argued that fixed costs should be ignored in the decision-making process, i.e. they are irrelevant to the decision. This is another argument in support of marginal costing rather than full costing.

The use of the full costing method can distort costing and the value placed upon products. Those who oppose full costing argue that the only costs that should be classified as product costs are those that are direct, which we are assuming in this analysis are only marginal costs. All other production costs, i.e. fixed overheads, are classified as period costs.

Although marginal costing of products is attractive and convenient, it implies that fixed costs are not incurred in the production process. This is clearly not true. Expenditure on fixed costs is just as essential in the manufacture of products as expenditure on marginal costs.

In recent years the case for inclusion of fixed costs in product costs has gained momentum as the proportion of fixed costs incurred in the manufacture of products has grown as a result of automation. Most of the costs associated with automation, such as the cost of machinery, are fixed costs. Another argument in support of full costing is that the omission of fixed costs causes the cost of products to be understated. For example, if the costs of a unit of production consist of $2 of marginal costs and $10 of fixed costs, the value given to this product for inventory valuation under the marginal-costing regime will be just $2. The cost of resources employed in the production of this unit, and thus its true value, is clearly more than $2! It is therefore not surprising that in practice firms tend to favour full costing for inventory valuation.

These methods of costing all have their virtues, and to some extent the method preferred is dependent on its application. For example, in the case of future decision making the arguments in favour of marginal costing as the preferred method are well documented, as we will see in Chapters 19 and 20. However, the preference is not so clear when other applications are considered. The preferred method depends on individual judgements regarding the strengths and weaknesses of the two methods.

Perhaps the most controversial debate regarding the use of full and marginal costing relates to inventory valuation and its effect on income measurement. It is therefore appropriate to examine these two methods of product costing in more detail.

Measuring income and valuing inventory

In Case Study 18.3, we consider a firm that produces only one product. In such a situation all the costs are by definition identifiable with the one product and therefore are classified as direct costs whether they are fixed or variable. However, in practice the distinction between these two classifications is still valid in this situation. The reason for this, as mentioned in the discussion on overhead absorption rates, is that many of the indirect costs are not known until some months after they have been incurred. For management purposes it is often preferable to absorb these costs using estimates, rather than waiting until the actual cost can be determined. In Case Studies 18.3 and 18.4 we treat fixed factory overheads in a similar way to their treatment in a multi-product firm.

Door Chime Company Ltd

The Door Chime Company Ltd manufactures and sells one design of door chime. The following are the costs of production for 20X1.

marginal costs (direct cost), $3.00 per unit
fixed factory overhead absorption rate, $2.00 per unit

The fixed factory overhead rate is based on estimates of overhead costs of $40 000 and an activity level of 20 000 units. Actual fixed overheads incurred in 20X1 were $40 000. The sales price is $8.00 per unit.

Sales and production data for 20X1 in units is as follows.

	Units
Opening inventory of finished goods	1 000
Production	20 000
Sales	20 000
Closing inventory of finished goods	1 000

During 20X1 selling expenses were $1600 and administration expenses not associated with production were $1000.

We will begin by producing a statement of financial performance for 20X1, using the absorption costing approach, and assume that any over- or under-absorption of overheads is charged or credited to the statement of financial performance as a period cost.

DOOR CHIME COMPANY LTD
STATEMENT OF FINANCIAL PERFORMANCE FOR
20X1 (USING ABSORPTION COSTING)

	$	$
Sales (20 000 @ $8)		160 000
Less Cost of goods sold		
Opening inventory of finished goods (1000 @ $5)	5 000	
Plus production (20 000 @ $5)	100 000	
Cost of goods available for sale	105 000	
Less Closing inventory of finished goods (1000 @ $5)	5 000	100 000
Gross Profit		60 000
Less Period costs		
Administration	1 000	
Selling	1 600	
Over- or under-absorption of overheads	—	2 600
Net Profit		57 400

The production and the opening and closing inventory of finished goods in this statement, using the absorption costing approach, are costed at the full cost of the product, i.e. the direct costs of $3 and the overheads absorbed at $2 per unit. You will also note that there are no movements in the opening and closing inventories during the year. This is because the units produced are equal to those sold.

The period costs are represented by selling and administration expenses; thus they are not included in the production cost.

There is no over- or under-absorption of overheads. This is because the total overheads absorbed ($2 per unit multiplied by the number of units produced, 20 000, i.e. $40 000) are the same as the actual overheads incurred during the year.

DOOR CHIME COMPANY LTD
STATEMENT OF FINANCIAL PERFORMANCE FOR 20X1
(USING MARGINAL COSTING)

	$	$
Sales		160 000
Less Cost of goods sold		
Opening inventory of finished goods (1000 @ $3)	3 000	
Production (20 000 @ $3)	60 000	
Cost of goods available for sale	63 000	
Less Closing inventory of goods sold (1000 @ $3)	3 000	
Contribution		60 000
		100 000
Less Period costs		
Fixed factory overheads	40 000	
Administration	1 000	
Selling	1 600	42 600
Net Profit		57 400

That is, the net profit is the same in both cases.

From these statements of financial performance it can be seen that the main differences between absorption and marginal costing are as follows.
- The product costs: the production costs and the values of opening and closing inventories of finished goods consist only of the direct costs of $3 per unit.
- Fixed factory overheads are classified as period costs under the marginal-costing approach and are not included as product costs.
- The summation of sales revenue less cost of goods sold represents the contribution; contribution was earlier defined as sales less marginal costs (see Chapter 17).
- Both methods of costing in this case study produce the same profit figure.

Now consider Case Study 18.4, where there is a movement in inventories over the two-year period. The units produced here are greater (20X2) or less (20X3) than those sold.

CASE STUDY 18.4

We assume that the costs and sales price are the same as in Case Study 18.3 for the following years 20X2 and 20X3.

Sales and production data, in terms of units, for 20X2 and 20X3 are as follows.

	20X2 Units	20X3 Units
Opening stock of finished goods	1 000	6 000
Production	22 000	16 000
Sales	17 000	21 000
Closing inventory of finished goods	6 000	1 000

We also assume that the overhead absorption rate, actual overheads incurred, administration and selling expenses are the same as in Case Study 18.3.

We begin our analysis by considering the absorption-costing method.

DOOR CHIME COMPANY LTD
STATEMENT OF FINANCIAL PERFORMANCE (USING ABSORPTION COSTING)

20X2	$	$	$
Sales (17 000 @ $8)		136 000	
Less Cost of goods sold			
Opening inventory of finished goods (1000 @ $5)	5 000		
Production (22 000 @ $5)	110 000		
Cost of goods available for sale	115 000		
Less Closing inventory of finished goods (6000 @ $5)	30 000	85 000	
Gross Profit		51 000	
Less Period costs			
Over-absorption of overheads—see note below	(4 000)		
Administration costs	1 000		
Selling costs	1 600	(1 400)	
Net Profit		52 400	

Over-absorption of overheads		
Overheads absorbed during the year (22 000 units @ $2)		44 000
Actual overheads incurred during the year		40 000
Over-absorption of overheads		4 000

NOTE: The $4000 represents the amount that we have overcharged to products during the period. That is, we have charged $44 000 through applying the absorption rate, which is based on estimates, while the actual overhead costs were $40 000. The difference will therefore be credited to the statement of financial performance.

20X3	$	$	$
Sales (21 000 @ $8)		168 000	
Less Cost of goods sold			
Opening inventory of finished goods (6000 @ $5)	30 000		
Production (16 000 @ $5)	80 000		
Cost of goods available for sale	110 000		
Less Closing inventory of finished goods (1000 @ $5)	5 000	105 000	
Gross Profit		63 000	
Less Period costs			
Under-absorption of overheads—see note below	8 000		
Administration	1 000		
Selling	1 600	10 600	
Net Profit		52 400	

Overheads absorbed during the year (16 000 @ $2)		32 000
Actual overheads incurred during the year		40 000
Under-absorption of overheads		8 000

NOTE: In this case we have absorbed less than we estimated by $8000 and this amount will therefore be charged to the statement of financial performance as a period cost.

DOOR CHIME COMPANY LTD
STATEMENT OF FINANCIAL PERFORMANCE (USING MARGINAL COSTING)

20X2	$	$
Sales		136 000
Less Cost of goods sold		
Opening inventory of finished goods (1000 @ $3)	3 000	
Production (22 000 @ $3)	66 000	
Cost of goods available for sale	69 000	
Less Closing inventory of finished goods (6000 @ $3)	18 000	51 000
Contribution		85 000
Less Period costs		
Fixed factory overheads	40 000	
Administration	1 000	
Selling	1 600	42 600
Net Profit		42 400

20X2	$	$
Sales		168 000
Less Cost of goods sold		
Opening inventory of finished goods (6000 @ $3)	18 000	
Production (16 000 @ $3)	48 000	
Cost of goods available for sale	66 000	
Less Closing inventory of finished goods (1000 @ $3)	3 000	63 000
Contribution		105 000
Less Period costs		
Fixed factory overheads	40 000	
Administration costs	1 000	
Selling	1 600	42 600
Net Profit		62 400

The following summarises the differences between the net profits of the methods used above.

	20X2 $	20X3 $
Marginal costing	42 400	62 400
Absorption costing	52 400	52 400
Net profit difference	(10 000)	10 000

The difference in the net profit over these two years is a direct result of the methods used. In the case of absorption costing, fixed costs are classified as product costs and are therefore included in the valuation of inventories. When there is an increase in inventories during a period (in 20X2), the fixed costs associated with these inventories are included in the inventory value rather than being included (recognised) as a cost in the 'cost of goods sold' computation. In contrast, when there has been a decrease in inventory during a period (in 20X3), which means a proportion of the goods sold (5000 units) has been obtained from the opening inventory rather than production, the fixed costs related to these inventories are realised as expenses and matched against sales. In the case of the marginal-costing approach, all fixed costs during a period, because they are classified as period costs, are charged in the statement of financial performance in the period in which they are incurred.

The following summarises the movement in inventories over the two-year period.

Movement in finished inventories	20X2 Units	20X3 Units
Opening	1 000	6 000
Closing	6 000	1 000
Difference	5 000	(5000)

In 20X2 there was an increase in inventories of 5000 units. Under the absorption-costing approach, the fixed cost element of these stocks (5000 units × $2 absorption rate = $10 000) is included as an asset in the period. But in the case of a marginal-costing approach, these fixed costs ($10 000) will be charged, as period costs, to the statement of financial performance in 20X2, i.e. when they were incurred. The net profit in the case of absorption costing is $10 000 more than the profit under the marginal-costing approach.

The reverse situation arises in 20X3. In this year the fixed costs associated with the decrease in inventories, under absorption costing, are released as costs and matched against the sales during the period. Thus 5000 units × $2 absorption = $10 000 is now recognised as a cost in the cost of goods sold. These fixed costs are excluded in the case of marginal costing because they were not incurred during the year: they relate to the previous year. Therefore the net profit calculated under absorption costing is $10 000 less than the profit under the marginal-costing method.

From the case studies we can summarise the differences between the methods as follows.

- When sales equal production (i.e. when there is no movement in inventory), marginal and absorption costing yield the same profit. The amount of fixed costs charged to the statement of financial performance is the same.
- When production exceeds sales (i.e. when inventories are increasing), absorption costing shows a higher profit than marginal costing does. Under absorption costing a portion of the fixed production costs is charged to inventories and thereby deferred to future periods.
- When sales exceed production, absorption costing shows a lower profit than marginal costing does. This is because the fixed costs included in the inventories are charged to the period in which the inventories are sold.

In the long run, the profit figures disclosed by the two methods must even out because sales cannot continuously exceed production, nor can production continuously exceed sales.

The differences in profits derived from the application of the two methods can be reconciled by the following arithmetical expression:

fixed overhead absorption rate × the movement in inventories during a period
= difference in profits

Summary

The determination of product costs for management information is clearly critical in the planning, control and decision-making process of organisations. However, the values given to products depend upon the form of costing method adopted. Two methods have been examined in this chapter—full costing and marginal costing. The main difference between them is the way in which production overheads are accounted for.

Under the full-costing method, production overheads are included as a product cost. In multi-product firms it is difficult, if not impossible, to trace overheads directly to products. There is therefore a need to adopt some system that equitably shares out the overheads to products. In this chapter we examined absorption costing as a means of sharing out overhead costs to products. It is important to recognise the advantages and the problems associated with this method, in particular the necessity of choosing a basis to apportion costs that by its very nature is discretionary but does have the advantage that it takes account of all the costs of production.

Activity-based costing involves allocating the overhead costs by using the most appropriate cost driver to determine the overhead absorption rate. The cost driver chosen is the one which has the highest correlation with the actual costs incurred by the production centre.

The marginal-costing method, in contrast, treats overheads as a period cost, and it follows that only expenses that are included in product costs are direct costs. While this method overcomes the problems associated with absorbing overheads, it does ignore a significant element of the production cost in the valuation of cost of sales and inventories.

The application of these costing methods was illustrated at the end of the chapter, applying both of them to inventory valuations. The example showed the differences in values and net profit obtained when these two methods were applied. It is important that you understand the reasons for these differences and appreciate the arguments for and against the application of the methods to product costing.

Further reading

Hilton, R., 1997. *Managerial Accounting*, 3rd edn, McGraw-Hill.

Hirsch, M.L., Louderback, J.G., and Smith, E., 1989. *Cost Accounting: Accumulation, Analysis and Use*, Thomas Nelson.

Horngren, C.T., Foster, G., and Datar, S., 1997. *Cost Accounting: A Managerial Emphasis*, 9th edn, Prentice-Hall.

Morse, W.J., and Roth, H.P., 1986. *Cost Accounting: Processing, Evaluating, and Using Cost Data*, 3rd edn, Addison-Wesley.

Review questions

1 Explain why it is important to determine the cost of products.

2 Define direct and indirect costs.

3 Give examples of expenditure that would be classified, in a manufacturing organisation, as direct costs and indirect costs.

4 What are period costs?

5 Explain why it is necessary to use estimates in determining an absorption rate for overheads.

6   Discuss the advantages and disadvantages of using marginal costing for product costing.

Problems for discussion and analysis

1   If a manager is paid a bonus based on profit earned, what might be the problems, in the short run, of using absorption costing?

2   Discuss how the use of marginal costing may ignore the impact of fixed costs.

3   Barclay Ltd uses a predetermined overhead rate in applying overheads to product costs, using direct labour costs for cost centre X and machine hours for cost centre Y. The following details the estimated forecasts for 20X1.

	X	Y
Direct labour costs	$100 000	$35 000
Production overheads	$140 000	$150 000
Direct labour hours	16 000	5 000
Machine hours	1 000	20 000

a   Calculate the predetermined overhead rate for cost centres X and Y.

b   BNH is one of the products manufactured by Barclay. The manufacturing process involves the two cost centres, X and Y. The following data relate to the resources that were used in the manufacture of the product during 20X1.

	X	Y
Direct materials	$20 000	$40 000
Direct labour	$32 000	$21 000
Direct labour hours	4 000	3 000
Machine hours	1 000	13 000

Determine the total production cost for product BNH, using full costing.

c   Assuming that product BNH consists of 20 000 units, what is the unit cost of BNH?

d   At the end of the year 20X1 it was found that actual production overhead costs amounted to $160 000 in cost centre X and $138 000 in cost centre Y. The total direct labour cost in cost centre X was $144 200 and the machine hours used were 18 000 in cost centre Y during the year. Calculate the over- or under-absorbed overhead for each cost centre.

4   Agent Orange Pty Ltd operates a factory with two production departments, P1 and P2, and one service department, S1. Estimates of factory overhead for the year commencing 1 July 20X3 were as follows.

	$	$
Fixed overhead		
Factory rates		7 500
Insurance (Buildings)		5 200
Maintenance		14 600
Depreciation (Equipment)		32 800
Variable overhead		
Electricity		12 000

(continued next page)

Indirect labour		
P1	18 000	
P2	23 500	
S1	44 000	85 500
Indirect materials		
P1	10 000	
P2	13 000	
S1	8 000	31 000

Other information available is as follows.

	Department		
	P1	P2	S1
Floor space (sq. m)	800	1 400	400
Value of equipment	$180 000	$100 000	$48 000
Machine hours	4 400	1 200	500
Direct labour hours	8 800	12 500	—
Allocation basis–S1	60%	40%	

Required:

a   Prepare overhead application rates for department P1 based on machine hours and for department P2 based on direct labour hours.

b   Calculate a single plant-wide overhead application rate based on direct labour hours.

(Adapted from *Management Accounting 1 Topic Questions*, University of Technology, Sydney, 1988, p. 9.)

5   Formula 500 Cars Ltd manufactured the metal frames of a small racing car called the Formula 500. It produced two different models, and the costs of direct material and direct labour for each model in February 20X1 were:

	Model ABC	Model XYZ
Direct materials	$200 000	$250 000
Direct labour	$400 000	$450 000

Formula 500 uses an activity-based costing system to allocate the overhead costs. The following details are available about cost drivers.

Activity	Cost driver
Welding	Number of welds (W)
Assembly	Number of direct labour hours (DLH)
Inspection	Time to inspect (IH)

The following schedule shows the projected costs and the amount of each cost driver for the year 20X1:

	Estimated costs	Estimated cost driver
Welding	$1 000 000	800 000 welds
Assembly	$800 000	400 000 DLH
Inspection	$500 000	20 000 IH
	$2 300 000	

During February 20X1 the actual amounts for each cost driver were:

	ABC	XYZ
Number of welds	30 000	40 000
Direct labour hours	15 000	20 000
Hours of inspection	600	1 000

Required:

    a   The total costs for ABC and XYZ for February.

    b   The cost per car for each model if, during February, 1500 of ABC and 1630 of XYZ were produced.

    c   If actual overhead for February was $190 000, determine if the factory overhead was under- or over-applied in February. How does the company report this under- or over-application of overhead?

6   JayDees Boats Ltd builds custom-designed company boats. The company uses an activity-based costing system for determining the costs of each boat it produces. The following activities and cost drivers apply to the construction of boats.

Activity	Cost Driver
Construction	Direct labour hours (DLH)
Inspection	Time to inspect (TTI)
Testing	Time to test (TTT)

At the beginning of 20X0, the following estimates were made for each activity and cost driver.

	Estimated costs for year $	Estimated cost driver hours
Construction	3 000 000	100 000 (DLH)
Inspection	1 000 000	20 000 (TTI)
Testing	500 000	8 000 (TTT)
	4 500 000	

During March 20X0, the actual direct materials and amounts for each cost driver for two boats—Mustang and Jaguar—were:

	Mustang	Jaguar
Direct materials	$160 000	$120 000
Direct labour hours	4 000	6 000
Inspection time	800	1 200
Testing time	200	300

Required:

    a   Determine the total cost for Mustang and Jaguar.

    b   If the actual overhead for March was $440 000, was the overhead under-or over-applied in March?

7   Briefly respond to each of the following comments. Indicate how management accounting information can assist managers in doing their jobs.

    a   Plant manager: 'Our accountants do a good job in keeping the shareholders informed about how our company has done in the past, but I don't see how they can help me run this plant.'

    b   Restaurant owner: 'There is no question that management accounting is useful in a manufacturing firm, but I run a restaurant. How can it help me?'

    c   City recreation director: 'Management accounting may be important in a non-profit organisation, but my job is to provide social services, not a profit. I should not be concerned with costs.'

    d   Production supervisor: 'I take a careful look at my department's performance report whenever we spend too much money and really chew out my staff for not doing a better job.'

e   Sales manager: 'Product pricing is a shot in the dark. You make an educated guess and then hope the product will sell, and, if it does, that the company will make a profit.'

f   Civil engineering student: 'My goal is to supervise the construction of highways, bridges and dams. I don't see why I should take a management accounting course.'

(Adapted from W.J. Morse and H.P. Roth, *Cost Accounting: Processing, Evaluating, and Using Cost Data,* 3rd edn, Addison-Wesley, 1986, p. 14.3.)

8   The Mosaic Company produces a single product. On 1 January 20X3 Mosaic had no work in progress or finished goods inventories. Unit production and sales information for the first three months of 20X3 are as follows.

	January	February	March
Production (units)	50 000	50 000	50 000
Sales (units)	30 000	50 000	70 000

Monthly fixed costs include manufacturing costs of $100 000, and selling and administration costs of $40 000. Variable costs are as follows.

Direct materials	$5.00 per unit
Direct labour	$5.00 per unit
Factory overhead	$10.00 per unit
Selling and administration	$3.00 per unit sold

Each unit sells for $30.00.

Required:

a   Prepare income statements, using full absorption costing for January, February and March.

b   Prepare income statements, using marginal costing for January, February and March.

c   Explain the differences between the full-absorption and marginal-costing methods for the three months.

(Adapted from W.J. Morse and P.H. Roth, *Cost Accounting: Processing, Evaluating and Using Cost Data*, 3rd edn, Addison-Wesley, 1986, p. 362.)

9   The Benzfor company manufactures cars. The following data covers the months of April, May and June 20X1.

	April	May	June
Car production			
Opening inventory	0	100	250
Production	600	800	650
Sales	500	650	350
	$	$	$
Variable costs			
Manufacturing costs per car	10 000	10 000	10 000
Marketing and administration	1 000	1 000	1 000
Fixed costs			
Manufacturing	500 000	500 000	500 000
Administration, etc.	85 000	90 000	85 000

The retail price for each car is $27 000.

Required:

a   Prepare a statement of financial performance for the three months using (i) marginal costing, and (ii) absorption costing.

b   Explain how and why the figures vary.

10 The managers of Absent Ltd have been studying the first three years' results of this newly formed company and are concerned about the figures. They think of profits as being directly related to the volume of sales, and find it confusing that for one year the reported sales are higher than those of the previous year but the reported net profit is lower.

The following figures apply to the years under consideration.

	20X1	20X2	20X3
Actual sales (units)	36 000	50 000	60 000
Actual production (units)	58 000	35 000	53 000

In each of the years the estimated production volume was 45 000 units and the estimated fixed overheads were $67 500.

The selling price was $4 per unit and variable costs were $1.50 per unit for three years.

Actual costs were equal to estimated costs in all years. Selling and administrative expenses for each year were $10 000. The company had no opening stock. The management accountant had difficulty explaining to the managers that fluctuations in profits resulted from differences between volume of sales and the volume of production within an accounting period, together with the system of product valuation used.

a   Prepare statements of financial performance for Absent Ltd using marginal costing and absorption costing for each of the three years to aid the management accountant's explanation.

b   Reconcile the net profit reported under the costing methods.

c   Which costing method would you recommend for management decision-making purposes, and why?

11 Drawrod Ltd has three manufacturing cost centres: Punching, Stamping and Assembly. In addition the company has two service cost centres: Maintenance and Inspection.

The following gives the estimated production overhead expenses for the year to 31 December 20X2.

	$	$
Indirect materials		
Punching	12 000	
Stamping	14 000	
Assembly	10 000	
Maintenance	8 000	
Inspection	4 000	48 000
Indirect labour		
Punching	24 000	
Stamping	30 000	
Assembly	14 000	
Maintenance	36 000	
Inspection	10 000	114 000

(continued next page)

Other overhead expenses

Electricity	56 000	
Rent	128 000	
Rates	32 000	
Insurance of buildings	32 000	
Insurance of machines	40 000	
Depreciation of machines	40 000	328 000
Total		490 000

The following are additional estimates relating to manufacturing for the year ended 31 December 20X2.

	Punching	Stamping	Assembly	Maintenance	Inspection	Total
Area occupied (sq. m)	18 000	12 000	24 000	3 000	3 000	60 000
Working hours	52 500	45 000	30 000	15 000	7 500	150 000
Book value of machines	200 000	140 000	60 000	–	–	400 000
Machine hours	51 200	64 000	44 800	–	–	160 000
Number of employees	180	150	240	30	60	660

The costs of the service cost centre are to be apportioned as follows.

	Maintenance %	Inspection %
Punching	40	20
Stamping	30	30
Assembly	30	50
	100	100

The company's bases for the absorption of overheads are as follows.

Punching: machine hours
Stamping: machine hours
Assembly: working hours

a Calculate the absorption rates for the Punching, Stamping and Assembly cost centres (to the nearest cent).

b Specify and explain the factors to be considered in determining whether to use a single factory-wide overhead absorption rate for all factory overheads or a separate rate for each manufacturing cost centre, with reference to the system applied to Drawrod Ltd.

Ethics case study

Digital Electronics Ltd manufactures specialised scientific instruments to customer specifications. It has contracts with government departments which are on a cost-plus basis. Under this arrangement the costs are defined as those costs which can be directly traced to the product, plus overheads based on a predetermined overhead rate, using an appropriate application base. Digital's other customers are in the non-government sector and are on a fixed-cost basis.

During February 20X1 the company worked on two main contracts—one with the defence department and the other with the Sarich Corporation. The two contracts were quite different, with the contract for the defence department requiring a large number of direct labour hours, while the contract for Sarich was the reverse.

The financial controller of the company has recommended to the general manager of Digital that the most appropriate base for the allocation of overheads is machine hours.

The general manager, however, decided in favour of using direct labour hours to allocate the overheads to both contracts.

Discuss:

a   why you think the general manager has chosen direct labour hours for the allocation of overheads instead of the machine hours recommended by the financial controller.

b   the ethical issues involved in this case. Should the financial controller take any further action?

Accounting for Decision Making: Without Resource Constraints

Learning objectives

At the end of this chapter you should be able to:

1   explain what is meant by 'sunk costs'

2   explain what is meant by 'differential or incremental costs'

3   understand what is meant by 'avoidable and unavoidable costs'

4   discuss the concept of opportunity costs, and its role in decision making

5   discuss the role of replacement cost in the application of opportunity costs

6   explain the costs and benefits that are relevant to specific decisions

7   explain and apply the contribution approach to decision making in cases with no resource constraints

8   understand how the same approach can be used in decisions involving whether to close unprofitable decisions.

Introduction

Management needs to make decisions about future business opportunities to ensure that the organisation's objectives are met. Many of these decisions relate to the short term and are expressed in financial terms in the organisation's budget (see Chapter 21). Management is also required to make decisions of a more immediate nature, which relate to opportunities that were not anticipated at the planning stage. To ignore profitable opportunities because they have not been specifically included in the budget would be irresponsible in a dynamic business environment. These decisions can be categorised as follows.

Decisions where there are no resource constraints

In these circumstances organisations are free to make a decision, knowing that it will not affect other opportunities. For instance, the introduction of a new product may not affect, in any way, the demand and production levels of other products. The decisions can also be simply described as 'accept or reject' decisions.

Decisions where there are resource constraints

This situation occurs when an organisation experiences a shortage of physical resources, e.g. a particular material. In such cases the organisation cannot accept all potentially desirable opportunities. To decide which of these opportunities to choose, it will be necessary to implement a priority (ranking) system.

Mutually exclusive decisions

These are decisions where the acceptance of one opportunity means that the others will be rejected. For instance, where management has to decide whether to make or buy a component to be embodied within one of the firm's products, the decision to make it means that the option to buy is rejected. Mutually exclusive decisions can include situations either with or without resource constraints.

In this chapter we examine the methods used by accountants to provide information for management to make efficient short-term decisions, and the application of these methods when there are no resource constraints. Decisions which are subject to resource constraints and mutually exclusive decisions are considered in the next chapter.

It is conventional to assume that short-term decisons are those that will affect the firm within a period of a year. It will also be assumed that the values of cash inflows and outflows throughout the year are of an equivalent value. This is naive, because clearly all individuals and firms prefer to receive, for example, cash today rather than in 11 months' time. For clarity it is convenient in our analyisis to make this assumption, because complexities arise when we begin to take account of the time value of money in the decision-making process.

Relevant costs and benefits

Decision making

Decisions relate to the future, and the function of decision making is to select courses of action that satisfy the objective of the firm. There is no opportunity to alter the past, although past experience might help us in future decisions. For example, the observation of past cost behaviour might help to determine future levels of cost.

Relevant costs and benefits can therefore be defined as those costs and benefits that result from making a specific decision. A more precise definition will be established after we have examined the underlying principles of relevant costs and benefits and considered some examples of the application of these principles.

The relevant costs for decision making are different from those used in accrual accounting. This is not surprising as the principles of traditional costing (e.g. overhead absorption methods) evolved from the need to report historical events, rather than to determine future costs and benefits. A number of methods adopted by accountants to account for decisions about the future are derived from economic theory and therefore might be familiar to you.

We now consider the principles underlying relevant costs for decision making and the application of these principles to specific types of decisions. The differences between the application of relevant costs and traditional costing will also be discussed.

Future and sunk (past) costs

Costs of a historical nature, which are normally referred to as sunk costs, are incurred as a result of a past decision and are therefore irrelevant to future decisions and should be ignored.

Key Concept 19.1

Sunk costs

Sunk costs or past costs can be easily identified in that they have been paid for or they are owed by the firm. The firm is committed to paying for them in the future.

CASE STUDY 19.1

A firm has an obsolete machine that was purchased and paid for two years ago. The net book value of the machine, as shown in the accounts of the firm, before it became obsolete, is $72 000. The alternatives now available to the firm are:

- to make alterations to the machine at an estimated cost of $20 000 and then sell it for $40 000
- to sell it for scrap, at an estimated selling price of $15 000.

The net book value of $72 000 represents the original cost of purchasing the machine less the accumulated depreciation (charge for depreciation over the two-year period). The original cost is the result of a past decision: it was incurred two years ago and therefore it is a sunk cost. It is irrelevant to the future decision whether to alter the machine and sell it, or sell it for scrap. The depreciation is also based on the original cost of the machine and is thus irrelevant to this future decision. The only relevant costs and benefits in this example are those related to the future; we can analyse these as follows.

	Alter $	Scrap $
Future benefits	40 000	15 000
Future costs	20 000	—
Future income	20 000	15 000

From the analysis of relevant costs and benefits it can be seen that the firm will be $5000 better off by altering the machine and selling it rather than selling it for scrap.

Differential (incremental) costs

Another important principle in the determination of relevant costs and benefits is that only differential (incremental) costs and benefits are relevant to future decisions. The application of the principles underlying differential costing is illustrated in Case Study 19.2, where a firm which has spare capacity is offered a special order. By comparing the costs and benefits associated with the opportunities available to the firm, we can identify differential costs and benefits. It is these costs and benefits that are relevant to decisions between competing opportunities.

Key Concept 19.2

Differential costs

Differential (incremental) costs are the differences in costs and benefits between alternative opportunities available to an organisation. It follows that when a number of opportunities are being considered, costs and benefits that are common to these alternative opportunities are irrelevant to the decision.

CASE STUDY 19.2

KT's Inc. manufactures hats and has a current capacity of 120 000 hats per year. However, it is predicted that in the forthcoming year sales will be only 90 000 hats. A mail-order firm offers to buy 20 000 hats at $7.50 each. The acceptance of this special order will not affect regular sales and it will take a year to complete. The managing director is reluctant to accept the order because $7.50 is below the factory unit cost of $8 per hat.

The following gives the predicted total income and the predicted income per unit, in a traditional costing format, if the order were not to be accepted.

	Total		Per unit	
	$	$	$	$
Sales: 90 000 hats at $10 each		900 000		10.00
Less factory expenses				
Variable	540 000		6.00	
Supervision	90 000		1.00	
Other fixed costs	90 000	720 000	1.00	8.00
Gross Profit		180 000		2.00
Selling expenses				
Variable	22 500		0.25	
Fixed	112 500	135 000	1.25	1.50
Profit		45 000		0.50

The management accountant, with the production and sales manager, is requested to review the costs of taking on the special order. These are their conclusions.
1   The variable costs of production relate to labour and materials and these will be incurred at the same rates as for the production of the normal production units.
2   There will be a need for additional supervision. However, it is anticipated that four of the current supervisors can cover this requirement if each of them works overtime of five hours per week. Supervisors are paid $10 per hour and overtime is paid at a premium of $2 per hour. There are 48 working weeks in the year. Therefore the additional costs are:

5 hours × $12 per hour × 48 weeks × 4 supervisors = $11 520

3 Other fixed costs are factory rent and the depreciation of plant. It is anticipated that these will remain the same if the order is accepted.
4 There will be a need to hire an additional machine, costing $10 000, if the contract is accepted.
5 The variable sales cost relates to salespersons' commission, and this cost will not be incurred on the special order.
6 The fixed sales expenses relate to the administering of sales. These costs will remain the same, except that a part-time clerk will be required to help with the additional workload if the special order is accepted. The salary will be $6000 per year.

Using the dfferential costing approach, we can compare the total income for the year for KT's Inc. if the order is accepted or rejected.

	Accept $	Reject $	Differential cost and revenue $
Sales	1 050 000	900 000	150 000
Factory expenses			
Variable costs	660 000	540 000	120 000
Supervision	101 520	90 000	11 520
Other fixed costs	90 000	90 000	—
Hire of plant	10 000	—	10 000
	861 520	720 000	141 520
Sales expenses			
Variable costs	22 500	22 500	—
Fixed costs	118 500	112 500	6 000
Total costs	1 002 520	855 000	147 520
Profit	47 480	45 000	2 480

From the differential analysis it can be seen that KT's will be $2480 better off if the special order is accepted. Also, it can be observed that a number of the costs are irrelevant in the decision analysis. That is, they are the same whether or not the order is accepted: for example, 'other fixed costs' are $90 000 for both the accept and the reject decisions. The analysis of data could have been simplified by considering only the differential costs and revenues related to the special order. If the differential analysis of costs and revenues results in a profit, then from a purely quantitative perspective, the order should be accepted.

Avoidable and unavoidable costs

There is an alternative way of determining whether a cost is relevant or irrelevant in decisions, such as the special order for the hats illustrated above. Instead of using the differential analysis, we ask the question: would a cost be avoided if the company did not proceed with the special order? If the answer is yes, the cost is relevant and should be included. For example, consider this question with regard to the cost of plant hire for the special order above: will the cost of plant hire be avoided if the company does not proceed with the order? The answer is yes, i.e. the cost is relevant to the decision because it will only be incurred if the order is accepted. A cost is described as unavoidable if it will be incurred regardless of the decision to accept or reject, i.e. the cost is irrelevant to the decision.

Opportunity cost

The economists' concept of opportunity cost has been adopted by accountants for decision-making purposes. This concept relates to the cost of using resources for alternative opportunities.

Key Concept 19.3

Opportunity cost

The opportunity cost of a resource is normally defined as the maximum benefit which could be obtained from that resource if it were used for some other purpose. If a firm uses a resource for alternative A rather than B, it is the potential benefits that are forgone by not using the resource for alternative B that constitute the opportunity cost. Therefore, the potential benefits forgone, the opportunity cost, are a relevant cost in the decision to accept alternative A.

The following is an example of the concept of opportunity costs. Jeff Jones, a qualified accountant, is a sole practitioner. He works 40 hours per week and charges clients $20 per hour. Jeff is already overworked and will not work any extra hours. A circus offers Jeff $1000 per week to become a clown. In the decision to become a clown Jeff must consider the benefits he would forgo from his accounting practice, i.e. $20 × 40 hours = $800 per week; this is the opportunity cost of Jeff's becoming a clown. Assuming that Jeff is concerned only with financial rewards, he will accept the offer because he will be $1000 − $800 = $200 per week better off.

Replacement costs

Where a resource was originally purchased for some purpose other than an opportunity currently under consideration, the relevant cost of using that resource is its replacement cost. This cost has come about as a direct result of the decision to use the resource for a purpose not originally intended and the need to replace the resource. The following example will help you to understand the application of this principle.

Easy Done Ltd has been approached by a customer who would like a special job done. The job would require the use of 500 kg of material Z. Material Z is used by Easy Done for a variety of purposes.

Currently the company holds 1000 kg in inventory which was purchased one month ago for $6 per kilogram. Since then, the price per kilogram has increased to $8. If 500 kg were used on this special job it would need to be replaced to meet the production demand from other jobs.

The relevant cost of using material Z on this special job is the replacement cost, 500 kg × $8 = $4000. This is because the material will need to be replaced as a result of its use, and the replacement will cost $4000. This cost has arisen as a direct result of accepting the special order and therefore it is relevant to the decision. It should be noted that the original cost of $6 per kilogram is irrelevant to the decision as it relates to a past decision and has already been incurred (i.e. it is a sunk cost).

Case Study 19.3 illustrates the application of the principles of relevant costs compared with traditional costing methods.

CASE STUDY 19.3

No Problem Ltd is considering whether to accept the offer of a contract to undertake some reconstruction work at a price of $73 000. The work will begin almost immediately and will take about a year to complete. The company's accountant has submitted the following statement.

	$	$
Contract price		73 000
Less Costs		
Cost of work already incurred in drawing up detailed costings		4 700
Materials		
A	7 000	
B	8 000	15 000
Labour		
Direct	21 000	
Indirect	12 000	33 000
Machinery		
Depreciation on machines owned	4 000	
Hire of special equipment	5 000	9 000
General overheads		10 500
Total cost		72 200
Expected profit		800

The management of the company doubts whether it is advisable to incur the inevitable risks involved for such a small profit margin. On making further enquiries, the following information becomes available.
1   Material A was bought two years ago for $7000. It would cost $8000 at today's prices. If not used on this contract, it could be sold for $6500. There is no alternative use for this material and no expected future use.
2   Material B was ordered for another job but will be used on this job if the contract is accepted. The replacement for the other job will cost $9000.
3   The trade union has negotiated a minimum wage agreement, as a result of which direct wages of $21 000 will be incurred whether the contract is undertaken or not. If not employed on this contract, these employees could be used to do much-needed maintenance work, which would otherwise be done by an outside contractor at an estimated cost of $18 500.
4   The indirect labour is the wage of a supervisor who will have to be taken on to supervise the contract. A suitable person is ready to take up the appointment at once.
5   The machine which is already owned is six years old. The final instalment of depreciation required to write off the balance on the asset account is $4000. There is no alternative use for the machine, and its scrap value is negligible, because of the high cost of dismantling and removal.
6   The general overhead absorption rate is 50 per cent of direct labour. Overheads are expected to rise by $4000 if the contract is accepted.
   With reference to this information and the principles of relevant costs, we can now consider the individual items of costs that should be accounted for in the decision whether to accept or reject the contract.
1   *Material A:* The $7000 originally paid for the material is a sunk cost and is thus irrelevant. We are told that the current replacement cost is $8000. However, the company can obtain only $6500 if it was sold, i.e. the net realisable value. This is the benefit the company forgoes (the opportunity cost) by using the material on this contract. Thus, $6500 is the relevant cost.

2   *Material B:* The fact that this material has already been ordered means that the company is committed to pay the supplier of the material. Thus, this cost of $8000 can also be considered as a sunk cost and is irrelevant to the decision. The only alternative is to use the material on the other job. If so, the company would have to purchase some more material at a cost of $9000. This is the opportunity cost of using the material on this contract.

3   *Direct labour:* These employees will be paid whether the contract is accepted or not; therefore this cost is unavoidable and irrelevant. However, if they were not employed on this contract the company would save $18 500 in fees to the outside contractor for maintenance. The $18 500 is therefore a relevant cost as this is the opportunity cost of using them on the contract.

4   *Indirect labour:* The cost of $12 000 for employing the supervisor is an incremental cost, i.e. it will be incurred only if the contract is accepted, and therefore is relevant to the contract.

5   *Depreciation on the machine owned:* The cost of depreciation relates to a past cost (i.e. sunk cost) and is thus irrelevant to the decision. A relevant benefit is the machine's scrap value. However, as this is negligible it is ignored.

6   *The hire of special equipment:* The cost of $5000 will be incurred only if the contract is accepted; it is an incremental cost and is relevant to the decision.

7   *General overhead:* The only cost that is relevant is the increase in cost of $4000 if the contract is accepted. This cost is incremental and is thus relevant to the decision. All the other costs related to general overheads are unavoidable and therefore irrelevant.

8   *Cost of work already incurred in drawing up costings ($4700, detailed at the beginning of the schedule):* This cost is irrelevant to the contract: it is a sunk cost and therefore should be excluded.

We are now in a position to draw up an amended statement of costs for the contract.

	Relevant costs $	Relevant benefits $
Contract price		73 000
Less Costs		
Materials		
A	6 500	
B	9 000	15 500
Labour		
Direct	18 500	
Indirect	12 000	30 500
Hire of special equipment		5 000
Overheads		4 000
Total costs		55 000
Expected profits		18 000

In this case study, it is apparent that, when we consider only costs that are relevant, the contract is more attractive to the company. In the original schedule of costs and revenues, which were based on traditional costing methods, the expected profit was only $800 compared with $18 000. It should be stressed that the higher profits yielded from the analysis of relevant costs and benefits compared with the traditional analysis is not always the rule. The result depends on the particular circumstances of the firm making the decisions.

The principles underlying the relevance of costs and benefits to decisions, described and illustrated in Case Study 19.3, focus on costs rather than revenues. However, the same principles apply to revenues: only those revenues that will be generated as a result of the decision are relevant to the decision and should be brought into the decision model. Relevant benefits, by their nature, relate to the future. All benefits that have been received or are due to be received from a prior commitment are irrelevant to future decisions.

Key Concept 19.4

Relevant costs and benefits

Relevant costs and benefits are those that relate to the future, and are additional costs and revenues that will be incurred or result from a decision.
Costs that are relevant to a decision might also be:
- the cost of replacing a resource that was orginally purchased for some other purpose
- the opportunity cost of using a resource that could be used for some alternative purpose.

The meaning of relevance

Earlier in this chapter relevant costs and benefits were defined, in general terms, as those costs and benefits that result from a specific decision. We are now in the position to derive a more precise definition.

There are also costs and revenues that are incurred or generated by an organisation that are irrelevant to a decision, i.e. are not affected by a decision. It is important to identify these costs and benefits so that we can eliminate them for our analysis.

Fixed and variable costs and the contribution approach

The concept of contribution was introduced in Chapter 17. The contribution is the difference between the sales revenue and the variable costs. We reintroduce the concept here in the context of relevant costs and decision making.

It is normally assumed that costs behave in a linear fashion: fixed costs are constant for all volumes and variable costs vary in direct proportion to volume. Often fixed costs are irrelevant to decisions because they remain the same whatever the decision is, i.e. they are unavoidable. When there are no scarce resources and the sales revenue exceeds the relevant variable costs, a decision to accept will be made. This rule applies to several types of decisions.

A word of caution: There are some situations when costs do not behave in a linear fashion, and so variations in unit variable costs or in fixed cost levels might occur. For example, the cost of new machinery specifically purchased for a future contract is classified as a fixed cost, but it is relevant to the contract because it is avoidable. When fixed costs are directly attributable to opportunites, they are relevant to the decision to accept or reject. However, unless you are given a clear indication to the contrary, you should always assume that costs behave in a linear fashion. It should be noted that this assumption was also adopted in Chapter 17.

The contribution approach can be applied to a number of types of decisions that management must take when running a business, as the following examples illustrate.

The range of products

The management of an organisation is confronted with a number of opportunities each year and has to decide which to embody in their plans. In Case Study 19.4 the products are independent of each other. We can derive a simple rule from this study: if a product makes a positive contribution, it is worth considering for acceptance in the firm's production program. The fixed costs have been apportioned to products. This is the convention under absorption costing, described in Chapter 18, where overheads are absorbed into products using predetermined rates based on budgeted figures for overhead costs and activity levels. Normally these overhead costs are unavoidable and thus not relevant, as in the case study below. Overhead costs are relevant only if they are incremental in nature.

CASE STUDY 19.4

A firm has the opportunity to manufacture and sell three products, 1, 2 and 3, in the forthcoming year. Here is a draft summary of the profit or loss on the products.

	Total	1	2	3
	$	$	$	$
Sales revenue	200 000	30 000	20 000	150 000
Variable costs	136 000	21 400	13 200	101 400
Fixed costs	44 000	3 400	7 400	33 200
Total costs	180 000	24 800	20 600	134 600
Profit (loss)	20 000	5 200	(600)	15 400

The fixed costs of $44 000 represent overhead costs which have been apportioned to the products and will remain the same whether or not all or some of the products are sold during the year.

Because of the loss shown by product 2, the management proposes to eliminate that product from its range.

The firm would be making a profit of $20 000 if all three products were manufactured and sold. However, if only 1 and 3 were sold, as the management suggests, the profit would be reduced.

	Total	1	3
		$	$
Sales	180 000	30 000	150 000
Variable costs	122 800	21 400	101 400
Contribution	57 200	8 600	48 600
Fixed costs	44 000		
Profit	13 200		

This reduction in profit is because product 2 makes a contribution of $6800 ($20 000 – $13 200) and the fixed costs remain the same at $44 000, whether or not 1, 2 or 3 are manufactured and sold.

Closing an unprofitable section

In a dynamic business environment, organisations regularly appraise the economic viability of their departments and divisions. Although the decision whether or not to close a department or division is very different from that involved in the determination of the range of products to be manufactured and sold, the same principles of relevance are adopted.

Invariably, in practice, there are a number of costs that are allocated to departments which are outside their control and relate to overheads that are incurred by the firm as a whole. A typical example is head office expenses, which relate to the administrative costs of running the business. These types of costs are irrelevant because they are unavoidable.

The rule to be applied in such decisions is that if a department makes a positive contribution, i.e. revenue exceeds variable costs, the department should remain open, and *vice versa*. However, when there are fixed costs that are directly attributable to a department, and therefore are avoidable, the rule can be amended as follows: if the revenue generated by a department exceeds the costs directly attributable to that department, it should remain open, and *vice versa*. An example of such a decision is given in Case Study 19.5.

Unfortunately, some organisations still ignore the principles of relevant costs and benefits in making future decisions. This distorts decision making and causes organisations to take wrong courses of action.

CASE STUDY 19.5

The following are the costs and revenues of three departments, Alpha, Beta and Gamma, summarised in a traditional costing format.

	Alpha $000	Beta $000	Gamma $000	Total $000
Revenue	80	40	60	180
Department costs	24	15	46	85
Apportioned costs	20	10	20	50
Total costs	44	25	66	135
Profit (loss)	36	15	(6)	45

The apportioned costs of $50 000 in total are unavoidable and relate to head office overhead costs.

From the way in which the data are presented, it could be argued that Department Gamma should be closed down because it makes a loss of $6000. Currently, the total profit of the three departments is $45 000. However, if Department Gamma were closed the profit would be reduced.

	Alpha $000	Beta $000	Total $000
Revenue	80	40	120
Less Department costs	24	15	39
Departmental profit	56	25	81
Less Apportioned costs			50
Profit			31

The reduction in profit to the firm as a whole of $14 000 is due to the closing of Department Gamma, which in fact makes a departmental profit of $14 000 ($60 000 – $46 000) which contributes to the head office overhead costs and the firm's overall profit. Thus Department Gamma should remain open.

Summary

In this chapter we considered decisions that organisations are required to make regarding future opportunities where there are no constraints in respect of physical resources. In the context of all the types of decisions considered, it is clear that the application of traditional costing methods will not result in organisations satisfying the assumed objective of maximising future cash flows. It was illustrated that the maximisation of cash flows will be satisfied only when the principles of relevant costs are applied to such decisions. The costs and benefits that are relevant were described and can be summarised thus:

- future costs and benefits
- differential and incremental costs and benefits
- avoidable costs
- replacement costs
- opportunity costs.

The main limitation of the analysis is that only quantitative information has been considered. In practice many of these decisions are made on the basis of qualitative criteria. This will be discussed at the end of Chapter 20, after we have examined the methods used to make decisions where there are scarce resources.

Further reading

Hilton, R., 1997. *Managerial Accounting*, 3rd edn, McGraw-Hill.

Hirsch, M.L., Louderback, J.G., and Smith, E., 1989. *Cost Accounting: Accumulation, Analysis and Use,* Thomas Nelson.

Horngren, C.T., Foster, G., and Datar, S., 1997. *Cost Accounting: A Managerial Emphasis,* 9th edn, Prentice-Hall.

Morse, W.J., and Roth, H.P., 1986. *Cost Accounting: Processing, Evaluating, and Using Cost Data*, 3rd edn, Addison-Wesley, p. 382.

Review questions

1   Discuss the reasons why accrual accounting methods are not appropriate to future decision making.

2   In the context of decision making explain the meaning of:
  a   sunk costs
  b   differential costs
  c   avoidable and unavoidable costs
  d   opportunity costs.

3   Depreciation is an important concept in the determination of profit. Discuss why it is classified as an irrelevant cost in decision making.

4   In the majority of cases fixed costs are irrelevant in decision making, but on some occasions they are relevant. Describe the circumstances when fixed costs are relevant to future decisions.

Problems for discussion and analysis

1   Calculators Ltd manufacture and sell pocket calculators. The price of these
    calculators is $22. The company's current output is 40 000 units per month,
    which represents 90 per cent of its productive capacity. Kodix, a chain-store
    customer who specialises in selling electronic goods, offers to buy 2000
    calculators as a special order at $16 each. The calculators would be sold under
    the name of Kodix.

    The total costs per month are $800 000 of which $192 000 are fixed costs.
    a   Advise Calculators Ltd whether it should accept the special order.
    b   Would your advice change if Kodix wanted 5000 calculators?

2   Sprinks Ltd produce three products, A, B and C. The following is an estimate of
    costs and revenues for the forthcoming year.

| | A | B | C |
	$	$	$
Sales	32 000	50 000	45 000
Total cost	36 000	38 000	34 000
Net profit (loss)	(4 000)	12 000	11 000

    The total cost of each product comprises one-third fixed costs and two-thirds
    variable costs. Fixed costs are constant whatever the volume of sales.

    The managing director argues that as product A makes a loss, production of it
    should be discontinued.

    Comment on the managing director's argument.

3   The Tinychip Co. produces a component used in the manufacture of
    microcomputers. Variable costs of producing and selling the component are
    $2 per unit. Fixed costs of providing the capacity to produce up to 100 000
    units per year are $50 000. The components are currently sold to a major
    computer manufacturer for $3.00 per unit and current sales are 60 000 units
    annually.

    A manufacturer of arcade video games believes the component can be used
    in the production of the games, and has offered to purchase 20 000 units from
    Tinychip at a price of $2.25 per unit. Since it is not known at this time if the
    manufacturer of the games will place additional orders, Tinychip considers this
    to be a once-only special order.

Required:

    a   Determine the differential revenues and differential costs of accepting the
        order.
    b   Should the special order be accepted? Explain.
    c   Would your answer to part (b) be different if current capacity were only
        60 000 units per year?

    (Adapted from W.J. Morse and H.P. Roth, *Cost Accounting: Processing,
    Evaluating, and Using Cost Data*, 3rd edn, Addison-Wesley, 1986, p. 674.)

4   Drake Pty Ltd currently manufacture a part which they use in the production of
    clocks. The part has the following unit costs at an annual volume of 40 000
    clocks.

	$
Direct materials	0.50
Direct labour	1.00
Variable overhead	0.50
Fixed overhead	2.00
Total	4.00

A supplier has offered to provide the part for Drake for $3.50 per unit.

Required:

a   If none of the fixed overheads can be reduced, should Drake continue to make the part or buy it from the supplier? If they buy, how much will the annual profits increase or decrease?

b   If all the fixed overheads can be eliminated, should Drake make or buy the part? If they buy, by how much will the annual profit increase or decrease?

(Adapted from W.J. Morse and H.P. Roth, *Cost Accounting: Processing, Evaluating, and Using Cost Data*, 3rd edn, Addison-Wesley, 1986, p. 675.)

5   Gallop Corporation Ltd has two divisions, production and assembly. The cost per unit charged by the production division to the assembly division is set to increase from $10 to $15. This is the same price as customers pay when they purchase directly from the production division. The manager of the assembly division is extremely upset and has expressed his intentions to buy the units from an outside supplier at a cost of $12 per unit.

The following data relate to the production division.

Units produced	100 000
Variable production costs per unit	$10
Indirect fixed costs allocated to the production division	$200 000
Normal profit per unit with production division	$3

Required:

a   What is the impact on overall profit for Gallop Corporation if the assembly division purchases units from outsiders? It normally purchases 50 000 units from the production division.

b   Discuss the implications of this decision for (i) the shareholders of Gallop, (ii) the management of Gallop Corporation, (iii) the heads of the production and assembly divisions.

6   Tredways Shoe Company produces three different types of shoes. The condensed results for the company for the past year are presented below.

	Scout $	Trouper $	Hounddog $
Sales	250 000	150 000	320 000
Cost of Goods Sold	210 000	155 000	250 000
Gross Profit	40 000	(5 000)	70 000
Operating Expenses	55 000	20 000	35 000
Net Income	(15 000)	(25 000)	35 000

The CEO believes Tredways should stop making Scouts and Troupers. However, before making a final decision he asks the accountant to provide more details about the cost items and these are presented below.

	Scout $	Trouper $	Hounddog $
Cost of Goods Sold			
Variable Manufacturing Costs	125 000	100 000	170 000
Fixed Manufacturing Costs	85 000	55 000	80 000
Operating Costs			
Variable	35 000	13 000	20 000
Fixed	20 000	7 000	15 000

Required:

Is the CEO correct? Should the information above lead to the company stopping the manufacture of Scouts and Troupers? What additional information do you need?

7 Sory Ltd manufacture a range of television sets. At present, the company is able to sell only 80 per cent of plant capacity of its 20-centimetre digital sets. These sets are sold to retailers for $200 per unit. With the present production, Sory sells 100 000 sets and has fixed costs of $7 500 000 and variable costs of $100 per unit.
   a   What is the present profit?
   b   If Sory reduced its price to retailers to $185 it believes it would operate at 100 per cent capacity. Should Sory take this step?
   c   Low Price Stores Ltd has offered to purchase 20 000 sets at $175. If Sory accepted this offer, the variable costs on the additional sets would be $95 as there would be no marketing costs. Given that Sory is operating at 80 per cent capacity, which of the three alternatives, (i), (ii) or (iii), produces the maximum profit?

8 Mikel Ltd manufactures components for bicycles. At the present time, sales are 100 000 units at $10 per unit. Fixed costs are $500 000 and variable costs are $5.50 per unit.

   If Mikel stopped production it would still have long-term fixed costs of $100 000.
   a   Should Mikel stop production? If not, what steps could the company consider to improve profit?
   b   Mikel has been offered a contract by ABC Ltd to supply 150 000 units at $9.00 per unit. Assuming Mikel has the capacity to produce these units at the same variable and fixed costs, should it accept the order?

9 Eatinatural Ltd is a company which specialises in the manufacture and sale of health foods. The company has just completed market research on a new type of organic toothpaste called Abrasive. The budget derived from the market research for one year's production and sales, which was presented to the board by the marketing manager, is as follows.

ABRASIVE TOOTHPASTE

	$	$
Cost of production (100 000 kg)		
Labour		
Direct wages	50 000	
Supervisory	30 000	80 000

(continued over page)

	$	$
Raw materials		
Ingredients X	17 000	
Ingredients Y	7 000	
Ingredients P	9 000	
Ingredients Z	1 000	34 000
Other variable costs		10 000
Fixed overheads (60% of direct labour)		30 000
Research and development		20 000
Total costs		174 000
Sales (100 000 kg at $1.60 per kg)		160 000
Loss		(14 000)

The board of directors is disappointed with this budget in view of the research and development costs already incurred of $20 000 and the need to make use of the spare capacity in the factory. Fred Sharpe, the managing director, suggests bringing in a consultant to examine the costs of the new product.

The following additional information is available.

i   It would be possible to transfer 60 per cent of the direct labour requirement from another department within the company. The monthly contribution of this department ($5000), subject to introduction of a special machine into the department at a hire cost of $4000 per year, would fall by only 20 per cent of its current level as a result of the reduction in the labour force. The remainder of the direct labour requirement would have to be recruited. It is anticipated that their wages will be the same as those of the workers transferred from the other department. In addition, it is estimated that the costs of recruitment, e.g. advertising, will be $3000.

ii Two supervisors would be required at a cost of $15 000 per year each. One would be recruited; the other, Reg Raven, would remain at work instead of retiring. The company will pay him a pension of $5000 per year on his retirement.

iii Inventories of ingredient X are currently available for a whole year's production of Abrasive, and are valued at their original cost. The price of this ingredient is subject to dramatic variations, and the current market price is double the original cost. It could be resold at the market price less 10 per cent selling expenses, or retained for use later in another new product to be manufactured by the company, by which time it is expected that the market price will have fallen by about 25 per cent.

iv Ingredient Y's price has been very stable and it is used for other products currently manufactured and sold by the company. There are no inventories available for the production of Abrasive.

v   Ingredient P is another commodity with a fairly static price. Half of the annual requirement is in inventory and the other half will have to be purchased during the year at an estimated cost of $4500. The materials in inventory could be resold for $4000 less 10 per cent selling expenses, or could be used to produce another product after some further processing. This processing, which would take 2000 hours in the Mixing Department where labour is paid $12 per hour, would save the company additional purchasing costs of $5000. The Mixing Department has sufficient idle capacity to do this amount of work only.

vi Ingredient Z was bought well in advance and is in inventory. It has no alternative use. Fred Sharpe is beginning to regret the decision to buy this ingredient in advance because it will deteriorate in store and might become dangerous before the end of the budget period. It cannot be sold and it will cost the company $500 to dispose of if it is not used to produce Abrasive.

vii The other variable costs can all be avoided if the contract is not accepted.

viii Fixed overheads of the company are expected to increase by $2000 per year as a result of manufacturing and selling Abrasive.

As the consultant employed by the company, you are requested to re-examine this statement, taking account of the additional information, and to recommend any necessary action. Clearly state any assumptions that you make.

10 The FitEquip Company manufacturers and sells four related product lines. Presented is a product line profitability statement for the year ended 30 June 20X3 which shows a loss for the baseball equipment line. A similar loss is projected for 20X4.

The management of FitEquip has requested a profitability study of the baseball equipment line to determine if it should be discontinued. The marketing department and the accounting department at the plant have developed the following additional data to be used in the study.

i   If the baseball equipment line is discontinued, the company will lose approximately 10 per cent of its sales in each of the other lines.

ii The plant now used in the manufacture of baseball equipment is quite specialised. Although the annual depreciation on the baseball plant is $115 000, it has a current salvage value of only $105 000 and a remaining useful life of five years. This plant cannot be used elsewhere in the company.

iii The company has been able to invest excess funds at 10 per cent per annum. If the baseball plant is sold, any proceeds will be invested at 10 per cent.

iv The space now occupied by the baseball plant could be closed off and rented for $175 000 per annum.

v   If the line is discontinued, the supervisor of the baseball equipment production, whose $30 000 salary is included in its fixed overhead, will be released.

vi All fixed manufacturing costs, except salaries of the line supervisors and depreciation, are common to all four product lines.

vii The fixed selling expenses are common to all products.

	Football $000	Baseball $000	Hockey $000	Misc. $000	Total $000
Sales	2 200	1 000	1 500	500	5 200
Cost of goods sold					
Material	400	175	300	90	965
Variable overhead	800	400	600	60	1 860
Fixed overhead	350	275	100	50	775
Less Total costs	1 550	850	1 000	200	3 600
Gross profit	650	150	500	300	1 600

(continued over page)

	Football $000	Baseball $000	Hockey $000	Misc. $000	Total $000
Selling expenses					
Variable	440	200	300	100	1 040
Fixed	100	50	100	50	300
Administration expenses	48	24	36	12	120
Less Total expenses	588	274	436	162	1 460
Product contribution	62	(124)	64	138	140

Required:

Should FitEquip discontinue the baseball equipment line? Support your answer with appropriate calculations.

(Adapted from W.J. Morse and H.P. Roth, 1986. *Cost Accounting: Processing, Evaluating, and Using Cost Data*, 3rd edn, Addison-Wesley, p. 383.)

11 General Grains Ltd has three major product lines: cereals, breakfast bars, and dog food. The income statement for the year ended 30 June 20X3, prepared by product line using full absorption costing, is as follows.

GENERAL GRAINS P/L
INCOME STATEMENT FOR THE YEAR ENDING 30 JUNE 20X3

	Cereals	Breakfast bars	Dog food	Total
Sales in kilograms	200 000	50 000	50 000	300 000
	$000	$000	$000	$000
Revenue from sales	1 000	400	200	1 600
Cost of sales				
Direct materials	330	160	100	590
Direct labour	90	40	20	150
Factory overhead	108	48	24	180
Less Total cost of sales	528	248	144	920
Gross Profit	472	152	56	680
Operating expenses				
Selling expenses				
Advertising	50	30	20	100
Commissions	50	40	20	110
Salaries	30	20	10	60
Total selling expenses	130	90	50	270
Administration expenses				
Licences	50	20	15	85
Salaries	60	25	15	100
Total administration expenses	110	45	30	185
Less Total operating expenses	240	135	80	455
Operating Income	232	17	(24)	225

The following additional information is available.

i   *Cost of sales:* All three products are produced with common facilities. The company's inventories of raw materials and finished products do not vary significantly from year to year. The inventories at 30 June 20X3 were essentially identical to those at 30 June 20X2.

Factory overhead was applied to products at 120 per cent of direct labour dollars. The factory overhead costs for the 20X2–X3 fiscal year were as follows.

	$
Variable indirect labour and supplies	15 000
Variable employee benefits	30 000
Supervisory salaries	35 000
Plant occupancy costs	100 000
Total	180 000

There was no over- or under-applied overhead for the year.

ii *Advertising:* The company has been unable to determine any direct causal relationship between the level of sales volume and the level of advertising expenditures. However, because management believes advertising is necessary, an annual advertising program is implemented for each product line. Each product is advertised independently of the others.

iii *Commissions:* Sales commissions are paid to the sales force at the rates of 5 per cent on the cereals and 10 per cent on the breakfast bars and dog food.

iv *Licences:* Various licences are required for each product line. These are renewed annually in each case.

v   *Salaries:* Sales and administrative personnel devote time and effort to each product line and to the company as a whole. Salaries and wages are allocated on the basis of management's estimates of the relative time spent on each product line. These costs are related to the company's overall activities rather than to any product line.

Required:

The controller of General Grains has recommended the company does a cost-volume-profit analysis of its operations. The controller has requested that you first prepare a revised income statement that employs a product contribution margin format that will be useful in CVP analysis. The statement should show the profit contribution for each product line and the net income (before taxes) for the company as a whole.

(Adapted from W.J. Morse and H.P. Roth, 1986. *Cost Accounting: Processing, Evaluating, and Using Cost Data*, 3rd edn, Addison-Wesley, p. 382.)

Ethics case study

Forpark Ltd is planning to add slides to the cubby houses they produce. Joe Clark, the accountant for Forpark, has just completed an analysis to see if the company should make or buy the slides. His analysis shows that, based on the written quotations received from two suppliers of the slides, the company should purchase the slides

The manager of Forpark agrees with Clark and they issue instructions to the purchasing department that orders should be placed for the slides as long as the price is not greater than $35 per unit.

A couple of days later, Clark is informed by the purchasing department that both suppliers have increased their price to $40 per unit. He discusses the situation with the manager and they decide that Forpark should now manufacture the slides. Clark thinks it is odd that both suppliers have increased their prices to the same figure.

Later in the week, Joe Clark is approached by his secretary, Jane Brown. Jane informs him that a friend of hers, who works for one of the suppliers of the slides, has told her about an agreement reached between the two suppliers of the slides. Essentially, the two suppliers have agreed to raise the price of their slides to $40 per unit. Jane does not want her friend to get into trouble for disclosing this type of confidential information, but at the same time she thinks she ought to tell Joe.

Discuss:

a   what Joe should do with the information received from Jane, remembering his responsibilities to the accounting profession, his company and to Jane

b   who is affected by the scheme to manipulate tenders in this manner.

Accounting for Decision Making: Resource Constraints and Mutual Exclusion

Learning objectives

At the end of this chapter you should be able to:

1. explain what is meant by decision making with constraints

2. explain and apply the contribution approach with one scarce resource

3. understand what is meant by 'internal opportunity cost' and the terms 'marginal product' and 'marginal return'

4. evaluate problems of whether entities should make or buy a product or a service in cases where there is spare capacity and when there is no spare capacity

5. discuss the role of qualitative factors in decision making with constraints

6. illustrate the impact of qualitative factors in relation to customers, employees, competitors, suppliers and legal constraints.

Introduction

In Chapter 19 we examined the principles of relevant costs and the application of these principles in making accounting decisions. These decisions related to situations where there were no resource constraints and acceptance or rejection did not affect the demand or production levels of any other products. In practice, however, a decision taken by an organisation often necessitates giving up other opportunities, either because of the lack of resources or because the decision is mutually exclusive (i.e. the acceptance of one opportunity means that others are rejected). In this chapter we examine decisions where there are resource constraints and the most common type of mutually exclusive decision for organisations, the make or buy decision.

In the case of decisions where there are resource constraints, we consider situations where there is only one scarce resource. Decision making when there are two or more scarce resources is outside the scope of this introductory text. The same principles apply, but when there are two or more scarce resources, more complex mathematical skills are required in the calculation of the solution.

In Chapter 19, in our analysis of short-term decisions, we assumed that only quantitative factors (e.g. costs and revenues) are relevant in the decision-making process. Initially, in this chapter we continue with this assumption. In reality, however, qualitative factors are also influential in the decision-making process. We conclude our examination of short-term decision making by considering the nature of qualitative factors and looking at some examples in which they influence the decision.

Decision making with constraints

For the situation where there are no constraints and fixed costs are unavoidable (i.e. irrelevant), as decribed in Chapter 19, we came to the following conclusion: all opportunities should be accepted if they make a positive contribution to fixed costs and profits.

Key Concept 20.1

Decision making with constraints: objectives

When there are resource constraints, the objective that should be applied is to establish the optimum output within the constraints to maximise contribution and thus profits.

However, if the availability of one or more resources is restricted, an organisation will be unable to accept every opportunity that yields a positive contribution. It is therefore necessary to formulate a decision-making rule that takes account of these resource constraints.

Before considering this process to determine the optimum output, it is appropriate to examine the nature of constraints that an organisation might be subjected to in the context of its operations.

Traditionally, in accounting textbooks, the constraints that are considered relate to shortages of manufacturing resources, such as particular types of materials, labour skills and the size of manufacturing plant. However, organisations in the service sector can similarly be restricted in their earning capacity as a result of such constraints. For example, an accounting practice could be restricted as to the number of clients it can accept for audit work because of the shortage of qualified accounting staff available to the practice. The principles to be applied when there are constraints are the same for both manufacturing and service sectors.

The constraints described relate to the short term and can invariably be eliminated in the long term. For example, a firm has the opportunity to manufacture and sell two products, Jack and Jill, both of which yield a positive contribution per unit. But due to a shortage of skilled machine operators the firm cannot satisfy the demand for these products. Clearly, this constraint is only a short-term phenomenon as the firm could train machine operators now to ensure that there will not be a shortage in the long term. However, in the short term this will be an effective constraint on production and ultimately on income.

The contribution approach with one scarce resource

In determining the optimum output, the analysis takes account only of quantitative factors. Qualitative factors often influence the final decision: for example, unprofitable products might be included in the range in order to maintain customer loyalty to all products sold by the firm. This should always be borne in mind when making such decisions.

To determine the optimum output with one constraint we must first determine the contribution. Secondly, we must establish the contribution per unit of the constraint for all those opportunities that yield a positive contribution. For example, say product Jack yields a positive contribution of $16 per unit and takes four labour hours to produce; assuming that labour is the only effective production constraint, then the contribution per labour hour in producing product Jack is $16 ÷ 4 hours = $4 per labour hour. This provides crucial information about the efficiency of the use of the constrained resource in terms of contribution and thus profitability.

The next stage is to rank these opportunities, preferring those that yield the highest contribution per constraint. If, for example, product Jill generates a positive contribution per labour hour of $3, product Jack will be ranked higher, in the absence of other factors, because it yields a contribution of $1 more per labour hour. The optimum plan can then be derived within the total resources available. In the example above, this will be total labour hours available to the firm in a defined period.

Example 20.1 illustrates the stages of this process.

Example 20.1: Troy Ltd

The directors of Troy Ltd are drawing up the production plan for the forthcoming year. There are five products that are under consideration: A, B, C, D and E. The following statement of the contribution per unit of these opportunities has been prepared by the company's accountant.

	A	B	C	D	E
	$	$	$	$	$
Selling price	10	24	48	13	22
Variable costs					
Materials	7	3	2	3	2
Labour	4	7	10	2	5
Total variable costs	11	10	12	5	7
Contribution per unit	(1)	14	36	8	15
Estimated demand in units	800	700	800	600	400
Labour hours per unit	4	7	10	2	5

For convenience of calculation, we will assume that all labour is paid at the rate of $1 per hour. The total of fixed costs for the year is estimated to be $14 990 and will vary with the range of products actually produced and sold.

Labour is scarce, and it is expected that only 7000 hours will be available next year.

We begin our analysis to determine the optimum production plan, within the labour constraint confronted by Troy Ltd, by accepting all opportunities that yield a positive contribution and rejecting those that yield a negative contribution. All the opportunities with the exception of product A yield a positive contribution. Product A, which has a negative contribution, will therefore, at this stage, be eliminated from the company's possible future range of products.

Before we continue it is wise to check whether the labour constraint of 7000 hours is an effective constraint on the company's activities. We do this by calculating the total labour hours required to meet the demand for the four products that yield positive contributions. We will begin with product B and follow alphabetical order.

Product	Demand		Labour hours	
	units	per unit	total	cumulative
B	700	7	4 900	4 900
C	800	10	8 000	12 900

It can be seen from the cumulative labour hours column that, if we satisfied the demand of only products B and C, the company would exceed the labour hours it has available (i.e. 7000 hours). Thus, we can conclude that labour hours are an effective constraint on the company's level of production and that the company will be unable to accept all the opportunities available to it.

We can now calculate, for the four remaining opportunities, the contribution per labour hour by dividing the labour hours per unit into the contribution per unit and ranking the opportunities in order of the highest contribution per labour hour.

	B	C	D	E
Contribution per labour hour	$14 ÷ 7 hours = $2	$36 ÷ 10 hours = $3.6	$8 ÷ 2 hours = $4	$15 ÷ 5 hours = $3
Ranking	4	2	1	3

Product D is ranked first because it yields the highest contribution per labour hour ($4), followed by product C with a contribution of $3.60 per hour, and then products E and B. This priority ranking can now be applied to determine the products that will be included in the optimum plan and to establish the total contribution that is generated by this plan.

Ranking	Product	Demand	Labour hours		Contribution	Total
		units	per unit	total	per unit	
1	D	600	2	1 200	$8	4 800
2	C	580	10	5 800	$36	20 880
				7 000		25 680

It can be seen that the company is able to satisfy the total demand for product D, which was ranked first, within the labour constraint, leaving 7000 − 1200 = 5800 hours available for the production of other products. Product C is the next product preferred within the ranking order and the total demand for C is estimated to be 800 units. However, to satisfy the demand for C will use up 800 units ¥ 10 hours per unit = 8000 hours, and we have only 5800 hours available. Therefore the company will be restricted to producing 5800 ÷ 10 = 580 units of product C because of the shortage of labour. Products B and E are excluded from the plan because there are no more labour hours available.

This is the optimal plan because it takes account of two important variables: contribution and the scarce resource, labour hours. If the production plan has been based on a priority ranking scheme that took account only of the contribution and ignored the labour constraint, the ranking order in terms of the highest contribution per unit would be as follows.

Ranking	Product
1	C
2	E
3	B
4	D

The total contribution that would be yielded from this ranking order would have been as follows.

Product	Demand units	Labour hours per unit	total	Contribution per unit	total
C	700	10	7 000	$36	$25 200

It can be seen that only product C, which was ranked first using the ranking order based on the highest contribution per unit, will be produced and sold by the company. This is because the maximum demand for product C is 800 units and, because of the restriction on labour hours available, only 700 units can be produced (i.e. 10 hours × 700 units = 7000 hours). The important point to recognise, however, is that the contribution of $25 200 generated from this ranking order is less than the contribution ($25 680) from using the order of ranking based on contribution per labour hour described earlier. The comparison of profitability using these two approaches clearly shows that if an organisation is to maximise its profits when there are resource constraints, these constraints must be taken into account in the decision process.

Contribution per unit and internal opportunity cost

The use of the contribution per unit of scarce resource in establishing an organisation's optimum production plan produces some interesting insights into the measurement of the opportunity cost of scarce resources. In Chapter 19 we defined the opportunity cost of a resource as 'the maximum benefit which could be obtained from that resource if it were used for some other purpose'. Invariably, the opportunity cost of a resource that is scarce will be greater than its purchase price. This is because there will be competing opportunities for the resource within the organisation. A number of examples were shown in the last chapter where the relevant cost of using a resource (the opportunity cost) exceeded the purchase price of the resource.

The concept of opportunity cost can also be applied in the selection of products to be included in an organisation's optimum production plan. We continue with the example of Troy Ltd to illustrate the application and to help us to understand further the role of opportunity costs in this type of decision.

In the case of Troy Ltd, labour was scarce, and there were competing alternative opportunities for this resource within the company. In particular, there were only enough labour hours to satisfy the demand for product D and partially to satisfy the demand for C, producing 580 units out of a total demand of 800. The contribution per labour hour of product C was $3.60. Opportunities that yield a higher contribution per labour hour are preferred, and in the case of products B and E, the contribution per labour hour was less; thus C was preferred. Indeed, if any new opportunities became available to Troy they would be included in the optimum production plan only if they generated a contribution per labour hour greater than $3.60.

Product C can therefore be described as the *marginal product* within the production plan, and the contribution per labour hour of $3.60 as the *marginal return* on one hour of labour. That is, if Troy had one more labour hour available the return on this hour would be $3.60, or conversely, if one hour fewer was available the company would lose $3.60, in terms of contribution. In terms of the production of product C, an extra labour hour will produce one-tenth of one unit of C, as it takes ten hours to produce one unit. We assume that product C is divisible, i.e. that we can make and sell one-tenth of a unit more or less of it. The following shows the increase in contribution from one more hour used in producing one-tenth of C.

	$
Selling Price ($48 ÷ 10)	4.80
Less Costs	
Materials ($2 ÷ 10)	0.20
Labour ($10 ÷ 10)	1.00
Total variable costs	1.20
Increase in contribution	3.60

This computation would be the same if one less hour were available, but would result in a loss in contribution of $3.60.

At this stage we summarise the three main points that have been derived from our analysis so far and examine their implications.

Implication 1

If one more labour hour becomes available it will contribute $3.60 per hour. In the case of Troy, the contribution of $3.60 per hour will be generated from an additional 2200 hours, if these hours are available. This figure is the number of hours that would be used in making another 220 units (220 × 10 hours per unit) of product C, the unsatisfied demand for C. (Remember, the total demand was 800 units, and 580 units can be produced within the original labour constraint.) If more than 2200 hours became available, assuming there were no new opportunities, labour would then be used to produce product E, which would generate $3 per hour. The number of units of E produced would clearly depend upon how many hours became available: 2000 hours would be required to satisfy the total demand for E. If any more hours were available, these would be employed on the least preferred product, B.

This information at the planning stage is extremely useful to managers in considering scenarios. For example, management might be unsure as to the exact number of hours available, and could ask the question: if 300 additional labour hours became available in the coming year, what would be the increased contribution? This can be quickly calculated when the contribution per labour hour is known, by multiplying the contribution per labour hour by the number of hours; in this example $3.60 × 300 hours = $1080.

Implication 2

If one less hour is available Troy would lose $3.60 per hour in contribution. The loss in contribution of $3.60 per hour would continue for every hour lost up to 5800 hours (580 × 10 hours per unit). These are the total hours required to satisfy the original constrained demand of 580 units of product C. This information, similarly, could be useful to management at the planning stage. For example, what would be the loss in contribution if 600 labour hours were lost due to machine breakdowns during the year? Knowing the loss in contribution for every hour lost, the calculation is simple: 600 hours $\times$ $3.60 = $2160.

Implication 3

If future opportunities became available they would have to contribute at least $3.60 per labour hour before they would be considered for inclusion in the future production plan. It would not be necessary, in such cases, to recalculate the contribution from each product and then to rank each product in coming to this conclusion. All that is necessary is to calculate the contribution per labour hour for any additional opportunities that become available. These are then compared with the contribution per labour hour generated from the current opportunities. If these new opportunities yield a higher contribution per labour hour, they will displace those currently in the plan. Once again this information is extremely useful to management.

We can conclude that knowledge of the contribution from the use of constrained resources is extremely useful to management in making decisions to ensure the future profitability of an organisation.

Internal opportunity cost

The contribution per labour hour is also known as the internal opportunity cost of labour. The term 'internal opportunity cost' is more appropriate when it is used in examining the efficient use of resources within an organisation. In the example of Troy, labour was paid $1 per hour, but there is the additional cost of labour (i.e. the internal opportunity cost of $3.60 per hour) that relates to its use within the organisation because there are competing opportunities for the use of the scarce resource. The cost of labour per hour is therefore represented by two elements of costs:

- cash cost of employing the labour, which can be described as the 'external opportunity cost'
- the internal opportunity cost, which reflects the cost of using the resource within the organisation itself due to competing opportunities.

These costs can be summarised as follows.

	$
Cash cost of employing labour (the external opportunity cost)	1.00
Internal opportunity cost for the use of labour in the organisation	3.60
Total cost of labour	4.60

The determination of the internal opportunity cost is extremely useful as it indicates how much Troy would be willing to pay to obtain one more labour hour. For example, to release more labour hours to produce additional units of product C, the manager decides to offer overtime to employees at a premium, but does not know what premium to offer. The total opportunity cost of $4.60 per hour is the maximum the company should be willing to pay for an additional labour hour. The payment of a higher rate will result in a loss. On the basis of this information, the company might decide to offer its employees $3 per hour (i.e. a premium of $2 per hour) for any overtime worked, which is $1.60 less than the maximum they can afford to pay. The contribution generated from one hour to produce one-tenth of product C will then be as follows.

	$	$
Selling price (one-tenth of $48)		4.80
Less Costs		
Materials ($2 ÷ 10)		0.20
Labour		
External opportunity cost	1.00	
Premium for overtime	2.00	3.00
Total costs		3.20
Contribution		1.60

If the company anticipated that employees would be willing to work 350 hours of overtime during the period, the additional total contribution will be $1.60 × 350 hours = $560.

In this analysis we have used the example of a labour constraint. The same principles apply to any situation where a resource is scarce: we must determine the opportunities that use these resources most efficiently.

CASE STUDY 20.1

India turns back to rail as oil prices soar

by Subramaniam Sharma and Anindya Mukherjee

NEW DELHI—Hindustan Lever is trying something new to get its products to customers faster and cheaper: taking the train.

Fed up with clogged roads and keen to avoid higher diesel fuel costs, the maker of everything from tea to toothpaste is transporting more gods via the colonial-era rail network and giving truckers less business.

'There is a definite benefit,' said P.K. Chattopadhyay, head of logistics at Hindustan Lever, a unit of Unilever NV of the Netherlands. The maker of Lux soap and Surf detergent will ship 10 per cent of its freight by rail this year from zero two years ago. The figure would be higher next year, he said.

Across India, manufacturers are eager to limit the increase in their costs from the 36 per cent surge in crude oil prices this year.

Fuel makes up 40 per cent of the cost of road freight charges compared to just 7 per cent for rail. Ram Naik, minister for petroleum and natural gas, said on Saturday that another fuel price rise might be essential by the end of the month.

'The oil price hike is a psychological factor,' said S.B. Roy, group general manager, domestic, at Container Corp of India, a state-owned company that is the sole provider of rail transport in large containers.

'It prompts the logistics manager to choose rail, which offers better stability, though not always better prices.'

Rail freight revenues rose 6.4 per cent in the five months to August from a year ago, after showing virtually no growth in the previous two years.

Forged by British rulers in the 19th century, India's rail network is the second-largest in the world after the US, where railways have been losing business to highways since the 1950s. With 62 000 kilometres of track spanning the subcontinent and 7000 stations, India's rail network still carries 40 per cent of all goods.

While a truck takes a week on average to move goods along the 2000-kilometre road between New Delhi and Chennai, rail takes less than five days. It's cheaper, too. A tonne of goods costs 2100 rupees (A$83) for the trip by road. It costs 1600 rupees to cover the same distance by rail.

Any savings from stable freight charges, in the face of rising fuel costs, will help industries such as cement and metal. Freight charges account for 25 per cent of total expenses for cement makers and about 15 per cent of costs for steel makers.

Rail transportation costs went up 4 per cent when diesel prices were raised 34 per cent in October last year, while truck freight rates rose 12 per cent.

'There is less impact on rail freight tariffs, as compared to trucking rates, when there is a diesel price hike,' said S.N. Singh, chief manager, traffic, at National Aluminium Company.

Asia's biggest aluminium producer saved six million rupees a year by favouring rail, Mr Singh said. He plans to move almost all of National's 5.6 million tonnes of finished aluminium by rail this year, up from about 90 per cent last year.

The lower costs are possible because 80 per cent of Indian Railways' trunk routes, which connect major cities with ports, are linked by electric trains.

New freight wagons also travel faster and need less maintenance, which has cut the time it takes to get goods across the country. Meanwhile, many of India's roads are falling into disrepair.

'Most of the highways in the country are two-lane and maintenance is poor, leading to inordinate delays in trucks being able to deliver on time,' said Shashanka Bhide, economist at the National Council of Applied Economic Research.

For now, at least, the government's rail system also has oil on its side.

BLOOMBERG/*Age,* 27 September 2000

Commentary

The article shows how increased fuel costs prompted Hindustan Lever to change its mode of transportation from road to rail. Other industries such as cement and steel makers are also changing as freight charges account for 25 per cent of total costs for cement makers and 15 per cent for steel makers. The change by Hindustan Lever will enable it to avoid significant cost increases since the cost of rail increased by only 4 per cent in the same period that diesel prices increased by 34 per cent. This case highlights effective decision making by management when confronted by significant price increases in one of the resources required to transport products to customers.

Make or buy decisions

An example of a make or buy decision is a decision whether an organisation should design and develop its own computer programs or whether an external software house should be hired to do the work.

The 'make' option gives the management of the organisation more direct control over the work. However, an external contractor often has specialist skills and expertise. As with most of the decisions considered in this chapter, make or buy decisions should not be made on the basis of cost alone. Qualitative factors will be considered in more depth at the end of this chapter.

Key Concept 20.2

Make or buy decisions

A make or buy decision involves the problem of an organisation choosing between making a product or carrying out a service using its own resources, and paying another external organisation to make a product or carry out a service for it.

We begin our analysis by first examining whether to make or buy when an organisation has spare capacity. We then consider the situation when capacity is restricted because of shortages of resources.

Where there is spare capacity

We assume that the organisation is not working at full capacity and thus has enough resources available to make a product or component, if it so wishes, without affecting the production of other products. Example 20.2 illustrates the principles that should be applied to make and buy decisions in this case.

Example 20.2: Leigh Ltd

Leigh Ltd is a company that is confronted with the problem of whether to make or buy three components, Bot, Lot and Tot. The respective costs are as follows.

	Bot	Lot	Tot
Production units	1 000	2 000	4 000
	$	$	$
Variable costs per unit			
Materials	4	5	2
Labour	10	12	5
Total variable cost	14	17	7

The fixed costs per annum that are directly attributable (avoidable costs) to the manufacture of the components and are apportioned (unavoidable costs) to components are as follows.

	$
Avoidable costs	
Bot	1 000
Lot	5 000
Tot	13 000
Apportioned fixed costs	30 000
	49 000

A subcontractor has offered to supply units of Bot, Lot and Tot for $12, $21 and $10 respectively.

The relevant costs to be taken into account in this decision are the differential costs associated with making and with buying. In this example the differential costs are the differences in unit variable costs and the directly attributable fixed costs. The following is a summary of the relevant costs.

	Bot	Lot	Tot
	$	$	$
Variable cost per unit, making	14	17	7
Cost per unit, buying	12	21	10
Additional cost per unit of buying	(2)	4	3
Production units per annum	1 000	2 000	4 000
Additional total variable cost of buying	(2 000)	8 000	12 000
Fixed costs saved by buying	1 000	5 000	13 000
Additional total cost of buying	(3 000)	3 000	(1 000)

The organisation would thus save $3000 per annum by subcontracting component Bot (this is because the variable cost per unit to make the component is greater than the purchase price), and $1000 per annum by subcontracting component Tot (this is due to the saving of $13 000 of fixed costs directly attributable to making the component). In the case of component Lot, the organisation will be $3000 better off making the component.

It should also be noted that the apportioned fixed costs are irrelevant to this decision because they are unavoidable.

In such decisions there will normally be another consideration. If components Bot and Tot are to be purchased from a subcontractor, it is likely that the organisation will have spare capacity which has some value to the organisation; for example, it might decide to let the space to an outside party, which would generate additional income. This additional income should be included as a relevant cost of making the components because the revenue will be forgone if the component is made. It is an opportunity cost.

Inevitably there will be qualitative factors that should be taken into account. In this example, the organisation might be concerned about the quality of the work of the subcontractor. This factor might lead the organisation to favour making components Bot and Tot, although in cost terms this policy would be unprofitable.

Where there is no spare capacity

A firm might be confronted with the decision whether to make or buy a component when it is currently working at full capacity. To make the component, it will be necessary for the firm to stop or restrict its current production output. In such cases the cost of making must include not only the costs directly attributed to making but also the loss in contribution of the production that has been displaced by the decision to make. The loss in contribution is the internal opportunity cost, which was discussed earlier.

Example 20.3 illustrates the application of the concept of the internal opportunity cost in the make or buy decision when capacity is restricted.

Example 20.3: Kellee Ltd

Kellee Ltd is in the process of deciding whether to make or buy a component of one of the products it manufactures and sells. Labour is in short supply and the factory is currently working at full capacity. The following are the estimated costs per unit to make the component; the assumption that labour is paid $4 per hour is made for convenience of calculation.

	Cost per unit
	$
Direct labour (5 hours @ $4 per hour)	20
Direct material	15
Fixed overheads	5
Total cost per unit	40

The fixed overhead costs are apportioned to the product and are unavoidable whether or not the component is made, so this cost is irrelevant to the decision. All the other costs are directly attributable to the cost of producing the component and are thus relevant. The relevant cost associated with making the component is therefore $35.

The alternative is to buy in the component from another firm. The cost of buying the component is $38 per unit.

If labour was not in short supply, the firm would make the component rather than buy it because the relevant costs of making ($35) are less than the purchase price of buying ($38).

However, in view of the shortage of labour we must consider the contribution forgone by the decision to make. To do so, we must account for the contribution generated from the current production activity that is to be restricted in deciding to make the component. The following data relate to the revenue and cost per unit associated with a product that is to be displaced by producing (making) the component.

| | | Cost per unit |
	$	$
Selling price		26
Less Costs		
Direct labour (3 hours @ $4 per hour)	12	
Direct material	8	20
Contribution per unit		6

The contribution per hour of labour generated from this product is $2 (i.e. contribution $6 divided by three hours' labour). This is the internal opportunity cost of using the labour on the manufacture of this product. If the labour is to be efficiently diverted to making the component instead of this product, it must therefore yield a contribution of at least $2 per hour. We can also conclude that the effective cost of labour employed on making the component consists of two elements: the cash paid to employees for their labour of $4 per hour (i.e. the external opportunity cost) plus the internal opportunity cost of $2 per hour. These two elements of cost should therefore be included in the calculation to decide whether to make or buy the component. The following summarises all the relevant costs in making the components.

	$	$
Direct labour		
Cash paid to employees (the external opportunity cost) ($4 x 5 hours)	20	
Internal opportunity cost ($2 x 3 hours)	6	26
Direct materials		15
Total relevant costs		41

The inclusion of the internal opportunity cost as relevant to the decision to make has resulted in a cost for making the component of $41. This exceeds the buying price of $38; thus, purely on financial grounds the decision should be to buy rather than to make.

The principle that the internal opportunity cost should be included in the relevant costs of a make or buy decision applies to all situations where there is no spare capacity because resources are scarce.

Qualitative factors

In our analysis of decision making in this and the previous chapter, all the decisions made were based only on financial criteria. Often qualitative factors are of great influence in such decisions. Indeed, on some occasions an opportunity would be rejected on purely quantitative (financial) criteria but for other, qualitative, reasons, the opportunity is accepted.

Qualitative factors are those which cannot be quantified in terms of costs and income. They might stem from either non-financial objectives or factors which could be quantified in money terms but have not been because there is insufficient information to make a reliable estimate.

The nature of these qualitative factors varies with the circumstances. The following are some examples of qualitative factors that might influence decisions.

Customers

The inclusion or exclusion of a product from the range offered or the quality of the product and after-sales service affects demand for the product and customer loyalty. For example, the exclusion of one product from a range because it is uneconomic to produce and sell, could affect the demand for other products. Products manufactured by firms are often interdependent and this interdependence should be considered when a decision is made.

Employees

Decisions involving the closure of part of a firm, or relocation, or changes in work procedures, require acceptance by the employees. If the changes are mishandled, problems between employees and management could lead to inefficiencies and losses.

Competitors

In a competitive market, decisions by one firm to enhance its competitive advantage might result in retaliation by competitors. For example, the decision to reduce selling prices in order to raise demand will not be successful if all competitors take similar action.

A firm might decide to produce an unprofitable product or to offer a service at a loss because it would otherwise be leaving the market to its competitors. The firm considers that continued service to customers will eventually affect the demand for its other products.

Legal constraints

An opportunity is sometimes rejected because of doubts about pending legislation. The decision to open a hotel, for example, might be influenced by pending legislation on safety requirements that would result in additional costs which are too complex to estimate.

Suppliers

A firm might rely heavily on a good relationship with a particular supplier for the prompt delivery of supplies. Some decisions might affect that relationship.

Summary

In this chapter we have developed a number of the concepts introduced in Chapter 19. In particular, the concept of opportunity cost was examined and the two elements of cost, the external and internal opportunity costs, were identified.

The concept of opportunity cost was shown to be a powerful tool in determining the optimal production plan when an organisation is experiencing a shortage of resources. In particular it ensures that scarce resources are used efficiently.

Lastly, we examined the qualitative factors that influence decisions. A number of examples were given which illustrate their importance in the decision-making process.

Further reading

Hilton, R., 1997. *Managerial Accounting*, 3rd edn, McGraw-Hill.

Hirsch, M.L., Louderback, J.G., and Smith, E., 1989. *Cost Accounting: Accumulation, Analysis and Use*, Thomas Nelson.

Horngren, C.T., Foster, G., and Datar, S. 1997. *Cost Accounting: A Managerial Emphasis*, 9th edn, Prentice-Hall.

Morse, W.J., and Roth, H.P., 1986. *Cost Accounting: Processing, Evaluating, and Using Cost Data*, 3rd edn, Addison-Wesley.

Review questions

1   Many organisations, at particular times, are subject to shortages of resources. These shortages effectively restrict their ability to meet the demand for their products or services. Describe four examples of these types of constraints, two for a manufacturing firm and two for a service firm.

2   Explain why a shortage of resources in an organisation is a short-term phenomenon.

3   Discuss the importance and usefulness of the concept of internal opportunity cost in the making of decisions.

4   The opportunity cost of a resource, in some circumstances, might be higher than the resource's purchase price. Explain why this might be the case.

5   Qualitative factors are often influential in the decision-making process. Describe the nature of qualitative factors and give three examples that might influence a decision to make a component rather than buy it from another firm.

Problems for discussion and analysis

1   Agro Company has been producing 10 000 units of part 7021 for its products. The unit cost for the part is as follows:

	$
Direct materials	5
Direct labour	10
Variable manufacturing overhead	6
Fixed manufacturing overhead	8
Total	29

Agro can purchase 10 000 units of part 7021 for $25 each. If the part is purchased, Agro can make another product and provide a contribution margin of $10 000. Indirect costs account for 75 per cent of the fixed manufacturing overhead costs, and these will remain even if the part is purchased.

Required:

Should Agro make or buy the part?

2 Advance Ltd manufactures two solar powered Frisbees, Wild One and Bold One. The company has only a limited supply of skilled labour, essential in the production process.

The following information is available:

	Wild One	Bold One
Contribution margin per unit	$15	$18
Units produced per hour	3	4

Anticipated sales exceed capacity for both products.

Total labour hours available: 12 000 hours.

Required:

Determine which product should be produced.

3 Coyle Ltd at present manufactures all the components that go to make up its finished products. A components supplier has offered to provide the firm's requirements of two components, the BC100 at $7.75 each and the BC200 at $2.00 each.

If the firm buys in components, the capacity utilised for these components at present would be unused. The firm currently manufactures 50 000 units of each component and the current costs of production are as follows:

	BC100	BC200
	$	$
Materials	2.50	1.00
Labour	3.00	1.25
Fixed overheads	3.50	1.75
Total cost per unit	9.00	4.00

a On a quantitative basis, should the firm continue to manufacture BC100 and BC200 or should it buy in one or both of the components?
b Discuss the qualitative factors which are likely to influence this decision.

4 XYZ Ltd manufactures two products. On average it sells 40 000 of product 1 and 60 000 of product 2 each year. This year the company has a restricted advertising budget of $50 000, which is only enough to effectively promote one of its products. The marketing department estimates that sales of product 1 will increase by 20 per cent if it is advertised, while product 2 will increase by 15 per cent if it is advertised.

The following data are provided:

	1	2
Selling price per unit	$20	$30
Variable cost per unit	10	14
Fixed cost per unit	5	10
Production time per unit (direct labour hours)	42	13

Required:

a Assuming unlimited direct labour hours, which product should it advertise?
b Assuming there are only 120 000 direct labour hours, would you change your decision?

5   The ABC company manufactures gas bottles for use in campervans and caravans. The costs per bottle are as follows.

	$
Direct materials	5.30
Direct labour	4.20
Variable overhead	0 35
Fixed overhead (per month)	$125 000

The company manufactures and sells 20 000 bottles per month and has the capacity, without increasing overhead costs, to manufacture 25 000.

Fixed costs are allocated on the basis of bottles manufactured.

Avco Ltd have offered to purchase 6000 bottles for $72 000. This is a one-off order and would not be repeated.
a   Should ABC accept the order? Why?
b   What problems might the company face if it accepts the order?

6   Pigeon Ltd proposes a production plan for 20X1, aiming to maximise profits. The following details are available.

	A	B	C	D	E	F
Labour hours per unit	6.4	7	4	9	5	12
Machine hours per unit	3	2	1	3	1	8
Maximum demand	2 500	1 200	700	1 100	900	2 900
	$	$	$	$	$	$
Selling price	20	28	8	36	16	40
Costs						
Direct materials	4	4	1.2	2.4	2.8	1.6
Direct labour	4	6	2.4	8.8	3.6	3.2
Fixed overhead	4	6	2.4	8.8	3.6	3.2
Total cost	12	16	6.0	20.0	10.0	8.0
Profit	8	12	2.0	16.0	6.0	32.0

Fixed overhead, which is estimated to cost $10 000 irrespective of what is produced and sold, is applied at 100 per cent of direct labour cost.

A maximum of 64 000 direct labour hours is expected to be available.
a   Calculate the optimal profit-maximising production plan and explain the reasons for your choice.
b   Explain the following hypothetical internal opportunity costs:
    i   direct labour hours $2.40
    ii machine hours $1.70

7   You have recently been appointed as a consultant to the Murphy Manufacturing Company. The management of the company has prepared a report showing certain data concerning the two products Mox and Tox. The following information has been extracted from this report:

	Mox	Tox
Monthly sales in units	1 000	2 000
	$	$
Selling Price	3.0	1.5
Costs		
Direct materials	0.8	0.5
Direct labour	1.0	0.2

(continued next page)

Fixed overheads	1.4	0.5
Total cost	3.2	1.2
Profit (loss)	(0.2)	0.3

In view of the poor results shown by Mox, the following changes have been proposed by the management.

- Abandon the production of Mox and buy in 1000 per month for $2800. The quality is identical and selling price will remain unchanged.
- Use the spare capacity to make Cox. It is estimated that 1000 units could be sold at $1 each. Material costs are $0.4 per unit and labour costs $0.2.

All overheads are fixed and are not expected to change from the present cost of $2000 per month. No inventories are held.

a   Comment on the suitability of the management's statement for assessing product profitability, and indicate any ways in which you think it could be improved.

b   Prepare a monthly statement of financial performance for the present and proposed new programs. Do the proposed changes appear to be profitable? Explain the reasons for any misunderstandings which might have arisen as a result of the management's proposal.

8   Flatlands Manufacturing produces a variety of motorised gardening tools. Management follows a pricing policy of full cost (including a fair share of selling and administrative costs) plus 15 per cent markup. In response to a request from Desperate Discounts stores, the following price has been developed for an order of 1000 Bush Turners (a small tilling machine).

	$
Manufacturing costs	
Direct materials	10 000
Direct labour	50 000
Factory overhead	20 000
Total	80 000
Selling and administrative costs	8 000
Total costs	88 000
Markup	13 200
Selling price	101 200

I.M. Desperate, the CEO of Desperate Discounts, rejected this price as too high and offered to purchase the 1000 Bush Turners at a price of $80 000.

The following additional information is available:

i   Flatlands Manufacturing has excess capacity.

ii   Factory overhead is applied on the basis of direct labour dollars.

iii Budgeted factory overhead is $400 000 for the current year, including $120 000 of fixed overhead.

iv   Budgeted production and sales for the current year total 40 000 units.

v   Fixed selling and administrative costs are $160 000 for the current year. In pricing computations, these costs are applied on the basis of the total number of units sold.

vi   Variable selling and administrative costs are believed to be a function of the total number of units sold.

Required:

   a   Determine the effect on income of accepting Desperate's offer.

   b   Briefly explain why you omitted certain costs from your analysis in part (a).

   c   How would your analysis in part (a) differ if Flatlands did not have excess capacity?

(Adapted from W.J. Morse and H.P. Roth, *Cost Accounting: Processing, Evaluating and Using Cost Data*, 3rd edn, Addison-Wesley, 1986, p. 683.)

9 Philco is a manufacturer of radios. The costs per radio, for a production run of 20 000 units, are as follows.

	$
Direct materials	27.00
Direct labour	13.00
Variable overhead	6.00
Fixed overhead	10.00

Fixed overhead is applied on a per unit basis.

Mikel Ltd has offered to supply the circuit board with components for $20.00 per unit. This would result in a saving of $10.00 in direct materials, $3.00 in direct labour and $4.00 in variable overhead. There would be no saving in fixed overhead. If Philco were to accept this offer, it would then have the capacity to manufacture 10 000 baby transistor radios. The costs for the transistors are as follows.

	$
Direct materials	4.00
Direct labour	3.00
Fixed overhead per unit	2.00

The fixed overhead for the transistors is in addition to the fixed overhead incurred on the radios. The transistor radio sells for $10.10.

Should Philco accept the outside help, assuming all production is sold?

10 Burco Ltd produces and sells two products, X and Y. During the last year 700 hours were worked and the operating results were as follows.

	X	Y	Total
Units sold	1 000	1 000	2 000
	$	$	$
Sales	1 000	2 000	3 000
Variable costs			
Labour	200	500	700
Materials	550	900	1 450
Total variable costs	750	1 400	2 150
Contribution	250	600	850
Fixed costs			600
Net income			250

All variable costs are a linear function of output. The material used for X is quite different from that used for Y, but both can be produced with the same labour force.

Five units of X can be made in one labour hour, while only two units of Y can be made in one labour hour. Labour hours are expected to be limited to 800 next year.

Information about the market for X and Y for the next year is set out below:

	X	Y
Maximum quantity that can be sold (units)	1 100	1 200
Minimum quantity that must be sold to retain market (units)	600	800

a   Assuming plant capacity is fully used, what is the optimum mix of X and Y?
b   Assuming that the price of material for Y decreases by 20 per cent, what is the optimal mix of X and Y? Assume no change in the price of X or Y.
c   Assuming that the cost of labour increases by 20 per cent, that prices can be put up by only 10 per cent without affecting sales limits and that the number of labour hours available is reduced to 600, what is the optimal mix of X and Y?
d   What is the net income in each of these three cases?
e   Discuss the limitations of your analysis.

11 The manufacturing capacity of the Gorgon Company's production facilities is 30 000 units of product per year. A summary of operating results for the year ended 30 June 20X4 is as follows.

	$
Sales (18 000 units @ $100)	1 800 000
Variable manufacturing and selling costs	-990 000
Contribution margin	810 000
Fixed costs	-495 000
Operating income	315 000

A foreign distributor has offered to buy 15 000 units at $90 each during 20X5. Assume that all of Gorgon's costs would be at the same levels and rates in 20X5 as in 20X4. If Gorgon accepts this offer, they will reject some business from regular customers so as not to exceed capacity.

Required:

a   Determine the differential revenues and costs of accepting the order.
b   What is the opportunity cost of accepting the order?
c   Should Gorgon accept or reject the order? Why?
d   If capacity were 45 000 units rather than 30 000 units, should Gorgon accept or reject the order?
e   What non-quantitative factors should Gorgon consider in making the decision?

(Adapted from W.J. Morse and H.P. Roth, *Cost Accounting: Processing, Evaluating and Using Cost Data*, 3rd edn, Addison-Wesley, 1986, p. 681.)

12   As company secretary, you have been directed by the managing director to prepare a confidential report on the possible closure of the Hobart factory and centralisation of activities at the Perth facility. The combination of an expected increase in rent of $15 000 and the desire of the managing director's daughter, who is married to the Hobart manager, to return to Perth, appears to be the major reason behind the request for the report.

Due to the nature of the report, information for the decision is difficult to obtain. However, the following data is available from corporate budgets for the ensuing year.

i   Fixed costs of the Hobart operations are at present $85 000, comprising the $50 000 salary of the Hobart manager, who will be transferred back to Perth, rent at $25 000, and the $10 000 salary of a part-time clerk whose services would be dispensed with.

ii   Variable costs at the Hobart factory are $125 000.

iii You have established that the sale of plant and other assets in Hobart will be sufficient to pay the termination of all Hobart staff including the part-time clerk.

iv   Additional space in Perth may be rented in steps of $10 000 per 10 000 units.

v   A common price policy has established the price of the sole product at $10.00. Budgeted figures call for 25 000 units to be produced at Hobart and 40 000 units to be produced at Perth. There are no inventories.

vi   Additional staff at Perth would need to be hired to meet the additional demands. This cost is expected to be $17 500. The cost to service the Hobart market from Perth would be $1.10 per unit in addition to the variable costs.

vii Variable costs at Perth have been budgeted at $160 000.

viii The Hobart factory has been allocated $45 000 of the head office costs.

ix   A local manufacturer in Hobart can supply the Hobart region and is willing to do so, a royalty of $2.00 per unit being paid to your company.

Required:

In your report, list alternatives available to your company, including a full and complete cost justification to support your recommendation. What factors should be considered besides the cost factor? List such qualitative factors in your report.

(Adapted from *Management Accounting 1 Topic Questions*, University of Technology, Sydney, 1988, pp. 331–2.)

Ethics case study

Orbital Machines Ltd is a company that has been manufacturing a revolutionary new engine for motor vehicles for ten years. It employs 1000 workers, and the economy of Winjarra is completely dependent on Orbital Machines.

On 10 July 20X0 the company won a major contract with the Ford Motor Company to provide orbital engines for all its cars from 1 January 20X1. In order to meet the production requirements, the company would need to make a significant investment in additional manufacturing equipment and employ more workers.

The costs of operating in Winjarra have increased because of higher rates and taxes, as well as wage demands flowing from a strong local trade union. The company would be reluctant to invest significant funds if increases in costs are likely to continue to be a problem.

The company has received an approach from the mayor of a small city 500 kilo-metres from Winjarra. The mayor would like Orbital to move its entire operation to his city, and he has offered the following incentives:

i   A large parcel of land with no rates and taxes for five years.

ii A work force where the average labour costs are 25 per cent lower than in Winjarra.

In return Orbital must employ local residents.

This move could allow Orbital to avoid the cost pressures in Winjarra, which in turn would allow it to compete more effectively in foreign markets.

Discuss:

a   who the stakeholders in this decision are

b   the quantitative and qualitative factors which are relevant to this decision

c   whether there are any ethical issues for the management of Orbital Machines to consider.

Budgets

Learning objectives

At the end of this chapter you should be able to:

1 discuss the various reasons for producing budgets

2 explain what is meant by the budget process

3 explain the stages and parties that are typically involved in the budget process

4 understand that budgets are typically set for responsibility centres

5 discuss the factors which influence the choice of the budget period

6 explain what is normally included in the master budget

7 discuss the role of sales and production budgets and the relationship between them

8 calculate budgets for materials purchased in units and in monetary terms; materials costs per unit manufactured and sold and for labour costs

9 explain why, in addition to budgets for materials and labour, it may also be important to construct budgets for overhead costs.

Introduction

In Chapter 15, four stages of the planning and control process were identified. The third stage, making operating decisions, focused on the use of resources and the individual decisions necessary to use them consistently within the overall objectives of an organisation. It was also stated that in this stage the decisions would be translated into a short-term plan, a budget, defined as 'a plan of action expressed in monetary terms'. In this chapter we examine the purpose of budgets, the budgeting process, and the preparation of budgets.

A budget must match the organisation's needs. In Chapter 15 we mentioned the application of contingency theory to all accounting information systems. The major contingency factors identified were technology, the commercial environment and the structure of the organisation. These factors affect the type of budget which is used by an organisation. For instance, in a retail organisation the budget deals mainly with the level of consumer sales and the purchases of goods necessary to satisfy these sales. In contrast, the budget of a manufacturing organisation focuses on the sales of products and the production activity necessary to meet these sales. There are some similarities between the two types of budget, and there is a common basis for preparing the budgets of different types of organisation. We concentrate in this chapter on large manufacturing organisations, which have relatively sophisticated budgets.

The purposes of budgets

Below are listed a number of the traditional purposes of budgets. The purpose of budgets, as we have said, depends on the type of organisation; those given below are common to most organisations.

To compel planning

The introduction of budgets within an organisation forces management to look ahead and set short-term targets. By looking to the future, management can anticipate potential problems. For example, the identification of shortages of cash at particular times in the budget period gives management the opportunity to make provisions to supplement this shortage, e.g. to negotiate an overdraft facility with the bank.

To co-ordinate functions within an organisation

The preparation of budgets tends to increase the co-ordination between departments and units within an organisation because it requires that the individual plans of managers are integrated. The managers are obliged to consider the relationships between various departments. For example, it is important that a purchasing department is aware of the material requirements for manufacture so that buying and inventory (stock) levels are maintained to service the needs of the manufacturing activity during the budget period.

As a form of communication

A budget is often a useful means by which top management can formally communicate objectives and strategies for the forthcoming period. This function is reinforced periodically through a control mechanism—referred to later—which reviews actual performance against the budget during the budget period.

To provide a basis for responsibility accounting

Individual managers are identified with their budget centres and are made responsible for achieving the budget targets. These targets are in terms of expenditure, income and output that are considered to be within the manager's control. Responsibility accounting was outlined in Chapter 15. Within the context of budgets, responsibility accounting represents an important feature of the delegation of responsibility within an organisation.

To provide a basis for a control mechanism

The budget provides a basis for comparing actual performance with a plan and identifying any deviation from that plan. The identification of these deviations gives management the opportunity to take corrective action so that such deviations do not persist in the future. When budgets are used as a control mechanism, it is described as 'budgetary control'.

To authorise expenditure

The budget can act as a formal authorisation of future expenditure from top management to the individuals who are responsible for the expenditure. If an item of expenditure is contained in the budget that has been approved by the top management of the organisation, it implies that the item has been approved, and generally no further authorisation is required.

To motivate employees

The budget can be used as a target to motivate employees to reach certain levels of attainment. For example, if during one budget period a salesperson achieves sales of products to the value of $30 000, management might in the next period set a target of $40 000, believing, rightly or wrongly, that this new target will motivate the salesperson to exceed the levels of the previous period.

Budgets mean different things to different people within an organisation. For example, a budget which is introduced by management with the aim of monitoring production costs might be perceived by production managers as a device to monitor their performance. Budgets can lead to much misunderstanding, frustration and friction within an organisation.

Key Concept 21.1

The budget process

The phrase 'the budget process' refers to the sequence of operations necessary to produce a budget for a particular organisation. The sequence of operations depends upon the type of organisation and its perceived requirements for planning and control.

The budget process

The following analysis focuses on the main features of the budget process. The products that are manufactured and sold in a budget period are determined via operating decisions, as previously described in Chapters 19 and 20. These decisions are initially made in isolation from functions within an organisation that are there to support the manufacture and sales of the products that have been chosen. In a manufacturing organisation these supportive functions relate to purchasing, production, marketing, administration and finance. Each of these functions also requires investment in resources, such as personnel.

It is at the beginning of the budget process that consideration is given to the operating decisions collectively and their interrelationships with these functions. At this stage the resource implications of the decisions are analysed to determine the extent to which they will draw upon the functions that were described above. From this analysis, guidelines are formulated for the preparation of the budgets. The guidelines represent a framework for people who prepare the budgets; they identify the overall levels of activity and the organisation's policies on performance criteria, e.g. productivity. The people involved at this stage are the top management of the organisation. They include those that have overall responsibility for the sales and production activities and those that are responsible for ensuring that the activities are co-ordinated, e.g. an accountant who has responsibility for the co-ordination of the accounting information input, often referred to as the budget accountant. Thus, the vitally important management task of co-ordinating the various interrelated aspects of decision making begins in the budgeting process.

In a manufacturing organisation, for example, the main task of co-ordination is concerned with the overall policy on the level of sales and production activities. The co-ordination of these activities involves ensuring that the level of production is sufficient to meet the sales demand for products plus any stock of finished goods that is required. For example, if the sales demand for a product is 150 units and the desired closing stock of finished goods is 30 units, assuming there are no opening stocks of finished goods available, 180 units will have to be manufactured to meet the sales and stock requirements in the budget period. The functions such as marketing and finance necessary to support these levels of output are also considered at this stage. So is the formulation of management policies on the levels of performance for the budget period.

When the output levels and associated policies have been determined by top management, they must be communicated to the preparers of the budgets, along with the guidelines. Budgets are prepared for the individual responsibility centres which have been defined by the organisation's hierarchy. These centres are managed by personnel who are responsible for particular functions within the organisation, e.g. generating sales, producing products and supporting the sales and production functions.

There is some debate on the extent to which managers who are responsible for spending and income-generating departments should be involved in the preparation of their own budgets, but they usually have some influence. The extent of influence varies from organisation to organisation and depends on management style. For example, the top management of some organisations might impose rules on subordinates without any discussion. Where a manager is solely responsible for the preparation of the budget, it is likely to be biased in favour of the manager; this is not in the best interests of the organisation as a whole. For example, a manager who is responsible for the sales of a particular product range will probably set budget targets that can easily be attained, thus gaining the favour of superiors.

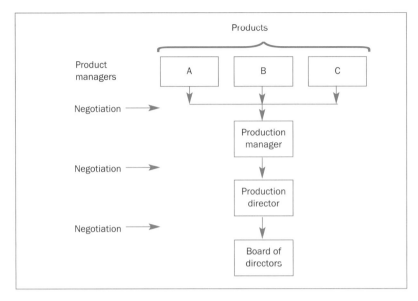

Figure 21.1 *A typical hierarchy for production management.*

It is likely, however, that a manager of a responsibility centre will have a greater degree of knowledge and understanding of the operation of the centre than any other personnel within the organisation, and this knowledge is important in the formulation of budgets. There is a strong case for some involvement by the manager of a responsibility centre in the preparation of the centre's budget.

Typically, in the budgeting process of an organisation, individual budgets for each responsibility centre are the subject of negotiations before they are approved and adopted by the organisation. The parties to the negotiations include the manager of the responsibility centre, the preparer of the budget (if not the manager) and the manager's superior. The accountant who is responsible for budgets within the organisation often acts as an intermediary in the negotiations. In large organisations the negotiation process has several stages as the budget moves up the management hierarchy for approval.

Figure 21.1 illustrates a typical hierarchy for the production management of an organisation and the stages of negotiation of the production budget for three groups of products. First, the production budgets in terms of costs and output levels are determined for products A, B and C. It has been assumed that a product manager is responsible for the production of each of the products. As mentioned, it is likely that each product manager will prepare his or her own budget or at least influence its content. When the budgets have been prepared, the first stage in negotiation takes place between the individual product managers and the production manager who has overall responsibility for this range of products. After the individual budgets have been agreed, the combined budgets for the range are then negotiated with the production director who has responsibility for all the production of the organisation. The negotiation of the production budget will be at board level where eventually the budget will be approved.

At each stage of the negotiation process, bargains are struck between the managers responsible for the budget and their immediate superiors. The negotiations between managers in the hierarchy of an organisation represent a bargaining process where the individual goals of managers are formulated for a forthcoming budget period.

At board level the fine-tuning of the respective budgets takes place. This process involves ensuring that all the budgets are consistent with each other, e.g. that the required material stock levels are sufficient to meet the production requirements throughout the year. When all the individual budgets have been finalised and approved at this level, they are summarised into what is commonly referred to as a master budget. The master budget is usually in the form of a budgeted statement of financial position and statement of financial performance for the budget period. The information in the master budget is in effect a summary of all the individual budgets, and thus represents the overall plan for an organisation. It clearly sets out the targets for the organisation in an easily understandable form and can later be compared with the actual statement of financial position and statement of financial performance.

After the final approval at board level, the budgets are passed down the organisation to the respective responsibility managers. It is these managers who carry out the plans contained within each individual budget.

Plans in the form of budgets are extremely useful to an organisation. Several of the purposes identified earlier for budgets highlight their usefulness. For example, they compel organisations to look ahead and thereby anticipate any particular problems that might arise in the future.

The nature of budgeting that has been described so far is static, in the sense that the planning process is based upon certain assumptions and events that will occur in the forthcoming budget period. However, the business environment in reality is dynamic, and thus events might not turn out as anticipated in the budget. Deviations from the budget might be harmful to the organisation; for example, the cost of producing a product might be greater than that anticipated in the budget, and losses might be made. It is therefore important that these actual events in a budget period are monitored against the budget so that action can be taken to alleviate any undesirable situations.

When undesirable deviations from the budget are caused by events which are within the control of the organisation, action can be taken to ensure that such deviations do not occur in the future. In contrast, events outside the control of the organisation, such as a downturn in the economy, could mean that the organisation has to reconsider its plans. Typically, this results in organisations 'trimming' their operations to lower levels of activity or diversifying into other markets. The point here is that undesirable situations can be averted if an efficient system of control is imposed, and if the actual and budgeted performances are compared frequently.

The budget period

The budget period normally employed by organisations is one year, which coincides with the periodic reporting requirements for published accounts regulated by the law. Most public companies, for example, are required by law to publish accounts annually. There is usually a link between the information in budgets and the annual accounts: a firm's budget normally includes the planned total sales for the period while the annual accounts show the actual sales achieved in the same period. Mainly for control purposes, the budget for the year is broken down into quarterly, monthly and weekly periods, depending on the needs of the particular organisation and the state of the economy. An organisation which operates in a very competitive market will want to monitor performance on a fairly frequent basis to ensure that it is maintaining its competitive position, as reflected in actual revenues, costs and outputs.

Preparing budgets

The master budget

Key Concept 21.2

Master budget

The master budget normally consists of the budgeted statement of financial performance and statement of financial position, representing a summary of the individual functional budgets of the organisation as a whole.

The master budget is defined in Key Concept 21.2. As we have said, it clearly sets out the objectives and the targets for the forthcoming budget period and provides a basis for co-ordinating individual functional budgets. In a medium-sized or large manufacturing organisation these functional budgets usually consist of sales, production, administration, distribution and cash budgets.

Frequently, for small organisations, the statement of financial performance, statement of financial position and cash budget are sufficient for the manager's needs. The information contained in these three budgeted statements provides a reasonable base to analyse the forthcoming period. In particular, a number of ratios and indicators can be derived such as those relating to profitability, liquidity and financing. The use of these ratios and indicators was discussed in Chapter 14.

We begin by considering the preparation of a statement of financial performance, statement of financial position and cash budget for a small firm just starting, in Example 21.1.

Example 21.1: Sivraj Ltd

Sivraj Ltd was formed on 1 July 20X2 with a share capital of $40 000. Of this, $24 000 was immediately invested in non-current assets, leaving $16 000 cash.

It is estimated that the non-current assets have a ten-year life, and will have no value at the end of that time. The company has decided to depreciate these assets using the straight-line method of depreciation. Therefore, the depreciation charge per year will be $24 000 ÷ 10 years = $2400, or, expressed in monthly terms, $2400 ÷ 12 months = $200.

Business plans have been formulated for the first months of operations. The cash budget for these plans is set out on page 493.

Sales for the six months are estimated to be $600 000. However, the company operates in a seasonal market and will also be allowing some of its customers to take credit. The company anticipates the following receipts of cash over the six months from sales.

	Cash receipts
	$
July	40 000
August	50 000
September	50 000
October	70 000
November	120 000
December	170 000
	500 000

From this breakdown of the anticipated cash received over the six-month period, it is apparent that at the end of the period there will be money owing from customers (i.e. debtors) of $600 000 – $500 000 = $100 000.

The materials required to meet the demand for sales are estimated to be $240 000. To enable the company to maintain a stock (to ensure against any shortages) $260 000 worth of materials will be purchased in the period. Because of the production cycle and the credit that the company will be obtaining from its suppliers, the pattern and amount paid to suppliers will be as follows:

	Payment to suppliers for materials $
July	60 000
August	60 000
September	20 000
October	20 000
November	20 000
December	20 000
	200 000

At the end of the six-month period the company has purchased materials costing $260 000 but has paid only $200 000 for them; thus it owes (i.e. has creditors of) $60 000 at the end of December 20X2.

The estimated labour cost that will be incurred over the six months will be $180 000. In addition, the firm anticipates that overheads (excluding depreciation) of $138 000 will also be incurred over this period. Overheads and wages will be paid evenly over the six-month period. We will assume that any cash deficits are financed by a bank overdraft.

To ensure that sufficient cash resources are available, the company wishes to calculate a cash budget (forecast) on a monthly basis as well as a budgeted statement of financial performance for the period and a statement of financial position at the end of the period.

We will begin by constructing the three budgeted statements from the information given. This will be followed by a commentary concerning the usefulness of these statements to management. The cash budget will be considered first.

SIVRAJ LTD
CASH BUDGET FOR SIX MONTHS

	July $	August $	September $	October $	November $	December $
Cash inflows						
Share capital	40 000					
Sales receipts	40 000	50 000	50 000	70 000	120 000	170 000
Total cash inflows	80 000	50 000	50 000	70 000	120 000	170 000
Cash outflows						
Materials	60 000	60 000	20 000	20 000	20 000	20 000
Wages	30 000	30 000	30 000	30 000	30 000	30 000
Overheads	23 000	23 000	23 000	23 000	23 000	23 000
Non-current assets	24 000					
Total cash outflows	137 000	113 000	73 000	73 000	73 000	73 000
Net cash flow	(57 000)	(63 000)	(23 000)	(3 000)	47 000	97 000
Bal. brought forward	—	(57 000)	(120 000)	(143 000)	(146 000)	(99 000)
Bal. carried forward	(57 000)	(120 000)	(143 000)	(146 000)	(99 000)	(2 000)

It can be seen from the cash budget for Sivraj that the inflows and outflows of cash are recorded in the budget statement when the cash is actually received or paid. There are a few main points to remember when constructing a cash budget.

- The dates of receipt and payment of cash and purchases are relevant; allowance must be made for any credit period given or received. For Sivraj the relevant sales figures are when the cash is actually received and not when the sales are earned in the period.
- Provisions should be excluded as they do not affect cash flows; for example depreciation on non-current assets is excluded because the cash flow associated with non-current assets occurs when the asset is paid for.
- Any inflows of capital and outflows such as drawings, payment of tax and dividends must be included. In the example of Sivraj, the only relevant item of this nature is the capital which was injected into the business when it began.
- The format of the cash budget is similar to the worksheets which were introduced in Chapter 6. In the case of cash budgets the column headings relate to the time period chosen for the budget. In this example, the requirement is monthly for six months to the end of December 20X2. The company could have chosen weeks, for example; in such a case there would be a column for each week of the six-month period. The time dimension depends upon the requirements of the managers of the organisation.

The statement of financial performance, for convenience, has been constructed in a summary form rather than through the use of a worksheet. Unlike the cash budget, the statement of financial performance is constructed by applying the concept of accrual accounting rather than cash flow accounting. Thus, in our example, the material cost is the cost of materials included in the sales rather than the cash paid for the materials. The depreciation charge for the six months is calculated by taking the monthly charge of $200 and multiplying by six.

SIVRAJ LTD
STATEMENT OF FINANCIAL PERFORMANCE
FOR THE SIX MONTHS ENDING 31 DECEMBER 20X2

	$	$
Sales		600 000
Cost of sales		
Materials	240 000	
Wages	180 000	420 000
Gross Profit		180 000
Depreciation	1 200	
Overheads	138 000	139 200
Net Profit		40 800

The statement of financial position, like the statement of financial performance, has been constructed without the use of a worksheet. We will briefly explain how the value of some of the assets and liabilities has been derived.

SIVRAJ LTD
STATEMENT OF FINANCIAL POSITION AT 31 DECEMBER 20X1

	$	$
Assets		
Current Assets		
Stock	20 000	
Debtors	100 000	
Total Current Assets		120 000
Non-current Assets		
Cost unspecified (at cost)	24 000	
Less Accumulated depreciation	(1 200)	
Total Non-current Assets		22 800
Total Assets		142 800
Liabilities		
Current Liabilities		
Bank overdraft	2 000	
Creditors	60 000	
Total Current Liabilities		62 000
Net Assets		80 800
Equity		
Share capital		40 000
Profit and loss		40 800
Total Equity		80 800

The stock figure represents the difference between materials purchased ($260 000) and materials consumed in the sales during the six-month period ($240 000). Debtors of $100 000 is the difference between the sales in the period and the cash received. The sum of $60 000 for creditors is the difference between the materials purchased ($260 000) and the cash paid at the end of the six months ($200 000). The bank overdraft is derived from the cash budget and is the balance at the end of December 20X2.

The use of worksheets in the construction of the statement of financial performance and the statement of financial position illustrates the interrelationships between these statements. Although worksheets were not used in this example, the interrelationships between these statements should still be apparent.

From a brief glance at these three budgeted statements for Sivraj, their usefulness for planning should be apparent. For example, it is predicted that, although the company anticipates making a profit of $40 800 for the six months, which appears reasonably healthy, there will be large deficits of cash during this period. The problem for Sivraj is the pattern of cash payments and receipts. High material costs are incurred in the first two months, as well as the payment for the non-current assets. In contrast, the major source of cash, sales, is greater in the later part of the period. Identifying this situation prior to trading is extremely useful because action can be taken to reduce these cash deficits while trying to obtain some additional funding. It might be possible to get receipts from sales in earlier, either by restricting the credit given to customers or by encouraging customers to pay more quickly by offering a discount for prompt payment. This would result in cash being received earlier and would reduce the cash deficit each month.

By identifying cash shortages at this stage, Sivraj is also in a better position to finance any deficits. The bank would look more favourably on an application for an overdraft after having some insight into the future profitability of the company. This situation can be contrasted with the negative attitude of the bank when an application for funding is made after a firm has gone into debt without any prior communication with the bank. Another alternative action to relieve the cash shortage is to raise additional share capital to fund the cash deficits of the business.

In the analysis of the budgets of Sivraj our main concern has been, not surprisingly, the cash deficits. If Sivraj had cash surpluses rather than deficits during the budget period, this information would also be useful to the business. By identifying surpluses at this early stage the firm would be in a better position to plan the investment of such funds, e.g. in short-term deposits, to obtain the maximum amount of interest.

As mentioned, a number of other characteristics of the business can be analysed through the use of ratio analysis. In general the major benefit of budgets of this nature to an organisation such as Sivraj is that events can be anticipated and action taken in the best interests of the organisation.

External funding organisations always require budgeted information from firms, similar to that produced for Sivraj, before they agree to lend money. This is particularly the case when small businesses, such as Sivraj, apply for funding from banks.

Sales and production budgets

The sales and production budgets prepared for manufacturing organisations reflect the respective targets for these functions in the forthcoming budget period. As previously mentioned, the summation of these budgets is embodied within the overall statement of financial performance and statement of financial position. Since these functions involve cash payments and receipts they are also the source for the overall cash budget.

In Example 21.2 we will concentrate on the sales and production budgets and subsequently determine a budgeted statement of financial performance. We also emphasise the importance of co-ordinating these different functions within an organisation, in particular the production output level to support the sales volume and desired stock levels.

Example 21.2: Nadia Ltd

Nadia Ltd has gathered the following data about future sales and production requirements for the year 20X2.

ESTIMATED SALES

Product	Units	Price $	Opening stock 1 January 20X2 Units	Desired closing stock 31 December 20X2 Units
A	20 000	55	8 000	10 000
B	50 000	50	15 000	15 000
C	30 000	65	6 000	6 000

MATERIALS USED IN MANUFACTURE

Stock no.	Unit	Amount per unit		
		A	B	C
54	component	3	—	5
32	metres	2	1	3
44	kilograms	—	2	—

ESTIMATED PURCHASE PRICE OF MATERIALS

Stock no.	Price
54	$3 per component
32	$2 per metre
44	$4 per kilogram

STOCK LEVELS OF MATERIALS

Stock no.	Opening stock 1 January 20X2	Closing stock 31 December 20X2
54	21 000 components	25 000 components
32	17 000 metres	23 000 metres
44	10 000 kilograms	8 000 kilograms

LABOUR REQUIREMENTS

Product	Hours per unit	Rate per hour $
A	4	7
B	5	5
C	5	6

Production overheads are estimated at $500 000 per year. For internal management purposes Nadia adopts a marginal costing system, and therefore treats these overheads as a period charge (see Chapter 18).

In this example, we presumed that the sales demand, in terms of volume, is the constraining factor. Thus the production volume will be dependent upon the sales demand.

The management of Nadia requires the following budgetary information for the forthcoming budget period:

- sales budget in monetary terms
- production budget in units
- materials purchased budget in units
- materials purchased budget in monetary terms
- materials cost per unit manufactured and sold
- the total labour hours worked during the period and the cost, plus the labour cost per unit manufactured and sold
- the unit contribution for each product
- the profit and loss for the budget period
- the value of closing finished stock at the end of the budget period.

Sales budget in monetary terms

We have been given the price per unit and the volume of units that it is estimated will be sold. To calculate the total sales revenue generated from these sales, we multiply these two variables.

Product	Unit × price $	Sales revenue $000
A	20 000 × 55	1 100
B	50 000 × 50	2 500
C	30 000 × 65	1 950
Total		5 550

Production budget in units

The production level during the budget period must not only satisfy the sales demand but must ensure that the stock levels are sufficient for the period. In the case of Nadia the opening and closing stock levels have been estimated, and we have been given the sales demand; from this information, with the help of a simple equation, we can determine the production level to satisfy this demand.

The equation we use, sometimes referred to as the inventory formula, is as follows (measured in units).

$$\text{production} + \text{opening stock} = \text{sales} + \text{closing stock}$$

It states that the units produced during the budget period plus what is in stock at the beginning of this period are equal to the units to be sold plus the units required as stock at the end of the period.

For our purposes, as there is only one unknown quantity (production), we need to rearrange the equation as follows.

$$\text{sales} + \text{closing stock} - \text{opening stock} = \text{production}$$

Applying this equation to the figures for Nadia, measured in units, we obtain the following:

Product	Sales	+	Closing stock	−	Opening stock	=	Production
A	20 000	+	10 000	−	8 000	=	22 000
B	50 000	+	14 000	−	15 000	=	49 000
C	30 000	+	6 000	−	6 000	=	30 000

The materials purchased budget measured in units

Three types of materials described by stock numbers (54, 32 and 44) are used in the production of A, B and C.

Materials required per unit of product	Product		
	A units	B units	C units
No. 54	3	—	5
No. 32	2	1	3
No. 44	—	2	—

Before determining how many units of these stocks will need to be purchased in the period we must first calculate the number of units of stock necessary to satisfy production requirements.

Production	Product		
Materials required	A	B	C
	units	units	units
	22 000	49 000	30 000
No. 54	66 000	—	150 000
No. 32	44 000	49 000	90 000
No. 44	—	98 000	—

The purchase of materials required for the forthcoming budget period can now be calculated using a similar equation to that used in determining the production level.

purchases + opening stocks = production + closing stocks

Purchases etc. in this equation are measured in terms of material units, e.g. components in the case of stock no. 54.

The equation states that the materials required for production during the period and closing stock at the end of the period will be met from the purchase of materials and the stock that is available at the beginning of the period.

In this example we are told the opening and closing stock requirements and we have calculated the materials required for production. Therefore, three of the four variables in the equation are known to us, and by rearranging the equation we can calculate the purchases figure.

production + closing stock – opening stock = purchases

Applying this equation to the information that has been given for the three stock numbers we obtain the following.

Stock no.	Production	+	Closing stock	–	Opening stock	=	Purchases
54	216 000	+	25 000	–	21 000	=	220 000
32	183 000	+	23 000	–	17 000	=	189 000
44	98 000	+	10 000	–	8 000	=	100 000

It should be remembered that the above purchases figures represent the units for the respective materials; thus, for example, in the case of stock no. 54 the purchases requirement will be 220 000 components.

The materials purchased in monetary terms

The calculation of purchases, measured in monetary terms, is straightforward. We multiply the purchases in terms of units by the cost per unit which was given at the beginning of the example.

Stock no.	Purchases units	Cost per unit $	Total cost $
54	220 000	3	660 000
32	189 000	2	378 000
44	100 000	4	400 000
			1 438 000

Materials cost per unit manufactured and sold

This information might be required by management to determine the profitability of each of the products sold and for stock valuation purposes. All the relevant information regarding this calculation has been given and it just remains for us to perform the calculation. For each unit of product we need to multiply the cost per unit of material by the amount of the material required to manufacture each product.

Stock no.	Cost per unit of stock	Products A	B	C
	$	$	$	$
54	3	9	–	15
32	2	4	2	6
44	4	–	8	–
Material cost per unit sold		13	10	21

Labour

Management requires to know the total labour worked in the period, the total cost, and the cost of labour per unit of goods manufactured and sold.

We begin by computing the labour cost per unit of goods manufactured and sold. This information will provide management with data that are useful to assess profitability and for stock valuation purposes. The arithmetic for the calculation is simple—to obtain the total labour cost per unit we multiply the hours per unit by the rate per hour.

Product	Hours per unit	Rate per hour	Total labour cost per unit
		$	$
A	4	7	28
B	5	5	25
C	5	6	30

For calculation of the total labour hours, the production units are multiplied by the hours per unit. If we then multiply the total labour by the rate per unit, we can determine the total cost. It is important to appreciate why production units are used in these calculations rather than sales units. The reason is that the objective here is to determine how many hours were actually worked and the cost of those hours during the year. If sales units were used we would be establishing the total hours that have been consumed in producing the sales. If there are changes between the opening and closing levels of finished stocks, the units produced will not equal the sales units sold. This was the case for products A and B, as can be seen when we determined the production levels for these two products earlier. In contrast, for product C the finished stock level remained unchanged and thus the production units and the sales units were the same, i.e. 30 000 units.

Product	Production units	Labour hours per unit	total	Rate per hour	Total cost
			$		$
A	22 000	4	88 000	7	616 000
B	49 000	5	245 000	5	1 225 000
C	30 000	5	150 000	6	900 000
			483 000		2 741 000

The unit contribution of each product

We have used the concept of contribution in earlier chapters relating, for example, to cost behaviour and cost-volume-profit analysis: the contribution per unit is equal to the sales price per unit, less variable costs per unit. The only variable costs in this example are materials and labour. These variable costs, you will remember, were determined earlier. Thus, the contribution per unit for these three products will be as follows.

	A		B		C	
	$	$	$	$	$	$
Sales price		55		50		65
Less Variable costs						
Material	13		10		21	
Labour	28	41	25	35	30	51
Contribution per unit		14		15		14

The profit or loss for the budget period

We begin by determining the total contribution for the three products and then deduct the overhead cost, which is the convention under the marginal costing regime.

Product	Contribution per unit	Units sold	
	$		$
A	14	20 000	280 000
B	15	50 000	750 000
C	14	30 000	420 000
Total contribution			1 450 000
Less overheads			500 000
Profit			950 000

Under the marginal costing regime, finished stock is valued at marginal cost (variable cost). From the information already obtained, we know the variable costs of each product; we multiply this cost by the number of units of finished stock, which was given at the beginning of this example.

Product	Finished stock in units	Marginal cost	Value of finished stock
		$	$
A	10 000	41	410 000
B	15 000	35	525 000
C	6 000	51	306 000
Total value of finished stock			1 241 000

These budgets act as a source of information in the construction of the statement of financial performance, statement of financial position and cash budget. The figures are broken down further to provide budgets for responsible departments, enabling the management of these departments to identify clearly the plans which affect them.

The budgets prepared for Nadia are not suitable for all manufacturing organisations, but the example illustrates the main principles in the preparation of budgets for manufacturing organisations.

Nadia overheads were given as one figure, i.e. $500 000 per year. Normally, as mentioned in the section on the budgeting process, organisations also prepare detailed budgets for overhead expenditure. These represent the planned costs associated with supporting the manufacturing function, such as machine maintenance, administration and sales. As new technology and automation are introduced into the manufacturing environment, overhead costs are tending to grow as a proportion of the total cost of operations. Organisations should be placing more emphasis on planning and control of these types of costs, but many of the systems that are in use have not been designed to cope with this phenomenon. There is considerable debate at present about the methods of costing and budgeting that should be introduced to monitor overhead costs.

CASE STUDY 21.1

Harvard Management Update

Rethinking: life without budgets

PICTURE this: it is 2004 and you are still working in a corporation, albeit a couple of rungs higher on the ladder. But every manager's job is different now. You no longer labour over budgets; in fact, your company does not use budgets at all. Of course, you are still held accountable for making your numbers, but 'the numbers' are nothing more than a few key performance indicators that you track in real time. You are starting to think that managing is like running your own little company. It is an apt analogy, because most of the units in your organisation do business with one another anyway.

Far-fetched? Not really. The seeds of these changes are being sown now. If they take root in a few years, as seems likely, they will change your work life as dramatically as anything you have experienced.

How many companies have attempted to re-engineer their budgeting? And how many find that budgeting still eats up week after dismal week of managerial time? Instead of reforming the budgetary beast, Jeremy Hope and Robin Fraser argue that companies should kill it, and learn to operate without budgets. What good are budgets anyway, when the market can render them obsolete so quickly?

Hope and Fraser are research directors of the Beyond Budgeting Round Table, a British-based consortium of 20 large companies investigating life without budgets. When companies get rid of budgeting, they say, good things happen. The politics, gaming, and sandbagging endemic to the process vanish overnight. As much as 20% of management

time is freed up for greater productivity, and companies learn to develop management methods more appropriate to today's mercurial world. They learn to allocate resources on the fly, in response to current market opportunities, rather than at an annual marathon session. They monitor performance by tracking trends and forecasts on a few critical indicators, rather than by tracking variances against a months-old budget.

A few pioneering companies are already harvesting these benefits. Svenska Handelsbanken, in Sweden, has been budget-less for decades, and now has the lowest cost structure of any bank in Europe. Volvo Cars gave up budgets about five years ago, replacing the process with rolling forecasts from a close monitoring of key indicators.

Only a handful of companies have rid themselves of budgets, but many have superimposed sophisticated performance-measurement tools on top of the budget. The tools include strategic systems such as the 'balanced scorecard' and operational systems such as automatic updates on daily shipments. The two are largely independent of each other, but that might be changing. New software makes it possible for managers to monitor a cascade of linked indicators. 'Strategic management and operational management are coming together,' says Laura Downing, vice-president of the US-based Balanced Scorecard Collaborative.

Even full financial information, usually not available until well after the close of a reporting period, can now be produced almost instantly. Fortune magazine reports that the chief financial officer of Cisco Systems can 'call up his company's revenues, margins, orders, discounts given on those orders, and top 10 customers—all for the previous day'. Soon, multi billion-dollar Cisco Systems expects to be closing its quarterly books in exactly one day. Such up-to-the-minute monitoring, of course, is one factor that makes it possible for companies to operate without budgets.

Some years back there was a flurry of interest in establishing markets for the goods and services provided and exchanged within a corporation. The idea did not take; decisions and transactions inside most companies take place on terms dictated from above. But internal markets are coming back, thanks, in part, to new interest in management through key indicators. If department heads do not have budgets, after all, they need some kind of profit-and-loss-style financials to assess their performance.

And there is nothing like the discipline of a market to ensure efficient, effective operations. At Lufthansa, for example, what was once a captive maintenance department is now a stand-alone unit that must bid for its parent company's business.

What will these developments mean? Take them together and you get a new picture of the manager's job. Front-line managers become something akin to real entrepreneurs, responsible for running their own chunks of the company. Middle managers coach them, and ensure that the responsibilities of a company's units are co-ordinated. Top management's role is to allocate resources, to monitor performance, and to provide the context and culture in which all this business activity can happen.

These new job descriptions are not likely to come into being overnight, but keep an eye out for them in the next few years. Managers who expect to thrive in the 21st century will need to learn the appropriate skills.

Business Review Weekly, 16 July 1999

Commentary

The article offers an alternative view to the importance of budgets. Companies like Volvo and Svenska Handelsbanken are operating without budgets. Savings in time and reductions in staff conflict are some of the advantages. There is a need for performance indicators and up-to-date financial information in order for companies to operate successfully without budgets, but clearly it is possible to provide this information.

Summary

We began this chapter by considering the main purposes of budgets:

- to compel planning
- to co-ordinate different functions
- as a form of communication
- to provide a basis for responsibility accounting
- to provide a basis for a control mechanism
- to authorise expenditure
- to motivate employees to improve performance.

From this list it is apparent that budgets are used for a variety of reasons. While it might appear that budgets can only be to the advantage of the organisation, they can create conflicts within it. For example, management might have introduced budgets for a positive reason, to motivate employees, but employees might see the budget in a negative light which has a demotivating effect. However, it will always be necessary to monitor performance. A sequence of operations is needed to implement a planning system, such as budgets, effectively. This sequence of operations is known as the budget process. It is important to understand this process because it links the reasons for the implementation of the budget and the preparation of budgets. It was also stressed that the budget process and form of budgets are dependent upon a number of contingent factors, such as the type of technology employed by the organisation.

The last section of the chapter focused on the preparation of budgets. Two examples were examined, which illustrated how the process of preparing budgets effectively co-ordinates the plans of separate functions of the organisation, e.g. the sales budget and its relationship with the production and stock budgets. It is important that you understand these principles in order to be able to prepare budgets.

Further reading

Hilton, R., 1997. *Managerial Accounting*, 3rd edn, McGraw-Hill.

Hirsch, M.L., Louderback, J.G., and Smith, E., 1989. *Cost Accounting: Accumulation, Analysis and Use*, Thomas Nelson.

Horngren, C.T., Foster, G., and Datar, S., 1997. *Cost Accounting: A Managerial Emphasis*, 9th edn, Prentice-Hall.

Wilson, R.M., and Chua, W.F., 1993. *Managerial Accounting: Method and Meaning*, 2nd edn, Chapman & Hall Ltd.

Review questions

1. What is a budget?
2. What are the main reasons for an organisation to introduce budgets?
3. Explain how budgets can mean different things to different people within an organisation, giving reasons.
4. Describe the main differences in the budgeting process for a small retail firm and a large manufacturing firm.
5. Discuss the interrelationships between the sales budget and the production budget in a manufacturing organisation.
6. Explain, giving examples, the main advantages of identifying cash surpluses and deficits in a cash budget.
7. What determines the budget time period?
8. What is a master budget? Describe its role in relation to other budgets.

Problems for discussion and analysis

1. What points need to be considered before preparing a budget?
2. Case Study 21.1 provides examples of companies that no longer prepare budgets. What are the main advantages and disadvantages of using a budget?
3. With reference to the example of Sivraj, prepare a statement of financial performance and statement of financial position from the data, using worksheets.

4   CJH Ltd is preparing its annual budget. The following data are available.

Product	Estimated sales Units	Opening stock Units	Closing stock Units
X	18	8	10
Y	50	15	15
Z	30	6	6

Material	Cost per unit $	Units of material used per unit of product			Opening stock Units	Closing stock Units
		X	Y	Z		
A	3	3	–	5	21	25
B	2	2	1	3	17	23
C	4	–	2	1	10	15

a   Prepare the production budget in units.
b   Give the total budgeted cost of materials used in the production of X, Y and Z.
c   Give the total cost of materials A, B and C purchased.

5   At the beginning of August 20X3 the Straw Tile Co. had 100 000 square metres of tiles and 400 000 kilos of raw materials on hand. Budgeted sales for the next three months are as follows.

	sq. m
August	200 000
September	180 000
October	150 000

The Straw Tile Co. wants to have sufficient raw materials on hand at the end of each month to meet 50 per cent of the following month's production requirements, and 40 per cent of the following month's budgeted sales. Five kilos of raw materials are required to produce one square metre of tiling. The standard cost per kilo of raw materials is $1.50.

Required:

a   Prepare a production budget for August and September.
b   Prepare a purchases budget in units for August.

(Adapted from W.J. Morse and H.P. Roth, *Cost Accounting: Processing, Evaluating, and Using Cost Data*, 3rd edn, Addison-Wesley, 1986, p. 413.)

6   The Natural Health Medical Centre is located in a summer resort community. During the summer months the Centre operates an outpatients' clinic for the treatment of minor injuries and illnesses. The clinic is administered as a separate department within the hospital. It has its own budget and maintains its own records. It refers all patients in need of extensive or intensive care to other hospital departments. An analysis of past monthly operating data reveals the following.
   i   *Staff:* Five base employees with monthly salaries totalling $20 000. One additional staff member is hired for every 500 patient visits, in excess of 3000, at a cost of $2000 per month.
   ii *Facilities:* Monthly maintenance costs total $1000. Monthly depreciation totals $500 on the clinic's facilities.

iii *Supplies:* The supplies expense averages $3 per patient. The Centre likes to keep a supplies inventory equal to 10 per cent of the following month's needs on hand at the end of each month. Supplies are purchased at cost from the hospital.

iv *Payments:* All staff and maintenance expenses are paid in the month the services are received. Supplies are paid for when received.

v *Collections:* The average bill for services rendered is $20. Of the total bills, 50 per cent are paid in cash at the time services are rendered, 10 per cent are never paid, and the remaining 40 per cent are covered by insurance. In the past, insurance companies have disallowed 10 per cent of the claims filed and paid the balance two months after services are rendered.

It is anticipated that the clinic will have 2000 patients in June, 3000 in July, and 4000 in August 20X3. As of 30 May, the clinic has $8000 in cash and $1200 in supplies.

Required:

a   Prepare a revenue and expense budget for June.

b   Prepare cash budgets for June and July.

(Adapted from W.J. Morse and H.P. Roth, *Cost Accounting: Processing, Evaluating and Using Cost Data*, 3rd edn, Addison-Wesley, 1986, p. 412.)

7   Borough Equipment Ltd produces two products, A and B, for sale to electrical wholesalers. The following information relates to the six months ending 31 December 20X3.

Product	Budgeted sales units	Price per unit $	Budgeted stocks 1 July 20X3 Units	Budgeted stocks 31 December 20X3 Units
A	16 200	14.35	5 100	8 100
B	11 800	12.20	2 600	6 600

Components bought in and used in manufacture:

Component	Amount used per unit of product A	B	Price $	Expected stocks 1 July 20X3	Expected stocks 31 December 20X3
X	5	3	0.68	38 000	46 000
Y	2	4	0.24	13 500	19 500

Labour:

Product	Hours per unit	Rate per hour $
A	2	4.50
B	1	4.00

Overheads for the six months are expected to be $25 000. The company uses a marginal-costing system and treats overheads as a period cost.

Prepare the following:

a   sales budget

b   production budget

c purchases budget in terms of components
d purchases budget in dollars
e the total labour hours and cost for the period
f the contribution per unit
g the profit and loss for the period.

Comment on the budgtets' usefulness for planning, decision making and control.

8 The owner of a business which sells fitness equipment for use in homes has requested a forecast of sales from her two salespeople for the next three months. She is trying to prepare a budgeted cash receipts and payments statement for the first quarter of 20X1/X2. The two salespeople provide the following sales forecast:

	Joe's estimates	Debbie's estimates
	$	$
July	100 000	90 000
August	150 000	200 000
September	170 000	300 000
October	160 000	400 000

The following details are available:
i Stock costs average 70 per cent of sales. Purchases are enough to cover the next month's sales and all purchases are paid in the month of purchase.
ii All sales are on account. Most customers pay the total within one month of the sale. Accounts receivable at 30 June 20X1 is $80 000.
iii Fixed expenses are $30 000 per month and variable expenses are 1 per cent of sales. All operating expenses are paid in the month in which they are incurred.
iv The company has cash in bank of $5000 at 1 July 20X0. The owner wants a minimum balance of cash on hand of $5000 at the end of every month starting in July.

Required:

a Prepare two budgeted cash receipts and payments statements for July to September 20X1 for the estimates provided by Joe and Debbie.
b Discuss what the owner should do in view of the differing sales estimates from Joe and Debbie.

9 In conjunction with the budgeting activities for the coming year, the Jeopardy Company developed the following information for 20X3:
i Sales (actual and budgeted):

	April (actual)	May (estimate)	June (estimate)	July (estimate)
Units sold	10 000	15 000	18 000	12 000
Sales revenue	$200 000	$300 000	$360 000	$240 000

ii All sales are on account. 40 per cent are collected in the month of sale, 58 per cent in the following month. A 2 per cent allowance for bad debts is established at the time of sale. There are no discounts for early payment.
iii At a monthly production volume of 15 000 units the standard cost is $12 per unit of final product:

	$
Direct materials (one unit at $4)	4
Direct labour (0.2 direct labour hours at $10 per hour)	2
Variable factory overhead (0.2 direct labour hours at $5 per hour)	1
Fixed factory overhead ($75 000 per month ÷ 3000 monthly direct labour hours × 0.2 direct labour hours per unit)	5
Total	12

iv   Selling and administrative expenses:

Variable, excluding estimated bad debts	$2 per unit sold
Fixed	$20 000 per month

v   Purchases are paid for at the time of acquisition. There are no purchase discounts.

vi   Non-cash fixed expenses total $25 000 per month, including $20 000 for manufacturing and $5000 for selling and administration. All other manufacturing costs and selling and administrative expenses are paid as incurred.

vii   The 1 May cash balance is $15 000.

viii Jeopardy desires to have ending finished goods equal to 20 per cent of the following month's sales and ending raw materials equal to 50 per cent of the following month's production requirements. The 1 May inventories are in line with this policy.

ix   There are no beginning or ending work-in-process inventories.

x   Any over-applied or under-applied fixed factory overhead is treated as an adjustment to total inventories on interim financial statements.

Required:

a   Prepare a production budget for May and June.

b   Prepare a manufacturing cost budget for May. Indicate the amount of any planned under-applied or over-applied fixed factory overhead.

c   Prepare a purchases budget in units and dollars for May.

d   Prepare a budgeted income statement for May.

e   Prepare a cash budget for May.

(Adapted from W.J. Morse and H.P. Roth, *Cost Accounting: Processing, Evaluating, and Using Cost Data*, 3rd edn, Addison-Wesley, 1986, p. 412.)

10   Alan Blue is considering going into business by opening a supermarket. Suitable premises have been found. Before granting him overdraft and lending facilities, his local bank has asked him to draw up a cash budget for the first three months of trading.

Alan has $100 000 of his own money, which he is willing to invest in the business. The premises will have to be leased one month before opening, and stock and staff need to be on hand two weeks prior to trading. The following information is relevant.

i   Expected sales for each of the first three months of trading are: $75 000, $90 000 and $110 000.

ii   Costs: staff costs, $1500 per week; rent, including rates, $2000 per week, payable one month in advance; utilities, $500 per week, payable a month in arrears; insurance, $10 000, payable a year in advance; administration, $200 per week; equipment, $45 000, to be bought when the premises are first rented and to be depreciated, straight line, over ten years with no residual value.

iii Alan is allowing a 25 per cent mark-up on all goods sold. As he is a new customer, all suppliers are insisting on being paid within seven days. Stock is ordered three weeks before it is required and there is a weekly delivery. It is assumed that sales are even throughout the four-week period.

iv The bank is prepared, if the cash budget indicates successful trading, to grant overdraft facilities to a maximum of $10 000, with interest set at 0.5 per cent per week. Further, the bank is prepared to grant a long-term loan of $50 000 with an interest rate of 12 per cent per annum, with interest to be paid quarterly (every 13 weeks). The long-term loan, if required, must be taken in full whether or not all the $50 000 is needed.

v Alan further estimates his weekly turnover in 12 months' time will be $175 000.

Required:

a Prepare a cash budget covering all operations until the end of the last week of the budget period.

b Given that the forecasts are reasonable, will the business be successful?

c Given that the turnover will increase, what other costs would you expect to increase?

11 The manager of a sports store wants to expand the size of his shop by renting the vacant premises next door. He approaches his bank with the following projections for the six months from 1 July 20X0.

STATEMENT OF FINANCIAL PERFORMANCE

	$	$
Sales		400 000
Inventory costs		225 000
Profit before expenses		175 000
Purchase of shelves, counters, etc.	80 000	
Salaries and dividends	60 000	140 000
Profit after expenses		35 000

CASH IN AND OUT

	$	$
Cash collections		400 000
Expenditures:		
Depreciation	30 000	
Six months' rent prepaid in June	6 000	
Cost of sales	185 000	
Repayment of note and interest	60 000	
Salaries and dividends	60 000	341 000
Difference		59 000

STATEMENT OF FINANCIAL POSITION

Debits	$
Cash	20 000
Furniture & fixtures	150 000
Total	170 000

Credits	
Accounts payable	50 000
Capital	40 000
Accumulated profits	80 000
Total	170 000

Required:

The manager has asked you for your opinion about these projections. What advice would you give him?

12   Faraday Ltd is a wholesaler. The management has been extremely worried about the firm's cash position over the last few years. In January 20X1 they sought your advice and asked you to prepare a cash budget for the forthcoming months of April, May and June 20X1. In addition they asked you to write a report on the cash position over this period, and in particular to identify ways in which it could be improved.

The following data are made available to you regarding the firm's operations.
i   Estimated sales for six months to June 20X1 are as follows.

Month	Credit sales $	Cash sales $
January	122 000	12 900
February	137 000	14 500
March	142 000	17 700
April	148 000	20 100
May	134 000	15 000
June	126 000	12 600

Cash is received immediately on cash sales. The firm allows customers one month's credit on sales other than for cash.

ii   Purchases of goods for resale are made on credit. The firm receives two months' credit on these purchases. The purchases for the six months to June 20X1 are as follows.

Month	$
January	62 000
February	58 000
March	71 000
April	80 000
May	54 000
June	48 000

iii   A stock check at the end of last year has revealed that $45 000 of stock, valued at cost, is considered obsolete. The firm is currently negotiating the sale of this stock for $9500 and expects payment in May 20X1.

iv   Faraday's manufacturing overheads are estimated to be $12 000 per month. This includes a charge for depreciation of $2000 per month. The company takes one month to pay these expenses.

v   Selling and distribution expenses are estimated to be $50 400 a year and are incurred evenly over the year. One month's credit is taken.

vi In June the firm anticipates paying $3880 tax to the Australian Taxation Office.

vii The firm has agreed to purchase new stock-handling equipment. The cost of $105 200 is payable in two equal instalments in April and May 20X1.

viii The firm expects in June to be able to buy adjacent property (costing $150 000) to expand its operation.

ix The firm is currently negotiating an advertising program with an agency. The cost will be $6300 in May and $7700 in June. Payments will be made in cash.

x   It is estimated that the cash balance at 1 April will be $16 000.

Ethics case study

Jetco Ltd manufactures and sells Tyrus, an automatic vacuum cleaner for swimming pools. Jetco employs ten salespeople and pays them a commission of $50 for each Tyrus they sell. In addition, if they meet the annual budget sales figure of 1000 units, they receive an annual bonus of $10 000.

Sue Clean is one of the sales staff and a close friend of Roger Pool, the accountant for Jetco. One day over lunch, Sue confides to Roger a problem that is hurting Jetco's profits. She explains that the sales target of 1000 is quite easy for the sales staff to achieve. Once achieved, there is no further financial incentive to increase sales in that year as the bonus is fixed at $10 000. Therefore, many sales staff commit customers to buy at the beginning of the following year which could mean a delay of four to eight weeks. This means that these sales are recorded next year and the salesperson is well on the way to achieving next year's target.

Discuss:

a   the problems for Jetco as a result of the strategies of the salespeople

b   what you should do with this information. Should he tell management or keep it confidential as Sue requested? If management discover that he knew of this practice and did not say anything, then he could lose his job. However, if he does say something then Sue could lose her job and Roger could lose a friend.

Appendix 1
Woolworths Limited
1999 Financial Report

Woolworths Limited
1999 financial report

The following financial statements, notes and declarations are reproduced from pages 42 to 75 of the 1999 financial report of Woolworths Limited.

Profit and Loss Statements*

	Note	Consolidated 52 weeks ended 27 June 99 $m	Consolidated 52 weeks ended 28 June 98 $m	Woolworths Limited 52 weeks ended 27 June 99 $m	Woolworths Limited 52 weeks ended 28 June 98 $m
Revenue from operating activities	2	18 765.5	17 106.3	6 524.7	6 004.2
Revenue from outside the operating activities	2	159.9	175.6	212.3	140.8
Total revenue		18 925.4	17 281.9	6 737.0	6 145.0
Earnings before interest, abnormal items and tax	3	539.4	516.2	395.7	345.5
Net finance costs	4	(45.5)	(42.8)	(45.2)	(43.0)
Operating profit before abnormal items and income tax		493.9	473.4	350.5	302.5
Abnormal items	5	(86.4)	(33.0)	(86.4)	(33.0)
Operating profit before income tax		407.5	440.4	264.1	269.5
Income tax expense	7	(150.2)	(160.8)	(35.0)	(44.7)
Operating profit after income tax		257.3	279.6	229.1	224.8
Outside equity interests in operating profit		(0.3)	(0.2)	—	—
Operating Profit Attributable to the Members of Woolworths Limited		257.0	279.4	229.1	224.8
Retained profits at beginning of the period		512.8	426.9	75.4	44.1
Dividends provided for or paid	8	(207.2)	(193.5)	(207.2)	(193.5)
Retained Profits at the End of the Financial Period		**562.6**	**512.8**	**97.3**	**75.4**
Earnings per share (EPS)					
Basic EPS		22.42	24.67		
Weighted average number of shares used in the calculation of basic EPS (million)		1 146.2	1 132.4		

Diluted EPS is not materially different from Basic EPS

The profit and loss statements should be read in conjunction with the notes to the financial statements on pages 46 to 73.

* From 1 July 2000 called statements of financial performance in Australia.

Balance Sheets*

	Note	Consolidated As at 27 June 99 $m	Consolidated As at 28 June 98 $m	Woolworths Limited As at 27 June 99 $m	Woolworths Limited As at 28 June 98 $m
CURRENT ASSETS					
Cash		232.6	150.3	200.9	139.7
Receivables	10	181.6	165.5	149.4	44.4
Inventories		1 652.6	1 562.4	544.3	523.9
Property, plant and equipment	13	86.0	127.6	—	—
Other	11	76.5	76.4	35.2	36.3
Total Current Assets		**2 229.3**	**2 082.2**	**929.8**	**744.3**
NON CURRENT ASSETS					
Receivables	10	30.5	17.3	1 381.7	1 171.1
Investments	12	1.7	1.3	71.8	71.8
Property, plant and equipment	13	2 130.3	1 762.6	463.7	406.8
Intangibles	14	133.9	81.3	80.7	54.1
Other	11	176.5	139.7	87.6	59.6
Total Non Current assets		**2 472.9**	**2 002.2**	**2 085.5**	**1 763.4**
Total Assets		**4 702.2**	**4 084.4**	**3 015.3**	**2 507.7**
CURRENT LIABILITIES					
Accounts payable		1 281.1	1 202.7	729.7	653.7
Accruals		318.7	277.7	156.4	139.2
Borrowings	15	6.1	6.7	0.2	—
Provisions	18	423.3	391.9	237.0	212.5
Total Current liabilities		**2 029.2**	**1 879.0**	**1 123.3**	**1 005.4**
NON CURRENT LIABILITIES					
Borrowings	15	957.9	671.5	940.5	665.6
Provisions	18	230.5	161.3	84.1	54.7
Total Non Current Liabilities		**1 188.4**	**832.8**	**1 024.6**	**720.3**
Total Liabilities		**3 217.6**	**2 711.8**	**2 147.9**	**1 725.7**
Net Assets		**1 484.6**	**1 372.6**	**867.4**	**782.0**
SHAREHOLDERS' EQUITY					
Share capital	19	721.4	285.0	721.4	285.0
Reserves	20	197.4	571.9	48.7	421.6
Retained profits		562.6	512.8	97.3	75.4
Shareholders' equity attributable to the members of Woolworths Limited		1 481.4	1 369.7	867.4	782.0
Outside equity interest in controlled entities:					
Reserves		0.9	0.9	—	—
Retained profits		2.3	2.0	—	—
Total outside equity interest		3.2	2.9	—	—
Total Shareholders' Equity		**1 484.6**	**1 372.6**	**867.4**	**782.0**

The balance sheets should be read in conjunction with the notes to the financial statements set out on pages 46 to 73.

* From 1 July 2000 called statements of financial position in Australia.

Notes to the Financial Statements

1 SIGNIFICANT ACCOUNTING POLICIES

The significant accounting policies that have been applied in the preparation of this general purpose financial report are as follows:

A) Basis of Preparation

This report has been prepared in accordance with Accounting Standards, Urgent Issues Group Consensus Views, other authoritative pronouncements of the Australian Accounting Standards Board and the Corporations Law.

It has been prepared on the basis of historical cost, except for certain assets which, as noted, are at valuation. The accounting policies adopted are consistent with those of the previous year except as noted below. Where necessary comparative information has been reclassified to achieve consistency in disclosure with current financial year amounts and other disclosures.

The financial periods of the Company end on the penultimate or last Sunday in June of each year. The financial period of the Company ended on 27 June 1999, which comprised 52 weeks and the corresponding Financial Statements to 28 June 1998 comprised 52 weeks.

Change in accounting policy

The Company and the Consolidated Entity applied the new Accounting Standard AASB1036 Borrowing Costs for the first time during the 52 weeks ended 27 June 1999. The standard requires borrowing costs relating to qualifying assets to be capitalised. All other borrowing costs are to be expensed as incurred. Qualifying assets are those that take more than 12 months to prepare for their intended use or sale.

In previous years, borrowing costs were not capitalised in respect of some assets which now meet the definition of qualifying assets in the standard. The new policy has been applied to all borrowing costs incurred after 28 June 1998.

This change in accounting policy resulted in an increase of $5.2 million in operating profit after income tax, and a reduction in net finance costs of $8.1 million. This effect is not considered to be material in the current year.

B) Principles of Consolidation

In these financial statements, Woolworths Limited is referred to as 'the Company' and the 'Consolidated' financial statements are those of the economic entity, comprising Woolworths Limited and its controlled entities.

All balances and the effects of all transactions, between controlled entities that are included in the consolidated financial statements have been eliminated.

Outside interests in the equity and results of controlled entities are shown as a separate item in the Consolidated financial statements.

C) Revenue Recognition

In general, revenue is recognised only when it is probable that the economic benefits comprising the revenue will flow to the entity and that the flow can be reliably measured. In addition to these general criteria, specific revenue recognition criteria apply as follows:

Sales revenue

Sales revenue represents the revenue earned from the provision of products and rendering of services to parties external to the economic entity. Sales revenue is only recognised when control of the products has passed to the buyer and for services when a right to be compensated has been attained and the stage of completion of the contract can be reliably measured.

Interest, rents and dividends

Interest, rental and dividend revenue is recognised when the economic entity has attained control of a right to be compensated for the provision of, or investment of, its assets. With interest and rents, control of the right to be compensated will accrue over time. For dividends the right to be compensated is usually attained with the approval of the dividend at a meeting of shareholders.

Proceeds from sale of assets

The gross proceeds of asset sales are recognised as revenue at the date that an unconditional contract of sale is exchanged with the purchaser.

D) Accounting for Acquisitions

Acquired businesses are accounted for using the cost method of accounting whereby fair values are assigned to all the identifiable underlying assets acquired and the liabilities assumed at the date of acquisition.

Goodwill is brought to account on the basis described in Note 1(M).

E) Income Tax

Tax effect accounting is applied using the liability method, whereby the income tax expense for the period is based on the accounting profit after adjustment for permanent differences.

The future income tax benefits or deferred income tax liabilities represent the net cumulative effect of items of income an expense that have been brought to account for tax and accounting purposes in different periods. Future income tax benefits pertaining to timing differences have only been brought to account where the benefits are expected to be realised beyond reasonable doubt.

F) Pre-opening Expenses

Pre opening expenses in connection with new stores are charged to the profit and loss account in the period in which they are incurred.

G) Stock Valuation of Finished Goods

Short life retail stocks are valued at the lower of average cost or net realisable value.

Long life retail stocks have been valued by the retail inventory method to arrive at cost, with subsequent adjustment of seasonal and slow moving lines which are discounted to provide normal profit margins when sold. Certain seasonal and slow moving items have been discounted below cost to values estimated to provide normal profit margins. Warehouse stocks are valued at average cost or net realisable value, whichever is the lower. These methods of valuation are considered to achieve a valuation reasonably approximating the lower of cost or net realisable value.

H) Purchase and Promotional Incentives

Purchase or promotional incentives are taken into income in the period to which the purchase or promotion relates, provided receipt of the incentive is reasonably assured.

I) Recoverable Amount

Non-current assets are not revalued to an amount in excess of their recoverable amount, and where carrying values exceed this recoverable amount assets are revalued to the recoverable amount.

In determining the recoverable amount expected future cash flows have not been discounted to their present values.

J) Valuation, Depreciation and Disposal of Property, Plant and Equipment

Valuation

Freehold properties were revalued by the Directors on 28 June 1998. It is the Board's intention to revalue the properties at approximate 3 yearly intervals. Accumulated depreciation on the revalued assets up to the date of revaluation is written back against the carrying value of the assets, and the surplus or deficit arising on revaluation is included in the carrying value of the assets and adjusted against the asset revaluation reserve. Potential capital gains tax on all revalued assets acquired after 19 September 1985 is not taken into account in determining the revalued amounts, except where a decision has been made to dispose of an asset being revalued, in which case the estimated capital gains tax liability or benefit applicable to the sale is brought to account.

Revaluations do not result in the carrying value of freehold or leasehold properties exceeding their recoverable amount.

Current Property, Plant and Equipment

Land and buildings purchased with the intent of development and sale within the next twelve months are classified as current assets.

Depreciation and Disposal

(i) Buildings, fixtures, fittings and plant

Buildings and plant comprising lifts, air conditioning, fire protection systems and other installations are depreciated on a straight line basis over the estimated useful life of the asset to the economic entity. Estimates of remaining useful lives are made on a regular basis for all assets.

The expected useful lives are as follows:

	1999	1998
Buildings	25–40 years	25–40 years
Fixtures, fittings and plant	3–40 years	3–40 years

(ii) Leasehold improvements

The cost of leasehold improvements is amortised, by charges against profit and loss, over the remaining period of the individual leases or the estimated useful life of the improvement to the economic entity, whichever is the shorter. Leasehold improvements held at the reporting date are being amortised over a maximum period of 20 years.

(iii) Plant, equipment and shop fittings

Plant, equipment and shop fittings (including application software) are depreciated on a straight line basis over the estimated useful life of the asset to the economic entity. Estimates of remaining useful lives are made on a regular basis for all assets.

The expected useful lives are as follows:

	1999	1998
Plant, equipment and fittings	2.5–40	2.5–40 years

(iv) Disposal of property, plant and equipment

Any surplus or deficit on the disposal of property, plant and equipment is brought to account in determining the operating profit.

K) Foreign exchange

Transactions

Transactions in foreign currencies within the consolidated entity are converted to local currency at the rate of exchange ruling at the date of the transaction.

Amounts payable to and by the entities within the consolidated entity that are outstanding at period end and are denominated in foreign currencies have been converted to local currency using rates of exchange ruling at the end of the financial period or, where applicable, the contractual exchange rate. The resulting gains or losses are credited or charged to the profit and loss account.

Specific Commitments

Exchange gains and losses, and costs, premiums and discounts on transactions intended to hedge the purchase of sale of goods or services are deferred up to the date of, and included in the measurement of the purchase or sale. In the case of hedges of monetary items, exchange gains and losses are brought to account in the period in which the exchange rates change. Gains or costs arising on entry into such hedging transactions are brought to account over the lives of the hedges.

Where a hedging transaction is terminated prior to maturity and the underlying transaction is still expected to occur, any gains or losses occurring prior to termination continue to be deferred and are brought to account in the measurement of the underlying transaction. Where the underlying transaction is no longer expected to occur, any previously deferred gains and losses are taken to profit and loss at the date of termination.

General Commitments

Exchange gains and losses on other hedge transactions are brought to account in the profit and loss account in the period in which the exchange rates change. Gains or costs arising on entry into these transactions are brought to account at the time of entry and amortised over the lives of the hedges.

Foreign Controlled Entities

All foreign controlled entities are self-sustaining, as each is financially independent of the Company.

The accounts of the foreign controlled entities are translated using the current rate method and any exchange differences are taken to the foreign currency translation reserve.

L) Receivables

Trade and Other Debtors

Trade and other debtors are carried at nominal amounts due less any provision for doubtful debts. Provision for doubtful debts is made when collection of the full nominal amount is no longer probable.

Short Term Deposits

Short term deposits are stated at the lower of cost and net realisable value. Interest income is brought to account in the period in which it is earned.

M) Intangibles

Liquor Licences

Liquor licences are valued at Directors' valuation at 21 June 1992 being the Directors' estimate of the recoverable amount of the licences. Independent valuation of each licence was obtained and the Directors' valuations did not exceed these values. Liquor licences are amortised on a straight-line basis over the estimated useful life of the licences, a period deemed to be 20 years. Subsequent purchases are recorded at cost.

Goodwill

Goodwill represents the excess of the purchase consideration over the fair value of identifiable net assets acquired at the time of acquisition of some, or all, of the assets or equity of another entity by entities within the economic entity.

Goodwill is amortised by the straight line method over the period during which benefits are expected to be received, a period deemed to be 20 years.

N) Investments

Interests in controlled entities are accounted for in the consolidated accounts as set out in Note 1(B).

Interests in partnerships are stated at cost, adjusted by the economic entity's share of movements in the net assets of the economic entity's share of movements in the net assets of the partnership. The economic entity's share of the profit or loss of the partnership is brought to account as it is earned.

Interests in semi-government securities are carried at amortised cost, calculated after accounting for the discount or premium on acquisition. Interest income is taken to account as revenue on an effective yield basis.

O) Leases

Operating lease payments, where the lessor effectively retains substantially all of the risks and benefits of ownership of the leased items, are charged to the profit and loss account in the periods in which they are incurred, as this represents the pattern of benefits derived from the leased assets.

The cost of improvements made on or to leasehold properties is accounted for as described in Note 1(J)(ii).

P) Trade Creditors and Accruals

These amounts represent liabilities for goods and services provided to the economic entity which were unpaid at the end of the period. The amounts are unsecured and are usually settled within 45 days of recognition.

Q) Borrowings

Loans and funds accepted on deposit are carried at their principal amounts, representing the present value of future cash flows associated with servicing of the debt. The amounts are unsecured. Interest is recognised as an expense of the period in which it accrues and recorded as an accrual in the balance sheet until it is paid.

R) Employee Entitlements

Wages and Salaries, Annual Leave and Sick Leave

Liabilities for wages and salaries, annual leave and vested sick leave are recognised, and are measured as the amount unpaid at period end at the current rates of pay in respect of employee's services up to that date.

Long Service Leave

A liability for long service leave is recognised, and is measured as the present value of expected future payments to be made in respect of services provided by employees up to period end. Consideration is given to expected future wage and salary levels, experience of employee departures and periods of service. The expected future cash flows are discounted, using interest rates attaching to Commonwealth government guaranteed securities which have terms to maturity, matching their estimated timing as closely as possible.

Employee Share Schemes

The cost of the employee share scheme described in Note 23 is not charged as an employee entitlement expense.

Superannuation

The Company has a Superannuation Plan that exists to provide defined benefit and/or accumulation type benefits to employees and their dependents on retirement, disability or death.

For funding purposes, actuarial valuations are carried out approximately every 3 years for the Company's liability for the defined benefit portion of the Plan. The Company's commitment in respect of accumulation benefits under the Plan is limited to making the specified contributions in accordance with the Rules of the Plan and/or any statutory obligations. The Company's contributions to the Superannuation Plan are expensed in the profit and loss account as incurred.

S) Borrowing Costs

Borrowing costs include interest, amortisation of discounts or premiums relating to borrowings, amortisation of ancillary costs incurred in connection with arrangement of borrowings and lease finance charges.

Borrowing costs are recognised as expenses in the period in which they are incurred, except where they are included in the cost of qualifying assets.

Qualifying assets are assets that take more than 12 months to prepare for their intended use or sale.

The capitalisation rate used to determine the amount of borrowing costs to be capitalised is the weighted average interest rate applicable to the entities outstanding borrowings during the year, in this case 6.35%.

This policy has changed as explained in Note 1(A).

T) Derivative Financial Instruments

The economic entity enters into forward foreign exchange contracts and interest rate swap agreements. Neither of these types of derivative financial instruments is recognised in the financial statements at inception.

Accounting for forward exchange contracts is in accordance with Note 1(K).

The net amount receivable or payable under interest rate swap agreements is progressively brought to account over the period to settlement. The amount recognised is adjusted against interest expense during the period.

U) Year 2000 Software Modification Costs

Costs relating to the testing and modification of computer software for year 2000 compatibility are charged as expenses when incurred and classified as an abnormal item in the profit and loss account.

V) Cash

For purposes of the statement of cash flows, cash includes deposits at call which are readily convertible to cash on hand and are subject to insignificant risk of changes in value, net of outstanding bank overdrafts.

W) Earnings per Share

Basic earnings per share is determined by dividing the operating profit after tax attributable to members of the Controlling Entity by the weighted average number of ordinary shares outstanding during the financial period, adjusted for bonus elements in ordinary shares issues during the period.

Diluted earnings per share adjusts the amounts used in the determination of basic earnings per share by taking into account any amounts unpaid on ordinary shares and any reduction in earnings per share that will probably arise from the exercise of options outstanding during the financial period.

	Consolidated		Woolworths Limited	
	52 weeks ended 27 June 99 $m	52 weeks ended 28 June 98 $m	52 weeks ended 27 June 99 $m	52 weeks ended 28 June 98 $m

2 REVENUE

REVENUE FROM OPERATING ACTIVITIES

Revenue from the sale of goods:

Related parties	—	—	112.6	104.8
Other parties	18 465.1	16 841.9	6 229.5	5 750.0
Rebates, discounts received and other operating income	300.4	264.4	182.6	149.4
	18 765.5	17 106.3	6 524.7	6 004.2

REVENUE FROM OUTSIDE OPERATING ACTIVITIES

Dividends:

Related parties	—	—	204.5	132.0
Interest:				
Related parties	—	—	0.2	0.2
Other parties	2.7	4.8	2.0	4.1
Rent:				
Related parties	—	—	1.7	3.2
Other parties	11.5	13.1	2.0	1.1
Gross proceeds from disposal of non-current assets	145.7	157.7	1.9	0.2
	159.9	175.6	212.3	140.8
Total Revenue	**18 925.4**	**17 281.9**	**6 737.0**	**6 145.0**

3 OPERATING INCOME AND EXPENSES

Operating profit before abnormal items, interest and income tax has been determined after:

CREDITING

Share of partnership result	1.3	0.9	—	—
Net gain on disposal of:				
Property, plant and equipment	9.1	—	—	—

CHARGING

Amounts provided for:

Bad and doubtful debts – trade	1.8	0.7	0.3	(0.4)
Bad and doubtful debts – other	0.5	(0.5)	0.2	—
Inventory obsolescence	2.1	1.5	1.5	1.5
Employee entitlements	151.4	141.7	52.2	48.7
Self-insured risks	45.2	28.2	22.9	11.2
Net loss on disposal of:				
Property, plant and equipment	—	1.4	2.2	1.8
Net foreign exchange losses:				
Non-speculative dealings	—	0.8	0.8	—
Depreciation of:				
Buildings	6.5	5.0	0	0
Plant and equipment	236.6	198.0	81.0	67.5
Amortisation of:				
Leasehold improvements	19.9	15.2	7.3	6.8
Liquor licences	2.0	1.7	1.2	1.7
Goodwill	4.9	2.8	3.2	2.4
Other intangibles	0.1	—	0.1	—

	Consolidated		Woolworths Limited	
	52 weeks ended 27 June 99 $m	52 weeks ended 28 June 98 $m	52 weeks ended 27 June 99 $m	52 weeks ended 28 June 98 $m

3 OPERATING INCOME AND EXPENSES (continued)

Contributions to defined benefit superannuation plans	41.5	32.7	24.7	14.2
Operating lease rental expenses:				
Leased premises and equipment				
– minimum lease payments	447.2	409.0	178.9	165.4
– contingent rentals	72.6	82.8	22.6	27.3
– sub-leases	7.9	0.7	—	—
	527.7	**492.5**	**201.5**	**192.7**

4 NET FINANCE COSTS

Interest income:				
Related parties	—	—	0.2	0.2
Other parties	2.7	4.8	2.0	4.1
	2.7	4.8	2.2	4.3
Interest expense:				
Other parties	(56.3)	(47.6)	(55.5)	(47.3)
Net interest expense	(53.6)	(42.8)	(53.3)	(43.0)
Less: borrowing costs capitalised (Note 1(S))	8.1	—	8.1	—
Net finance costs	**(45.5)**	**(42.8)**	**(45.2)**	**(43.0)**

5 ABNORMAL ITEMS

Operating profit after income tax includes the following items that are considered abnormal by virtue of their size and effect:

Costs relating to Year 2000 testing and remedial software modifications	(22.2)	(25.2)	(22.2)	(25.2)
Cost relating to rationalisation of warehousing and distribution functions	(34.2)	(7.8)	(34.2)	(7.8)
Writedown in value of assets to recoverable amount	(30.0)	—	(30.0)	—
Aggregate abnormal items before income tax	**(86.4)**	**(33.0)**	**(86.4)**	**(33.0)**
Aggregate tax effect	31.1	11.9	31.1	11.9
Aggregate abnormal items after income tax	**(55.3)**	**(21.1)**	**(55.3)**	**(21.1)**

6 AUDITORS' REMUNERATION

Audit services:				
BDO Nelson Parkhill	0.565	0.547	0.555	0.532
Other services:				
BDO Nelson Parkhill	0.050	0.490	0.050	0.490
	0.615	**1.037**	**0.605**	**1.022**

| | Consolidated | | Woolworths Limited | |
	52 weeks ended 27 June 99 $m	52 weeks ended 28 June 98 $m	52 weeks ended 27 June 99 $m	52 weeks ended 28 June 98 $m

7 TAXATION

Prima facie income tax expense on the current period operating profit calculated at 36%	146.7	158.5	95.0	97.0
Tax effect of permanent differences:				
Amortisation of intangibles	2.5	1.7	1.5	1.5
Depreciation of buildings	2.4	1.9	0.1	0.1
Building allowance deduction	(1.4)	(1.2)	—	—
Rebatable dividend income	—	—	(73.6)	(47.5)
Recoupment of carry forward tax capital losses	(2.0)	—	—	—
Tax capital losses not recognised as a deduction	—	1.0	0	0.1
Other permanent differences reducing tax payable	(0.2)	(0.4)	(0.1)	(0.1)
Other permanent differences increasing tax payable	0.4	0.5	0.5	0.1
Income tax expense on current year's operating profit	148.4	162.0	23.2	51.2
Over provision in prior period	—	(1.0)	—	(2.5)
Adjustment to deferred tax balances	1.8	(0.2)	11.8	(4.0)
Income tax expense attributable to operating profit	**150.2**	**160.8**	**35.0**	**44.7**
Income tax expense attributable to operating profit comprises:				
Provision for current income tax liability	161.3	159.6	47.2	58.0
Provision for deferred tax liability	25.9	19.1	15.8	0.2
Future income tax benefit	(37.0)	(16.9)	(28.0)	(11.0)
Over provision in prior period	—	(1.0)	—	(2.5)
	150.2	**160.8**	**35.0**	**44.7**

On 14 September 1992 the Company entered into a Subvention Agreement under which the tax losses within IEL were used to reduce taxes that the Company and certain of its controlled entities otherwise would have been required to pay to the Australian Tax Office (ATO) in respect of its 1991 and 1992 operating profit. The agreement ensures that the Company and certain of its controlled entities will either make a subvention payment to IEL or to the ATO to the extent that the ATO does not allow IEL losses to be grouped against taxable income of the Company and those controlled entities. These financial statements have been prepared on the assumption that these taxes will be paid to the ATO. This basis is consistent with the prior period.

8 DIVIDENDS PAID OR PROVIDED

Final dividend of 10 cents (1998 – 9 cents) per fully paid ordinary share proposed to be paid 5 October 1999 (1998 – 9 October 1998) Franked at 36%	115.3	102.6	115.3	102.6
Interim dividend of 8 cents (1998 – 8 cents) per fully paid ordinary share paid 30 April 1999 (1998 – 24 April 1998) Franked at 36%	91.9	90.9	91.9	90.9
Total dividends provided for or paid	**207.2**	**193.5**	**207.2**	**193.5**
Dividends paid in cash or satisfied by the issue of new shares under the dividend reinvestment plan during the years ended 27 June 1999 and 28 June 1998 were as follows:				
Paid in cash	154.1	153.3	154.1	153.3
Satisfied by the issue of new shares	40.4	38.7	40.4	38.7
	194.5	**192.0**	**194.5**	**192.0**

	Consolidated		Woolworths Limited	
	52 weeks ended 27 June 99 $m	52 weeks ended 28 June 98 $m	52 weeks ended 27 June 99 $m	52 weeks ended 28 June 98 $m

FRANKED DIVIDENDS

The franked portions of the dividends proposed as at 27 June 1999 will
be franked out of existing franking credits or out of franked credits arising
from the payment of income tax in the year ending June 2000.

Franking credits available for the subsequent financial year	571.5	509.5	153.4	71.3

The above amounts represent the balances of the franking accounts as at the end of the financial period, adjusted for:

(a) Franking credits that will arise from the payment of income tax payable at the end of the financial period

(b) Franking debits that will arise from the payment of dividends proposed at the end of the financial period

9 SEGMENT DISCLOSURES

	Supermarkets		General Merchandise		Wholesale		Consolidated	
	1999 $m	1998 $m	1999 $m	1998 $m	1999 $m	1998 $m	1999 $m	1998 $m
INDUSTRY SEGMENTS								
Sales to customers outside the economic entity	15 398.6	14 179.8	2 610.7	2 388.8	455.8	273.3	18 465.1	16 841.9
Unallocated revenue							460.3	440.0
Total Revenue	**15 398.6**	**14 179.8**	**2 610.7**	**2 388.8**	**455.8**	**273.3**	**18 925.4**	**17 281.9**
Segment operating profit	514.7	514.0	90.0	79.3	(4.2)	(10.9)	600.5	582.4
Unallocated expenses							(61.1)	(66.2)
Net finance costs							(45.5)	(42.8)
Operating profit before abnormal items and income tax							**493.9**	**473.4**
Abnormal items							(86.4)	(33.0)
Operating profit before income tax							**496.5**	**440.4**
Segment assets	2 579.4	2 138.5	750.5	716.4	151.5	101.2	3 481.4	2 956.1
Unallocated							1 220.8	1 128.3
Total Assets							**4 702.2**	**4 084.4**

Inter-segment pricing is determined on an arm's length basis.

The economic entity operates predominantly in the retailing industry within Australia. More than 99% of revenue, operating profit before income tax and total assets relate to operations within Australia.

The periods reported are for the 52 weeks ended 27 June 1999 and the 52 weeks ended 28 June 1998, respectively.

	Consolidated		Woolworths Limited	
	As at 27 June 99 $m	As at 28 June 98 $m	As at 27 June 99 $m	As at 28 June 98 $m

10 RECEIVABLES

CURRENT

Trade receivables	115.2	92.3	22.1	18.1
Less: provision for doubtful debts	(2.9)	(2.8)	(0.4)	(0.5)
	112.3	**89.5**	**21.7**	**17.6**
Other receivables	65.4	68.9	124.2	25.8
Less: provision for doubtful debts	(0.9)	(0.6)	(0.6)	(0.5)
	64.5	**68.3**	**123.6**	**25.3**
Short term deposits	2.1	7.2	1.5	—
Staff and other advances	2.7	0.5	2.6	1.5
	181.6	**165.5**	**149.4**	**44.4**

NON-CURRENT

Other debtors	1.1	0.6	1.0	0.4
Employee loans	29.4	16.7	29.4	16.7
Loans to controlled entities	—	—	1 351.3	1 154.0
	30.5	**17.3**	**1 381.7**	**1 171.1**

11 OTHER ASSETS

CURRENT

Prepayments	76.4	76.3	35.1	36.2
Borrowing costs	0.3	0.2	0.3	0.2
Less: Amortisation	(0.2)	(0.1)	(0.2)	(0.1)
	76.5	**76.4**	**35.2**	**36.3**

NON-CURRENT

Borrowing costs	0.6	0.8	0.7	0.8
Future income tax benefits	175.9	138.9	86.9	58.8
	176.5	**139.7**	**87.6**	**59.6**

12 INVESTMENTS

NON-CURRENT

Controlled entities:				
Unlisted shares at cost	—	—	71.3	71.3
Other corporations:				
Unlisted shares at cost				
Interest in partnership	1.2	0.8	—	—
Semi-Government Securities, at cost	0.5	0.5	0.5	0.5
	1.7	**1.3**	**71.8**	**71.8**

Semi-Government Securities

The Semi-Government Securities which were acquired on 6 February 1999 represents NSW Treasury Inscribed Stock. The principal is $500 000 and maturity is 25 August 1999. The current interest rate is 4.85% p.a.

	Consolidated		Woolworths Limited	
	As at	As at	As at	As at
	27 June 99	28 June 98	27 June 99	28 June 98
	$m	$m	$m	$m

13 PROPERTY, PLANT AND EQUIPMENT

CURRENT

Land and buildings held for development and resale:

Land at cost	19.3	—	—	
Land at directors' valuation 28 June 1998	35.0	61.2	—	—
Development costs	31.7	66.4	—	—
	86.0	**127.6**	—	—

NON-CURRENT

Property, Plant and Equipment

Freehold land and buildings:

At cost	110.0	—	—	
At directors' valuation 28 June 1998	361.4	393.3	—	—
	471.4	393.3	—	—
Less: accumulated depreciation on buildings	(4.4)	—	—	
	467.0	393.3	—	—

Leasehold improvements:

At cost	174.5	112.0	60.0	45.6
At directors' valuation 25 June 1995	79.7	79.7	40.6	40.6
	254.2	191.7	100.6	86.2
Less: accumulated amortisation	(51.4)	(34.1)	(19.9)	(14.7)
	202.8	157.6	80.7	71.5

Plant and equipment:

At cost	2 738.1	2 312.0	840.4	744.1
Less: accumulated depreciation	(1 277.6)	(1 100.3)	(457.4)	(408.8)
	1 460.5	**1 211.7**	**383.0**	**335.3**
	2 130.3	**1 762.6**	**463.7**	**406.8**
Total property, plant and equipment – net book value	**2 216.3**	**1 890.2**	**463.7**	**406.8**

Revaluations:

Freehold land and buildings

The freehold land and buildings owned by the economic entity are stated at Directors' valuation at 28 June 1998 and at cost. Arriving at their valuation the Directors obtained independent valuations of all major properties, which amounted to approximately 40% in value of all properties and utilised cost for all warehouse development properties which amount to 32% in value of all properties. Using the independent valuation results as a guide and accepting cost for warehouse and certain development properties, the Directors appraised the value of all remaining properties. The Directors' valuation of freehold land and buildings is the aggregate of the independent valuations of major properties, the cost of warehouse and certain development properties and the Directors' appraisal of all other properties.

The independent valuations were carried out by the following lead valuers:

Name	Company	Qualifications
C Long	Richard Ellis	AAPI (Reg #2321)
A Cubbins	Harrison Humphreys	FAPI (Reg #106)

Leasehold improvements

The leasehold improvements are stated at Directors' valuation at 25 June 1995 and at cost. The Directors believe that these values do not exceed the recoverable amount of these assets.

	Consolidated		Woolworths Limited	
	As at	As at	As at	As at
	27 June 99	28 June 98	27 June 99	28 June 98
	$m	$m	$m	$m

14 INTANGIBLES

Liquor licences:				
At cost	16.0	12.0	10.5	9.8
At directors' valuation 1992	25.6	25.6	14.2	14.2
	41.6	37.6	24.7	24.0
Accumulated amortisation	(11.0)	(9.0)	(6.6)	(9.0)
	30.6	28.6	18.1	15.0
Goodwill – at cost	113.2	57.8	70.5	43.9
Accumulated amortisation	(9.9)	(5.1)	(7.9)	(4.8)
	103.3	52.7	62.6	39.1
	133.9	**81.3**	**80.7**	**54.1**

Liquor licences were revalued downwards by the directors at 21 June 1992, to the amount at which the licences could be realised.

Independent valuation of each licence was obtained and the directors' valuations did not exceed these values.

15 BORROWINGS

CURRENT

Unsecured

Funds accepted on short term deposit	6.1	6.7	0.2	—
	6.1	6.7	0.2	—

NON-CURRENT

Unsecured

Bank loans	655.0	380.1	655.0	380.1
Other loans	285.5	285.5	285.5	285.5
	940.5	**665.6**	**940.5**	**665.6**

Secured

Bank loans	17.4	5.9	—	—
	957.9	**671.5**	**940.5**	**665.6**

Bank loans

Unsecured bank loans represents a 5 year $800 million revolving credit facility, comprising a series of bilateral loan agreements. Each drawdown under the facility has a term of between one and six months, and may be rolled over on maturity. Interest is payable on rollover, at a rate calculated as the Bank Bill Swap yield plus a margin. The facility is subject to a negative pledge agreement.

Other loans comprise Medium Term Notes of $80 million and $70 million which were issued into the domestic market and mature on 20 August 2007. Interest is payable on these issues, quarterly at the Bank Bill Swap rate plus a margin and semi-annually at a fixed rate on a bond basis, respectively. Senior Notes of $100 million US dollars were issued in the United States capital markets, maturing on 1 September 2007. Under the principal agreement, interest is payable on this debt semi-annually in US dollars, at a fixed rate. The Company has entered into cross currency swaps in respect of these borrowings (refer Note 26) which eliminate all foreign currency exposures.

Secured bank loans represent drawdowns on a multi option facility secured by a mortgage over land and buildings and an equitable charge over the assets of a controlled entity. Interest is payable on this facility at both fixed and variable rates.

Funds accepted on short term deposit

Funds accepted on short term deposit represent retention monies held on certain construction projects and amounts received from certain employees.

	Consolidated		Woolworths Limited	
	As at 27 June 99 $m	As at 28 June 98 $m	As at 27 June 99 $m	As at 28 June 98 $m

16 FINANCING ARRANGEMENTS

Unrestricted access was available at balance date to the following lines of credit:

	Consolidated		Woolworths Limited	
Total facilities				
Bank overdrafts	11.0	11.0	11.0	11.0
Bank loans facilities	867.5	817.5	850.0	800.0
	878.5	828.5	861.0	811.0
Used at balance date:				
Bank overdrafts				
Bank loans facilities	672.4	386.0	655.0	380.1
	672.4	386.0	655.0	380.1
Unused at balance date:				
Bank overdrafts	11.0	11.0	11.0	11.0
Bank loans facilities	195.1	431.5	195.0	419.9
	206.1	442.5	206.0	430.9

Bank loans facilities may be drawn at any time, subject to the covenants of the lending agreements. All facilities are denominated in Australian dollars.

The bank overdraft facilities are unsecured and may be drawn at any time.

17 FOREIGN CURRENCY RECEIVABLES AND PAYABLES

The Australian dollar equivalents of unhedged amounts receivable and payable in foreign currencies, calculated at year end exchange rates, are as follows:

	Consolidated		Woolworths Limited	
Amounts receivable:				
Current				
– United States dollars	0.6	–	0.5	–
Amounts payable:				
Current				
– United States dollars	2.4	2.6	1.2	0.9
– New Zealand dollars	–	0.2	–	–
– Hong Kong dollars	0.3	0.1	–	–
– Japanese yen	0.2	–	–	–

	Consolidated		Woolworths Limited	
	As at	As at	As at	As at
	27 June 99	28 June 98	27 June 99	28 June 98
	$m	$m	$m	$m

18 PROVISIONS

CURRENT

Current income tax liability	78.8	98.4	17.4	36.5
Employee entitlements	169.3	156.0	61.4	60.1
Self-insured risks	30.0	34.9	13.0	13.3
Asset writedown	30.0	—	30.0	—
Dividends	115.2	102.6	115.2	102.6
	423.3	**391.9**	**237.0**	**212.5**

NON-CURRENT

Deferred income tax liability	125.5	93.1	45.7	29.9
Employee entitlements	77.3	68.2	26.9	24.8
Self-insured risks	27.7	—	11.5	—
	230.5	**161.3**	**84.1**	**54.7**
Total provisions	**653.8**	**553.2**	**321.1**	**267.2**

19 SHARE CAPITAL

ISSUED AND PAID-UP CAPITAL

Fully paid ordinary shares:

1 152 827 897 (1998: 1 139 992 315 of 25 cents par value)	721.5	285.0	721.4	285.0

From 1 July 1998, the Company's share capital does not have a fixed nominal (par) value, as a result of the Company Law Review Act 1998.

Movements in issued ordinary share capital during the period

- On 1 July 1998, $372.9 million representing the balance standing to the credit of the share premium reserve was transferred to issued share capital as a result of the abolition of par value by the Company Law Review Act 1998.
- The issue under the Dividend Reinvestment Plan of 8 160 635 ordinary shares (1998: 8 608 178) for a total value of $40.8 million (1998: $38.7 million).
- The issue of 3 030 226 (1998: 31 526) ordinary shares under the Employee Share Plan at a total value of $16.7 million (1998: $NIL).
- There were 405 782 (1998: 1 344 863) ordinary shares at a value of $2.1 million (1998: $5.8 million), issued as a result of the Share Purchase Plan.
- There were 1 238 939 (1998: 6 467 355) ordinary shares issued at a total value of $3.8 million (1998: $17.5 million) as a result of options exercised under the Executive Share Option Plan and Senior Executive Service Contracts in the current period.

	Consolidated		Woolworths Limited	
	As at 27 June 99 $m	As at 28 June 98 $m	As at 27 June 99 $m	As at 28 June 98 $m

20 RESERVES

CAPITAL PROFITS RESERVE

Balance at beginning of the period	68.8	59.5	2.6	2.6
Transfer from asset revaluation reserve on disposal of non-current assets	(0.2)	9.3	–	–
Balance at end of the period	68.6	68.8	2.6	2.6

ASSET REVALUATION RESERVE

Balance at beginning of the period	84.4	94.2	0.6	0.6
Transfer to capital profits reserve	0.2	(9.3)	–	–
Revaluation of freehold properties	–	(0.5)	–	–
Balance at end of the period	84.6	84.4	0.6	0.6

GENERAL RESERVE

Balance at beginning of the period	46.9	46.9	45.5	45.5
Balance at end of the period	46.9	46.9	45.5	45.5

SHARE PREMIUM RESERVE

Balance at beginning of the period	372.9	315.0	372.9	315.0
Premium on shares issues	–	57.9	–	57.9
Transfer to issued ordinary share capital (Note 19)	(372.9)	–	(372.9)	–
Balance at end of the period	–	372.9	–	372.9

FOREIGN CURRENCY TRANSLATION RESERVE

Balance at beginning of the period	(1.1)	(0.2)	–	–
Net exchange differences on translation of controlled foreign entities	(1.6)	(0.9)	–	–
Balance at end of the period	(2.7)	(1.1)	–	–
Total Reserves	**197.4**	**571.9**	**48.7**	**421.6**

	Consolidated		Woolworths Limited	
	As at	As at	As at	As at
	27 June 99	28 June 98	27 June 99	28 June 98
	$m	$m	$m	$m

21 CONTINGENT LIABILITIES

The details and estimated maximum amounts of contingent liabilities
which may become payable are shown below. No provision has been
made in the financial statements in respect of these contingencies.

Guarantees

Trading guarantees	11.8	16.3		
Workers' compensation self-insurance guarantees	20.1	18.7		
Unsecured guarantees in respect of performance covenants in tenancy and other contracts. The total amount of these guarantees is indeterminable but no event has or is anticipated to occur that would result in crystallisation of the liability	–	–		
Under the terms of a Deed of Cross Guarantee, the Company has guaranteed the debts of certain controlled entities, thereby relieving them of the need to prepare financial statements under ASIC Class Order 98/100	–	–		

Litigation

Litigation in progress or threatened against the Company and certain of its controlled entities	4.5	1.5		

Other

Outstanding letters of credit issued to suppliers	17.2	6.5		

22 COMMITMENTS FOR EXPENDITURE

Capital expenditure commitments

Estimated capital expenditure under firm contracts, not provided for in these financial statements, payable:

Not later than one year	94.0	271.4	32.0	96.5
Later than one, not later than two years	3.3	1.1	0.8	1.1
	97.3	**272.5**	**32.8**	**97.6**

Operating lease commitments

Future minimum rentals under non-cancellable operating leases, not provided for in these financial statements, payable:

Not later than one year	489.6	422.5	187.4	167.9
Later than one year, not later than two years	467.1	404.3	177.8	159.2
Later than two years, not later than five years	1 253.5	1 088.2	456.8	406.4
Later than five years	3 400.2	3 099.8	1 379.2	1 205.4
Total future minimum lease payments not provided for	**5 610.4**	**5 014.8**	**2 201.2**	**1 938.9**

The commitments set out above do not include contingent
turnover rentals which are charged on many of the retail
premises leased by the Company and its controlled
entities. These rentals are calculated as a percentage of
the turnover of the store occupying the premises, with the
percentage and turnover threshold at which the additional
rentals commences varying with each lease agreement.

Future minimum lease payments expected to be received in relation to non-cancellable sub-leases of operating leases	0.9	1.0	0.7	0.7

The Company and economic entity leases retail premises and warehousing facilities for periods of up to 70
years. Generally the lease agreements are for an average term of 5 years and include renewal options for an
additional 5 years. Under most leases, the Company is responsible for property taxes, insurance, maintenance
and expenses related to the leased properties.

23 EMPLOYEE ENTITLEMENTS

Superannuation plans

All permanent salaried employees of the Company and its controlled entities are eligible to join the Woolworths Group Superannuation Scheme (Woolworths Super). This Scheme provides lump sum accumulation benefits to members on retirement, disability or death. The right to receive lump sum defined benefits based on years of service and final average salary has been preserved for former members of defined benefit categories of superannuation funds previously sponsored by the Company.

The Company and certain of its controlled entities are legally obliged to contribute to Woolworths Super at fixed rates as set out in the trust deed and rules of the Scheme. Members contribute to the Scheme at fixed rates dependent upon their membership category.

The Company is also obliged to contribute at fixed rates to defined contribution retirement plans for certain employees under awards, industrial agreements and superannuation legislation.

The Company and its controlled entities contributed to Woolworths Super and to various industry based superannuation funds during the current financial period.

Actuarial assessments of Woolworths Super are made at intervals of no more than three years. The last actuarial assessment was as at 31 August 1996. In a report dated 23 May 1997 by Mr P Hughes, FIA, FIAA, the actuary concluded that the available net assets of the Scheme were sufficient to meet all benefits payable in the event of the Scheme's winding up, or the voluntary or compulsory termination of the employment of each member with the Company and its controlled entities.

The Scheme assets at net market value, accrued benefits and the vested benefits of Woolworths Super based on the last actuarial report, and the last annual financial report of the Scheme dated 31 August 1998, are set out below. Accrued benefits are those which the Scheme is presently obliged to pay at some later date, based on membership of the Scheme. Vested benefits are those benefits that would be currently payable to members on resignation from the Scheme, that do not depend on any other factor. Accrued benefits are measured as at 31 August 1998.

	1999 $m	1998 $m
Scheme assets at net market value	485.3	445.5
Total accrued benefits	*477.9	**430.0
Excess of scheme assets over accrued benefits	7.4	15.5
Vested benefits	469.5	416.9

* Total accrued benefits as at 31 August 1998
** Estimated total accrued benefits as at 31 August 1997

Employee Share Plan ('Share Plan')

The Share Plan has been established to enable all non-managerial and managerial employees (excluding executives) the opportunity to participate in the Share Plan at market price but with an interest free loan from the Company to finance the acquisition.

Eligibility: All permanent employees (excluding executives) of Woolworths with 2 years full time service, or its part-time or casual equivalent, are eligible to participate in the Share Plan. The Directors may permit offers to employees with less service. The number of Shares currently offered to each eligible employee ranged from 100 to 5 000 depending on the employee's position with Woolworths, salary and years of service.

Loans: The Company makes an interest free loan to the trustee of the Plan as agent for each participant to finance the acquisition of shares. Loans are limited in recourse to the proceeds of sale of shares acquired. Dividends and other distributions on the shares are applied to repay the loan. The loan may be repaid at any time after 3 years and in any event must be repaid when the employee ceases employment with Woolworths or after 10 years or when a takeover offer is accepted for the shares, whichever is the earlier. If loans are not repaid, the shares will be sold and the funds received after payment of costs and expenses will be applied to repay the loan.

Entitlement to shares: Shares are allotted at the average market price of the shares in the Company traded on the ASX in the 5 trading days before the date of the offer. All shares acquired under the Share Plan are held by a wholly owned subsidiary of the Company (Woolworths Custodian Pty Limited) as trustee of the Share Plan. At any time after 3 years from the date of acquisition a participant may request the trustee to transfer the shares, but only if the loan made to acquire those shares is repaid in full. Shares may be transferred earlier at the discretion of the Directors on the employee's death or retirement but only if the loan made to acquire the shares is repaid in full. The trustee may exercise the voting rights attached to the shares in the manner directed by the Directors until they are transferred to the participant.

At 27 June 1999, there were 24 024 (1998: 18 679) participating employees who held a total of 10 988 754 (1998: 8 795 678) shares. During the 52 week period 3 030 226 (1998: NIL) shares were issued.

The total amount receivable by the Company in relation to these shares was $31 315 288 at 27 June 1999 (1998: $17 990 574).

Share Option Plan (Option Plan)

The Option Plan has been established to enable executive employees to acquire an initial allocation of options in the Company and, thereafter, annually, subject to the achievement of certain profit targets, as outlined below.

General offers: Under the Option Plan in 1993 an initial offer of 6 835 000 options was made to 218 executive employees of Woolworths. The number of options offered to each executive was based on the executive's management level. Upon appointment as an executive (or promotion to a more senior level) the executive may be offered options or further options.

Price and exercise: There is no amount paid in respect of the grant of options. They may normally only be exercised after 4 years from the date of grant of the options. At the Company's discretion, options may be exercised at an earlier date in proportion to the time elapsed if a takeover bid is made for shares in the Company or, if the participant retires, is made redundant or voluntarily ceases employment with Woolworths. If an executive resigns or is dismissed the options will generally lapse. Options expire after 5 years from the date of issue. Options may not be transferred. Each option is to subscribe for one fully paid ordinary share in the Company and, when issued, the shares will rank equally with all other fully paid ordinary shares. The exercise price per share for those options issued initially under the Option Plan is $2.695. For options issued subsequently, the exercise price will be the greater of the par value of the ordinary shares in the Company and the prevailing market price when the option is granted.

At 27 June 1999, there were 7 424 000 (1998: 7 644 000) options outstanding. During the 52 week period ended 27 June 1999 2 250 000 (1998: 3 144 000) options were granted at an exercise price of $5.16.

Employee Share Purchase Plan (Share Purchase Plan)

The Share Purchase Plan has been established to enable all permanent employees of Woolworths to acquire shares in the Company on an annual basis at a discount to the prevailing market price. Offers have been made under the Share Purchase Plan during the 52 week period ended 27 June 1999.

Offers: Each year the Directors offer to issue fully paid ordinary shares to all permanent employees of Woolworths. The subscription price is the greater of the par value of ordinary shares in the Company and 95% of the prevailing market price provided that if the Dividend Reinvestment Plan discount rate is reduced, the Share Purchase Plan discount rate will also be reduced, to the same rate.

The number of shares offered to each employee are determined in accordance with a formula based on the employee's position with Woolworths and wage or salary at 30 September in each year.

Loans: Woolworths do not provide employees with any loans to assist in the acquisition of the shares under the Share Purchase Plan.

Rights attaching to shares: Shares issued under the Share Purchase Plan rank equally with all other fully paid ordinary shares.

Limit: The number of shares which may be offered in any year under the Share Purchase Plan may not exceed 1% of the total number of issued ordinary shares of the Company at that time.

During the 52 week period ended 27 June 1999, 405 782 (1998: 1 344 863) shares were issued at a market price of $5.58 (1998: $4.34).

Executive Service Contracts

The Company has, since 1993, entered into various Service Contracts with certain Senior Executives as an incentive for them to remain with the Company. As part of the consideration under these Contracts, options to acquire unissued shares in the Company were granted to each Executive. For all of those options the terms and conditions are in all material respects the same as those offered under the Share Option Plan detailed above.

At 27 June 1999, there were 590 000 (1998: 1 715 000) options outstanding. During the 52 week period no (1998: 435 000) options were granted.

Service Contracts, by way of replacement for or in lieu of the previous Contracts, were also entered into during the period with Senior Executives as well as new Contracts in respect of certain other Executives. The Contracts provide for payment of a cash bonus equivalent to the Executive's salary at 1 January 1999, provided the Executive remains employed on expiry of the Senior Executive Contracts on 1 January 2002 and the remaining Executive Contracts on 1 January 2004 or 1 January 2006, as applicable. The Board may elect to convert the cash bonus to shares or options in the Company, subject to shareholder approval at the 1999 AGM. The total amount of the cash bonus payable on 1 January 2002 is $6 855 000, on 1 January 2004 is $2 801 000 or alternatively on 1 January 2006 is $4 650 000.

24 RELATED PARTIES

Directors

The names of each person holding office as a director of Woolworths Limited during the 52 weeks ended 27 June 1999 are Messrs J C Dahlsen, L M L'Huillier, M J Phillips, R J Clairs, R C Corbett and J C Ballard, and Prof A E Clarke and Ms D J Grady. Mr R J Clairs retired as a director on 31 December 1998.

Details of directors' remuneration and retirement benefits are disclosed at Note 25 and the Directors' Statutory Report.

Apart from the details disclosed in this note, no director has entered into a material contract with the Company or the economic entity since the end of the previous financial period and there were no material contracts involving directors' interests existing at the end of the period.

Directors' holdings of shares and options

The interests of directors and their director-related entities in shares and options within the consolidated entity as at 27 June 1999 are shown below:

	Consolidated	
	As at	As at
	27 June 1999	28 June 1998
	Number held	Number held
Woolworths Limited:		
Ordinary shares	221 609	197 669
Options over ordinary shares	319 000	845 000

Directors' transactions in shares and options

During the 52 weeks ended 27 June 1999, the aggregate numbers of shares and share options acquired or disposed of by directors of the Company and their director-related entities was as follows:

	Consolidated	
	52 weeks	52 weeks
	ended	ended
	27 June 1999	28 June 1998
Woolworths Limited		
Acquisitions		
Ordinary shares	529 782	584 771
Options over ordinary shares	48 000	323 000

The terms and conditions and number of options and shares granted under the Executive Share Option Plan, Share Purchase Plan and Senior Executive Service Contracts as set out on page 62 and in Note 23 were on the same basis as outlined in the Prospectus dated 19 May 1993. All other transactions relating to shares issued were as a result of the Dividend Reinvestment Plan and were on the same basis as transactions by other shareholders.

Other transactions with directors and their director-related entities

Mr J C Dahlsen is a director of the Australian and New Zealand Banking Group Limited ('ANZ'). The ANZ Group has provided funds to the Company via a number of facilities and funds have also been placed on deposit with the ANZ Group at various times during the period. All transactions were conducted in the ordinary course of business.

Mr J C Dahlsen is a consultant to the legal firm of Corrs Chambers Westgarth ('Corrs'). This firm renders legal advice to the Company and its controlled entities in the ordinary course of business.

Mr J C Dahlsen is a director of Southern Cross Broadcasting (Aust.) Limited. During the period this company supplied the Company with television and radio advertising airtime both directly and via charges to the company's advertising agency.

Mr J C Dahlsen is a director of the Melbourne Business School Ltd. During the period, this company provided education and training services for which it was paid.

Mr J C Dahlsen is a director of The Graduate School of Management Ltd. During the period, this company provided education and training services for which it was paid.

Mr M J Phillips is the chairman of IBJ Australia Bank Limited ('IBJ'). At various times during the period the Company had funds on deposit and on loan with IBJ in the short term money market, as part of IBJ's normal banking business.

Mr M J Phillips is a director of QBE Insurance Limited 'QBE'). QBE supplies the economic entity with industrial special risk insurance and public and product liability insurance as a co-insurer.

Mr M J Phillips is a director of The Australian Gas Light Company ('AGL'), which supplies the Company with various gas products.

Mr W B Croome is an independent director of a controlled entity of the Company, Statewide Independent Wholesalers Limited ('Statewide'). Mr Croome has a significant interest in a supermarket in Tasmania that is supplied with products for resale by Statewide.

Ms D J Grady is a director of Lend Lease Corporation ('Lend Lease'). Lend Lease is the owner of various shopping centres in which the Company is a tenant and for which the company pays market-based rentals.

Prof A E Clarke is a director of AMP Limited which is the owner of various shopping centres in which the Company is a tenant and for which market-based rental is paid.

Ms D J Grady and Mr J C Ballard are directors of Wattyl Limited, which supplies the Company with paint products for resale and its own use.

Ms D J Grady was for part of the period a director and Mr L M L'Huillier is a director of MLC Limited ('MLC'). The Company or its related entities lease retail premises from MLC at market-based rentals.

Mr L M L'Huillier is a director of Fortis Australia Limited ('Fortis') and was for the period an advisor to PriceWaterhouseCoopers Australasia. During the period the Company paid market-based rentals to Fortis in respect of retail premises. PriceWaterhouseCoopers has provided the Company with professional accounting services during the period for which it was paid.

The terms and conditions of all transactions with directors and their director-related entities were determined in the ordinary course of business, on a basis that was no more favourable than those available, or which would be reasonably expected to be made available, on similar transactions made on an arms-length basis.

The value of transactions during the period with directors and their director-related entities were as follows:

Director	Director-related entity		1999 $'000	1998 $'000
A E Clarke	AMP Limited	Premises rentals	14 111	9 102
		Superannuation	6	–
J C Ballard/D J Grady	Wattyl Limited	Inventory purchases	2 050	1 734
J C Dahlsen	ANZ Banking Group Limited	Interest and fees paid	4 538	4 485
		Interest received	304	189
		Loans advanced	223 131	436 781
		Loans repaid	29 255	47 868
	Corrs Chambers Westgarth	Legal services	1 197	793
	Melbourne Business School Ltd	Education expenses	7	–
	Southern Cross Broadcasting (Aust) Ltd	Advertising	95	165
	The Graduate School of Management Ltd	Education expenses	2	–
L M L'Huillier	Fortis Australia Limited	Premises rentals	1 517	659
	MLC Limited	Premises rentals/superannuation	1	3 237
	PriceWaterhouseCoopers Australasia	Accounting services	511	10
L M L'Huillier/D J Grady	Lend Lease Corporate Services Limited	Premises rentals	25 074	29 733
M J Phillips	Australian Gas Light Company	Gas supplies	130	162
	IBJ Australia Bank Limited	Interest paid	264	181
		Interest received	76	220
	QBE Insurance Group Limited	Insurance premiums	11	55
R C Corbett	Australian Retailers Association	Membership fees	8	6
W B Croome	Croome Investments Pty Limited	Sales of inventory	867	899

The aggregate amounts payable to and receivable from directors and their director-related entities at balance dates arising from these transactions were as follows:

Current liabilities	248	245
Non-current liabilities	100 000	70 000

WHOLLY-OWNED GROUP

The ultimate parent entity is Woolworths Limited, a company incorporated in New South Wales.

The wholly-owned group consists of Woolworths Limited and its wholly-owned controlled entities. During the financial period and previous financial periods, Woolworths Limited advanced and repaid loans to and received loans from, and provided treasury, accounting, taxation and administrative services to, other entities within the wholly-owned group. Entities within the wholly-owned group also exchanged goods and services in sale and purchase transactions. All transactions occurred on the basis of normal commercial terms and conditions.

The details of sales, dividends and lease rentals transacted within the wholly-owned group are disclosed at Notes 2 and 3. Ownership interests in controlled entities are disclosed at Note 28 and the balances of loans payable to/receivable from controlled entities is shown in Note 10.

	Consolidated		Woolworths Limited	
	52 weeks ended 27 June 99 $ thousand	52 weeks ended 28 June 98 $ thousand	52 weeks ended 27 June 99 $ thousand	52 weeks ended 28 June 98 $ thousand

25 REMUNERATION OF DIRECTORS AND EXECUTIVES

DIRECTORS' REMUNERATION

Income paid or payable, or otherwise made available, to directors by the Company	**5 170**	**3 648**	**5 170**	**3 648**

Details of options granted to and exercised by directors during the year are set out in Note 24. It is the Company's belief that options issued are not a cost to the Company.

The number of directors whose remuneration is disclosed above, falls within the following bands for the 52 weeks ended 27 June 1999 and 52 weeks ended 28 June 1998 are as follows:

$	1999	1998	$	1999	1998
40 000–49 999	–	2	970 000–979 999	–	1
70 000–79 999	–	2	990 000–999 999	–	1*
80 000–89 999	4	–	1 160 000–1 169 999	1	–
100 000–109 999	–	1	1 190 000–1 199 999	–	1
130 000–139 000	1	–	3 320 000–3 329 999	1*	–
140 000–149 999	–	1			
210 000–219 999	1	–			

Two executives were also directors of Woolworths Limited for which they received no separate remuneration.

* Includes lump sum payments made on retirement or termination.

	Consolidated		Woolworths Limited	
	52 weeks ended 27 June 99 $ thousand	52 weeks ended 28 June 98 $ thousand	52 weeks ended 27 June 99 $ thousand	52 weeks ended 28 June 98 $ thousand

RETIREMENT BENEFITS PAID TO DIRECTORS

Benefit paid to the estate of Mr J A Illiffe in consequence of his death whilst a director of Woolworths Limited	–	210	–	210

EXECUTIVES' REMUNERATION

The amount received and receivable by executive officers of the economic entity and the Company in the current period whose remuneration is $100 000 or more is $36 364 389 (1998: $30 764 202). The average amount received by executive officers was $255 730 (1998: $240 345).

Executive officers are deemed to be all executive directors of Woolworths Limited and any of its controlled entities, and all salaried employees that are engaged in the strategic management of the business operations of the Woolworths Group, including executive grade operational personnel. This definition is a variation from that which was adopted in previous periods, and comparatives have been adjusted accordingly. Previously, the Company disclosed all employees whose total remuneration was in excess of $100 000 as executive officers. This was clearly not the intent of the applicable accounting standard and the definition has been changed to one more in keeping with the meaning of the term 'executive officer'.

A summary of the numbers of options granted to and exercised by executive officers with income of at least $100 000 are set out below. The terms and conditions relating to the options are set out in Note 23.

Granted	1 426 000
Exercised	539 230
Forfeited	1 163 770
Outstanding	5 242 000

$	1999	1998	$	1999	1998
100 000–109 999	6	1	380 000–389 999	1	–
110 000–119 999	4	2	400 000–409 999	1	–
120 000–129 999	4	5	410 000–419 999	1	2
130 000–139 999	6	5	420 000–429 999	1	–
140 000–149 999	12	9	430 000–439 999	1	2
150 000–159 999	6	12	440 000–449 999	2	–
160 000–169 999	9	13	450 000–459 999	–	1
170 000–179 999	13	11	460 000–469 999	–	–
180 000–189 999	14	11	470 000–479 999	2	–
190 000–199 999	10	6	480 000–489 000	–	1
200 000–209 999	8	10	490 000–499 999	1	–
210 000–219 999	3	6	500 000–509 999	–	1
220 000–229 999	6	3	510 000–519 000	1	1
230 000–239 999	5	4*	530 000–539 000	–	1
240 000–249 999	3	4	540 000–549 999	–	1
250 000–259 999	4	–	550 000–559 000	1	–
260 000–269 999	1	–	560 000–569 999	–	1
270 000–279 999	1	1	580 000–589 999	1	–
280 000–289 999	2	–	610 000–619 999	1*	–
290 000–299 999	–	1	650 000–659 000	–	1
300 000–309 999	2	–	660 000–669 999	2	–
310 000–319 999	–	1	670 000–679 000	–	1
320 000–329 999	–	2*	830 000–839 999	1	–
330 000–339 999	2	1	970 000–979 000	–	1
340 000–349 999	1	1	990 000–999 999	–	1*
350 000–359 999	–	2	1 169 000–1 169 999	1	–
360 000–369 000	–	1	1 190 000–1 200 000	–	1
370 000–379 999	1	–	3 320 000–3 329 999	1*	–

* Includes lump sum payments made on retirement or termination.

26 FINANCIAL INSTRUMENTS

Off-Balance Sheet Derivative Instruments

Woolworths Limited is party to financial instruments with off-balance sheet risk in order to hedge exposure to fluctuations in interest and foreign exchange rates. The interest rate instruments include swaps and forward rate agreements. Foreign exchange instruments include forward contracts, cross currency swaps and options.

Interest Rate Instruments

Bank Loans of the economic entity currently bear an average variable interest rate of 5.04% (1998: 5.29%). It is policy to protect part of the loans from exposure to increasing interest rates. Accordingly, the economic entity has entered into interest rate swap agreements.

Interest Rate Swap Agreements

Under the swap agreements the economic entity will receive interest at variable rates and pay interest at fixed rates. The contracts are used to protect against rising interest rates on the variable interest component of the underlying debt. The contracts are settled on a net basis, and the net amount receivable or payable on the contract is adjusted against interest expense in the period in which settlement takes place. The swaps that were executed in respect of the Domestic Medium Term Notes are matched according to coupon payment dates and maturity. All other swap contracts are settled on a quarterly basis to approximately match the dates on which the interest is payable on the Revolving Credit Facility.

Swap agreements in place at 27 June 1999 cover approximately 45% of the principal outstanding on the Revolving Credit Facility, and 30% of the principal outstanding on the Domestic Medium Term Notes. The continued total of domestic notes subject to fixed rates, including the effect of the interest rate swaps is $115 million.

Forward Rate Agreements

At the end of the previous financial period the economic entity had entered into forward rate agreements covering a nominal amount of $20 million. There are no similar agreements in place as at the end of the current financial period.

At 27 June 1999, the notional principal amounts and periods of expiry of the interest rate swap agreements and forward rate agreements are as follows:

	As at 27 June 1999 $ million	As at 28 June 1998 $ million
Less than 1 year	45	140
1–2 years	70	55
2–3 years	95	25
3–4 years	85	55
4–5 years	—	85
Greater than 5 years	45	45
	340	405

Foreign Currency Instruments

The economic entity has exposure to movements in foreign currency exchange rates through term borrowings, and anticipated sales of inventory and purchases of inventory and equipment, which are denominated in foreign currencies. In order to hedge against part of this exposure, the economic entity enters into forward exchange contracts and cross currency swap agreements. The term borrowings re fully hedged.

Forward Exchange Contracts and Foreign Currency Options

Under these agreements the economic entity has contracted to buy or sell foreign currencies in exchange for Australian dollars at a pre-determined rate to be settled at a future date. The maturity dates of the contracts are timed to match the anticipated timing of major foreign currency receipts and payments that are expected to occur within the ensuing financial period.

At period end, the details of outstanding forward contracts and options are (Australian dollar equivalents):

	27 June 1999 $ million		28 June 1998 $ million		27 June 1999 $ million	28 June 1998 $ million
	Buy	Sell	Buy	Sell	Exchange rate	Exchange rate
Maturing:						
Within 6 months:						
– United States dollars	54.9	—	55.3	—	0.65	0.61
— Japanese yen	—	0.6	—	7.1	80.13	83.81
— Swedish krona	—	—	3.3	—	—	5.74
— Hong Kong dollars	9.4	—	6.5	—	4.99	4.74
— Finnish marks	5.4	—	—	—	3.22	—

Where these contracts are used to hedge specific anticipated future transactions, any unrealised gains or losses on the contracts are deferred and will be recognised in the measurement of the underlying transactions when they occur. Amounts receivable and payable on open contracts are included in other debtors and other creditors respectively.

No material gains, losses and costs have been deferred as at 27 June 1999.

Cross Currency Swap Agreements

As part of a $100 million issue of US dollars denominated Senior Notes during the financial period, the economic entity entered into two cross currency swap agreements to fully hedge the US dollar value of the notes issued. The effect of the cross currency swaps is to offset all of the foreign currency and (US dollar) interest rate exposure on both interest and principal payments associated with the notes, which mature on 1 September 2007. The maturity and settlement dates under the swaps match the maturity and coupon payments for the term of the notes. The exposure to the economic entity is in Australian dollars with 50% of the notes at a fixed rate coupon of 7.104% paid semi-annually, and 50% at a variable rate of the Bank Bill Swap rate plus a margin, paid quarterly. At balance date the effective variable rate was 5.323% (1998: 5.355%).

CREDIT RISK EXPOSURE

The credit risk on financial assets of the economic entity which have been recognised on the balance sheet, other than investments in shares, is generally the carrying amount, net of any provisions for doubtful debts.

The recognised financial assets of the economic entity include amounts receivable arising from unrealised gains on derivative financial instruments. For off-balance sheet financial instruments, including derivatives, which are deliverable, credit risk may also arise from the potential failure of the counterparties to meet their obligations under the respective contracts at maturity. As at 27 June 1999, no material credit risk exposure existed in relation to potential counterparty failure on deliverable off-balance sheet financial instruments.

INTEREST RATE RISK EXPOSURE

The economic entity's exposure to interest rate risk and the effective average interest rate for each class of financial assets and financial liabilities as at 27 June 1999 is set out below.

Exposure will arise predominantly from assets and liabilities bearing variable interest rates as the economic entity intends to hold fixed rate assets and liabilities to maturity.

Fixed interest maturing in:

1999	Floating interest rate $ million	1 year or less $ million	1 to 5 years $ million	Over 5 years $ million	Non-interest bearing $ million	Total $ million	Average interest Rate %
Financial assets							
Cash and deposits	216.2	–	–	–	16.4	232.6	4.76
Receivables	–	–	–	–	181.6	181.6	–
	216.2	–	–	–	198.0	414.2	
Financial liabilities							
Trade creditors	–	–	–	–	1 281.1	1 281.1	–
Accrued expenses	–	–	–	–	318.7	318.7	–
Revolving bilateral loan facility	655.0	–	–	–	–	655.0	5.04
Multi option facility							
– fixed	–	–	–	9.5	–	9.5	6.80
– variable	8.0	–	–	–	–	8.0	4.98
Variable rate domestic notes	80.0	–	–	–	–	80.0	5.38
Fixed rate domestic notes	–	–	–	70.0	–	70.0	7.25
USD notes	–	–	–	134.0	–	134.0	6.76
Interest rate swaps*	(340.0)	45.0	250.0	45.0	–	–	5.87
Cross currency swaps:							
– fixed/floating	67.0	–	–	(67.0)	–	–	5.36
	470.0	45.0	250.0	191.5	1 599.8	2 556.3	
Net financial assets (liabilities)	(253.8)	(45.0)	(250.0)	(191.5)	(1 401.8)	(2 142.1)	

* Notional principal amounts

Fixed interest maturing in:

1998	Floating interest rate $ million	1 year or less $ million	1 to 5 years $ million	Over 5 years $ million	Non-interest bearing $ million	Total $ million	Average interest Rate %
Financial assets							
Cash and deposits	135.9	—	—	—	14.4	150.3	5.06
Receivables	—	—	—	—	165.5	165.5	—
Financial liabilities							
Trade creditors	—	—	—	—	1 202.7	1 202.7	—
Accrued expenses	—	—	—	—	277.7	277.7	
Revolving bilateral loan facility	380.1	—	—	—	—	380.1	5.29
Bill facility	5.9	—	—	—	—	5.9	5.23
Variable rate domestic notes	80.0	—	—	—	—	80.0	5.42
Fixed rate domestic notes	—	—	—	70.0	—	70.0	7.25
USD notes	—	—	—	134.0	—	134.0	6.76
Interest rate swaps*	(385.0)	120.0	220.0	45.0	—	—	7.09
Forward rate agreements*	(20.0)	20.0	—	—	—	—	4.89
Cross currency swaps:							
– fixed/floating	67.0	—	—	(67.0)	—	—	5.36
	128.0	140.0	220.0	182.0	1 480.4	2 150.4	
Net financial assets (liabilities)	7.9	(140.0)	(220.0)	(182.0)	(1 300.5)	(1 834.6)	

* Notional principal amounts

NET FAIR VALUE OF FINANCIAL ASSETS AND LIABILITIES

On-balance sheet

The carrying value of cash and cash equivalents and non-interest bearing monetary financial assets and liabilities of the economic entity approximates their net fair value and as such they have been omitted from these disclosures.

The net fair value of other monetary financial assets and liabilities is based upon market prices where a market exists or the expected future cash flows, discounted where appropriate by current interest rates for assets and liabilities with similar risk profiles.

Off-balance sheet

The net fair value of financial assets or liabilities arising from interest rate swap and forward rate agreements, and forward foreign currency contracts and swap agreements has been determined as the carrying value which represents the amount currently receivable or payable at period end.

For forward rate agreements, and interest rate and cross currency swaps, the net fair value has been determined by the net present value of cash flows due under the contracts, using a discount rate appropriate to the type and maturity of the contract.

For forward currency contracts, the net fair value is taken to be the unrealised gain or loss at period end calculated by reference to the current forward rates for contracts with similar maturity profiles.

| | As at 27 June 1999 | | As at 28 June 1998 | |
	Carrying amount $m	Net fair value $m	Carrying amount $m	Net fair value $m
On-balance sheet financial instruments				
FINANCIAL LIABILITIES				
Bank loans	672.4	672.4	386.0	386.0
Other loans	285.5	291.3	285.5	312.4
	957.9	**963.7**	**671.5**	**698.4**
Off-balance sheet financial instruments				
FINANCIAL ASSETS				
Forward exchange contracts	–	–	0.3	1.9
FINANCIAL LIABILITIES				
Interest rate swaps	0.3	(1.0)	0.7	4.4
Forward exchange contracts	–	1.9	–	–
Cross currency swaps	1.8	3.5	1.8	17.1
	2.1	**2.5**	**2.5**	**21.5**

None of the classes of financial assets are readily traded on organised markets in standardised form.

27 DEED OF CROSS GUARANTEE

Pursuant to ASIC Class Order 98/1418, the wholly-owned subsidiaries listed below are relieved from the Corporations Law requirements for preparation, audit and lodgement of financial reports.

It is a condition of the class order that the Company and each of the subsidiaries enter into a deed of cross guarantee. Under the deed the Company guarantees the payment of all debts of each of the subsidiaries in full, in the event of a winding up. The subsidiaries in turn guarantee the payment of the debts of the Company in full in the event that it is wound up.

The subsidiaries that are party to the deed are:

Woolworths Properties Pty Limited
Woolworths (Victoria) Pty Limited
Woolworths (WA) Pty Limited
Woolworths Managers Superannuation Scheme Pty Limited
Woolworths (Publishing) Pty Limited
Rockmans Stores Pty Limited
Australian Independent Retailers Pty Limited
SPAR Australia Pty Limited
Barmos Pty Limited
Nalos Pty Limited
Josona Pty Limited
Woolstar Pty Limited
QFD Pty Limited
Queensland Property Investments Pty Limited
Philip Leong Stores Pty Limited
Woolies Liquor Stores Pty Limited
Calvartan Pty Limited
Australian Safeway Stores Pty Limited
Dick Smith Electronics Staff Superannuation Fund Pty Limited
Weetah Pty Limited

Woolworths (Q'land) Pty Limited
Woolworths (South Australia) Pty Limited
Australian Liquor & Grocery Wholesalers Pty Limited
Woolworths Staff Superannuation Scheme Pty Limited
Charmtex Pty Limited
Grocery Wholesalers Pty Limited
Dick Smith Electronics Holdings Pty Limited
Woolworths Custodian Pty Limited
Fabcot Pty Limited
Barjok Pty Limited
Australian Independent Wholesalers Pty Limited
Woolworths (R&D) Pty Limited
Dentra Pty Limited
Jack Butler & Staff Pty Limited
Woolworths Group Superannuation Scheme Pty Ltd
Woolworths Executive Superannuation Scheme Pty Ltd
Mac's Liquor Stores Pty Limited
Dick Smith Electronics Pty Limited
Dick Smith (Wholesale) Pty Limited
Dick Smith Management Pty Limited
Dick Smith Electronics Franchising Pty Limited

A consolidated profit and loss statement and consolidated balance sheet for the closed group representing the Company and the subsidiaries noted above, which are party to the deed, as at 27 June 1999 is set out below:

	As at 27 June 1999 $ million
PROFIT AND LOSS STATEMENT	
Operating profit before income tax	401.7
Income tax expense	(146.7)
Operating profit after income tax	255.0
Extraordinary items after income tax	—
Net Profit	255.0
Retained earnings at the beginning of the period	503.8
Transfers to reserves	—
Transfers from reserves	—
Dividends provided for or paid	(207.2)
Retained earnings at the end of the period	551.6
BALANCE SHEET	
CURRENT ASSETS	
Cash	211.3
Receivables	174.2
Inventories	1 623.1
Property, plant and equipment	86.0
Other	76.2
Total Current Assets	2 170.8
NON-CURRENT ASSETS	
Receivables	29.5
Investments	15.7
Property, plant and equipment	2 107.4
Intangibles	133.9
Other	175.9
Total Non-Current Assets	2 462.4
Total Assets	4 633.2
CURRENT LIABILITIES	
Accounts payable	1 256.1
Accruals	315.5
Borrowings	1.9
Provisions	424.5
Total Current Liabilities	1 998.0
NON-CURRENT LIABILITIES	
Borrowings	940.5
Provisions	223.1
Total Non-Current Liabilities	1 163.6
Total Liabilities	3 161.6
Net Assets	1 471.6
SHAREHOLDERS' EQUITY	
Share capital	721.4
Reserves	198.6
Retained earnings	551.6
Total Shareholders' Equity	1 471.6

28 CONTROLLED ENTITY DISCLOSURES

Name	Legend	Place of incorporation	Investment of the company 1999 $m	Investment of the company 1998 $m	Beneficial percentage held by economic entity 1999 %	Beneficial percentage held by economic entity 1998 %
Woolworths Limited		NSW	—	—	—	—
Controlled entities of Woolworths Limited:						
Woolworths Properties Pty Limited	a	NSW	23.5	23.5	100	100
Woolworths (Q'land) Pty Limited	a	NSW	10.0	10.0	100	100
Woolworths (Victoria) Pty Limited	a	VIC	4.0	4.0	100	100
Woolworths (South Australia) Pty Limited	a	SA	4.0	4.0	100	100
Woolworths (WA) Pty Limited	a	WA	2.5	2.5	100	100
Australian Liquor & Grocery Wholesalers Pty Ltd	a	NT	0.2	0.2	100	100
Woolworths Managers Superannuation Scheme Pty Limited	a,d	NSW	—	—	100	100
Woolworths Staff Superannuation Scheme Pty Limited	a,d	NSW	—	—	100	100
Woolworths (Publishing) Pty Ltd	a,d	QLD	—	—	100	100
Charmtex Pty Limited	a	NSW	0.5	0.5	100	100
Rockmans Stores Pty Limited	a	NSW	0.1	0.1	100	100
Grocery Wholesalers Pty Ltd	a	NSW	0.2	0.2	100	100
Australian Independent Retailers Pty Ltd	a	VIC	0.1	0.1	100	100
Dick Smith Electronics Holdings Pty Limited	a	NSW	20.6	20.6	100	100
SPAR Australia Pty Limited	a,d	NSW	—	—	100	100
Woolworths Custodian Pty Ltd	a,d	NSW	—	—	100	100
Barmos Pty Ltd	a,d	NSW	—	—	100	100
Fabcot Pty Limited	a,d	NSW	—	—	100	100
Nalos Pty Limited	a,d	NSW	—	—	100	100
Barjok Pty Ltd	a,d	NSW	—	—	100	100
Josona Pty Ltd	a,d	NSW	—	—	100	100
Woolstar Investments Ltd	c,d	NZ	—	—	100	100
Woolworths Insurance Pty Ltd	c	Singapore	1.2	1.2	100	100
DSE Merge Corporation	c	USA	—	—	100	100
DSE Investments Inc.	c	USA	3.8	3.8	100	100
Australian Independent Wholesalers Pty Ltd	a,d	NSW	—	—	100	100
Woolstar Pty Limited	a	ACT	0.6	0.6	100	100
Woolworths (R&D) Pty Limited	a,d	NSW	—	—	100	100
Controlled entities of Woolworths Properties Pty Limited:						
QFD Pty Limited:	a,d	ACT	—	—	100	100
Dentra Pty Limited	a,d	ACT	—	—	100	100
Controlled entities of Woolworths (Q'land) Pty Limited:						
Queensland Property Investments Pty Ltd	a,d	QLD	—	—	100	100
Philip Leong Stores Pty Limited	a,d	QLD	—	—	100	100
Controlled entity of Woolworths (South Australia) Pty Limited:						
Woolies Liquor Stores Pty Ltd	a,d	SA	—	—	100	100
Controlled entities of Woolworths (Victoria) Pty Limited:						
Statewide Independent Wholesalers Limited	b,d	TAS	—	—	60	60
Calvartan Pty Limited	a,d	ACT	—	—	100	100
Controlled entities of Calvartan Pty Limited:						

28 CONTROLLED ENTITY DISCLOSURES (continued)

Name	Legend	Place of incorporation	Investment of the company 1999 $m	1998 $m	Beneficial percentage held by economic entity 1999 %	1998 %
Jack Butler & Staff Pty Ltd	a,d	QLD	—	—	100	100
Controlled entities of Jack Butler and Staff Pty Ltd:						
Woolworths Group Superannuation Scheme Pty Ltd	a,d	QLD	—	—	100	100
Woolworths Executive Superannuation Scheme Pty Limited	a,d	QLD	—	—	100	100
Australian Safeway Stores Pty Ltd	a,d	VIC	—	—	100	100
Controlled entity of Australian Safeway Stores Pty Ltd:						
Mac's Liquor Stores Pty Limited	a,d	QLD	—	—	100	100
Controlled entities of Dick Smith Electronics Holdings Pty Limited:						
Dick Smith Electronics Pty Limited	a,d	NSW	—	—	100	100
Dick Smith (Wholesale) Pty Ltd	a,d	NSW	—	—	100	100
Dick Smith Management Pty Ltd	a,d	NSW	—	—	100	100
Dick Smith Electronics Franchising Pty Ltd	a,d	NSW	—	—	100	100
Dick Smith Electronics (HK) Ltd	c,d	Hong Kong	—	—	100	100
DSE (NZ) Limited	b,d	NZ	—	—	100	100
Dick Smith Electronics Ltd	b,d	UK	—	—	100	100
Dick Smith Electronics Staff Superannuation Fund Pty Limited	a,d	NSW	—	—	100	100
Controlled entities of DSE (NZ) Limited:						
Como Imports (NZ) Ltd	b,d	NZ	—	—	100	100
David Reid Electronics (1992) Limited	b,d	NZ	—	—	100	100
Controlled entities of Dentra Pty Limited:						
Weetah Pty Limited	a,d	NT	—	—	100	100
			71.3	71.3	—	—

a) These controlled entities have been granted relief from the Corporations Law requirements for preparation, audit and lodgement of financial statements, pursuant to ASIC Class Order 98/1418. Full details of this relief are set out in Note 27.

b) Controlled entities audited or reviewed by other BDO Nelson Parkhill firm affiliates.

c) Controlled entities audited by another firm of auditors.

d) As a result of rounding, the investment by the Company in these controlled entities is not displayed.

Directors' Declaration

The Directors declare that the financial statements and notes set out on pages 42 to 73:

a) comply with Accounting Standards and the Corporations Regulations and other mandatory professional reporting requirements; and

b) give a true and fair view of the Company's and consolidated entity's financial position as at 27 June 1999 and of their performance, as represented by the results of their operations and their cash flows, for the financial period ended on that date.

In the Directors' opinion:

a) the financial statements and notes are in accordance with the Corporations Law; and

b) there are reasonable grounds to believe that the Company will be able to pay its debts as and when they become due and payable; and

c) at the date of this Declaration, there are reasonable grounds to believe that the Company and the subsidiaries identified in Note 27 will be able to meet any obligations or liabilities to which they are, or may become, subject by virtue of the Deed of Cross Guarantee described in Note 27.

This Declaration is made on 20th day of September 1999 in accordance with a resolution of the Directors.

J C Dahlsen

Chairman

R C Corbett

Group Managing Director

Independent Audit Report

To the members of Woolworths Limited

Scope

We have audited the financial statements of Woolworths Limited for the financial year ended 27 June 1999 as set out on pages 42 to 74. The financial statements include the consolidated financial statements of the consolidated entity comprising the Company and the entities it controlled at the year's end or from time to time during the financial year. The Company's directors are responsible for the preparation and presentation of the financial statements. We have conducted an independent audit of these financial statements in order to express an opinion on them to the members of the Company.

Our audit has been conducted in accordance with Australian Auditing Standards to provide reasonable assurance as to whether the financial statements are free of material misstatement. Our procedures included examination, on a test basis, of evidence supporting the amounts and other disclosures in the financial statements, and the evaluation of accounting policies and significant accounting estimates. These procedures have been undertaken to form an opinion as to whether, in all material respects, the financial statements are presented fairly in accordance with Accounting Standards, other mandatory professional reporting requirements and statutory requirements so as to present a view which is consistent with our understanding of the Company's and the consolidated entity's financial position, the results of their operations and their cash flows.

The audit opinion expressed in this report has been formed on the above basis.

Audit opinion

In our opinion, the financial statements of Woolworths Limited are in accordance with:

a) the Corporations Law, including:

    (i) giving a true and fair view of the Company's and the consolidated entity's financial position as at 27 June 1999 and of their performance for the year ended on that date; and

    (ii) complying with Accounting Standards and the Corporations Regulations; and

b) other mandatory professional reporting requirements.

BDO Nelson Parkhill

Chartered Accountants

Stephen La Greca

Partner

Dated at Sydney this 20th day of September 1999

Appendix 2
An Introduction to
Financial Mathematics

An introduction to financial mathematics

Interest can be either simple or compound. Simple interest is calculated only on the original principal. If $1000 is deposited in a bank at a rate of 10 per cent simple interest per annum for three years, the interest per year is $100, i.e. 10 per cent of $1000. So, after three years, the interest earned is $300.

Compound interest

Compound interest is calculated both on the principal and on any interest previously earned. So, if the bank in the above example pays 10 per cent interest compounded annually, how much interest will be earned in three years? The following table shows one way of calculating this.

	Balance at start	Interest	Balance at end
Year 1	$1 000	$100	$1 100
Year 2	$1 100	$110	$1 210
Year 3	$1 210	$121	$1 331

Therefore the compound interest is $331 compared to $300 simple interest.

Future value

Fortunately, we do not need to work through such calculations as the balance, or future value, at the end of the time period can be determined by using the formula:

$$FV = A (1+R)^n$$

where
A = amount at the start
R = interest rate per annum ÷ 100
n = number of years
FV = future value after n years

Key Concept A2.1

Future value of $1

The future value of $1 is the value of $1 after n years at r per cent compound interest per annum. This is given by
$(1 + R)^n$, where $R = r ÷ 100$

Returning to our example, we see that A = 1000, R = 10 ÷ 100 = 0.1 and n = 3. Therefore:

$$FV = 1000 (1 + 0.1)^3$$
$$= 1000 (1.1)^3$$
$$= 1000 \times 1.331$$
$$= \$1331$$

Calculators and computers make the task of carrying out these calculations far easier.

Note that there are several ways to calculate that $(1.1)^3 = 1.331$. Firstly, $(1.1)^3 = 1.1 \times 1.1 \times 1.1$. Many calculators have an x^y key to perform this calculation quickly. Also, tables have been compiled which show the future value of $1. Such a table is provided in Appendix 3 (pp. 555–6).

Example A2.1

Use Appendix 3 to find the future value of $1, and hence calculate how much $10 000 invested at 12 per cent per annum compounded annually will amount to in ten years.

$$FV = A(1+R)^n$$
$$= A \times \text{future value of \$1}$$

From Table 1 in Appendix 3, we see that the future value of $1 after ten years at 12 per cent is 3.1058. Hence:

$$FV = 10\ 000 \times 3.1058$$
$$= \$31\ 058$$

The simple interest would only have been 12 per cent of $10 000 × 10 years = $12 000, and the future value would be $22 000. This example illustrates the benefit of the compounding of interest compared with simple interest. However, note that we have not considered inflation or other charges.

Present value

In the previous section we looked at how much an amount would grow to in time. We often want to reverse the situation and ask how much needs to be invested now in order to receive a certain amount in the future. This is particularly important in the calculation of capital projects which provide cash flows over several years. This is known as present value. To calculate present value, we use the formula:

$$PV = A\left[\frac{1}{(1+R)^n}\right]$$

where
- A = future amount
- R = interest rate per annum ÷ 100
- n = number of years
- PV = present value, i.e. the amount which needs to be invested

To show that the above formula works, we will reverse the first compound interest question we considered.

Key Concept A2.2

Present value of $1

The present value of $1 is the amount which needs to be invested now, at r per cent per annum compound interest, in order to compound to $1 after n years. This is given by

$$\frac{1}{(1+R)^n}, \text{ where } R = r \div 100$$

Example A2.2

What is the present value of $1331 received in three years' time, at 10 per cent per annum compound interest?

$$PV = A\left[\frac{1}{(1+R)^n}\right]$$

$$= 1331\left[\frac{1}{(1.10)^3}\right]$$

$$= 1331 \times 0.7513$$

$$= \$1000$$

This confirms that we need to invest $1000 today to accumulate $1331 in three years at the compound interest rate of 10 per cent. Therefore, $1000 is the present value of $1331 received in three years at a discount rate of 10 per cent.

There are tables which give the present value of $1 for a range of interest rates and years. Table 2 in Appendix 3 (pp. 557–8) provides these values.

Example A2.3

Use Table 2 to find the present value of $1 and hence the present value of $31 058 received after ten years at 12 per cent compound interest per annum.

$$PV = A\left[\frac{1}{(1+R)^n}\right]$$

$$= A \times \text{present value of } \$1$$

From Table 2, we see that the present value of $1 after ten years at 12 per cent is 0.32197. Hence:

$$PV = 31\ 058 \times 0.32197$$

$$= \$9999.74$$

If we refer back to Example A2.1 then the answer we would expect is $10 000. The difference of 26 cents is what we describe as a rounding error. It occurs because the interest factors in the tables are rounded to four or five decimal places.

Annuities

Future value

In the previous examples we either calculated the future value of a single amount invested today, or we determined the present value of a sum to be received in the future. In many instances, money will be invested or withdrawn regularly over the investment period. Where the same amount is invested or withdrawn on a regular basis, we have an annuity. There are different types of annuities. An ordinary annuity is where each of the equal payments is made at the end of each compounding period. An annuity due is where each of the equal payments is made at the beginning of each compounding period.

Example A2.4

Troy wants to invest $1000 at the end of each year for five years at a compound interest rate of 10 per cent per annum. How much will Troy's investment be worth in five years?

We could perform five calculations and then add these together. However, we can determine the sum of an annuity by using the formula:

$$FVA = A [1 + (1 + R) + (1 + R)^2 + \ldots + (1 + R)^{n-1}]$$

or $$FVA = A \left[\frac{(1+R)^n - 1}{R} \right]$$

where
$$A = \text{amount of annuity}$$
$$R = \text{interest rate per annum} \div 100$$
$$n = \text{number of years}$$
$$FVA = \text{future value of annuity}$$

Once again, there are tables which provide future value of ordinary annuity factors. Table 3 in Appendix 3 (pp. 559–60) shows the future value of $1 per period.

Key Concept A2.3

Future value of $1 per period

The future value of $1 per period is the value of an investment after n time periods, given that $1 is invested at the end of each time period, at a compound interest rate of r per cent. The future value of $1 per period is

$$\frac{(1 + R)^n - 1}{R}, \text{ where } R = r \div 100$$

For Example A2.4 we have A = 1000, R = 0.1 and n = 5.

$$
\begin{aligned}
FVA &= 1000 \left[\frac{(1.10)^5 - 1}{0.10} \right] \\
&= 1000 \times \text{future value per \$1 period} \\
&= 1000 \times 6.1051 \\
&= \$6105.10
\end{aligned}
$$

Example A2.5

If Stacey invests $500 at the end of each year at 8 per cent per annum compounded annually, how much will she have at the end of five years? (Use Table 3.)

$$
\begin{aligned}
FVA &= A \left[\frac{(1+R)^n - 1}{R} \right] \\
&= A \times \text{future value of \$1 per period}
\end{aligned}
$$

From Table 3, the future value of $1 per period after five years at 8 per cent is 5.8666. Hence:

$$
\begin{aligned}
FVA &= 500 \times 5.8666 \\
&= \$2933.30
\end{aligned}
$$

Present value

We can also reverse Example A2.5 and imagine that Stacey wishes to provide her daughter with an annuity of $500 for five years. How much should Stacey invest now, at 8 per cent per annum, compounded annually, so that the daughter can withdraw $500 at the end of each year for the next five years? This amount is called the present value of an annuity.

The formula is:

$$PVA = A \left[\frac{1}{1+R} + \frac{1}{(1+R)^2} + \ldots + \frac{1}{(1+R)^n} \right]$$

or

$$PVA = A \left[\frac{1 - \frac{1}{(1+R)^n}}{R} \right]$$

where
- A = amount paid out per year
- R = interest rate ÷ 100
- n = number of years
- PVA = present value of annuity, i.e. amount to be invested now

Table 4 in Appendix 3 shows the present value of $1 per period.

Key Concept A2.4

Present value of $1 per period

The present value of $1 per period is the amount which needs to be invested now, at r per cent per annum compound interest, so that a sum of $1 can be withdrawn at the end of each year, for n years. The present value of $1 per period is

$$\frac{1 - (1+R)^n}{R}$$

where R = r ÷ 100

$$PVA = 500 \left[\frac{\frac{1}{(1 + 0.08)^5}}{0.08} \right]$$

$$= 500 \times \text{present value of \$1 per period}$$
$$= 500 \times 3.9927$$
$$= \$1996.35$$

Therefore, Stacey needs to invest $1996.35 now at 8 per cent compound interest per annum, for five years, in order for her daughter to receive $500 a year for five years.

More frequent compounding

The tables make the solution to financial mathematical problems reasonably easy. However, what do we do when the interest is compounded quarterly, monthly or daily? We illustrate what can be done by using the equations for future value and present value.

Future value

$$FV = A \left[1 + \frac{R}{m} \right]^{m \times n}$$

where
A = amount
R = interest rate per annum ÷ 100
n = number of years
m = number of times per year that interest is compounded
FV = future value

Example A2.6

How much will $1000 amount to in five years at 12 per cent per annum, compounded quarterly?

$$FV = 1000 \left[1 + \frac{0.12}{4} \right]^{5 \times 4}$$

$$= 1000 \, (1.03)^{20}$$
$$= 1000 \times 1.8061$$
$$= \$1806.10$$

Note that, using Table 1, we look up a 3 per cent interest rate with n = 20.

Present value

$$PV = A \left[\frac{1}{\left[1 + \dfrac{R}{m} \right]^{m \times n}} \right]$$

where
A = amount
R = interest rate per annum ÷ 100
n = number of years
m = number of times interest is compounded per year
PV = present value

Using the data from Example A2.6, what is the present value of $1000 to be received in five years' time?

$$PV = 1000 \times \left[\frac{1}{\left[1 + \dfrac{0.12}{4} \right]^{5 \times 4}} \right]$$

$$= 1000 \left[\frac{1}{(1.03)^{20}} \right]$$

$$= 1000 \times 0.55367$$
$$= \$553.67$$

(Use 3% and n = 20 in Table 2.)

Appendix 3
Present and Future Value
Factor Tables

TABLE 1: FUTURE VALUE OF $1 = (1+R)^n

n	0.25%	0.5%	0.66%	0.75%	1.0%	1.5%	1.75%	2.0%	2.5%	3.0%	3.5%	n
1	1.002 50	1.005 00	1.006 67	1.007 50	1.010 00	1.015 00	1.017 50	1.020 00	1.025 00	1.030 00	1.035 00	1
2	1.005 01	1.010 03	1.013 38	1.015 06	1.020 10	1.030 23	1.035 31	1.040 40	1.050 63	1.060 90	1.071 23	2
3	1.007 52	1.015 08	1.020 13	1.022 67	1.030 30	1.045 68	1.053 42	1.061 21	1.076 89	1.092 73	1.108 72	3
4	1.010 04	1.020 15	1.026 93	1.030 34	1.040 60	1.061 36	1.071 86	1.082 43	1.103 81	1.125 51	1.147 52	4
5	1.012 56	1.025 25	1.033 78	1.038 07	1.051 01	1.077 28	1.090 62	1.104 08	1.131 41	1.159 27	1.187 69	5
6	1.015 09	1.030 38	1.040 67	1.045 85	1.061 52	1.093 44	1.109 70	1.126 16	1.159 69	1.194 05	1.229 26	6
7	1.017 63	1.035 53	1.047 61	1.053 70	1.072 14	1.109 84	1.129 12	1.148 69	1.188 69	1.229 87	1.272 28	7
8	1.020 18	1.040 71	1.054 59	1.061 60	1.082 86	1.126 49	1.148 88	1.171 66	1.218 40	1.266 77	1.316 81	8
9	1.022 73	1.045 91	1.061 63	1.069 56	1.093 69	1.143 39	1.168 99	1.195 09	1.248 86	1.304 77	1.362 90	9
10	1.025 28	1.051 14	1.068 70	1.077 58	1.104 62	1.160 54	1.189 44	1.218 99	1.280 08	1.343 92	1.410 60	10
11	1.027 85	1.056 40	1.075 83	1.085 66	1.115 67	1.177 95	1.210 26	1.243 37	1.312 09	1.384 23	1.459 97	11
12	1.030 42	1.061 68	1.083 00	1.093 81	1.126 83	1.195 62	1.231 44	1.268 24	1.344 89	1.425 76	1.511 07	12
13	1.032 99	1.066 99	1.090 22	1.102 01	1.138 09	1.213 55	1.252 99	1.293 61	1.378 51	1.468 53	1.563 96	13
14	1.035 57	1.072 32	1.097 49	1.110 28	1.149 47	1.231 76	1.274 92	1.319 48	1.412 97	1.512 59	1.618 69	14
15	1.038 16	1.077 68	1.104 80	1.118 60	1.160 97	1.250 23	1.297 23	1.345 87	1.448 30	1.557 97	1.675 35	15
16	1.040 76	1.083 07	1.112 17	1.126 99	1.172 58	1.268 99	1.319 93	1.372 79	1.484 51	1.604 71	1.733 99	16
17	1.043 36	1.088 49	1.119 58	1.135 44	1.184 30	1.288 02	1.343 03	1.400 24	1.521 62	1.652 85	1.794 68	17
18	1.045 97	1.093 93	1.127 05	1.143 96	1.196 15	1.307 34	1.366 53	1.428 25	1.559 66	1.702 43	1.857 49	18
19	1.048 58	1.099 40	1.134 56	1.152 54	1.208 11	1.326 95	1.390 45	1.456 81	1.598 65	1.753 51	1.922 50	19
20	1.051 21	1.104 90	1.142 13	1.161 18	1.220 19	1.346 86	1.414 78	1.485 95	1.638 62	1.806 11	1.989 79	20
21	1.053 83	1.110 42	1.149 74	1.169 89	1.232 39	1.367 06	1.439 54	1.515 67	1.679 58	1.860 29	2.059 43	21
22	1.056 47	1.115 97	1.157 40	1.178 67	1.244 72	1.387 56	1.464 36	1.545 98	1.721 57	1.916 10	2.131 51	22
23	1.059 11	1.121 55	1.165 12	1.187 51	1.257 16	1.408 38	1.490 36	1.576 90	1.764 61	1.973 59	2.206 11	23
24	1.061 76	1.127 16	1.172 89	1.196 41	1.269 73	1.429 50	1.516 44	1.608 44	1.808 73	2.032 79	2.283 33	24
25	1.064 41	1.132 80	1.180 71	1.205 39	1.282 43	1.450 95	1.542 98	1.640 61	1.853 94	2.093 78	2.363 24	25
30	1.077 78	1.161 40	1.220 59	1.251 27	1.347 85	1.563 08	1.682 80	1.811 36	2.097 29	2.427 26	2.806 79	30
35	1.091 32	1.190 73	1.261 82	1.298 90	1.416 60	1.683 88	1.835 29	1.999 89	2.373 21	2.813 86	3.333 59	35
40	1.105 03	1.220 79	1.304 45	1.348 35	1.488 86	1.814 02	2.001 60	2.208 04	2.685 06	3.262 04	3.959 26	40
45	1.118 92	1.251 62	1.348 52	1.399 68	1.564 81	1.954 21	2.182 98	2.437 85	3.037 90	3.781 60	4.702 36	45
50	1.132 97	1.283 23	1.394 07	1.452 96	1.644 63	2.105 24	2.380 79	2.691 59	3.437 11	4.383 91	5.584 93	50
60	1.161 62	1.348 85	1.489 85	1.565 68	1.816 70	2.432 20	2.831 82	3.281 03	4.399 79	5.891 60	7.878 09	60

(continued over page)

TABLE 1 (CONTINUED)

n	4.0%	4.5%	5.0%	6.0%	7.0%	8.0%	10.0%	12.0%	15.0%	20.0%	n
1	1.040 00	1.045 00	1.050 00	1.060 00	1.070 00	1.080 00	1.100 00	1.120 0	1.150	1.200	1
2	1.081 60	1.092 03	1.102 50	1.123 60	1.144 90	1.166 40	1.210 00	1.254 4	1.322	1.440	2
3	1.124 86	1.141 17	1.157 63	1.191 01	1.225 04	1.259 71	1.331 00	1.404 9	1.521	1.728	3
4	1.169 86	1.192 52	1.215 51	1.262 47	1.310 79	1.360 48	1.464 10	1.573 5	1.749	2.074	4
5	1.216 65	1.246 18	1.276 28	1.338 22	1.402 55	1.469 32	1.610 51	1.762 0	2.011	2.488	5
6	1.265 32	1.302 26	1.340 10	1.418 51	1.500 73	1.586 87	1.771 56	1.973 8	2.313	2.938	6
7	1.315 93	1.360 86	1.407 10	1.503 63	1.605 78	1.713 82	1.948 72	2.210 7	2.660	3.583	7
8	1.368 57	1.422 10	1.477 46	1.593 84	1.718 18	1.850 93	2.143 59	2.476 0	3.059	4.300	8
9	1.423 31	1.486 10	1.551 33	1.689 47	1.838 45	1.999 00	2.357 95	2.773 1	3.518	5.160	9
10	1.480 24	1.552 97	1.628 89	1.790 84	1.967 15	2.158 92	2.593 74	3.105 8	4.046	6.192	10
11	1.539 45	1.622 85	1.710 34	1.898 29	2.104 85	2.331 63	2.853 12	3.478 5	4.652	7.430	11
12	1.601 03	1.695 88	1.795 86	2.012 19	2.252 19	2.518 17	3.138 43	3.896 0	5.350	8.916	12
13	1.665 07	1.772 20	1.885 65	2.132 92	2.409 84	2.719 62	3.452 27	4.363 5	6.153	10.699	13
14	1.731 68	1.851 94	1.979 93	2.260 90	2.578 53	2.937 19	3.797 50	4.887 1	7.076	12.839	14
15	1.800 94	1.935 28	2.078 93	2.396 55	2.759 03	3.172 16	4.177 25	5.473 6	8.137	15.407	15
16	1.872 98	2.022 37	2.182 87	2.540 35	2.952 16	3.425 94	4.594 97	6.130 3	9.358	18.488	16
17	1.947 90	2.113 38	2.292 02	2.692 77	3.158 81	3.700 01	5.054 47	6.866 1	10.761	22.186	17
18	2.025 82	2.208 48	2.406 62	2.854 33	3.379 93	3.996 01	5.559 92	7.690 0	12.375	26.623	18
19	2.106 85	2.307 86	2.526 95	3.025 59	3.616 52	4.315 70	6.115 91	8.612 8	14.232	31.945	19
20	2.191 12	2.411 71	2.653 30	3.207 13	3.869 68	4.660 95	6.727 50	9.646 3	16.367	38.338	20
21	2.278 77	2.520 24	2.785 96	3.399 56	4.140 56	5.033 83	7.400 25	10.803 8	18.821	46.005	21
22	2.369 92	2.633 65	2.925 26	3.603 53	4.430 40	5.436 54	8.140 27	12.100 3	21.645	55.206	22
23	2.464 72	2.752 17	3.071 52	3.819 74	4.740 52	5.871 46	8.954 30	13.552 3	24.891	66.247	23
24	2.563 30	2.876 01	3.225 10	4.048 93	5.072 36	6.341 18	9.849 73	15.178 6	28.625	79.497	24
25	2.665 84	3.005 43	3.386 35	4.291 87	5.427 43	6.848 47	10.834 71	17.000 1	32.919	95.396	25
30	3.243 40	3.745 32	4.321 94	5.743 49	7.612 25	10.062 65	17.449 40	29.960 0	66.212	237.376	30
35	3.946 09	4.667 35	5.516 02	7.686 08	10.676 58	14.785 34	28.102 44	52.800 0	133.175	590.668	35
40	4.801 02	5.816 36	7.039 99	10.285 71	14.974 45	21.724 52	45.259 26	93.051 0	267.862	1 469.771	40
45	5.841 18	7.248 25	8.985 01	13.764 61	21.002 45	31.920 44	72.890 48	163.987 6	538.767	3 657.258	45
50	7.106 68	9.032 64	11.477 40	18.420 15	29.457 02	46.901 61	117.390 85	289.002 1	1 083.652	9 100.427	50
60	10.519 63	14.027 41	18.679 19	32.987 69	57.946 43	101.257 06	304.481 64	897.596 9	4 383.999	56 347.514	60

TABLE 2: PRESENT VALUE OF $1 = $\dfrac{1}{(1+R)^n}$

n	0.25%	0.50%	0.66%	0.75%	1.0%	1.5%	2.0%	2.5%	3.0%	3.5%	n
1	0.997 51	0.995 02	0.993 38	0.992 56	0.990 09	0.985 22	0.980 39	0.975 60	0.970 87	0.966 18	1
2	0.995 02	0.990 07	0.986 80	0.985 17	0.980 29	0.970 66	0.961 16	0.951 81	0.942 59	0.933 51	2
3	0.992 54	0.985 15	0.980 26	0.977 83	0.970 59	0.956 31	0.942 32	0.928 59	0.915 14	0.901 94	3
4	0.990 06	0.980 25	0.973 77	0.970 55	0.960 98	0.942 18	0.923 84	0.905 95	0.888 48	0.871 44	4
5	0.987 59	0.975 37	0.967 32	0.963 33	0.951 46	0.928 26	0.905 73	0.883 85	0.862 60	0.841 97	5
6	0.985 13	0.970 52	0.960 92	0.956 16	0.942 04	0.914 54	0.887 97	0.862 29	0.837 48	0.813 50	6
7	0.982 67	0.965 69	0.954 55	0.940 94	0.932 71	0.901 02	0.870 56	0.841 26	0.813 09	0.785 99	7
8	0.980 22	0.960 89	0.948 23	0.941 98	0.923 48	0.887 71	0.853 49	0.820 74	0.789 40	0.759 41	8
9	0.977 78	0.956 10	0.941 95	0.934 96	0.914 33	0.874 59	0.836 75	0.800 72	0.766 41	0.733 73	9
10	0.975 34	0.951 35	0.935 71	0.928 00	0.905 28	0.861 66	0.820 34	0.781 19	0.744 09	0.708 91	10
11	0.972 91	0.946 61	0.929 52	0.921 09	0.896 32	0.848 93	0.804 26	0.762 14	0.722 42	0.684 94	11
12	0.970 48	0.941 91	0.923 36	0.914 24	0.887 44	0.836 38	0.788 49	0.743 55	0.701 37	0.661 78	12
13	0.968 06	0.937 22	0.917 25	0.907 43	0.878 66	0.824 02	0.773 03	0.725 42	0.680 95	0.639 40	13
14	0.965 65	0.932 56	0.911 17	0.900 68	0.869 96	0.811 84	0.757 87	0.707 72	0.661 11	0.617 78	14
15	0.963 24	0.927 92	0.905 14	0.893 97	0.861 34	0.799 85	0.743 01	0.690 46	0.641 86	0.596 89	15
16	0.960 84	0.923 30	0.899 14	0.887 32	0.852 82	0.788 03	0.728 44	0.673 62	0.623 16	0.576 70	16
17	0.958 44	0.918 71	0.893 19	0.880 71	0.844 37	0.776 38	0.714 16	0.657 19	0.605 01	0.557 20	17
18	0.956 05	0.914 14	0.887 27	0.874 16	0.836 01	0.764 91	0.700 15	0.641 16	0.587 39	0.538 36	18
19	0.953 67	0.909 59	0.881 40	0.867 65	0.827 73	0.753 60	0.686 43	0.625 52	0.570 28	0.520 15	19
20	0.951 29	0.905 06	0.875 56	0.861 19	0.819 54	0.742 47	0.672 97	0.610 27	0.553 67	0.502 56	20
21	0.948 92	0.900 56	0.869 76	0.854 78	0.811 43	0.731 49	0.659 77	0.595 38	0.537 54	0.485 57	21
22	0.946 55	0.896 08	0.864 00	0.848 42	0.803 39	0.720 68	0.646 83	0.580 86	0.521 89	0.469 15	22
23	0.944 19	0.891 62	0.858 28	0.842 10	0.795 44	0.710 03	0.634 15	0.566 69	0.506 69	0.453 28	23
24	0.941 84	0.887 19	0.852 60	0.835 83	0.787 56	0.699 54	0.621 72	0.552 87	0.491 93	0.437 95	24
25	0.939 49	0.882 77	0.846 95	0.829 61	0.779 76	0.689 20	0.609 53	0.539 39	0.477 60	0.423 14	25
30	0.927 83	0.861 03	0.819 27	0.799 19	0.741 92	0.639 76	0.552 07	0.476 74	0.411 98	0.356 27	30
35	0.916 32	0.839 82	0.792 50	0.769 88	0.705 91	0.593 86	0.500 02	0.421 37	0.355 38	0.299 97	35
40	0.904 95	0.819 14	0.766 61	0.741 65	0.671 65	0.551 26	0.452 89	0.372 43	0.306 55	0.252 57	40
45	0.893 72	0.798 96	0.741 56	0.714 45	0.639 05	0.511 71	0.410 19	0.329 17	0.264 43	0.212 65	45
50	0.882 63	0.779 29	0.717 32	0.688 25	0.608 03	0.475 00	0.371 52	0.290 94	0.228 10	0.179 05	50
60	0.860 87	0.741 37	0.671 21	0.638 70	0.550 45	0.409 30	0.304 78	0.227 28	0.169 73	0.126 93	60

(continued over page)

TABLE 2 (CONTINUED)

n	4.0%	4.5%	5.0%	6.0%	7.0%	8.0%	10.0%	12.0%	15.0%	20.0%	n
1	0.961 53	0.956 93	0.952 38	0.943 39	0.934 57	0.925 92	0.909 09	0.892 86	0.869 57	0.833 33	1
2	0.924 55	0.915 72	0.907 02	0.889 99	0.873 43	0.857 33	0.826 45	0.797 19	0.756 14	0.694 44	2
3	0.888 99	0.876 29	0.863 83	0.839 61	0.816 29	0.793 83	0.751 31	0.711 78	0.657 52	0.578 70	3
4	0.854 80	0.838 56	0.822 70	0.792 09	0.762 89	0.735 02	0.683 01	0.635 52	0.571 75	0.482 25	4
5	0.821 92	0.802 45	0.783 52	0.747 25	0.712 98	0.680 58	0.620 92	0.567 43	0.497 18	0.401 88	5
6	0.790 31	0.767 89	0.746 21	0.704 96	0.666 34	0.630 16	0.564 47	0.506 63	0.432 33	0.334 90	6
7	0.759 91	0.734 82	0.710 68	0.665 05	0.622 74	0.583 49	0.513 16	0.452 35	0.375 94	0.279 08	7
8	0.730 69	0.703 18	0.676 83	0.627 41	0.582 00	0.540 26	0.466 51	0.403 88	0.326 90	0.232 57	8
9	0.702 58	0.672 90	0.644 60	0.591 89	0.543 93	0.500 24	0.424 10	0.360 61	0.284 26	0.193 81	9
10	0.675 56	0.643 92	0.613 90	0.558 39	0.508 34	0.463 19	0.385 54	0.321 97	0.247 18	0.161 51	10
11	0.649 58	0.616 19	0.584 67	0.526 78	0.475 09	0.428 88	0.350 49	0.287 48	0.214 94	0.134 59	11
12	0.624 59	0.589 66	0.556 83	0.496 96	0.444 01	0.397 11	0.318 63	0.256 67	0.186 91	0.112 16	12
13	0.600 57	0.564 27	0.530 32	0.468 83	0.414 96	0.367 69	0.289 66	0.229 17	0.162 53	0.093 46	13
14	0.577 47	0.539 97	0.505 06	0.442 30	0.387 81	0.340 46	0.263 33	0.204 62	0.141 33	0.077 89	14
15	0.555 26	0.516 72	0.481 01	0.417 26	0.362 44	0.315 24	0.239 39	0.182 70	0.122 89	0.064 91	15
16	0.533 90	0.494 46	0.458 11	0.393 64	0.338 73	0.219 89	0.217 63	0.163 12	0.106 86	0.054 09	16
17	0.513 37	0.473 17	0.436 29	0.371 36	0.316 57	0.270 26	0.197 84	0.145 64	0.092 93	0.045 07	17
18	0.493 62	0.452 80	0.415 52	0.350 34	0.295 86	0.250 24	0.179 86	0.130 04	0.080 80	0.037 56	18
19	0.474 64	0.433 30	0.395 73	0.330 51	0.276 50	0.231 71	0.163 51	0.116 11	0.070 26	0.031 30	19
20	0.456 38	0.414 64	0.376 88	0.311 80	0.258 41	0.214 54	0.148 64	0.103 67	0.061 10	0.026 08	20
21	0.438 83	0.396 78	0.358 94	0.294 15	0.241 51	0.198 65	0.135 13	0.092 56	0.053 13	0.021 74	21
22	0.421 95	0.379 70	0.341 84	0.277 50	0.225 71	0.183 94	0.122 85	0.082 64	0.046 20	0.018 11	22
23	0.405 72	0.363 35	0.325 57	0.261 79	0.210 94	0.170 31	0.111 68	0.073 79	0.040 17	0.015 09	23
24	0.390 12	0.347 70	0.310 06	0.246 97	0.197 14	0.157 69	0.101 53	0.065 88	0.034 93	0.012 58	24
25	0.375 11	0.332 73	0.295 30	0.232 99	0.184 24	0.146 01	0.092 30	0.058 82	0.030 38	0.010 48	25
30	0.308 31	0.267 00	0.231 37	0.174 11	0.131 36	0.099 37	0.057 31	0.033 38	0.015 10	0.004 21	30
35	0.253 41	0.214 25	0.181 29	0.130 10	0.093 66	0.067 63	0.035 58	0.018 94	0.007 51	0.001 69	35
40	0.208 28	0.171 92	0.142 04	0.097 22	0.066 78	0.046 03	0.022 09	0.010 74	0.003 73	0.000 68	40
45	0.171 19	0.137 96	0.111 29	0.072 65	0.047 61	0.031 32	0.013 72	0.006 10	0.001 86	0.000 27	45
50	0.140 71	0.110 70	0.087 20	0.054 28	0.033 94	0.021 32	0.008 52	0.003 46	0.000 92	0.000 11	50
60	0.095 06	0.071 29	0.053 54	0.030 31	0.017 26	0.009 88	0.003 28	0.001 11	0.000 23	0.000 02	60

TABLE 3: FUTURE VALUE OF $ 1 PER PERIOD $= \dfrac{(1+R)^n - 1}{R}$

n	0.25%	0.5%	0.66%	0.75%	1.0%	1.5%	2.0%	2.5%	3.0%	3.5%	n
1	1.000 00	1.000 00	1.000 00	1.000 00	1.000 00	1.000 00	1.000 00	1.000 0	1.000 0	1.000 0	1
2	2.002 50	2.005 00	2.006 67	2.007 50	2.010 00	2.015 00	2.020 00	2.025 0	2.030 0	2.035 0	2
3	3.007 51	3.015 03	3.020 04	3.022 56	3.030 10	3.045 23	3.060 40	3.075 6	3.090 9	3.106 2	3
4	4.015 03	4.030 10	4.040 18	4.045 23	4.060 40	4.090 90	4.121 61	4.152 5	4.183 6	4.214 9	4
5	5.025 06	5.050 25	5.067 11	5.075 56	5.101 01	5.152 27	5.204 04	5.256 3	5.309 1	5.362 5	5
6	6.037 63	6.075 50	6.100 89	6.113 63	6.152 02	6.229 55	6.308 12	6.387 7	6.468 4	6.550 2	6
7	7.052 72	7.105 88	7.141 57	7.159 48	7.213 54	7.322 99	7.434 28	7.547 4	7.662 5	7.779 4	7
8	8.070 35	8.141 41	8.189 18	8.213 18	8.285 67	8.432 84	8.582 97	8.736 1	8.892 3	9.051 7	8
9	9.090 53	9.182 12	9.243 77	9.274 78	9.368 53	9.559 33	9.754 63	9.954 5	10.159 1	10.368 5	9
10	10.113 25	10.228 03	10.305 40	10.344 34	10.462 21	10.702 72	10.949 72	11.203 4	11.463 9	11.731 4	10
11	11.138 54	11.279 17	11.374 10	11.421 92	11.566 83	11.863 26	12.168 72	12.483 5	12.807 8	13.142 0	11
12	12.166 38	12.335 56	12.449 93	12.507 59	12.682 50	13.041 21	13.412 09	13.795 6	14.192 0	14.602 0	12
13	13.196 80	13.397 24	13.532 93	13.601 39	13.809 33	14.236 83	14.680 33	15.140 4	15.617 8	16.113 0	13
14	14.229 79	14.464 23	14.623 15	14.703 40	14.947 42	15.450 38	15.973 94	16.519 0	17.086 3	17.677 0	14
15	15.265 37	15.536 55	15.720 63	15.813 68	16.096 90	16.682 14	17.293 42	17.931 9	18.598 9	19.295 7	15
16	16.303 53	16.614 23	16.825 54	16.932 28	17.257 86	17.932 37	18.639 29	19.380 2	20.156 9	20.971 0	16
17	17.344 29	17.697 30	17.937 61	18.059 27	18.430 44	19.201 36	20.012 07	20.864 7	21.761 6	22.705 0	17
18	18.387 65	18.785 79	19.057 19	19.194 72	19.614 75	20.489 38	21.412 31	22.386 3	23.414 4	24.499 7	18
19	19.433 62	19.879 72	20.184 24	20.338 68	20.810 89	21.796 72	22.840 56	23.946 0	25.116 9	26.357 2	19
20	20.482 20	20.979 12	21.318 80	21.491 22	22.019 00	23.123 67	24.297 37	25.544 7	26.870 4	28.279 7	20
21	21.533 41	22.084 01	22.460 93	22.652 40	23.239 19	24.470 52	25.783 32	27.183 3	28.676 5	30.269 5	21
22	22.587 24	23.194 43	23.610 66	23.822 30	24.471 59	25.837 58	27.298 98	28.862 9	30.536 8	32.328 9	22
23	23.643 71	24.310 40	24.768 07	25.000 96	25.716 30	27.225 14	28.844 96	30.584 4	32.452 9	34.460 4	23
24	24.702 82	25.431 96	25.933 19	26.188 47	26.973 46	28.633 52	30.421 86	32.349 0	34.426 5	36.666 5	24
25	25.764 57	26.559 12	27.106 08	27.384 88	28.243 20	30.063 02	32.030 30	34.157 8	36.459 3	38.949 9	25
30	31.113 31	32.280 02	33.088 85	33.502 90	34.784 89	37.538 68	40.568 08	43.902 7	47.575 4	51.622 7	30
35	36.529 24	38.145 38	39.273 73	39.853 81	41.660 28	45.592 09	49.994 48	54.928 2	60.462 1	66.674 0	35
40	42.013 20	44.158 85	45.667 54	46.446 48	48.886 37	54.267 89	60.401 98	67.402 6	75.401 3	84.550 3	40
45	47.566 06	50.324 16	52.277 34	53.290 11	56.481 07	63.614 20	71.892 71	81.516 1	92.719 9	105.781 7	45
50	53.188 68	56.645 16	59.110 42	60.394 26	64.463 18	73.682 83	84.579 40	97.484 3	112.796 9	130.997 9	50
60	64.646 71	69.770 03	73.476 86	76.424 14	81.669 67	96.214 65	114.051 54	135.991 6	163.053 4	196.516 9	60

(continued over page)

TABLE 3 (CONTINUED)

n	4.0%	4.5%	5.0%	6.0%	7.0%	8.0%	10.0%	12.0%	15.0%	20.0%	n
1	1.000 0	1.000 0	1.000 0	1.000 0	1.000 0	1.000 0	1.000 0	1.000	1.000	1.00	1
2	2.040 0	2.045 0	2.050 0	2.060 0	2.070 0	2.080 0	2.100 0	2.120	2.150	2.20	2
3	3.121 6	3.137 0	3.152 5	3.183 6	3.214 9	3.246 4	3.310 0	3.374	3.472	3.64	3
4	4.246 5	4.278 2	4.310 1	4.374 6	4.439 9	4.506 1	4.641 0	4.779	4.993	5.36	4
5	5.416 3	5.470 7	5.525 6	5.627 1	5.750 7	5.866 6	6.105 1	6.353	6.742	7.44	5
6	6.633 0	6.716 9	6.801 9	6.975 3	7.153 3	7.335 9	7.715 6	8.115	8.754	9.93	6
7	7.898 3	8.019 2	8.142 0	8.393 8	8.654 0	8.922 8	9.487 2	10.089	11.067	12.92	7
8	9.214 2	9.380 0	9.549 1	9.897 5	10.259 8	10.636 6	11.435 9	12.300	13.727	16.50	8
9	10.582 8	10.802 1	11.026 6	11.491 3	11.978 0	12.487 6	13.579 5	14.776	16.786	20.80	9
10	12.006 1	12.288 2	12.577 9	13.180 8	13.816 4	14.486 6	15.937 4	17.549	20.304	25.96	10
11	13.486 4	13.841 2	14.206 8	14.971 6	15.783 6	16.645 5	18.531 2	20.655	24.349	32.15	11
12	15.025 8	15.464 0	15.917 1	16.869 9	17.888 5	18.977 1	21.384 3	24.133	29.002	39.58	12
13	16.626 8	17.159 9	17.713 0	18.882 1	20.140 6	21.495 3	24.522 7	28.029	34.352	48.50	13
14	18.291 9	18.932 1	19.598 6	21.015 1	22.550 5	24.214 9	27.975 0	32.393	40.505	59.20	14
15	20.023 6	20.784 1	21.578 6	23.276 0	25.129 0	27.152 1	31.772 5	37.280	47.580	72.04	15
16	21.824 5	22.719 3	23.657 5	25.672 5	27.888 1	30.324 3	35.949 7	42.753	55.717	87.44	16
17	23.697 5	24.741 7	25.840 4	28.212 9	30.840 2	33.750 2	40.544 7	48.884	65.075	105.93	17
18	25.645 4	26.855 1	28.132 4	30.905 7	33.999 0	37.450 2	45.599 2	55.750	75.836	128.12	18
19	27.671 2	29.063 6	30.539 0	33.760 0	37.379 0	41.446 3	51.159 1	63.440	88.212	154.74	19
20	29.778 1	31.371 4	33.066 0	36.785 6	40.995 5	45.762 0	57.275 0	72.052	102.443	186.69	20
21	31.969 2	33.783 1	35.719 3	39.992 7	44.865 2	50.422 9	64.002 5	81.699	118.810	225.03	21
22	34.248 0	36.303 4	38.505 2	43.392 3	49.005 7	55.456 8	71.402 8	92.502	137.631	271.03	22
23	36.617 9	38.937 0	41.430 5	46.995 8	53.436 1	60.893 3	79.543 0	104.603	159.276	326.24	23
24	39.082 6	41.689 2	44.502 0	50.815 6	58.176 7	66.764 8	88.497 3	118.155	184.167	392.48	24
25	41.645 9	44.565 2	47.727 1	54.864 5	63.249 0	73.105 9	98.347 1	133.334	212.793	471.98	25
30	56.084 9	61.570 6	66.438 8	79.058 2	94.460 8	113.283 2	164.494 0	241.532	434.744	1 181.88	30
35	73.652 2	81.496 6	90.320 3	111.434 8	138.236 9	172.316 8	271.024 4	431.663	881.168	2 948.34	35
40	95.025 5	107.030 3	120.799 8	154.762 0	199.635 1	259.056 5	442.592 6	767.088	1 779.090	7 343.95	40
45	121.029 4	138.850 0	159.700 2	212.743 5	285.749 3	386.505 6	718.904 8	1 358.224	3 585.128	18 281.31	45
50	152.667 1	178.503 0	209.348 0	290.335 9	406.528 9	573.770 2	1 163.908 5	2 400.008	7 217.716	45 497.19	50
60	237.990 7	289.498 0	353.583 7	533.128 1	813.520 4	1 253.213 3	3 034.816 4	7 471.641	29 219.992	281 732.57	60

$$\text{TABLE 4: PRESENT VALUE OF \$1 PER PERIOD} = 1 - \frac{1}{(1+R)^n}\Big/R$$

n	0.25%	0.5%	0.66%	0.75%	1.0%	1.5%	2.0%	2.5%	3.0%	3.5%	n
1	0.997 51	0.995 02	0.993 38	0.992 56	0.990 10	0.985 22	0.980 39	0.975 6	0.970 9	0.966 2	1
2	1.992 52	1.985 10	1.980 18	1.977 72	1.970 40	1.955 88	1.941 56	1.927 4	1.913 5	1.899 7	2
3	2.985 06	2.970 25	2.960 44	2.955 56	2.940 99	2.912 20	2.883 88	2.856 0	2.828 6	2.801 6	3
4	3.975 12	3.950 50	3.934 21	3.926 11	3.901 97	3.854 38	3.807 73	3.762 0	3.717 1	3.673 1	4
5	4.962 72	4.925 87	4.901 54	4.889 44	4.853 43	4.782 65	4.713 46	4.645 8	4.579 7	4.515 1	5
6	5.947 85	5.896 38	5.862 45	5.845 60	5.795 48	5.697 19	5.601 43	5.508 1	5.417 2	5.328 6	6
7	6.930 52	6.862 07	6.817 01	6.794 64	6.728 19	6.598 21	6.471 99	6.349 4	6.230 3	6.114 5	7
8	7.910 74	7.822 96	7.765 24	7.736 61	7.651 68	7.485 93	7.325 48	7.170 1	7.019 7	6.874 0	8
9	8.888 52	8.779 06	8.707 19	8.671 58	8.566 02	8.360 52	8.162 24	7.970 9	7.786 1	7.607 7	9
10	9.863 86	9.730 41	9.642 90	9.599 58	9.471 30	9.222 19	8.982 54	8.752 1	8.530 2	8.316 6	10
11	10.836 77	10.677 03	10.572 42	10.520 67	10.367 63	10.071 12	9.786 85	9.514 2	9.252 6	9.001 6	11
12	11.807 25	11.618 93	11.495 78	11.434 91	11.255 08	10.907 51	10.575 34	10.257 8	9.954 0	9.663 3	12
13	12.775 32	12.556 15	12.413 03	12.342 35	12.133 74	11.731 53	11.348 37	10.983 2	10.635 0	10.302 7	13
14	13.740 96	13.488 71	13.324 20	13.243 02	13.003 70	12.543 38	12.106 25	11.690 9	11.296 1	10.920 5	14
15	14.704 20	14.416 62	14.229 34	14.136 99	13.865 05	13.343 23	12.849 26	12.381 4	11.937 9	11.517 4	15
16	15.665 04	15.339 93	15.128 48	15.024 31	14.717 87	14.131 26	13.577 71	13.055 0	12.561 1	12.094 1	16
17	16.623 48	16.258 63	16.021 67	15.905 02	15.562 25	14.907 65	14.291 87	13.712 2	13.166 1	12.651 3	17
18	17.579 53	17.172 77	16.908 94	16.779 18	16.398 27	15.672 56	14.992 03	14.353 4	13.753 5	13.189 7	18
19	18.533 20	18.082 36	17.790 34	17.646 83	17.226 01	16.426 17	15.678 46	14.978 9	14.323 8	13.709 8	19
20	19.484 49	18.987 42	18.665 90	18.508 02	18.045 55	17.168 64	16.351 43	15.589 2	14.877 5	14.212 4	20
21	20.433 40	19.887 98	19.535 66	19.362 80	18.856 98	17.900 14	17.011 21	16.184 5	15.415 0	14.698 0	21
22	21.379 95	20.784 06	20.399 67	20.211 21	19.660 38	18.620 83	17.658 05	16.765 4	15.936 9	15.167 1	22
23	22.324 14	21.675 68	21.257 95	21.053 31	20.455 82	19.330 86	18.292 20	17.332 1	16.443 6	15.620 4	23
24	23.265 98	22.562 87	22.110 54	21.889 15	21.243 39	20.030 41	18.913 93	17.885 0	16.935 5	16.058 4	24
25	24.205 47	23.445 64	22.957 49	22.718 76	22.023 16	20.719 61	19.523 46	18.424 4	17.413 1	16.481 5	25
30	28.867 87	27.794 05	27.108 85	26.775 08	25.807 71	24.015 84	22.396 46	20.930 3	19.600 4	18.392 0	30
35	33.472 43	32.035 37	31.124 55	30.682 66	29.408 58	27.075 60	24.998 62	23.145 2	21.487 2	20.000 7	35
40	38.019 86	36.172 23	35.009 03	34.446 94	32.834 69	29.915 85	27.355 48	25.102 8	23.114 8	21.355 1	40
45	42.510 88	40.207 20	38.766 58	38.073 18	36.094 51	32.552 34	29.490 16	26.833 7	24.518 7	22.495 5	45
50	46.946 17	44.142 79	42.401 34	41.566 45	39.196 12	34.999 69	31.423 61	28.362 3	25.729 8	23.455 6	50
60	55.652 36	51.725 56	49.318 43	48.173 37	44.955 04	39.380 27	34.760 89	30.908 7	27.675 6	24.944 7	60

(continued over page)

TABLE 4 (CONTINUED)

n	4.0%	4.5%	5.0%	6.0%	7.0%	8.0%	10.0%	12.0%	15.0%	20.0%	n
1	0.9615	0.9569	0.9524	0.9433	0.9345	0.9259	0.9091	0.8929	0.8695	0.8333	1
2	1.8861	1.8727	1.8594	1.8333	1.8080	1.7832	1.7355	1.6901	1.6257	1.5278	2
3	2.7751	2.7490	2.7232	2.6730	2.6243	2.5770	2.4868	2.4018	2.2832	2.1065	3
4	3.6299	3.5875	3.5460	3.4651	3.3872	3.3121	3.1698	3.0373	2.8549	2.5887	4
5	4.4518	4.3900	4.3295	4.2123	4.1001	3.9927	3.7907	3.6048	3.3521	2.9906	5
6	5.2421	5.1579	5.0757	4.9173	4.7665	4.6228	4.3552	4.1114	3.7844	3.3255	6
7	6.0021	5.8927	5.7864	5.5823	5.3892	5.2063	4.8684	4.5638	4.1604	3.6046	7
8	6.7327	6.5959	6.4632	6.2097	5.9712	5.7466	5.3349	4.9676	4.4873	3.8372	8
9	7.4353	7.2688	7.1078	6.8016	6.5152	6.2468	5.7590	5.3282	4.7715	4.0310	9
10	8.1109	7.9127	7.7217	7.3600	7.0235	6.7100	6.1445	5.6502	5.0187	4.1925	10
11	8.7605	8.5289	8.3064	7.8868	7.4986	7.1389	6.4950	5.9377	5.2337	4.3271	11
12	9.3851	9.1186	8.8633	8.3838	7.9426	7.5360	6.8136	6.1944	5.4206	4.4392	12
13	9.9856	9.6829	9.3936	8.8526	8.3576	7.9037	7.1033	6.4235	5.5831	4.5327	13
14	10.5631	10.2228	9.8986	9.2949	8.7454	8.2442	7.3666	6.6282	5.7244	4.6106	14
15	11.1184	10.7395	10.3797	9.7122	9.1079	8.5594	7.6060	6.8109	5.8473	4.6755	15
16	11.6523	11.2340	10.8378	10.1058	9.4466	8.8513	7.8237	6.9740	5.9542	4.7296	16
17	12.1657	11.7072	11.2741	10.4772	9.7632	9.1216	8.0215	7.1196	6.0471	4.7746	17
18	12.6593	12.1600	11.6896	10.8276	10.0590	9.3718	8.2014	7.2497	6.1279	4.8122	18
19	13.1339	12.5933	12.0853	11.1581	10.3355	9.6035	8.3649	7.3658	6.1982	4.8435	19
20	13.5903	13.0079	12.4622	11.4699	10.5940	9.8181	8.5135	7.4694	6.2593	4.8696	20
21	14.0292	13.4047	12.8212	11.7640	10.8355	10.0168	8.6486	7.5620	6.3124	4.8913	21
22	14.4511	13.7844	13.1630	12.0415	11.0612	10.2007	8.7715	7.6446	6.3586	4.9094	22
23	14.8568	14.1478	13.4886	12.3033	11.2721	10.3710	8.8832	7.7184	6.3988	4.9245	23
24	15.2470	14.4955	13.7986	12.5503	11.4693	10.5287	8.9847	7.7843	6.4337	4.9371	24
25	15.6221	14.8282	14.0939	12.7833	11.6535	10.6747	9.0770	7.8431	6.4641	4.9476	25
30	17.2920	16.2889	15.3725	13.7648	12.4090	11.2577	9.4269	8.0552	6.5659	4.9789	30
35	18.6646	17.4610	16.3742	14.4982	12.9476	11.6545	9.6441	8.1755	6.6166	4.9915	35
40	19.7928	18.4016	17.1591	15.0462	13.3317	11.9246	9.7790	8.2438	6.6417	4.9966	40
45	20.7200	19.1563	17.7741	15.4558	13.6055	12.1084	9.8628	8.2825	6.6542	4.9986	45
50	21.4822	19.7620	18.2559	15.7618	13.8007	12.2334	9.9148	8.3045	6.6605	4.9995	50
60	22.6235	20.6380	18.9293	16.1614	14.0392	12.3766	9.9672	8.3240	6.6651	4.9999	60

Glossary

AAS (AUSTRALIAN ACCOUNTING STANDARDS) (Chapter 2) The standards issued by the Australian Accounting Research Foundation on behalf of CPA Australia and the Institute of Chartered Accountants in Australia for guidance in professional accountancy practice in Australia.

ABSENTEE OWNERS (Chapter 14) The shareholders in large businesses.

ABSORPTION COSTING (full costing) (Chapter 18) The method whereby the cost of inventories is determined so as to include the appropriate share of both variable and fixed costs, the latter being allocated on the basis of normal operating capacity (*AASB 1019*).

ABSORPTION OF OVERHEADS (Chapter 18) The term used for the process of sharing out indirect costs to products.

ABSORPTION RATE (Chapter 18) An absorption rate is normally used to charge out overheads to units of production on an equitable basis. It is determined by dividing the total overheads of a production cost centre by the level of activity.

ACCOUNT (Chapter 2) A device used to provide a record of increases and decreases in each item that appears in a firm's financial statements.

ACCOUNTING (Chapter 1) The process of identifying, measuring and communicating economic information to permit informed judgement and decisions by users of the information.

ACCOUNTING PROFIT (Chapter 11) The amount of profit as determined by application of Australian Accounting Standards and Concepts.

ACCOUNTING RATE OF RETURN (Chapter 16) A method of project evaluation which involves dividing average net income by either average book value of investment or total initial investment.

ACCOUNTING SYSTEM (Chapter 1) A collection of source documents, records, procedures, management policies and data-processing methods used to convert economic data into useful information.

ACCOUNTING THEORY MONOGRAPH (Chapter 2) A series prepared by various authors which explores conceptual matters of relevance to the development of Accounting Standards.

ACCRUAL BASIS (of accounting) (Chapter 2) The method of accounting whereby revenues and expenses are identified with a specific period of time, such as a month or year, and are recorded as incurred, along with acquired assets, without regard to the date of receipt or payment of cash.

ACCRUALS (Chapter 8) Accruals are amounts owing at a point in time, the amounts of which are not known with any certainty.

AGED DEBTORS ANALYSIS (Chapter 8) An analysis prepared by management which examines debts in terms of how old they are in order to reach a decision on the probability of receipt of payment.

ALLOCATED (Chapter 18) In the context of product costing, a cost that can be directly traced to a cost centre.

AMORTISE (Chapters 9, 18) To systematically write off a portion or all of an asset over a period of years. This normally applies to intangible assets.

ANNUITY (Chapter 16) Stream of equal cash flows received or paid over a number of periods.

APPORTIONING (Chapter 18) The term 'apportioning', in the context of product costing, describes the sharing out of overhead costs that cannot be directly traced to a cost centre.

ASSETS (Chapters 2, 4, 9) Future economic benefits controlled by the entity as a result of past transactions or other past events (*SAC 4, 14*).

AUDIT (Chapter 13) The examination of a company's general-purpose financial reports by an independent external observer (the auditor) to ensure that they present a 'true and fair' representation of the company's financial status. The auditor's findings are presented in the auditor's report.

AUDITOR'S REPORT (Chapter 13) A report required by the Corporations Law, prepared by an auditor and included with a company's financial statements, stating whether the company's financial statements comply with the requirements of the Corporations Law, whether they provide a true and fair view of the state of affairs of the company, and whether they are in accordance with applicable Accounting Standards.

AUSTRALIAN ACCOUNTING RESEARCH FOUNDATION (AARF) (Chapters 1, 13) A body, jointly established and sponsored by CPA Australia and the Institute of Chartered Accountants in Australia.

AVERAGE COST (Chapter 7) A method of inventory valuation where an average cost is calculated by dividing the total costs of goods available for sale by the number of units available for sale. Two variations of the average cost method are moving average and weighted average.

AVOIDABLE COST (Chapter 19) An avoidable cost is a cost that will not have to be paid if a company does not proceed with a decision, e.g. delivery of a special order. Such a cost is relevant and should be included in the decision.

BAD DEBTS (Chapter 8) Credit sales of a business for which the revenue is not collected due to the debtor(s) not paying. Two ways in which this non-payment can be accounted for are by direct write-off and the provision for doubtful debts.

BANK OVERDRAFT (Chapters 4, 10) A common source of short-term funds whereby a business negotiates with a bank to establish a limit to which the business can write cheques that will be accepted even though there is no money in the account. Normally an overdraft can be terminated by the bank at short notice.

BREAKEVEN CHART (Chapter 17) A method used in CVP analysis which illustrates the relationship between cost, volume and profits by plotting these variables on a graph. The breakeven point and areas of profit and loss can clearly and quickly be identified, enabling management to establish the effects of changing one of the variables.

BREAKEVEN POSITION (Chapter 17) The sales volume at which revenues and total costs are equal, with no net profit or loss.

BUDGET (Chapters 16, 21) A short- and long-term plan of action for the future operating activities of a business, expressed in monetary terms.

BUDGET PERIOD (Chapter 21) The timeframe of the budget, normally one year. The reason for choosing this period relates to the periodic reporting requirements for published accounts regulated by law.

BUDGET PROCESS (Chapter 21) The sequence of operations necessary to produce a budget for a particular organisation. The operations depend upon the type of organisation and its perceived requirements for planning and control.

BUDGETARY CONTROL (Chapter 21) This describes the use of budgets as a control mechanism, e.g. actual performance can be compared with the budget to identify any deviations so that management can take corrective action.

BUSINESS ENTITY PRINCIPLE (Chapter 4) This states that transactions, assets and liabilities that relate to the enterprise are accounted for separately. It applies to all types of enterprises, irrespective of the fact that the enterprise may not be recognised as a separate legal or taxable entity.

BUSINESS RISK (Chapter 14) The risk resulting from factors in the uncertain commercial environment affecting the operations of a business. Also referred to as commercial risk, it is a function of many variables and differs from industry to industry.

CAPITAL BUDGETING (Chapter 16) Analysis of proposed investments in assets with a long life.

CASH (Chapter 12) Cash on hand and cash equivalents.

CASH EQUIVALENTS (Chapter 12) Highly liquid investments which are readily convertible to cash on hand at the investor's option and which a company or an economic entity uses in its cash management function on a day-to-day basis; and borrowings which are integral to the cash management function and which are not subject to a term facility.

CASH FLOWS (Chapter 12) Cash movements resulting from transactions with parties external to the company (or economic entity).

CASH FLOW STATEMENT (Chapter 12) A financial statement showing the cash inflows and cash outflows for an accounting period.

CASH ON HAND (Chapter 12) Notes and coins held, and deposits held at call with a bank or financial institution.

COMMON-SIZE STATEMENTS (Chapter 14) A financial statement in which the amount reported of each item in the statement is stated as a percentage of some specific amount also reported in the statement.

COMPANY (Chapter 11) An entity incorporated, or taken to be incorporated, under the Corporations Law (Corporations Law, section 9). It is recognised as a separate legal entity.

COMPOUND INTEREST (Chapter 16) Interest based on principal plus interest previously earned.

CONCEPTUAL FRAMEWORK (Chapters 1, 2) The Conceptual Framework is a set of interrelated concepts which define the nature, subject, purpose and broad content of general-purpose financial reports.

CONSERVATISM (Chapter 2) The concept of conservatism is described in *SAC 3*, paragraph 26, as 'a deliberate bias toward understatement of revenues or assets and/or maximum recognition of expenses or liabilities'.

CONSOLIDATED FINANCIAL STATEMENTS (Chapter 12) The name given to the financial reports prepared on behalf of an economic entity which enable users to examine the performance and financial position of both the parent entity on its own and the combination of the parent entity and the other entities it controls.

CONSTANT CHAIN OF REPLACEMENT (Chapter 16) Where it is assumed that funds are reinvested in assets identical to the one being used.

CONTRA ACCOUNT (Chapters 7, 9) An account that is deducted from a related account.

CONTRIBUTION MARGIN METHOD (Chapter 17) A method widely used in CVP analysis to aid managers in making decisions. The contribution margin is equal to the sales price per unit, less the variable cost per unit. The contribution margin is also described as the contribution per unit.

CONTROL (Chapter 12) The capacity of an entity to dominate decision making, directly or indirectly, in relation to the financial and operating policies of another entity so as to enable that other entity to operate with it in pursuing the objectives of the controlling entity (*AASB 1024*).

CORRELATION (Chapter 17) Correlation in a general sense denotes the interdependence between quantitative and qualitative data. In a narrower sense, correlation describes the relationship between two or more measurable variables.

COST ESTIMATION (Chapter 17) Cost estimation relates to methods that are used to measure past (historical) costs at varying activity levels. These costs will then be employed as the basis to predict future costs that will be used in decision making.

COST FUNCTION (Chapter 17) A graphical representation of the relationship between a dependent cost variable (y) and an independent cost variable (x), where the vertical axis is the dependent cost variable and the horizontal axis is the independent cost variable. Points are plotted on the graph to produce a cost function. The function may be linear or non-linear.

COST OF A NON-CURRENT ASSET (Chapter 9) The cost of a non-current asset includes: (a) all reasonable and necessary costs incurred to place the asset in a position and condition ready for use; (b) all costs incurred which enhance the future economic benefits of the asset beyond those initially expected at acquisition.

COST OF CAPITAL (Chapter 16) Minimum rate of return required of a project before it is accepted.

COST VOLUME PROFIT (CVP) ANALYSIS (Chapter 17) A technique used by organisations to help them make decisions by examining the interrelationships between cost, volume and profits.

CREDITOR (Chapters 1, 8) A person or entity to whom a debt is owed.

CURVILINEAR REGRESSION (Chapter 17) A regression which is not linear.

DEBENTURES (Chapter 10) The term given to secured transferable loan stock that can be listed on the stock exchange. Debentures can be secured over specific assets, or by way of a floating charge over all assets.

DEBTORS (Chapter 8) Debtors arise when a business sells goods or services to a third party on credit terms.

DEPENDENT VARIABLE (Chapter 17) In a cost function, the dependent variable is expressed as variable y and is the cost to be predicted—the total cost for an activity.

DEPRECIABLE AMOUNT (Chapter 9) The historical cost of a depreciable asset, or other revalued amount substituted for historical cost, in the financial report, less in either case the net amount expected to be recovered on disposal of the asset at the end of its useful life (*AASB 1021*).

DEPRECIABLE ASSET (Chapter 9) A non-current asset having a limited useful life (*AASB 1021*).

DEPRECIATION EXPENSE (Chapters 2, 3, 5, 9) An expense recognised systematically for the purpose of allocating the depreciable amount of a depreciable asset over its useful life (*AASB 1021*).

DIFFERENTIAL COSTS (incremental costs) (Chapter 19) The differences in costs and benefits between alternative opportunities available to an organisation. It follows that when a number of opportunities are being considered, costs and benefits that are common to these alternative opportunities are irrelevant to the decision.

DIRECT COSTS (Chapter 18) A direct cost is one that is traceable, and thus attributable, to a product.

DIRECT WRITE-OFF (Chapter 8) A method of accounting for bad debts where the amount owing by the debtor is eliminated when it is determined the debtor will not pay. The debtor's balance is reduced and the other side of the transaction is the recognition of an expense.

DIRECTORS' REPORT (Chapter 13) A report required by the Corporations Law, prepared by a company's directors and included with the company's financial statements, providing information including the directors' names, activities of the company, profit or loss for the year, amount of dividends, review of operation and many other matters in relation to the company.

DIRECTORS' STATEMENT (Chapter 13) A statement required by the Corporations Law, signed by at least two directors and included with a company's financial statements, outlining whether, in their opinion, the statement of financial performance and the statement of financial position present a true and fair view, whether the company will be able to pay its debts as they fall due, and whether the financial statements comply with applicable Accounting Standards.

DISCOUNTING (Chapters 3, 16) Present value of a sum to be received in x period given y interest rate.

DIVIDEND COVER (Chapter 14) Number of times the net profit after tax covers the ordinary dividend payment.

DOUBLE-ENTRY BOOKKEEPING (Chapter 6) The system developed for recording accounting information based on the concept that every transaction affects two or more components of the statement of financial position (accounting) equation.

DUE PROCESS (Chapter 13) The name of the process which has been designed to allow all interested parties maximum opportunity to comment on proposed Accounting Standards.

ECONOMIC CONSEQUENCES (Chapter 1) The impact of accounting policy changes on the economic position of various parties affected by the change.

ECONOMIC VALUE (Chapter 3) The value of the expected earnings from using an item, discounted at an appropriate rate to give a present-day value.

EFFICIENT MARKETS HYPOTHESIS (Chapter 14) A market is efficient if it reacts immediately and without bias to reflect new information in asset prices.

ENTITY (Chapters 1, 12) A fictional or notional being, such as a business, club, company, partnership, etc., in respect of which financial transactions occur and accounts are kept.

EQUITY (Chapters 2, 4) The residual interest in the assets of an entity after deduction of its liabilities (*SAC 4*, 67).

EQUITY INVESTORS (Chapter 4) The ordinary shareholder in a company, or the owner or partner in a sole proprietorship or partnership.

ETHICAL (Chapter 1) To behave in an honest and morally correct manner.

EXPECTATION GAP (Chapter 13) The difference between what an auditor is required to do and what is expected by users.

EXPENSES (Chapters 2, 5) Consumptions or losses of future economic benefits in the form of reductions in assets or increases in liabilities of the entity, other than those relating to distributions to owners, that result in a decrease in equity during the reporting period (*SAC 4*, 117).

EXPOSURE DRAFT (ED) (Chapter 2) A document circulated by the AASB to interested groups for comment and amendment before a standard is produced.

EXTRAORDINARY ITEMS (Chapter 11) Items of revenue and expense which are attributable to events or transactions of a type that are outside the ordinary operations of the reporting entity and are not of a recurring nature (*AASB 1018*).

FACTORING (Chapter 10) Where amounts owing by debtors are sold to a collection agency.

FEASIBLE REGION (Chapter 15) Where the boundaries of the activity spaces of each group involved with an organisation overlap, i.e. the acceptable activity is common to more than one group.

FINAL DIVIDENDS (Chapter 11) Dividends proposed by the directors at the annual general meeting. The shareholders can approve the dividend or lower it, but they cannot raise it.

FINANCE LEASE (Chapter 10) A lease which effectively transfers from the lessor to the lessee substantially all the risks and benefits incident to ownership of the leased property (*AASB 1008*).

FINANCIAL ACCOUNTING (Chapter 1) That part of an accounting system that tries to meet the needs of various external user groups.

FINANCIAL RISK (Chapters 5, 10, 14) The risk that a business might not be able to repay borrowed funds or interest as they fall due.

FINANCIAL STATEMENTS (Chapter 1) The means of conveying to management and to interested outside parties a concise picture of the profitability and financial position of the business. The most widely used financial statements are the statement of financial position, statement of financial performance and the statement of cash flows.

FINISHED GOODS (Chapter 7) Goods that have been through the complete production or assembly cycle and are ready for resale to the customer.

FIRST IN, FIRST OUT (FIFO) (Chapter 7) A method of inventory valuation based on the artificial assumption that the first goods bought are first sold. The inventory held at the end of the period is assumed to be that purchased most recently.

FIXED ASSETS (Chapter 4) A term previously in use to describe those assets of an entity which were acquired with the view to be held by the entity, for the purpose of generating income over a number of years. Today, fixed assets are commonly referred to as non-current assets.

FIXED CHARGE (Chapter 14) In relation to a creditor, means the creditor has a charge against specific assets and normally holds a mortgage or other security over the asset.

FIXED COSTS (Chapter 17) A cost is fixed if it does not change in response to changes in the level of activity within the relevant range of activity.

FLOATING CHARGE (Chapter 14) In relation to a creditor, the security over the assets does not relate to a specific asset but to all assets in general.

FRANKED DIVIDENDS (Chapter 11) Dividends paid by a company which have been subject to company taxation.

FULL COSTING (absorption costing) (Chapter 18) The full cost of a product consists of the direct and indirect costs of production.

GENERAL-PURPOSE FINANCIAL REPORT (Chapter 13) A financial report intended to meet the information needs common to users who are unable to command the preparation of reports so as to satisfy, specifically, all of their needs (*SAC 2*, 5).

GOAL CONGRUENCE (Chapter 15) The alignment of organisational goals with the personal and group goals of the individuals within an organisation.

GOING CONCERN (Chapter 1) The assumption that a business will continue to operate in the future without any intention to liquidate or to significantly reduce its scale of operations.

GOODWILL (Chapter 2) Goodwill is the future benefits from unidentifiable assets (*AASB 1013*).

GROUP (Chapter 12) The term applied to a parent company and its subsidiaries for which consolidated financial statements are prepared. The group is an economic entity and not a legal entity.

HIRE PURCHASE (Chapter 10) A financial institution buys an asset and hires it to the prospective buyer. Ownership remains with the financial institution until the hirer makes the final payment.

HISTORIC COST (Chapter 3) The cost incurred by an individual or enterprise in acquiring an item, measured at the time of the originating transaction.

INCOME (Chapters 3, 9) The total payments received, usually in a year, from salary or wages, investments, rents, business operations, etc. That amount which an individual can consume and still be as well off at the end of the period as he or she was at the start of the period.

INCOME TAX EXPENSE (Chapter 12) The amount of income tax which would be payable on the pre-tax accounting profit adjusted for permanent differences. The term 'income tax benefit' is used to describe this amount where it is a net credit (*AASB 1020*, para. 15.1).

INDEPENDENT PROJECTS (Chapter 16) The acceptance or rejection of one project has no effect on other projects.

INDEPENDENT VARIABLE (Chapter 17) In a cost function, the independent variable is expressed as variable x and is the level of activity.

INDIRECT COSTS (overhead costs) (Chapter 18) Costs that cannot be easily and conveniently identified with a particular product.

INTANGIBLE ASSETS (Chapter 9) Non-current assets which lack physical substance and are not used for investment purposes.

INTEREST (Chapters 1, 16) A charge made for the use of money.

INTEREST COVER (Chapter 14) The number of times net profit before interest and tax covers the interest payment.

INTERIM DIVIDENDS (Chapter 11) Dividends declared and paid part way through the accounting period in anticipation of a final profit.

INTERNAL RATE OF RETURN (Chapter 16) The rate of return which discounts the cash flows of a project so that the present value of cash inflows equals the present value of cash outflows.

INVENTORIES (Chapter 7) Goods, other property and services: (a) held for sale in the ordinary course of business; (b) in the process of production for such sale; or (c) to be used up in the production of goods, other property or services for sale, including consumable stores and supplies (*AASB 1019*).

IRREVOCABLE CONTRACT (Chapter 2) A legal or formal agreement made between two or more people that cannot be changed without incurring significant penalties.

JUST-IN-TIME MANAGEMENT (Chapter 7) A management technique designed to lower the costs of holding high levels of stock.

LAST IN, FIRST OUT (LIFO) (Chapter 7) A method of inventory valuation based on the assumption that the last goods bought are the first sold. Ending inventory is assumed to consist of the cost of the earliest units purchased.

LEASE (Chapter 10) A contractual agreement between two parties whereby one party (the lessee) obtains the rights to use an item, such as a machine, in exchange for a series of lease payments to the other party (the lessor).

LENDERS (Chapter 14) Persons or organisations which permit the temporary use of money, etc., in return for payment.

LESSEE (Chapter 10) The person or company obtaining the rights to use leased property.

LESSOR (Chapter 10) The owner of the property which is leased out.

LIABILITIES (Chapters 2, 4) Future sacrifices of economic benefits that an entity is presently obliged to make to other entities as a result of past transactions or other past events (*SAC 4*, 48).

LINEAR COST FUNCTION (Chapter 17) A linear cost function is a straight-line cost function which can be mathematically expressed as $y = a + bx$ where y is the total cost to be predicted; a is a constant (or 'fixed cost'); b is the cost that will be the same for each unit of activity and thus as the activity varies so will the cost (this cost is known as 'variable cost'); x is the level of activity measured in units of output.

LIQUIDITY (Chapters 1, 14) The ability of a business to satisfy its short-term obligations. Liquidity refers to the ease with which assets can be converted to cash in the normal course of business.

LONG TERM FINANCE (Chapter 10) For periods greater than three to five years.

MAKE OR BUY DECISION (Chapter 20) The decision made by an organisation which must choose between making a product or carrying out a service using its own resources, and paying another external organisation to make the product or carry out the service for it.

MANAGEMENT ACCOUNTING (Chapters 1, 15) That part of an accounting system that tries to meet the needs of management and internal users.

MARGINAL COSTING (Chapters 7, 18) A method of valuing inventory based on establishing how much it would cost a firm to produce one extra unit of its product. The marginal cost of a product consists of only the direct costs of production.

MARGINAL PRODUCT (Chapter 20) The change in output (production) associated with a unit change in one of an organisation's scarce resources, e.g. labour.

MARGINAL RETURN (Chapter 20) The contribution or economic value of a marginal unit of a particular scarce resource used by an organisation in the production of a specific product.

MASTER BUDGET (Chapter 21) The budgeted statement of financial performance and statement of financial position, representing a summary of the individual functional budgets of the organisation as a whole.

MATERIALITY (Chapter 9) Broadly, an item can be said to be material if its non-disclosure would cause the accounts to be misleading in some way.

MATERIALITY TEST (Chapter 2) Assesses whether omission, misstatement or non-disclosure of an item of relevant and reliable information could affect decision making about the allocation of scarce resources by the users of the general-purpose financial reports of an entity (SAC 3, 28).

MEDIUM-TERM FINANCE (Chapter 10) Generally for periods of one to three or five years.

MORTGAGE LOAN (Chapter 10) A loan which is secured by real property such as land and buildings.

MULTIPLE REGRESSION (Chapter 17) The regression of a dependent variable on more than one independent or predicted variable.

MUTUALLY EXCLUSIVE PROJECTS (Chapter 16) Where the acceptance of one project results in the rejection of the other project.

NET PRESENT VALUE (Chapter 16) The figure that results from discounting all cash flows of a project at a minimum rate of return and summing the resultant present values.

NET REALISABLE VALUE (Chapters 3, 7) The estimated proceeds of sales, less, where applicable, all further costs to the stage of completion, and less all costs to be incurred in marketing, selling and distribution to customers (AASB 1019).

NON-CANCELLABLE LEASE (Chapter 10) A contract which cannot be cancelled allowing a person or entity to use or occupy property in return for rent.

NON-CURRENT ASSETS (Chapters 4, 9) All assets other than current assets (AASB 1040, para. 9.1).

NON-CURRENT LIABILITIES (Chapter 4) Liabilities which are not current liabilities (AASB 1040, para. 9.1).

NON-REDEEMABLE PREFERENCE SHARE (Chapters 10, 14) Preference shares which cannot be redeemed out of the company's profits or out of the proceeds of a new share issue.

OBJECTIVE OF FINANCIAL REPORTING (Chapter 2) The objective of general-purpose financial reporting is to 'provide information useful to users for making and evaluating decisions about the allocation of scarce resources' (SAC 2, 43).

OPERATING CYCLE (Chapter 4) The average period between the purchase of merchandise and the conversion of this merchandise back into cash.

OPERATING DECISIONS (Chapter 15) Decisions that focus on the efficient use of the resources available to a firm in the short term.

OPERATING LEASE (Chapter 10) A short-term lease under which most of the risks and rewards associated with ownership of the property remain with the lessor.

OPPORTUNITY COST (Chapters 19, 20) The opportunity cost of a resource is normally defined as the maximum benefit which could be obtained from that resource if it were used for some alternative purpose. If a firm uses a resource for alternative A rather than B, it is the potential benefits that are forgone by not using the resource for alternative B that constitute the opportunity cost. The potential benefits forgone, the opportunity cost, are a relevant cost in the decision to accept alternative A. The opportunity cost reflects the cost of the most valuable alternative given up.

ORDINARY SHAREHOLDER (Chapters 10, 14) A person holding a class of shares that have no preferences relative to other classes.

ORIGINAL COST (Chapter 3) The cost of an item at the time of the transaction between the buyer and the seller.

OVER-RECOVERY OF OVERHEAD (Chapter 18) A statement of financial performance which credits the difference between actual overhead cost and the estimate on which the absorption rate is based. The difference is classified as a period revenue because it is not identified with any of the units of production produced during the year.

PARENT ENTITY (Chapter 12) One which controls another entity.

PARTNERSHIP (Chapters 1, 11) The relationship which exists between persons carrying on a business in common with a view to profit (*Partnership Act 1892*, Section 1(1)).

PAYBACK (Chapter 16) The time required to recover the initial investment.

PERIOD COSTS (Chapter 18) Costs which relate to the period in question. They are recognised in the statement of financial performance in the accounting period when they are incurred and cannot justifiably be carried forward to future periods because they do not represent future benefits, or the future benefits are so uncertain as to defy measurement.

PERIODIC METHOD (Chapter 7) A method of accounting for inventory where an accurate record of purchases is kept and an annual inventory count is conducted to establish the cost of goods sold during a period. This annual inventory count is carried out at the statement of financial position date; thus the inventory figure in the statement of financial position represents a snapshot of the inventory level at that particular point in time.

PERMANENT DIFFERENCES (Chapter 12) The items which arise as a result of the different rules for income tax and accounting, causing permanent differences between taxable income and accounting profit.

PERPETUAL METHOD (Chapter 7) A method of accounting for inventory that operates at the point of every sale: the inventory records of a business are updated every time a sale occurs. The perpetual method is applied by entities with sophisticated computer systems and by certain types of businesses in which it is easy to keep track of inventories.

PLANNING AND CONTROL (Chapter 15) Planning involves the determination of objectives and of means by which to obtain them. The control process is the means of ensuring that the plans are achieved.

PREFERENCE SHAREHOLDER (Chapters 10, 14) One who holds a class of shares which receive preferential treatment over ordinary shares, e.g. preference in dividend distribution.

PREPAYMENTS (Chapter 8) Prepayments are payments in advance.

PRESENT-DAY VALUE (Chapters 3, 16) The value today of a given amount or item.

PRINCIPLE OF DUALITY (Chapter 4) The basis of the double-entry bookkeeping system on which accounting is based. It states that every transaction has two opposite and equal components.

PRODUCT COST (Chapter 18) The cost of producing an item. When firms manufacture only one product, the process of product costing is straightforward. When firms manufacture more than one product (multi-product firms), the process of product costing can be complex. Two approaches used in determining product costs in multi-product firms are marginal costing and full costing.

PRODUCTION BUDGET (Chapter 21) An estimate of the number of units that will be manufactured by an organisation during the budget period.

PRODUCTION COST CENTRE (Chapter 18) Production cost centres are departments where the manufacturing activity physically takes place.

PROFIT (Chapter 3) The difference between the wealth at the start and at the end of a period. It is a measure of flow which summarises activity over a period.

PROVISION FOR DOUBTFUL DEBTS (Chapter 8) A contra debtors' account which shows the estimated total of future bad debts.

QUALITATIVE (Chapter 1) The nature or characteristics of information.

QUANTITATIVE (Chapter 1) The amount or size of information.

REALISE (Chapter 5) Convert to cash or a legal claim to cash.

RECOGNISE (Chapter 5) To record an item in the financial statements.

REDEEMABLE PREFERENCE SHARE (Chapters 10, 14) Preference shares that can be redeemed out of the company's profits or out of the proceeds of a new share issue.

REDUCING-BALANCE METHOD (Chapter 9) A method of depreciation which results in a decreasing depreciation charge over the useful life of the depreciable asset. Depreciation expense is calculated for each period through the application of a predetermined depreciation rate to the declining undepreciated cost of the asset, called the written-down value or net book value. The following formula is used to determine the annual depreciation rate.

$$\text{depreciation rate} = 1 - \sqrt[n]{\frac{r}{c}}$$

where n = estimated useful life (in years), r = estimated residual value, and c = original cost (in dollars).

REGRESSION ANALYSIS (Chapter 17) A sophisticated method of cost estimation which involves making a number of observations from past cost behaviour and statistically analysing the data to produce a line of best fit through plotted cost points on a graph. Patterns of behaviour can be identified from the linear regression model and conclusions drawn about the correlation between cost and the activity being analysed.

RELEVANCE (Chapter 2) For financial information to be relevant it must have value in assisting users to make decisions about the allocation of scarce resources and to assess the rendering of accountability by preparers (SAC 3, 8).

RELEVANT RANGE OF ACTIVITY (Chapter 17) The levels of activity that a firm has experienced in past periods. It is assumed that in this range the relationship between the independent variables will be similar to that previously experienced.

RELIABILITY (Chapter 2) The reliability of financial information is determined by the degree of correspondence between what that information conveys to users and the underlying transactions and events that have occurred and been measured and displayed. Reliable information, without bias or undue error, faithfully represents those transactions and events (SAC 3, 16).

REPLACEMENT COST (Chapter 3) The amount that would have to be paid at today's prices to purchase an item similar to the existing item. The cost that has come about as a direct result of the decision to use a resource for a purpose not originally intended and the need to replace the resource.

REPORTING ENTITY (Chapter 2) Entities (including economic entities) in respect of which it is reasonable to expect the existence of users dependent on general-purpose financial reports for information which will help them to make and evaluate decisions about the allocation of scarce resources (SAC 1, 40).

RESERVES (Chapter 11) Amounts set aside out of profits and other surpluses which are not designed to meet any liability, contingency, commitment or diminution in value of assets known to exist at the date of the statement of financial position.

RESIDUAL VALUE (Chapter 9) The residual value of a non-current asset is an estimate of the net amount recoverable on ultimate disposal of the asset when it is no longer viable to use in the business.

RESPONSIBILITY ACCOUNTING (Chapter 15) An approach used to monitor performance whereby personnel in an organisation who incur expenditure and generate revenues are identified and made responsible for these costs and revenues.

RESPONSIBILITY CENTRES (Chapter 15) The various decision centres throughout an organisation, normally departments or divisions, recognised in the responsibility accounting management approach. The manager's knowledge of the centre places him or her in an advantageous position within the organisation to ensure that budget targets are achieved.

REVENUES (Chapters 2, 5) Inflows or other enhancements or savings in outflows of future economic benefits in the form of increases in assets or reductions in liabilities of the entity, other than those relating to contributions by owners, that result in an increase in equity during the reporting period (*SAC 4*, 111).

SAC (Chapter 2) Statements of Accounting Concepts which are prepared by the Public Sector Accounting Standards Board and the Australian Accounting Standards Board.

SALES BUDGET (Chapter 21) The conversion of the sales forecast for a budget period of an organisation into detailed information concerning the products or services that are anticipated to be sold.

SECURED LENDER (Chapters 10, 14) Someone who has a legal charge over the assets of a business and can claim those assets if the business does not repay or service the loan in accordance with the agreement.

SERVICE COST CENTRE (Chapter 18) Those decision centres which are primarily engaged in servicing the production function, but are not directly involved in the production activity.

SHORT-TERM FINANCE (Chapter 10) Finance for a period of less than one year.

SIMPLE INTEREST (Chapter 16) Interest based on original principal only.

SOLE TRADER (Chapter 11) A one-owner business.

SOLVENCY (Chapter 14) The ability of a business to repay borrowed funds or interest as they fall due. An insolvent firm is unable to meet its commitments.

SPARE CAPACITY (Chapter 20) An organisation which has enough resources available to make another product or component, without affecting the production of other products, is said to have spare capacity.

STANDARDS OVERLOAD (Chapter 2) A problem concerned with the time and costs involved in preparing general-purpose financial reports which must comply with a large number of accounting standards.

STATEMENT OF FINANCIAL PERFORMANCE (Chapters 1, 5) A financial report listing the revenues, expenses and net profit or net loss of a business (entity) for a time period.

STATEMENT OF FINANCIAL POSITION (Chapters 1, 4) A statement which shows all the resources controlled by an enterprise and all the obligations due by the enterprise at one point in time.

STATEMENTS OF ACCOUNTING STANDARDS (Chapters 1, 2, 13) Standards which prescribe certain accounting and disclosure requirements for certain types of transactions. They are more specific than Accounting Concepts.

STEWARDSHIP (Chapter 1) The need to protect a firm's economic resources (normally referred to as assets) from theft, fraud, wastage, etc.

STOCK EXCHANGE (Chapter 1) A market for the buying and selling of stocks and shares in which supply and demand governs price.

STRAIGHT-LINE METHOD (Chapter 9) A method of depreciation which allocates an equal amount of depreciation to all the periods over the useful life of the depreciable asset. The depreciation charge for each period is determined by dividing the cost of the asset, less the estimate of any residual value at the end of the asset's life, by the useful life of the asset.

STRATEGIC DECISIONS (Chapter 15) Decisions that determine the long-term policies of a firm and that are necessary if the firm is to meet its objectives.

SUBSIDIARY (Chapter 12) An entity which is controlled by a parent entity.

SUNK COSTS (past costs) (Chapter 19) Costs which have been paid or which are owed by a firm. The firm is committed to paying for them in the future.

T ACCOUNT (Chapter 11) Under the traditional approach to accounting, an account format shaped like the letter T. Debits are recorded on the left-hand side and credits on the right-hand side.

TAX-EFFECT ACCOUNTING METHOD (Chapter 12) Accounting for the timing differences between taxable income and accounting profit adjusted for permanent differences.

TAX-PAYABLE METHOD (Chapter 12) The accounting method for calculating income tax expense, where taxable income is multiplied by the tax rate to give income tax expense.

TAXABLE INCOME (Chapter 12) The amount of profit as determined by the Tax Commissioner on which the current income tax liability is calculated.

TIMING DIFFERENCES (Chapter 12) A revenue or expense item that enters into the calculation of accounting profit and taxable income but in different periods.

TRADE CREDIT (Chapter 10) The finance available from suppliers selling goods on credit.

TREND ANALYSIS (Chapter 14) A technique commonly used in financial statement analysis to assess a business's growth prospects.

TRIAL BALANCE (Chapter 11) The preparation of a statement which lists all of the financial accounts and their respective debit or credit balances to ensure the equality of debits and credits made to the accounts.

UNAVOIDABLE COST (Chapter 19) A cost which will be incurred whether or not a decision (e.g. delivery of a special order) is accepted or rejected, i.e. the cost is irrelevant to the decision.

UNDER-RECOVERY OF OVERHEAD (Chapter 18) A statement of financial performance which records the difference between actual overhead cost and the estimate on which the absorption rate is based. The difference is classified as a period cost because it is not identified with any of the units of production produced during the year.

UNITS-OF-OUTPUT METHOD (Chapter 9) A method of depreciation which relates depreciation to use rather than to time. It is appropriate to use for an asset where usage will materially affect its lifespan. The depreciation charge is determined by dividing the cost of the asset, less the estimate of the asset's residual value, by the estimated number of output units expected from the asset during its estimated useful life. Output units can be expressed in numerous ways, e.g. kilometres, operating hours. The result of the calculation is a depreciation rate per output unit which, when multiplied by the number of units used or produced during the period, gives the depreciation expense for a period.

UNREALISED GAIN (Chapter 2) A gain which is yet to be realised by way of a transaction. For example, an increase in the value of an asset represents an unrealised gain until the asset is sold, at which time the gain would be realised.

UNREALISED LOSS (Chapter 2) A loss which is yet to be realised by way of a transaction. For example, a decrease in the value of an asset represents an unrealised loss until the asset is sold, at which time the loss would be realised.

UNSECURED CREDITOR (Chapters 10, 14) Someone who does not have a legal charge on the assets of a business.

UNSECURED NOTE (Chapters 10, 14) A debt instrument which is not secured by a charge over property.

USEFUL LIFE (Chapter 9) For a non-current asset, the time period the asset is expected to be used to produce goods or services.

USER GROUP (Chapter 14) The classes of person for whom the financial statement analysis is being undertaken.

UTILITY Usefulness.

VALUE (Chapter 3) An item's equivalence in money.

VARIABLE COSTS (Chapter 17) Costs that are the same per unit of activity within the relevant range of activity; therefore total variable costs increase and decrease in direct proportion to the increase and decrease in the activity level. The activity level depends upon what is being measured, i.e. production output or sales output.

WEALTH (Chapter 3) A static measure representing a stock at a particular point in time.

WORK IN PROGRESS (Chapters 7, 18) Products and services that are at an intermediate stage of completion.

WORKSHEET (Chapter 6) An arrangement of columns on a sheet of paper, used by accountants to gather and organise the information from which financial statements can be prepared.

WRITTEN-DOWN COST (Chapter 3) The historic cost after an adjustment for usage (commonly referred to as depreciation).

WRITTEN-DOWN VALUE (net book value) (Chapter 9) The cost of a non-current asset less the total depreciation to date.

Index